NOLO *Your Legal Companion*

"In Nolo you can trust." —**THE NEW YORK TIMES**

OUR MISSION
Make the law as simple as possible, saving you time, money and headaches.

Whether you have a simple question or a complex problem, turn to us at:

NOLO.COM

Your all-in-one legal resource

Need quick information about wills, patents, adoptions, starting a business—or anything else that's affected by the law? **Nolo.com** is packed with free articles, legal updates, resources and a complete catalog of our books and software.

NOLO NOW

Make your legal documents online

Creating a legal document has never been easier or more cost-effective! Featuring Nolo's Online Will, as well as online forms for LLC formation, incorporation, divorce, name change—and many more! Check it out at **http://nolonow.nolo.com**.

NOLO'S LAWYER DIRECTORY

Meet your new attorney

If you want advice from a qualified attorney, turn to Nolo's Lawyer Directory—the only directory that lets you see hundreds of in-depth attorney profiles so you can pick the one that's right for you. Find it at **http://lawyers.nolo.com**.

ALWAYS UP TO DATE

Sign up for NOLO'S LEGAL UPDATER

Old law is bad law. We'll email you when we publish an updated edition of this book—sign up for this free service at nolo.com/legalupdater.

Find the latest updates at NOLO.COM

Recognizing that the law can change even before you use this book, we post legal updates during the life of this edition at **nolo.com/updates**.

Is this edition the newest? ASK US!

To make sure that this is the most recent available, just give us a call at **800-728-3555**.

(Please note that we cannot offer legal advice.)

7th Edition

Nolo's Encyclopedia of Everyday Law

Answers to Your Most Frequently Asked Legal Questions

by Shae Irving, J.D.
& Nolo editors

SEVENTH EDITION   JANUARY 2008

Editor   SHAE IRVING

Production   SUSAN PUTNEY

Index   THÉRÈSE SHERE

Proofreader   ROBERT WELLS

Printer   DELTA PRINTING SOLUTIONS, INC.

Nolo's encyclopedia of everyday law : answers to your most frequently asked legal questions / by Shae Irving & Nolo editors. -- 7th ed.

        p. cm.

  Includes index.

  ISBN 978-1-4133-0560-9 (pbk.)

  1. Law--United States--Popular works. 2. Law--United States--Miscellanea. I. Irving, Shae. II. Nolo (Firm)

KF387.N65 2008
349.73--dc22

        2007031791

Quantity sales: For information on bulk purchases or corporate premium sales, please contact the Special Sales department. For academic sales or textbook adoptions, ask for Academic Sales, 800-955-4775. Nolo, 950 Parker St., Berkeley, CA 94710.

Dedication

For Edward F. Dolan

Acknowledgments

Thanks to Jake Warner for inspiring and supporting this project. And thanks to all the Nolo editors and hardworking production folks who keep the book on track. For this edition, we'd particularly like to acknowledge **Kathleen Michon**, **Susan Putney**, and **Robert Wells**.

We're also grateful to every Nolo author whose fine work has shaped these pages. You'll find many of these talented individuals listed in the Contributors section on the following page. But we want to give special thanks to:

Paul Bergman and **Sara Berman-Barrett**, authors of *Represent Yourself in Court* and *The Criminal Law Handbook*

David W. Brown, author of *Beat Your Ticket: Go to Court and Win!*

Denis Clifford, author of many Nolo titles, including *The Quick & Legal Will Book*, *Nolo's Simple Will Book*, and *Make Your Own Living Trust*, and coauthor of *Plan Your Estate* and *A Legal Guide for Lesbian & Gay Couples*

Frederick W. Daily, author of *Stand Up to the IRS* and *Tax Savvy for Small Business.*

Stephen R. Elias, author of numerous Nolo books, including *The New Bankruptcy: Will It Work for You?*, *Special Needs Trusts: Protect Your Child's Financial Future*, *How to File for Chapter 7 Bankruptcy*, and *Legal Research: How to Find & Understand the Law*

Cora Jordan, author of *Neighbor Law: Fences, Trees, Boundaries & Noise* and coauthor (with Denis Clifford) of *Plan Your Estate*

Mimi E. Lyster, author of *Building a Parenting Agreement That Works: How to Put Your Kids First When Your Marriage Doesn't Last.*

Anthony Mancuso, author of *Incorporate Your Business*, *How to Form a Nonprofit Corporation* (national and California editions), *Form Your Own Limited Liability Company*, *The Corporate Records Handbook*, and *LLC or Corporation?*

Joseph Matthews, author of *How to Win Your Personal Injury Claim* and *Long-Term Care: How to Plan & Pay for It,* and coauthor (with Dorothy Matthews Berman) of *Social Security, Medicare & Government Pensions*

Fred S. Steingold, author of *The Legal Guide for Starting & Running a Small Business* and *The Employer's Legal Handbook.*

Contributors

Ilona Bray Illona's legal background includes solo practice as well experience in the nonprofit and corporate worlds. She has written or coauthored several Nolo titles, including *Effective Fundraising for Nonprofits, Becoming a U.S. Citizen*, and *Nolo's Essential Guide to Buying Your First Home*.

Catherine Caputo Before joining Nolo, Cathy was an attorney in private practice assisting start-up and small business clients with a wide range of legal needs. She edits small business books and software and also focuses on issues affecting seniors, such as Social Security benefits and retirement. Cathy received her law degree, with honors, from the University of San Francisco School of Law.

Amy DelPo Amy has been an editor at Nolo since January 2000. She specializes in workers' rights, sexual harassment law, employment law, criminal law, and civil litigation. She brings more than six years of criminal and civil litigation experience to her work at Nolo, having litigated cases in all levels of state and federal courts, including the California Supreme Court and the United States Supreme Court. Amy received her law degree, with honors, from the University of North Carolina at Chapel Hill.

Emily Doskow Emily is a Nolo author and editor, and a mediator and attorney in private practice in Berkeley, California, specializing in adoption and family law, especially for same-sex couples. She is the coauthor of several Nolo books, including *Nolo's Essential Guide to Divorce, Becoming a Mediator, Do Your Own California Adoption*, and *How to Change Your Name in California*.

Diana Fitzpatrick Diana worked on municipal finance issues at the San Francisco City Attorney's office before joining Nolo. She also worked at a law firm in New York for several years before moving to the Bay Area. Diana is a graduate of New York University School of Law and Barnard College.

Lisa Guerin During her years as a law student at Boalt Hall School of Law at the University of California at Berkeley, Lisa worked for Nolo as a research and editorial assistant. After a stint as a staff attorney at the U.S. Court of Appeals for the Ninth Circuit, Lisa has worked primarily in the field of employment law, in both government and private practice. Lisa rejoined Nolo in 2000 and is the coauthor of several employment titles, including *Create Your Own Employee Handbook* and *Dealing With Problem Employees*.

Shae Irving Shae graduated from Boalt Hall School of Law at the University of California at Berkeley in 1993 and began working for Nolo in 1994. She has written extensively on durable powers of attorney, health care directives, and other estate planning issues. She is the managing editor for *Nolo's Quicken WillMaker Plus* software.

Bethany K. Laurence Beth graduated from Hastings College of the Law at the University of California in 1993. She spent several years working for a corporate legal publisher before coming to Nolo. She joined Nolo's editorial staff in 1997 and has never been happier. Beth is the coauthor of Nolo's *Business Buyout Agreements* and the editor of many of Nolo's small business books.

Janet Portman Janet received undergraduate and graduate degrees from Stanford University and a law degree from the University of Santa Clara. She was a public defender before coming to Nolo. Janet is Nolo's managing editor, the author of *Every Landlord's Guide to Finding Great Tenants*, and the coauthor of many Nolo titles, including *Every Landlord's Legal Guide, Every Tenant's Legal Guide, Renters' Rights*, and *Negotiating the Best Lease for Your Business.*

Mary Randolph Mary has been editing and writing Nolo books and software for more than a decade. She earned her law degree from Boalt Hall School of Law at the University of California at Berkeley, and her undergraduate degree at the University of Illinois. She is the author of *Deeds for California Real Estate, The Executor's Guide*, and other Nolo materials.

Alayna Schroeder Alayna graduated from the University of California, Hastings College of the Law, and worked as an employment attorney before joining Nolo's staff in 2005. In addition to editing employment and real estate titles, she is coauthor of *Nolo's Essential Guide to Buying Your First Home.*

Betsy Simmons-Hannibal Betsy is a Nolo editor specializing in estate planning books and software. She graduated with honors from Golden Gate University School of Law where she was research editor of the law review. Prior to joining Nolo, she trained at two private law firms as well as the San Francisco Superior Court and the Federal District Court of Northern California. When she's not working, you might find her playing soccer, traveling with her husband, or doting on her curious dog.

Marcia Stewart Marcia is an expert on landlord-tenant law, buying and selling houses, and other issues of interest to consumers. She is the coauthor of Nolo's *Every Landlord's Legal Guide, Every Tenant's Legal Guide, Renters' Rights*, and *Leases & Rental Agreements*, and editor of Nolo's *LeaseWriter* software for landlords.

Richard Stim Rich graduated from the University of San Francisco Law School and worked in private practice for 16 years until joining Nolo as an editor in 2000. He is the author of *Profit From Your Idea, Getting Permission*, and *Music Law*, and is the coauthor of *Patent Pending in 24 Hours.*

Ralph Warner Ralph is a cofounder of Nolo. He is the author (or coauthor) of a number of Nolo books, including *Every Landlord's Legal Guide, Everybody's Guide to Small Claims Court, Form a Partnership*, and *Get a Life: You Don't Need a Million to Retire Well.* Ralph is a lawyer who became fed up with the legal system and dedicated his professional life to making law more accessible and affordable to all Americans.

Table of Contents

About This Book

Whether we like it or not, the law touches our personal lives in many ways each day. We may not think much about the laws that affect us as we carry out simple tasks such as driving a car, making a telephone call, or buying milk at the corner grocery store. But every now and again, we're sure to need an answer to a common legal question that arises in the course of daily life:

What can I do about my noisy neighbor?

What are my rights if I'm fired from my job?

Do I really need to make a will?

What should I do if I can't pay the child support I owe?

And so on.

This book provides answers to frequently asked questions about more than 100 subjects you might encounter in your personal life—topics that range from buying a house to getting a divorce, from paying your debts to starting and running a small business. Obviously, we can't answer every question on a particular subject, but we've answered many common ones to get you started. Throughout each chapter, you'll find resource boxes listing sources for more information about a particular subject.

In addition, for those of you who are computer savvy, each chapter contains a list of online sites that will help you learn more about a particular area of the law. Look for the "Online Help" icon as you read. And if you need more information about finding the law, the appendix contains a section that shows you how to do basic legal research—with a focus on using the Internet.

Think of this book as a desk reference—a little encyclopedia that explains what the law really means in a language you can understand. But remember that the law changes constantly, as legislatures pass new statutes and courts hand down their rulings. We will publish new, revised editions of this book periodically, but it will never be perfectly current. It's always your responsibility to be sure a law is up to date before you rely on it. Check for legal updates on our website at www.nolo.com for the most current legal information affecting Nolo books and software.

Houses

Home is heaven for beginners.

—CHARLES H. PARKHURST

Buying or selling a house is a both exciting and demanding. To do it right, you need to understand how houses are priced, financed, and inspected; how to find and work with a real estate agent; how to protect your interests when negotiating a contract; and how legal transfer of ownership takes place. This chapter covers many of the basic topics that buyers, sellers, and owners need to understand.

Buying a House

Before you fall in love with a house, it's essential to determine how much you can afford to pay and what your financing options are. You'll also need to choose a good real estate agent or broker, decide whether to buy an old house, new house, or condo, and finally, even if you think you've found your dream home, you'll need to understand house inspections and insure your new home against unforeseen problems.

I'm a first-time home buyer. How do I determine how much house I can afford?

Don't rely on abstract formulas to determine how much you can pay. Instead, take a close look at how much of your monthly income you can realistically set aside after you stop paying rent. Then, when considering a particular house, total up the estimated monthly loan payments (including principal and interest) plus one-twelfth of your yearly bill for property and homeowners' insurance. Now compare that to your monthly income.

Lenders have historically wanted you to make all monthly housing payments with 28% to 38% of your gross monthly income (before taxes). The exact percentage depends on the amount of your down payment, the interest rate on the type of mortgage you want, your credit score, the level of your long-term debts, and other factors. However, if you have a good credit history, many lenders are happy to help you get even deeper into debt.

It's best to run the numbers yourself before you talk to a bank or lender. Various online mortgage calculators, such as those on the websites listed at the end of this chapter, will help you get a realistic picture.

Once you've done the basic calculations, you can ask a lender or loan broker for a prequalification letter saying that you are likely to be approved for a loan of a specified amount based on your income and credit history.

However, unless you're in a very slow market, with lots more sellers than buyers, you'll want to do more than prequalify—you'll want to be guaranteed for a specific loan amount. This means that the lender actually evaluates your financial situation, runs a credit check, and preapproves you for a loan. Having lender pre-approval makes you more financially attractive to sellers than simple loan prequalification and is crucial in competitive markets.

How important is my credit history in getting loan approval?

Your credit history plays a vital role in determining the type and amount of loan lenders offer you. When reviewing loan applications, lenders typically request your credit score from the credit bureaus. This score is a statistical summary of the information in your credit report, including:

- your history of paying bills on time
- the level of your outstanding debts
- how long you've had credit
- your credit limit
- the number of inquiries for your credit report (too many of a certain kind can lower your score), and
- the types of credit you have.

The higher your credit score, the easier it will be to get a loan. If your score is low, a lender may either reject your loan application altogether or insist on a very large down payment or high interest rate to lower the lender's risk.

To avoid problems, always check your credit report and clean up your file if necessary—before, not after, you apply for a mortgage. For information on how to order and clean up your credit report, see Chapter 9.

How can I find the best home loan or mortgage?

Banks, credit unions, savings and loans, insurance companies, mortgage bankers, and others make home loans. Lenders and terms change frequently as new companies appear, old ones merge, and market conditions fluctuate. To get the best deal, compare loans and fees from at least a half-dozen lenders. This information is published in the real estate sections of most metropolitan newspapers and is widely available on the Internet.

Mortgage rate websites come in two basic flavors: those sites that don't offer loans (called "no-loan" sites) and those that do. No-loan sites are a great place to examine mortgage programs, learn mortgage lingo, and crunch numbers with online mortgage calculators.

Many online mortgage sites also offer direct access to loans from one or more lenders. However, many customers report dissatisfaction with online mortgage services and prefer to complete their transaction with a "live" lender or broker.

See the end of this chapter for addresses of some mortgage websites.

To avoid all the legwork involved in shopping for mortgages on your own, you can also work with a loan broker, someone who specializes in matching house buyers with an appropriate mortgage lender. Given the increasing variety of loan types—as discussed further on in this section—an experienced broker can also help you decide which is best for you. (But check the broker's qualifications carefully—not all brokers are licensed.) Loan brokers usually collect their fee from the lender, not from you.

What are my other options for home loans?

You may also be eligible for a government-guaranteed loan, offered by:

- the Federal Housing Administration (FHA), an agency of the Department of Housing and Urban Development (HUD) (see www.hud.gov)
- the U.S. Department of Veterans Affairs (see www.homeloans.va.gov), or
- a state or local housing agency.

Government loans usually have low down payment requirements and sometimes offer better-than-market interest rates as well.

Also, ask banks and other private lenders about any "first-time buyer programs" that offer low down-payment plans and flexible qualifying guidelines to low- and moderate-income buyers with good credit.

Finally, don't forget private sources of mortgage money—parents, other relatives, friends, or even the seller of the house you want to buy. Borrowing money privately is usually the most cost-efficient method of all.

What's the difference between a fixed and an adjustable rate mortgage?

With a fixed rate mortgage, the interest rate and the amount you pay each month remain the same over the entire mortgage term, traditionally 15 or 30 years. A number of variations are available, including five- and seven-year fixed rate loans with balloon payments at the end.

With an adjustable rate mortgage (ARM), your interest rate will fluctuate in step with the interest rates in the economy. Initial interest rates of ARMs are usually offered at a discounted ("teaser") rate, which is lower than those for fixed rate mortgages. Over time, however, initial discounts are filtered out. To avoid constant and drastic changes, ARMs typically regulate (cap) how much and how often the interest rate and/or payments can change in a year and over the life of the loan.

A number of variations are available for ARMs, including hybrids that change from a fixed to an adjustable rate after a period of years; interest-only loans; and loans that offer a menu of payment options each month.

How do I decide between a fixed and an adjustable rate mortgage?

Because interest rates and mortgage options change often, your choice of a fixed or an adjustable rate mortgage should depend on the interest rates and mortgage options available when you're buying, how much you can afford in the short term, your view of the future (generally, high inflation will mean that ARM rates will go up and lower inflation means that they will fall), and how willing you are to take a risk.

Very risk-averse people usually choose the certainty of a fixed rate mortgage, even when balanced against the possibility that an ARM might be cheaper in the long run. However, some people can't afford the relatively higher interest rates at which fixed rate mortgages usually begin.

Keep in mind that if you take out a loan now, and several years from now interest rates have dropped, refinancing may be an option.

To make sure you can refinance in the future, you'll want to avoid prepayment penalties on your first mortgage.

What's the best way to find and work with a real estate agent or broker?

Get recommendations from people who have purchased a house in the past few years and whose judgment you trust. Don't work with an agent you meet at an open house or find in the Yellow Pages or on the Internet unless and until you call references and thoroughly check the person out.

The agent or broker you choose should be in the full-time business of selling real estate and should have the following five traits: integrity, business sophistication, experience with the type of services you need, knowledge of the area where you want to live, and sensitivity to your tastes and needs.

All states regulate and license real estate agents and brokers. You may have different options as to the type of legal relationship you have with an agent or broker; typically, the seller pays the commission of the real estate salesperson who helps the buyer locate the seller's house. The commission is a percentage (usually 5%) of the sales price of the house. What this means is that your agent or broker has a built-in conflict of interest: Unless you've agreed to pay the agent separately, he or she won't get paid until you buy a home, and the more you pay for a house, the bigger the agent's cut.

To offset this conflict, you need to become knowledgeable about the house-buying process, your ideal affordable house and neighborhood, your financing needs and options, your legal rights, and how to evaluate comparable prices.

What's the best way to get information on homes for sale and details about the neighborhood?

Most people begin their search on the Internet, scanning online listings to see which homes are worth a visit, how much they cost, and what amenities they offer. Virtual tours of new homes often include floor plans and photographs.

Once you identify a house you like, you can email the address or identification number to your agent, the listing agent, or the owner (if it's a listing by a FSBO—for sale by owner) to obtain additional information or to set up an appointment to see the home.

The list of websites at the end of this chapter includes some of the major national real estate listing sites. Your state or regional realty association or multiple listing service (MLS) may also have a website listing homes for sale. Major real estate companies, including ERA, RE/MAX, Coldwell Banker, Prudential, and others offer home listings on their websites.

Virtually all online editions of newspapers offer a homes-for-sale classifieds section that works much like an online listing site. On most newspaper sites, you can browse all the listings or customize your search by typing in your criteria, such as price range, location, and number of bedrooms and baths. Check the Newspaper Association of America (www.naa.org) for a link to your newspaper. (Under "NAA Resources," click "NewsVoyager.")

Advice on relocation decisions and details about your new community and its services are also readily available online. For valuable information about cities, communities, and neighborhoods, including schools, housing costs, demographics, crime rates, and jobs, see the websites listed at the end of this chapter.

Keep in mind that the Internet is no substitute for your own legwork. Ask your friends and colleagues, walk and drive around neighborhoods, talk to local residents, read local newspapers, visit the local library and planning department, and do whatever it takes to help you get a better sense of a neighborhood or city.

My spouse and I want to buy a $450,000 house. We have good incomes and can make high monthly payments, but we don't have $90,000 to make a 20% down payment. Are there other options?

Assuming you can afford (and qualify for) high monthly mortgage payments and have an excellent credit history, you should be able to find a low- (10% to 15%) or even no-down-payment loan for a $450,000 house. However, you may have to pay a higher interest rate and loan fees (points) than someone making a higher down payment.

In addition, a buyer who puts less than 20% down may be required to purchase private mortgage insurance (PMI), which is designed to reimburse a mortgage lender up to a certain amount if a buyer defaults and the foreclosure sale price is less than the amount owed the lender (the mortgage plus the costs of the foreclosure sale). To avoid PMI, it may be worth taking out a second mortgage, even at a higher interest rate.

PMI premiums are usually paid monthly and typically cost less than one-half of one percent of the mortgage loan. You can ordinarily drop PMI once your equity in the house reaches 22%, if you've made timely mortgage payments.

I want to buy a newly built house. Is there anything special I need to know?

The most important factor in buying a newly built house is not what you buy (that is, the particular model), but rather from whom you buy. New is not always better, especially if the house is slapped together in a hurry. And as the first person to live in the house, you could be in for unpleasant surprises, such as water pipes that aren't connected to the sewer or light switches that don't work.

Shop for an excellent builder—someone who builds quality houses, delivers on time, and stands behind the work. To check out a particular builder, talk to existing owners in the development you're considering, or ask an experienced contractor to look at other houses the developer is building. Keep tabs on the builder as the work is done, by scheduling regular home inspections. (You'll need to negotiate for these in your purchase contract.)

Many developers of new housing will help you arrange financing; some will also pay a portion of your monthly mortgage or subsidize your interest payments for a short period of time (called a "buydown" of the mortgage). As with any loan, be sure you comparison shop before arranging financing through a builder.

Also, be sure to negotiate the prices of any add-ons and upgrades, such as a spa or higher-quality appliances. These can add substantially to the cost of a new home.

Is there anything I need to know before buying a home in a development run by a homeowners' association?

When you buy a home in a new subdivision or planned unit development, chances are good that you also automatically become a member of an exclusive club—the homeowners' association, whose members are the people who own homes in the same development. The homeowners' association will probably exercise a lot of control over how you use and what you do to your property.

Deeds to houses in new developments almost always include restrictions—from the size of your dog to the colors you can paint your house to the type of front yard landscaping you can do to where (and what types of vehicles) you can park in your driveway. Usually, these restrictions, called covenants, conditions, and restrictions (CC&Rs), put decision-making rights in the hands of a homeowners' association. Before buying, study the CC&Rs carefully to see if they're compatible with your lifestyle. If you don't understand something, ask for more information and seek legal advice if necessary.

It's not easy to get out from under overly restrictive CC&Rs after you move in. You'll likely have to submit an application (with fee) for a variance, get your neighbors' permission, and possibly go through a formal hearing. And if you want to make a structural change, such as building a fence or adding a room, you'll probably need formal permission from the association in addition to complying with city zoning rules.

How can I make sure that the house I'm buying is in good shape?

In some states, you may have the advantage of a law that requires sellers to disclose considerable information about the condition of the house. (See *Selling Your House*, below.) Regardless of whether the seller provides disclosures, however, you should have the property inspected for defects or malfunctions in the building's structure.

Start by conducting your own inspection. To help you learn what to look for, see *Nolo's Essential Guide to Buying Your First Home*, by Ilona Bray, Alayna Schroeder, and Marcia Stewart. Ideally, you should inspect a house before you make a formal written offer to buy it so that you can save yourself the trouble should you find serious problems.

If a house passes your inspection, hire a general contractor to check all major house systems from top to bottom, including the roof, plumbing, electrical and heating systems, and drainage. This will take two or three hours and cost you anywhere from $200 to $500 depending on the location, size, age, and type of home. Accompany the inspector during the examination so that you can learn more about the maintenance and preservation of the house and get answers to any questions you may have, including which problems are important and which are relatively minor. Depending on the property, you may want to arrange specialized inspections for pest damage (your mortgage lender may require a pest inspection), hazards from floods, earthquakes, and other natural disasters and environmental health hazards such as asbestos, mold, and lead.

In most states, professional inspections are done after you and the seller have signed a purchase agreement. (Your purchase should be contingent upon the house passing one or more inspections.) To avoid confusion and disputes, be sure you get a written report of each inspection.

If the house is in good shape, you can proceed, knowing that you're getting what you paid for. If an inspector discovers problems—such as an antiquated plumbing system or a major termite infestation—you can negotiate for the seller to pay for necessary repairs. Finally, you can back out of the deal if an inspection turns up problems, assuming your purchase contract is properly written to allow you to do so.

I'm making an offer to buy a house, but I don't want to lock myself into a deal that might not work out. How can I protect myself?

Real estate contracts almost always contain contingencies—events that must happen within a certain amount of time (such as 30 days) in order to finalize the deal. For example, you may want to make your offer contingent on your ability to qualify for financing, the house passing certain physical inspections, or even your ability to sell your existing house first. Be aware, however, that the more contingencies you want, the less likely the seller is to accept your offer or sign the purchase agreement. See *Selling Your House*, below, for more on real estate offers.

When should I start looking for homeowners' insurance?

A house may be the biggest investment you make in your life, so you'll want to fully insure it against damage (by fire, wind, vandalism, earthquakes, floods, and mold, for example). A com-

prehensive homeowners' insurance policy should cover the replacement value of your house and other structures, and partial replacement of valuable items of personal property like art and computers. But beware: So-called "replacement cost coverage" for your house pays you only a preset amount, so you'll want to make sure that's enough to cover your actual rebuilding costs. You'll probably want some liability coverage as well, in case visitors to your property slip and fall or are otherwise injured.

Start shopping for homeowners' insurance soon after your purchase agreement has been signed. Don't make the mistake of putting this off until escrow is about to close—finding a good policy at a reasonable price is getting harder and harder, due to recent losses and clampdowns in the insurance industry.

The problem is particularly acute in states such as California and Texas, where expensive mold claims have pushed the industry into a state of panic. Homebuyers who have filed past claims for water damage (a precursor to mold) or who are buying a house with a history of mold problems may find themselves unable to get any insurance at all. Homebuyers with a history of making frequent claims on their insurance policies have similar problems. Some homebuyers now add a contingency to their purchase contract stating that the deal can be cancelled if they can't find adequate insurance.

Shop carefully—and if you're in a state with a troubled insurance industry, buy a policy with a high deductible. This will lower your premium cost and prevent you from racking up a history of claims that could endanger your ability to renew your policy or get future insurance.

Strategies for Buying an Affordable House

To find a good house at a comparatively reasonable price, you must learn about the housing market and what you can afford, make some sensible compromises as to size and amenities, and above all, be patient. Here are some proven strategies to meet these goals:

1. Buy a fixer-upper cheap (preferably one that needs mostly cosmetic fixes).

2. Buy a small house (with remodeling potential) and add on later.

3. Buy a house at an estate or probate sale.

4. Buy a house subject to foreclosure (when a homeowner defaults on the mortgage).

5. Buy a shared-equity house, pooling resources with someone other than a spouse or partner.

6. Rent out a room or two in the house.

7. Buy a duplex, triplex, or house with an in-law unit.

8. Lease a house you can't afford to buy now with an option to buy later.

9. Buy a limited-equity house built by a nonprofit organization.

10. Buy a house at an auction.

More Information About Buying a Home

Nolo's Essential Guide to Buying Your First Home, by Ilona Bray, Alayna Schroeder, and Marcia Stewart, provides everything you need to select the best house, mortgage, agent, inspections, and much more.

How to Buy a House in California, by Ralph Warner, Ira Serkes, and George Devine (Nolo), explains all the details of the California house-buying process and contains tear-out contracts and disclosure forms.

Your New House: The Alert Consumer's Guide to Buying and Building a Quality Home, by Alan & Denise Fields (Windsor Peak Press), offers valuable advice for those who want to buy or build a new home.

Inspecting a House, by Rex Cauldwell (Taunton Press), shows professional inspectors how to inspect a house in order to discover major problems, such as a bad foundation, leaky roof, or malfunctioning fireplace, and it's written in language a layperson can understand.

Selling Your House

If you're selling a home, you need to time the sale properly, price the home accurately, and understand the laws (such as disclosure requirements) that cover house transactions. These questions and answers will get you started.

I don't need to sell in a hurry. When are the best and worst times to put a house on the market?

Too many people rush to sell their houses and lose money because of it. Ideally, you should put your house on the market when there's a large pool of buyers—causing prices to go up. This may occur in the following situations:

• Your area is considered especially attractive—for example, because of the schools, low crime rate, employment opportunities, weather, or proximity to a major city.

• Mortgage interest rates are low.

- The economic climate of your region is healthy, and people feel confident about the future.
- There's a jump in house-buying activity, as often occurs in spring.

Of course, if you have to sell immediately—because of financial reasons, a divorce, a job move, or an imperative health concern—and you don't have any of the advantages listed above, you may have to settle for a lower price, or help the buyer with financing, in order to make a quick sale.

I want to save on the real estate commission. Can I sell my house myself without a real estate broker or agent?

Usually, yes. This is called a FSBO (pronounced "fizzbo")—for sale by owner. You must be aware, however, of the legal rules that govern real estate transfers in your state, such as who must sign the papers, who can conduct the actual transaction, and what to do if and when any disputes or other problems arise. You also need to be aware of any state-mandated disclosures as to the physical condition of your house. (See the discussion below.)

If you want to go it alone, be sure you have the time, energy, and ability to handle all the details—from setting a realistic price to negotiating offers and closing the deal. Also, be aware that FSBOs are usually more feasible in hot or sellers' markets, where there's more competition for homes, or when you're not in a hurry to sell. And you may not be able to save the whole 5%.

For example, a buyer who is represented by an agent may approach you and agree to complete the transaction only if you pay the commission for the buyer's agent. (Traditionally, that's one-half of the total 5%.)

For more advice on FSBOs, including the involvement of attorneys and other professionals in the house transaction, contact your state department of real estate. Also, check online at www.owners.com.

If you're in California, check out *For Sale by Owner,* by George Devine (Nolo). This book provides step-by-step advice on handling your own sale in California.

Is there some middle ground where I can use a broker on a more limited (and less expensive) basis?

Yes. You might consider doing most of the work yourself—such as showing the house—and hiring a real estate broker for such crucial tasks as:

- setting the price of your house
- advertising your home in the local multiple listing service (MLS) of homes for sale in the area, an online database managed by local boards of realtors, and
- handling some of the more complicated paperwork when the sale closes.

If you work with a broker in a limited way, you may be able to negotiate a reduction of the typical 5% commission, or you may be able to find a real estate agent who charges by the hour for specified services.

Preparing Your House for Sale

Making your house and garden look as attractive as possible may put several thousand dollars in your pocket. At a minimum, sweep the sidewalk; mow and fertilize the lawn; put some pots of blooming flowers by the front door; clean the windows; and fix chipped or flaking paint. Clean and tidy up all rooms and remove both clutter and some furniture, to make them look bigger. Be sure the house smells good—hide the kitty litter box and bake some cookies. Check for loose steps, slick areas, or unsafe fixtures, and deal with everything that might cause injury to a prospective buyer. Take care of minor maintenance issues that might make buyers think you've taken poor care of the house, such as a cracked window, overgrown front yard, leaking faucet, or loose doorknob. You can improve the look of your house without spending much money—a new shower curtain and towels might really spruce up your bathroom, and freshly cut flowers will improve every room. Or you can spend several thousand dollars to have a professional "stage" your house with rented furniture and accessories, a technique some real estate agents swear by.

How much should I ask for my house?

No matter how much you love your house, or how much work you've put into it, you must objectively determine how much your property will fetch on the market—called "appraising" a house's value. The most important appraisal factors are recent sales prices of similar properties in the neighborhood (called "comps").

Real estate agents have access to sales data for the area and can give you a good estimate of what your house should sell for. Many real estate agents will offer this service free, hoping that you will list your house with them. You can also hire a professional real estate appraiser to give you a documented opinion as to your house's value. A number of companies offer detailed comparable sales prices online. See the list of recommended websites at the end of this chapter. Public record offices, such as the county clerk or recorder's office, may also have information on recent house sales.

The asking prices of houses still on the market can also provide guidance (adjusting for the fact that asking prices are typically 10% or more above the usual sales price in slow markets and up to 25% below the selling price in hot markets). To find out asking prices, go to open houses and check newspaper real estate classified ads and online listings of homes for sale.

Do I need to take the first offer that comes in?

You're under no obligation to accept the first or any other offer. In fact, offers, even very attractive ones, are rarely accepted as written. More typically, you will negotiate to accept some, maybe even most, of the offer terms, but propose certain changes, for example:

- price—you want more money
- financing—you want a larger down payment
- occupancy—you need more time to move out
- buyer's sale of current house—you don't want to wait for this to occur
- inspections—you want the buyer to schedule them more quickly.

A contract is formed when either you or the buyer accept all of the terms of the other's offer or counteroffer in writing within the time allowed.

What are my obligations to disclose problems about my house, such as a basement that floods in heavy rains?

In most states, it is illegal to fraudulently conceal major physical defects in your property, such as your troublesome basement. And states are increasingly requiring sellers to take a proactive role by making written disclosures on the condition of the property.

California, for example, has stringent disclosure requirements. California sellers must give buyers a disclosure form listing such defects as a leaky roof, faulty plumbing, deaths that occurred within the last three years on the property, even the presence of neighborhood nuisances, such as a dog that barks every night. In addition, California sellers must disclose potential hazards from floods, earthquakes, fires, environmental hazards (such as mold, asbestos, and lead) and other problems. The form for this is called a Natural Hazard Disclosure Statement. California sellers must also tell buyers about a database maintained by law enforcement authorities on the location of registered sex offenders.

Generally, you are responsible for disclosing only information within your personal knowledge. However, many sellers hire a general contractor to inspect the property. The inspection report will help you determine which items need repair or replacement and will assist you in preparing any required disclosures. The report is also useful in pricing your house and negotiating with prospective buyers.

Full disclosure of any property defects will also help protect you from legal problems from a buyer who seeks to rescind the sale or sues you for damages suffered because you carelessly or intentionally withheld important information about your property.

Check with your real estate broker or attorney, or your state department of real estate, for disclosures required in your state and any special forms you must use. Also, be aware that real estate brokers are increasingly insisting that sellers complete disclosure forms, regardless of whether it's legally required.

What are home warranties, and should I buy one?

Home warranties are service contracts that cover major housing systems—electrical wiring, built-in appliances, heating, plumbing, and the like—for one year from the date the house is sold. Most warranties cost $300 to $500 and are renewable. If something goes wrong with any of the covered systems after the sale closes, the repairs are paid for (minus a modest service fee)—and the new buyer saves money. Many sellers find that adding a home warranty to the deal makes their house more attractive and easier to sell.

Before buying a home warranty, be sure you don't duplicate coverage. You don't need a warranty for the heating system, for example, if your furnace is just six months old and still covered by the manufacturer's three-year warranty.

Your real estate agent or broker can provide more information on home warranties.

Sellers Must Disclose Lead-Based Paint and Hazards

If you are selling a house built before 1978, you must comply with the federal Residential Lead-Based Paint Hazard Reduction Act of 1992 (42 U.S.Code § 4852d), also known as Title X (Ten). You must:

- disclose all known lead-based paint and hazards in the house
- give buyers a pamphlet prepared by the U.S. Environmental Protection Agency (EPA) called *Protect Your Family From Lead in Your Home*
- include certain warning language in the contract, as well as signed statements from all parties verifying that all disclosures (including giving the pamphlet) were made
- keep signed acknowledgments for three years as proof of compliance, and
- give buyers a ten-day opportunity to test the house for lead.

If you fail to comply with Title X, the buyer can sue you for triple the amount of damages suffered—for example, three times the cost of repainting a house previously painted with lead-based paint.

For more information, contact the National Lead Information Center, 800-424-LEAD (phone) or www.epa.gov/lead.

What is the "house closing"?

The house closing is the final transfer of ownership from the seller to the buyer. It occurs after both you and the buyer have met all the terms of the contract and the deed is recorded. (See *Deeds*, below). Closing also refers to the time when the transfer will occur, such as "The closing on my house will happen on January 27 at 10:00 a.m."

Do I need an attorney for the house closing?

This varies depending on state law and local custom. In some states, attorneys are not typically involved in residential property sales, and an escrow or title company handles the entire closing process. In many other states, particularly in the eastern part of the country, attorneys have a more active role in all parts of the house transaction; they handle all the details of offer contracts and house closings. Check with your state department of real estate or your real estate broker for advice.

I'm selling my house and buying another. What are some of the most important tax considerations?

If you sell your home, you may exclude up to $250,000 of your profit (capital gain) from tax. For married couples filing jointly, the exclusion is $500,000. (Unmarried co-owners may also divide the profit and each take a $250,000 exclusion.)

The law applies to sales after May 6, 1997. To claim the whole exclusion, you must have owned and lived in your residence an aggregate of at least two of five years before the sale. You can claim the exclusion once every two years.

Even if you haven't lived in your home a total of two years out of the last five, you are still eligible for a partial exclusion of capital gains if you sold because of a change in employment or health, or due to unforeseen circumstances. You get a portion of the exclusion, based on how long you lived in the house. To calculate it, take the number of months you lived there before the sale and divide it by 24.

For example, if you're an unmarried taxpayer who's lived in your home for 12 months, and you sell it for health reasons at a $100,000 profit, the entire amount would be excluded from capital gains. Because you lived in the house for half of the two-year period, you could claim half the exclusion, or up to $125,000. (12/24 x $250,000 = $125,000.)

For more information on current tax laws involving real estate transactions, see Publication 523, *Selling Your Home*, available from the IRS at 800-829-1040 or at their website, www.irs.gov.

Deeds

Castles in the air are the only property you can own without the intervention of lawyers. Unfortunately, there are no title deeds to them.
—J. FEIDOR REES

Remember playing Monopoly as a kid, where amassing deeds to property—those little color-coded cards—was all-important? Real-life deeds aren't nearly so colorful, but they're still very, very important. Here are some questions commonly asked about deeds.

What is a deed?

A deed is the document that transfers ownership of real estate. It contains the names of the old and new owners and a legal description of the property, and is signed by the person transferring the property.

Do I need a deed to transfer property?

Almost always. You can't transfer real estate without having something in writing.

I'm confused by all the different kinds of deeds—quitclaim deed, grant deed, warranty deed. Does it matter which kind of deed I use?

Probably not. Usually, what's most important is the substance of the deed: the description of the property being transferred and the names of the old and new owners. Here's a brief run-down of the most common types of deeds:

A **quitclaim deed** transfers whatever ownership interest you have in the property. It makes no guarantees about the extent of your interest. Quitclaim deeds are commonly used by divorcing couples; one spouse signs over all his rights in the couple's real estate to the other. This can be especially useful if it isn't clear how much of an interest, if any, one spouse has in property that's held in another spouse's name.

A **grant deed** transfers your ownership and implies certain promises—that the title hasn't already been transferred to someone else or been encumbered, except as set out in the deed. This is the most commonly used kind of deed, in most states.

A **warranty deed** transfers your ownership and explicitly promises the buyer that you have good title to the property. It may make other promises as well, to address particular problems with the transaction.

Does a deed have to be notarized?

Yes. The person who signs the deed (the person who is transferring the property) should take the deed to a notary public, who will sign and stamp it. The notarization means that a notary public has verified that the signature on the deed is genuine. The signature must be notarized before the deed will be accepted for recording. And in some states, deeds must be witnessed, just like wills.

After a deed is signed and notarized, do I have to put it on file anywhere?

Yes. You should "record" (file) the deed in the land records office in the county where the property is located. This office goes by different names in different states; it's usually called the county recorder's office, land registry office, or register of deeds. In most counties, you'll find it in the courthouse.

Recording a deed is simple. Just take the signed, original deed to the land records office. The clerk will take the deed, stamp it with the date and some numbers, make a copy, and give the original back to you. The numbers are usually book and page numbers, which show where the deed will be found in the county's filing system. There will be a small fee, probably about $5 a page, for recording. However, if you're buying or selling a house, the escrow company will normally take care of this for you.

What's a trust deed?

A trust deed (also called a deed of trust) isn't like the other types of deeds; it's not used to transfer property. It's really just a version of a mortgage, commonly used in some states.

A trust deed transfers title to land to a "trustee," usually a trust or title company, which holds the land as security for a loan. When the loan is paid off, title is transferred to the borrower. The trustee has no powers unless the borrower defaults on the loan; then the trustee can sell the property and pay the lender back from the proceeds, without first going to court.

More Information About Deeds

Deeds for California Real Estate, by Mary Randolph (Nolo), contains tear-out deed forms and instructions for transferring California real estate.

For information about deeds in other states, check your local law library.

Online Help

www.nolo.com
Nolo offers information on a wide variety of legal topics, including real estate matters. The website also has several real estate calculators, at www.nolo.com/calculators.

www.homefair.com
Homefair offers lots of information and calculators that will help you move and make relocation decisions. It's especially useful if you're deciding where to live based on home prices, schools, crime, salaries, and other factors.

www.bestplaces.net
Run by Bert Sperling, the guru of "Best of" lists, this site will tell you everything from the best towns for affordable housing to the worst for getting a good night's sleep.

http://realestate.msn.com
This site helps with all aspects of buying or selling a home—from listings and financing to home improvements.

www.ashi.org
The American Society of Home Inspectors offers information on buying a home in good shape, including referrals to local home inspectors.

www.inman.com

Real estate columnist Brad Inman provides the latest real estate news. Also, see www.deadlinenews.com by real estate writer Broderick Perkins.

www.realtylocator.com

Realty Locator provides over 100,000 real estate links nationwide, including property listings, agents, lenders, neighborhood data, real estate news, and resources on everything from home improvement to mortgage calculators.

www.fanniemae.com

Fannie Mae, the nation's largest source of home mortgage loans, offers several useful home affordability mortgage calculators. See the "For Home Buyers & Homeowners" section. It also provides a wide range of consumer information.

www.hsh.com

HSH Associates publishes detailed information on mortgage loans available from lenders across the United States.

www.realtor.com

The official website of the National Association of Realtors lists over one and a half million homes for sale throughout the United States and provides links to real estate broker websites and a host of related realty services.

www.move.com

This website lists new homes and developments in major metropolitan areas.

www.owners.com

This site lists homes sold without a broker, also known as FSBOs (for sale by owner). It also provides useful information for anyone considering selling their home without a real estate agent.

www.escrowhelp.com

Sandy Gadow, author of *The Complete Guide to Your Real Estate Closing* (McGraw-Hill), offers FAQs and articles on this key part of the purchase process.

www.homegain.com

HomeGain is geared toward home sellers. It provides an agent-evaluator service to help you find a real estate agent, a home-valuation tool to help price your home, calculators for a wide variety of tasks, and other resources.

www.domania.com

This site's free Home Price Check service allows you to enter an address and see what other houses in the neighborhood have sold for.

Neighbors

*People have discovered that they can fool the devil,
but they can't fool the neighbors.*

—EDGAR WATSON HOWE

Years ago, problems between neighbors were resolved informally, perhaps with the help of a third person respected by both sides. These days, neighbors—who may not know each other well, if at all—are quicker to head for court. Usually, of course, lawsuits only cost everyone money and exacerbate bad feelings, which makes it even harder for neighbors to coexist peacefully. But knowing the legal ground rules is important; it can help you figure out who's right, who's wrong, and what your opinions are—without having to call in a judge.

Boundaries

Most of us don't know, or care, exactly where our property boundaries are located. But if you or your neighbor wants to fence the property, build a structure, or cut down a tree close to the line, you need to know where the boundary actually runs.

How can I find the exact boundaries of my property?

You can hire a licensed land surveyor to survey the property and place official markers on the boundary lines. A simple survey usually costs about $500; if no survey has been done for a long time, or if the maps are unreliable and conflicting, be prepared to spend $1,000 or more.

My neighbor and I don't want to pay a surveyor. Can't we just make an agreement about where we want the boundary to be?

You and the neighbor can decide where you want the line to be, and then make it so by signing deeds that describe the boundary. If you have a mortgage on the property, consult an attorney for help in drawing up the deeds. You may need to get the permission of the mortgage holder before you give your neighbor even a tiny piece of the land.

Once you have signed a deed, you should record (file) it at the county land records office, usually called the county recorder's office, land registry office, or something similar. Deeds are discussed in more detail in Chapter 1.

What can I do if a neighbor starts using my property?

If a neighbor starts to build on what you think is your property, do something immediately. If the encroachment is minor—for instance, a small fence in the wrong place—you may think you shouldn't worry. But you're wrong. When you try to sell your house, a title company might refuse to issue insurance because the neighbor is on your land.

Also, if you don't act promptly, you could lose part of your property. A person who uses another's land for a long enough time can gain a legal right to continue to do so and, in some circumstances, gain ownership of the property.

Talk to your neighbor right away. Most likely, a mistake has been made because of a conflicting description in the neighbor's deed or just an erroneous assumption about the boundary line. Try to get your neighbor to agree to share the cost of a survey. If your neighbor is hostile and insists on proceeding without the survey, state that you will sue if necessary. Then send a firm letter—or have a lawyer send one on letterhead. If the building doesn't stop, waste no time in having a lawyer get a judge's order to temporarily stop the neighbor until you can bring a civil lawsuit for trespass before the judge. (Usually, mediation is a good way to resolve neighbor issues, but time is of the essence in this situation so you need to call a lawyer right away if you can't agree.)

A Little Common Sense

If you are having no trouble with your property and your neighbors, yet you feel inclined to rush out and determine your exact boundaries just to know where they are, please ask yourself a question. Have you been satisfied with the amount of space that you occupy? If the answer is yes, then consider the time, money, and hostility that might be involved if you pursue the subject.

If a problem exists on your border, keep the lines of communication open with the neighbor, if possible. Learn the law and try to work out an agreement. Boundary lines simply don't matter that much to us most of the time; relationships with our neighbors matter a great deal.

Fences

Local fence ordinances are usually strict and detailed. Most regulate height and location, and some control the material used and even the fence's appearance. Residents of planned unit developments and subdivisions are often subject to even pickier rules. On top of all this, many cities require you to obtain a building permit before you begin construction.

Fence regulations apply to any structure used as an enclosure or a partition. Usually, they include hedges and trees.

How high can I build a fence on my property?

In residential areas, local rules commonly restrict artificial (constructed) backyard fences to a height of six feet. In front yards, the limit is often four feet.

Height restrictions may also apply to natural fences—fences of bushes or trees—if they meet the ordinance's general definition of fences. Trees that are planted in a row and grow together to form a barrier are usually considered a fence. When natural fences are specifically mentioned in the laws, the height restrictions commonly range from five to eight feet.

If, however, you have a good reason (for example, you need to screen your house from a noisy or unsightly neighboring use, such as a gas station), you can ask the city for a one-time exception to the fence law, called a variance. Talk to the neighbors before you make your request, to explain your problem and get them on your side.

My neighbor is building a fence that violates the local fence law, but nothing's happening. How can I get the law enforced?

Cities are not in the business of sending around fence-inspection teams, and as long as no one complains, a nonconforming fence may stand forever.

Tell the neighbor about the law as soon as possible. If the fence is still being built, your neighbor may be able to modify it at a low cost. If the neighbor suggests that you mind your own business, alert the city. All it takes in most circumstances is a phone call to the planning or zoning department or the city attorney's office. If the neighbor refuses to conform, the city can impose a fine and even sue.

My neighbor's fence is hideous. Can I do anything about it?

As long as a fence doesn't pose a threat of harm to neighbors or those passing by, it probably doesn't violate any law just because it's ugly. Occasionally, however, a town or subdivision allows only certain types of new fences—such as board fences—in an attempt to create a harmonious architectural look. Some towns also prohibit certain materials—for example, electrically charged or barbed wire fences.

Even without such a specific law, if a fence is so poorly constructed that it is an eyesore or a danger, it may be prohibited by another law, such as a blighted property ordinance. And if the fence was erected just for meanness—it's high, ugly, and has no reasonable use to the owner—it may be a "spite fence," which means you can sue the neighbor to get it torn down.

The fence on the line between my land and my neighbor's is in bad shape. Can I fix it or tear it down?

Unless the property owners agree otherwise, fences on a boundary line belong to both owners as long as both are using the fence. Both owners are responsible for keeping the fence in good repair, and neither may remove it without the other's permission.

A few states impose harsh penalties on neighbors who refuse to chip in for maintenance after a reasonable request from the other owner. Connecticut, for example, allows one neighbor to go ahead and repair the fence, then sue the other owner for double the cost.

Of course, it's rare that a landowner needs to resort to a lawsuit. Your first step should be to talk to the neighbor about how to tackle the problem. Your neighbor will probably be delighted that you're taking the initiative to fix the fence. When you and your neighbor agree on how to deal with the fence and how much you'll each contribute to the labor and material costs, put your agreement in writing. You don't have to make a complicated contract. Just note the specifics of your agreement and sign your names.

Trees

Woodman, spare that tree.
Touch not a single bough:
In youth it sheltered me,
And I'll protect it now.
— GEORGE POPE MORRIS

We human beings exhibit some complicated, often conflicting, emotions about trees. This is especially true when it comes to the trees in our own yards. We take ownership of our trees and their protection very seriously in this country, and this is reflected in the law.

Can I trim the branches of the neighbor's tree that hang over my yard?

You have the legal right to trim tree branches up to the property line. But you may not go onto the neighbor's property or destroy the tree itself.

Deliberately Harming a Tree

In almost every state, a person who intentionally injures someone else's tree is liable to the owner for two or three times the amount of actual monetary loss. These penalties protect tree owners by providing harsh deterrents to would-be loggers.

Most of a big oak tree hangs over my yard, but the trunk is on the neighbor's property. Who owns the tree?

Your neighbor. It is accepted law in all states that a tree whose trunk stands wholly on the land of one person belongs to that person.

If the trunk stands partly on the land of two or more people, it is called a boundary tree, and in most cases it belongs to all the property owners. All the owners are responsible for caring for the tree, and one co-owner may not remove a healthy boundary tree without the other owners' permission.

My neighbor dug up his yard, and in the process killed a tree that's just on my side of the property line. Am I entitled to compensation for the tree?

Yes. The basic rule is that someone who cuts down, removes, or hurts a tree without permission owes the tree's owner money to compensate for the harm done. You can sue to enforce that right—but you probably won't have to, once you tell your neighbor what the law is.

My neighbor's tree looks like it's going to fall on my house any day now. What should I do?

You can trim back branches to your property line, but that may not solve the problem if you're worried about the whole tree coming down.

City governments often step in to take care of dangerous trees or make the owner do so. Some cities have ordinances that prohibit maintaining any dangerous condition—including a hazardous tree—on private property. To enforce such an ordinance, the city can demand that the owner remove the tree or pay a fine. Some cities will even remove such a tree for the owner. To check on your city's laws and policies, call the city attorney's office.

You might also get help from a utility company, if the tree threatens its equipment. For example, a phone company will trim a tree that hangs menacingly over its lines.

If you don't get help from these sources, and the neighbor refuses to take action, you can sue. The legal theory is that the dangerous tree is a "nuisance" because it is unreasonable for the owner to keep it in its current state, and it interferes with your use and enjoyment of your property. You can ask the court to order the owner to prune or remove the tree. You'll have to sue in regular court (not small claims court) and prove that the tree really does pose a danger to you.

Views

The privilege of sitting in one's home and gazing at the scenery is a highly prized commodity. And it can be a very expensive one. Some potential buyers commit their life savings to properties, assuming that a stunning view is permanent. However, that isn't always the case.

If a neighbor's addition or growing tree blocks my view, what rights do I have?

Unfortunately, you have no right to light, air, or view unless it has been granted in writing by a law or subdivision rule. The exception to this general rule is that someone may not deliberately and maliciously block another's view with a structure that has no reasonable use to the owner.

This rule encourages building and expansion, but the consequences can be harsh. If a view becomes blocked, the law will help only if:

• a local law protects views
• the obstruction violates private subdivision rules, or
• the obstruction violates some other specific law.

How can a view ordinance help?

A few cities that overlook the ocean or other desirable vistas have adopted view ordinances. These laws protect property owners from having their view (usually, the view that they had when they bought the property) obstructed by growing trees. The laws don't cover buildings or other structures that block views.

The ordinances allow someone who has lost a view to sue the tree owner for a court order requiring him or her to restore the view. A neighbor who wants to sue must first approach the tree owner and request that the tree be cut back. The complaining person usually bears the cost of trimming or topping, unless the tree was planted after the law became effective or the owner refuses to cooperate.

Some view ordinances contain extensive limitations that take away much of their power. Some examples:

• Certain species of trees may be exempt, especially if they grew naturally.
• A neighbor may be allowed to complain only if the tree is within a certain distance from the neighbor's property.
• Trees on city property may be exempt.

Cities Without View Ordinances

If your city (like most) doesn't have a view ordinance, you might find help from other local laws. Here are some laws that may help restore your view:

Fence height limits. If a fence is blocking your view, it may violate a local law. Commonly, local laws limit artificial (constructed) fences in back yards to six feet high and in front yards to three or four feet. Height restrictions may also apply to natural fences, such as hedges.

Tree laws. Certain species of trees may be prohibited—for example, trees that cause allergies or tend to harm other plants. Laws may also forbid trees that are too close to a street (especially an intersection), to power lines, or even to an airport.

Zoning laws. Local zoning regulations control the size, location, and uses of buildings. In a single-family area, buildings are usually limited to heights of 30 or 35 feet. Zoning laws also usually require a certain setback (the distance between a structure and the boundary lines). They also limit how much of a lot can be occupied by a structure. For instance, many suburban cities limit a dwelling to 40% to 60% of the property.

I live in a subdivision with a homeowners' association. Will that help me in a view dispute?

Often, residents of subdivisions and planned unit developments are subject to a detailed set of rules called covenants, conditions, and restrictions (CC&Rs). They regulate most matters that could concern a neighbor, including views. For example, a rule may state that trees can't obstruct the view from another lot, or may simply limit tree height to 15 feet.

If someone violates the restrictions, the homeowners' association may apply pressure (for example, by taking away swimming pool or clubhouse privileges) or even sue. A lawsuit is costly and time-consuming, however, and the association may not want to sue unless there have been serious violations of the rules.

If the association won't help, you can take the neighbor to court yourself, but be prepared for a lengthy and expensive ordeal.

I want to buy a house with a great view. Is there anything I can do to make sure I won't ever lose the view—and much of my investment?

First, ask the property owner or the city planning and zoning office whether the property is protected by a view ordinance. Then check with the real estate agent to see whether neighbors are subject to restrictions that would protect your view. Also, if the property is in a planned unit development, find out whether a homeowners' association actively enforces the restrictions.

Check local zoning laws for any property that might affect you. Could the neighbor down the hill add a second-story addition?

Finally, look very closely from the property to see which trees might later obstruct your view. Then go introduce yourself to their owners and explain your concerns. A neighbor who also has a view will probably understand your concern. If someone is unfriendly and uncooperative, you stand warned.

How to Approach a View Problem

Before you approach the owner of a tree that has grown to block your view, answer these questions:

- Does the tree affect the view of other neighbors? If it does, get them to approach the tree owner with you. You could all pitch in to cover trimming costs.

- Which part of the tree is causing view problems for you—one limb, the top, or one side?

- What is the least destructive action that could be taken to restore your view? Maybe the owner will agree to a limited and careful pruning.

- How much will the trimming cost? Be ready to pay for it. Remember that every day you wait and grumble is a day for the trees to grow and for the job to become more expensive. The loss of your personal enjoyment is probably worth more than the trimming cost, not to mention the devaluation of your property (which can be thousands of dollars).

Noise

Nothing so needs reforming as other people's habits.
                                —MARK TWAIN

If you are a reasonable person and your neighbor is driving you wiggy with noise, the neighbor is probably violating a noise law.

Do I have any legal recourse against a noisy neighbor?

You bet. The most effective weapon you have to maintain your peace and quiet is your local noise ordinance. Almost every community prohibits excessive, unnecessary, and unreasonable noise, and police enforce these laws.

Most laws designate certain "quiet hours"— for example, from 10 p.m. to 7 a.m. on weekdays, and until 8 or 9 a.m. on weekends. So running a power mower may be perfectly acceptable at 10 a.m. on Saturday, but not at 7 a.m. Many towns also have decibel level noise limits. When a neighbor complains, they measure the noise with electronic equipment. To find out what your town's noise ordinance says, ask at the public library or the city attorney's office.

Once you've figured out that your neighbor is in fact violating a noise ordinance, try approaching the neighbor in a friendly way and letting the neighbor know the noise is disturbing you. It's always possible that you'll get an apology and the noise will stop. The next step would be to ask the neighbor to attend a mediation session and try to work it out. (To learn about mediation, see Chapter 16.) If all else fails and your neighbor keeps disturbing you, you can also sue and ask the court to award you money damages or to order the neighbor to stop the noise ("abate the nuisance," in legal terms). For money damages alone, you can use small claims court. For a court order telling somebody to stop doing something, you'll have to sue in regular court.

Of course, what you really want is for the nuisance to stop. But getting a small claims court to order your neighbor to pay you money can be amazingly effective. And suing in small claims court is easy and inexpensive, partly because you don't need a lawyer.

Noise that is excessive and deliberate may also violate state criminal laws against disturbing the peace or disorderly conduct. This means that, in very extreme circumstances, the police can arrest your neighbor. Usually, these offenses are punishable by fines or short jail sentences.

The neighbor in the apartment next to mine is very noisy. Isn't the landlord supposed to keep tenants quiet?

In addition to the other remedies all neighbors have, you have another arrow in your quiver: You can lean on the landlord to quiet the neighbor. Standard rental and lease agreements contain a clause entitled "Quiet Enjoyment." This clause gives tenants the right to occupy their apartments in peace, and also imposes upon them the responsibility not to disturb their neighbors. It's the landlord's job to enforce both sides of this bargain.

If the neighbor's stereo is keeping you up every night, the tenants are probably violating the rental agreement, and could be evicted. Especially if several neighbors complain, the landlord will probably order the tenant to comply with the lease or face eviction. For more information about your rights as a tenant, see Chapter 3.

Tips for Handling a Noise Problem

- Know the law and stay within it.
- Be reasonably tolerant of your neighbors.
- Communicate with your neighbors—both the one causing the problem and the others affected by it.
- Assert your rights.
- Ask the police for help when it is appropriate.
- Use the courts when necessary.

My neighbor's dog barks all the time, and it's driving me crazy. What can I do?

Usually, problems with barking dogs can be resolved without resorting to police or courts. If you do eventually wind up in court, however, a judge will be more sympathetic if you made at least some effort to work things out first. Here are the steps to take when you're losing patience (or sleep) over a neighbor's noisy dog:

1. Ask your neighbor to keep the dog quiet. Sometimes owners are blissfully unaware that there's a problem. If the dog barks for hours every day—but only when it's left alone—the owner may not know that you're being driven crazy.

If you can establish some rapport with the neighbor, try to agree on specific actions to alleviate the problem: for example, that your neighbor will take the dog to obedience school, get the dog a citronella collar to prevent barking, or consult with an animal behavior specialist, or that the dog will be kept inside after 10 p.m. After you agree on a plan, set a date to talk again in a couple of weeks.

2. Try mediation. Mediators, both professionals and volunteers, are trained to listen to both sides, identify problems, keep everyone focused on the real issues, and suggest compromises. A mediator won't make a decision for you but will help you and your neighbor agree on a resolution.

Many cities have community mediation groups that train volunteers to mediate disputes in their own neighborhoods. Or ask for a referral from:

- the small claims court clerk's office
- the local district attorney's office—the consumer complaint division, if there is one
- radio or television stations that offer help with consumer problems, or
- a state or local bar association.

For more information on mediation, see Chapter 16.

3. Look up the law. In some places, barking dogs are covered by a specific state or local ordinance. If there's no law aimed specifically at dogs, a general nuisance or noise ordinance makes the owner responsible. Local law may forbid loud noise after 10 p.m., for example, or prohibit any "unreasonable" noise. And someone who allows a dog to bark after numerous warnings from police may be arrested for disturbing the peace.

To find out what the law is where you live, go to a law library and check the state statutes and city or county ordinances yourself. Look in the index under "noise," "dogs," "animals," or "nuisance." For more information on how to do this, see the appendix. Or call the local animal control agency or city attorney.

4. Ask animal control authorities to enforce local noise laws. Be persistent. Some cities have special programs to handle dog complaints.

5. Call the police if you think a criminal law is being violated. Generally, police aren't too interested in barking dog problems. And summoning a police cruiser to a neighbor's house obviously will not improve your already-strained relations. But if nothing else works, and the relationship with your neighbor is shot anyway, give the police a try.

My neighbor just started giving piano lessons at her home—very loud lessons, starting at 7 a.m. on the weekends. What can I do about this?

The first thing you should do is figure out whether your neighbor is breaking any laws. Check your local zoning law to find out whether your neighborhood is zoned for residential use only—if so, your neighbor is in violation. Next, find out whether your neighborhood imposes "quiet hours," during which neighbors can't make excessive noise. Typically, quiet is enforced until at least 8 a.m. on weekends.

Once you know your rights, talk to the other folks on your block (and perhaps those who live behind your noisy neighbor). Are others also bothered by the noise? If so, approach the piano teacher as a group. Explain the problem and present some possible solutions. For example, perhaps your neighbor can soundproof her practice room and agree to hold her first lesson of the day at 9 a.m.

If your neighbor is breaking the law, make that clear—but also emphasize that you have not yet spoken to the police or any other local authority, and that you'd like to work the problem out informally. Don't let yourself get pushed around, however—if your neighbor refuses to be reasonable, explain that you know your legal rights and are prepared to enforce them. And remember, even if your neighbor isn't violating a particular zoning or noise regulation, she may be creating a nuisance.

If your neighbor agrees to your proposed solution, great. (For information about mediation, see Chapter 16.) If not, you might try to solve the problem through neighborhood mediation. If all efforts at compromise fail, you can either complain to local authorities (such as the zoning board, if your neighbor is violating the zoning laws, or the police if your neighbor is breaking a noise ordinance) or take your neighbor to court.

More Information About Neighbor Law

Neighbor Law: Fences, Trees, Boundaries & Noise, by Cora Jordan (Nolo), explains laws that affect neighbors and shows how to resolve common disputes without lawsuits.

Every Dog's Legal Guide, by Mary Randolph (Nolo), is a guide to the laws that affect dog owners and their neighbors.

Online Help

www.nolo.com
Nolo offers information about a wide variety of legal topics, including neighbor law.

www.statelocalgov.net/index.cfm
Piper Resources maintains State and Local Government on the Net, a comprehensive index of websites for states, counties, cities, and towns. Check here first for the local laws that are so important in neighbor disputes.

Landlords and Tenants

*Property has its duties as well
as its rights.*

—THOMAS DRUMMOND

Thirty years ago, custom, not law, controlled how most landlords and tenants interacted with each other. This is no longer true. Today, whether you focus on leases and rental agreements; habitability; discrimination; the amount, use and return of security deposits; how and when a landlord may enter a rental unit; or a dozen other issues, both landlord and tenant must understand their legal rights and responsibilities.

Because landlord-tenant laws vary significantly depending on where you live, remember to check your state and local laws for specifics. A list of state landlord-tenant statutes is included at the end of this chapter. You can find and read the state statutes online. (See "Finding Statutes and Regulations Online" in the appendix.)

Leases and Rental Agreements

It's important to carefully read—and fully understand—the terms of your lease or rental agreement. This piece of paper is the contract that describes many important aspects of the landlord-tenant relationship.

Why is it important to sign a lease or rental agreement?

The lease or rental agreement is the key document of the tenancy. A thorough lease or rental agreement will cover important issues such as:

- the length of the tenancy
- the amount of rent and deposits the tenant must pay

- the number of people who can live on the rental property
- who pays for utilities
- whether the tenant may have pets
- whether the tenant may sublet the property
- the landlord's access to the rental property, and
- who pays attorneys' fees if there is a lawsuit over the meaning or implementation of the agreement.

Leases and rental agreements should always be in writing, even though oral agreements are enforceable for up to one year in most states. Though oral agreements can be easy and informal, they often lead to disputes. If a tenant and landlord later disagree about key issues, such as whether the tenant can sublet, the result is all too likely to be a court argument over who said what to whom, when, and in what context.

What's the difference between a rental agreement and a lease?

The biggest difference is the length of occupancy. A written rental agreement provides for a tenancy of a short period (often 30 days). The tenancy automatically renews at the end of this period unless the tenant or landlord ends it by giving written notice, typically 30 days. For these month-to-month rentals, the landlord can change the terms of the agreement with proper written notice, subject to any rent control laws. This notice is usually 30 days, but it can be shorter in some states if the rent is paid weekly or biweekly or if the landlord and tenant agree to a shorter notice period. In some states, the notice period is longer.

A written lease, on the other hand, gives a tenant the right to occupy a rental unit for a set term—most often for six months or a year, but sometimes longer—as long as the tenant pays the rent and complies with other lease provisions. Unlike a rental agreement, when a lease expires it does not usually automatically renew itself. A tenant who stays on with the landlord's consent usually becomes a month-to-month tenant (with the same terms and conditions that were present in the lease).

In addition, with a fixed-term lease, the landlord cannot raise the rent or change other terms of the tenancy during the lease, unless the changes are specifically provided for in the lease or the tenant agrees.

What happens if a tenant breaks a lease?

As a general rule, a tenant may not legally move out during the lease period unless the landlord consents or has significantly violated its terms—for example, by failing to make necessary repairs, or by failing to comply with an important law concerning health or safety. A few states have laws that allow tenants to break a lease because health problems or a job relocation require a permanent move. A tenant who begins active military service or service in the Public Health Service, National Oceanic and Atmospheric Administration, or National Guard (for more than a month at a time), may break a lease after giving 30 days' notice.

A tenant who breaks a lease without a legally recognized cause will be responsible for the remainder of the rent due under the lease term. In most states, however, a landlord has a legal duty to try to find a new tenant reasonably quickly—no matter what the tenant's reason for leaving—rather than charge the tenant for the total remaining rent due under the lease. Once the next tenant starts paying rent, the old tenant's responsibility for the rent will stop.

When can a landlord legally break a lease and end a tenancy?

A landlord may legally break a lease if a tenant significantly violates its terms or the law—for example, by paying the rent late, keeping a dog in violation of a no-pets clause in the lease, substantially damaging the property, or participating in illegal activities on or near the premises, such as selling drugs.

To end the tenancy for these reasons, the landlord sends the tenant a notice stating that the tenancy has been terminated. State laws are very detailed as to how a landlord must write and deliver (serve) a termination notice. The termination notice may state that the tenancy is over and advise the tenant to vacate the premises or face an eviction lawsuit. Or, the notice may give the tenant a few days to remedy the problem—for example, pay the rent or find a new home for the dog—and thus avoid termination of the tenancy. If a tenant doesn't comply with the termination notice, the landlord can file a lawsuit to evict the tenant.

Tenant Selection

Choosing tenants is the most important decision any landlord makes. To do it well, landlords need a reliable system that helps weed out tenants who will pay their rent late, damage the rental unit, or cause legal or practical problems later.

What's the best way for landlords to screen tenants?

Savvy landlords should ask all prospective tenants to fill out a written rental application that asks for the following information:

- employment, income, and credit history
- identification, such as a driver's license number or Individual Taxpayer Identification Number (ITIN)
- details on past evictions and bankruptcies, and
- references.

Before choosing tenants, landlords should check with previous landlords and other references; verify income, employment, and bank account information; and obtain a credit report. The credit report is especially important because it will indicate whether an applicant has a history of paying rent or bills late, has gone through bankruptcy, or has a heavy debt load compared to income.

How can a landlord avoid discrimination lawsuits when choosing a tenant?

Fair housing laws specify clearly illegal reasons to refuse to rent to a tenant. (For details, see *Housing Discrimination*, below.) Landlords are legally free to choose among prospective tenants as long as their decisions comply with these laws and are based on legitimate business criteria. For example, a landlord is entitled to reject someone with a poor credit history, insufficient income to pay the rent, or past behavior—such as damaging rental property—that makes the person a bad risk. A reasonable occupancy policy limiting the number of people per rental unit—one that is clearly tied to health and safety—can also be a legal basis for refusing tenants.

Housing Discrimination

Not so long ago, a landlord could refuse to rent to an applicant, or could evict a tenant, for almost any reason. If a landlord didn't like your race or religion, or the fact that you had children, you might find yourself out on the street. But times have changed. To protect everyone's right to be treated fairly and to help people find adequate housing, Congress and state legislatures passed laws prohibiting discrimination, most notably the federal Fair Housing Acts.

Examples of Housing Discrimination

The Fair Housing Act and Fair Housing Amendments Act prohibit landlords from taking any of the following actions based on race, religion, or any other protected category:

- advertising or making any statement that indicates a preference based on group characteristic, such as skin color
- falsely saying that a rental unit is no longer available
- setting more restrictive standards, such as higher income requirements, for certain tenants
- refusing to rent to members of certain groups
- failing to accommodate the needs of disabled tenants, such as refusing to allow a guide dog or other service animal
- setting different terms for some tenants, such as adopting an inconsistent policy of responding to late rent payments, or
- terminating a tenancy for a discriminatory reason.

What types of housing discrimination are illegal?

The federal Fair Housing Act and Fair Housing Amendments Act prohibit landlords from choosing or rejecting tenants (or treating tenants differently) on the basis of a group characteristic such as:

- race
- religion
- ethnic background or national origin
- sex
- familial status (including age)
- the fact that the prospective tenant has children (except in certain designated senior housing), or
- mental or physical disability.

In addition, some state and local laws prohibit discrimination based on a person's marital status, sexual orientation, or gender identity; or because an applicant or tenant receives financial assistance from the government. And some cities and counties have added other criteria, such as one's personal appearance.

On the other hand, landlords are allowed to select tenants using criteria that are based on valid business reasons, such as requiring a minimum income or positive references from previous landlords, as long as these standards are applied equally to all tenants.

How does a tenant file a discrimination complaint?

A tenant who thinks that a landlord has broken a federal fair housing law should contact the U.S. Department of Housing and Urban Development (HUD), the agency that enforces the Fair Housing Act. To find the nearest office, call HUD's Fair Housing Information Clearinghouse at 800-343-3442, or check the HUD website at www.hud.gov. HUD will provide a complaint form and will decide whether to pursue the claim. A tenant must file a complaint within one year of the alleged discriminatory act. If HUD decides that the complaint may have merit, it will appoint a mediator to negotiate with the landlord and tenant and reach a settlement (called a "conciliation"). If a settlement can't be reached, the fair housing agency will hold an administrative hearing to determine whether discrimination has occurred.

If the discrimination is a violation of a state fair housing law, the tenant may file a complaint with the state agency in charge of enforcing the law. (In California, for example, the Department of Fair Employment and Housing enforces the state's two fair housing laws.)

Instead of filing a complaint with HUD or a state agency, tenants may file lawsuits directly in federal or state court. If a state or federal court or housing agency finds that discrimination has taken place, a tenant may be awarded damages, including any higher rent the tenant had to pay as a result of being turned down, and damages for humiliation and emotional distress.

Rent and Security Deposits

Landlords may charge whatever the market will bear for rent, except in areas covered by rent control. Many states do, however, have rules as to when and how tenants must pay the rent and how landlords may increase it.

Security deposits are more strictly regulated by state law. Most states dictate how much money a landlord can require, how the funds can be used—for example, whether they can be applied to clean a unit—and when and how the deposit must be returned.

What laws cover rent due dates, late rent, and rent increases?

By custom, leases and rental agreements usually require the tenant to pay rent monthly, in advance. Often rent is due on the first day of the month. However, it is legal for a landlord to require rent to be paid at different intervals or on a different day of the month. Unless state law or the lease or rental agreement specifies otherwise, there is no legally recognized grace period—in other words, if a tenant hasn't paid the rent on time, the landlord can usually terminate the tenancy the day after it is due. Some landlords charge fees for late payment of rent or for bounced checks; these fees are usually legal if they are reasonable. The laws on late fees are in your state's landlord-tenant statutes, listed at the end of this chapter.

For month-to-month rentals, the landlord can raise the rent (subject to any rent control laws) with proper written notice, typically 30 days. With a fixed-term lease, the landlord may not raise the rent during the lease, unless the increase is specifically called for in the lease or the tenant agrees.

How much security deposit can a landlord charge?

All states allow landlords to collect a security deposit when the tenant moves in. Landlords use the deposit to cover unpaid rent and damages or cleaning beyond ordinary wear and tear.

Half the states limit the amount landlords can charge, usually to not more than a month or two's worth of rent.

Many states require landlords to put deposits in a separate account, and some require landlords to pay tenants interest on deposits.

How Rent Control Works

Communities in only four states—California, Maryland, New Jersey, and New York—and the District of Columbia have laws that limit the amount of rent landlords may charge. Rent control ordinances also limit the circumstances in which rent may be increased. Many rent control laws require landlords to have a legal or just cause (that is, a good reason) to terminate a tenancy—for example, if the tenant doesn't pay rent or if the landlord wants to move a family member into the rental unit. Landlords and tenants in New York City, Newark, San Francisco, and other cities with rent control should get a current copy of the ordinance and any regulations interpreting it. Check the phone book for the address and phone number of the local rent control board, or go online to your city's website (all cities with rent control ordinances post them online).

What are the rules for returning security deposits?

The rules vary from state to state, but landlords usually have a set amount of time in which to return deposits, usually 14 to 30 days after the tenant moves out.

Landlords may deduct from a tenant's security deposit as long as they do it correctly and for an allowable reason. Many states require landlords to provide a written, itemized accounting of deductions for unpaid rent and for repairs for damage that was beyond normal wear and tear, together with payment for any deposit balance.

A tenant may sue a landlord who fails to return the deposit in the time and manner required; or who violates other provisions of security deposit laws (such as interest requirements). Tenants often bring these lawsuits in small claims court. If the landlord has intentionally and flagrantly violated the ordinance, in some states a tenant may recover the entire deposit—sometimes even two or three times this amount—plus attorneys' fees and other damages.

The rules for keeping and returning security deposits are in state landlord-tenant statutes, listed at the end of this chapter.

Tenants' Privacy Rights

In most states, landlords have a legal responsibility to keep fairly close tabs on the condition of the property. Tenants however, have the right to be left alone. To balance landlords' responsibilities with tenants' rights to privacy in their homes, laws in many states set rules about when and how landlords may legally enter rented premises.

Under what circumstances may a landlord enter rental property?

Typically, a landlord has the right to legally enter rented premises in cases of emergency, in order to make needed repairs, or to show the property to prospective tenants or purchasers.

Several states allow landlords the right of entry during a tenant's extended absence (often defined as seven days or more), to maintain the property as necessary, and to inspect for damage and needed repairs. In most cases, a landlord may not enter just to check up on the tenant or the rental property.

Must landlords provide notice of entry?

States typically require landlords to provide advance notice (usually 24 hours) before entering a rental unit. Without advance notice, a landlord or manager may enter rented premises while a tenant is living there only in an emergency, such as a fire or serious water leak, or when the tenant gives permission.

To find out how much notice a landlord must give a tenant before entering, check your state's landlord-tenant statutes, listed at the end of this chapter.

Is it legal for a landlord to answer questions about a tenant's credit?

Creditors, banks, and prospective landlords may ask a landlord to provide credit or other information about a current or former tenant. A landlord who sticks to the facts that are relevant to the tenant's creditworthiness (such as whether the tenant paid rent on time) may respond to these inquiries without fear of legal liability. To be extra careful, some landlords insist that tenants sign a release giving the landlord permission to respond to such requests.

Cable Access and Satellite Dishes

The range of entertainment services available from cable companies and wireless providers is growing steadily. But in order for tenants to take advantage of these offerings, they need a building wired with coaxial cable (for cable TV) or an antenna—typically a pizza-sized dish—mounted near their television (for satellite or other wireless TV reception). Many buildings already have cable throughout, and tenants can activate service with a phone call to the cable provider. But if a tenant wants cable in a building that isn't cable-ready, or wants to install a satellite dish or other antenna, the situation gets a little more complicated.

Installing cable or an antenna is known as an "improvement"—and most landlords specify, in their lease or rental agreement, that alterations or improvements require the consent of the landlord. This is just one aspect of the general right landlords have to control their property. However, the rules are a bit different when it comes to telecommunications improvements. The Federal Communications Act (47 U.S.C. §§ 151 and following) decrees that all Americans should have as much access as possible to information that comes through a cable or over the air on wireless transmissions. Landlords cannot unreasonably interfere with that access.

Can a tenant force a landlord to provide cable TV access?

In this situation, the Telecommunications Act doesn't vary the general rule allowing landlords to control their property. If a building is not already wired for cable TV, the landlord can refuse a tenant's request for access. Of course, this would be a short-sighted decision because, in the long run, properties without access will be less desirable and will command a lower rent than properties that offer cable.

Can a tenant demand different cable service than the one offered by the landlord?

Many buildings—particularly multiunit properties—are already wired for cable. In competitive markets, many landlords have secured attractive deals with cable service providers, passing the savings on to tenants. Many landlords have signed "exclusive" contracts with these providers, in which they promise not to allow other cable companies into the building. In most states, residential landlords are free to enter into these contracts. They are also free to simply refuse access to a second provider, even if they haven't signed an exclusive contract with another. In short, if a landlord has decided on a specific provider and wants only that company's cables or services in the building, the tenants' choice will be to sign on with that provider or go without cable altogether.

Does a tenant have a right to install a satellite dish?

The Federal Communications Commission has provided considerable guidance on tenants' rights to install satellite dishes and other antennas. Broadly speaking, tenants may install antennas as long as they are situated within their own rented space and do not pose a safety or structural danger. For example, bolting a dish to the living room wall would normally be permitted. But landlords are free to prohibit placement on an exterior wall or in common areas (such as walkways, roofs, or hallways). Landlords may also refuse permission if the dish presents a danger of injury or violates fire codes, and can require tenants to purchase renters' insurance, which will cover a claim if the device falls or otherwise injures someone.

Can tenants place a dish or other antenna so that reception is optimal?

Under the law, tenants have the right to place an antenna where they'll receive an "acceptable quality" signal. But reception devices that need to maintain a line-of-sight contact with a transmitter, or view a satellite, may not work if they're stuck behind a wall or below the roofline. In particular, a dish must be on a south wall, because satellites are in the southern hemisphere. So what can a tenant whose apartment is too low or has no southern exposure do to get "acceptable" reception?

Tenants in multifamily rentals may mount a dish on a mast as long as it does not extend beyond their exclusive rented space. For example, in a two-story rental, a mast that goes into the space opposite the second story would be acceptable, but one that extended above the roofline would not. Tenants in single-family rentals may use a mast as long as it is not higher than 12 feet above the roofline and is installed in a safe way.

**More Information on
Cable TV and Satellite Dishes**

The Federal Communications Commission (FCC) is the government agency responsible for interpreting the Federal Communications Act. For complete details on the FCC's rule on satellite dishes and other antennas (called the "Over-the-Air Reception Devices Rule"), go to the FCC's website at www.fcc.gov/mb or call the FCC at 888-CALLFCC (toll free). You can find the text of the rule itself at 47 C.F.R. § 1.4000.

Repairs and Maintenance

In 1863, an English judge wrote that "Fraud apart, there is no law against letting [leasing] a tumble-down house." But in 21st century America, it's no longer legal to be a slumlord. Landlords must repair and maintain their rental property or face financial losses and legal problems from tenants—who may withhold rent and pursue other legal remedies—and from government agencies that enforce housing codes.

What are the landlord's repair and maintenance responsibilities?

Under most state and local laws, rental property owners must offer and maintain housing that satisfies basic habitability requirements, such as adequate weatherproofing; available heat, water, and electricity; and clean, sanitary, and structurally safe premises. Local building or housing codes typically set specific standards, such as the minimum amounts of light, ventilation, and electrical wiring. Many cities require

the installation of smoke detectors in residential units and specify security measures involving locks and keys.

To find out more about state laws on repair and maintenance responsibilities, check your state's landlord-tenant statutes listed at the end of this chapter. Your local building or housing authority and health or fire department can provide information on local housing codes and penalties for violations.

What are a tenant's rights if the landlord refuses to maintain the property?

If a landlord doesn't meet his or her legal responsibilities, a tenant usually has several options, depending on the state. These options include:

- paying less rent
- withholding the entire rent until the problem is fixed
- making necessary repairs or hiring someone to make them and deducting the cost from the next month's rent
- calling the local building inspector, who can usually order the landlord to make repairs, or
- moving out, even in the middle of a lease.

A tenant who has lived under substandard conditions can also sue the landlord for a partial refund of rent paid during that time. In some circumstances, the tenant can sue for the discomfort, annoyance, and emotional distress caused by the substandard conditions.

Tenants should check state and local laws and understand available remedies before taking any action, especially before using "repair and deduct" and withholding rent.

What must tenants do to keep the rental property in good shape?

All tenants have the responsibility to keep their own living quarters clean and sanitary. A landlord can usually delegate his repair and maintenance tasks to the tenant in exchange for a reduction in rent. If the tenant fails to do the job well, however, the landlord is not excused from his responsibility to maintain habitability. In addition, tenants must carefully use common areas and facilities, such as lobbies, garages, and pools.

Is a landlord liable if a tenant or visitor is injured on the rental property?

A landlord may be liable to the tenant—or others—for injuries caused by dangerous or defective conditions on the rental property. In order to hold the landlord responsible, the tenant must prove that the landlord was negligent and that the landlord's negligence caused an injury. To do this, the injured person must show that:

- the landlord had control over the problem that caused the injury
- the accident was foreseeable
- fixing the problem (or at least giving adequate warnings) would not have been unreasonably expensive or difficult
- a serious injury was the probable consequence of not fixing the problem
- the landlord failed to take reasonable steps to avert the accident
- the landlord's failure—his negligence—caused the tenant's accident, and
- the tenant was genuinely hurt.

For example, if a tenant falls and breaks his ankle on a broken front door step, the landlord will be liable if the tenant can show that:

- it was the landlord's responsibility to maintain the steps (this would usually be the case, because the steps are part of the common area, which is the landlord's responsibility)
- an accident of this type was foreseeable (falling on a broken step is highly likely)
- a repair would have been easy or inexpensive (fixing a broken step is a minor job)
- the probable result of a broken step is a serious injury (a fall certainly qualifies)
- the landlord failed to take reasonable measures to maintain the steps (this will be easy to prove if the step was broken for weeks, or even days, but less so if the step broke five minutes earlier and showed no previous signs of weakening)
- the broken step caused the injury (this is easy to prove if the tenant has a witness to the fall, but might be hard if there are no witnesses and the landlord claims that the tenant really got hurt somewhere else and is attempting to pin the blame on the landlord), and
- the tenant is really hurt (in the case of a broken bone, this is easy to establish).

A tenant can file a personal injury lawsuit for medical bills, lost earnings, pain and other physical suffering, permanent physical disability, disfigurement, and emotional distress. A tenant can also sue for property damage that results from faulty maintenance or unsafe conditions.

**More Information About
Personal Injury Lawsuits**

How to Win Your Personal Injury Claim, by Joseph L. Matthews (Nolo), provides step-by-step details on how to understand what a claim is worth, prepare a claim for compensation, negotiate a fair settlement, and manage a case without a lawyer.

How can property owners minimize financial losses and legal problems related to repairs and maintenance?

Landlords who offer and maintain housing in excellent condition can avoid many problems. Here's how:

- Clearly set out responsibilities for repair and maintenance in the lease or rental agreement.
- Use a written checklist to inspect the premises and fix any problems before new tenants move in.
- Encourage tenants to immediately report plumbing, heating, weatherproofing, or other defects or safety or security problems—whether in the tenant's unit or in common areas such as hallways and parking garages.
- Keep a written log of all tenant complaints and repair requests, with details as to how and when problems were addressed.
- Handle urgent repairs as soon as possible. Take care of major inconveniences, such as a plumbing or heating problem, within 24 hours. For minor problems, respond in 48 hours. Always keep tenants informed as to when and how the repairs will be made and the reasons for any delays.
- Twice a year, give tenants a checklist on which to report potential safety hazards or maintenance problems that might have

been overlooked. Use the same checklist to inspect all rental units once a year.

Landlord Liability for Criminal Acts and Activities

Can a law-abiding landlord end up financially responsible for the criminal acts of a total stranger? Yes—especially if the crime occurred on rental property where an assault or other crime occurred in the recent past. Rental property owners are being sued with increasing frequency by tenants injured by criminals.

What are the landlord's responsibilities for tenant safety and security?

Property owners are responsible for keeping their premises reasonably safe for tenants and guests. Landlords in most states now have at least some degree of legal responsibility to protect their tenants from would-be assailants and thieves and from the criminal acts of fellow tenants. Landlords must also protect the neighborhood from their tenants' illegal activities, such as drug dealing. These legal duties stem from building codes, ordinances, statutes, and, most frequently, court decisions.

How can a landlord limit responsibility for crime committed by strangers on the rental property?

Effective preventive measures are the best ways to avoid being held liable for others' criminal acts and activities. The following steps will not only limit the likelihood of crime but also reduce the risk that the property owner will be found responsible if a criminal assault or robbery does occur. A landlord should:

- Meet or exceed all state and local security laws that apply to the rental property, such as requirements for deadbolt locks on doors, good lighting, and window locks.

- Realistically assess the crime situation in and around the rental property and neighborhood and implement a security that provides reasonable protection for the tenants—both in individual rental units and in common areas such as parking garages and elevators. Local police departments, the landlord's insurance company, and private security professionals can all provide useful advice on security measures. Often, the most effective measures are the easiest and cheapest, like properly trimming trees and bushes and installing adequate lights. If additional security requires a rent hike, the landlord should discuss the situation with the tenants. Many tenants will pay more for a safer place to live.

- Educate tenants about crime problems in the neighborhood and describe the security measures provided by the landlord—including their limitations.

- Maintain the rental property and conduct regular inspections to spot and fix any security problems, such as broken locks or burned out exterior floodlights. Asking tenants for their suggestions as part of an ongoing repair and maintenance system is also a good idea.

- Handle tenant complaints about dangerous situations, suspicious activities, or broken security items immediately. Failing to do this may saddle a landlord with a higher level of legal liability should a tenant be injured by a criminal act after the landlord learned of a complaint.

The Costs of Crime

The money a landlord spends today on effective crime-prevention measures will pale in comparison to the costs that may result from crime on the premises. Settlements paid by landlords' insurance companies for horrific crimes such as rape and assault are likely to be hundreds of thousands of dollars; jury awards are even larger.

What kinds of legal trouble do landlords face from tenants who deal drugs on the property?

Drug-dealing tenants can cause landlords all kinds of practical and legal problems:

- It will be difficult to find and keep good tenants, and the value of the rental property will plummet.

- Anyone who is injured or annoyed by drug dealers—be it other tenants or people in the neighborhood—may sue the landlord on the grounds that the property is a public nuisance that seriously threatens public safety or morals.

- Local, state, or federal authorities may levy stiff fines against the landlord for allowing the illegal activity to continue.

- Law enforcement authorities may initiate eviction proceedings on their own against drug-dealing tenants. They can also seek criminal penalties against the landlord for knowingly allowing drug dealing on the rental property.

• In extreme cases, the presence of drug dealers may result in government confiscation of the rental property.

How can a property owner avoid legal problems from tenants who deal drugs or otherwise break the law?

There are several practical steps landlords can take to avoid trouble from tenants and limit their legal exposure:

• Screen tenants carefully and choose tenants who are likely to be law-abiding and peaceful citizens. Weed out violent or dangerous individuals to the extent allowable under privacy and antidiscrimination laws, which may limit questions about a tenant's past criminal activity, drug use, or mental illness.

• Don't accept a cash deposit or rental payments.

• Do not tolerate tenants' disruptive behavior. Include an explicit provision in the lease or rental agreement prohibiting drug dealing and other illegal activity by tenants or guests, and promptly evict tenants who violate the clause.

• Be aware of suspicious activity, such as heavy traffic in and out of the rental premises.

• Respond to tenant and neighbor complaints about drug dealing on the rental property. Get advice from police immediately upon learning of a problem.

• Consult with security experts to do everything reasonable to discover and prevent illegal activity on the rental property.

Landlord Liability for Lead Poisoning

Landlords are increasingly likely to be held liable for tenant health problems resulting from exposure to lead and other environmental toxins, even if the landlord didn't cause—or even know about—the danger.

What are a landlord's legal responsibilities regarding lead in rental property?

Because of the health problems caused by lead poisoning, the federal Residential Lead-Based Paint Hazard Reduction Act was enacted in 1992. This law is commonly known as Title X (ten). Environmental Protection Agency (EPA) regulations implementing Title X apply to rental property built before 1978.

Under Title X, before signing or renewing a lease or rental agreement, and before undertaking any renovation, a landlord must give every tenant the EPA pamphlet, *Protect Your Family From Lead in Your Home,* or a state-approved version of this pamphlet. At the start of the tenancy, both the landlord and tenant must sign an EPA-approved disclosure form to prove that the landlord told the tenants about any known lead-based paint hazards on the premises. Property owners must keep this disclosure form as part of their records for three years after the tenancy begins.

A landlord who fails to comply with EPA regulations faces penalties of up to $10,000 for each violation. And a landlord who is found liable for tenant injuries from lead may have to pay three times what the tenant suffered in damages.

 More Information About Lead Hazard Resources

You can get information on the evaluation and control of lead dust, and copies of *Protect Your Family From Lead in Your Home,* by calling the National Lead Information Center at 800-424-LEAD, or checking its website at www.epa.gov/opptintr/lead/nlic.htm. In addition, state housing departments have information on state laws and regulations governing the evaluation and control of lead hazards.

Are there any rental properties exempt from Title X regulations?

These properties are not covered by Title X:

- housing for which a construction permit was obtained, or on which construction was started, after January 1, 1978
- housing certified as lead-free by a state-accredited lead inspector

- lofts, efficiencies, and studio apartments
- short-term vacation rentals of 100 days or less
- a single room rented in a residential dwelling
- housing designed for persons with disabilities, unless any child under the age of six lives there or is expected to live there, and
- retirement communities (housing designed for seniors, where one or more tenants is at least 62 years old), unless children under the age of six are present or expected to live there.

Landlord's Liability for Exposure to Asbestos and Mold

In addition to lead, property owners may be liable for tenant health problems caused by exposure to other environmental hazards, such as asbestos and mold.

Regulations concerning asbestos are issued by the Occupational Safety and Health Administration (OSHA). They set strict standards for the testing, maintenance, and disclosure of asbestos in buildings constructed before 1981. For information, call the nearest OSHA office or check OSHA's website at www.osha.gov.

Mold is the newest environmental hazard fueling lawsuits against rental property owners. Across the country, tenants have won multimillion-dollar cases against landlords for claims of significant health problems—such as rashes, chronic fatigue, nausea, cognitive losses, hemorrhaging, and asthma—allegedly caused by exposure to "toxic molds" in their building. In a typical case, the Delaware Supreme Court, in May 2001, upheld a $1.4 million award to two tenants who suffered asthma and other health problems allegedly caused by mold that grew when the landlord refused to fix leaks in their apartment.

There are no federal or state laws or regulations that set permissible exposure to mold, though California has directed its Department of Health Services to study the issue. New York City's Department of Health has developed guidelines for indoor air quality, which landlords in New York City should follow. In fact, any landlord would be wise to consult them. You can read them online at www.ci.nyc.ny.us (search for "facts about mold"). San Francisco has added mold to its list of nuisances, thereby allowing tenants to sue landlords under private and public nuisance laws if they fail to clean up serious outbreaks (San Francisco Health Code § 581).

Insurance

Both tenants and landlords need insurance to protect their property and bank accounts. Without adequate insurance, landlords risk losing hundreds of thousands of dollars of property to fire or other hazards. While tenants may not have as much at stake financially, they also need insurance—especially tenants with expensive personal belongings. Tenant losses from fire or theft are not covered by the landlord's insurance policy.

How can insurance help protect a rental property business?

A well-designed insurance policy can protect rental property from losses caused by many perils, including fire, storms, burglary, and vandalism. (Earthquake and flood insurance are typically separate and, in some areas, coverage for mold claims may not even be available.) A comprehensive policy will also include liability insurance, covering injuries or losses suffered by others as the result of defective conditions on the property.

Equally important, liability insurance covers the cost (including lawyer's bills) of defending personal injury lawsuits.

Here are some tips on choosing insurance:

• Purchase enough coverage to protect the value of the property and assets.

• Be sure the policy covers not only physical injury but also libel, slander, discrimination, unlawful and retaliatory eviction, and invasion of privacy suffered by tenants and guests.

• Carry liability insurance on all vehicles used for business purposes, including the manager's car or truck.

• Make sure your policy is "occurrence based," not "claims based." Here's the difference: a claims-based policy must be in effect on the date you make the claim—even if it was in place when the incident leading to the claim occurred. Under an occurrence-based arrangement, you can make the claim after the policy has ended, as long as the claim arose while the policy was in effect—which is obviously to your advantage.

If you need more information, *The Legal Guide for Starting & Running a Small Business*, by Fred S. Steingold (Nolo), contains a detailed discussion of small business law, including how to insure your rental property.

What does renter's insurance cover?

The average renter's policy covers tenants against losses to their belongings that occur as a result of fire and theft, up to the amount stated on the face of the policy, such as $25,000 or $50,000.

Most renter policies include deductible amounts of $250 or $500. This means that if a tenant's apartment is burglarized, the insurance company will pay only for the amount of the loss over and above the deductible amount.

In addition to fire and theft, most renter's policies include personal liability coverage ($100,000 is a typical amount) for injuries or damage caused by the tenant—for example, when a tenant's garden hose floods and ruins the neighbor's cactus garden, or a tenant's guest is injured on the rental property due to the tenant's negligence.

Renter's insurance is a package of several types of insurance designed to cover tenants for more than one risk. Each insurance company's package will be slightly different—types of coverage offered, exclusions, the dollar amounts specified, and the deductibles will vary. Tenants who live in a flood- or earthquake-prone area will need to pay extra for coverage. Policies covering flood and earthquake damage can be hard to find; tenants should shop around until they find the type of coverage that they need. There's lots of information on the Web—type "renter's insurance" into your favorite search engine to learn more.

Resolving Disputes

Legal disputes—actual and potential—come in all shapes and sizes for landlords and tenants. Whether it's a disagreement over a rent increase, responsibility for repairs, or return of a security deposit, rarely should lawyers and litigation be the first choice for resolving a landlord-tenant dispute.

How can landlords and tenants avoid disputes?

Both landlords and tenants should follow these tips to avoid legal problems:

- Know your rights and responsibilities under federal, state, and local law.
- Make sure the terms of your lease or rental agreement are clear.
- Keep communication open. If there's a problem—for example, a disagreement about the landlord's right to enter a tenant's apartment—see if you can resolve the issue by talking it over, without running to a lawyer.
- Keep copies of any correspondence, and make notes of conversations about any problems. For example, a tenant should ask for repairs in writing and keep a copy of the letter. The landlord should keep a copy of the repair request and note when and how the problem was repaired.

We've talked about the problem and still don't agree. What should we do next?

If you can't work out an agreement on your own but want to continue the rental relationship, consider mediation by a neutral third party. Unlike a judge, the mediator has no power to impose a decision but will simply work with you both to help find a mutually acceptable solution to the dispute. Mediation is often available at little or no cost from a publicly funded program.

State Landlord-Tenant Statutes

Here are some of the key statutes pertaining to landlord-tenant law in each state. In some states, important legal principles are contained in court opinions, not codes or statutes. Court-made law is not reflected in this chart.

Alabama	Ala. Code §§ 35-9-1 to 35-9-100	**Maryland**	Md. Code Ann. [Real Prop.] §§ 8-101 to 8-604
Alaska	Alaska Stat. §§ 34.03.010 to 34.03.380	**Massachusetts**	Mass. Gen. Laws Ann. ch. 186, §§ 1 to 22
Arizona	Ariz. Rev. Stat. Ann. §§ 12-1171 to 12-1183; §§ 33-1301 to 33-1381; 33-301 to 33-381	**Michigan**	Mich. Comp. Laws §§ 554.131 to .201 & 554.601 to 554.641
Arkansas	Ark. Code Ann. §§ 18-16-101 to 18-16-306; 18-16-501 to 18-16-508	**Minnesota**	Minn. Stat. Ann. §§ 504B.001 to 504B.471
California	Cal. Civ. Code §§ 1925 to 1954, 1961 to 1962.7	**Mississippi**	Miss. Code Ann. §§ 89-7-1 to 89-8-27
Colorado	Colo. Rev. Stat. §§ 38-12-101 to 38-12-104, 38-12-301 to 38-12-302, 13-40-101 to 13-40-123	**Missouri**	Mo. Rev. Stat. §§ 441.005 to 441.880, §§ 535.150 to 535.300
Connecticut	Conn. Gen. Stat. Ann. §§ 47a-1 to 47a-74	**Montana**	Mont. Code Ann. §§ 70-24-101 to 70-26-110
Delaware	Del. Code Ann. tit. 25, §§ 5101 to 5907	**Nebraska**	Neb. Rev. Stat. §§ 76-1401 to 76-1449
Dist. of Columbia	D.C. Code Ann. §§ 42-3201 to 42-3610; D.C. Mun. Regs., tit. 14, §§ 300 to 311	**Nevada**	Nev. Rev. Stat. Ann. §§ 118A.010 to 118A.520; 40-215 to 40.280
Florida	Fla. Stat. Ann. §§ 83.40 to 83.682	**New Hampshire**	N.H. Rev. Stat. Ann. §§ 540:1 to 540:29, 540-A:1 to 540-A:8
Georgia	Ga. Code Ann. §§ 44-7-1 to 44-7-81	**New Jersey**	N.J. Stat. Ann. §§ 46:8-1 to 46:8-50; 2A:42-1 to 42-96
Hawaii	Haw. Rev. Stat. §§ 521-1 to 521-78	**New Mexico**	N.M. Stat. Ann. §§ 47-8-1 to 47-8-51
Idaho	Idaho Code §§ 6-201 to 6-324, §§ 55-208 to 55-308	**New York State**	N.Y. Real Prop. Law §§ 220 to 238; Real Prop. Acts §§ 701 to 853; Mult. Dwell. Law (all); Mult. Res. Law (all); Gen. Oblig. Law §§ 7-103 to 7-108
Illinois	735 Ill. Com. Stat. §§ 5/9-201 to 321 & 765 Ill. Comp. Stat. §§ 705/0.01 to 742/30	**North Carolina**	N.C. Gen. Stat. §§ 42-1 to 42-14.2, 42-25.6 to 42-76
Indiana	Ind. Code Ann. §§ 32-31-1-1 to 32-31-8-6	**North Dakota**	N.D. Cent. Code §§ 47-16-01 to 47-16-41
Iowa	Iowa Code Ann. §§ 562A.1 to 562A.36	**Ohio**	Ohio Rev. Code Ann. §§ 5321.01 to 5321.19
Kansas	Kan. Stat. Ann. §§ 58-2501 to 58-2573	**Oklahoma**	Okla. Stat. Ann. tit. 41, §§ 101 to 136
Kentucky	Ky. Rev. Stat. Ann. §§ 383.010 to 383.715	**Oregon**	Or. Rev. Stat. §§ 90.100 to 91.225
Louisiana	La. Rev. Stat. Ann. §§ 9:3251 to 9:3261; La. Civ. Code Ann. art. 2668 to 2729	**Pennsylvania**	68 Pa. Cons. Stat. Ann. §§ 250.101 to 250.510-B, §§ 399.1 to 399.18
Maine	Me. Rev. Stat. Ann. tit. 14, §§ 6001 to 6046	**Rhode Island**	R.I. Gen. Laws §§ 34-18-1 to 34-18-57

State Landlord-Tenant Statutes, cont'd.			
South Carolina	S.C. Code Ann. §§ 27-40-10 to 27-40-940	Virginia	Va. Code Ann. §§ 55-218.1 to 55-248.40
South Dakota	S.D. Codified Laws Ann. §§ 43-32-1 to 43-32-30	Washington	Wash. Rev. Code Ann. §§ 59.04.010 to 59.04.900, 59.18.010 to 59.18.911
Tennessee	Tenn. Code Ann. §§ 66-28-101 to 66-28-521	West Virginia	W.Va. Code §§ 37-6-1 to 37-6-30
Texas	Tex. Prop. Code Ann. §§ 91.001 to 92.354	Wisconsin	Wis. Stat. Ann. §§ 704.01 to 704.50; Wis. Admin. Code §§ 134.01 to 134.10
Utah	Utah Code Ann. §§ 57-17-1 to 57-17-5, 57-22-1 to 57-22-6	Wyoming	Wyo. Stat. §§ 1-21-1201 to 1-21-1211, §§ 34-2-128 to 34-2-129
Vermont	Vt. Stat. Ann. tit. 9, §§ 4451 to 4468		

More Information About Mediation

For information on local mediation programs, call your mayor's or city manager's office and ask for the staff member who handles "landlord-tenant mediation matters" or "housing disputes." That person should refer you to the public office, business, or community group that handles landlord-tenant mediations.

You can learn more about mediation in Chapter 16 of this book.

If mediation doesn't work, is there a last step before going to a lawyer?

If you decide not to mediate your dispute, or mediation fails, it's time to pursue other legal remedies. If the disagreement involves money, such as return of the security deposit, you can take the case to small claims court. A few states use different names for this type of court (such as "landlord-tenant court"), but the purpose is the same for all: to provide a speedy, inexpensive resolution of disputes that involve relatively small amounts of money.

Keep in mind that your remedy in small claims court may be limited to an award of money damages. The maximum amount you can sue for varies from $1,500 to $10,000, depending on your state.

You can find more information about small claims court in Chapter 16.

More Information About Landlord-Tenant Law

From the landlord's point of view:
Every Landlord's Legal Guide, by Marcia Stewart, Ralph Warner, and Janet Portman (Nolo). This 50-state book provides extensive legal and practical information on leases, tenant screening, rent, security deposits, privacy, repairs, property managers, discrimination, roommates, liability, tenancy termination, and much more. It includes more than 30 legal forms and agreements as tear-outs and on disk.

LeaseWriter Plus (Nolo)(CD-ROM for Windows). This software program generates a customized legal residential lease or rental agreement, plus more than a dozen key documents and forms every landlord and property manager needs. It includes a database to track tenants and rental properties, and a log for rental payments, repairs, and problems. The program gives you instant access to state-specific landlord-tenant information and extensive online legal help.

Every Landlord's Tax Deduction Guide, by Stephen Fishman (Nolo). This book explains the many tax write-offs available to landlords and provides advice on maximizing deductions, claiming credit and losses, filling out necessary tax forms, and much more.

Every Landlord's Guide to Finding Great Tenants, by Janet Portman (Nolo). This book gives you a system (including detailed forms) for finding, choosing—and legally rejecting—tenants.

From the tenant's point of view:

Every Tenant's Legal Guide, by Janet Portman and Marcia Stewart (Nolo). This book gives tenants in all 50 states the legal and practical information they need to deal with their landlords and protect their rights when things go wrong. It covers all important issues of renting, including signing a lease, getting a landlord to make needed repairs, fighting illegal discrimination, protecting privacy rights, dealing with roommates, getting the security deposit back fairly, moving out, and much more.

Renters' Rights, by Janet Portman and Marcia Stewart (Nolo). A concise, highly accessible guide for tenants in every state, loaded with tips and strategies.

For both landlords and tenants:

Everybody's Guide to Small Claims Court, by Ralph Warner (National and California Editions)(Nolo). The book explains how to evaluate your case, prepare for court, and convince a judge you're right. It also tells you what remedies (money only, or en-

forcement of the lease) are available in your state.

Mediate, Don't Litigate, by Peter Lovenheim and Lisa Guerin (Nolo), explains how to choose a mediator, prepare a case, and navigate the mediation process. (Available only as an eBook from www. nolo.com.)

Additionally, tenants' unions and rental property owners' associations are good sources of advice. Look in your telephone book's white pages for names of these organizations.

For tenants renting commercial property:

Negotiate the Best Lease for Your Business, by Janet Portman and Fred S. Steingold (Nolo). Gives commercial tenants the information they need to understand and negotiate a commercial lease, plus tips on finding suitable space, choosing and working with brokers and lawyers, and bargaining effectively for the best terms and conditions.

 Online Help

www.nolo.com
Nolo offers information about a wide variety of legal topics, including landlord-tenant law, and provides links to federal and state statutes.

http://tenant.net
TenantNet provides information about landlord-tenant law, with a focus on tenants' rights. TenantNet is designed primarily for tenants in New York City, but the site offers information about the law in many other states. The site also provides the text of the federal fair housing law.

www.statelocalgov.net
This directory has links to many cities that have posted their ordinances (and often their rent control laws) online.

Workplace Rights

I like work; it fascinates me.
I can sit and look at it for hours.

—JEROME K. JEROME

If you're like most workers, you have experienced occasional job-related problems or have questions about whether you are being treated fairly—and legally—on the job. Here are several common problems:

- You were not hired for a job and you suspect it was because of your race, national origin, age, sex, sexual orientation, religion, or disability.

- Your employer promoted a less-qualified person to fill a position you were promised.

- You are regularly forced to work overtime but are not given extra pay, or you are paid for your overtime hours at your regular pay rate (rather than time-and-a-half).

- You need to take a leave of absence from your job to care for a sick parent, but you are concerned that this will jeopardize your job or your eligibility for a promotion.

- You have been called to serve on a jury and wonder if your employer must pay you for this time.

- You want to know whether your employer can read your emails or monitor your telephone conversations.

- You have been laid off and you want to know whether you're entitled to unemployment compensation or severance pay, and when you will get your final paycheck.

Federal laws provide a number of basic guarantees for most workers—such as the right to work free from discrimination, to take leave for certain reasons, and to be notified in advance if you will lose your job due to a plant closing or large-scale layoff. Many states give workers additional rights—for example, to receive a higher minimum wage or to take time off to attend a child's school conference or serve on a jury. And some local governments provide even more protections. Your employer must follow whichever law—federal, state, or local—provides you the most protection.

Fair Pay and Time Off

*I do not like work even when
someone else does it.*

—MARK TWAIN

These days, most of us spend at least half of our waking hours working. Ideally, this time will be spent on jobs that are fulfilling. But whether or not we enjoy our work, all of us want to be paid fairly and on time—and to be able to take time off to tend to important obligations and emergencies. Fortunately, both state and federal laws protect these rights.

Which laws cover pay and work hours?

The Fair Labor Standards Act (FLSA), is the major federal law that covers wages and hours of work (29 U.S.C. §§ 201-219). It regulates how much workers must be paid, how many hours they can be required to work, and the special rules that apply to younger workers. The law includes provisions on:

- minimum wage
- hours worked
- overtime, and
- child labor.

The FLSA applies to most employers, including the federal government, state and local governments, schools, and virtually all private employers.

In addition, your state probably has a wage and hour law that covers the same basic topics. Many state laws give workers more rights than the federal law, so it's always a good idea to become familiar with what your state requires. And a few municipalities also impose rules on local employers, including rules setting a higher minimum wage. Your employer must follow whichever law is most beneficial to you.

What is the minimum wage?

The current federal minimum wage is $5.85 per hour. On July 24, 2008 it will increase to $6.55, and on July 24, 2009 it will go up again, to $7.25 per hour. Additionally, states have their own minimum wage laws that require a higher rate of pay. For example, Rhode Island's current minimum wage is $7.40 per hour. Employers must pay whichever minimum wage rate—federal or state—is higher. To find out the minimum wage rates in the 50 states, the District of Columbia, Puerto Rico, and Guam, go to www.dol.gov/esa/minwage/america.htm, a page on the U.S. Department of Labor's website that lists each state's minimum wage. You can also contact your state labor department for information.

In addition, some cities and counties have enacted so-called "living wage" ordinances, which require certain employers to pay a higher minimum wage. Many of these laws cover only employers that have contracts with, or receive subsidies from, the state or county, but some apply more broadly to private employers in the area. To find out whether your area has a living wage ordinance, contact your local government offices or go to the website of the Economic Policy Institute at www.epinet.org and click "living wage."

How can I figure out whether I am entitled to overtime pay?

First, check to see whether your employer is covered by the FLSA or your state's wage and hour law. Because the coverage of these laws is so broad, you can be pretty sure that your employer must comply with them. The next step is to figure out whether you are considered an "exempt" employee under these laws—if you are exempt, then you are not entitled to overtime.

The following workers are exempt (and, therefore, not entitled to overtime):

- outside salespeople

- independent contractors

- certain computer specialists, including computer system analysts, programmers, and software engineers, as long as they are paid at least $27.63 per hour or at least $455 per week

- employees of seasonal amusement or recreational businesses

- farmworkers

- transportation workers

- newspeople

- employees of motion picture theaters, and

- commissioned employees of retail or service businesses, if their regular rate of pay is more than one and a half times the minimum wage and more than half their pay comes from commissions.

The largest categories of exempt workers—and the categories employers are most likely to try to shoehorn their workers into—are executive, administrative, and professional workers. If you earn a salary of at least $455 per week and you routinely exercise discretion, supervise other employees, make high-level decisions, and/or work in a professional or creative field, you probably fall within one of these exemptions. However, some employers—in an effort to avoid paying overtime—claim that their employees fall into one of these categories even though the employees actually perform fairly routine tasks. For example, a fast-food restaurant may classify many of its employees as assistant managers (and schedule them to work lots of unpaid overtime) but assign them the same basic tasks as the rest of its workforce. Employers can face significant penalties—and costly lawsuits—for relying on this type of ruse.

If you are not exempt, then you are probably entitled to overtime if you work more than 40 hours in a week or, in a few states, more than eight hours in a day. To learn more about your state's overtime requirements, contact your state department of labor.

Does my employer have to pay me overtime if I work more than eight hours in a day?

Under the FLSA, your employer does not have to pay you overtime if you work more than eight hours in any given day. The federal law is interested only in weeks, not days—as long as you work less than 40 hours in a week, you aren't entitled to overtime.

In this area, however, it's definitely worth checking to see what your state law has to say on the subject. Some states, such as California, require employers to pay overtime to employees who work more than eight hours in a day. Your employer must comply with whichever law—federal or state—is most beneficial to you.

Can my employer require me to take time off instead of paying me time-and-a-half for overtime hours?

Most workers are familiar with compensatory or comp time—the practice of offering employees time off from work in place of cash payments for overtime.

However, compensatory time is generally illegal under federal law, except for state and federal government employees. Some states allow private employers to give employees comp time instead of cash. But there are complex, often conflicting laws about how and when it may be given. A common control, for example, is that employees must voluntarily request in writing that comp time be given instead of overtime pay—before the extra hours are worked. Check with your state's labor department for special laws on comp time in your area.

Many employers and employees routinely violate the rules governing the use of compensatory time in place of cash overtime wages. However, such violations are risky. Employees can find themselves unable to collect money due them if a company goes out of business or they are fired. And employers can end up owing large amounts of overtime pay to employees as the result of a labor department prosecution of compensatory time violations.

If you would prefer to have time off rather than overtime pay, you can ask your employer to rearrange your work hours to accomplish this without violating the law. For example, if you usually work eight hours a day, five days a week, you could work four ten-hour days and take the fifth day off (as long as your state doesn't have a daily overtime standard—that is, doesn't count anything over eight hours in a day as overtime). Or, your employer can use the time-and-a-half overtime pay to cover hours you take off during the same pay period. For example, if you usually work 40 hours a week and are paid every two weeks, you could work 50 hours in one week and 25 the next, without changing your weekly pay amount. Because you would be entitled to

be paid for 15 extra hours for the first week (ten hours at time-and-a-half pay = 15 hours of pay), you could simply take 15 hours off the next week and come out even.

Can my boss force me to work overtime?

Under the federal FLSA, your employer can force you to work overtime and can even fire you if you refuse to do so.

The FLSA does not limit the number of hours in a day or days in a week that an employer can schedule an employee to work. It only requires employers to pay nonexempt employees overtime (time and a half the worker's regular rate of pay) for any hours over 40 that the employee works in a week.

However, your state law may provide additional rights, such as the daily overtime standard explained above. Contact your state labor department to learn more.

My boss says that because I earn tips on the job, he can pay me less than the minimum wage. Is this true?

It depends on how generous your customers are. Generally, employers must pay all employees at least the minimum wage. But the calculations become tricky when an employee routinely receives at least $30 per month in tips. Under federal law, employers are allowed to credit a portion of those tips against the minimum wage requirement, which, under federal law, is currently $5.85 per hour (on July 24, 2008 it adjusts to $6.55, and on the same date in 2009 it rises to $7.25). Employers can pay you as litle as $2.13 an hour, as long as you earn enough in tips to bring your hourly pay up to at least the minimum wage.

EXAMPLE: Alphonse is employed as a waiter and earns more than $10 per hour in tips. Denis, the restaurant's owner, is required to pay Alphonse at least $2.13 per hour on top of his tips for the first 40 hours worked in each week.

If business slows and Alphonse's tips dip to, say, $1 an hour, Denis must pay at least $4.85 per hour, which is the additional salary required to make up the full amount of minimum wage Alphonse is owed: $5.85 an hour.

Some states don't allow employers to pay tipped employees less than the minimum wage, no matter how much the employees earn in gratuities. If you work in one of those states, your employer may not take a tip credit and must pay you at least the minimum hourly wage. Contact your state labor department for information on your state's law.

I am required to carry a beeper 24 hours a day, every day of the week for my job. I am occasionally called on my vacation, holidays, and other days off. Am I entitled to be paid anything for on-call time?

Under federal law, vacation days, holidays, and other paid days off work should be just that—days off work—and you are entitled to enjoy them free from the reins of your beeper. When your employer requires you to be on call but does not require you to stay on the company's premises, the following two rules generally apply:

- On-call time that you control and use for your own enjoyment or benefit is not counted as payable time.

- On-call time over which you have little or no control and which you cannot use for your own enjoyment or benefit is payable time.

Disputes usually boil down to the meaning of control and use of time. If the occasional beep beckons you only to call in to give advice, but you are otherwise free to spend your time any way you want, your employer need only pay for the time you spend answering the beeper. However, if your employer insists that you be available to return to work on demand and puts constraints on your behavior between beeper calls—you cannot consume alcohol, or you must stay within a certain radius of work, for example—you may be entitled to compensation for your on-call time.

Similarly, if you receive five or six beeper calls on every day off, and if each of those beeps requires you to come into the office or be in a specific place, then a court will likely see that your time isn't your own and will require that your employer compensate you.

And—as always—be sure to check with your state labor department to see whether your state has different rules.

What laws ensure my right to take vacations?

Here's a surprising legal truth that most workers would rather not learn: No federal law requires employers to pay you for time off, such as vacation or holidays. This means that if you receive a paid vacation, it's because of custom, not law.

And just as vacation benefits are discretionary with each employer, so are the rules about how and when they accrue. For example, it is perfectly legal for an employer to require a certain length of employment—six months or a year are common—before an employee is entitled to take any vacation time. It is also legal for employers to prorate vacations for part-time employees, or to deny them the benefit completely. Employers are also free to set limits on how much paid time off employees may earn before it must be taken.

However, some states prohibit "use it or lose it" vacation policies, which take away accrued vacation hours if employees don't use their time off by a certain deadline (often, the end of the year). To find out whether your state has such a rule, contact your state labor department.

Even with this kind of rule, it may still be legal for your employer to prohibit you from accumulating more hours once you have a certain number of hours in the bank.

If I lose or leave my job, when will I receive my final paycheck?

State law, not federal law, determines when employees must receive their final paychecks, so the answer to this question depends on where you live. Final-paycheck laws usually distinguish between employees who quit and those who are fired—the latter are often entitled to receive their paycheck a bit sooner. For example, a state might mandate that a fired employee receive all accrued wages and vacation pay immediately, but require an employee who quits to wait 72 hours—or even until the next regularly scheduled payday. To find out what your state's law requires, contact your state labor department.

Independent Contractors Are Exempt

The Fair Labor Standards Act covers only employees, not independent contractors, who are considered independent businesspeople. Whether a person is an employee for purposes of the FLSA, however, generally turns on whether that worker is employed by a single employer, and not on the sometimes more lax Internal Revenue Service definition of an independent contractor.

If nearly all of your income comes from one company, a court would probably rule that you are an employee of that company for purposes of the FLSA, regardless of whether other details of your worklife would appear to make you an independent contractor.

The FLSA was passed to clamp down on employers who cheated workers of their fair wages. As a result, employee status is broadly interpreted so that as many workers as possible are protected by the law. In recent cases on this issue, courts have tended to classify workers as employees rather than independent contractors.

Courts are more likely to find that workers are employees when:

- the relationship appears to be permanent
- the worker lacks bargaining power with regard to the terms of his or her employment, and
- the individual worker is economically dependent upon the business to which he or she provides services.

Am I entitled to take time off from work if I get sick?

No federal law requires an employer to offer *paid* time off for illness (although a handful of states have temporary disability programs that offer workers some wage replacement if they must miss work for specified reasons). However, the Family and Medical Leave Act (FMLA), a federal law passed in 1993, gives workers some rights to *unpaid* leave for qualifying medical reasons, or to bond with a new child. Under the FMLA, you may be eligible for up to 12 weeks of unpaid leave during a 12-month period. Your employer can count your accrued paid benefits—vacation, sick leave, and personal leave days—toward the 12 weeks of leave allowed under the law. But many employers give employees the option of deciding whether or not to include paid leave time as part of their 12 weeks of sick leave.

The FMLA applies to all private and public employers with 50 or more employees—an estimated one-half of the workforce. To be covered under the law, you must:

- be employed within a 75-mile radius of 50 or more employees of the same company
- work for the employer for a year or more, and
- work at least 1,250 hours (about 24 hours a week) during the year preceding the leave.

There are a number of loopholes in the FMLA. For example, schoolteachers and instructors who work for educational agencies and private elementary or secondary schools may have restrictions on their FMLA leave. If you and your spouse both work for the same employer, your total leave allotment may be restricted when taking leave to bond with a new child. And if you are among the highest-paid 10% of employees, you may not be entitled to reinstatement as normally required.

A number of states have passed their own versions of family leave laws—and most of them give workers more liberal leave rights. A number of laws apply, for example, to smaller workplaces and extend to workers who have been on the job only a short time. Check with your state's department of labor for more information.

What if a member of my family gets sick—can I take time off to care for him or her?

Possibly. Workers' rights under the FMLA—or under your state's version of it—also apply if a member of your immediate family has a qualifying condition. And your state may allow you to use at least some of your paid sick leave (if your employer provides it) to care for a sick family member. Contact your state's department of labor to find out whether it has this kind of leave law.

My employer refused to grant me the time off for sick leave guaranteed by the FMLA. What can I do?

The FMLA is enforced by the U.S. Department of Labor. If you have specific questions about this law, including how to file a claim against your employer for failing to comply, contact your local Department of Labor office. You can find a list of local offices at the Department of Labor's website at www.dol.gov.

You generally must file a claim under the FMLA within two years of an employer's violation. If the violation was willful (intentional), you'll have up to three years to file.

Does my employer have to pay me for time I spend on jury duty?

No federal law requires employers to pay employees for jury duty, but some state laws do. Most states prohibit employers from penalizing an employee who is called for jury duty or actually serves on a jury. However, relatively few states require private employers to pay their workers for this time. And some of these states place limits on the amount an employer must pay—for example, by allowing the employer to pay only for a certain number of days off or to subtract any amounts the employee receives from the court from his or her regular wages. To find out about any protections offered in your state, contact your state labor department.

Can I take time off work to vote?

This is another state law issue. Many states require employers to give employees some time off to cast their ballots—and prohibit employers from disciplining employees who take time off for this purpose—but a number of restrictions apply. For example, some states give an employee the right to take time off only if the employee otherwise wouldn't have enough time, before or after work, to make it to the polls. Some states require employers to pay workers for this time; others do not. And a few states allow employers to require workers to give advance notice or provide proof that they actually voted to take advantage of these legal protections. For information on your state's rules, contact your state labor department.

If I am called to serve in the military, does my employer have to hold my job open for me until I return?

Federal and state laws provide strong protections for workers who must leave their jobs for military service. Under the Uniformed Services Employment and Reemployment Rights Act of 1994 (USERRA), employers may not discriminate against employees who are called to serve in the armed forces, National Guard, or Reserve. (38 U.S.C. §§ 4301 and following.)

USERRA also entitles an employee who takes time off to serve in the armed forces to job reinstatement, if the employee meets these conditions:

- the employee must have given notice, before taking leave, that the leave was for military service
- the employee must have spent no more than five years on leave for military service (with some exceptions)
- the employee must have been released from military service under honorable conditions, and
- the employee must report back or apply for reinstatement within specified time limits (these limits vary depending on the length of the employee's leave).

Workers must be returned to the position they would have held had they been continuously employed throughout their leave, as long as they are otherwise qualified for that job. This means that you are entitled to more than simple reinstatement to your old position; you also have the right to receive any promotions, increased pay, or additional job responsibilities you would have gotten had you never taken leave—but only if you are qualified to do that job. If you are not qualified, your employer must try to get you qualified. You are also entitled to the benefits and seniority you would have earned had you been continuously employed. For purposes of your employer's benefits plans and leave policies, the time you spent on leave must be counted as time worked.

Returning members of the military receive one additional benefit: You cannot be fired without cause for up to one year after you are reinstated (the exact length of this protection depends on the length of your military service), regardless of your employer's policies or practices.

To find out more about USERRA, check out the website of the Department of Labor, at www.dol.gov. For lots of free information on the law, see the website of the National Committee for Employer Support of the Guard and Reserve, at www.esgr.com.

In addition to these federal protections, almost every state has a law prohibiting discrimination against those in the state's militia or National Guard—and some of these laws provide the same protections available under USERRA. Most state laws also require employers to grant leave to employees for certain types of military service. Some states require leave only for those employees called to active duty; other states require leave for those called for training as well. Employees who take military leave are not generally entitled to pay, although many private employers choose to pay at least a portion of the employee's salary for time spent on leave. To find out about your state's law, contact your state department of labor.

Can I take time off work to attend school conferences with my child's teacher?

Although the federal leave laws do not require employers to provide time off for their employees to attend school events, some state laws do. These laws vary in their particulars, including which employees are eligible for leave, which employers have to provide leave, and how much time an employee may take off during the course of a year. To find out whether your state has a leave law that applies to school activities, check with your state's department of labor.

More Information About Wages, Hours, and Time Off

You can check into your employer's wage and payment policies by calling the local U.S. Labor Department, Wage and Hour Division office, listed in the federal government section of your telephone directory.

Most of the exemptions to FLSA coverage are listed in the statute at 29 U.S.C. § 213. The most direct way to become familiar with these exemptions is to read about them in an annotated edition of the U.S. Code, which is what your local law library (or even a large public library) is most likely to have. You can also find this law through Nolo's Legal Research Center at www.nolo.com/statute/federal. cfm. You can also read a summary of the law's provisions in *The Essential Guide to Federal Employment Laws*, by Amy DelPo & Lisa Guerin (Nolo).

The Department of Labor's website (www.dol. gov) offers many helpful materials, including the full text of the FLSA and its regulations, fact sheets on federal wage, hour, and leave laws, information on state wage and hour laws, and links to other resources.

Workplace Health and Safety

Several laws establish basic safety standards aimed at reducing the number of illnesses, injuries, and deaths in workplaces. Because most workplace safety laws rely for their effectiveness on employees who are willing to report job hazards, most laws also prevent employers from firing or discriminating against employees who report unsafe conditions to proper authorities.

Do I have any legal rights if I feel that my workplace is unsafe or unhealthy?

Federal and state laws protect you from an unsafe workplace. The Occupational Safety and Health Act of 1970 (OSHA) is the main federal law covering threats to workplace safety. (29 U.S.C. §§ 651 and following.) OSHA requires employers to provide a workplace that is free of dangers that could physically harm employees.

In addition to the basic right to a safe workplace, OSHA gives you the following rights:

- You can get training from your employer on the health and safety standards that your employer must follow.
- You can get training from your employer on any dangerous chemicals you are exposed to and on ways you can protect yourself from harm.
- You can get training from your employer on any other health and safety hazards (such as construction hazards or blood-borne pathogens) that might exist in your workplace.
- You can request information from your employer about OSHA standards, worker injuries and illnesses, job hazards, and workers' rights.
- You can ask your employer to cure any hazards or OSHA violations.
- You can file a complaint about unsafe working conditions with OSHA.
- You can request that OSHA inspect your workplace.
- You can find out the results of an OSHA inspection.
- You can file a complaint with OSHA if your employer retaliates against you for asserting your rights under the act.
- You can request the federal government to research possible workplace hazards.

Most states also have their own OSHA laws, most of which offer protections similar to the federal law.

How do I assert my rights to a safe workplace?

If you feel that your workplace is unsafe, your first action should be to make your supervisor aware of the danger. If your employer doesn't take prompt action, follow up in writing. Then, if you are still unsuccessful in getting your company to correct the safety hazard, you can file a complaint at the nearest OSHA office. Look under the U.S. Labor Department in the federal government section of your local telephone directory. You can also file a complaint online at www.osha.gov.

If you feel that a workplace hazard poses an imminent danger (a danger that could immediately cause death or serious physical harm), you should immediately call the agency's hotline at 800-321-OSHA.

Can I refuse to do work that puts me in danger?

OSHA gives you a very limited right to refuse to do a job if you have a reasonable, good faith belief that you will be exposed to imminent danger. As you might imagine, not every unsafe condition qualifies as an imminent danger. A workplace danger is imminent if:

- you face a threat of death or serious physical injury, and
- the threat is immediate—that is, you believe that death or serious injury could occur

within a short time period, before OSHA could take any steps to remedy the situation.

If you are facing an imminent danger, you should ask your employer to correct the problem, ask your employer for other work, tell your employer that you won't perform the work until the problem is resolved, and remain at the workplace unless and until asked to leave by your employer. You should also immediately call OSHA's hotline at 800-321-OSHA.

What to Do After an Injury

Workplace hazards often become obvious only after they cause an injury. For example, an unguarded machine part that spins at high speed may not seem dangerous until someone's clothing or hair gets caught in it. But even after a worker has been injured, employers sometimes fail—or even refuse—to eliminate the danger.

If you have been injured at work by a hazard that should be eliminated before it injures someone else, take the following steps as quickly as possible after obtaining the proper medical treatment:

- Immediately file a claim for workers' compensation benefits so that your medical bills will be paid and you will be compensated for your lost wages and injury. In some states, the amount you receive from a workers' comp claim will be larger if a violation of a state

workplace safety law contributed to your injury. (For more information about workers' compensation, see the next series of questions in this chapter.)

- Tell your employer that a continuing hazard or dangerous condition exists. As with most workplace safety issues, the odds of getting meaningful results will be greater if other employees join in your complaint.

- If your employer does not eliminate the hazard promptly, file a complaint with OSHA and any state or local agency that you think may be able to help. You can obtain a list of state health and safety agencies on the OSHA website at www.osha.gov. For example, if your complaint is about hazardous waste disposal, you may be able to track down a specific local group that has been successful in investigating similar complaints in the past.

Does OSHA protect against the harmful effects of tobacco smoke in the workplace?

OSHA rules apply to tobacco smoke only in rare and extreme circumstances, such as when contaminants created by a manufacturing process combine with tobacco smoke to create a dangerous workplace air supply that fails OSHA standards. Workplace air-quality standards and measurement techniques are so technical that typically only OSHA agents or consultants who specialize in environmental testing are able to determine when the air quality falls below allowable limits.

If OSHA won't protect me from secondhand tobacco smoke at work, is there anything I can do to limit or avoid exposure?

If you are bothered by coworkers' smoking, there are a number of steps you can take.

Check local and state laws. A growing number of local and state laws prohibit or place significant restrictions on smoking in the workplace. Most of them also set out specific procedures for pursuing complaints. Your state's labor department should have up-to-date information about these laws. If you can't find local laws that prohibit smoking in workplaces, check with a national nonsmokers' rights group, such as Americans for Nonsmokers Rights, 2530 San Pablo Avenue, Suite J, Berkeley, CA 94702, 510-841-3032, www.no-smoke.org.

Ask your employer for an accommodation. If you have a disability caused or aggravated by smoke, you may be entitled to a reasonable accommodation. Successful accommodations to smoke-sensitive workers have included installing additional ventilation systems, restricting smoking to outdoor areas or special rooms, and segregating smokers and nonsmokers. See *Discrimination*, below, for more information on disabilities and reasonable accommodation.

Consider income-replacement programs. If you are unable to work out a plan to resolve a serious problem with workplace smoke, you may be forced to leave the workplace. But you may qualify for workers' compensation or unemployment insurance benefits. See *Losing Your Job*, below.

 More Information About Workplace Health and Safety

The Occupational Safety and Health Administration, 200 Constitution Avenue, NW, Washington, DC 20210, 202-693-1999, publishes pamphlets about workplace safety laws. You can also visit OSHA online at www.osha.gov.

You can also read a summary of OSHA in *The Essential Guide to Federal Employment Laws*, by Amy DelPo & Lisa Guerin (Nolo).

Workers' Compensation

If you are injured on the job—or suffer a work-related illness or disease that prevents you from working—you may be eligible to receive benefits from your state workers' compensation program. You also may be entitled to free medical care. If your disability is classified as permanent or results in death, additional benefits may be available to you and/or your family. If you receive workers' compensation benefits, however, you lose your right to sue your employer for the injury.

Who pays workers' compensation benefits?

In most states, employers are required to purchase insurance for their employees from a workers' compensation insurance company (also called an insurance carrier). In some states, larger employers who are clearly solvent are allowed to self-insure or act as their own insurance companies, while small companies (with fewer than three or four employees) are not required to carry workers' compensation insurance at all. When a worker is injured, his or her claim is filed with the insurance company—or self-insuring employer—who pays medical and disability benefits according to a state-approved formula.

Are all on-the-job injuries covered by workers' compensation?

The workers' compensation system is designed to provide benefits to injured workers, even if an injury is caused by the employer's or employee's carelessness. But there are some limits. Usually, injuries caused by an employee's intoxication or use of illegal drugs are not covered by workers' compensation. Coverage may also be denied for:

- self-inflicted injuries (including those caused by a person who starts a fight)
- injuries suffered while a worker was committing a serious crime
- injuries suffered while an employee was not on the job, and
- injuries suffered when an employee's conduct violated company policy.

If your employer's conduct is especially egregious (for example, your employer did something intentional or reckless that injured you), you may be allowed to bypass the workers' compensation system and sue your employer in court—for much larger amounts of money than you could collect through workers' compensation.

Does workers' compensation cover only injuries, or does it also cover long-term problems and illnesses?

Your injury does not need to be caused by an accident—such as a fall from a ladder—to be covered. Many workers, for example, receive compensation for repetitive stress injuries, including carpal tunnel syndrome and back problems, that are caused by overuse or misuse over a long period of time. You may also be compensated for some illnesses and diseases that are the gradual result of work conditions—for example, heart conditions, lung disease, and stress-related digestive problems.

Do I have to be injured at my workplace to be covered by workers' compensation?

No. As long as your injury is job-related, it's covered. For example, you'll be covered if you are injured while traveling on business, doing a work-related errand, or even attending a required, business-related social function.

How do I claim workers' compensation benefits?

First, promptly report the work-related injury or sickness to your employer. Most states require you to do this within two to 30 days following an injury. If an injury occurs over time (for example, a breathing problem or carpal tunnel syndrome), you must report your condition soon after you discover it and realize that it is caused by your work.

Next, get the medical treatment you need and follow the doctor's instructions exactly. (This may include an "off-work order" or a "limited-duties work order.") Then, file a claim with your workers' compensation carrier. Your employer must give you the necessary forms; ask someone in the personnel or benefits department.

Finally, make sure you save copies of all correspondence with your employer, its insurance carrier, and your doctor concerning your workers' compensation claim. You might need this paperwork if you run into problems later.

Are You Covered by Workers' Compensation?

Most workers are eligible for workers' compensation coverage, but every state excludes some workers. Exclusions often include:

- business owners
- independent contractors
- casual workers
- domestic employees in private homes
- farmworkers
- maritime workers
- railroad employees, and
- unpaid volunteers.

Check the workers' compensation law of your state to see whether these exclusions affect you.

Federal government employees are also excluded from state workers' compensation coverage, but they receive workers' compensation benefits under a separate federal law.

In addition, some states don't require smaller employers—those with fewer than three to five employees, depending on the state's rules—to carry workers' compensation insurance. If you work for one of these employers, you may be excluded from the state program.

What kind of benefits will I receive?

The workers' compensation system provides replacement income, medical expenses, and sometimes vocational rehabilitation benefits—that is, job training, schooling, or job placement assistance if you are unable to return to your former position. The benefits paid through workers' compensation, however, are almost always relatively modest.

If you become temporarily unable to work, you'll usually receive two-thirds of your average wage up to a fixed ceiling. But because these payments are tax-free, if you received decent wages prior to your injury, you'll fare reasonably well in most states. You will be eligible for these wage-loss replacement benefits as soon as you've lost a few days of work because of an injury or illness that is covered by workers' compensation.

If you become permanently unable to do the work you were doing prior to the injury, or unable to work at all, you may be eligible to receive long-term or lump-sum benefits. The amount of the payment will depend on the nature and extent of your injuries. If you anticipate a permanent work disability, contact your local workers' compensation office as soon as possible; these benefits are rather complex and may take a while to process.

Can I be treated by my own doctor?

In some states, you have a right to see your own doctor if you make this request in writing before the injury occurs. More typically, however, injured workers are referred to a doctor or health plan recruited and paid for by their employer.

The doctor's report will have a big impact upon the benefits you receive. While it's crucial that you tell the doctor the truth about both your injury and your medical history (your benefits may be denied based on fraud if you don't), be sure to clearly identify all possible job-related medical problems and sources of pain. This is no time to downplay or gloss over your injuries.

Keep in mind that a doctor paid for by your employer's insurance company is not your friend. The desire to get future business may motivate a doctor to minimize the seriousness of your injury or to identify it as a preexisting condition.

Social Security Benefits for the Permanently Disabled

If you're permanently unable to return to work, you may qualify for Social Security disability benefits. Social Security will, over the long run, provide more benefits than workers' compensation—but be forewarned that these benefits are hard to get. They are reserved for seriously injured workers. To qualify, your injury or illness:

- must prevent you from doing any "substantial gainful work," and

- must be expected to last at least 12 months, or to result in death.

If you think you may meet the above requirements, contact your local Social Security office. For more information about Social Security benefits, see Chapter 13.

If I am initially treated by an insurance company doctor, do I have a right to see my own doctor at some point?

State workers' compensation systems establish technical and often tricky rules in this area. Often, you have the right to ask for another doctor at the insurance company's expense if you clearly state that you don't like the one the insurance company provides, although there is sometimes a waiting period before you can get a second doctor. Also, if your injury is serious, you usually have the right to a second opinion. And in some states, after you are treated by an insurance company's doctor for a certain period (90 days is typical), you may have the automatic right to transfer your treatment to your own doctor or health plan—and the workers' comp insurance company will have to pick up the tab.

To understand your rights, contact your state worker's compensation office (sometimes called the industrial relations office). You can also get a copy of your state's rules—or, if necessary, research your state workers' compensation laws and regulations in the law library. The appendix explains how to do your own legal research.

Will I be covered if I suffer an injury to a part of my body that had been injured previously?

If the previous injury was also work-related, workers' compensation should provide full coverage. If it wasn't, you may receive lower-level benefits.

If your earlier injury occurred at a former job, it's generally up to your current employer's insurance company and your former employer to sort out who's responsible for paying your benefits—sometimes they will split the costs between them.

How do I find a good workers' compensation lawyer—and how much will it cost?

You usually don't need a lawyer unless you suffer a permanent disability or all or part of your workers' compensation claim is denied. If you find yourself in one of these situations, you'll probably want to do some research to learn your rights and duties. For example, many claims are denied based on a doctor's report claiming that you are not injured. If you dispute the report, you may have a right to obtain a second doctor's opinion paid for by the workers' compensation insurer.

If your claim is denied, consider hiring an experienced workers' compensation lawyer to help you navigate the appeals process. The best way to find a good lawyer is often through word of mouth—talk to other injured workers or check with a local union or other workers' organization.

In most states, fees for legal representation in workers' compensation cases are limited to between 10% and 15% of any eventual award. Because these fees are relatively modest, workers' compensation lawyers customarily take on many clients and, as a result, do not have time to provide much individual attention. Most of your contacts with your attorney's office will be with paralegals and other support personnel. This is not a bad thing in itself, if the office is well run by support staff. Be sure that the office is able to stay on top of paperwork and filing deadlines, and that a knowledgeable person is available to answer your questions clearly and promptly.

What to Do When the Insurance Company Won't Pay

Some workers' compensation carriers take an aggressive stance and deny legitimate claims for workers' compensation. When this happens, it's often because the insurer claims you haven't been injured or, if you have, that it's not serious enough to qualify you for temporary or total disability. Commonly, this is done after a private investigator hired by the insurance company follows you and takes photographs showing you engaging in fairly strenuous physical activity, such as lifting a box or mowing the lawn, despite claiming a disabling injury.

If your legitimate benefits are denied, you should immediately file an appeal with your state appeals agency—called the industrial accidents board, the workers' compensation appeals board, or something similar. You may also want to hire an attorney to help you press your claim.

If I receive workers' compensation, can I also sue my employer in court?

Generally, no. The workers' compensation system was established as part of a legal trade-off. In exchange for giving up the right to sue an employer in court, you get workers' compensation benefits no matter who was at fault. Before the workers' compensation system was in place, if you went to court, you stood to recover a large amount of money, but only if you could prove the injury was caused by your employer.

Today, you may be able to sue in court if your injury was caused by someone other than your employer (a visitor or outside contractor, for example) or if it was caused by a defective product (such as a flaw in the construction of the equipment you were using).

You might also be able to sue your employer in court if your injury was caused by intentional, reckless, or illegal conduct on your employer's part.

What if my employer tells me not to file a workers' compensation claim or threatens to fire me if I do?

In most states, it is a violation of the workers' compensation laws to retaliate against an employee for filing a workers' compensation claim. If this happens, immediately report it to your local workers' compensation office.

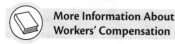
More Information About Workers' Compensation

California Workers' Comp: How to Take Charge When You're Injured on the Job, by Christopher Ball (Nolo), includes all of the forms and instructions you need to file a workers' compensation claim in California. The book is also useful for people who live elsewhere, given the absence of self-help resources for other states. It provides a good overview of how the system works.

Online Help

www.workerscompensation.com is a private website that provides information on state workers' compensation laws. Use the "select a state" box to find information about your state's rules.

Discrimination

Sometimes, I feel discriminated against, but it does not make me angry. It merely astonishes me. How can any deny themselves the pleasure of my company? It's beyond me.

—ZORA NEALE HURSTON

Since 1964, when the landmark federal law prohibiting certain types of workplace discrimination was enacted, most employees have been protected from being fired or disciplined because of their race, color, national origin, sex, or religion. And more recent federal laws protect against discrimination based on age, disability, and citizenship status. Despite these laws and similar laws in many states, however, workplace discrimination is still with us.

What is discrimination?

Legally, discrimination is treating someone differently because of a protected characteristic—a trait that the law has determined should not be the basis for employment decisions. Protected characteristics under federal law include race, color, national origin, religion, sex, disability, and age. Many states and local governments have enacted antidiscrimination laws that include additional protected characteristics, such as marital status, sexual orientation, and gender identity.

What laws protect employees from discrimination?

The major federal law that prohibits discrimination is the Civil Rights Act of 1964 (usually referred to as Title VII). (42 U.S.C. § 2000e.) This law protects employees from discrimination based on race, national origin, color, sex, and religion. Other federal antidiscrimination laws include the Age Discrimination in Employment Act (ADEA), which prohibits age discrimination against employees who are at least 40 years old (29 U.S.C. §§ 621-634), the Americans with Disabilities Act (ADA), which prohibits disability discrimination (42 U.S.C. §§ 12101 and following), the Equal Pay Act, which requires employers to pay men and women equally for doing the same work (29 U.S.C. § 206(d)), and the Immigration Reform and Control Act (IRCA), which prohibits employers from discriminating against employees who are eligible to work in the United States based on their citizenship status (8 U.S.C. § 1324 (a) and (b)).

In addition to these federal laws, all states prohibit some forms of discrimination in employment. Many of these laws mimic the federal protections, but some also protect against discrimination based on other characteristics, such as sexual orientation, marital status, height or weight, and AIDS or HIV status. And some city and local governments also prohibit additional types of discrimination.

Are all employees protected from discrimination?

Some employees who work for smaller employers may not be protected from discrimination. For example, Title VII and the ADA apply only to employers who have at least 15 employees. The ADEA applies only to employers who have at least 20 employees. The IRCA applies to employers with four or more employees.

Even if you are not covered by these federal laws, however, you may be protected by other antidiscrimination laws. Many states have enacted laws that apply to smaller employers, as

have many local governments. Contact your state's fair employment practices agency to find out more about your state's law. For information about local laws, contact your local government agency that deals with discrimination issues.

What should I do if I think I'm being discriminated against?

Your first step is to let your employer know that you believe you are a victim of discrimination. If your employer has a complaint procedure, make sure you follow it. If there's no formal complaint procedure, ask the human resources department or a manager how to complain. Filing a complaint will not only give your employer an opportunity to fix the problem, it will also protect your right to collect damages from your employer if you decide to file a lawsuit.

If complaining within the company isn't effective, you can file a discrimination charge at a government agency. The Equal Employment Opportunity Commission (EEOC) is the federal agency that handles discrimination complaints. To get information about how to file a charge—and to find an EEOC office near you—go to the agency's website at www.eeoc.gov. Most states also have an agency that deals with employment discrimination (sometimes called "fair employment practices," or FEP, agencies). You must file your charge within a certain amount of time, which might be as short as 180 days after the incident you believe was discriminatory. Therefore, it is important to act as soon as you realize that you might be the victim of discrimination; if you don't, you might lose your rights.

You must file a charge with an administrative agency first, if you want to sue your employer for discrimination. The agency may decide to investigate your complaint, propose that you and your employer try to settle or mediate the complaint, dismiss your complaint, or bring a lawsuit on your behalf in court.

In many cases, the agency will simply authorize you to file a lawsuit on your own. If you decide to go this route, you should talk to an experienced employment lawyer first. (For information on finding the right lawyer, see Chapter 16.)

My boss seems to promote only white employees to work with customers, while African-American and Latino employees hold mostly stockroom jobs with little customer contact. Is this legal?

If your employer is making these decisions based on race, this is illegal employment discrimination. Segregating employees based on race or preferring employees of one race for certain positions is discriminatory. Some employers try to justify this type of practice by claiming that their customers are "more comfortable" with employees of a particular race, or by making staffing decisions based on the race of their customers (for example, by hiring only Asian-Americans to work in stores in Asian-American neighborhoods). However, this kind of logic won't stand up in court—the EEOC has stated that these are not valid reasons for distinguishing among employees.

Can a company ask my race on its employment application?

No. Because an employer can't make hiring decisions based on race, it should not ask for this information on an employment application. If an employer has a legitimate need to keep track of the race of applicants and employees—for purposes of complying with an affirmative action plan, for example—it should keep these statistics separately. Some employers accomplish this by asking applicants to state their race on a separate sheet of paper—one that does not contain their name or other identifying information.

What is reverse discrimination?

In the context of race discrimination, "reverse discrimination" is a term sometimes used to describe discrimination against white employees or applicants. Because race discrimination laws traditionally were enacted to prevent discrimination against groups that were historically mistreated or denied opportunities, some employers believe that white employees are not protected by these laws. This belief is incorrect, however. Any time an employer makes a decision based on race, it commits illegal discrimination. So, for example, it is discriminatory for the owner of a Chinese restaurant or an African clothing boutique to refuse to hire white applicants based solely on their race.

Can my employer refuse to promote me to a customer service position because I speak with an accent?

There are two competing interests at work in this situation. On the one hand, diction and accent are closely associated with a person's nationality, so making employment decisions based on accent could constitute national origin discrimination. On the other hand, employers have a legitimate interest in making sure that their employees can communicate effectively with customers.

The law resolves the issue this way: an employer can make job decisions based on accent if the employee's accent materially interferes with his or her ability to do the job. If the job truly requires strong English communication skills (as many customer service positions do), the employer may refuse to hire or promote an employee with an accent only if the accent substantially impairs the employee's ability to communicate and be understood. If an employee's accent is so strong that customers cannot understand what he or she is saying, an employer is probably justified in refusing to place that employee in a position that requires extensive communication with customers. If, however, an employee has a perceptible foreign accent but can communicate clearly in English, an employer may not make decisions based on the employee's accent.

Can my employer impose a dress code that prohibits me from wearing traditional ethnic clothing?

An employer can require employees to follow a dress code, but the rules cannot single out particular types of ethnic dress. For example, a dress code that explicitly prohibited saris, turbans, or garments made of Kente cloth would be discriminatory. However, a uniform dress code that required, for example, no loose clothing or jewelry for those operating machinery is acceptable.

Gather Your Evidence

If you believe you are being discriminated against, you should take some steps to make sure you will be able to prove your claims. Here are a few tips:

- **Take notes.** Start writing down every incident or statement that is offensive—or just seems fishy. For example, you might make a log of every racist comment your supervisor makes, or note discriminatory statements made by company officials in speeches or presentations. And keep track of key employment decisions that you suspect could be discriminatory—like how many female workers have been promoted to a particular position. Make sure to date your entries.

- **Collect documents.** Keep copies of any documents that seem to indicate discrimination. For example, print out copies of email messages that contain religious slurs or jokes about older workers. Also keep copies of any discriminatory notes or items posted on company bulletin boards. You might also want to take pictures of discriminatory graffiti or cartoons on the walls. But make sure you don't take or copy any documents you are not entitled to have—if you steal or copy confidential company documents, you may lose your right to sue for money damages (and lose your job).

- **Talk to other employees.** If you have been discriminated against or harassed based on a protected characteristic, you may not be alone. Talk to your coworkers to find out whether they have faced similar problems—or have seen or heard of any discriminatory behavior towards other employees.

Can my employer require me to speak only English at work?

Courts will take a very close look at English-only rules to determine whether they are discriminatory. Because the language we speak is closely connected to our nationality, English-only rules may very well discriminate on the basis of national origin.

Generally, employers have to show that there is a business necessity for the policy—that the policy is necessary for the employer to operate safely and efficiently. For example, if an employer can show that safety requires all workers to speak a common language, or that an English-only rule is necessary to serve customers who speak only English, that would constitute a business necessity.

Even if an employer has a good reason for requiring employees to speak English, however, it cannot adopt a policy that is too broad. For example, requiring employees to speak English to customers might pass muster; prohibiting employees from speaking any other language even while on breaks and making personal phone calls might not.

Can an employer refuse to hire me because of my religion—or because I'm not religious?

No. Title VII of the Civil Rights Act of 1964 prohibits employers from treating an employee less favorably because of the employee's religion—or the fact that an employee is not religious. For example, an employer commits illegal discrimination if it refuses to hire Jews, refuses to allow Sikhs to work with customers, or promotes only those who share the owner's religious beliefs.

However, in limited situations, employers are actually required to take an employee's religion into account. The law requires employers to accommodate an employee's religious beliefs and practices, if they can reasonably do so. Examples of reasonable accommodations might include allowing an employee to wear traditional religious garb or allowing an employee to take time off during the workday to pray.

My employer requires all of us to attend a weekly meeting, where he says prayers and reads from the Bible. Is this legal?

No. An employer cannot require an employee to participate in religious observances or activities as a condition of employment. This prohibition extends to mandatory workplace programs that use yoga, meditation, biofeedback, or similar practices, if the program conflicts with an employee's religious beliefs.

I belong to a small religious group that isn't well-known—am I still protected from discrimination?

Yes. You don't have to belong to a mainstream or traditional religion to be protected. In fact, you don't even have to be a member of any recognized or organized religion. The EEOC defines religious beliefs as moral or ethical beliefs about right and wrong that are held sincerely, with the strength of traditional religious beliefs. Even if you can't point to an established religious group that holds the same beliefs, you are still protected.

Can my employer force me to work on my Sabbath day?

Employers are required to make reasonable accommodations for their employees' religious beliefs or practices unless doing so would create an undue hardship on the employer's business operations. For example, if your employer can arrange a voluntary job swap, shift change, flexible schedule, or job transfer that would allow you to take the day off, that might be a reasonable accommodation.

However, if the employer cannot give you the day off without incurring costs beyond ordinary administrative expenses, infringing on the rights of other employees, or diminishing workplace efficiency, it is not required to accommodate your request.

Can I proselytize in the workplace?

This is a complicated issue. Because employers are not allowed to make employment decisions based on religion, they may not single out employees of a particular religion for different treatment. In the context of workplace proselytizing, this means that an employer cannot clamp down on expressions of religious belief if the employer allows other kinds of personal expression at work.

On the other hand, an employer is obligated to prevent religious harassment—and proselytizing can cross this line if other workers find your religious discussions offensive based on their own religious beliefs (or the fact that they are not religious). For this reason, many employers prohibit employees from engaging in any type of personal expression that disrupts the workplace, from religious testifying to political discussions to displaying artwork that some might find offensive.

My boss rarely promotes women to positions requiring overnight travel—he says they won't want to spend time away from their families. Is this legal?

No. Title VII of the Civil Rights Act of 1964 prohibits sex discrimination, and this includes discrimination based on stereotypes about men and women. So, for instance, an employer can't refuse to promote women to sales positions based on a belief that women are less aggressive than men, and an employer can't promote only women to management positions based on a belief that women are more nurturing and better at promoting teamwork than men. In your situation, your employer seems to be making a number of assumptions about male and female employees' feelings about their jobs and families—including that female employees have family obligations in the first place, which some may not.

My employer pays software salespeople—who tend to be men—more than employees who train customers on how to use the software—who tend to be women. Is this legal?

It depends on how similar the two jobs are. Under the Equal Pay Act, employers must pay men and women equally for doing substantially equal work in the same establishment. In deciding whether work is substantially equal, courts will look at the skill, effort, responsibility, and working conditions each job requires. Only jobs that are quite similar will qualify as substantially equal. And even for substantially equal jobs, differences in pay are allowed if they are based on merit, seniority, quantity or quality of work, or any other factor that isn't related to sex.

At first glance, it seems that salespeople have different job responsibilities (selling) than trainers (teaching), and that different skills are required for each job. However, some employers are in the habit of calling similar jobs by different titles—for example, male employees who handle appointments, telephone calls, correspondence, and other office work for more senior employees might be called "administrative assistants," while women who perform the same work might be called "secretaries." It doesn't matter what the jobs are called—if they are substantially equal, men and women must receive equal pay for doing them.

Can my employer require me to take time off during my pregnancy?

Not if you are able to work. In days gone by, employers routinely required women to stop working when they reached a certain stage of pregnancy or when they were "showing." Today, however, antidiscrimination laws prohibit these practices. An employer may not require a woman to take time off during her pregnancy or prohibit her from returning to work for a set period of time after she gives birth.

Are all workers protected from age discrimination?

No. There are limits on both the employees and the employers who are covered. The federal Age Discrimination in Employment Act (ADEA) protects workers over the age of 40 from age discrimination in any employment decision. The ADEA doesn't apply to workers under the age of 40—or to workplaces with fewer than 20 employees. The ADEA applies to federal employees, private sector employees, and labor union employees. It also protects state employees from discrimination, although they cannot file a lawsuit against the state to vindicate their rights.

There are several other exceptions to the broad protection of the ADEA:

- Executives or people "in high policy-making positions" can be forced to retire at age 65 if they would receive annual retirement pension benefits worth $44,000 or more.

- There are special exceptions for police and fire personnel, tenured university faculty, and certain federal employees having to do with law enforcement and air traffic control. If you are in one of these categories, check with your personnel office or benefits plan office for details.

Almost every state also has a law against age discrimination in employment, and these laws often provide greater protection than the federal law. For example, some states provide age discrimination protection to workers before they reach age 40, and some protect against the actions of employers with fewer than 20 employees. In addition, employees who work for the state can sue the state directly for age discrimination under their state law—although they don't enjoy this right under federal law.

To find out more about the laws of your own state, contact your state fair employment practices department.

Out From Under the Golden Parachute

A growing number of employers ask older workers to sign waivers—also called releases or agreements not to sue. In return for signing the waiver, the employer offers the employee an incentive to leave the job voluntarily, such as a significant amount of severance pay. The Older Workers Benefit Protection Act places a number of restrictions on such waivers:

- Your employer must make the waiver understandable to the people who are likely to use it.

- The waiver may not cover any rights or claims that you become aware of after you sign it, and it must specify that it covers your rights under the ADEA.

- Your employer must offer you something of value (such as severance pay)—over and above what is already owed to you—in exchange for your signature on the waiver.

- Your employer must advise you, in writing, that you have the right to consult an attorney before you sign the waiver.

- If the offer is being made to a group or class of employees, your employer must inform you in writing how the class of employees is defined; the job titles and ages of all the individuals to whom the offer is being made; and the ages of all the employees in the same job classification or unit of the company to whom the offer is not being made.

- Your employer must give you at least 21 days to consider the waiver (or 45 days, if the offer is made to a group of employees). You also have the right to revoke the agreement for up to seven days after you sign it.

I've noticed a pattern where I work: Older workers tend to be laid off just before their pension rights lock in or vest. Is that legal?

Using various ploys like this one to cheat workers out of their promised pensions is a technique some employers use to save money. But it's not legal. The federal Older Workers Benefit Protection Act forbids:

- using an employee's age as the basis for discrimination in benefits, and

- targeting older workers for their staff-cutting programs.

Can my employer force me to take early retirement?

No employer can require you to retire because of your age. An early-retirement plan is legal only if it gives you a choice between two options: keeping things as they are or choosing to retire under a plan that leaves you better off than you previously were. This choice must be a genuine one; you must be free to reject the offer.

What laws protect disabled workers from workplace discrimination?

The Americans with Disabilities Act (ADA) prohibits employment discrimination on the basis of workers' disabilities. Generally, the ADA prohibits employers from:

- discriminating on the basis of physical or mental disability

- asking job applicants questions about their past or current medical conditions

- requiring job applicants to take medical exams, and

- creating or maintaining worksites that include substantial physical barriers to the movement of people with physical disabilities.

The ADA covers companies with 15 or more employees. Its coverage broadly extends to private employers, employment agencies, and labor organizations. A precursor of the ADA, the Vocational Rehabilitation Act, prohibits discrimination against disabled workers in state and federal government.

In addition, many state laws protect against discrimination based on physical or mental disability. To find out about your state's anti-discrimination laws, contact your state fair employment practices agency.

Whom does the ADA protect?

The ADA's protections extend to disabled workers—defined as people who:

- have a physical or mental impairment that substantially limits a major life activity
- have a record or history of impairment, or
- are regarded as having an impairment.

An impairment includes physical disorders, such as cosmetic disfigurement or loss of a limb, as well as mental and psychological disorders.

The ADA protects job applicants and employees who, although disabled as defined above, are still qualified for a particular job. In other words, they must be able to perform the essential functions of a job with or without some form of accommodation, such as wheelchair access, a voice-activated computer, or a customized workspace. As with other workers, whether a disabled worker is deemed qualified for a given job depends on whether he or she has appropriate skill, experience, training, or education for the position.

If I am disabled, how do I get my employer to accommodate my disability?

The first step is simple, but often overlooked: Ask. The ADA places the burden on you to tell your employer that you have a disability and that you need an accommodation.

When you ask for an accommodation, you do not need to use formal legal language or even do it in writing (though it's always a good idea to document your request). Just tell your employer what your disability is and why you need an accommodation.

Once you request the accommodation, your employer should engage in an informal process of determining whether and how it can accommodate you. As part of this process, your employer is allowed to ask you for documentation, or proof, of your disability. It is important that you comply with this request to the best of your ability; if you don't, then you will lose your right to an accommodation.

If an accommodation is not "reasonable" (see below), your employer does not have to provide it. Nor does your employer have to provide you with the accommodation that you want, as long as it provides another one that is effective. If you don't accept a particular accommodation, be prepared to defend your choice on the grounds that the accommodation isn't effective. If a court decides that the offered accommodation was reasonable, you may no longer be qualified for the job, and your employer can terminate you.

Accommodations Don't Need to Cost a Bundle

According to ergonomic and job accommodation experts, the cost of accommodating a particular worker's disability is often surprisingly low.

- 31% of accommodations cost nothing.
- 50% cost less than $50.
- 69% cost less than $500.
- 88% cost less than $1,000.

The Job Accommodation Network (JAN), which provides information about how to accommodate people with disabilities, gives the following examples of inexpensive accommodations:

- Glare on a computer screen caused an employee with an eye disorder to get eye fatigue. The problem was solved with a $39 antiglare screen.
- A deaf medical technician couldn't hear the buzz of a timer, which was necessary for laboratory tests. The problem was solved with an indicator light at a cost of $26.95.

To contact JAN, call 800-526-7234 or visit its website at www.jan.wvu.edu.

How can I tell if the accommodation my employer offers is reasonable?

The ADA points to several specific accommodations that are likely to be deemed reasonable—some of them changes to the physical setup of the workplace, some of them changes to how or when work is done. They include:

- making existing facilities usable by disabled employees—for example, by modifying the height of desks and equipment, installing computer screen magnifiers, or installing telecommunications devices for the deaf
- restructuring jobs—for example, allowing a ten-hour/four-day workweek so that a worker can receive weekly medical treatments
- modifying exams and training materials—for example, allowing more time for taking an exam, or allowing it to be taken orally instead of in writing
- providing a reasonable amount of additional unpaid leave for medical treatment
- hiring readers or interpreters to assist an employee, and
- providing temporary workplace specialists to assist in training.

These are just a few possible accommodations. The possibilities are limited only by an employee's and employer's imaginations—and the reality that might make one or more of these accommodations financially or otherwise impossible in a particular workplace.

When can an employer legally refuse to provide a particular accommodation?

The ADA does not require employers to make accommodations that would cause them an undue hardship—defined in the ADA as "an action requiring significant difficulty or expense." Additionally, an employer isn't required to provide the specific reasonable accommodation you request, if it would rather grant a different, but effective, reasonable accommodation.

The Equal Employment Opportunity Commission (EEOC), the federal agency responsible for enforcing the ADA, has set out some of the factors that will determine whether a particular accommodation presents an undue hardship on a particular employer:

- the nature and cost of the accommodation
- the financial resources of the employer (a large employer may be expected to foot a larger bill than a mom-and-pop business)
- the nature of the business (including size, composition, and structure of the workforce), and
- the impact providing the accommodation will have on the employer's operations.

It is not easy for employers to prove that an accommodation is an undue hardship, as financial difficulty alone is not usually sufficient. Courts will look at other sources of money, including tax credits and deductions available for making some accommodations, as well as the disabled employee's willingness to pay for all or part of the costs.

Can I be fired because I'm gay?

No federal law protects nongovernment workers from discrimination based on their sexual orientation, so it depends on the laws of the state and local government where you work. To date, 20 states and the District of Columbia prohibit private employers from making employment decisions based on sexual orientation. And more than a hundred local governments also prohibit this type of discrimination. To find out more, go to the website of Lambda Legal at www.lambdalegal.org, and click "State by State" for information on state and local laws prohibiting sexual orientation discrimination.

Can my employer refuse to promote me to a position in which I would be supervised by my spouse?

It depends on your state's laws. Relatively few states prohibit marital status discrimination in the first place, so most employers are free to make employment decisions based on the fact that you are married, single, or divorced. Even if your state prohibits discrimination on the basis of marital status, employers may still be allowed to prohibit spouses from reporting to one another, in the interests of promoting efficiency and preventing favoritism (or the appearance of it).

To find out whether your state has a law prohibiting marital status discrimination (and if so, what the law requires), contact your state fair employment practices agency.

Harassment

Sexual harassment on the job took a dramatic leap into public awareness in October 1991, when Professor Anita Hill made known her charges against Judge Clarence Thomas after his nomination to the U.S. Supreme Court. Many other incidents have erupted since then, from the Tailhook incident in the ranks of the U.S. Navy to Paula Jones's harassment claims against former President Clinton. And more recently, Mitsubishi Motors agreed to pay a record $34 million settlement to hundreds of women harassed at its auto-assembly plant.

Although sexual harassment tends to get the most media coverage, other types of workplace harassment are also illegal—including harassment based on race, disability, and religion.

What is harassment?

Legally speaking, harassment is unwelcome conduct that creates an intimidating, hostile, or offensive work environment or otherwise interferes with an employee's work performance.

Like discrimination, harassment is illegal only if it is based on a person's protected characteristic. Under federal law, protected characteristics include race, color, national origin, sex, religion, age, disability, and citizenship status.

Harassment can take many forms, from racial or religious slurs and jokes to X-rated graffiti to cruel practical jokes played on disabled employees.

What is sexual harassment?

In legal terms, sexual harassment is any unwelcome sexual advance or conduct on the job that creates an intimidating, hostile, or offensive working environment. In real life, sexually harassing behavior ranges from repeated X-rated or belittling jokes to a workplace full of offensive pornography to an outright sexual assault.

What laws prohibit workplace harassment?

The same federal laws that protect employees from discrimination also prohibit harassment. This means that you are protected from harassment only if your employer is subject to the federal antidiscrimination laws discussed in *Discrimination,* above. For example, if you work for an employer that has only 15 employees, your employer does not have to comply with the federal laws that prohibit discrimination based on age—so you are not protected from harassment based on your age.

Many state laws also prohibit harassment. Some of them work like the federal laws—in other words, the same laws that prohibit discrimination also prohibit harassment. In other states, separate laws or provisions prohibit harassment, and these laws may apply to different employers. For example, California prohibits harassment by all employers regardless of size,

while only those employers with at least five employees are prohibited from discriminating.

My coworkers like to tease me about my accent and nationality —when does this kind of joking around cross the line into harassment?

There's no clear point at which teasing becomes illegal harassment. Courts and the Equal Employment Opportunity Commission (EEOC), the federal agency that enforces federal laws prohibiting harassment, have said that one or two isolated jokes don't constitute harassment. On the other hand, repeated and offensive jokes—such as using racial slurs or belittling you because of your nationality—probably do. The test is whether the harassing conduct unreasonably interferes with your work performance or creates an intimidating, hostile, or offensive work environment. The more your coworkers tease you—and the more offensive their jokes are—the more likely you are facing illegal harassment.

I'm being harassed at work. What is the first thing I should do?

Consider telling the harasser to stop. Surprisingly often, this works. Speaking directly to the harasser is especially likely to be effective if it's possible that the harasser doesn't realize how damaging the behavior is. For example, a coworker who doesn't understand that his jokes about your religion or his comments about your appearance are offensive might be embarrassed to learn that his behavior is upsetting you—and more than willing to change his ways.

If you are afraid to confront the harasser(s), go directly to your supervisor, human resources department, or other manager and make a complaint. The benefit of complaining directly to the harasser(s) is that doing so lets the harasser know that the behavior is unwelcome. Conduct is harassing only if it is not welcome to the person on the receiving end. This can be a disputed issue, particularly in sexual harassment cases—if you have participated in sexual banter in the workplace or have a prior dating relationship with the harasser; for example, the harasser may later argue (to your employer or in court) that he or she didn't know you were offended. Telling the harasser directly that you are upset is a sure-fire way to be clear about this.

However, if the conduct is severely disturbing or offensive, you may sensibly believe that the harasser must know that you are upset by it. For example, if you have been threatened with racial violence or sexual assault, there is no need to sit down with your persecutor and explain why you are upset.

Also, document what's going on by keeping a diary or journal noting important facts like what occured, the full names of any witnesses, and the dates that events took place. Your case will be stronger if you can later prove that the harassment continued after you confronted the harasser.

What should I do if the harasser keeps it up—or I'm too intimidated to tell the harasser to stop?

Complain, complain, complain. Start by finding out whether your company has a complaint procedure in place (check your employee handbook or ask a manager). If so, use that process to make a formal complaint. If your company doesn't have a complaint policy or procedure, talk to your supervisor, someone in your company's human resources department, or another manager. When you make your complaint, be thorough and honest—don't leave anything out

or exaggerate any details. If the person taking your complaint asks you to sign or fill out a written complaint, make sure everything in the document is accurate—and that nothing important has been omitted—before you sign.

You may be afraid to complain about harassment, perhaps because the harasser is your supervisor or has made threats against you. The laws that prohibit harassment also prohibit your employer from retaliating against you for complaining about harassment. Although this might be cold comfort if you fear for your job or your safety, the fact is that your legal rights might be limited if you fail to complain. An employer who can successfully argue that it didn't know about the harassment has a defense to a harassment lawsuit—and the best way to nip this argument in the bud is to complain to someone in authority, using the company's designated procedures.

What legal steps can I take to end harassment?

If complaining to the harasser and/or company officials doesn't stop harassment, your next step is to file a charge of harassment at the federal EEOC or your state's fair employment practices agency. These agencies enforce federal and state laws prohibiting harassment, and they are empowered to take complaints, investigate, try to settle or mediate the problem, and even sue on the employee's behalf, if they think the case warrants their involvement.

If you are considering suing your employer, you absolutely must file a charge of harassment with a government agency first: In most circumstances, courts will not allow your harassment lawsuit to go forward unless you have first filed with one of these agencies. And the deadlines for filing can be short—you might have only 180 days after the harassing incidents to file a charge.

Although these agencies don't often sue an employer on an employee's behalf, the results can be tremendous when they do. In January 2005, for example, the EEOC announced that it had negotiated a settlement of $2,750,000 for 12 African-American dockworkers who were subjected to a racially hostile work environment, including assaults, threats of physical harm, racially offensive graffiti, property damage, and hanging nooses in the workplace. The EEOC had filed a lawsuit on the workers' behalf before brokering the deal.

More commonly, however, the agency will choose not to get involved and instead will issue you a document referred to as a "right-to-sue" letter. This document allows you to take your case to court. If you decide to file a lawsuit, you will almost certainly want to hire an attorney to represent you.

More Information About Harassment

For more information about your right to be free of discrimination and harassment, check out *Your Rights in the Workplace*, by Barbara Kate Repa (Nolo). The website of the EEOC, at www.eeoc. gov, has many helpful materials on harassment, as well as information on how to file a charge of harassment with the agency.

9to5 is a national nonprofit membership organization for working women. It provides counseling, information, and referrals for problems on the job, including family leave, pregnancy disability, termination, compensation, and sexual harassment.

9to5 also offers a newsletter and publications. There are local chapters throughout the country.

9to5, National Association of Working Women
207 E. Buffalo Street #21K
Milwaukee, WI 53202
414-274-0925
800-522-0925 (hotline)
www.9to5.org

Workplace Privacy

The common law secures to each individual the right of determining, ordinarily, to what extent his thoughts, sentiments, and emotions shall be communicated to others.

—SAMUEL WARREN & LOUIS BRANDEIS

Technology has made it possible—sometimes even easy—to pry into people's lives, habits, and communications. Testing, background checks, electronic monitoring, and surveillance equipment all make it possible for employers to find out more about you than you ever dreamed possible. As a result, many employees are understandably concerned about protecting their privacy.

At the same time, employers sometimes have good reasons to take a close look at what their employees are doing. If one employee is harassing another through the company's email or telephone system, for example, the employer has a legal obligation to look into it—which might include monitoring employee communications. And employers have a legitimate interest in hiring workers who are truly qualified for the position—and have the experience, educational background, and skills they claimed on their applications.

Can a prospective employer run a background check on me?

Yes, within limits. A prospective employer doesn't have the right to dig into all of your personal affairs, and generally shouldn't be investigating things that have no bearing on your ability to do the job. However, a prospective employer certainly has the right to verify the information on your resume and/or application by, for example, checking to make sure that you hold the degrees, licenses, and certifications you claim to have, and calling former employers to confirm that you really did work for them.

In some cases, a prospective employer might want to take things a step further. For example, if you are applying for a delivery job, the employer will probably want to check your driving record. If you are applying for a position working with vulnerable clients—young children or the elderly, for example—the employer may want to make sure that you don't have a criminal record.

There are some limits on the information a prospective employer can gather. For example, federal law makes academic records confidential, so an employer might not be able to get your transcripts unless you consent or provide them. An employer also has to get your consent to order a copy of your credit report—and if the employer decides not to hire you based on the report, it must give you a copy of the report and let you know how to challenge its contents. And, to get any but the most basic information about your military service, your employer must have your consent.

Can a prospective employer ask whether I have a criminal record—and do I have to answer?

State laws determine whether a prospective employer can ask about prior arrests and convictions. Some states prohibit employers from asking about (or considering in their hiring decisions) arrests that did not lead to conviction, criminal records that have been sealed or expunged, convictions that are more than ten years old, or juvenile convictions. And some states allow employers to consider an applicant's criminal record only for certain positions (most commonly, child care workers, private detectives, nurses, and other jobs requiring a license) or only if the conviction has some relationship to the job. To find out more about your state's rules, contact your state department of labor.

Can my employer require me to take a drug test?

It depends on the laws of your state. Although most states allow employers to require job applicants to submit to drug testing, some states limit an employer's right to require current employees to take a drug test. Although some states allow employers to test employees generally, most impose some restrictions—for example, that the employer may test only employees who work in certain safety-sensitive positions, employees who have been in workplace accidents, or employees whom the employer reasonably suspects of illegal drug use. To find out whether your state has a drug-testing law, contact your state department of labor.

Can I refuse to take a lie detector test?

In most cases, yes. The federal Employee Polygraph Protection Act prohibits all private employers from requiring their workers to submit to lie detector tests—and from firing or otherwise disciplining employees who refuse to take a test—in most circumstances. (29 U.S.C. §§ 2001 and following.) Certain employers—those who are authorized by the federal Drug Enforcement Administration (DEA) to manufacture, distribute, or dispense certain controlled substances and those who provide security services—have a very limited right to require employees to submit to polygraph testing, in a few situations.

The only exception that applies generally to all employers has to do with workplace investigations. An employer may ask an employee to take a polygraph (and may fire the employee for refusing to do so) if the employer is investigating theft or loss of property, the employee had access to the property, the employer has a reasonable suspicion that the employee was involved, and the employer provides detailed information to the employee, before the test, about these facts. Unless you are facing this situation, you may legally refuse to take a lie detector test, and your employer may not take action against you based on your refusal.

Can my employer read my email?

In most situations, yes. Employers generally have the right to read employee email messages sent and received on the employer's system. Even if your employer gives you some reason to believe that your email messages are private—for example, by providing a system that allows you to mark certain messages "confidential" or allowing employees to create their own passwords that the company doesn't have access to—a court would probably uphold the employer's right to read employee email.

As a result, the best course of action for employees is to follow your employer's email policy carefully—and never to send an email on company equipment that you wouldn't want your boss to read.

My employer monitors our phone calls—is this legal?

Probably, as long as your employer has notified you of its monitoring. Under federal law, employers generally have the right to monitor employee conversations with clients or customers for quality control. Some states prohibit secret monitoring, and employers in those states must inform the parties to the call—by announcement or by signal (such as a beeping noise)—that someone is listening in.

Under federal law, once an employer realizes that a particular call is personal, it must immediately stop monitoring. However, if your employer has designated particular phones for business use only, it is probably within its rights to monitor all calls on those phones.

Can my employer monitor my Internet surfing?

Yes. Technology exists that allows employers to track the sites employees visit—and how much time they spend there. Although employers should inform their employees about any Internet rules and monitoring systems they use, employers generally have the right to monitor what employees do on the company's computer system.

Given this state of affairs—and the possibility that your employer might be monitoring without your knowledge—it's best to limit Internet activities on the job to work-related sites, and save the surfing, shopping, and instant messaging for another time.

Losing Your Job

It is easier for a man to be thought fit for an
employment that he has not, than for one he
stands already possessed of.

—FRANÇOIS, DUC DE LA ROCHEFOUCAULD

The fear of being laid off or fired looms large
for many workers. Employers have traditionally
had a free hand to hire and fire, but a number
of recent laws and legal rulings restrict these
rights. If you do lose your job—or decide to
leave it—you have certain legal rights on your
way out the door.

For what reasons can I be fired?

Unless you have an employment contract with
your employer, your employment is probably at
will, which means that your employer can fire
you for any reason that isn't illegal. Examples of
illegal reasons for firing include firing a worker
because of his or her race, religion, and so on
(see *Discrimination,* above); firing someone for
filing a health and safety complaint or a charge
of sexual harassment; or firing a worker for
exercising a legal right, such as taking family
and medical leave or taking leave to serve in
the military. Even if you are employed at will,
you can't be fired for reasons like these, which
courts and legislatures have put off limits even
to at-will employers.

If you are employed at will, your employer
can fire you for reasons that are job-related
(incompetence, excessive absences, violating
certain laws or company rules) or whimsical
(your voice is abrasive, you tell corny jokes, you
love Broadway musicals).

If you have an employment contract, the
terms of your contract will determine the reasons for which you can be fired. Sometimes,
contracts list reasons for which the employee
can be fired (common examples include criminal acts, serious misconduct, or the employer's
bankruptcy). Other contracts leave the issue
open. In such a situation, the law usually says
that you can only be fired for a legitimate,
business-related reason (sometimes called "just
cause" or "good cause"). If your contract says
that you are employed at will, however, you are
stuck in the same boat as those without a contract, and your employer can fire you for any
legal reason.

How do I know if I have an employment contract?

When most people think about contracts, they
think of a formal written document. And many
contracts do take that form. There are other
kinds of contracts, however. You and your
employer can make an oral agreement that is
never put in writing, and it will still be a valid
contract in the right circumstances. And if your
employer promises you something, that promise may create a contract as well.

If you fit into the following situations and
are fired for questionable reasons, then you
may have a legal claim against your employer
for breach of contract—and you might want to
consider talking to an attorney:

• Your employer, supervisor, or manager
promised you that you would only be fired
for certain reasons—for example, poor
performance or serious misconduct.

• Your employer, manager, or supervisor
promised you that you would have a long
and secure career at the company.

- You and your employer, manager, or supervisor agreed orally on the terms or length of your employment.

What are illegal reasons for firing?

Employers do not have the right to discriminate against you in violation of state or federal fair employment laws. In addition to protecting against the traditional forms of discrimination based on race, color, religion, national origin, disability, and age, many states also protect against discrimination based on sexual orientation, marital status, gender identity, receipt of public funds, and other factors.

Separate state and federal laws protect workers from being fired for taking advantage of laws intended to protect them from unsafe working conditions. State and federal laws also protect whistleblowers. In addition, many states protect workers from being fired for exercising a legal right or for refusing to comply with an illegal request by their employer—for example, to falsify tax records or rip off customers.

What can I do to protect any legal rights I might have before leaving my job?

Even if you decide not to challenge the legality of your firing, you will be in a much better position to enforce all of your workplace rights if you carefully document what happened. For example, if you apply for unemployment insurance benefits and your former employer challenges that application, you will typically need to prove that you were dismissed for reasons other than serious misconduct.

There are a number of ways to document what happened. The easiest is to keep an employment diary where you record and date significant work-related events such as performance reviews, commendations or reprimands, salary increases or decreases, and even informal comments your supervisor makes to you about your work. Note the date, time, and location for each event, which members of management were involved, and whether or not witnesses were present.

Whenever possible, back up your log with materials issued by your employer, such as copies of the employee handbook, memos, brochures, employee orientation videos, and any written evaluations, commendations, or criticisms of your work. However, don't take or copy any documents that your employer considers confidential—this will come back to haunt you if you decide to file a lawsuit.

If a problem develops, ask to see your personnel file. If possible, make a copy of all reports and reviews in it. Some states require employers to allow employees to copy at least some of the documents in their files; others don't. Also make a list of every single document the file contains. That way, if your employer later adds anything, you will have proof that it was created after the fact.

Am I entitled to severance pay if I am fired or laid off?

It depends on your employer's policies and practices. No law requires every employer to provide severance pay. Nevertheless, some employers give laid-off workers one or two months' salary. And some employers are more generous to long-term employees, basing severance on a formula such as one or two weeks' pay for every year an employee has worked for the company.

Your employer may be legally obligated to give you severance pay if you were promised it, as evidenced by:

- a written employment contract stating that you would receive severance
- a promise of severance pay in an employee handbook
- a long history of the company paying severance to other employees in your position, or
- an oral promise to pay you severance—although you may have trouble proving the promise was ever made.

What rights do I have if I get laid off?

In addition to any right to severance pay you may have (see above), you may have the right to advance notice of a layoff—or payment of up to 60-days' wages if your employer doesn't provide this notice.

The federal Worker Adjustment and Retraining Notification Act (WARN Act) requires employers that have at least 100 full-time employees to give written notice to workers, 60 days in advance, that they are going to lose their jobs in a plant closing or mass layoff. (29 U.S.C. §§ 2101 and following.) The WARN Act applies only if at least 50 workers—and at least 1/3 of the company's workforce—are going to lose their jobs. There are a lot of exceptions to the WARN Act as well; as a result, lots of employees aren't subject to its protections.

The WARN Act only requires employers to give notice, not to pay severance. However, if an employer violates the law, a court can order it to pay back wages for every day that it failed to give notice, up to 60 days of pay. Some states have similar laws, and a few of them require employers to pay laid off workers a small amount of money. Contact your state labor department to find out whether your state has a plant-closing law.

Do I have the right to continued health insurance coverage after I get fired?

Ironically, workers have more rights to health insurance coverage after they lose their jobs than while they were employed. Under the Consolidated Omnibus Budget Reconciliation Act (COBRA), employers with 20 or more employees must offer departing workers the option to continue coverage under the company's group health insurance plan at the workers' own expense for a specific period—usually 18 months. (29 U.S.C. §§ 1161 and following.) Family coverage is also included. In some circumstances, such as the death of the employee, the employee's surviving dependents can continue coverage for up to 36 months.

Your employer (or the administrator that deals with your employer's insurance plan) is required to give you COBRA paperwork, allowing you to choose to continue your coverage, shortly after your employment ends. If you don't receive this paperwork, contact your former employer and ask for it.

Am I entitled to unemployment benefits if I get fired?

Fired employees can claim unemployment benefits if they were terminated because of financial cutbacks or because they were not a good fit for the job for which they were hired. They can also receive benefits if the employer had a good reason to fire but the infractions were relatively minor, unintentional, or isolated.

In most states, however, an employee who is fired for "misconduct" will not be able to receive unemployment benefits. Although you may think that any action that leads to termination would constitute misconduct, the unemployment laws don't look at it that way. Not all actions that result in termination are serious enough to qualify as misconduct—and justify denying benefits.

Common actions that often result in firing but do not constitute misconduct are poor performance because of lack of skills, good faith errors in judgment, off-work conduct that does not have an impact on the employer's interests, and poor relations with coworkers.

What qualifies as misconduct? Generally speaking, an employee engages in misconduct if he or she willfully does something that substantially injures the employer's business interests. Revealing trade secrets or sexually harassing coworkers is misconduct; simple inefficiency or an unpleasant personality is not. Other common types of misconduct include extreme insubordination, chronic tardiness, numerous unexcused absences, intoxication on the job, and dishonesty.

 Online Help

www.nolo.com

Nolo offers information about a wide variety of legal topics, including workplace rights.

www.eeoc.gov

The U.S. Equal Employment Opportunity Commission is the federal agency responsible for enforcing federal antidiscrimination laws, including Title VII (which outlaws discrimination in employment based on race, gender, religion, and national origin), the Equal Pay Act, the Age Discrimination in Employment Act, and the Americans with Disabilities Act. The agency's website provides plenty of information about these laws. Among other things, it includes information on your workplace rights, the text of the fair employment laws, and instructions on how to file a charge against your employer.

www.dol.gov

The U.S. Department of Labor enforces many of the laws that govern your relationship with your employer, including wage and hour laws, health and safety laws, leave laws, and benefits laws. This website offers information about your rights under all of the laws enforced by the department, and it contains links to state labor department websites.

www.osha.gov

The federal Occupational Safety and Health Administration interprets and enforces workplace safety laws. Its website offers information on the requirements of OSHA, provides detailed guidelines on a number of workplace safety topics, and explains how to file a complaint about unsafe working conditions.

www.law.cornell.edu

The Legal Information Institute at Cornell Law School provides information about discrimination in the workplace, including relevant codes and regulations.

www.privacyrights.org

The Privacy Rights Clearinghouse provides fact sheets, links, and other resources on privacy issues, including workplace privacy rights.

Small Businesses

Business is never so healthy as when, like a chicken,
it must do a certain amount of scratching for what it gets.

—HENRY FORD

For all sorts of personal and economic reasons, more Americans are starting and running their own businesses today than ever before. This trend has been helped by the increasing availability of powerful and affordable data-storage and communications equipment, most notably the personal computer and the Internet. Because of this accessible technology, today's savvy small-time operator can often accomplish tasks that just a few decades ago could be tackled only by large corporations.

But not all change has been positive. When it comes to the law, the relatively informal world of just 40 years ago—where deals were often sealed with a handshake—has given way to a world where legal rules affect almost every small business relationship, including organizing the business, dealing with co-owners, hiring and supervising employees, and relating to customers and suppliers. Staying on top of all these rules is as necessary as it is challenging. Fortunately, by using affordable, good-quality

self-help legal resources and getting additional help from a knowledgeable small business lawyer, you can master the laws you need to know to keep your business healthy.

Before You Start

Your imagination is your preview of life's coming attractions.

—ALBERT EINSTEIN

No matter what type of business you want to start, there are some practical and legal issues you'll face right away, including choosing a name and location for your business, deciding whether or not to hire employees, writing a business plan, choosing a legal structure (sole proprietorship, partnership, corporation, or limited liability company), establishing a system for reporting and paying taxes, and adopting policies to deal with your customers. This section addresses many of these concerns. As you read, don't be discouraged by the details. If you have chosen a business that you will truly enjoy and, after creating a tight business plan, are confident you'll make a decent profit, your big jobs are done. Furthermore, many people and affordable sources of information are available to help you cope with the practical details we discuss here.

I'm thinking of starting my own business. What should I do first?

Be sure you are genuinely interested in what the business does. If you aren't, you are unlikely to succeed in the long run—no matter how lucrative your work turns out to be. Yes, going into business with a firm plan to make a good living is important, but so too is choosing a business that fits your life goals in an authentic way. Here are a few things you might want to consider before you take the leap:

- Do you know how to accomplish the principal tasks of the business? (Don't open a transmission-repair shop if you hate cars, or a restaurant if you can't cook.)

- If the business involves working with others, do you do this well? If not, look into the many opportunities to begin a one-person business.

- Do you understand basic business tasks, such as how to keep the books and prepare a profit-and-loss forecast and cash-flow analysis? If not, learn before—not after—you begin.

- Does the business fit your personality? If you are a shy introvert, stay away from businesses that require lots of personal selling. If you are easily bored, find a business that will allow you to deal with new material on a regular basis (publishing a newsletter, for example).

What should I keep in mind when choosing a name for my business?

First, assume that you will have competitors and that you will want to market your products or services under the name you choose. (This will make your name a trademark.) For marketing purposes, the best names are those that customers will easily remember and associate with your business. Also, if the name is memorable, it will be easier to stop others from using it in the future.

Most memorable business names are made-up words, such as Exxon and Kodak, or are somehow fanciful or surprising, such as Double Rainbow ice cream and Penguin Books. And some notable names are cleverly suggestive, such as The Body Shop (a store that sells personal hygiene products) and Accuride tires.

Names that tend to be forgotten by consumers are common names (names of people), geographic terms, and names that literally describe some aspect of a product or service. For instance, Steve's Web Designs may be very pleasing to Steve as a name, but it's not likely to help Steve's customers remember his company when faced with competitors such as Sam's Web Designs and Sheri's Web Designs. Similarly, names like Central Word Processing Services or Robust Health Foods are not particularly memorable.

Of course, over time even a common name can become memorable through widespread use and advertising, as with Ben and Jerry's Ice Cream. And unusual names of people can sometimes be very memorable indeed, as with Fuddrucker's (restaurants and family entertainment centers).

Choosing a Domain Name

If your business will have a website, part of choosing your business name will be deciding on a domain name. Using all or part of your business name in your domain name will make your website easier for potential customers to find. But many domain names are already taken, so you'll want to see what's available before you settle on a business name. After you pick an appropriate domain name, you'll need to register it with a registrar such as Alldomains.com.

How do I find out whether I'm legally permitted to use the business name I've chosen?

Your first step depends on whether you plan to form a corporation or a limited liability company (LLC). If you do, you should check with the secretary of state's office in your state to see whether your proposed name is the same or confusingly similar to an existing corporate or LLC name in your state. If it is, you'll have to choose a different name.

If you don't plan to incorporate or form an LLC, check with your county clerk to see whether your proposed name is already on the list maintained for fictitious or assumed business names in your county. In the states where assumed business name registrations are statewide, check with your secretary of state's office. (The county clerk should be able to tell you whether you'll need to check the name at the state level.) If you find that your chosen name or a very similar name is listed on a fictitious or assumed name register, you shouldn't use it.

If my proposed business name isn't listed on a county or state register, am I free to use it however I like?

Not necessarily. Even if you are permitted to use your chosen name as a corporate, LLC, or assumed business name in your state or county, you might not be able to use the name as a trademark or servicemark. To understand the distinction, consider the potential functions of a business name:

- A business name may be a trade name that describes the business for purposes of bank accounts, invoices, taxes, and the public.
- A business name may be a trademark or servicemark used to identify and distinguish products or services sold by the business (for example, Ford Motor Co. sells Ford automobiles, and McDonald's Corporation offers McDonald's fast food services).

While your corporate or assumed business name registration may legally clear the name for the first purpose, it doesn't speak to the second. For example, if your business is organized as a limited liability company or corporation, you may get the green light from your secretary of state to use IBM Toxics as your business name (if no other corporation or LLC in your state is using it or something confusingly similar). But if you try to use that name out in the marketplace, you're asking for a claim of trademark violation from the IBM general counsel's office.

To find out whether you can use your proposed name as a trademark or servicemark, you will need to do what's known as a trademark search. (See Chapter 8 for information.)

I've found out that the name I want to use is available. What do I need to do to reserve it for my business?

If you are forming a corporation or an LLC, every state has a procedure—operated by the secretary of state's office—under which a proposed name can be reserved for a certain period of time, usually for a fee. You can usually extend the reservation period for an additional fee. (For more information about corporations and LLCs, see *Legal Structures for Small Businesses*, below.)

If you are not forming a corporation or an LLC, then you may need to file a fictitious or assumed business name statement with the agency that handles these registrations in your state (usually the county clerk, but sometimes the secretary of state). Generally speaking, you need to file a fictitious business name statement only if your business name does not include the legal names of all the owners.

If you plan to use your business name as a trademark or servicemark and your service or product will be marketed in more than one state (or across territorial or international borders), you can file an application with the U.S. Patent and Trademark Office to reserve the name for your use. (See Chapter 8 for information.)

What should I keep in mind when choosing a location for my business?

Commercial real estate brokers are fond of saying that the three most important factors in establishing a business are location, location, and location. While true for some types of businesses—such as a retail sandwich shop that depends on lunchtime walk-in trade—locating in a popular, high-cost area is a mistake for many businesses. For example, if you design computer software, repair tile, import jewelry from Indonesia, or do any one of ten thousand other things that don't rely on foot traffic, your best bet is to search out convenient, low-cost, utilitarian surroundings. And even if yours is a business that many people will visit, consider the possibility that a low-cost, offbeat location may make more sense than a high-cost, trendy one.

What about zoning and other rules that restrict where a business may locate?

Never sign a lease without being absolutely sure you will be permitted to operate your business at that location. If the rental space is in a shopping center or other retail complex, this involves first checking carefully with management, because many have contractual restrictions (for example, no more than two pizza restaurants in the Mayfair Mall). If your business will not be located in a shopping center, you'll need to be sure that you meet applicable zoning rules, which typically divide a municipality into residential, commercial, industrial, and mixed-use areas.

You'll also need to find out whether any other legal restrictions will affect your operations. For example, some cities limit the number of certain types of business—such as fast food restaurants or coffee bars—in certain areas, and others require that a business provide off-street parking, close early on weeknights, limit advertising signs, or meet other rules as a condition of getting a permit. Fortunately, many cities have business development offices that help small business owners understand and cope with these kinds of restrictions.

Selling Goods and Services on Consignment

Many small business people, especially those who produce art, crafts, and specialty clothing items, sell on consignment. In a consignment agreement, the owner of goods (in legal jargon, the consignor) puts the goods in the hands of another person or business—usually a retailer (the consignee)—who then attempts to sell them. If the goods are sold, the consignee receives a fee, which is usually a percentage of the purchase price, and the rest of the money is sent to the consignor. For example, a sculptor (the consignor) might place his or her work for sale at an art gallery (the consignee) with the understanding that if the artwork sells, the gallery keeps 50% of the sale price. Or a homeowner might leave old furniture with a resale shop that will keep one-third of the proceeds if the item sells. Typically, the consignor remains the owner of the goods until the consignee sells them.

As part of any consignment of valuable items, the consignor (owner) wants to be protected if the goods are lost or stolen while in the consignee's possession. The key here is to make sure that the consignee has an insurance policy that will cover any loss. When extremely valuable items are being consigned, it's often appropriate for the consignor to be named as a coinsured who can receive a share of the insurance proceeds if a loss occurs.

If you're a consignee, check your insurance coverage. Before you accept the risk of loss or theft, make sure your business insurance policy covers you for loss of "personal property of others" left in your possession—and that the amount of coverage is adequate. Getting full reimbursement for the selling price of consigned goods may require an added supplement (called an endorsement) to your insurance policy. Check with your insurance agent or broker.

For a consignment contract, including detailed instructions and guidance, as well as small business forms and contracts, see Nolo's business software, *Quicken Legal Business Pro*.

What is a business plan, and do I need to write one?

A business plan is a written document that describes the business you want to start and how it will become profitable. The document usually starts with a statement outlining the purpose and goals of your business and how you plan to realize them, including a detailed marketing plan. It should also contain a formal profit-and-loss projection and cash-flow analysis designed to show that the business will be profitable if it develops as expected.

Your business plan enables you to explain your business prospects to potential lenders and investors in a language they can understand. Even more important, the intellectual rigor of creating a tight business plan will help you see whether the business you hope to start is likely to meet your personal and financial goals. Many budding entrepreneurs who take an honest look at their financial numbers see that hoped-for profits are unlikely to materialize. One of the most important purposes of writing a good business plan is to talk yourself out of starting a bad business.

I plan to sell products and services directly to the public. What do I need to know to comply with consumer-protection laws?

Many federal and state laws regulate the relationship between a business and its customers. These laws cover such things as advertising, pricing, door-to-door sales, written and implied warranties, and, in a few states, layaway plans and refund policies. You can find out more about consumer-protection laws by contacting the Federal Trade Commission, 600 Pennsylvania Avenue, NW, Washington DC 20580, 202-326-2222, www.ftc.gov, and by contacting your state's consumer protection agency.

Although it's essential to understand and follow the rules that protect consumers, most successful businesses regard them as only a foundation for building friendly customer service policies designed to produce a high level of customer satisfaction. For example, many enlightened businesses tell their customers they can return any purchase for a full cash refund at any time for any reason. Not only does this encourage existing customers to continue to patronize the business but it also can be a highly effective way to get customers to talk up the business to their friends.

 More Information About Starting Your Small Business

Legal Guide for Starting & Running a Small Business, by Fred S. Steingold (Nolo), provides clear, plain-English explanations of the laws that affect business owners every day. It covers partnerships, corporations, limited liability companies, leases, trademarks, contracts, franchises, insurance, hiring and firing, and much more.

Legal Forms for Starting & Running a Small Business, by Fred S. Steingold (Nolo), contains the forms and instructions you need to accomplish many routine legal tasks, such as borrowing money, leasing property, and contracting for goods and services.

Negotiate the Best Lease for Your Business, by Fred S. Steingold and Janet Portman (Nolo), gives you all the information you need to choose the right spot and negotiate a commercial lease.

Working for Yourself: Law & Taxes for Independent Contractors, Freelancers & Consultants, by Stephen Fishman (Nolo), covers every aspect of starting your own business, including information on taxes, choosing the right location, bookkeeping, and more.

The Small Business Start-Up Kit, by Peri H. Pakroo (Nolo), shows you how to choose from among the basic types of business organizations, write an effective business plan, file the right forms in the right place, acquire good bookkeeping and accounting habits, and get the proper licenses and permits.

Small Time Operator, by Bernard Kamoroff, C.P.A. (Bell Springs Publishing), is a good source of practical information on getting a small business off the ground—from business licenses, to taxes, to basic accounting. It includes ledgers and worksheets to get you started.

Quicken Legal Business Pro, (software by Nolo), contains over 60 interactive forms and contracts that all small businesses should have, plus the text of five best-selling Nolo business titles.

How to Write a Business Plan, by Mike McKeever (Nolo), shows you how to write the business plan necessary to finance your business and make it work. It includes up-to-date sources of financing.

Guerrilla Marketing, by Jay Conrad Levinson (Houghton Mifflin), contains hundreds of ideas and strategies to help you market your business.

Marketing Without Advertising, by Michael Phillips and Salli Rasberry (Nolo), shows you how to generate sales and encourage customer relations without spending a lot of money on advertising.

Legal Structures for Small Businesses

There is no one legal structure that's best for all small businesses. Whether you're better off starting as a sole proprietor or choosing one of the more complicated organizational structures, such as a partnership, corporation, or limited liability company (LLC), usually depends on several factors, including the size and profitability of your business, how many people will own it, and whether it will face liability risks not covered by insurance.

If I'm the only owner, what's the easiest way to structure my business?

The vast majority of small business people begin as sole proprietors, because it's cheap, easy, and fast. With a sole proprietorship, there's no need to draft an agreement or go to the trouble and expense of registering a corporation or limited liability company (LLC) with your state regulatory agency. Usually, all you have to do is get a local business license and, unless you are doing business under your own name, file and possibly publish a fictitious name statement.

If it's so simple, why aren't all businesses sole proprietorships?

There are several reasons why doing business as a sole proprietor is not right for everyone. First, a sole proprietorship is possible only when a business is owned by one person (unless you live in a community property state where spouses can be sole proprietors of a jointly owned business). Second, the owner of a sole proprietorship is personally responsible for all business debts, whereas limited liability companies and corporations normally shield their owners' assets from such debts. And finally, unlike a corporation (or an LLC that elects to be taxed as a corporation), which is taxed separately from its owners (something that can result in lower taxes for some small businesses—see below), a sole proprietor and his or her business are considered to be the same legal entity for tax purposes. This means you'll report all of the business's income, expenses, and deductions on your individual tax return.

I'm starting my business with several other people. What are the advantages and disadvantages of forming a general partnership?

One big advantage of a general partnership is that you usually don't have to register it with your state and pay an often hefty fee, as you do to establish a corporation or limited liability company. And because a partnership is a "pass-through" tax entity (the partners, not the partnership, are taxed on the partnership's profits), filing income tax returns is easier than it is for a regular corporation, where separate tax returns must be filed for the corporate entity and its owners. But because the business-related acts of one partner legally bind all others, it is essential that you go into business with a partner or partners you completely trust. It is also essential that you prepare a written partnership agreement establishing, among other things, each partner's share of profits or losses and day-to-day duties as well as what happens if one partner dies or retires.

Finally, a major disadvantage of doing business as a partnership is that all partners are personally liable for business debts and liabilities (for example, a judgment in a lawsuit). Of course, a good insurance policy can do much to reduce lawsuit worries, and many small, savvy businesses do not face debt problems. However, businesses that face significant risks in either of these areas should probably organize themselves as a corporation or LLC in order to benefit from the limited liability these business structures provide.

What exactly is limited liability—and why is it so important?

Some types of businesses—corporations and limited liability companies are the most common—shield their owners from personal responsibility for business debts. For instance, if the business goes bankrupt, its owners are not usually required to use their personal assets to make good on business losses—unless they voluntarily assume responsibility. Other types of businesses—sole proprietorships and general partnerships—do not provide this shield, which means their owners are personally responsible for business liabilities. To see how this works, assume someone obtains a large court judgment against an incorporated business. Because corporate stockholders are not personally liable for business debts, their houses and other personal assets can't be taken to pay the judgment, even if the corporation files for bankruptcy. By comparison, if a sole proprietorship or partnership gets

into the same kind of trouble, the houses, bank accounts, and other valuable personal assets of the business's owners (and possibly their spouses) can be attached and used to satisfy the debt.

Why do so many small business owners choose not to take advantage of limited liability protection?

Many small businesses simply don't have major debt or lawsuit worries, so they don't need limited liability protection. For example, if you run a small service business (perhaps you are a graphic artist, management consultant, or music teacher), your chances of being sued or running up big debts are low. And when it comes to liability for many types of debts, creating a limited liability entity makes little practical difference for new businesses. Often, if you want to borrow money from a commercial lender or establish credit with a vendor, you will be required to pledge your personal assets or personally guarantee payment of the debt, even if you've chosen a limited liability business structure.

Finally, organizing your business to achieve limited liability status is no substitute for purchasing a good business insurance policy, especially if your business faces serious and predictable financial risks (for instance, the risk that a customer may trip and fall on your premises or that your products may malfunction). After all, if a serious injury occurs and you don't have insurance, all the assets of your business—which will probably amount to a large portion of your net worth—can be grabbed to satisfy any resulting court judgment. If you purchase comprehensive business insurance, your personal assets may not be at significant risk, and you may therefore conclude you don't need limited liability status.

Small Business Structures: An Overview		
TYPE OF ENTITY	**MAIN ADVANTAGES**	**MAIN DRAWBACKS**
Sole Proprietorship	Simple and inexpensive to create and operate Owner reports profit or loss on his or her personal tax return	Owner personally liable for business debts and liabilities
General Partnership	Relatively easy and inexpensive to create and operate Owners (partners) report their share of profit or loss on their personal tax returns	Owners (partners) personally liable for business debts Must prepare and file separate partnership tax return
Limited Partnership	Limited partners have limited personal liability for business debts as long as they don't participate in management General partners can raise cash without involving outside investors in management of business	General partners personally liable for business debts More expensive to create than a general partnership Suitable mainly for companies that invest in real estate or other businesses
Regular Corporation	Owners have limited personal liability for business debts Owners' fringe benefits (such as health insurance and pension plans) can be deducted as business expenses Owners can split corporate profit among owners and corporation, sometimes	More expensive to create than partnership or sole proprietorship Paperwork can seem burdensome to some owners Separate taxable entity that must prepare and file a separate corporate tax return paying a lower overall tax rate
S Corporation	Owners have limited personal liability for business debts Owners report their share of corporate profit or loss on their personal tax returns Owners can use corporate loss to offset personal income	More expensive to create than partnership or sole proprietorship More paperwork than for a limited liability company, which offers some of the same advantages Income must be allocated to owners in proportion to their ownership interests Fringe benefits deductible only for owners who own more than 2% of shares
Professional Corporation	Owners have no personal liability for malpractice of other owners	More expensive to create than partnership or sole proprietorship Paperwork can seem burdensome to some owners All owners must generally belong to, and often be licensed to practice in, the same profession

Small Business Structures: An Overview, cont'd.		
TYPE OF ENTITY	**MAIN ADVANTAGES**	**MAIN DRAWBACKS**
Nonprofit Corporation	Corporation doesn't pay income taxes Contributions to charitable corporations are tax-deductible Fringe benefits can be deducted as business expense	Full tax advantages available only to groups organized for charitable, scientific, educational, literary, or religious purposes Property transferred to corporation stays there; if corporation ends, property must go to another nonprofit
Limited Liability Company	LLCs can be organized with only one member Owners have limited personal liability for business debts even if they participate in management Owners report their share of profit or loss on their personal tax returns IRS rules allow LLCs to choose between being taxed as partnership or corporation	More expensive to create than partnership or sole proprietorship Laws for creating LLCs in a few states may not reflect latest federal tax changes
Professional Limited Liability Company	Same advantages as a regular limited liability company Gives state-licensed professionals a way to enjoy those advantages	Same as for a regular limited liability company Members must all belong to the same profession At least one state (California) does not permit professionals to organize as an LLC
Limited Liability Partnership	Mostly of interest to partners in old-line professions such as law, medicine, and accounting Owners (partners) usually aren't personally liable for the malpractice of other partners Owners report their share of profit or loss on their personal tax returns	Owners (partners) are usually personally liable for many business debts Not available in all states Often limited to a short list of professions

Given all its limitations, when is it wise for a small business person to seek limited liability status?

You should consider forming a business that offers its owners limited liability if:

- your business subjects you to a risk of lawsuits in an area where insurance coverage is unaffordable or incomplete, or

- your business will incur significant debts, is well established, and has a good credit rating so that you no longer need to personally guarantee every loan or credit application.

The easiest and most popular way to gain limited liability status is to form a corporation or a limited liability company (LLC).

Is forming a corporation difficult?

No. As long as you and close associates and family members will own all of the stock, and none of the stock will be sold to the public, the necessary documents—principally your articles of incorporation and corporate bylaws—can usually be prepared in a few hours.

While most states use the term "articles of incorporation" to refer to the basic document creating the corporation, some states use the term "certificate of incorporation," "certificate of formation," or "charter."

The first step is to check with your state's corporate filing office (usually either the secretary of state or department of corporations) and conduct a trademark search to be sure the name you want to use is legally available.

You then fill in the blanks in a preprinted form (available from most states' corporate filing offices or websites) listing the purpose of your corporation, its principal place of business, and the number and type of shares of stock. You'll file these documents with the appropriate office, along with a registration fee that will usually be between $200 and $1,000, depending on the state.

You'll also need to complete, but not file, corporate bylaws. These will outline a number of important corporate housekeeping details, such as when annual shareholder meetings will be held, who can vote, and how shareholders will be notified if there is need for an additional special meeting.

Fortunately, a good self-help book can make it easy and safe to incorporate your business without a lawyer.

What about operating my corporation? Aren't ongoing legal formalities involved?

Assuming your corporation has not sold stock to the public, conducting corporate business is remarkably straightforward and uncomplicated. Often it amounts to little more than recording key corporate decisions (for example, borrowing money or buying real estate) and holding an annual meeting. Even these formalities can often be done by written agreement and don't usually require a face-to-face meeting between the directors.

How are corporations taxed?

Corporate taxation is complicated; we'll be able to cover only the main points here. Most types of businesses—sole proprietorships, partnerships, corporations that have qualified for subchapter S status, and limited liability companies that have not elected to be taxed as regular, or C, corporations—are pass-through tax entities. This means that all business profits and losses "pass through" the business and are reported on the individual tax returns of the owners. For example, if a sole proprietor's convenience store turns a yearly profit of $85,000, this amount goes right on his or her personal tax return. By contrast, a regular profit corporation (and any LLC that elects to be taxed like a corporation) is a separate tax entity—meaning that the business files a tax return and pays its own taxes.

This corporate tax structure creates the possibility of double taxation—the corporation pays tax on its profit, then the owners pay tax again when those profits are paid to them as dividends. But corporate profits won't always be taxed twice. That's because owners of most incorporated small businesses are also employees of those businesses; the money they receive in the form of salaries and bonuses is tax-deductible to the corporation as an ordinary and necessary business expense. If the corporation pays surplus money to owners in the form of reasonable salaries, along with bonuses and other fringe benefits, a corporation does not have to show a profit, and therefore will pay no corporate income tax. In addition, most small corporations don't pay dividends, so there's no double taxation.

Are there tax advantages to forming a corporation?

Frequently, yes. Corporations pay federal income tax at a lower rate than do most individuals for the first $75,000 of their profits—15% of the first $50,000 of profit and 25% of the next $25,000. (Professional corporations are charged a flat 35% tax rate.) By contrast, in a sole proprietorship or partnership, where the business owner(s) pay taxes on all profits at their personal income tax rates, they could pay more.

A corporation can often reduce taxes by paying its owner-employees a decent salary (which, of course, is tax-deductible to the corporation but taxable to the employee), and then retaining additional profits in the business (say, for future expansion). The additional profits will be taxed at the lower corporate tax rates. Under IRS rules, however, the maximum amount of profits most corporations are allowed to retain without an additional tax is $250,000, and some professional corporations are limited to $150,000.

Recently I've heard a lot about limited liability companies. How do they work?

For many years, small business people have been torn between operating as sole proprietors (or, if several people are involved, as partnerships) or incorporating. On the one hand, many owners are attracted to the tax-reporting simplicity of being a sole proprietor or partner. On the other, they desire the personal liability protection offered by incorporation. Until the mid-1990s, it was possible to safely achieve these dual goals only by forming a corporation and then complying with a number of technical rules to gain S-corporation status from the IRS. Then the limited liability company (LLC) was introduced and slowly gained full IRS acceptance.

LLCs have many of the most popular attributes of both partnerships (pass-through tax status) and corporations (limited personal liability for the owners). You can form an LLC by filing a document, usually called "articles of organization," with your state's corporate filing office (often the secretary or department of state).

Can any small business register as a limited liability company?

Most small businesses can be run as LLCs because limited liability companies are recognized by all states. And all states permit one-owner LLCs, which means that sole proprietors can easily organize their businesses as LLCs to obtain both limited liability and pass-through tax status.

Are there any drawbacks to forming a limited liability company?

Very few, beyond the fact that LLCs require a moderate amount of paperwork at the outset and a filing fee. You must file articles of organization with your state's secretary of state, along with a filing fee that will range from a few hundred dollars in some states to almost $1,000 in others.

More Information About Choosing a Structure for Your Small Business

LLC or Corporation?, by Anthony Mancuso (Nolo), explains everything you need to know to choose the best legal structure for your business.

Legal Guide for Starting & Running a Small Business, by Fred S. Steingold (Nolo), explains what you need to know to choose the right form for your business and shows you what to do to get started.

Legal Forms for Starting & Running a Small Business, by Fred S. Steingold (Nolo), provides all the forms you'll need to get your business up and running, no matter what ownership structure you choose.

LLC Maker, by Anthony Mancuso (Nolo), is interactive software containing all the information and forms you'll need to set up an LLC on your own.

Form Your Own Limited Liability Company, by Anthony Mancuso (Nolo), explains how to set up an LLC in any state, without the aid of an attorney.

Incorporate Your Business, by Anthony Mancuso (Nolo), explains how to set up a corporation in any state.

Incorporator Pro, by Anthony Mancuso (Nolo), is interactive software that gives you all the forms and instructions necessary to incorporate your business in any state.

Nonprofit Corporations

In the long run you hit only what you aim at. Therefore, though you should fail immediately, you had better aim at something high.

—HENRY DAVID THOREAU

A nonprofit corporation is a group of people who join together to do some activity that benefits the public, such as running a homeless shelter, an artists' performance group, or a low-cost medical clinic. Making an incidental profit from these activities is allowed under legal and tax rules, but the primary purpose of the organization should be to do good work, not to make money. Nonprofit goals are typically educational, charitable, or religious.

How do nonprofit organizations begin?

Most nonprofits start out as small, informal, loosely structured organizations. Volunteers perform the work, and the group spends what little money it earns to keep the organization afloat. Formal legal papers (such as a nonprofit charter or bylaws) are rarely prepared in the beginning. Legally, groups of this sort are considered nonprofit associations, and each member can be held personally liable for organizational debts and liabilities.

Once a nonprofit association gets going and starts to make money, or wishes to obtain a tax exemption to attract public donations and qualify for grant funds, the members will formalize its structure. Usually the members decide to incorporate, but forming an unincorporated nonprofit association by adopting a formal association charter and operating bylaws is an alternative.

Most groups form a nonprofit corporation because it is the traditional form—the IRS and grant agencies are very familiar with it. Also, once incorporated, the individual members of the nonprofit are not personally liable for debts of the organization—a big legal advantage over the unincorporated association.

Will my association benefit from becoming a nonprofit corporation?

Here are some circumstances that might make it worth your while to incorporate and get tax-exempt status:

- **You want to solicit tax-deductible contributions.** Contributions to nonprofits are generally tax deductible for those who make them. If you want to solicit money to fund your venture, you'll make it more attractive to potential donors if their contributions are tax-deductible.

- **Your association makes a taxable profit from its activities.** If your association will generate any kind of income from its activities, it's wise to incorporate so that you and your associates don't have to pay income tax on this money.

- **You want to apply for public or private grant money.** Without federal tax-exempt status, your group is unlikely to qualify for grants.

- **Your members want some protection from legal liability.** By incorporating your association, you can generally insulate your officers, directors, and members from liability for the activities they engage in on behalf of the corporation

- **Your advocacy efforts might provoke legal quarrels.** If, for instance, your association is taking aim at a powerful industry (such as tobacco companies), it might be worth incorporating so that your association's officers and directors will have some protection from the spurious lawsuits that are sure to come—and will also receive compensation for their legal fees.

Forming a nonprofit corporation brings other benefits as well, such as lower nonprofit mailing rates and local real estate and personal property tax exemptions.

Is forming a nonprofit corporation difficult?

Legally, no. To form a nonprofit corporation, one of the organization's founders prepares and files standard articles of incorporation—a short legal document that lists the name and the directors of the nonprofit plus other basic information. The articles are filed with the secretary of state's office for a modest filing fee. After the articles are filed, the group is a legally recognized nonprofit corporation.

Is there more to forming a nonprofit than this simple legal task?

Taxwise, there is more. In addition to filing your articles, you will want to apply for and obtain federal and state nonprofit tax exemptions. Many groups don't want to form a nonprofit unless they can qualify for tax-exempt status. Unfortunately, you must form your corporation before you submit your federal tax exemption application. Why? Because the IRS requires that you submit a copy of your filed articles with the exemption application. Still, you should carefully review the tax exemption application before you submit your corporation papers. Doing so will give you a good idea of whether your organization will qualify for a tax exemption or not.

What type of tax exemption do most nonprofits get?

Most organizations obtain a federal tax exemption under Section 501(c)(3) of the Internal Revenue Code, for charitable, educational, religious, scientific, or literary purposes. States typically follow the federal lead and grant state tax-exempt status to nonprofits recognized by the IRS as 501(c)(3) organizations.

How can my organization get a 501(c)(3) tax exemption?

You'll need to get the IRS Package 1023 exemption application. This is a lengthy and technical application with many references to the federal tax code. Most nonprofit organizers need help in addition to the IRS instructions that accompany the form. But you can do it on your own if you have a good self-help resource by your side, such as Nolo's *How to Form Your Own Nonprofit Corporation,* by Anthony Mancuso, which shows you, line by line, how to complete your application.

Are there any restrictions imposed on 501(c)(3) nonprofits?

You must meet the following conditions to qualify for a 501(c)(3) IRS tax exemption:

- The assets of your nonprofit must be irrevocably dedicated to charitable, educational, religious, or similar purposes. If your 501(c)(3) nonprofit dissolves, any assets it owns must be transferred to another 501(c)(3) organization. (In your organizational papers, you don't have to name the specific organization that will receive your assets—a broad dedication clause will do.)

- Your organization cannot campaign for or against candidates for public office, and

political lobbying activity is restricted.

- If your nonprofit makes a profit from activities unrelated to its nonprofit purpose, it must pay taxes on the profit (but up to $1,000 of unrelated income can be earned tax-free).

More Information About Nonprofit Corporations

How to Form a Nonprofit Corporation, by Anthony Mancuso (Nolo), shows you how to form a tax-exempt corporation in all 50 states. In California, look for *How to Form a Nonprofit Corporation in California,* also by Anthony Mancuso (Nolo).

The Law of Tax Exempt Organizations, by Bruce Hopkins (Wiley), is an in-depth guide to the legal and tax requirements for obtaining and maintaining a 501(c)(3) tax exemption and public charity status with the IRS.

Small Business Taxes

The taxpayer—that's someone who works for the federal government but doesn't have to take the civil service examination.

—RONALD REAGAN

Taxes are a fact of life for every small business. Those who take the time to understand and follow the rules will have little trouble with tax authorities. By contrast, those who are sloppy or dishonest are likely to be dogged by tax bills, audits, and penalties. The moral is simple: Meeting your obligations to report business information and pay taxes is one of the cornerstones of operating a successful business.

Record-Keeping Basics

Keep all receipts and canceled checks for business expenses. It will help if you separate your documents by category, such as:

- auto expenses
- rent
- utilities
- advertising
- travel
- entertainment, and
- professional fees.

Organize your documents by putting them into individual folders or envelopes, and keep them in a safe place. If you are ever audited, the IRS is most likely to zero in on business deductions for travel and entertainment, and car expenses. Remember that the burden will be on you to explain your deductions. If you're feeling unsure about how to get started or what documents you need to keep, consult a tax professional familiar with record keeping for small businesses.

I want to start my own small business. What do I have to do to keep out of trouble with the IRS?

Start by learning a new set of "3 Rs"—record keeping, record keeping, and (you guessed it) record keeping. IRS studies show that poor records—not dishonesty—cause most small business people to lose at audits or fail to comply with their tax-reporting obligations, with resulting fines and penalties. Even if you hire someone to keep your records, you need to know your obligations—if your bookkeeper or accountant goofs up, you'll be held responsible.

I don't have enough money in my budget to hire a business accountant or tax preparer. Is it safe and sensible for me to keep my own books?

Yes, if you remember to keep thorough, current records. Consider using a check register–type computer program such as *Quicken* (Intuit) to track your expenses, and if you are doing your own tax return, use Intuit's companion program, *TurboTax for Business* or *TurboTax for Home & Business* (for sole proprietors). To ensure that you're on the right track, it's a good idea to run your bookkeeping system by a savvy small business tax professional, such as a CPA. With just a few hours of work, a tax pro can help you avoid the most common mistakes and show you how to dovetail your bookkeeping system with tax-filing requirements.

When your business is firmly in the black and your budget allows for it, consider hiring a bookkeeper to do your day-to-day payables and receivables. And hire an outside tax pro to handle your heavy-duty tax work—not only are the fees a tax-deductible business expense, but chances are your business will benefit if you put more of your time into running it and less into completing paperwork.

What is—and isn't—a tax-deductible business expense?

Just about any "ordinary, necessary and reasonable" expense that helps you earn business income is deductible. These terms reflect the purpose for which the expense is made. For example, buying a computer, or even a sound system, for your office or store is an "ordinary and necessary" business expense, but buying the same items for your family room obviously isn't. The property must be used in a "trade or business," which means it is used with the expectation of generating income.

In addition to the "ordinary and necessary" rule, a few expenses are specifically prohibited by law from being tax deductible—for instance, you can't deduct a bribe paid to a public official. Other deduction no-nos are traffic tickets and clothing you wear on the job, unless it is a required uniform. As a rule, if you think it is necessary for your business, it is probably deductible. Just be ready to explain it to an auditor.

Business Costs That Are Never Deductible

A few expenses are not deductible even if they are business-related, because they violate public policy (IRC § 162). These expenses include:

- any type of government fine, such as a tax penalty paid to the IRS, or even a parking ticket
- bribes and kickbacks
- any kind of payment made for referring a client, patient, or customer, if it is contrary to a state or federal law, and
- expenses for lobbying and social club dues.

Thankfully, very few other business expenses are affected by these rules.

If I use my car for business, how much of that expense can I write off?

You must keep track of how much you use your car for business in order to figure out your deduction. (You'll also need to produce these records if you're ever audited.) Start by keeping a log showing the miles for each business use, always noting the purpose of the trip. Then, at the end of the year, you will usually be able to figure your deduction by using either the "mileage method" (for the year 2007 you can take 48.5¢ per mile deduction for business usage) or the "actual expense" method (you can take the total you pay for gas and repairs plus depreciation according to a tax code schedule, multiplied by the percentage of business use). Figure the deduction both ways and use the method that benefits you most.

Can I claim a deduction for business-related entertainment?

You may deduct only 50% of expenses for entertaining clients, customers, or employees, no matter how many martinis or Perriers you swigged. (Yes, in the old days, you could write off more.)

The entertainment must be either directly related to the business (such as a catered business lunch) or "associated with" the business, meaning that the entertainment took place immediately before or immediately after a business discussion. Qualified business entertainment includes taking a client to a ball game, a concert, or dinner at a fancy restaurant, or just inviting a few of your customers over for a Sunday barbecue at your home.

Parties, picnics, and other social events you put on for your employees and their families are an exception to the 50% rule—such events are 100% deductible. Keep in mind that if you are audited, you must be able to show some proof that it was a legitimate business expense. So, keep a guest list and note the business (or potential business) relationship of each person entertained.

Commonly Overlooked Business Expenses

Despite the fact that most people keep a sharp eye out for deductible expenses, it's not uncommon to miss a few. Some overlooked routine deductions include:

- advertising giveaways and promotions
- audio- and videotapes related to business skills
- bank service charges
- business association dues
- business gifts
- business-related magazines and books (like this one)
- casual labor and tips
- casualty and theft losses
- charitable contributions
- coffee service
- commissions
- consultant fees
- credit bureau fees
- education to improve business skills
- interest on credit cards for business expenses
- interest on personal loans used for business purposes
- office supplies
- online computer services related to business
- parking and meters
- petty cash funds
- postage
- promotion and publicity
- seminars and trade shows
- taxi and bus fare, and
- telephone calls away from the business.

Must some types of business supplies and equipment be deducted over several years?

Current expenses, which include the everyday costs of keeping your business going, such as office supplies, rent, and electricity, can be deducted from your business's total income in the year you incurred them. But expenditures for things that will generate revenue in future years—for example, a desk, copier, or car—must be "capitalized," that is, written off or amortized over their useful life (usually three, five, or seven years, according to IRS rules). There is one important exception to this rule, discussed next.

If I buy business equipment this year, can I take the whole deduction at once?

Normally the cost of "capital equipment"— equipment that has a useful life of more than one year—must be deducted over a number of years. There is one major exception. Section 179 of the Internal Revenue Code allows you to deduct a certain amount of capital assets each year against your business income. This amount is $108,000 for 2007 through 2009 (with an annual adjustment for inflation) and $25,000 for 2010 and later. Even if you buy the equipment on credit, with no money down, you can still qualify for this deduction.

A friend told me that corporations get the best tax breaks of any type of business, so I am thinking of incorporating my start-up. What do you recommend?

There's a seed of truth in what your friend told you, but keep in mind that most tax benefits flow to profitable, established businesses, not to startups in their first few years. For example, corporations can offer more tax-flexible pension plans and greater medical deductions than sole proprietors, partnerships, or LLCs, but few start-ups have the cash flow needed to take full advantage of this tax break. Similarly, the ability to split income between a corporation and its owners—thereby keeping income in lower tax brackets—is effective only if the business is solidly profitable. And incorporating adds state fees, as well as legal and accounting charges, to your expense load. So unless you are sure that substantial profits will begin to roll in immediately, hold off.

For more information about choosing the right structure for your business, see *Legal Structures for Small Businesses*, above.

I am thinking about setting up a consulting business with two of my business associates. Do we need to have partnership papers drawn up? Does it make any difference taxwise?

If you go into business with other people and split the expenses and profits, under the tax code you are in partnership whether you have signed a written agreement or not. This means that you will have to file a partnership tax return every year, in addition to your individual tax return.

Even though a formal partnership agreement doesn't affect your tax status, it's essential to prepare one to establish all partners' rights and responsibilities vis-à-vis each other, and to provide for how profits and losses will be allocated to each partner. For more information about partnerships, see *Legal Structures for Small Businesses*, above.

> **Business Assets That Must Be Capitalized**
>
> Buildings
>
> Cellular phones and beepers
>
> Computer components and software
>
> Copyrights and patents
>
> Equipment
>
> Improvements to business property
>
> Inventory
>
> Office furnishings and decorations
>
> Small tools and equipment
>
> Vehicles
>
> Window coverings.

I am a building contractor with a chance to land a big job. If I get it, I'll need to hire people quickly. Should I hire independent contractors or employees?

If you will be telling your workers where, when, and how to do their jobs, you should treat them as employees, because that's how the IRS will classify them. Generally, you can treat workers as independent contractors only if they have their own businesses and offer their services to several clients—for example, a specialty sign painter with his own shop.

When in doubt, err on the side of treating workers as employees. While classifying your workers as independent contractors might save you money in the short run (you wouldn't have to pay the employer's share of payroll taxes or have an accountant keep records and file payroll tax forms), it may get you into big trouble if the IRS later audits you. The IRS is very aware of the tax benefits of misclassifying an employee as an independent contractor and regularly audits companies that hire large numbers of independent contractors. If your company is audited, the IRS may reclassify your "independent contractors" as employees—and slap you with hefty back taxes, penalties, and interest.

I am planning a trip to attend a trade show. Can I take my family along for a vacation and still deduct the expenses?

If you take others with you on a business trip, you can deduct business expenses for the trip no greater than if you were traveling alone. If your family rides in the back seat of the car and stays with you in one standard motel room, then you can fully deduct your automobile and hotel expenses. You can also fully deduct the cost of your air tickets even if they feature a two-for-one or "bring along the family" discount. You can't claim a deduction for your family's meals or jaunts to Disneyland or Universal Studios, however. And if you extend your stay and partake in some of the fun after the business is over, the expenses attributed to the nonbusiness days aren't deductible, unless you extended your stay to get discounted airfare (the "Saturday overnight" requirement). In this case, your hotel room and your own meals would be deductible.

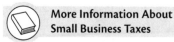

More Information About Small Business Taxes

Tax Savvy for Small Business, by Frederick W. Daily (Nolo), tells small business owners what they need to know about federal taxes and shows them how to make the right tax decisions.

Deduct It!, by Stephen Fishman (Nolo), provides invaluable information on business deductions for small business owners.

Working With Independent Contractors, by Stephen Fishman (Nolo), explains who qualifies as an independent contractor, describes applicable tax rules, and shows employers how to set up effective working agreements with independent contractors.

Working for Yourself: Law & Taxes for Independent Contractors, Freelancers & Consultants, by Stephen Fishman (Nolo), is designed for the estimated 20 million Americans who are self-employed and offer their services on a contract basis.

Home-Based Businesses

As technology advances, it becomes more and more convenient and economical to operate a business from home. Depending on local zoning rules, as long as the business is small, quiet, and doesn't create traffic or parking problems, it's usually legal to do so. But as with any other business endeavor, it pays to know the rules before you begin.

Is a home-based business legally different from other businesses?

No. The basic legal issues, such as picking a name for your business and deciding whether to operate as a sole proprietorship, partnership, limited liability company, or corporation, are the same. Similarly, when it comes to signing contracts, hiring employees, and collecting from your customers, the laws are identical whether you run your business from home or the top floor of a high-rise.

Are there laws that restrict a person's right to operate a business from home?

Municipalities have the legal right to establish rules about what types of activities can be carried out in different geographic areas. For example, laws and ordinances often establish zones for stores and offices (commercial zones), factories (industrial zones), and houses (residential zones). In some residential areas—especially in affluent communities—local zoning ordinances absolutely prohibit all types of business. In the great majority of municipalities, however, residential zoning rules allow small nonpolluting home businesses, as long as the home is used primarily as a residence and the business activities don't negatively affect neighbors.

How can I find out whether residential zoning rules allow the home-based business I have in mind?

Get a copy of your local ordinance from your city or county clerk's office, the city attorney's office, or your public library, and read it carefully. Zoning ordinances are worded in many different ways to limit business activities in residential areas. Some are extremely vague, allowing "customary home-based occupations." Others allow homeowners to use their houses for a broad—but, unfortunately, not very specific—list of business purposes (for example, "professions and domestic occupations, crafts, or services"). Still others contain a detailed list of approved occupations, such as "law, dentistry, medicine, music lessons, photography, cabinetmaking."

If you read your ordinance and still aren't sure whether your business is okay, you may be tempted to talk to zoning or planning officials. But until you figure out what the rules and politics of your locality are, it may be best to do this without identifying and calling attention to yourself. (For example, have a friend who lives nearby make inquiries.)

The business I want to run from home is not specifically allowed or prohibited by my local ordinance. What should I do to avoid trouble?

Start by understanding that in most areas zoning and building officials don't actively search for violations. The great majority of home-based businesses that run into trouble do so when a neighbor complains—often because of noise or parking problems, or even because of the unfounded fear that your business is doing something illegal, such as selling drugs.

It follows that your best approach is often to explain your business activities to your neighbors and make sure that your activities are not worrying or inconveniencing them. For example, if you teach piano lessons or do physical therapy from your home and your students or clients will often come and go, make sure your neighbors are not bothered by noise or losing customary on-street parking spaces.

Do zoning ordinances include rules about specific activities, such as making noise, putting up signs, or having employees?

Many ordinances—especially those that are fairly vague about what types of businesses you can run from your home—restrict how you can carry out your business. The most frequent rules limit your use of on-street parking, prohibit outside signs, limit car and truck traffic, and restrict the number of employees who can work at your house on a regular basis (some prohibit employees altogether). In addition, some zoning ordinances limit the percentage of your home's floor space that can be devoted to the business. Again, you'll need to study your local ordinance carefully to see how these rules will affect you.

I live in a planned development that has its own rules for home-based businesses. Do these control my business activities, or can I rely on my city's home-based business ordinance, which is less restrictive?

In an effort to protect residential property values, most subdivisions, condos, and planned unit developments create special rules—typically called covenants, conditions and restrictions (CC&Rs)—that govern many aspects of property use. Rules pertaining to home-based businesses are often significantly stricter than those found in city ordinances. As long as the rules of your planned development are reasonably clear and consistently enforced, you must follow them.

Will maintaining a home office help me show the IRS that I'm an independent contractor?

No. An independent contractor is a person who controls both the outcome of a project and the means of accomplishing it, and who offers services to a number of businesses or individual purchasers. Although having an office or place of business is one factor the IRS looks at in determining whether an individual qualifies as an independent contractor, it makes no difference whether your office is located at home or in a traditional business setting.

Are there tax advantages to working from home?

Almost all ordinary and necessary business expenses (everything from wages to computers to paper clips) are tax deductible, no matter where they are incurred—in a factory or office, while traveling or at home.

But if you operate your business from home and qualify under IRS rules, you may be able to deduct part of your rent from your income taxes—or if you own your home, to take a depreciation deduction.

You may also be eligible to deduct a portion of your total utility, home repair and maintenance, property tax, and house insurance costs, based on the percentage of your residence you use for business purposes.

To qualify for home-office deductions, the IRS requires you to meet two legal tests:

- you must use your business space regularly and exclusively for business purposes, and
- your home office must be the principal place where you conduct your business. This rule is satisfied if your office is used for administrative or managerial activities, as long as these activities aren't often conducted at another business location. Alternatively, you must meet clients at home or use a separate structure on your property exclusively for business purposes.

The amount of your deduction can't exceed your home-based business's total profit.

Insuring Your Home-Based Business

Don't rely on a standard homeowner's or renter's insurance policy to cover your home-based business. These policies often exclude or strictly limit coverage for business equipment and injuries to business visitors. For example, if your computer is stolen or a client or business associate trips and falls on your steps, you may not be covered.

Fortunately, it's easy to avoid these nasty surprises. Sit down with your insurance agent and fully disclose your planned business operation. You'll find that it's relatively inexpensive to add business coverage to your homeowner's policy—and it's a tax-deductible expense. But be sure to check prices—some insurance companies provide special, cost-effective policies designed to protect both your home and your home-based business.

How big will my home office tax deduction be if my business qualifies under IRS rules?

To determine your deduction, you first need to figure out how much of your home you use for business as compared to other purposes. Do this by dividing the number of square feet used for your home business by the total square footage of your home. The resulting percentage determines how much of your rent (or, if you are a homeowner, depreciation), insurance, utilities, and other expenses are deductible. But remember, you can't deduct more than the profit your home-based business generates. (Additional technical rules apply to calculating depreciation on houses you own to allow for the fact that the structure, but not the land, depreciates.) For more information, see IRS Publication 587,

Business Use of Your Home (you can view it online at www.irs.gov).

Do I need to watch out for any tax traps when claiming deductions for my home office?

Claiming a home office deduction increases your audit risk slightly, but this needn't be a big fear if you carefully follow the rules.

Keep in mind that if you sell your house, you will have to pay tax on the depreciation portion of the home-based office deductions you have previously taken (up to a maximum of 25%), whether you made a profit or not. And you can't use the $250,000 per person "capital gains exclusion" on the sale of a home to offset this tax. For example, if your depreciation deductions total $5,000 for the last seven years, you have to pay tax on this amount in the year you sell your house. Despite this tax, it's generally wise to continue to take your home office deductions each year. Especially for people who don't plan to sell their houses anytime soon, it's usually beneficial to receive a tax break today that you won't have to repay for many years. You can use your tax savings to help your business grow.

I have a full-time job, but I also operate a separate part-time business from home. Can I claim a tax deduction for my home-based business expenses?

Yes, as long as your business meets certain IRS rules. It makes no difference that you work only part-time at your home-based business or that you have another occupation. But your business must be more than a disguised hobby—it has to pass muster with the IRS as a real business.

The IRS defines a business as "any activity engaged in to make a profit." If a venture makes money—even a small amount—in three of five consecutive years, it is presumed to possess a profit motive. (IRC § 183(d).) However, courts have held that some activities that don't meet this three-profitable-years-out-of-five test still qualify as a business if they are run in a businesslike manner. When determining whether an unprofitable venture qualifies for a deduction, courts may look at whether you kept thorough business records, had a separate business bank account, prepared advertising or other marketing materials, and obtained any necessary licenses and permits (a business license from your city, for example).

 More Information About Home-Based Business

Home Business Tax Deduction: Keep What You Earn, by Stephen Fishman (Nolo), explains how to take advantage of the many tax write-offs available to those who run a business from home.

Tax Savvy for Small Business, by Frederick W. Daily (Nolo), shows you how to take the home office deduction, including depreciation and household expenses.

The Best Home Businesses for the 21st Century, by Paul & Sarah Edwards (J.P. Tarcher), profiles over 100 workable home-based businesses, including information about how each business works and what skills and opportunities are necessary to succeed.

Working for Yourself: Law & Taxes for Independent Contractors, Freelancers & Consultants, by Stephen Fishman (Nolo), shows independent contractors how to meet business startup requirements, comply with strict IRS rules, and make sure they get paid in full and on time.

Employers' Rights & Responsibilities

At some point during your business venture, you may need to hire people to help you manage your workload. When you do, you'll have to follow a host of state and federal laws that regulate your relationship with your employees. Among the things you'll need to know and understand are:

- proper hiring practices, including how to write appropriate job descriptions, conduct interviews, and respect applicants' privacy rights
- paperwork requirements, including tax obligations, verifying your employees' immigration status, and more
- wage and hour laws, as well as the laws that govern retirement plans, health care benefits, and life insurance benefits
- workplace safety rules and regulations
- how to write an employee handbook and conduct performance reviews, including what you should and shouldn't put in an employee's personnel file
- how to avoid sexual harassment as well as discrimination based on several factors, including gender, age, race, pregnancy, religion, disability, and national origin, and
- how to avoid trouble if you need to fire an employee.

This section provides you with an overview of your role as an employer, and you can find more guidance elsewhere in this book. Employee's rights—including questions and answers about wages, hours, and workplace safety—are discussed in Chapter 4; retirement plans are covered in Chapter 13.

There Are a Number of Pitfalls to Avoid in Job Ads:

Don't Use	Use
Salesman	Salesperson
College Student	Part-time Worker
Handyman	General Repair Person
Gal Friday	Office Manager
Married Couple	Two-Person Job
Counter Girl	Retail Clerk
Waiter	Wait Staff
Young	Energetic

First things first. How can I write advertisements that will attract the best pool of potential employees—without getting in legal hot water?

The best way to write an ad that meets legal requirements is to stick to the job skills needed and the basic responsibilities. Some examples:

"Fifty-unit apartment complex seeks experienced manager with general maintenance skills."

"Midsized manufacturing company has opening for accountant with tax experience to oversee interstate accounts."

"Cook trainee position available in new vegetarian restaurant. Flexible hours."

Many small employers get tripped up when summarizing a job in an advertisement. This can easily happen if you're not familiar with the legal guidelines. Nuances in an ad can be used as evidence of discrimination against applicants—for example, based on gender, age, or marital status.

Help Wanted ads placed by federal contractors must state that all qualified applicants will receive consideration for employment without regard to race, color, religion, sex, or national origin. Ads often express this with the phrase, "An Equal Opportunity Employer." To show your intent to be fair, you may want to include this phrase in your ad even if you're not a federal contractor.

Any tips on how to conduct a good interview that gets me the information I need, while avoiding questions that cause legal trouble?

Good preparation is your best ally. Before you begin to interview applicants for a job opening, write down a set of questions focusing on the job duties and the applicant's skills and experience. For example:

"Tell me about your experience in running a mailroom."

"How much experience did you have making cold calls on your last job?"

"Explain how you typically go about organizing your workday."

"Have any of your jobs required strong leadership skills?"

By writing down the questions and sticking to the same format at all interviews for the position, you reduce the risk that a rejected applicant will later complain about unequal treatment. It's also smart to summarize the applicant's answers for your files—but don't get so involved in documenting the interview that you forget to listen closely to the applicant. And don't be so locked in to your list of questions that you don't follow up on something significant that an applicant has said, or try to pin down an ambiguous or evasive response.

To break the ice, you might start by giving the applicant some information about the job—the duties, hours, pay range, benefits, and career opportunities. Questions about the applicant's work history and experience that may be relevant to the job opening are always appropriate. But don't encourage the applicant to divulge the trade secrets of a present or former employer—especially a competitor. That can lead to a lawsuit. And be cautious about an applicant who volunteers such information or promises to bring secrets to the new position; that person will probably play fast and loose with your own company's secrets, given the chance.

I've heard horror stories about employers who get sued for discriminating—by employees and even by people they've interviewed but decided not to hire. How can they do that?

Federal and state laws prohibit many employers from discriminating against an employee or applicant because of race, color, gender, religious beliefs, national origin, disability, or age (if the person is at least 40 years old). Also, many states and cities have laws prohibiting employment discrimination based on other characteristics, such as marital status, sexual orientation, or gender identity. Often, these laws apply only if you have a minimum number of employees, such as five.

A particular form of discrimination becomes illegal when Congress, a state legislature, or a city council decides that a characteristic—race, for example—bears no legitimate relationship to employment decisions. As an employer, that means you must be prepared to show that your hiring and promotion decisions have been based on objective criteria and that the more-qualified applicant has always succeeded.

Still, when hiring, you can exercise a wide range of discretion based on business considerations. You remain free to hire, promote, discipline, and fire employees and to set their duties and salaries based on their skills, experience, performance, and reliability—factors that are logically tied to valid business purposes.

The law also prohibits employer practices that seem neutral but have a disproportionate impact on a particular group of people. Again, a policy is legal only if there's a valid business reason for its existence. For example, refusing to hire people who don't meet a minimum height and weight is permissible if it's clearly related to the physical demands of the particular job—felling and hauling huge trees, for instance. But applying such a requirement to exclude applicants for a job as a cook or receptionist wouldn't pass legal muster.

Can I run a background check on a prospective employee?

As an employer, you likely believe that the more information you have about job applicants, the better your hiring decisions will be. But make sure any information you seek is actually related to the job. It's often a waste of time and effort to acquire and review transcripts and credit reports—although occasionally they're useful. If you're hiring a bookkeeper, for example, previous job experience is much more important than the grades the applicant received in a community college bookkeeping program ten years ago. On the other hand, if the applicant is fresh out of school and has never held a bookkeeping job, a transcript may yield some insights.

If you pay someone outside of your company (such as a private investigator or background search company) to look into an applicant's background, or if you request a report from a credit agency about an applicant, you must comply with a federal law called the Fair Credit Reporting Act or FCRA (15 U.S.C. § 1681). Among other things, this law requires you to get the applicant's consent to the investigation and give the applicant a copy of the background check or investigative report if you decide not to hire the applicant based on its contents. You can find a summary of the FCRA and tips for compliance in *The Essential Guide to Federal Employment Laws*, by Amy DelPo and Lisa Guerin (Nolo).

Finally, it's usually not wise to resort to screening applicants through personality tests; most state laws and court rulings restrict your right to use them.

Can I require job applicants to pass a drug test?

It depends on the laws of your state. Although many states allow employers to test all applicants for illegal drug use, some states allow testing only for certain jobs—those that require driving, carrying a weapon, or operating heavy machinery, for example. Before requiring any applicant to take a drug test, you should check with your state's department of labor to find out what the law allows.

In general, you will be on safest legal ground if you have a strong, legitimate reason for testing applicants—especially if your reason involves protecting the public's safety. Be careful when testing current employees, however—the rules are usually different.

Is drug use a disability?

When it passed the Americans with Disabilities Act (ADA), Congress refused to recognize illegal drug use or current drug addiction as a disability. Therefore, if an applicant fails a legally administered drug test, you will not violate the ADA by refusing to hire that applicant.

However, the ADA does protect applicants who no longer use illegal drugs and have successfully completed (or are currently attending) a supervised drug rehabilitation program. Although you can require these applicants to take a drug test or show you proof of their participation in a rehabilitation program, you cannot refuse to hire them solely because they used to take illegal drugs.

What paperwork do I have to complete when I hire a new employee?

There are a few steps you are legally obligated to take when you hire someone new. Federal and state laws impose these requirements:

- **Report the employee to your state's new hire reporting agency.** The new hire reporting program requires employers to report information on new employees for the purpose of locating parents who owe child support. For more information, go to the Administration for Children & Families website at www.acf.dhhs.gov, which also provides the name and address of your state's new hire reporting agency. Most states provide a form you can use to provide the necessary information.

- **Fill out Form I-9,** *Employment Eligibility Verification.* U.S. Citizenship and Immigration Services (USCIS, formerly known as the INS) requires employers to use this form to verify that every employee they hire is eligible to work in the United States. (You don't have to file this form with the USCIS, but you must keep it in your files for three years and make it available for inspection by officials of the USCIS.) You can obtain the form online at www.uscis.gov.

• **Have the employee fill out IRS Form W-4, *Withholding Allowance Certificate.*** On this form, employees tell you how many allowances they are claiming for tax purposes, so that you can withhold the correct amount of tax from their paychecks. (You don't have to file the form with the IRS.) You can find this form at www.irs.gov.

You may choose to have a new employee fill out additional paperwork—for example, to acknowledge receipt of your company's employee handbook—but such documents aren't legally required.

How do I avoid legal problems when giving employee evaluations?

Be consistent, honest, and objective in employee evaluations. If a fired employee initiates a legal action against you, a judge or jury will probably see those evaluations—and will want to see that your words and actions are consistent. For example, a jury will sense that something is wrong if you consistently rate a worker's performance as poor or mediocre—but continue to hand out generous raises or perhaps even promote the person. The logical conclusion: You didn't take seriously the criticisms in your evaluation report, so you shouldn't expect the employee to take them seriously, either.

It's just as important to be honest in evaluations. It can be damaging to include only positive remarks or praise in report after report if that isn't the full picture. Even if your intentions are good, if all your written accounts suggest the employee is doing a great job and you later discipline or fire the employee, your actions will look unfair to both the employee and an objective outsider. And employers who appear unfair often lose court fights, especially in situations where a sympathetic employee appears to have been treated harshly.

Finally, keep your comments objective. Make sure your evaluation is tied to the employee's job performance. Avoid expressing general thoughts or ideas and, whenever possible, cite objective facts instead. For example, if an employee is chronically late, write "you were late seven times in the last month (time records attached)" instead of "you're late all the time."

If your system is working, employees with excellent evaluations should not need to be fired for poor performance. And employees with poor performance shouldn't be getting big raises or feeling surprised when you impose discipline.

As a small employer, what should I keep in personnel files—and what right do employees have to see what's inside?

Create a file for each employee in which you keep all job-related information, including:

• job description
• job application
• offer of employment
• IRS form W-4, the *Employee's Withholding Allowance Certificate*
• receipt or acknowledgment form for employee handbook
• periodic performance evaluations
• sign-up forms for employee benefits
• complaints from customers and coworkers
• awards or citations for excellent performance
• warnings and disciplinary actions, and
• notes on an employee's attendance or tardiness.

Experts recommend keeping one separate file for all of your employees' USCIS I-9 *Employment Eligibility Verification* forms—the forms you have to complete for new employees demonstrating that they are authorized to work in the United States. There are two practical reasons for keeping these forms in their own file—and out of your workers' personnel files. First, this will limit the number of people who know an employee's immigration status. If the I-9 is in the employee's personnel file, anyone who reviews that file (a supervisor, human resources employee, or payroll administrator) will know whether or not the employee is a citizen. This could lead to problems later, if the employee claims to have been discriminated against based on immigration status. If you keep the forms in a separate file, fewer people will be aware of the employee's immigration status—and the employee will have a much tougher time trying to prove that important employment decisions were made on that basis.

Second, if the U.S. Citizenship and Immigration Service (formerly the INS) decides to audit you, it is entitled to see I-9 forms as they are kept in the normal course of business. If you keep these forms in each employee's personnel file, that means the government will rummage through all of these files—causing inconvenience for you and privacy concerns for your employees. On the other hand, if you keep your forms in a single folder, you can simply hand over that folder if the government comes knocking.

Many states have laws giving employees—and former employees—the right to see their own personnel files. The rules vary from state to state. Typically, if your state allows employees to see their files, you can insist that a supervisor is present to make sure nothing is taken, added, or changed. Some state laws allow employees to obtain copies of items in their files, but not necessarily all items. For example, a law may limit the employee to copies of documents that he or she has signed. If an employee is entitled to a copy of an item in the file or if you're inclined to let the employee have a copy of any document in the file, you—rather than the employee—should make the copy.

Usually, you won't have to let the employee see sensitive items such as information assembled for a criminal investigation, reference letters, and information that might violate the privacy of other people. In a few states, employees may insert rebuttals to information in their personnel files with which they disagree.

Am I required to offer my employees paid vacation, disability, maternity, or sick leave?

No federal law requires you to offer paid vacation time or paid sick or disability leave to your employees. In 2002, however, California became the first state to provide some paid sick and family leave for employees (the law didn't take effect until 2004). And other states—or even cities or local governments—may follow suit.

If you decide to adopt a policy that gives your employees paid vacation or sick time, you must apply the policy consistently to all employees. If you offer some employees a more attractive package than others, you are opening yourself up to claims of unfair treatment.

The same rules apply to pregnancy and maternity leave. If you offer paid vacation, sick, or disability leave, you must allow pregnant women and women who have just given birth to make use of these policies. For example, a new mother who is physically unable to work following the birth of her child must be allowed to use paid disability leave if such leave is available to other employees.

Special Rules for Medical Records

The Americans with Disabilities Act (ADA) and the Family and Medical Leave Act (FMLA) impose very strict limitations on how you must handle information from medical examinations and inquiries. You must keep the information in medical files that are separate from nonmedical records, and you must store the medical files in a separate locked cabinet. To further guarantee the confidentiality of medical records, designate one person to be in charge of those files.

The ADA and FMLA allow very limited disclosure of medical information. You may:

- inform supervisors about necessary restrictions on an employee's duties and about necessary accommodations
- inform first aid and safety workers about a disability that may require emergency treatment and about specific procedures that are needed if the workplace must be evacuated, or
- provide medical information required by government officials.

Otherwise, don't disclose medical information about employees. The best policy is to treat all medical information about all employees as confidential.

Must I offer my employees unpaid leave?

There are two situations in which you might be legally required to offer unpaid leave to your employees. First, if the employee requesting leave qualifies as disabled under the Americans with Disabilities Act (see below), and requests the leave as a reasonable accommodation for the disability, you may be required to grant the leave request. For example, an employee who needs time off to undergo surgery or treatment for a disabling condition is probably entitled to unpaid leave, unless you can show that providing the leave would be an undue hardship to your business.

Second, your employees might be entitled to unpaid leave under the Family and Medical Leave Act (FMLA) or a similar state statute. See Chapter 4 for an explanation of when you must provide leave under the FMLA.

What am I legally required to do for my disabled employees?

The Americans with Disabilities Act (ADA) prohibits employers from discriminating against disabled applicants or employees. However, the ADA does not require employers to hire or retain workers who can't do their jobs. Only "qualified workers with disabilities"—employees who can perform all the essential elements of the job, with or without some form of accommodation from their employers—are protected by the law.

An employee is legally disabled if any one of the following is true:

- The employee has a physical or mental impairment that substantially limits a major life activity (such as the ability to walk, talk, see, hear, breathe, reason, or take care of oneself). Courts tend not to categorically characterize certain conditions as disabilities—instead, they consider the effect of the particular condition on the particular employee.

- The employee has a record or history of impairment.
- The employee is regarded by the employer as disabled, even if the employer is incorrect.

The ADA also requires employers to make reasonable accommodations for their disabled employees. This means you may have to provide some assistance or make some changes in the job or workplace to enable the worker to do the job. For example, an employer might lower the height of a workspace or install ramps to accommodate a worker in a wheelchair, provide voice-recognition software for a worker with a repetitive stress disorder, or provide TDD telephone equipment for a worker with impaired hearing.

It is your employee's responsibility to inform you of his or her disability and request a reasonable accommodation—you don't have to be psychic to follow the law. Once an employee raises the issue, you must engage in a dialogue with the worker to try to figure out what kinds of accommodations might be effective and practical. Although you don't have to provide the precise accommodation your worker requests, you do have to work together to come up with a reasonable solution.

Employers don't have to provide an accommodation if it would cause their business to suffer "undue hardship"— essentially, if the cost or effect of the accommodation would be excessive. There are no hard and fast rules about when an accommodation poses an undue hard-

ship. When faced with this issue, courts consider a number of factors, including:

- the cost of the accommodation
- the size and financial resources of the employer
- the structure of the employer's business, and
- the effect the accommodation would have on the business.

Employees With Mental Disabilities

The ADA applies equally to employees with physical disabilities and employees with mental or psychiatric disabilities. Therefore, workers who suffer from severe depression, bipolar disorder, schizophrenia, attention deficit disorder, and other mental conditions may be covered by the ADA, if the condition meets the ADA's definition of a disability.

Workers with mental disabilities are also entitled to reasonable accommodations. For example, you might allow an employee whose antidepressant medication causes drowsiness in the morning to come in a few hours late, or provide an office with soundproofed walls to reduce distractions for an employee who suffers from attention deficit disorder.

One of my employees just told me that she was sexually harassed by a coworker. What should I do?

Most employers feel anxious when faced with complaints of sexual harassment. And with good reason: Such complaints can lead to workplace tension, government investigations, and even costly legal battles. If the complaint is mishandled, even unintentionally, an employer may unwittingly put itself out of business.

Here are some basics to keep in mind if you receive a complaint:

- **Educate yourself.** Do some research on the law of sexual harassment—learn what sexual harassment is, how it is proven in court, and what your responsibilities are as an employer. An excellent place to start is the website for the Equal Employment Opportunity Commission (www.eeoc.gov), the federal agency responsible for administering many employment laws.

- **Follow established procedures.** If you have an employee handbook or other documented policies relating to sexual harassment, follow those policies. Don't open yourself up to claims of unfair treatment by bending the rules.

- **Interview the people involved.** Start by talking to the person who complained. Then talk to the employee accused of harassment and any witnesses. Get details: what was said or done, when, where, and who else was there.

- **Look for corroboration or contradiction.** Usually, the accuser and accused offer different versions of the incident, leaving you with no way of knowing who's telling the truth. Turn to other sources for clues. For example, schedules, time cards, and other attendance records (for trainings, meetings, and so on) may help you determine if each party was where they claimed to be. Witnesses may have seen part of the incident. And in some cases, documents will prove one side right. After all, it's hard to argue with an X-rated email.

- **Keep it confidential.** A sexual harassment complaint can polarize a workplace. Workers will likely side with either the complaining employee or the accused employee, and the rumor mill will start working overtime. Worse, if too many details about the complaint are leaked, you may be accused of damaging the reputation of the alleged victim or alleged harasser—and get slapped with a defamation lawsuit. Avoid these problems by insisting on confidentiality, and practicing it in your investigation. But don't promise the accused person that you'll keep the complaint confidential. After all, you will probably have to discuss it with the accuser, and perhaps with witnesses or your superiors.

- **Document everything.** Take notes during your interviews, including important and objective information like the person's full name, the date, and what the person said. Before the interview is over, go back through your notes with the interviewee, to make sure you got it right. Write down the steps you have taken to learn the truth, including interviews you have conducted and documents you have reviewed. Document any action taken against the accused, or the reasons for deciding not to take action. This written record will protect you later if your employee claims that you ignored a complaint or conducted a one-sided investigation.

- **Cooperate with government agencies.** If the accuser makes a complaint with a government agency (either the federal Equal Employment Opportunity Commission (EEOC) or an equivalent state agency), that agency may investigate. Try to provide the agency with the materials it requests, but remember that the agency is gathering evidence that could be used against you later. This is a good time to consider hiring a lawyer to advise you.

- **Don't retaliate.** It is against the law to punish someone for making a sexual harassment complaint. The most obvious forms of retaliation are termination, discipline, demotion, pay cuts, or threats of any of these actions. More subtle forms of retaliation may include changing the shift hours or work area of the accuser, changing the accuser's job responsibilities or reporting relationships, or leaving the accuser out of meetings and other office functions.

- **Take appropriate action against the harasser.** Once you have gathered all the information available, sit down and figure out what really happened. If you conclude that some form of sexual harassment occurred, decide how to discipline the harasser appropriately. Once you have decided on an appropriate action, take it quickly, document it, and notify the accuser.

My employees' religious differences are causing strife in the workplace. What am I required to do?

This is a tricky area. An increasing number of employees are claiming religious discrimination. And unfortunately, the law in this delicate area is unclear.

First, make sure you aren't imposing your religious beliefs on your employees. You have the legal right to discuss your own religious beliefs with an employee, if you're so inclined, but you can't persist to the point that the employee feels you're being hostile, intimidating, or offensive.

So if an employee objects to your discussion of religious subjects or you get even an inkling that your religious advances are unwelcome, back off. Otherwise, you may find yourself embroiled in a lawsuit or administrative proceeding.

If employees complain to you that a coworker is badgering them with religious views, you have a right—if not a duty—to intervene, although you must, of course, use the utmost tact and sensitivity.

While you may feel that the best way to resolve these knotty problems is to simply banish religion from the workplace, that's generally not a viable alternative. You're legally required to accommodate the religious needs of employees—for example, allowing employees to pick and choose the paid holidays they would like to take during the year. You don't, however, have to make an accommodation that would impose an undue hardship, such as requiring more than ordinary administrative costs or diminishing efficiency in other jobs.

Some of my employees insist they have a right to smoke during breaks and at lunch, and another group claims they'll quit if I allow smoking on the premises. I'm caught in the middle. What should I do?

It's well established that second-hand tobacco smoke can harm the health of nonsmokers. Consequently, in many states and municipalities, employers are legally required to limit or prohibit smoking in the workplace. And a number of locales have specific laws that ban or limit smoking in public places; if your workplace falls within the legal definition of a public place—a bar, restaurant, or hotel, for example—your legal rights and responsibilities will be clearly spelled out in the law.

Given the scientific facts and the general direction in which the law is moving, your safest legal course is to restrict smoking in the workplace—and a total ban may be the only practical solution. That's because in many modern buildings, it's too expensive—maybe even impossible—to provide a separate ventilation system for a smokers' room.

In addition to meeting the specific requirements of laws and regulations that limit or prohibit smoking in the workplace, be aware that you may be legally liable to nonsmoking employees if you don't take appropriate actions on their complaints.

It's been a bad year for my business—and it looks as though I may have to lay off some workers. Are there legal problems to avoid?

Generally, you're free to lay off or terminate employees because business conditions require it. But if you do cut back, don't leave your business open to claims that the layoffs were really a pretext for getting rid of employees for illegal reasons.

Be sensitive to how your actions may be perceived. If the layoff primarily affects workers of a particular race, women, or older employees, someone may well question your motives. Make sure that you have sound business reasons for each employee you decide to lay off.

Larger employers—those with at least 100 employees—are legally required to give employees 60-days' notice before a plant closing or mass layoff. This requirement is set out in the federal Workers Adjustment and Retraining Notification Act (WARN Act). There are plenty of exceptions to the WARN Act, however—most notably, that it applies only if a large number of employees are being let go. Many states have passed similar laws, and some

of these laws apply to smaller employers and/or smaller layoffs. A few states require more than notice—for example, employers may have to pay a small severance or continue paying for health insurance coverage for laid-off workers.

How can I make sure that my employees don't reveal my company's trade secrets to a competitor—especially after they leave the company?

You should take two steps to protect your trade secrets from disclosure by former employees: always treat your trade secrets as confidential, and require any employee who will learn your trade secrets to sign a nondisclosure agreement.

A trade secret is any information that provides its owner with a competitive advantage in the market, and is treated as a secret—that is, handled in a manner that can reasonably be expected to prevent others from learning about it. Examples of trade secrets might include recipes, manufacturing processes, customer or pricing lists, and ideas for new products. If you own a trade secret, you have the legal right to prevent anyone from disclosing, copying, or using it, and you can sue anyone who violates these rights to your disadvantage.

Always keep your trade secrets confidential. For example, you should mark documents containing trade secrets "confidential" and limit their circulation, disclose trade secret material only to those employees with a real need to know, keep materials in a safe place, and have a written policy stating that trade secrets are not to be revealed to outsiders.

In addition to taking steps to keep your trade secrets confidential, you should also require any employee who will deal with your trade secrets to sign a nondisclosure agreement (NDA) promising not to reveal your secrets. You can find more information and sample NDA forms in *Nondisclosure Agreements*, by Richard Stim and Stephen Fishman (Nolo).

What are my legal obligations to an employee who is leaving the company?

Surprisingly, your responsibility to your employees doesn't necessarily end when the employment relationship ends. Even after an employee quits or is fired, you may have to:

- **Provide the employee's final paycheck in accordance with state law.** Most states require that an employee receive this check fairly quickly, sometimes immediately after getting fired.

- **Provide severance pay.** No law requires employers to provide severance pay (although a few states require employers to pay severance to workers fired in a plant closure). But if you promise it, you must pay it to all employees who meet your policy's requirements.

- **Give information on continuation of health insurance, under a federal law called the Consolidated Omnibus Budget Reconciliation Act (COBRA).** If you offer your employees health insurance, and your company has 20 or more employees, you must offer departing employees the option to continue their coverage under the company's group health insurance plan, at their own expense, for a specified period.

- **Allow former employees to view their personnel files.** Most states give employees and former employees the legal right to see their personnel files, and to receive copies of some of the documents relating to their jobs. State laws vary as to how long employers must keep these records for former employees.

I have to give a reference for a former employee I had to fire. I don't want to be too positive about him, but I am also afraid he might sue me for unflattering remarks. Advice?

The key to protecting yourself is to stick to the facts and act in good faith. You'll get in trouble only if you exaggerate or cover up the truth—or are motivated by a desire to harm your former employee.

Former employees who feel maligned can sue for defamation—called slander if the statements were spoken or libel if they were written. To win a defamation case, a former employee must prove that you intentionally gave out false information and that the information harmed his or her reputation. If you can show that the information you provided was true, the lawsuit will be dismissed.

And even if it turns out that the information provided is untrue, employers in most states are entitled to some protection in defamation cases. This protection is based on a legal doctrine called "qualified privilege." To receive the benefits, you will probably have to show that either a former employee or that employee's prospective employer asked you to provide a reference; that you limited your comments to truthful, job-related statements; and that your comments weren't motivated by ill will or malice toward the employee.

A practical policy—and one that gives you a high degree of legal protection—is simply not to discuss an employee with prospective employers if you can't say something positive. Just tell the person inquiring that it's not your policy to comment on former workers.

Where an employee's record is truly mixed, it's usually possible to accent the positive while you try to put negative information into a more favorable perspective. If you do choose to go into detail, don't hide the bad news. In very extreme cases (in which the former employee committed a serious crime or engaged in dangerous wrongdoing), you could be sued by the new employer for concealing this information.

Do I have the same legal obligations to independent contractors as I do to employees?

Generally, an employer has more obligations, both legally and financially, to employees than to independent contractors. The workplace rights guaranteed to employees do not protect independent contractors, for the most part. And an employer must make certain contributions to the government on behalf of its employees, while independent contractors are expected to make these payments themselves.

Here are a number of rules that apply only to employees:

- **Antidiscrimination laws.** Most laws prohibiting employers from discriminating against employees or applicants for employment based on such characteristics as race, gender, national origin, religion, age, or disability do not protect independent contractors.

- **Wage and hour laws.** Independent contractors are not covered by laws governing the minimum wage, overtime pay, and the like.

- **Medical and parental leave laws.** You are not required to offer independent contractors medical or parental leave.

- **Workers' compensation laws.** You do not have to provide workers' compensation for independent contractors.

- **Unemployment insurance.** You do not have to contribute to your state's unemployment insurance fund for independent contractors.

- **Social Security taxes.** You are not required to make any Social Security or Medicare payments on behalf of independent contractors.

- **Wage withholding.** You are not required to withhold state or federal income tax, or state disability insurance payments (where applicable) from the paychecks of independent contractors.

When can I classify a worker as an independent contractor?

Different government agencies use different tests to decide whether workers should be classified as independent contractors or employees. Generally, these tests are intended to figure out whether an independent contractor is truly a self-employed businessperson offering services to the general public. The more discretion a worker has to decide how, when, and for whom to perform work, the more likely that the worker is an independent contractor. For example, an independent contractor might do similar work for other companies, provide the tools and equipment to do the job, decide how to do the job (including when, where, and in what order to do the work), and hire employees or assistants to help out with big projects. On the other hand, a worker who works only for you, under conditions determined by you, is more likely to be classified as an employee.

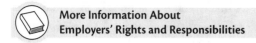

More Information About Employers' Rights and Responsibilities

The Employer's Legal Handbook, by Fred Steingold (Nolo), explains employers' legal rights and responsibilities in detail.

The Job Description Handbook, by Margie Mader-Clark (Nolo), helps you write job descriptions that are effective and legal.

Dealing With Problem Employees, by Amy DelPo and Lisa Guerin (Nolo), offers employers advice and step-by-step instructions for handling problems in the workplace, from giving effective performance evaluations to terminating employment when things who don't work out.

The Essential Guide to Federal Employment Laws, by Amy DelPo and Lisa Guerin (Nolo), summarizes every important federal workplace law and provides compliance tips, resources, record-keeping requirements, and more.

The Manager's Legal Handbook, by Lisa Guerin and Amy DelPo (Nolo), provides all the basic information, tips, and real-world examples employers need to answer their employment law questions.

The Performance Appraisal Handbook, by Amy DelPo (Nolo), gives information, advice, and instructions that will help you give legal, effective performance evaluations.

Create Your Own Employee Handbook, by Lisa Guerin and Amy DelPo (Nolo), shows you all the practical information, sample policies, and forms you need to make an employee handbook that works for your company.

The Essential Guide to Workplace Investigations, by Lisa Guerin (Nolo), provides step-by-step instructions for investigating common problems—and taking effective action to stop them.

The Progressive Discipline Handbook, by Margie Mader-Clark and Lisa Guerin (Nolo), gives more information on how to effectively discipline employees while avoiding legal pitfalls.

The Essential Guide to Family & Medical Leave, by Lisa Guerin and Deborah England (Nolo), covers the ins and outs of the Family and Medical Leave Act (FMLA).

Information on independent contractors can be found in *Working With Independent Contractors*, by Stephen Fishman (Nolo).

Consultant and Independent Contractor Agreements, by Stephen Fishman (Nolo), helps you draft legal agreements with independent contractors after you've decided to hire them.

For information on federal discrimination laws and lists of state resources, contact the Equal Employment Opportunity Commission, 1801 L St., NW, Washington, DC, 20507, 800-669-4000, www.eeoc.gov.

For information on wage and hour laws, workers' compensation, and family and medical leave, contact the Department of Labor, 200 Constitution Ave., NW, Washington, DC, 20210, 866-487-2365, www.dol.gov.

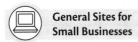

General Sites for Small Businesses

www.nolo.com
Nolo offers free information and small business books, software, and forms on a wide variety of subjects, including starting and running your small business.

www.americanexpress.com/smallbusiness
The American Express Small Business Exchange provides information and resources for your small business. Click "Articles & Discussions" to get started.

www.nfib.com
The National Federation of Independent Business provides news, workshops, and action alerts for small business owners. The NFIB is the nation's largest advocacy organization for small and independent businesses.

www.sba.gov
The Small Business Administration provides information about starting, financing, and expanding your small business.

http://smallbusiness.yahoo.com
Yahoo offers an abundance of links to resources for small business people.

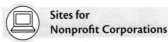

Sites for Nonprofit Corporations

www.igc.org
The Institute for Global Communication offers an extensive list of links to resources for activism and nonprofit development.

www.boardsource.org
BoardSource, formerly the National Center for Nonprofit Boards, provides information and publications to help you run a successful nonprofit organization.

Patents

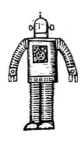

*To invent, you need a good
imagination and a pile of junk.*

—THOMAS EDISON

Many of us muse about the million-dollar idea: the invention that will make life easier for others and more lucrative for us. Most of these ideas never get off the ground, however; we decide it's not really worth the time and effort to create the perfect dog toothbrush, clothes hanger, or juice squeezer. But every now and then we may hit on a winner—an idea worth developing, marketing, and protecting. In these situations, we must turn to the patent laws for help.

This chapter addresses the basic legal issues that arise in the patent area, answering questions such as:

- What is a patent?
- When does a particular invention qualify for a patent?
- How do you get a patent in the United States or abroad?
- How are patent rights enforced?
- How can you profit from your patent?

Qualifying for a Patent

There is nothing which persevering effort and unceasing and diligent care cannot accomplish.

—SENECA

A patent is a document issued by the U.S. Patent and Trademark Office (PTO) that grants a monopoly for a limited period of time on the right to manufacture, use, and sell an invention.

What types of inventions can be patented?

The PTO issues three different kinds of patents: utility patents, design patents, and plant patents.

Design patents last for 14 years from the date the patent issues. Plant and utility patents last for 20 years from the date of filing.

To qualify for a utility patent—by far the most common type of patent—an invention must be:

- a process or method for producing a useful, concrete, and tangible result (such as a genetic engineering procedure, an investment strategy, or computer software)
- a machine (usually something with moving parts or circuitry, such as a cigarette lighter, sewage treatment system, laser, or photocopier)
- an article of manufacture (such as an eraser, tire, transistor, or hand tool)
- a composition of matter (such as a chemical composition, drug, soap, or genetically altered life form), or
- an improvement of an invention that fits within one of the first four categories.

Often, an invention will fall into more than one category. For instance, a laser can usually be described both as a process (the steps necessary to produce the laser beam) and a machine (a device that implements the steps to produce the laser beam). Regardless of the number of categories into which a particular invention fits, it can receive only one utility patent.

If an invention fits into one of the categories described above, it is known as "statutory subject matter" and has passed the first test in qualifying for a patent. But an inventor's creation must overcome several additional hurdles before the PTO will issue a patent. The invention must also:

- have some utility, no matter how trivial
- be novel (that is, it must be different from all previous inventions in some important way), and
- be nonobvious (a surprising and significant development) to somebody who understands the technical field of the invention.

For design patents, the law requires that the design be novel, nonobvious, and nonfunctional. For example, a new shape for a car fender, bottle, or flashlight that doesn't improve how it functions would qualify.

Finally, plants may qualify for a patent if they are both novel and nonobvious. Plant patents are issued less frequently than any other type of patent.

More Examples of Patentable Subject Matter

The following items are just some of the things that might qualify for patent protection: biological inventions; carpet designs; new chemical formulas, processes, or procedures; clothing accessories and designs; computer hardware and peripherals; computer software; containers; cosmetics; decorative hardware; electrical inventions; electronic circuits; fabrics and fabric designs; food inventions; furniture design; games (board, box, and instructions); housewares; jewelry; laser light shows; machines; magic tricks or techniques; mechanical inventions; medical accessories and devices; medicines; methods of doing business; musical instruments; odors; plants; recreational gear; and sporting goods (designs and equipment).

What types of inventions cannot be patented?

Some types of inventions will not qualify for a patent, no matter how interesting or important they are. For example, mathematical formulas, laws of nature, newly discovered substances that occur naturally in the world, and purely theoretical phenomena—for instance, a scientific principle like superconductivity without regard to its use in the real world—have long been considered unpatentable. This means, for example, that you can't patent a general mathematical approach to problem solving or a newly discovered painkiller in its natural state.

In addition, the following categories of inventions don't qualify for patents:

- processes done entirely by human motor coordination, such as choreographed dance routines or a method for meditation

- most protocols and methods used to perform surgery on humans

- printed matter that has no unique physical shape or structure associated with it

- unsafe new drugs

- inventions useful only for illegal purposes, and

- nonoperable inventions, including "perpetual motion" machines (which are presumed to be nonoperable because to operate they would have to violate certain bedrock scientific principles).

Can computer software qualify for patent protection?

Yes. Even though you can't get a patent on a mathematical formula per se, you may be able to get protection for a specific application of a formula. Thus, software may qualify for a patent if it produces a useful, concrete, and tangible result. For example, the PTO will not issue a patent on the complex mathematical formulae that are used in space navigation but will grant a patent for the software and machines that translate those equations and make the space shuttle go where it's supposed to go.

Can a business method qualify for a utility patent?

A business method is a series of steps that express some business activity. Examples include a method of calculating an interest rate or a system for evaluating employee performance. Before 1988, the PTO rarely granted patents for methods of doing business. Then, in 1988, the United States Court of Appeals for the Federal Circuit changed this. (*State Street Bank & Trust Co. v. Signal Financial Group, Inc.* 149 F.3d 1368 (Fed. Cir. 1998).) The court ruled that patent laws were intended to protect business methods, so long as the method produced a "useful, concrete and tangible result."

In response to the development of these new methods, the PTO created a new classification for such applications: "Data processing: financial, business practice, management or cost/price determination."

Is it possible to obtain a patent on forms of life?

Forms of life, from bacteria to cows, that are genetically altered to have new and useful characteristics or behaviors may qualify for utility patents. Also patentable are sequences of DNA that have been created to test genetic behaviors and the methods used to accomplish this sequencing. With the advent of cloning techniques and the ability to mix genes across species—for example, the human immune system genetic code transplanted into a mouse for testing purposes—the question of what life forms can and cannot be patented promises to be a subject of fierce debate for years to come.

What makes an invention novel?

In the context of a patent application, an invention is considered novel when it is different from all previous inventions (called "prior art") in one or more of its constituent elements. When deciding whether an invention is novel, the PTO will consider all prior art that existed as of the date the inventor files a patent application on the invention or, if necessary, as of the date the inventor can prove he or she first built and tested the invention. If prior art is uncovered, the invention may still qualify for a patent if the inventor can show that he or she conceived of the invention before the prior art existed and was diligent in building and testing the invention or filing a patent application on it.

An invention will flunk the novelty test if it was described in a published document or put to public use more than one year before the patent application was filed. This is known as the one-year rule.

When is an invention considered nonobvious?

To qualify for a patent, an invention must be nonobvious as well as novel. An invention is considered nonobvious if someone who is skilled in the particular field of the invention would view it as an unexpected or surprising development.

For example, in August 2006, Future Enterprises invents a portable, high-quality wireless scanner that can be worn like eyeglasses. A computer engineer would most likely find this invention to be surprising and unexpected. Even though it isn't generally that surprising when computer-based technology becomes more portable, the specific way in which the portability is accomplished by this invention (placing the scanner at eye level) would be a breakthrough in the field—and thus unobvious. Contrast this with a bicycle developer who uses a new, light but strong metal alloy to build his bicycles. Most people skilled in the art of bicycle manufacturing would consider the use of the new alloy in the bicycle to be obvious, given that low weight is a desirable aspect of high-quality bicycles.

Figuring out whether an invention will be considered nonobvious by the PTO is difficult because it is such a subjective exercise—what one patent examiner considers surprising another may not. In addition, the examiner will usually be asked to make the nonobviousness determination well after the date of the invention, because of delays inherent in the patent process. The danger of this type of retroactive assessment is that the examiner may unconsciously be affected by intervening technical improvements. To avoid this, the examiner generally relies only on the prior-art references (documents describing previous inventions) that existed as of the date of invention.

As an example, assume that in 2008, Future Enterprises' application for a patent on the 2006 invention is being examined in the PTO. Assume further that by 2008 you can find a portable "eyeglass scanner" in any consumer electronics store for under $200. The patent examiner will have to go back to when the scanner was invented to fully appreciate how surprising and unexpected it was when it was first conceived—and ignore the fact that in 2008 the technology of the invention is very common.

What makes an invention useful?

Patents may be granted for inventions that have some type of usefulness (utility), even if the use is humorous. For example, there may not be many people who need a musical condom or a motorized spaghetti fork, but both items have some use. However, the invention must work—at least in theory. Thus, a new approach to manufacturing superconducting materials may qualify for a patent if it has a sound theoretical basis—even if it hasn't yet been shown to work in practice. But a new drug that has no theoretical basis and hasn't been tested will not qualify for a patent.

The inventor need not show utility to qualify for a design or plant patent.

Are You the First?

As discussed above, patents are awarded only on new and nonobvious inventions. How can an inventor find out whether his or her invention is really new? Start by finding out whether it has ever been patented. Although a number of great inventions have never received a patent, most have. A quick spin through the patent database can provide a good head start on finding out just how innovative an invention really is.

The Internet can be used for free access to patents issued since 1971. The U.S. Patent and Trademark Office (www.uspto.gov) and the European Patent Office (EPO) (http://ep.espacenet.com) both provide free online databases where you simply type in keywords that describe your invention.

Commercial, fee-based databases often offer more choices than the free USPTO site. Below are some fee-based patent databases and a brief description of their contents.

- **MicroPatent** (www.micropatent.com). You can search U.S. and Japanese patents from 1976 to the present, International patents issued under the Patent Cooperation Treaty (PCT) from 1983, and European patents from 1988.

- **Delphion** (www.delphion.com). You can search U.S. patents from 1971 to the present, full-text patents from the European Patent Office and the World Intellectual Property Organization PCT collection, and abstracts from Derwent world patent index.

- **LEXPAT** (www.lexis-nexis.com). You can search U.S. patents from 1971 to the present. In addition, the LEXPAT library offers extensive searching capability of technical journals and magazines (to find prior art).

- **QPAT** (www.qpat.com) and **Questel/Orbit** (www.questel.orbit.com). You can search U.S. patents from 1974 to the present and full-text European patents from 1987 to the present.

Sometimes an inventor needs to search for patents issued before 1971. All patents issued since the founding of the United States count when deciding whether an invention is sufficiently new to deserve a patent. And if the invention involves timeless technology (another way to core an apple), these pre-1971 patents are as important as those that were issued later.

A great resource for complete patent searching—from the first patent ever issued to the latest—is a network of special libraries called Patent and Trademark Depository Libraries (PTDLs). Every state but Connecticut has at least one. While a complete patent search can be done for free in these libraries, many of them also offer computer searches for a reasonable fee. Consult the PTO website at www.uspto.gov to find the PTDL nearest you.

Obtaining a Patent

Many times a day I realize how much my own outer and inner life is built upon the labors of my fellow men, both living and dead, and how earnestly I must exert myself in order to give in return as much as I have received.

—ALBERT EINSTEIN

Because a patent grants the inventor a monopoly on his or her invention for a relatively long period of time, patent applications are rigorously examined by the Patent and Trademark Office (PTO). Typically, a patent application travels back and forth between the applicant and the patent examiner until both sides agree on which aspects of an invention the patent will cover, if any. During this process, the inventor may have to amend some of the patent claims—the descriptions of exactly what the invention is and what it does—to distinguish the invention from the prior art. This process typically takes a year or two.

If an agreement is reached, the PTO "allows" the application and publishes a brief description of the patent in a weekly online publication called the *Official Gazette*. (You can access it on the PTO website at www.uspto.gov.) If no one objects to the patent as published, and the applicant pays the required issuance fee, the PTO provides the applicant with a document called a patent deed, which we colloquially refer to as a patent. The patent deed consists primarily of the information submitted in the patent application, as modified during the patent-examination process.

What information is typically included in a patent application?

There is no such thing as an automatic patent through creation or usage of an invention. To receive patent protection, an inventor must file an application, pay the appropriate fees, and obtain a patent. To apply for a U.S. patent, the inventor must file the application with a branch of the U.S. Department of Commerce known as the U.S. Patent and Trademark Office, or PTO. A U.S. patent application typically consists of:

- an information disclosure statement—that is, an explanation of how the invention differs from all previous and similar developments (the "prior art")
- a detailed description of the structure and operation of the invention (called a patent specification) that explains how to build and use the invention
- a precise description of the aspects of the invention to be covered by the patent (called the patent claims)
- all drawings that are necessary to fully explain the specification and claims
- a patent application declaration—a statement under oath that the information in the application is true, and
- the filing fee.

In addition, small inventors often include a declaration asking for a reduction in the filing fee.

Understanding the Provisional Patent Application

Often inventors want to have a patent application on file when they show their invention to prospective manufacturers, to discourage ripoffs. Also, inventors like to get their invention on record as early as possible in case someone else comes up with the same invention. To accomplish both of these goals, an inventor may file what is known as a provisional patent application (PPA). The PPA need only contain a complete description of the structure and operation of an invention and any drawings that are necessary to understand it—it need not contain claims, formal drawings, a patent application declaration, or an information disclosure Statement.

An inventor who files a regular patent application within one year of filing a PPA can claim the PPA's filing date for the regular patent application. If the regular patent application includes any new matter (technical information about the invention) that wasn't in the PPA, the inventor won't be able to rely on the PPA's filing date for the new matter. The PPA's filing date doesn't affect when the patent on the invention will expire; it still expires 20 years from the date the regular patent application is filed. So, the PPA has the practical effect of delaying examination of a regular patent application and extending—up to one year—the patent's expiration date.

What happens if there are multiple applications for the same invention?

If a patent examiner discovers that another application is pending for the same invention and that both inventions appear to qualify for a patent, the patent examiner will declare that a conflict (called an interference) exists between the two applications. In that event, a hearing is held to determine who is entitled to the patent.

Who gets the patent depends on who first conceived the invention and worked on it diligently, who first built and tested the invention, and who filed the first provisional or regular patent application. Because of the possibility of a patent interference, it is wise to document all invention-related activities in a signed and witnessed inventor's notebook so that you can later prove the date the invention was conceived and the steps you took to build and test the invention. The notebook will also help you put together your patent application.

How are U.S. patents protected abroad?

Patent rights originate in the U.S. Constitution and are implemented exclusively by federal laws passed by Congress. These laws define the kinds of inventions that are patentable and the procedures that must be followed to apply for, receive, and maintain patent rights for the duration of the patent.

All other industrialized countries offer patent protection as well. Though patent requirements and rules differ from country to country, several international treaties (including the Patent

Cooperation Treaty and the Paris Convention) allow U.S. inventors to obtain patent protection in other countries that have adopted the treaties if the inventors take certain required steps, such as filing a patent application in the countries on a timely basis and paying required patent fees.

Enforcing a Patent

Once a patent is issued, it is up to the owner to enforce it. If friendly negotiations fail, enforcement involves two basic steps:

- making a determination that the patent is being illegally violated (infringed), and
- filing a federal court action to enforce the patent.

Because enforcing a patent can be a long and expensive process, many potential patent infringment suits never get filed. Instead, the patent owner often settles with the infringer. Frequently, an infringer will pay a reasonable license fee that allows the infringer to continue using the invention.

What constitutes infringement of a patent?

To decide whether an inventor is violating a patent, you must carefully examine the patent's claims (most patents contain more than one of these terse statements of the scope of the invention) and compare the elements of each claim with the elements of the accused infringer's device or process. If the elements of a patent claim match the elements of the device or process (called "reading on" or "teaching" the device or process), an infringement has occurred. Even if the claims don't literally match the infringing device, it is possible that a court would find an infringement by applying what's

known as the "doctrine of equivalents." In these cases, the invention in the patent and the allegedly infringing device or process are sufficiently equivalent in what they do and how they do it to warrant a finding of infringement.

For example, Steve invents a tennis racket with a scorekeeper embedded in the racket handle's end. The invention is claimed as a tennis racket handle that combines grasping and scorekeeping functions. Steve receives a patent on this invention. Later, Megan invents and sells a tennis racket with a transparent handle that provides a more sophisticated scorekeeping device than Steve's racket. Even though Megan's invention improves on Steve's invention in certain respects, it will most likely be held to be an infringement of Steve's invention, for one of two reasons:

- Megan's invention teaches the same elements as those claimed in Steve's patent (a tennis racket handle with two functions), or
- considering what it is and how it works, Megan's invention is the substantial equivalent of Steve's invention (the doctrine of equivalents).

You can't always rely on the doctrine of equivalents to protect your invention from infringers, however. If you amended your patent claims during the application process (something the patent examiner might ask you to do), you cannot use the doctrine of equivalents to go after infringers unless:

- your amendment involved a feature of the invention that was unforeseeable when you originally filed the application, or
- your amendment could not be included in the original claim for some other reason.

These rules are based on a Supreme Court case from 2002 (*Festo v. Shoketsu Kinzoku Kabushiki Co. Ltd.*, 122 S.Ct. 1831).

What remedies are available for patent infringement?

A patent owner may enforce the patent by bringing a patent infringement action (lawsuit) in federal court against anyone who uses the invention without permission. If the lawsuit is successful, the court will take one of two approaches. It may issue a court order (called an injunction) preventing the infringer from any further use or sale of the infringing device and award damages to the patent owner. Or, the court may work with the parties to hammer out an agreement under which the infringing party will pay the patent owner royalties in exchange for permission to use the infringing device.

Bringing a patent infringement action can be tricky, because it is possible for the alleged infringer to defend by proving to the court that the patent is really invalid (most often by showing that the PTO made a mistake in issuing the patent in the first place). In a substantial number of patent infringement cases, the patent is found invalid and the lawsuit dismissed, leaving the patent owner in a worse position than before the lawsuit.

When does patent protection end?

Patent protection usually ends when the patent expires. For all utility patents filed before June 8, 1995, the patent term is 17 years from the date of issuance. For utility patents filed on or after June 8, 1995, the patent term is 20 years from the date of filing. For design patents, the period is 14 years from date of issuance. For plant patents, the period is 17 years from date of issuance.

A patent may expire if its owner fails to pay required maintenance fees. Usually this occurs because attempts to commercially exploit the underlying invention have failed and the patent owner chooses not to throw good money after bad.

Patent protection ends if a patent is found to be invalid. This may happen if someone shows that the patent application was insufficient or that the applicant committed fraud on the PTO, usually by lying or failing to disclose the applicant's knowledge about prior art that would legally prevent issuance of the patent. A patent may also be invalidated if someone shows that the inventor engaged in illegal conduct when using the patent—such as conspiring with a patent licensee to exclude other companies from competing with them.

Once a patent has expired, the invention described by the patent falls into the public domain: It can be used by anyone without permission from the owner of the expired patent. The basic technologies underlying television and personal computers are good examples of valuable inventions that are no longer covered by in-force patents.

The fact that an invention is in the public domain does not mean that subsequent developments based on the original invention are also in the public domain. New inventions that improve public domain technology are constantly being conceived and patented. For example, televisions and personal computers that roll off today's assembly lines employ many recent inventions that are covered by in-force patents.

The Life of an Invention

Although most inventors are concerned with the rights a patent grants during its monopoly or in-force period (from the date the patent issues until it expires), the law actually recognizes five "rights" periods in the life of an invention. These five periods are as follows:

1. **Invention conceived but not yet documented.** When an inventor conceives an invention but hasn't yet made any written, signed, dated, and witnessed record of it, the inventor has no rights whatsoever.

2. **Invention documented but patent application not yet filed.** After making a proper signed, dated, and witnessed documentation of an invention, the inventor has valuable rights against any inventor who later conceives the same invention and applies for a patent. The invention may also be treated as a "trade secret"—that is, kept confidential. This gives the inventor the legal right to sue and recover damages from anyone who immorally learns of the invention—for example, through industrial spying.

3. **Patent pending (patent application filed but not yet issued).** During the patent pending period, including the one-year period after a provisional patent application is filed, the inventor's rights are the same as they are in Period 2, above, with one exception. If the patent owner intends to also file for a patent abroad, the PTO will publish the application 18 months after the earliest claimed filing date. An inventor whose application is published before a patent issues may obtain royalties from an infringer from the date of publication, as long as the application later issues as a patent and the infringer had actual notice of the published application. Otherwise, the inventor has no rights whatsoever against infringers—only the hope of a future monopoly, which doesn't commence until a patent issues.

   By law, the PTO must keep all patent applications secret until the application is published or the patent issues, whichever comes first. The patent pending period usually lasts from one to three years.

4. **In-force patent (patent issued but hasn't yet expired).** After the patent issues, the patent owner can bring and maintain a lawsuit for patent infringement against anyone who makes, uses, or sells the invention without permission. The patent's in-force period lasts from the date it issues until it expires. Also, after the patent issues, it becomes a public record or publication that prevents others from getting patents on the same or similar inventions—that is, it becomes "prior art" to anyone who files a subsequent patent application.

5. **Patent expired.** After the patent expires, the patent owner has no further rights, although infringement suits can still be brought for any infringement that occurred during the patent's in-force period as long as the suit is filed within the time required by law. An expired patent remains a valid "prior-art reference" forever.

Putting a Patent to Work

Our aspirations are our possibilities.

—ROBERT BROWNING

On its own, a patent has no value. A patent becomes valuable only when a patent owner takes action to profit from his or her monopoly position. There are several basic approaches to making money from a patent.

How can an inventor make money with a patent?

Some inventors start new companies to develop and market their patented inventions. This is not typical, however, because the majority of inventors would rather invent things than run a business. More often, an inventor makes arrangements with an existing company to develop and market the invention. This arrangement usually takes the form of a license (contract) authorizing the developer to commercially exploit the invention in exchange for paying the patent owner royalties for each invention sold. Or, in a common variation of this arrangement, the inventor may sell all the rights to the invention for a lump sum.

What does it mean to license an invention?

A license is written permission to use an invention. A license may be exclusive (if only one manufacturer is licensed to develop the invention) or nonexclusive (if a number of manufacturers are licensed to develop it). The license may be for the entire duration of the patent or for a shorter period of time.

The developer itself may license other companies to market or distribute the invention. The extent to which the inventor will benefit from these sublicenses depends on the terms of the agreement between the inventor and the developer. Especially when inventions result from work done in the course of employment, the employer-business usually ends up owning the patent rights and receives all or most of the royalties based on subsequent licensing activity. (See the next question.)

In many cases, a developer will trade licenses with other companies—called cross-licensing—so that companies involved in the trade will benefit from each other's technology. For example, assume that two computer companies each own several patents on newly developed remote-controlled techniques. Because each company would be strengthened by being able to use the other company's inventions as well as its own, the companies might agree to swap permissions to use their respective inventions.

Can inventors who are employed by a company benefit from their inventions?

Typically, inventor-employees who invent in the course of their employment are bound by employment agreements that automatically assign all rights in the invention to the employer. While smart research and development companies give their inventors bonuses for valuable inventions, they aren't legally obligated to do so (unless the contract requires it).

If there is no employment agreement, the employer may still own rights to an employee-created invention under the "employed to invent" rule. If an inventor is employed—even without a written employment agreement—to accomplish a defined task, or is hired or directed to create an invention, the employer will own all rights to the subsequent invention.

If there is no employment agreement and the inventor is not employed to invent, the inventor may retain the right to exploit the invention, but the employer is given a nonexclusive right to use the invention for its internal purposes (this is called a shop right). For example, Robert is a machinist in a machine shop and invents a new process for handling a particular type of metal. If Robert isn't employed to invent and hasn't signed an employment agreement giving the shop all rights to the invention, Robert can patent and exploit the invention for himself. The shop, however, would retain the right to use the new process without having to pay Robert.

How Patents Differ From Copyrights and Trademarks

In some cases, a design may be subject to patent, trademark, and copyright protection all at the same time.

How do patents differ from copyrights?

With the exception of innovative designs, patents are closely associated with things and processes that are useful in the real world. Almost at the opposite end of the spectrum, copyright applies to expressive arts such as novels, fine and graphic arts, music, photography, software, video, cinema, and choreography. While it is possible to get a patent on technologies used in the arts, it is copyright that keeps one artist from stealing another artist's creative work.

An exception to the general rule that patents and copyright don't overlap can be found in product designs. It is possible to get a design patent on the purely ornamental (nonfunctional) aspects of a product design and also claim a copyright in the same design. For example, the stylistic fins of a car's rear fenders may qualify for both a design patent (because they are strictly ornamental) and copyright (as to their expressive elements).

For more information about copyright law, see Chapter 7.

What's the difference between patent and trademark?

Generally speaking, patents allow the creator of certain kinds of inventions that contain new ideas to keep others from making commercial use of those ideas without the creator's permission. Trademark, on the other hand, is not concerned with how a new technology is used. Rather, it applies to the names, logos, and other devices—such as color, sound, and smell—that are used to identify the source of goods or services and distinguish them from their competition.

Generally, patent and trademark laws do not overlap. When it comes to a product design, however—say, jewelry or a distinctively shaped musical instrument—it may be possible to obtain a patent on a design aspect of the device while invoking trademark law to protect the design as a product identifier. For example, a surfboard manufacturer might receive a patent for a surfboard design that mimics the design used in a popular surfing film. If the design is intended to be—and actually is—used to distinguish the particular type of surfboard in the marketplace, trademark law may kick in to protect the appearance of the board.

For more information about trademarks, see Chapter 8.

**More Information
About Patents**

Patent It Yourself, by David Pressman (Nolo), takes you step by step through the process of getting a patent without hiring a patent lawyer.

Patent Pending in 24 Hours, by Richard Stim and David Pressman (Nolo), explains how to prepare and file a provisional patent application.

Patent Savvy for Managers, by Kirk Teska (Nolo), explains how to use a cost-benefit analysis to determine whether to pursue a patent.

How to Make Patent Drawings, by Jack Lo and David Pressman (Nolo), takes you step by step through the process of making your own patent drawing.

Profit From Your Idea, by Richard Stim (Nolo), explains how to realize your invention's commercial potential.

Patent, Copyright & Trademark, by Richard Stim (Nolo), provides concise definitions and examples of the important words and phrases commonly used in patent law.

Nolo's Patents for Beginners, by David Pressman and Richard Stim (Nolo), explains all of the essential patent principles in plain English.

What Every Inventor Needs to Know About Business & Taxes, by Stephen Fishman (Nolo), gives inventors all the information they need to start and run an invention business, pay taxes, and license and protect their inventions.

Online Help

www.nolo.com
Nolo offers information about a wide variety of legal topics, including patent law.

www.uspto.gov
The U.S. Patent and Trademark Office is the place to go for recent policy and statutory changes and transcripts of hearings on various patent law issues. The U.S. Patent and Trademark Office maintains a serarchable electronic database of the front page of all patents issued since 1971. This site is an excellent way to initiate a search for relevant patents.

www.inventionconvention.com
The National Congress of Inventor Organizations (NCIO) maintains this invention website that includes links, trade show information, and advice for inventors.

www.freshpatents.com
FreshPatents.com provides the latest published U.S. patent applications each week before the USPTO decides whether to grant or deny the patent.

Copyrights

People seldom improve when they have no other model but themselves to copy after.

—OLIVER GOLDSMITH

It has long been recognized that everyone benefits when creative people are encouraged to develop new intellectual and artistic works. When the U.S. Constitution was written in 1787, the framers took care to include a copyright clause (Article I, Section 8) giving Congress the power to "promote the Progress of Science and useful Arts" by passing laws that give creative people exclusive rights in their own artistic works for a limited period of time.

Copyright laws are not designed to enrich creative artists but to promote human knowledge and development. These laws encourage artists in their creative efforts by giving them a mini-monopoly over their works, called a copyright. But this monopoly is limited when it conflicts with the overriding purpose of encouraging people to create new works of scholarship or art.

This chapter introduces you to copyright law and guides you through the first steps of creating, owning, and protecting a copyright. To learn about how copyrights differ from—and work with—patents and trademarks, see Chapters 6 and 8.

Copyright Basics

It is necessary to any originality to have the courage to be an amateur.

—WALLACE STEVENS

Copyright is a legal device that gives the creator of a work of art or literature, or a work that conveys information or ideas, the right to control how that work is used. The Copyright Act of 1976—the federal law providing for copyright protection—grants authors a bundle of exclusive rights over their works, including the right to reproduce, distribute, adapt, or perform them.

An author's copyright rights may be exercised only by the author—or by a person or entity to whom the author has transferred all or part of those rights. If someone wrongfully uses the material covered by a copyright, the copyright owner can sue and obtain compensation for any losses suffered.

What types of creative work does copyright protect?

Copyright protects works such as poetry, movies, video games, videos, DVDs, plays, paintings, sheet music, recorded music performances, novels, software code, sculptures, photographs, choreography, and architectural designs.

To qualify for copyright protection, a work must be "fixed in a tangible medium of expression." This means that the work must exist in some physical form for at least some period of time, no matter how brief. Virtually any form of expression will qualify as a tangible medium, including a computer's random access memory (RAM), the recording media that capture all radio and television broadcasts, and the scribbled notes on the back of an envelope that contain the basis for an impromptu speech.

In addition, the work must be original—that is, independently created by the author. It doesn't matter if an author's creation is similar to existing works, or even if it is arguably lacking in quality, ingenuity, or aesthetic merit. As long as the author toils without copying from someone else, the results are protected by copyright.

Finally, to receive copyright protection, a work must be the result of at least some creative effort on the part of its author. There is no hard and fast rule as to how much creativity is enough. As one example, a work must be more creative than a telephone book's white pages, which are simply an alphabetical listing of telephone numbers rather than a creative selection of listings.

Does copyright protect an author's creative ideas?

No. Copyright shelters only fixed, original, and creative expression, not the ideas or facts upon which the expression is based. For example, copyright may protect a particular song, novel, or computer game about a romance in space, but it cannot protect the underlying idea of having a love affair among the stars. Allowing authors to monopolize their ideas would thwart the underlying purpose of copyright law, which is to encourage people to create new work.

For similar reasons, copyright does not protect facts—whether scientific, historical, biographical, or news of the day. Any facts that an author discovers in the course of research are in the public domain, free to all. For instance, anyone is free to use information included in a book about how the brain works, an article about the life and times of Neanderthals, or a TV documentary about the childhood of former President Clinton—as long as they express the information in their own words.

Facts are not protected even if the author spends considerable time and effort discovering things that were previously unknown. For example, the author of the book on Neanderthals takes ten years to gather all the necessary materials and information for her work. At great expense, she travels to hundreds of museums and excavations around the world. But after the book is published, any reader is free to use the results of this ten-year research project to write his or her own book on Neanderthals—without paying the original author.

Is the Work Published?

In the complicated scheme of copyright laws, which law applies to a particular work depends on when that work is published. A work is considered published when the author makes it available to the public on an unrestricted basis. This means that it is possible to distribute or display a work without publishing it if there are significant restrictions placed on what can be done with the work and when it can be shown to others. For example, Andres Miczslova writes an essay called "Blood Bath" about the war in Iraq and distributes it to five human rights organizations under a nonexclusive license that places restrictions on their right to disclose the essay's contents. "Blood Bath" has not been "published" in the copyright sense. If Miczslova authorizes them to post the essay on the Internet, however, it would likely be considered published.

How long does a copyright last?

For works published after 1977, the copyright lasts for the life of the author plus 70 years. However, if the work is a work for hire (that is, the work is done in the course of employment or has been specifically commissioned) or is published anonymously or under a pseudonym, the copyright lasts between 95 and 120 years, depending on the date the work is published.

All works published in the United States before 1923 are in the public domain. Works published after 1922, but before 1964, are protected for 95 years from the date of publication, if a renewal was filed with the Copyright Office during the 28th year after publication. If no renewal was filed, such works are in the public domain. Works published from 1964 to 1977 are protected for 95 years whether or not a renewal was filed. If the work was created, but not published, before 1978, the copyright lasts for the life of the author plus 70 years. And if such a work was published before 2003, the copyright lasts until December 31, 2047.

Copyright Ownership

He who can copy, can do.

—LEONARDO DA VINCI

A copyright is initially owned by a creative work's author or authors. But under the law, a person need not actually create the work to be its "author" for copyright purposes. A protectible work created by an employee as part of his or her job is initially owned by the employer—that is, the employer is considered to be the work's author. Such works are called "works made for hire." Works created by non-employees (independent contractors) may also be works made for hire if the contractors sign written agreements to that effect and the work falls within one of eight enumerated categories (see below).

Like any other property, a copyright can be bought and sold. Transfers of copyright ownership are unique in one respect, however: Authors or their heirs have the right to terminate any transfer of copyright ownership 35 to 40 years after it is made.

What are the exceptions to the rule that the creator of a work owns the copyright?

Copyrights are generally owned by the people who create the works of expression, with some important exceptions:

- If a work is created by an employee in the course of his or her employment, the employer owns the copyright.
- If the work is created by an independent contractor, and the independent contractor signs a written agreement stating that the work shall be "made for hire," the commissioning person or organization owns the copyright only if the work is (1) a part of a larger literary work, such as an article in a magazine or a poem or story in an anthology; (2) part of a motion picture or other audiovisual work, such as a screenplay; (3) a translation; (4) a supplementary work such as an afterword, an introduction, chart, editorial note, bibliography, appendix, or index; (5) a compilation; (6) an instructional text; (7) a test or answer material for a test; or (8) an atlas. Works that don't fall within one of these eight categories are works made for hire only if created by an employee within the scope of his or her employment.
- If the creator has sold the entire copyright, the purchasing business or person becomes the copyright owner.

Who owns the copyright in a joint work?

When two or more authors prepare a work with the intent to combine their contributions into inseparable or interdependent parts, the work is considered a joint work, and the authors are considered joint copyright owners. The most common example of a joint work is when a book or article has two or more authors. However, if a book is written primarily by one author but another author contributes a specific chapter to the book and is given credit for that chapter, then this probably wouldn't be a joint work because the contributions aren't inseparable or interdependent.

The U.S. Copyright Office considers joint copyright owners to have an equal right to register and enforce the copyright. Unless the joint owners make a written agreement to the contrary, each copyright owner has the right to commercially exploit the copyright, as long as the other copyright owners get an equal share of the proceeds.

Can two or more authors provide contributions to a single work without being considered joint authors?

Yes. If, at the time of creation, the authors did not intend their works to be part of an inseparable whole, combining their works later does not create a joint work. Rather, the result is considered a collective work. In this case, each author owns a copyright in only the material he or she added to the finished product. For example, in 1980, Vladimir writes a famous novel full of complex literary allusions. In 2007, his publisher issues a student edition of the work with detailed annotations written by an English professor. The student edition is a collective work. Vladimir owns the copyright in the novel, but the professor owns the annotations.

What rights do copyright owners have?

The Copyright Act of 1976 grants a number of exclusive rights to copyright owners, including:

- reproduction right—the right to make copies of a protected work

- distribution right—the right to sell or otherwise distribute copies to the public
- right to create adaptations (called derivative works)—the right to prepare new works based on the protected work, and
- performance and display rights—the rights to perform a protected work (such as a stageplay) or to display a work in public.

This bundle of rights allows a copyright owner to be flexible when deciding how to realize commercial gain from the underlying work; the owner may sell or license any or all of these rights.

Can a copyright owner transfer some or all of his rights?

Yes. When a copyright owner wishes to commercially exploit the work covered by the copyright, the owner typically transfers one or more of these rights to the person or entity who will be responsible for getting the work to market, such as a book or software publisher. It is also common for the copyright owner to place some limitations on the exclusive rights being transferred. For example, the owner may limit the transfer to a specific period of time, allow the right to be exercised only in a specific part of the country or world, or require that the right be exercised only through certain media, such as hardcover books, audiotapes, magazines, or computers.

If a copyright owner transfers all of these rights unconditionally, it is generally termed an "assignment." When only some of the rights associated with the copyright are transferred, it is known as a "license." An exclusive license exists when the transferred rights can be exercised only by the owner of the license (the licensee) and no one else—including the person who granted the license (the licensor). If the license allows others (including the licensor) to exercise the same rights being transferred in the license, the license is said to be nonexclusive.

The U.S. Copyright Office allows buyers of exclusive and nonexclusive copyright rights to record the transfers in the U.S. Copyright Office. This helps to protect the buyer in case the original copyright owner later tries to transfer the same rights to another party.

Copyright Protection

Copyright protection automatically comes into existence when the protected work is created. However, the degree of protection that copyright laws extend to a protected work can be influenced by later events.

Do I have to include a copyright notice on my work?

Until 1989, a published work had to contain a valid copyright notice to receive protection under the copyright laws. But this requirement is no longer in force—works first published after March 1, 1989, need not include a copyright notice to gain protection under the law.

But even though a copyright notice is not required, it's still important to include one. When a work contains a valid notice, an infringer cannot claim in court that he or she didn't know the work was copyrighted. This makes it much easier to win a copyright infringement case and perhaps collect enough damages to make the cost of the case worthwhile. And the very existence of a notice might discourage infringement.

Including a copyright notice may also make it easier for a potential infringer to track down a copyright owner and legitimately obtain permission to use the work.

International Copyright Protection

Copyright protection rules are fairly similar worldwide, due to several international copyright treaties. The most important international treaty is the Berne Convention. Under this treaty, all member countries—and there are more than 100, including virtually all industrialized nations—must afford copyright protection to authors who are nationals of any member country. This protection must last for at least the life of the author plus 50 years and must be automatic, without the need for the author to take any legal steps to preserve the copyright.

In addition to the Berne Convention, the GATT (General Agreement on Tariffs and Trade) treaty contains a number of provisions that affect copyright protection in signatory countries. Together, the Berne Copyright Convention and the GATT treaty allow U.S. authors to enforce their copyrights in most industrialized nations, and allow the nationals of those countries to enforce their copyrights in the United States.

What is a valid copyright notice?

A copyright notice should contain:

- the word "copyright"
- a "c" in a circle (©)
- the date of publication, and
- the name of either the author or the owner of all the copyright rights in the published work.

For example, the correct copyright for the ninth edition of *The Copyright Handbook,* by Stephen Fishman (Nolo), is *Copyright © 2006 by Stephen Fishman.*

When can I use a work without the author's permission?

When a work becomes available for use without permission from a copyright owner, it is said to be "in the public domain." Most works enter the public domain because their copyrights have expired.

To determine whether a work is in the public domain and available for use without the author's permission, you first have to find out when it was published. Then you can apply the periods of time set out earlier in this chapter. (See "How long does a copyright last?" above.) If the work was published between 1923 and 1963, however, you must check with the U.S. Copyright Office to see whether the copyright was properly renewed. If the author failed to renew the copyright, the work has fallen into the public domain and you may use it.

The Copyright Office will check renewal information for you, for a fee. (Call the Reference & Bibliography Section at 202-707-6850.) You can also hire a private copyright search firm to see if a renewal was filed. Finally, you may be able to conduct a renewal search yourself. The renewal records for works published from 1950 to the present are available online at www.copyright. gov. Renewal searches for earlier works can be conducted at the Copyright Office in Washington, DC, or at one of the many government depository libraries throughout the country. Call the Copyright Office for more information.

With one important exception, you should assume that every work is protected by copyright (and therefore off limits) unless you can establish otherwise. As mentioned above, you can't rely on the presence or absence of a copyright notice (©) to make this determination, because a notice is not required for works published after March 1, 1989. And even for works published before 1989, the absence of a copyright notice doesn't mean the copyright isn't valid—for example, if the author made diligent attempts to correct the situation, the copyright may still be in force.

The exception to the general rule that you can't use a copyrighted work without the author's permission is called the "fair use rule." This rule recognizes that society can often benefit from the unauthorized use of copyrighted materials when the purpose of the use serves the ends of scholarship, education, or an in-

---

If You Want to Use Material on the Internet

Each day, people post vast quantities of creative material on the Internet—material that is available for downloading by anyone who has the right computer equipment. Because the information is stored somewhere on an Internet server, it is fixed in a tangible medium and potentially qualifies for copyright protection. Whether it does, in fact, qualify depends on other factors that you would have no way of knowing about, such as when the work was first published (which affects the need for a copyright notice), whether the copyright in the work has been renewed (for works published before 1964), whether the work is a work made for hire (which affects the length of the copyright), and whether the copyright owner intends to dedicate the work to the public domain.

As a general rule, it is wise to operate under the assumption that all materials are protected by either copyright or trademark law unless conclusive information indicates otherwise. A work is not in the public domain simply because it has been posted on the Internet (a popular fallacy) or because it lacks a copyright notice (another fallacy). As a general rule, you need permission to reproduce copyrighted materials, including photos, text, music, and artwork. It's best to track down the author of the material and ask for permission.

The most useful sources for finding information and obtaining permission are copyright collectives or clearinghouses. These are organizations that organize and license works by their members. For example, the Copyright Clearinghouse (www.copyright.com), and RSicopyright (www.icopyright.com) provide permissions for written materials. You can use an Internet search engine to locate other collectives for music, photos, and artwork.

If you want to use only a very small portion of text for educational or nonprofit purposes, the fair use rule may apply (see above).

formed public. For example, scholars must be free to quote from their research resources in order to comment on the material. To strike a balance between the public's need to be well informed and the rights of copyright owners to profit from their creativity, Congress passed a law authorizing the use of copyrighted materials in certain circumstances deemed to be "fair"—even if the copyright owner doesn't give permission.

Often, it's difficult to know whether a court will consider a proposed use to be fair. The fair use statute requires the courts to consider the following questions in deciding this issue:

- Is it a competitive use? If the use potentially affects the sales of the copied material, it's probably not fair.

- How much material was taken compared to the entire work of which the material was a part? The more someone takes, the less likely that the use is fair.

- How was the material used? Did the defendant change the original by adding new expression or meaning? Did the defendant add value to the original by creating new information, new aesthetics, new insights, and understandings? If the use was transformative, this weighs in favor of a fair use finding. Criticism, comment, news reporting, research, scholarship, and nonprofit educational uses are also likely to be judged fair uses. Uses motivated primarily by a desire for a commercial gain are less likely to be fair use.

As a general rule, if you are using a small portion of somebody else's work in a noncompetitive way for the purpose of benefitting the public, you're on pretty safe ground. On the other hand, if you take large portions of someone else's expression for your own purely commercial reasons, the rule usually won't apply.

Copyright Registration and Enforcement

Although every work published after 1989 is automatically protected by copyright, you can strengthen your rights by registering your work with the U.S. Copyright Office. This registration makes it possible to bring a lawsuit to protect your copyright if someone violates (infringes) it. The registration process is straightforward and inexpensive, and can be done without a lawyer.

Why should I register my work with the U.S. Copyright Office?

You must register your copyright with the U.S. Copyright Office before you are legally permitted to bring a lawsuit to enforce it.

You can register a copyright at any time, but filing promptly may pay off in the long run. "Timely registration"—that is, registration within three months of the work's publication date or before any copyright infringement actually begins—makes it much easier to sue and recover money from an infringer. Timely registration creates a legal presumption that your copyright is valid and allows you to recover up to $100,000 (and possibly lawyer's fees) without having to prove that you suffered actual monetary losses because of the infringement.

How do I register a copyright?

You can register your copyright by filing a simple form and depositing one or two samples of the work (depending on what it is) with the U.S. Copyright Office. There are different forms for different types of works—for example, form TX is for literary works while form VA is for a visual art work. You can get forms and instructions from the U.S. Copyright Office by telephone, 202-707-9100, or online at www.copyright.gov. Registration currently costs $45 per work. If you're registering several works that are part of one series, you may be able to save money by registering the works together (called "group registration").

As a result of legislation in 2005, the Copyright Office instituted a preregistration procedure for certain works that have a history of prerelease infringement—for example, movies, music, books, computer programs, and advertising photographs. Preregistration offers protection under limited circumstances, primarily when a copyright owner needs to sue for infringement while a work is still being prepared for commercial release. It is not a substitute for registration; it simply indicates that you intend to register the work after you have completed and/or published it. To find out whether your work is eligible for preregistration, contact the U.S. Copyright Office using the information above.

How are copyrights enforced?

If someone violates the rights of a copyright owner, the owner is entitled to file a lawsuit in federal court asking the court to:

- issue orders (restraining orders and injunctions) to prevent further violations
- award money damages if appropriate, and
- in some circumstances, award attorneys' fees.

Whether the lawsuit will be successful and whether damages will be awarded depends on whether the alleged infringer can raise one or more legal defenses to the charge. Common legal defenses to copyright infringement are:

- too much time has elapsed between the infringing act and the lawsuit (the statute of limitations defense)
- the infringement is allowed under the fair use doctrine (discussed above)
- the infringement was innocent (the infringer had no reason to know the work was protected by copyright)
- the infringing work was independently created (that is, it wasn't copied from the original), or
- the copyright owner authorized the use in a license.

Someone who has good reason to believe that a use is fair—but later ends up on the wrong end of a court order—is likely to be considered an innocent infringer at worst. Innocent infringers usually don't have to pay any damages to the copyright owner, but they do have to cease the infringing activity or pay the owner for the reasonable commercial value of that use.

More Information About Copyrights

The Copyright Handbook: What Every Writer Needs to Know, by Stephen Fishman (Nolo), is a complete guide to the law of copyright. The book includes forms for registering a copyright.

Patent, Copyright & Trademark: An Intellectual Property Desk Reference, by Stephen Elias and Richard Stim (Nolo), provides concise definitions and examples of the important words and phrases commonly used in copyright law.

Getting Permission: How to License & Clear Copyrighted Materials Online & Off, by Richard Stim (Nolo), spells out how to obtain permission to use art, music, writing, or other copyrighted works and includes a variety of permission and licensing agreements.

The Public Domain: How to Find & Use Copyright-Free Writings, Music, Art & More, by Stephen Fishman (Nolo), is an authoritative book that explains what is protected by copyright law.

Online Help

www.nolo.com
Nolo offers information about a wide variety of legal topics, including copyright law.

www.copyright.gov
The U.S. Copyright Office offers regulations, guidelines, forms, and links to other helpful copyright sites.

http://fairuse.stanford.edu
This is one of the leading websites for measuring fair use. It provides academic fair use links and guidelines.

www.benedict.com
The Copyright Website has articles, good links, and slick design. Best of all, you can examine actual examples from real cases.

www.ipmall.fplc.edu
The Intellectual Property Mall provided by the Franklin Pierce Law Center is a source of ever-changing links and information about copyrights, trademarks, and patents.

Trademarks

A good name lost is seldom regained.

—JOEL HAWES

Most of us encounter many trademarks each day; we might eat Kellogg's cornflakes for breakfast, then drive our Ford car to work, where we sit down at an IBM computer. But as we go about our daily tasks, we rarely think about the laws behind the familiar words and images that identify the products and services we use.

Trademark law sets the legal rules that govern how businesses may:

- distinguish their products or services in the marketplace to prevent consumer confusion, and
- protect the means they've chosen to identify their products or services against use by competitors.

This chapter will introduce you to trademark law and answer common questions about choosing, using, and protecting a trademark.

Types of Trademarks

The term "trademark" is commonly used to describe many different types of devices that label, identify, and distinguish products or services in the marketplace. The basic purpose of all these devices is to inform potential customers of the origin and quality of the underlying products or services.

What is a trademark?

A trademark is a distinctive word, phrase, logo, graphic symbol, slogan, or other device that is used to identify the source of a product and to distinguish a manufacturer's or merchant's products from others. Some examples are Nike sports apparel, Gatorade beverages, and Microsoft software. In the trademark context, "distinctive" means unique enough to help customers recognize a particular product in the marketplace. A mark may either be inherently distinctive (the mark is unusual in and of itself, such as Milky Way candy bars) or may become distinctive over time because customers come to associate the mark with the product or service (for example, Beef & Brew restaurants).

Consumers often make their purchasing choices on the basis of recognizable trademarks. For this reason, the main purpose of trademark law is to make sure that trademarks don't overlap in a manner that causes customers to become confused about the source of a product. However, in the case of trademarks that have become famous—for example, McDonald's—the courts are willing to prohibit a wider range of uses of the trademark (or anything close to it) by anyone other than the famous mark's owner. For instance, McDonald's was able to prevent the use of the mark McSleep by a motel chain because McSleep traded on the McDonald's mark reputation for a particular type of service (quick, inexpensive, standardized). This type of sweeping protection is authorized by federal and state statutes (referred to as antidilution laws) designed to prevent the weakening of a famous mark's reputation for quality.

What is a service mark?

For practical purposes, a service mark is the same as a trademark—but while trademarks promote products, service marks promote services and events. As a general rule, when a business uses its name to market its goods or services in the Yellow Pages, on signs, or in advertising copy, the name qualifies as a service mark. Some familiar service marks: Jack in the Box (fast food service), Kinko's (photocopying service), ACLU (legal service), Blockbuster (video rental service), CBS's stylized eye in a circle (television network service), and the Olympic Games' multicolored interlocking circles (international sporting event).

What is a certification mark?

A certification mark is a symbol, name, or device used by an organization to vouch for products and services provided by others—for example, the "Good Housekeeping Seal of Approval." This type of mark may cover characteristics such as regional origin, method of manufacture, product quality, and service accuracy. Some other examples of certification marks: Stilton cheese (a product from the Stilton locale in England), Carneros wines (from grapes grown in the Carneros region of Sonoma/Napa counties), and Harris tweeds (a special weave from a specific area in Scotland).

What is a collective mark?

A collective mark is a symbol, label, word, phrase, or other mark used by members of a group or organization to identify goods, members, products, or services they render. Collective marks are often used to show membership in a union, association, or other organization.

The use of a collective mark is restricted to members of the group or organization that owns the mark. Even the group itself—as opposed to its members—cannot use the collective mark on any goods it produces. If the group wants to identify its product or service, it must use its own trademark or service mark.

EXAMPLE: The letters "ILGWU" on a shirt label is the collective mark that identifies the shirt as a product of a member of the International Ladies Garment Workers Union. If, however, the ILGWU wanted to start marketing its own products, it could not use the ILGWU collective mark to identify them; the union would have to get a trademark of its own.

What is trade dress?

In addition to a label, logo, or other identifying symbol, a product may come to be known by its distinctive packaging—for example, Kodak film or the Galliano liquor bottle—and a service by its distinctive decor or shape, such as the decor of Gap clothing stores. Collectively, these types of identifying features are commonly termed "trade dress." Because trade dress often serves the same function as a trademark or service mark—the identification of goods and services in the marketplace—trade dress can be protected under the federal trademark laws and in some cases registered as a trademark or service mark with the Patent and Trademark Office.

What kinds of things can be considered trademarks or service marks?

Most often, trademarks are words or phrases that are clever or unique enough to stick in a consumer's mind. Logos and graphics that become strongly associated with a product line or service are also typical. But a trademark or service mark can also consist of letters, numbers, a sound, a smell, a color, a product shape, or any other nonfunctional but distinctive aspect of a product or service that tends to promote and distinguish it in the marketplace. Titles, character names, or other distinctive features of movies, television, and radio programs can also serve as trademarks or service marks when used to promote a service or product. Some examples of unusual trademarks are the pink color of housing insulation manufactured by Owens-Corning and the shape of the Absolut vodka bottle.

What's the difference between a business name and a trademark or service mark?

The name that a business uses to identify itself is called a "trade name." This is the name the business uses on its stock certificates, bank accounts, invoices, and letterhead. When used to identify a business in this way—as an entity for nonmarketing purposes—the business name is given some protection under state and local corporate and fictitious business name registration laws, but it is not considered a trademark or entitled to protection under trademark laws.

If, however, a business uses its name to identify a product or service produced by the business, the name will then be considered a trademark or service mark and will be entitled to protection if it is distinctive enough. For instance, Apple Computer Corporation uses the trade name Apple as a trademark on its line of computer products.

Although trade names by themselves are not considered trademarks for purposes of legal protection, they may still be protected under federal and state unfair competition laws against a confusing use by a competing business.

If my trade name is registered with the secretary of state as a corporate name, or placed on a fictitious business name list, can I use it as a trademark?

Not necessarily. When you register a corporate name with a state agency or place your name on a local fictitious business name register, there is no guarantee that the name has not already been taken by another business as a trademark. This means that before you start using your business name as a trademark, you will need to make sure it isn't already being used as a trademark by another company in a way that prevents you from using it. For more information about trademark searches, see *Conducting a Trademark Search,* below.

Trademark Protection

If a trademark or service mark is protected, the owner of the mark can:

- prevent others from using it in a context where it might confuse consumers, and
- recover money damages from someone who used the mark knowing that it was already owned by someone else.

Trademark law also protects famous marks by allowing owners to sue to prevent others from using the same or a similar mark, even if customer confusion is unlikely.

Not all marks are entitled to an equal amount of protection, however—and some aren't entitled to any protection at all.

What laws offer protection to trademark owners?

The basic rules for resolving disputes over who is entitled to use a trademark come from decisions by federal and state courts (the common law). These rules usually favor the business that first used the mark when the second use would be likely to cause customer confusion. A number of additional legal principles that protect owners against improper use of their marks derive from federal statutes known collectively as the Lanham Act (Title 15 U.S.C. §§ 1051 to 1127). And all states have statutes that govern the use and protection of marks within the state's boundaries.

In addition to laws that specifically protect trademark owners, all states have laws that protect one business against unfair competition by another business, including the use by one business of a name already used by another business in a context that's likely to confuse customers.

What types of marks are entitled to the most legal protection?

Trademark law grants the most legal protection to the owners of names, logos, and other marketing devices that are distinctive—that is, memorable because they are creative or out of the ordinary, or because they have become well known to the public through their use over time or because of a marketing blitz.

Inherently Distinctive Marks

Trademarks that are unusually creative are known as inherently distinctive marks. Typically, these marks consist of:

- unique logos or symbols (such as the McDonald's Golden Arch and the Nike swoosh)
- made-up words or words that have no dictionary meaning, such as Exxon or Kodak (called "fanciful" or "coined" marks)
- words that are surprising or unexpected in the context of their usage, such as *Time* magazine or Diesel Bookstore (called "arbitrary marks"), and
- words that cleverly connote qualities about the product or service, such as Slenderella diet food products (called "suggestive or evocative marks").

Which marks receive the least protection?

Trademarks and service marks consisting of common or ordinary words are not considered inherently distinctive and receive less protection under federal and state laws. Typical examples of trademarks using common or ordinary words are:

- people's names, such as Pete's Muffins or Smith Graphics

- geographic terms, such as Northern Dairy or Central Insect Control, and

- descriptive terms—that is, words that attempt to literally describe the product or some characteristic of the product, such as Rapid Computers, Clarity Video Monitors, or Ice Cold Ice Cream.

However, nondistinctive marks may become distinctive through use over time or through intensive marketing efforts.

What about Ben and Jerry's Ice Cream? Even though Ben and Jerry are common names, isn't the Ben and Jerry's trademark entitled to maximum protection?

Absolutely. Even if a mark is not inherently distinctive, it may become distinctive if it develops great public recognition through long use and exposure in the marketplace. A mark that becomes protected in this way is said to have acquired a "secondary meaning." In addition to Ben and Jerry's, examples of otherwise common marks that have acquired a secondary meaning and are now considered to be distinctive include Sears (department stores) and Park 'n Fly (airport parking services.)

What cannot be protected under trademark law?

There are five common situations in which there is no trademark protection. In any of these situations, the intended trademark cannot be registered, and the owner has no right to stop others from using a similar name. Generally, when speaking of what *cannot* be protected under trademark law, we are referring to the standards established under the Lanham Act

(the federal statute that provides for registration of marks and federal court remedies in case a mark is infringed).

- **Nonuse.** An owner may lose trademark protection by "abandoning" a trademark. This can happen in many ways. The most common is when the mark is no longer used in commerce and there is sufficient evidence that the owner intends to discontinue its use. Under the Lanham Act, a trademark is presumed to be abandoned after three years of nonuse. But an owner who can prove that he or she intended to resume commercial use of the mark will not lose trademark protection.

- **Generics and genericide.** A generic term describes a type of goods or services; it is not a brand name. Examples of generic terms are "computer," "eyeglasses," and "eBook." Consumers are used to seeing a generic term used in conjunction with a trademark (for example, Avery labels or Hewlett-Packard printers). On some occasions, a company invents a new word for a product (for example, Kleenex for a tissue) that functions so successfully as a trademark that the public eventually comes to believe that it is the name of the item. This is called genericide. When that happens, the term loses its trademark protection. Other famous examples of genericide are "aspirin," "yo-yo," "escalator," "thermos," and "kerosene."

- **Confusingly similar marks.** A mark will not receive trademark protection if it is so similar to another existing trademark that it causes confusion among consumers. This standard, known as likelihood of confusion, is a foundation of trademark law.

Many factors are weighed when considering "likelihood of confusion." The most important are: the similarity of the marks, the similarity of the goods, the degree of care exercised by the consumer when making the purchase, the intent of the person using the similar mark, and any actual confusion that has occurred.

- **Weak marks.** A weak trademark will not be protected unless the owner can prove that consumers are aware of the mark. There are three types of weak marks: descriptive marks, geographic marks that describe a location, and marks that are primarily surnames (last names). When an applicant attempts to register a weak mark, the PTO will permit the applicant to submit proof of distinctiveness or to move the application from the Principal Register to the Supplemental Register. (See *Registering a Trademark,* below, for more information about the different benefits these registers offer.)

- **Functional features.** Trademark law, like copyright law, will not protect functional features. Generally, a functional feature is something that is necessary for the item to work. The issue usually arises with product packaging or shapes. For instance, the unique shape of the Mrs. Butterworth syrup bottle is not a functional feature because it is not necessary for the bottle to work. Therefore, it is eligible for trademark protection.

Are Internet domain names—names for sites on the World Wide Web—protected by trademark law?

Domain name registration, by itself, does not permit you to stop another business from using the same name for its business or product. Instead, it gives you only the right to use that specific Internet address. To protect your domain name as a trademark, the name must meet the usual trademark standards. That is, the domain name must be distinctive or must achieve distinction through customer awareness, and you must be the first to use the name in connection with your type of service or product. An example of a domain name that meets these criteria and has trademark protection is Amazon.com. Amazon.com was the first to use this distinctive name for online retail sales, and the name has been promoted to customers through advertising and sales.

Using and Enforcing a Trademark

Generally, a trademark is owned by the business that first uses it in a commercial context—that is, attaches the mark to a product or uses the mark when marketing a product or service. A business may also obtain trademark protection if it files for trademark registration before anyone else uses the mark. (Trademark registration is discussed in more detail in *Registering a Trademark,* below.)

Once a business owns a trademark, it may be able to prevent others from using that mark, or a similar one, on their goods and services.

What does it mean to "use" a trademark?

In trademark law, "use" means that the mark is at work in the marketplace, identifying the underlying goods or services. This doesn't mean that the product or service actually has to be sold, as long as it is legitimately offered to the public under the mark in question. For example, Robert creates a website where he offers his new invention—a humane mousetrap—for sale under the trademark MiceFree. Even if Robert doesn't sell any traps, he is still "using" the trademark as long as "MiceFree" appears on the traps or on tags attached to them and the traps are ready to be shipped when a sale is made. Similarly, if Kristin, a trademark attorney, puts up a website to offer her services under the service mark Trademark Queen, her service mark will be in use as long as she is ready to respond to customer requests for her advice.

How can a business reserve a trademark for future use?

It is possible to acquire ownership of a mark by filing an "intent-to-use" (ITU) trademark registration application with the U.S. Patent and Trademark Office before someone else actually uses the mark. The filing date of this application will be considered the date of first use of the mark if the applicant actually uses the mark within the required time limits—six months to three years after the PTO approves the mark, depending on whether the applicant seeks and pays for extensions of time.

For more information about trademark registration, see *Registering a Trademark,* below.

When can the owner of a trademark stop others from using it?

Whether the owner of a trademark can stop others from using it depends on such factors as:

- whether the trademark is being used on competing goods or services (goods or services compete if the sale of one is likely to affect the sale of the other)
- whether consumers would likely be confused by the dual use of the trademark, and

- whether the trademark is being used in the same part of the country or is being used on related goods (goods that will probably be noticed by the same customers, even if they don't compete with each other).

In addition, under federal and state laws known as "antidilution statutes," a trademark owner may go to court to prevent its mark from being used by someone else if the mark is famous and the later use would dilute the mark's strength—that is, weaken its reputation for quality (called "tarnishment") or render it common through overuse in different contexts (called "blurring").

Antidilution statutes can apply even if there is no way customers would be likely to confuse the source of the goods or services designated by the later mark with the famous mark's owner. For instance, consumers would not think that Microsoft Bakery is associated with Microsoft, the software company, but Microsoft Bakery could still be forced to choose another name under federal and state antidilution laws.

Certain acts are not considered dilution, including comparing goods in an advertisement; parodying, criticizing, or commenting upon a famous mark owner or the owner's goods or services; reporting news; and any noncommercial use of a mark.

How does a trademark owner prevent others from using the mark?

Typically, the owner will begin by sending a letter, called a "cease and desist letter," to the wrongful user, demanding that it stop using the mark. If the wrongful user continues to infringe the mark, the owner can file a lawsuit to stop the improper use. The lawsuit is usually filed in federal court if the mark is used in more than one state or country, and in state court if the dispute is between purely local marks. In addition to preventing further use of the mark, a trademark owner can sometimes obtain money damages from the wrongful user.

When can a trademark owner get money from someone who has infringed the owner's mark?

If a trademark owner proves in federal court that the infringing use is likely to confuse consumers and that it suffered economically as a result of the infringement, the competitor may have to pay the owner damages based on the loss. And if the court finds that the competitor intentionally copied the owner's trademark, or at least should have known about the mark, the competitor may have to give up the profits it made by using the mark as well as pay other damages, such as punitive damages, fines, or attorneys' fees. On the other hand, if the trademark's owner has not been damaged, a court can allow the competitor to continue to use the trademark under limited circumstances designed to avoid consumer confusion.

Do I have the right to use my last name as a mark even if someone else is already using it for a similar business?

It depends on the name. A mark that is primarily a surname (last name) does not qualify for protection under federal trademark law unless the name becomes well known as a mark through advertising or long use. If this happens, the mark is said to have acquired a "secondary meaning."

If a surname acquires a secondary meaning, it is off limits for all uses that might cause customer confusion, whether or not the name is registered. Sears, McDonald's, Hyatt, Champion, Howard Johnson's, and Calvin Klein are just a few of the hundreds of surnames that have become effective and protected marks over time.

Also, a business that tries to capitalize on the name of its owner to take advantage of an identical famous name being used as a trademark may be forced, under the state or federal anti-dilution laws, to stop using the name. This may happen if the trademark owner files a lawsuit.

TM and ®: What do they mean?

Many people like to put a "TM" (or "SM" for service mark) next to their mark to let the world know that they own it. However, it is not legally necessary to provide this type of notice; the use of the mark itself is the act that confers ownership.

The "R" in a circle (®) is a different matter entirely. This notice may not be put on a mark unless it has been registered with the U.S. Patent and Trademark Office—and it should accompany a mark after registration is complete. Failing to put the notice on a registered trademark can greatly reduce your chances of recovering significant damages if you later have to file a lawsuit against an infringer.

Conducting a Trademark Search

If you want to find out whether the trademark you've chosen for your products or services is available, you'll need to conduct a trademark search—an investigation to discover potential conflicts between your desired mark and any existing marks. Ideally, the search should be done before you begin to use a mark; this will help you avoid the expensive mistake of infringing a mark belonging to someone else.

Why do I need to conduct a trademark search?

The consequences of failing to conduct a reasonably thorough trademark search may be severe, depending on how widely you intend to use your mark and how much it would cost you to change it if a conflict later develops. If the mark you want to use has been federally registered by someone else, a court will presume that you knew about the registration—even if you did not. You will be precluded from using the mark in any context where customers might become confused. And if you do use the mark improperly, you will be cast in the role of a "willful infringer." Willful infringers can be held liable for large damages and payment of the registered owner's attorneys' fees; they can also be forced to stop using the mark altogether.

My business is local. Why should I care what name or mark someone else in another part of the country is using?

Most small retail or service-oriented business owners well know the mantra for success: location, location, location. But as the Internet takes firm hold, the concept of location takes on a whole new meaning. Instead of being rooted in physical space, businesses are now required to jockey for locations in the virtual or electronic space known as the Internet.

Vast numbers of businesses—even local enterprises—are putting up their own websites, creating a new potential for competition (and confusion) in the marketplace. Because of this, every business owner must pay attention to whether a proposed name or mark has already been taken by another business, regardless of the location or scope of that business.

Can I do my own trademark search?

Yes. Although the most thorough trademark searches are accomplished by professional search firms such as Thomson & Thomson, it is also possible to conduct a preliminary online trademark search to determine whether a trademark is distinguishable from other federally registered trademarks. You can accomplish this with the PTO's trademark databases (www.uspto.gov), which provide free access to records of federally registered marks or marks that are pending. In addition, privately owned fee-based online trademark databases often provide more current PTO trademark information. Below are some private fee-based online search companies:

Saegis (www.thomson-thomson.com). Provides access to all TrademarkScan databases (state, federal, and international trademark databases), domain name databases, common law sources on the Internet, and newly filed United States federal trademark applications. Saegis also provides access to Dialog services, discussed next.

Dialog (www.dialog.com). Provides access to TrademarkScan databases, including state and federal registration and some international trademarks, and allows searching of news databases.

Trademark.com (www.trademark.com). Provides access to current federal registration information.

LexisNexis (www.lexisnexis.com). Lexis provides access to federal and state registrations.

You can also search for nonregistered trademarks through its Nexis news services. The PTO uses Nexis to evaluate descriptive and generic terms.

You can also visit one of the Patent and Trademark Depository libraries available in every state. These libraries offer a combination of hardcover directories of federally registered marks and an online database of both registered marks and marks for which a registration application is pending. To find the Patent and Trademark Depository library nearest you, consult the PTO website at www.uspto.gov.

You should also search for marks that have not been registered. This is important because an existing mark, even if it's unregistered, would preclude you from:

- registering the same or a confusingly similar mark in your own name, and

- using the mark in any part of the country or any commercial transaction where customers might be confused.

You can search for unregistered marks in the Patent and Trademark Depository libraries and on the Internet. In the libraries, use the available product guides and other materials. On the Internet, look for online shopping websites and review the inventory for items similar to yours. For example, go to eToys (www.etoys.com) to find hundreds of trademarked toys. You can also search for unregistered marks by using an Internet search engine. Enter your proposed name in the search field of an Internet search engine (such as Google or Alta Vista). You will get a report of every time that name appears on Web pages indexed by that engine. Because no search engine is 100% complete, you should do this same search on several different search engines.

How can I find out whether a mark I want to use is already being used as a domain name (the name of a website)?

Every website is identified by a unique phrase known as a "domain name." For example, the domain name for Nolo is Nolo.com. Because so much business is now being done online, most people will want to be able to use their proposed mark as a domain name so that their customers can easily locate them on the Web.

The easiest way to find out if a domain name is already in use is to check with one of the dozens of online companies that have been approved to register domain names. You can access a listing of these registrars through InterNIC's site at www.internic.net or the site of the Internet Corporation of Assigned Names and Numbers (ICANN) at www.icann.org. ICANN is the organization that oversees the process of approving domain name registrars.

Should I have a professional firm conduct my trademark search?

Many people prefer to pay a professional search firm to handle a trademark search. This makes sense if your financial plans justify an initial outlay of several hundred dollars, the minimum cost for a thorough professional search for both registered and unregistered marks. Depending on the search firm, you may also get a legal opinion as to whether your proposed mark is legally safe to use in light of existing registered and unregistered marks. Obtaining a legal opinion may provide important protection down the road if someone later sues you for using the mark.

How do I find a professional search firm?

There are many trademark search services in the United States. Here are two of the most well known:

Trademark Express (www.tmexpress.com). Trademark Express is a private company that, in addition to other trademark-related services, offers a full choice of trademark searches.

Thomson & Thomson (www.thomson-thomson.com). Thomson & Thomson is the trademark search service of choice for the legal professional.

If you don't like doing business at a distance, you can find trademark search services in your area by looking in the Yellow Pages of the nearest good-sized city under "trademark consultants" or "information brokers." If that yields nothing, consult the advertisements in a local legal journal or magazine. You can also find a good list of trademark search firms at www.ggmark.com.

Registering a Trademark

It is possible to register certain types of trademarks and service marks with the U.S. Patent and Trademark Office (PTO). Federal registration puts the rest of the country on notice that the trademark is already taken and makes it easier to protect a mark against would-be copiers.

How does a mark qualify for federal registration?

To register a trademark with the PTO, the mark's owner first must put it into use "in commerce that Congress may regulate." This means the mark must be used on a product or service that crosses state, national, or territorial lines or that affects commerce crossing such lines—for example, a catalogue business or a restaurant or motel that caters to interstate or international customers. Even if the owner files an intent-to-use (ITU) trademark application (ITU applications are discussed in *Using and Enforcing a Trademark,* above), the mark will not actually be registered until it is used in commerce.

Once the PTO receives a trademark registration application, the office must answer the following questions:

- Is the trademark the same as or similar to an existing mark used on similar or related goods or services?
- Is the trademark on the list of prohibited or reserved names?
- Is the trademark generic—that is, does the mark describe the product itself rather than its source?
- Is the trademark too descriptive (not distinctive enough) to qualify for protection?

If the answer to each question is "no," the trademark is eligible for registration and the PTO will continue to process the application.

I know the PTO won't register a mark if it's not distinctive or already in use. But are there other types of marks that are ineligible for federal registration?

Yes. The PTO won't register any marks that contain:

- names of living persons without their consent
- the U.S. flag
- other federal and local governmental insignias
- the name or likeness of a deceased U.S. president without his widow's consent
- words or symbols that disparage living or deceased persons, institutions, beliefs, or national symbols, or
- marks that are judged immoral, deceptive, or scandalous.

As a general rule the PTO takes a liberal view of the terms "immoral" and "scandalous" and will rarely refuse to register a mark on those grounds.

If the PTO decides that a mark is eligible for federal registration, what happens next?

Next, the PTO publishes the trademark in the *Official Gazette* (a publication of the U.S. Patent and Trademark Office). The *Gazette* states that the mark is a candidate for registration; this provides existing trademark owners with an opportunity to object to the registration. If someone objects, the PTO will schedule a hearing to resolve the dispute.

Is it possible to federally register a mark made up of common or ordinary words?

Yes, if the combination of the words is distinctive. But even if the entire mark is judged to lack sufficient distinctiveness, it can be placed on a list called the Supplemental Register. (Marks that are considered distinctive—either inherently or because they have become well known—are placed on a list called the Principal Register.) Marks on the Supplemental Register receive far less protection than do those on the Principal Register. The benefits granted by each type of registration are discussed in more detail below.

What are the benefits of federal trademark registration?

It depends on which register carries the mark. Probably the most important benefit of placing a mark on the Principal Register is that anybody who later starts using the same or a confusingly similar trademark may be presumed by the courts to be a "willful infringer" and therefore liable for large money damages.

Placing a trademark on the Supplemental Register produces significantly fewer benefits but still provides notice of ownership. This notice makes it far less likely that someone will use that identical mark; the fear of being sued for damages should keep potential infringers away. Also, if the trademark remains on the Supplemental Register for five years—meaning that the registration isn't canceled for some reason—and the mark remains in use during that time, it may be moved to the Principal Register under the secondary meaning rule (secondary meaning will be presumed).

Even if a mark is not registered, it is still possible for the owner to sue the infringer under a federal statute that forbids use of a "false designation of origin" (Title 15 U.S.C. § 1125). It is usually much easier to prove the case and collect large damages, however, if the mark has been registered.

How long does federal registration last?

Once a trademark or service mark is placed on the Principal Register, the owner receives a certificate of registration good for an initial term of ten years. The registration may lapse before the ten-year period expires, however, unless the owner files a form within six years of the registration date (called the Section 8 Declaration) stating that the mark is either still in use in commerce or that the mark is not in use for legitimate reasons.

The Section 8 Declaration is usually combined with a Section 15 Declaration, which effectively renders the trademark incontestable except for limited reasons.

The original registration may be renewed indefinitely for additional ten-year periods if the owner files the required renewal applications (called a Section 9 Declaration) with the U.S. Patent and Trademark Office. A Section 8 Declaration must also be filed at the time of trademark renewal. Failure to renew a registration does not void all rights to the mark, but if the owner fails to reregister, the special benefits of federal registration will be lost.

What happens if there is a conflict between an Internet domain name and an existing trademark?

The answer depends on the nature of the conflict. There are three reasons a conflict may develop between the owner of a trademark and the owner of a domain name:

The domain name registrant is a cybersquatter. If a domain name is registered in bad faith—for example, someone registers the name with the intent of selling it back to a company with the same name—the domain name can be taken away under federal law or under international arbitration rules for domain name owners. A victim of cybersquatting in the United States can now sue under the provisions of the Anticybersquatting Consumer Protection Act (ACPA) or can fight the cybersquatter using an international arbitration system created by ICANN. The ICANN arbitration system is usually faster and less expensive than suing under the ACPA. In addition, it does not require an attorney. For information on the ICANN policy, visit the organization's website at www.icann.org.

The domain name infringes an existing trademark. If a domain name is likely to confuse consumers because it is similar to an existing trademark, the owner of the federally owned trademark can sue for infringement in federal court. For example, it's likely that the Adobe company, makers of graphics software, would be able to prevent another software company from using the domain name of www.adoobie.com.

The domain name dilutes a famous trademark. If a domain name dilutes the power of a famous trademark, the trademark owner can sue under federal laws to stop the continued use. Dilution occurs when the domain name blurs or tarnishes the reputation of a famous trademark. For example, Gucci could probably prevent a company from using the domain name "guccigoo.com" for the purpose of selling baby diapers.

How to Register Your Trademark

For most trademarks already in use, federal registration is a relatively straightforward process. The PTO, www.uspto.gov, has an excellent online system for filing an application for trademark registration, known as TEAS (Trademark Electronic Application System). In order to encourage applicants to file their trademark using TEAS, the PTO has stopped supplying blank trademark application forms. To further discourage paper applications, the PTO charges more for paper filings: $375, as opposed to $325 for a TEAS application. When you complete your registration form online, you will have to:

- describe your mark
- state when it was first used
- describe the products or services on which the mark will be used, and
- suggest the classification under which the mark should be registered (there are approximately 40 classifications for goods and services; the PTO can help you figure out which one is right for your mark).

In addition, you must submit:

- a "drawing" of your mark (for word marks, this simply involves setting the mark out in the middle of a page in capital letters)
- a sample of how your proposed mark is being used, and
- the registration fee.

If you are applying to register your mark on the basis of its intended use, then you needn't provide the samples or the date of first use, but you can't complete your registration until you put your mark into actual use and file some additional paperwork with the PTO.

The PTO website also offers plain-English instructions for completing the online application. For more information about registering your trademark, see the resource list at the end of this chapter.

Can a business register its mark at the state level?

It is possible to register a mark with the state trademark agency, although the state registration does not offer the same level of protection provided by federal law. The main benefit of state registration is that it notifies anyone who checks the list that the mark is owned by the registrant.

This will lead most would-be users of the same mark to choose another one rather than risk a legal dispute with the registered mark's owner. If the mark is also federally registered, this notice is presumed, and state registration isn't necessary. If, however, the mark is used only within the state and doesn't qualify for federal registration, state registration is a good idea.

How Trademarks Differ From Patents and Copyrights

Trademarks are often mentioned in the same breath as copyrights and patents. Though these terms do sometimes apply to the same thing, they're more often defined by their differences. It's important to understand how trademark law differs from other laws protecting creative works (collectively called "intellectual property laws").

How does trademark differ from copyright?

Copyright protects original works of expression, such as novels, fine and graphic arts, music, photography, software, video, cinema, and choreography by preventing people from copying or commercially exploiting them without the copyright owner's permission. But the copyright laws do not protect names, titles, or short phrases. That's where trademark law comes in. Trademark protects distinctive words, phrases, logos, symbols, slogans, and any other devices used to identify and distinguish products or services in the marketplace.

There are, however, areas where both trademark and copyright law may be used to protect different aspects of the same product. For example, copyright laws may protect the artistic aspects of a graphic or logo used by a business to identify its goods or services, while trademark may protect the graphic or logo from use by others in a confusing manner in the marketplace. Similarly, trademark laws are often used in conjunction with copyright laws to protect advertising copy. The trademark laws protect the product or service name and any slogans used in the advertising, while the copyright laws protect the additional creative written expression contained in the ad.

For more information about copyright law, see Chapter 7.

What's the difference between patent and trademark?

Patents allow the creator of certain kinds of inventions that contain new ideas to keep others from making commercial use of those ideas without the creator's permission. For example, Tom invents a new type of hammer that makes it very difficult to miss the nail. Not only can Tom keep others from making, selling, or using the precise type of hammer he invented, but he may also be able to apply his patent monopoly rights to prevent people from making commercial use of any similar type of hammer during the time the patent is in effect (20 years from the date the patent application is filed).

Generally, patent and trademark laws do not overlap. When it comes to a product design, however—say, jewelry or a distinctively shaped musical instrument—it may be possible to obtain a patent on a design aspect of the device while invoking trademark law to protect the design as a product identifier. For instance, an auto manufacturer might receive a design patent for the stylistic fins that are part of a car's rear fenders. Then, if the fins were intended to be—and actually are—used to distinguish the particular model car in the marketplace, trademark law may kick in to protect the appearance of the fins.

For more information about patent law, see Chapter 6.

More Information About Trademarks

Trademark: Legal Care for Your Business & Product Name, by Stephen Elias (Nolo), shows you how to choose a legally strong business and product name, register the name with state and federal agencies, and sort out any name disputes that arise.

Patent, Copyright & Trademark: An Intellectual Property Desk Reference, by Stephen Elias and Richard Stim (Nolo), provides concise definitions and examples of the important words and phrases commonly used in trademark law.

The following associations of trademark lawyers offer a number of helpful publications. Write, call, or visit online for a list of available materials.

International Trademark Association (INTA)
1133 Avenue of the Americas
New York, NY 10036
212-768-9887
www.inta.org

American Intellectual Property Law
Association (AIPLA)
2001 Jefferson Davis Highway, Suite 203
Arlington, VA 22202
703-415-0780
www.aipla.org

Online Help

www.nolo.com
Nolo offers information about a wide variety of legal topics, including trademarks.

www.inta.org
The International Trademark Association (INTA) provides trademark services, publications, and online resources.

www.uspto.gov
The U.S. Patent and Trademark Office provides new trademark rules and regulations, free trademark searching, and lots of useful links to trademark-related sites.

www.schwimmerlegal.com
Martin Schwimmer's trademark blog is one of the most interesting (and popular) sources of daily trademark news.

www.ggmark.com
This site, maintained by a trademark lawyer, provides basic trademark information and a fine collection of links to other trademark resources.

Your Money

*Too many people spend money they haven't
earned, to buy things they don't want,
to impress people they don't like.*

—WILL ROGERS

America's economy is driven by consumer spending. When we open any newspaper or magazine, turn on the radio or television, or take a drive across town, we're bombarded with ads urging us to spend our hard-earned dollars. And we respond by pulling out our cash, checks, credit cards, and debit cards.

What the ads don't tell you is what to do when things go wrong—for example, when the item you buy is defective, when you lose your credit card, when you need extra time to pay, or when you fall behind and the bill collectors start calling.

Fortunately, many federal (and some state) laws provide some protections to consumers; this chapter describes some of the most important. While no law substitutes for common sense, comparison shopping, and avoiding offers that sound too good to be true, many laws can help you if you run into trouble.

Purchasing Goods and Services

*I did not have three thousand pairs of shoes:
I had one thousand and sixty.*

—IMELDA MARCOS

While 19th century business relationships were governed by the doctrine "caveat emptor" or "let the buyer beware," the notion that a buyer-seller arrangement should be fair gained ground in the 20th century. As a result, you now have a right to receive goods and services that meet certain minimum standards.

When I buy something, is it covered by a warranty?

Generally, yes. A warranty (also called a guarantee) is an assurance about the quality of goods or services you buy and is intended to protect you if something you purchase fails to live up to what you were promised.

An express warranty is one that is actually stated, usually in writing. Most express warranties state something such as "this product is warranted against defects in materials or workmanship" for a specified time. Most either come directly from the manufacturer or are included in the sales contract you sign with the seller. But an express warranty may also be in an advertisement or on a sign in a store ("all dresses 100% silk"), or in a salesperson's oral description of a product's features.

An implied warranty is not spoken or written but is based on reasonable consumer expectations. There are two implied warranties—one for "merchantability" and one for "fitness." The implied warranty of merchantability is an assurance that a new item will work if you use it for a reasonably expected purpose (for example, that a toaster will toast bread or a power drill will drill holes). This warranty applies only to the product's ability to perform its basic purpose, not to everything that could possibly go wrong with the product. For used items, the warranty of merchantability is a promise that the product will work as expected, given its age and condition.

The implied warranty of fitness applies when you buy an item with a specific (even unusual) purpose in mind. If you communicated your specific needs to the seller, the implied warranty of fitness assures you that the item will meet these needs.

How long does a warranty last?

An express warranty lasts for the term stated in the language of the warranty—for example, "three years after the date of purchase." The lifespan of an implied warranty depends on state law. Some states limit an implied warranty to a period of time—one or two years, for example. Others say that an implied warranty lasts only as long as any express warranty made about a product.

Can a seller avoid a warranty by selling a product "as is"?

The answer depends on whether the warranty is express or implied and on the laws of the state where you live. Sellers cannot avoid express warranties by claiming the product is sold "as is." On the other hand, if there is no express warranty, sellers can sometimes avoid an implied warranty by selling the item "as is." Some states prohibit all "as is" sales. And in all states, the buyer must know that the item is sold "as is" in order for the seller to avoid an implied warranty.

How do I enforce a warranty if something is wrong with the product I bought?

Most of the time, a defect in an item will show up immediately, and you can ask the seller or manufacturer to fix or replace it. It's best to make this request in a letter that states when you purchased the item, what you paid for it, and what's wrong with it. If the seller refuses, try to mediate the dispute through a community or Better Business Bureau mediation program. (For more information about mediation, see Chapter 16.) You can also contact your state or local consumer protection agency.

If all else fails, you can sue. If the seller or manufacturer won't make good under a warranty, you must sue within one to four years of when you discovered the defect, depending on your state's laws.

Do I have any recourse if the item breaks after the warranty expires?

Usually not. But in most states, if the item gave you some trouble while it was under the warranty and you had it repaired by someone authorized by the manufacturer to make repairs, the manufacturer must extend your original warranty for the amount of time the item sat in the shop. If you think you're entitled to an extension, call the manufacturer and ask to speak to the department that handles warranties.

You may have other options as well. If your product was trouble-free during the warranty period, the manufacturer may offer a free repair for a problem that arose after the warranty expired if the problem is widespread. Many manufacturers have secret "fix-it" lists—items with defects that don't affect safety and therefore don't require a recall but that the manufacturer will repair for free. It can't hurt to call and ask.

I just bought a stereo system, and the salesclerk tried to sell me an extended warranty contract. Should I have bought it?

Probably not. Merchants encourage you to buy extended warranties (also called service contracts) because they are a source of big profits for stores, which pocket up to 50% of the amount you pay.

Rarely will you have the chance to exercise your rights under an extended warranty, however. Name-brand electronic equipment and appliances usually don't break down during the first few years (and if they do, they're covered by the original warranty), and they often have a lifespan well beyond the length of the extended warranty.

How to File a Complaint for Fraud

The National Fraud Information Center (NFIC), a project of the National Consumer's League, can help you if you've been defrauded. NFIC provides:

- assistance in filing a complaint with appropriate federal agencies
- recorded information on current fraud schemes
- tips on how to avoid becoming a fraud victim, and
- consumer publications in English or Spanish.

You can contact NFIC at 800-876-7060, or online at www.fraud.org.

Also contact your local prosecutor (such as the District Attorney's office) to find out if it investigates consumer fraud complaints. Finally, contact any local newspaper, radio station, or television station "action line." Especially in metropolitan areas, these folks often have an army of volunteers ready to pursue consumer complaints.

I think I was the victim of a scam. Can I get my money back?

Federal and state laws prohibit "unfair or deceptive trade acts or practices." If you think you've been cheated, *immediately* let the appropriate government offices know. Although any government investigation will take some time, these agencies often have the resources to go after unscrupulous merchants. And the more agencies you notify, the more likely someone will take notice of your complaint and act on it.

Unfortunately, government agencies are rarely able to get you your money back. If the business is a reputable one, however, it may refund your money when a consumer fraud law enforcement investigator shows up. It certainly can't hurt to complain.

If you can't get relief from a government agency, consider suing the company in small claims court. *Everybody's Guide to Small Claims Court,* by Ralph Warner (Nolo), provides extensive information on how to sue in small claims court. (See Chapter 16.)

I received some unordered merchandise in the mail, and now I'm getting billed. Do I have to pay?

You don't owe any money if you receive an item you never ordered. It's considered a gift. If you get bills or collection letters from a seller who sent you something you never ordered, write to the seller stating your intention to treat the item as a gift. If the bills continue, insist that the seller send you proof of your order. If this doesn't stop the bills, notify the state consumer protection agency in the state where the merchant is located.

If you sent for something in response to an advertisement claiming a "free" gift or "trial" period, and are now being billed, be sure to read the fine print of the ad. It may say something about charging shipping and handling; or worse, you may have inadvertently joined a club or subscribed to a magazine. Write the seller, cancel your membership or subscription, offer to return the merchandise, and state that you believe the ad was misleading.

I just signed a contract to have carpeting installed in my house, and I changed my mind. Can I cancel?

Possibly. Under the Federal Trade Commission's "cooling-off rule," you have until midnight of the third day (not including Sundays and federal holidays) after a contract was signed to cancel either of the following:

- door-to-door sales contracts for more than $25, or
- a contract for more than $25 made anywhere other than the seller's normal place of business—for instance, at a sales presentation at a hotel or restaurant, outdoor exhibit, computer show, or trade show (other than public car auctions and craft fairs).

These are situations where you are especially vulnerable to deception and high-pressure sales tactics.

This cooling-off period does not apply to contracts to buy a car, truck, van, or camper. If your dealer says otherwise, be sure to get it in writing.

Do I have the right to cancel any other kinds of contracts?

The federal Truth in Lending Act lets you cancel some loans up until midnight of the third day (not including Sundays or federal holidays) after you signed the contract. It applies only to loans for which you pledged your home as security, as long as the loan is not a first mortgage. For example, the Act applies to home improvement loans, home equity loans, and second mortgages. If the lender never notified you of the three-day right to cancel, you have even longer to cancel your loan.

The federal Credit Repair Organization Act gives you three days to cancel a contract with a credit repair organization.

In addition, many states have laws that allow you to cancel written contracts covering the purchase of certain goods or services within a few days of signing, including contracts for dance or martial arts lessons, credit repair services, health club memberships, dating services, weight loss programs, time share properties, and hearing aids. In a few states, you can also cancel a contract if you negotiated the transaction in a language other than English but the seller did not give you a copy of the contract in that language. Contact your state consumer protection agency to find out what contracts, if any, are covered in your state.

I ordered some clothes through a catalogue, and there's a delay in shipping. Can I cancel my order?

If you order goods online or by mail, phone, or fax (other than magazine subscriptions, seeds, or plants), the Federal Trade Commission's "Mail or Telephone Order Rule" requires that the seller ship to you within the time promised or, if no time was stated, within 30 days. If the company didn't promise a shipping time and you are applying for credit to pay for the item, the company has 50 days to ship.

If the seller cannot ship within those time frames, the seller must send you a notice with a new shipping date and offer you the option of canceling your order and getting a refund, or accepting the new date. If the seller can't meet the second deadline, it must send a notice requesting your signature to agree to yet a third date. If you don't return the notice, the seller must automatically cancel your order and refund your money.

Do I have the right to a cash refund after I make a purchase?

Generally, no. A seller isn't required to offer refunds or exchanges, though many do.

But some states (including California and Florida) require merchants to post their refund or exchange policies, particularly if the seller doesn't offer a full cash refund. Merchants that don't follow these rules have to allow customers to return items for a full refund, as long as the customer does so within the time limits set by state law.

More Information About Purchasing Goods and Services

Everybody's Guide to Small Claims Court, by Ralph Warner (Nolo), has extensive information on pursuing your rights in the event a seller or manufacturer won't make good on a warranty.

Solve Your Money Troubles, by Robin Leonard and John Lamb (Nolo), explains how to handle debts for defective goods or services.

The Federal Trade Commissions's website, www.ftc. gov, has lots of information about goods and services, including fact sheets and links to consumer groups.

The Direct Marketing Association is a membership organization made up of mail-order companies and other direct marketers. If you have a complaint about a particular company, contact Ethics and Consumer Affairs, c/o DMA, 1615 L Street, NW, Washington, DC 20036, 202-955-5030, www. dmaconsumers.org. DMA may contact the mail-order company and try to resolve your problem.

Using Credit and Charge Cards

Today, most Americans have six or seven credit cards. Buying on credit has become a cornerstone of the American economy. But buying on credit can be very expensive—the interest rate charged by bank credit card companies averages more than 13%; on gasoline company and department store cards, it's significantly higher. Only traditional charge cards (also called travel and entertainment cards), such as American Express and Diners Club, generally don't impose interest because you must pay off the entire balance each month. However, even these companies now offer terms that look like regular credit card accounts.

My credit card debt is consuming my life. How can I cut credit card costs?

If you have more than one card, pay down the balances with the highest interest rates and then use (or obtain) a card with a low rate. Because there is great competition among credit card issuers, you might get a rate reduction simply by asking for one from your current credit card company.

I'm always getting credit card offers with low interest rates in the mail. Should I sign up and transfer the balance from my current card to the new card?

It depends. Check the fine print of the offer. Many credit card companies offer a "teaser" rate—a low rate that lasts for a short period of time. Once the "teaser" period is over, a much higher rate kicks in. Also be sure to consider any annual fees, grace periods, and nuisance fees before you switch.

Which Cards Should You Keep?

When you think about the costs of using your credit cards, you may decide that you're better off canceling most of them. If so, you'll have to decide which cards to keep. If you don't carry a monthly balance, keep a card with no annual fee, but make sure it has a grace period. If you carry a balance each month, get rid of the cards that come with the worst of the following features:

- **High interest rates.**
- **Unfair interest calculations.** Avoid cards that charge interest on the average daily balance, not the balance due. Here's why: Let's say you pay $1,200 of your $1,500 balance in January. If your bank uses the average daily balance method, in February it will charge you interest on the $1,500 average daily balance from January, not on the $300 you still owe.
- **No grace period.** This means you pay interest from the time of purchase until the time of payment, even if you pay your balance in full.
- **Nuisance fees.** If you can, get rid of cards with late-payment fees, over-the-limit fees, inactivity fees, fees for not carrying a balance or for carrying a balance under a certain amount, or a flat monthly fee that's a percentage of your credit limit.

I can't afford the minimum payment required on my statement. Can I pay less?

Most card companies insist that you make the monthly minimum payment, which is usually 2% to 2.5% of the outstanding balance. If you can convince the card issuer that your financial situation is desperate, the issuer may cut your payments in half. In some cases, the issuer may waive payments altogether for a few months. This courtesy is usually extended only to people who have never made late payments.

Bear in mind that paying nothing or very little on your credit card should be a temporary solution only. The longer you pay only a small amount, the quicker your balance will increase due to interest charges.

My wallet was stolen. Will I have to pay charges that the thief made using my credit cards?

No. Federal law limits your liability for unauthorized charges made on your credit or charge card after it has been lost or stolen. If you notify the card issuer within a reasonable time after you discover the loss or theft, you're not responsible for any charges made after the notification and are liable for only the first $50 of charges made before you notified the card issuer. Some card issuers don't even charge the $50.

I purchased an item using my credit card and the item fell apart. Can I refuse to pay?

Maybe. Under federal law, you must first attempt in good faith to resolve the dispute with the merchant. If that fails, you can withhold payment on non-seller-issued cards only if the purchase was for more than $50 and was made within your home state or within 100 miles of your home. This limitation applies only if you used a card not issued by the seller, such as a MasterCard. There is no $50, 100-mile, or instate limitation if you use a seller's card, such as your Sears card.

The 100-mile limitation is easy to calculate when purchases are made in person. But if you order through the mail, over the telephone, or using your computer, the law is unclear as to where the purchase took place. Your best bet is to claim that the purchase was made in the state where you live (even if the catalogue company is on the other side of the country) because you placed the order from home.

My credit card billing statement contains an error. What should I do?

Immediately write a letter to the customer service department of the card issuer. Give your name, account number, an explanation of the error, and the amount involved. Enclose copies of supporting documents, such as receipts showing the correct amount of the charge. You must act quickly—the issuer must receive your letter within 60 days after it mailed the bill to you.

Be sure to use the correct "billing error" address (you can find it in the tiny print on the back of your statement), not the address where you send your regular payments.

Under the federal Fair Credit Billing Act, the issuer must acknowledge receipt of your letter within 30 days, unless it corrects the bill within that time. Furthermore, the issuer must, within two billing cycles (but in no event more than 90 days), correct the error or explain why it believes the amount to be correct.

During the two-billing-cycle/90-day period, the issuer cannot report the amount to credit bureaus or other creditors as delinquent. The issuer can charge you interest on the amount you dispute during this period, but if it later agrees that you were correct, it must drop the interest accrued.

Must I give my phone number when I use a credit card?

Probably not. Several states, including California, bar merchants from writing down personal information when you use a credit card (unless it's needed for shipping, billing, installation, or special orders). Furthermore, merchant agreements with Visa and MasterCard prohibit them from requiring a customer to furnish a phone number when paying with one of these cards.

I took out a cash advance using my credit card and feel I was gouged. What are all those fees?

Cash advances usually come with the following fees:

- *Transaction fees.* Most banks charge a transaction fee of up to 4% for taking a cash advance.
- *No grace period.* Most banks charge interest from the date the cash advance is posted, even if you pay it back in full when your bill comes.
- *Interest rates.* The interest rate is often higher on cash advances than it is on ordinary credit card charges.

Using an ATM or Debit Card

A bank is a place where they lend you an umbrella in fair weather and ask for it back when it begins to rain.

—ROBERT FROST

Banks issue ATM cards to allow customers to withdraw money, make deposits, transfer money between accounts, find out their balances, get cash advances, and even make loan payments at all hours of the day or night.

Debit cards combine the functions of ATM cards and checks. Debit cards are issued by banks but can be used at stores. When you pay with a debit card, the money is automatically deducted from your checking account.

What are the advantages of using an ATM or debit card?

There are generally two advantages:

- You don't have to carry your checkbook and identification, but you can make purchases directly from your checking account.
- You pay immediately—without running up interest charges on a credit card bill.

Are there disadvantages?

Yes. You don't have 20 to 25 days to pay the bill, as you would if you paid by credit card. Also, you don't have the right to withhold payment (the money is immediately removed from the account) in the event of a dispute with the merchant over goods or services. Finally, many banks charge transaction fees when you use an ATM or debit card at locations other than those owned by the bank.

Do I have to pay if there's a mistake on my statement or receipt?

Although ATM statements and debit receipts don't usually contain errors, mistakes do happen. If you find an error, you have 60 days from the date of the statement or receipt to notify the bank. Always call first and follow up with a letter. If you don't notify the bank within 60 days, it has no obligation to investigate the error, and you're out of luck.

The bank has ten business days from the date of your notification to investigate the problem and tell you the result. If the bank needs more time, it can take up to 45 days, but only if it deposits or recredits the disputed amount of money into your account. If the bank later determines that there was no error, it can take the money back, but it must first send you a written explanation.

If Your ATM Card Is Lost or Stolen

If your ATM or debit card is lost or stolen (never, never, never keep your personal identification number—PIN—near your card), call your bank immediately and follow up with a confirming letter. Under federal law, your liability is:

- $0 for charges made after you report the card missing
- up to $50 if you notify the bank within two business days after you realize the card is missing (unless you were on extended travel or in the hospital)
- up to $500 if you fail to notify the bank within two business days after you realize the card is missing (unless you were on extended travel or in the hospital), but do notify the bank within 60 days after your bank statement is mailed to you listing the unauthorized withdrawals
- unlimited if you fail to notify the bank within 60 days after your bank statement is mailed to you listing the unauthorized withdrawals (unless you were on extended travel, in the hospital, or had similar good reasons for the delay).

In response to consumer complaints about the possibility of unlimited liability, Visa and MasterCard now cap the liability on debit cards at $50. A few states have capped the liability for unauthorized withdrawals on an ATM or debit card at $50 as well. And some large debit card issuers won't charge you anything if unauthorized withdrawals appear on your statement.

More Information About Credit, Charge, ATM, and Debit Cards

Solve Your Money Troubles, by Robin Leonard and John Lamb (Nolo), contains extensive information on credit, charge, ATM, and debit card laws, and practical usage tips.

The Federal Deposit Insurance Corporation, 550 17th Street, NW, Washington, DC 20429, 877-275-3342, www.fdic.gov, publishes free pamphlets.

The Federal Trade Commission, CRC-240, 600 Pennsylvania Ave., NW, Washington, DC 20580, 877-FTC-HELP (382-4357), www.ftc.gov, offers lots of consumer information on billing errors, credit problems, and credit and ATM cards.

Strategies for Repaying Debts

If you think nobody cares if you're alive, try missing a couple of car payments.

—EARL WILSON

Today, many people are either unemployed or forced to work harder than ever (often in more than one job), earning less, saving little, and struggling with debt. If this story sounds familiar to you, you're not alone. Here are some specific suggestions for dealing with debts.

I feel completely overwhelmed by my debts and don't know where to begin. What should I do?

Take a deep breath and realize that for the most part your creditors want to help you pay them. Whether you're behind on your bills or are afraid of getting behind, call your creditors. Let them know what's going on—job loss, reduction in hours, medical problem, or other issues—and ask for help. Suggest possible solutions such as a temporary reduction of your payments, skipping a few payments and tacking them on at the end of a loan or paying them off over a few months, dropping late fees and other charges, or even re-writing a loan. If you need help negotiating with your creditors, consider contacting a nonprofit debt counseling organization.

To find an agency in your area, go to the web-site of the United States Trustee (www.usdoj. gov/ust) and click "Credit Counseling and Debtor Education"; you'll find a list of agencies the Trustee's office has approved to provide the counseling debtors must now complete before filing for bankruptcy.

I'm afraid I might miss a car payment—should I just let the lender repossess?

No. Before your car payment is due, call the lender and ask for extra time. If you're at least six months into the loan and haven't missed any payments, the lender may let you miss one or two months' payments and tack them on at the end. If you don't pay or make arrange-ments with the lender, the lender can repossess without warning, although many will warn you and give you a chance to pay what's due.

If your car is repossessed, you can get it back by paying the entire balance due and the cost of repossession or, in some cases, by paying the cost of the repossession and the missed payments, then making payments under your contract. If you don't get the car back, the lender will sell it at an auction for far less than it's worth. You'll owe the lender the difference between the balance of your loan and what the sale brings in.

If you are far behind on your car payments and can't catch up, think hard about whether you can really afford the car. If you decide to give up your car, there are two options that are almost always better than waiting for the dealer to repossess it. First, you can sell the car yourself and use the proceeds to pay off the loan (or most of the loan). You'll get more for the car if you sell it yourself than the dealer will by sell-ing it at an auction after repossession—which means you'll be able to pay off more of the loan. Or, you can voluntarily "surrender" your car to the dealer before repossession. This will save you repossession costs and attorneys' fees. Because it also makes life easier for dealers, many will agree to waive any deficiency balance or prom-ise not to report the default or repossession to credit bureaus if you work out a deal.

How soon after I miss a house payment will the bank begin foreclosure proceedings?

This varies from state to state and lender to lender, but most lenders don't start foreclosure proceedings until you've missed several pay-ments. Before taking back your house, a lender would usually rather rewrite the loan, suspend principal payments for a while (have you pay interest only), reduce your payments, or even let you miss a few payments and spread them out over time.

If your loan is owned by one of the giant U.S. mortgage holders, Fannie Mae or Freddie Mac, foreclosure could come even more slowly. Fannie Mae and Freddie Mac often work with homeowners to avoid foreclosure when a loan is delinquent.

If your loan is insured by a federal agency such as the Department of Housing and Urban Development (HUD), the Federal Housing

Administration (FHA), the Veterans Administration (VA), or the Farmers Home Administration (FmHA), the lender may be required to try to help you avoid foreclosure. Contact the federal agency to find out more.

Might I be better off just selling my house?

You're certainly better off selling the house than having it go to foreclosure. If you can find a buyer who will offer to pay at least what you owe your lender, take the offer. If the offer is for less than you owe your lender, your lender can block the sale. But many lenders will agree to a "short sale"—one that brings in less than you owe the lender—and agree to forgo the rest. Some lenders require documentation that you are experiencing financial or medical hardship before they will agree to a short sale.

Can I just walk away from the house?

If you get no offers for your house or the lender won't approve a short sale, you can walk away from your house. To do this, you transfer your ownership interest in your home to the lender using a deed in lieu of foreclosure. Keep in mind that with a deed in lieu, you won't get any cash back, even if you have lots of equity in your home. The deed in lieu may also appear on your credit report as a negative mark. If you opt for a deed in lieu, try to get concessions from the lender—after all, you are saving it the expense and hassle of foreclosing on your home. For example, ask the lender to eliminate negative references on your credit report or give you more time to stay in the house.

My utility bill was huge because of a very cold winter. Do I have to pay it all at once?

Maybe not. Many utility companies offer cus-

tomers an amortization program. This means that if your bills are higher in certain months than others, the company averages your yearly bills so you can spread out the large bills. Also, if you are elderly, disabled, or earn a low income, you may be eligible for reduced rates—ask your utility company.

I'm swamped with student loans and can't afford my payments. What can I do to avoid default?

First, know that you're right to do all you can to avoid default, rather than ignoring your loans and hoping they'll just go away. If you default, the amount you owe will probably skyrocket.

To avoid default, contact the companies that service your student loans and tell them why you can't make your payments. You may be eligible for a deferment or forbearance—ways of postponing repayment. In very limited circumstances, you may be able to cancel a loan. Also talk to your loan holders about flexible payment options—many now offer payments geared to borrowers' incomes.

Another option is consolidating your student loans. With loan consolidation, you can lower your monthly payments by extending your repayment period; you may also be able to lower your interest rate. Most loan consolidators offer flexible repayment options based on your income, and you may be able to consolidate even if one or more of your loans is in default. Consolidation terms and eligibility vary slightly from lender to lender. For information on consolidation, including potential disadvantages, go to www.studentloanborrowerassistance.org.

Finally, if you can prove that repayment would cause you extreme hardship, you may be able to discharge your student loans in bankruptcy.

Beware of the IRS

IRS regulations might require you to pay higher taxes if you settle a debt or a creditor writes off money you owe. The rules state that if a creditor agrees to forgo a debt you owe, you must treat the amount you didn't pay as income. Similarly, if a creditor ceases collection efforts, declares a debt uncollectible, and reports it as a tax loss to the IRS, you must treat this amount as income. This includes any amount owed after a house foreclosure or property repossession, or on a credit card bill.

The rule applies to a debt or part of a debt for $600 or more forgiven by any bank, credit union, savings and loan, or other financial institution. The institution must send you and the IRS a Form 1099-C at the end of the tax year. These forms report that income, which means that when you file your tax return for the tax year in which your debt was forgiven, the IRS will check to make sure that you report the amount on the Form 1099-C as income.

There are some exceptions to this rule, however. Even if you receive a Form 1099-C, you don't have to report the amount in these situations:

- The debt was canceled as a result of Hurricane Katrina (this applies only to nonbusiness debts).
- The debt was a student loan and was canceled because you worked in a profession and for an employer as promised when you took out the loan.
- The debt would have been deductible had you paid it.
- The cancellation of the debt is intended as a gift (this would be unusual).
- You discharge the debt in Chapter 11 bankruptcy.
- You were insolvent before the creditor agreed to waive the debt.

You are insolvent if your debts exceed the value of your assets.

Let's say your assets are worth $35,000 and your debts total $45,000. You are insolvent to the tune of $10,000. If a creditor forgives or writes off debts up to that amount, you will not have to include it as income on your tax return.

On the other hand, let's say your assets and debts are $35,000 and $45,000 respectively, but your creditor forgives or writes off a $14,000 debt. Now, you can ignore $10,000 of the Form 1099-C income (the amount of your insolvency), but you will have to report the remaining $4,000 on your tax return. If you don't report all or a portion of a canceled debt because of insolvency, you must complete and file IRS Form 982, *Reduction of Tax Attributes Due to Discharge of Indebtedness*, with your tax return.

I defaulted on a student loan a long time ago, and I just received collection letters. I can't afford very much, but I can pay something. Any suggestions?

Federal law allows you to rehabilitate your student loan by agreeing with your lender on a "reasonable and affordable" payment plan based on your income and expenses. Once you've made nine consecutive monthly payments, your loan will come out of default. The default notation will come off your credit report, and if you return to school, you can apply for an in-school deferment to postpone your payments.

If you do not return to school, after you make nine consecutive monthly payments, the holder of your loan will sell it back to a regular loan-servicing company. (This is called loan rehabilitation.) Your new loan servicer will put you on a standard ten-year repayment plan, which may cause your monthly payments to increase dramatically. If you can't afford them, you will need to apply for a deferment (if you are eligible) or request a flexible repayment option.

I paid off my student loan a long time ago, but the Department of Education recently wrote me saying I still owe it. Help!

You need documentation. First, contact your school and ask for its Department of Education report showing the loan's status. Then, think about ways you can show that you paid the loan: Do you have canceled checks or old bank statements? Can you get microfiche copies of checks from your bank or a government regulatory agency if your bank is out of business? Does an old roommate remember seeing you write a check every month? Can you get old credit reports (check with lenders from whom you've borrowed in years past) that may show a payment status on an old loan? Get old tax returns (from the IRS, if necessary) showing that you itemized the interest deduction on student loan payments back when that was permitted. The last holder of the loan might have a copy of the signed promissory note. Any of these things will help you prove to the Department of Education that you paid your loan.

To find out more about the status of your loan, visit the Department of Education's website at www.ed.gov or the National Student Loan Data System's website at www.nslds.ed.gov. Or call the federal Student Aid Information Center at 800-4-FED-AID (800-433-3243) or the student loan ombudsman at 877-557-2575 (www.ombudsman.ed.gov).

When can a creditor garnish my wages, place a lien on my house, seize my bank account, or take my tax refund?

For the most part, a creditor must sue you, obtain a court judgment, and then solicit the help of a sheriff or other law enforcement officer to garnish wages. Even then, the maximum the creditor can take is 25% of your net pay or the amount by which your weekly net earnings exceed 30 times the federal minimum wage ($5.85 until July 24, 2008, then $6.55 until July 24, 2009, then $7.25), whichever is less.

In two situations your wages may be garnished without your being sued:

- Most federal administrative agencies (including the IRS and the Department of Education) can garnish your wages to collect debts owed to that agency.
- Up to 50% of your wages can be garnished to pay child support or alimony (even more if you don't currently support any dependents or if you are in arrears).

To place a lien on your house or empty your bank account, almost all creditors must first sue you, get a judgment, and then use a law enforcement officer. A few creditors, such as an unpaid contractor who worked on your house, can put a lien on your house without suing. And again, the IRS is an exception—it can place a lien or empty your bank account without suing first.

Your tax refund can never be taken unless the Treasury Department receives such a request from the IRS, the Department of Education, or a child support collection agency.

If You Bounce a Check

In every state, writing a bad check is a crime. Aggressive district attorneys don't hesitate to prosecute, especially given that an estimated 450 million rubber checks are written each year. If you are prosecuted, you may be able to avoid a trial if your county has a "diversion" program, where you attend classes for bad check writers. You must pay the tuition and make good on the bad checks you wrote.

Even if you escape criminal prosecution, you'll be charged a bad check "processing" fee by your bank. Many banks charge more than $30. In addition, most creditors who receive a bad check can sue for damages. Before suing you, the creditor usually must first make a written demand that you make good on the bad check. If you don't pay up within approximately 30 days, the creditor can sue you. Damages recoverable by the merchant vary from state to state but are often a minimum of $50, and in most states more like a few hundred or a thousand dollars.

Can I go to jail for not paying my debts?

Debtor's prisons were eliminated in the United States by 1850. However, you can still be jailed in connection with a debt if: you willfully violate a court order, especially an order to pay child support; you are convicted of willfully refusing to pay income taxes; or you are about to conceal yourself or your property to avoid paying a debt for which a creditor has a judgment against you.

More Information About Repaying Debts

Solve Your Money Troubles, by Robin Leonard and John Lamb (Nolo), explains your legal rights and offers practical strategies for dealing with debts and creditors.

The Student Loan Borrower Assistance Project, www.studentloanborrowerassistance.org, offers free, detailed information on student loan consolidation, repayment options, defaults, and much more.

The Ultimate Credit Handbook, by Gerri Detweiler (Plume), provides tips on improving your credit and cutting your debt.

Surviving Debt: A Guide for Consumers, by Gary Klein, Deanne Loonin, and Odette Williamson (National Consumer Law Center), contains tips on dealing with debt collectors and repaying debts.

Myvesta.org, 800-680-3328, www.myvesta.org, offers free publications, recommended books, a forum for posting your debt questions, information on obtaining your credit report, and special programs to help you get out of debt.

National Foundation for Credit Counseling, 800-388-2227, www.nfcc.org, can put you in contact with the consumer credit counseling service office located nearest you.

The Federal Student Aid Information Center, 800-4-FED-AID, (433-3243) provides information about federal student loan programs.

The Federal Trade Commission, CRC-240, 600 Pennsylvania Ave., NW, Washington, DC 20580, 877-FTC-HELP (382-4357), www.ftc.gov, publishes nearly 50 free pamphlets on debts and credit. Go to the FTC website and click on "Consumer Protection," or call or write and ask for a complete list.

Dealing With the IRS

*Of all debts men are least willing
to pay the taxes.*

—RALPH WALDO EMERSON

No three letters bring more fear to the average American than IRS. Yet, at one time or
another in our lives, nearly everyone will owe
a tax bill they can't pay, need extra time to file
a tax return, or even get audited. This section
suggests several strategies for dealing with the
government's tax collectors.

How long should I keep my tax papers?

Keep anything related to your tax return—W-2
and 1099 forms, receipts and canceled checks for
deductible items—for at least three years after
you file. The IRS usually has three years from the
day you file your return to audit you. For example, if you filed your 2005 tax return on April
15, 2006, keep those records until at least April
16, 2009. To be completely safe, you should
keep your records for six years. The reason is
that the IRS can audit you up to six years after
you file if the IRS believes you underreported
your income by 25% or more.

One last caution: Keep records showing
purchase costs and sales figures for real estate,
stocks, or other investments for at least three
years after you sell these assets. You must be
able to show your taxable gain or loss to an
auditor.

If I can't pay my taxes, should I file a return anyway?

Absolutely. The consequences of filing and not
paying are less severe than those for simply not

filing. If you don't file a tax return, the IRS
will assess a penalty of up to 25% of the tax
due, plus interest. In addition, the IRS could
criminally charge you for failing to file a return
(although it isn't likely to). By contrast, if you
file a return but can't pay, you'll only be on
the hook for interest and penalties of ½% per
month of the tax you owe.

Who has access to my IRS files?

Under federal law, tax files are confidential.
This was an attempt by Congress to correct the
abuses of power uncovered in the Watergate
scandal. Even IRS officials cannot rummage
willy-nilly through your tax files unless they
are involved in some kind of case regarding
you and your taxes. Consequently, individuals,
businesses, and credit reporting agencies do not
have access to your tax information unless you
authorize its release to the IRS in writing.

The privacy law has exceptions, however,
and IRS security is sometimes lax. Your IRS
files are shared with other federal and state
agencies that can demonstrate a "need to
know." This usually occurs when your affairs
are being investigated by a law enforcement
agency. In fairness to the IRS, many leaks
are the result of sloppiness by other federal
or state agencies granted access to IRS files.
Furthermore, computer hackers have broken
into IRS and government databases and re-
trieved private tax information.

Do many people cheat on their taxes? And what will happen to me if I cheat on mine?

No one really knows how many people cheat
the IRS, but several years ago an independent
poll found that 20% of Americans admitted to
cheating. This is somewhat in line with govern-

ment studies showing that 82% of us faith-fully file and pay our taxes every year. The IRS claims that most cheating is by self-employed small business people who do not have taxes withheld by their employers.

If you are caught in some major cheating, the government can (but rarely does) throw you in jail. Very few people are jailed in the United States for tax crimes—and many of those who are also are charged with drug crimes.

The IRS would much rather collect money than put anyone in prison. More likely, if you're caught cheating, you'll be assessed heavy penalties and will probably be audited for several years.

I am faced with a tax bill that I can't pay. Am I completely at the IRS's mercy, or do I have some options?

There are six ways to deal with a tax bill you can't pay:

- Borrow from a financial institution, family, or friends and pay the tax bill in full.
- Negotiate a monthly payment plan with the IRS. Your payments will include interest and penalty charges. (See IRS Form 9465, *Install-ment Agreement Request.*)
- File for Chapter 13 bankruptcy to set up a payment plan for your debts, including your taxes.
- Find out whether you can wipe out the debt in a Chapter 7 bankruptcy (only cer-tain tax debts are dischargeable).
- Make an offer in compromise—that is, ask the IRS to accept less than the full amount due—by filing IRS Form 656, *Offer in Com-promise.*
- Ask the IRS to designate your debt tempo-rarily uncollectible if you are out of work or your income is very low. This will buy you

time to get back on your feet before dealing with the IRS. But interest and penalties will continue to accrue.

Tax-Avoidance Schemes Don't Work

Dozens of tax-avoidance schemes emerge every decade. Some promoters are very persuasive, particularly if you are predisposed to believing that it's possible to opt out of the tax system. Sad to say, these promoters are all snake-oil salesmen, the most successful of whom make millions peddling their products at expensive seminars and through under-ground publications. One recent scheme involves holding your assets in multiple fam-ily trusts, limited partnerships, and offshore banks. While these artifices may put your as-sets beyond the reach of your creditors, they won't beat the IRS.

I made a mistake on my tax return and am now being billed for the taxes, plus interest and penalties. Do I have to pay it all?

Maybe not. The IRS must charge you interest on your tax bill, but penalties are discretionary. The IRS abates (cancels) one-third of all penal-ties it charges. The trick is to convince the IRS that you had "reasonable cause" (a good excuse) for failing to observe the tax law. Here are some reasons that might work:

- serious illness or a death in the family
- destruction of your records by a flood, fire, or other catastrophe
- wrong advice from the IRS over the phone
- bookkeeper or accountant error, or
- your being in jail or out of the country at the time the tax return was due.

You can ask anyone at the IRS to cancel a penalty, in person or over the phone. And you can ask for a penalty to be canceled even if you already paid it. The best way to get the IRS's attention is to use IRS Form 843, *Claim for Refund and Request for Abatement.* Send this form to your IRS Service Center.

Can the IRS take my house if I owe back taxes?

The IRS can seize just about anything you own—including your home and pension plans. There is a list of items exempt by federal law from IRS seizures, but it is hardly generous, and it doesn't include your residence. Moreover, state homestead-protection laws don't apply to the IRS. With that said, the good news is that the federal Taxpayer Bill of Rights discourages the IRS from taking homes of people who owe back taxes. In addition, the IRS doesn't like the negative publicity generated when it takes a home, unless of course it is the home of a notorious public enemy.

Nevertheless, if the IRS collection division has tried—and failed—to get any cooperation from a tax debtor (for example, if the debtor has not answered correspondence or returned phone calls, or has made threats, lied about income, or hidden assets), the IRS may go after a residence as a last resort. An IRS tax collector can't make the decision on his or her own— it must come from top IRS personnel.

If the IRS lets you know that it plans to take your house, your Congressperson may be able to intervene and put some pressure on the IRS to stop the seizure. And if the seizure would add you and your family to the ranks of the homeless, you can plead that the seizure would create a substantial hardship.

In the unhappy event the IRS does seize your home, all may not be lost. The IRS must sell the home at public auction, usually held about 45 days after the seizure. Then, the high bidder at auction must wait 180 days to get clear title. In this interim period, you have the right to redeem (buy back) the home by coming up with the bid price plus interest.

What are my chances of getting through an audit without owing additional taxes?

Although only about 1% of all tax returns are audited (the percentage is higher for those who own a small business), the IRS has a pretty high success rate. Fewer than 15% of all IRS audit victims make a clean getaway. This is primarily because the IRS's sophisticated computer selection process makes it likely that the agency will audit returns in which adjustments are almost a certainty.

If you receive an audit notice, focus on limiting the damage rather than getting off scot-free. Most adjustments made following an audit result from poor taxpayer records, so make sure you have organized documentation to back up your deductions, exemptions, and other claims. Ignore the tales about dumping a box of receipts on the auditor's desk in the hope that she will throw up her hands and let you off rather than go through the mess. It doesn't work like that. If you have any significant worries, get a tax pro to represent you or help you navigate through the perilous audit waters.

Can I challenge the IRS if I get audited and don't agree with the result?

Yes, you do not have to accept any audit report. In most cases, you can appeal by sending a protest letter to the IRS within 30 days after receiving the audit report. If you request an appeals consideration, you will be granted a meeting with an appeals officer who is not part of the IRS division that performed your audit. See IRS Publication 5, *Your Appeal Rights and How to Prepare a Protest If You Don't Agree.*

If your appeal fails, you still can file a petition in tax court. This is a fairly inexpensive and simple process if the audit bill is for less than $50,000. If it's for more, you will most likely need the help of a tax attorney.

Generally, it pays to contest an audit report by appealing and going to court. About half the people who challenge their audit report succeed in lowering their tax bill.

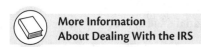

**More Information
About Dealing With the IRS**

Stand Up to the IRS, by Frederick W. Daily (Nolo), explains your legal rights and offers practical strategies for dealing with the IRS.

Surviving an IRS Tax Audit, by Frederick W. Daily (Nolo), provides a wealth of information for minimizing the damage when you are audited.

Debt Collections

Laws prohibit debt collectors from using abusive or deceptive tactics to collect a debt. Unfortunately, many collectors ignore the rules and don't play fair. In addition, creditors and debt collectors have powerful collection tools once they have won a lawsuit for the debt. Here are some frequently asked questions and answers to help you deal with debt collectors.

Collection agencies have been calling me all hours of the day and night. Can I get them to stop contacting me?

It's against the law for a bill collector who works for a collection agency (as opposed to working in the collections department of the creditor itself) to call you at an unreasonable time. The law presumes that calls before 8 a.m. or after 9 p.m. are unreasonable. But other hours may be unreasonable too, such as daytime hours for a person who works nights. The law, the federal Fair Debt Collection Practices Act (FDCPA), also bars collectors from calling you at work if you ask them not to, harassing you, using abusive language, making false or misleading statements, adding unauthorized charges, and many other practices. Under the FDCPA, you can demand that the collection agency stop contacting you, except to tell you that collection efforts have ended or that the creditor or collection agency will sue you. You must put your request in writing.

I'm getting calls from the collections department of a local merchant I did business with. Can I tell that collector to stop contacting me?

Usually not. The FDCPA applies only to bill collectors who work for collection agencies. Though many states have laws prohibiting all debt collectors—including those working for the creditor itself—from harassing, abusing, or threatening you, these laws usually don't give you the right to demand that the collector stop contacting you.

A bill collector insisted that I wire the money I owe through Western Union. Am I required to do so?

No, and it could be expensive if you do. Many collectors, especially when a debt is more than 90 days past due, will suggest several "urgency payment" options, including:

* *Sending money by express or overnight mail.* This will add at least $10 to your bill; a first class stamp is fine.
* *Wiring money through Western Union's Quick Collect or American Express's Moneygram.* This is another $10 down the drain.
* *Putting your payment on a credit card.* You'll never get out of debt if you do this.

You Can Run, But You Can't Hide

In this technological age, it's easy to run from collectors—but hard to hide. Collectors use many different resources to find debtors. They may contact relatives, friends, neighbors, and employers, posing as long-lost friends to get these people to reveal your new whereabouts. In addition, collectors often get information from post office change of address forms, state motor vehicle registration information, voter registration records, former landlords, and banks.

Can a collection agency add interest to my debt?

In most cases, yes. But only if either:

* the original agreement allows for additional interest during collection proceedings, or
* state law authorizes the addition of interest.

Virtually all states do allow this interest.

A collection agency sued me and won. Will I still get calls and letters demanding payment?

Probably not. Before obtaining a court judgment, a bill collector generally has only one way of getting paid: to demand payment. This is done with calls and letters. You can ignore the phone calls and throw out your mail, and the collector can't do much else short of suing you. Once the collector (or creditor) sues and gets a judgment, however, you can expect more aggressive collection actions. If you have a job, the collector will try to garnish up to 25% of your net wages. The collector may also try to seize any bank or other deposit accounts you have. If you own real property, the collector will probably record a lien, which will have to be paid when you sell or refinance your property. Even if you're not currently working or have no property, you're not home free. Depending on the state, court judgments can last up to 20 years and, in many states, can be renewed so they last even longer.

What can I do if a bill collector violates the FDCPA?

Document the violation as soon as it occurs. Write down what happened, when it happened, and who witnessed it. In some states, you can tape-record phone conversations with debt collectors without their knowledge. But beware. In other states, including California, this is illegal. Instead, try to have a witness present (or on another phone extension) the next time you talk to the collector.

Then file a complaint with the Federal Trade Commission (the address and phone number are at the end of this section). Also complain to your state consumer protection agency. And send a copy of your complaint to the creditor who hired the collection agency. If the violations are severe enough, the creditor may stop the collection efforts.

Also, you can sue a collection agency (and the creditor that hired the agency) in small claims court for violating the FDCPA. You are less likely to win if you can prove only a few minor violations. If the violations are outrageous, you can sue the collection agency and creditor in regular civil court. One Texas jury awarded a debtor $11 million when a debt collector made death and bomb threats against her and her husband that frightened them into moving out of the county.

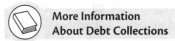

More Information About Debt Collections

Solve Your Money Troubles, by Robin Leonard and John Lamb (Nolo), explains your legal rights and offers practical strategies for dealing with debts and creditors.

The Federal Trade Commission, CRC-240, 600 Pennsylvania Ave, NW, Washington, DC 20580, 877-FTC-HELP (382-4357), www.ftc.gov, publishes free pamphlets on debts and credit, including a few on the Fair Debt Collections Practices Act. It also takes complaints about collection agencies.

Bankruptcy

Where everything is bad it must be good to know the worst.

—FRANCIS HERBERT BRADLEY

If you are seriously in debt, you might consider filing for bankruptcy. And because bankruptcy law has changed—to the detriment of debtors—it's more important than ever to know exactly what you're getting yourself into.

What exactly is bankruptcy?

Bankruptcy is a federal court process designed to help consumers and businesses eliminate their debts or repay them under the protection of the bankruptcy court. Bankruptcy's roots can be traced to the Bible. (Deuteronomy 15:1-2 — "Every seventh year you shall practice remission of debts. This shall be the nature of the remission: Every creditor shall remit the due that he claims from his neighbor; he shall not dun his neighbor or kinsman.")

Aren't there different kinds of bankruptcy?

Yes. Bankruptcies can generally be described as "liquidation" or "reorganization."

Liquidation bankruptcy is called Chapter 7. Under Chapter 7 bankruptcy, a consumer or business asks the bankruptcy court to wipe out (discharge) the debts owed. Certain debts cannot be discharged—these are discussed below. In exchange for the discharge of debts, the business assets or the consumer's nonexempt property are sold—that is, liquidated—and the proceeds are used to pay off creditors. The property a consumer might lose is discussed below.

In a reorganization bankruptcy, you file a plan with the bankruptcy court that proposes how you will repay your creditors. Some debts must be repaid in full; others you pay only in part; others aren't paid at all. Some debts you have to pay with interest; some are paid at the beginning of your plan and some at the end.

There are several types of reorganization bankruptcy. Consumers with secured debts of less than $1,010,650 and unsecured debts of less than $336,900 can file for Chapter 13. Family farmers can file for Chapter 12. Businesses, or consumers with debts in excess of the Chapter 13 debt limits, can file for Chapter 11—a complex, time-consuming, and expensive process.

Who can file for Chapter 7 bankruptcy?

Not everyone is eligible to use Chapter 7. For example, you may not file for Chapter 7 bankruptcy if your debts were discharged in another Chapter 7 case within the last eight years, or in a Chapter 13 case within the last six years. You also won't be allowed to file if you had a previous Chapter 7 case dismissed within the last 180 days for specified reasons. And, the court may dismiss your Chapter 7 case if you have tried to defraud your creditors.

As of 2005, there is a new eligibility rule for using Chapter 7: If the court determines, based on income and expense figures you provide, that you have enough money to pay off at least some of your debts, you will be required to use Chapter 13 if you file for bankruptcy. This new rule, called "the means test," can get quite complicated. Here are the basic steps you have to follow:

1. Calculate your average monthly income in the six months before you file for bankruptcy.

2. Compare your income to your state's median income for a family of your size (you can find median income figures at the website of the U.S. Trustee, www.usdoj. gov/ust).

3. If your income is equal to or less than the median, you may use Chapter 7. If your income is more than the median, you'll have to add up your expenses—in some cases, using amounts allowed by the IRS rather than what you actually spend—and compare them to your income. If these figures show that you would have enough money left over to pay a portion of your debts, you may not be allowed to use Chapter 7.

If your income exceeds your state's median income, you'll need help doing the additional calculations necessary to take the means test. You can find it at www.legalconsumer.com, which offers a free online means test calculator.

How does a Chapter 7 bankruptcy case generally proceed?

You will file a packet of forms with the bankruptcy court listing your income, expenses, assets, debts, and property transactions for the past couple of years. You must also file a certificate showing that you've completed a credit counseling course, and pay a filing fee, currently about $300.

Once your case is filed, a bankruptcy trustee will be appointed by the court to oversee your case. Shortly after you file, you must attend a brief "meeting of creditors," where the trustee reviews your forms and asks questions about the information you supplied. (Creditors rarely attend this meeting, despite its name.) If you have any nonexempt property, you must give it (or its cash value) to the trustee.

Three to six months later, after you complete a second required course (this one on debt management), you will receive a notice from the court that your qualified debts were discharged, and your case will be over.

How does a Chapter 13 bankruptcy case typically proceed?

To file for Chapter 13 bankruptcy, you'll have to file forms listing income, expenses, debts, assets, and property transactions for the past couple of years. You'll also have to file a proposed repayment plan, in which you describe how you intend to repay your debts over the next three to five years. You'll have to get credit counseling from a nonprofit agency before you file.

The court will appoint a trustee to oversee your case. The trustee will call a meeting of creditors (creditors often attend this meeting, especially if they want something more than you're offering in your repayment plan). Then, you'll attend a hearing before a bankruptcy judge who will either confirm or deny your plan. If your plan is confirmed, and you make all of the payments called for under the plan, any remaining balance on dischargeable debts will be wiped out at the end of your case.

Nondischargeable Debts

Certain debts cannot be discharged—that is, they will not be wiped out if you file for bankruptcy. If you file for Chapter 7, you will still owe these debts even after your bankruptcy case is over. If you file for Chapter 13, you will have to pay these debts in full as part of your repayment plan. Nondischargeable debts include:

- Tax debts
- Debts you owe for child or spousal support
- Debts for personal injury or death caused by your drunk operation of a car or other vehicle
- Student loans, in most cases
- Fines and penalties imposed for breaking the law, and
- Certain cash advances and debts for luxury goods incurred shortly before filing for bankruptcy.

What property might I lose if I file for bankruptcy?

You lose no property (other than the income you use to fulfill your repayment plan) in Chapter 13, unless you choose to sell it to pay a debt or give it back to the seller. In Chapter 7, you select property you are eligible to keep from a list of exemptions provided by your state; in some states, you have the option of instead using exemptions provided in the federal Bankruptcy Code.

Certain kinds of property are exempt in almost every state, while others are almost never exempt. The following are items you can typically keep (exempt property):

- motor vehicles, to a certain value
- reasonably necessary clothing (no mink coats)
- reasonably needed household furnishings and goods (the second TV may have to go)
- household appliances
- jewelry, to a certain value
- personal effects
- life insurance (cash or loan value, or the proceeds of life insurance), to a certain value
- pensions
- part of the equity in your home
- tools of your trade or profession, to a certain value
- portion of unpaid but earned wages, and
- public benefits (welfare, Social Security, unemployment compensation) accumulated in a bank account.

Items you must typically give up (nonexempt property) include:

- expensive musical instruments (unless you're a professional musician)
- stamp, coin, and other collections
- family heirlooms
- cash, bank accounts, stocks, bonds, and other investments
- second car or truck, and
- second or vacation home.

 More Information About Bankruptcy

How to File for Chapter 7 Bankruptcy, by Stephen Elias, Albin Renauer, and Robin Leonard (Nolo), provides all of the information you need to file for Chapter 7 bankruptcy, including required forms.

Chapter 13 Bankruptcy: Repay Your Debts, by Robin Leonard and Stephen Elias (Nolo), contains the forms and instructions necessary to file for Chapter 13 bankruptcy.

The New Bankruptcy: Will It Work for You?, by Stephen Elias (Nolo), helps you decide whether to file for bankruptcy and, if so, which type is best for you.

The website of the U.S. Trustee, www.usdoj.gov/ust, provides lists of approved credit and debt counseling agencies, median income amounts for each state, information on the means test, and a complete set of the most current bankruptcy forms.

Legal Consumer, at www.legalconsumer.com, provides a wealth of free information on bankruptcy, including lists of state and federal exemptions, filing requirements, an online means test calculator, and much more

Rebuilding Credit

People who have been through a financial crisis—bankruptcy, repossession, foreclosure, history of late payments, IRS lien or levy, or something similar—may think they will never get credit again. Not true. By following some simple steps, you can rebuild your credit in just a couple of years.

What's the first step in rebuilding credit?

To avoid getting into financial problems in the future, you must understand your flow of income and expenses. Some people call this making a budget. Others find the term "budget" too restrictive and use the term "spending plan." Whatever you call it, write down every expenditure you make for at least two months. At each month's end, compare your total expenses with your income. If you're overspending, you have to cut back or find more income. As best you can, plan how you'll spend your money each month. If you have trouble putting together your own budget, consider getting help from a nonprofit consumer credit counseling agency, that provides budgeting help for free or at a low cost. You can find a list of agencies by state at www.usdoj.gov/ust.

Okay, I've made my budget. What do I do next?

Now it's time to clean up your credit report. Credit reports are compiled by credit bureaus—private, for-profit companies that gather information about your credit history and sell it to banks, mortgage lenders, credit unions, credit card companies, department stores, insurance companies, landlords, and even employers.

Credit bureaus get most of their data from creditors. They also search court records for lawsuits, judgments, and bankruptcy filings. And they go through county records to find recorded liens (legal claims against property).

To create a credit file for a given person, a credit bureau searches its computer files until it finds entries that match the name, Social Security number, and any other available identifying information. All matches are gathered together to make the report.

Noncredit data in a credit report usually includes names you previously used, past and present addresses, Social Security number, employment history, marriages, and divorces. Your credit history includes the names of your creditors, type and number of each account, when each account was opened, your payment history for the previous 24 to 36 months, your credit limit or the original amount of a loan, and your current balance. The report will show if an account has been turned over to a collection agency or is in dispute.

What should I do if I find mistakes in my report?

As you read through your report, make a list of everything out of date. Check for the following:

- Lawsuits, paid tax liens, accounts sent out for collection, late payments, and any other adverse information more than seven years old.
- Bankruptcies more than ten years after the discharge or dismissal. (Credit bureaus often list Chapter 13 bankruptcies for only seven years, but they can stay for as many as ten.)
- Credit inquiries (requests by companies for a copy of your report) more than two years old.

Next, look for incorrect or misleading information. According to a 2004 study by the Public Interest Research Group (PIRG), one in four credit reports contains errors serious enough to cause someone to be denied credit, a loan, a mortgage, or a job. Check your report for:

- incorrect or incomplete name, address, phone number, Social Security number, or employment information
- bankruptcies not identified by their specific chapter number
- accounts not yours or lawsuits in which you were not involved
- incorrect account histories—such as late payments when you paid on time
- closed accounts listed as open—it may look as if you have too much open credit, and
- any account you closed that doesn't say "closed by consumer."

After reviewing your report, complete the "request for reinvestigation" form the credit bureau sent you or send a letter listing each item that is incorrect or too old to be reported. Once the credit bureau receives your request, it must investigate the items you dispute and contact you within 30 days (45 days if you send the bureau additional information within the 30-day period). If you don't hear back within the time limit, send a follow-up letter.

If you are right, or if the creditor who provided the information can no longer verify it, the credit bureau must remove the information from your report. Credit bureaus sometimes remove an item on request without an investigation if rechecking the item is more bother than it's worth.

If the credit bureau insists that the information is correct, call the bureau to discuss the problem:

- Experian: 888-397-3742
- TransUnion: 800-888-4213
- Equifax: 800-685-1111.

If you don't get anywhere with the credit bureau, contact the creditor directly and ask that the information be removed. If the information was reported by a collection agency, send the agency a copy of your letter too.

If a credit bureau is including the wrong information in your report, or you want to explain a particular entry, you have the right to put a brief explanatory statement in your report. The credit bureau must give a copy of your statement—or a summary—to anyone who requests your report. Be clear and concise; use the fewest words possible.

I've been told that I need to use credit to rebuild my credit. Is this true?

Yes. The one type of positive information creditors most like to see in credit reports is credit payment history. If you have a credit card, use it every month. (Make small purchases and pay them off to avoid interest charges.) If you don't have a credit card, apply for one. If your application is rejected, try to find a cosigner or apply for a secured card—where you deposit some money into a savings account, then get a credit card with a line of credit close to the amount you deposited. But don't apply for new credit before getting back on your feet. Defaulting on new credit will only make matters worse.

What else can I do to rebuild my credit?

After you've cleaned up your credit report, work on getting positive information into your record. Here are two suggestions:

- If your credit report is missing accounts you pay on time, send the credit bureaus a recent account statement and copies of canceled checks showing your payment history. Ask that these be added to your report. The credit bureau doesn't have to add anything, but often will.

- Creditors like to see evidence of stability, so if any of the following information is not in your report, send it to the bureaus and ask that it be added: your current employment, your previous employment (especially if you've been at your current job fewer than two years), your current residence, your date of birth, and your checking account number. Again, the credit bureau doesn't have to add these, but often will.

How long does it take to rebuild credit?

If you follow the steps outlined above, it will take about two years to rebuild your credit to the point that you won't be turned down for a major credit card or loan. After approximately four years, you may be able to qualify for a mortgage.

 **More Information
About Rebuilding Your Credit**

Credit Repair, by Robin Leonard and John Lamb (Nolo), is a quick guide to lawfully rebuilding your credit. It contains several strategies for improving credit, sample credit reports with explanations of how to read them, and the text of the federal and many state credit reporting laws.

Solve Your Money Troubles, by Robin Leonard and John Lamb (Nolo), explains your legal rights and offers practical strategies for dealing with debts and creditors, including rebuilding your credit.

The Federal Trade Commission, CRC-240, 600 Pennsylvania Ave., NW, Washington, DC 20580, 877-FTC-HELP (382-4357), www.ftc.gov, publishes free fact sheets and information on debts and

credit, including how to get a free copy of your credit reports and deal with errors in those reports.

 Online Help

www.nolo.com

Nolo offers information about a wide variety of legal topics, including advice about consumer law, debts, and credit. It also has free online calculators for credit, mortgage, savings, debt, retirement, and more.

www.ftc.gov

The Federal Trade Commission has dozens of helpful publications on consumer issues, enforcement guidance, tips on spending and using credit wisely, and much more.

www.fraud.org

The National Fraud Information Center helps you file a complaint with federal agencies if you've been defrauded. It also offers information on how to avoid becoming the victim of a scam.

www.bbb.org

The Better Business Bureau provides general information on its programs and services, including alerts, warnings, and updates about businesses. You can also find information about filing a complaint against a business and using the BBB's dispute resolution program.

www.pueblo.gsa.gov

The Federal Citizen Information Center provides the latest in consumer news as well as many publications of interest to consumers, including the *Consumer Information Catalog*.

www.irs.gov

The Internal Revenue Service provides tax information, forms, and publications.

Cars and Driving

*When Solomon said that there was a time
and a place for everything, he had not encountered
the problem of parking an automobile.*

—BOB EDWARDS

Plainly, Americans love their cars—that's why we own more cars per person than the rest of the world, on average. For the privilege of owning and operating a new vehicle, we pay an average of more than $8,000 per year. We also expend plenty of time and energy figuring out which cars to buy, how to insure and maintain them, and how to keep out of trouble on the road. This chapter provides answers to many common questions about owning a car and driving responsibly.

Buying a New Car

These days, the average new car costs more than $28,000. For that amount of money, you would hope for a hassle-free buying experience and a safe and reliable product. Unfortunately, new car buyers are frequently overwhelmed by the pressure to buy immediately or spend more than planned. What's worse, the product you bring home might be plagued with problems ranging from annoying engine "pings," to frequent stalls, to safety hazards such as poor acceleration or carbon monoxide leaks.

I want to get a good deal on a new car. What make and model should I buy?

There are several good resources to help you comparison shop when you're looking for a new car. *Consumer Reports* magazine publishes an annual car-buying issue that compares price, features, service history, resale value, and reliability. Another helpful source of information is *Motor Trend* magazine. Finally, many websites provide price and feature information. To start, try www.carprices.com or www.edmunds.com.

When deciding what car to buy, resist the urge to buy more car than you can afford—and don't talk yourself into a more expensive car by financing it over four or five years. You'll pay a bundle in interest that way.

Do you have any tips for negotiating with a car dealer?

Negotiating price with a dealer is almost never a pleasant experience. And, if you don't do it well, you are likely to pay hundreds or thousands of dollars more for a car. Here are some tips for getting the best deal.

- Know which car you want (or a few you are interested in), which features you want, and what you can afford to pay before you walk into the dealership. Then, stick to your guns.

- Know the dealer's cost for the car before you start negotiating. Use this figure as the starting point from which you negotiate up. The dealer invoice price is how much the dealer paid for the car. Many websites list dealer invoice prices. But the dealer's final cost is often even lower, because manufacturers offer dealers behind-the-scenes financial incentives. To find out the car's true cost to the dealer, you can order a report from *Consumer Reports* (www.consumerreports. org or 800-888-8275) for a small fee.

- Don't buy in a hurry. You need time to compare prices. And usually, the longer you take and the more times you walk away, the lower the price will fall.

- Contact local dealerships via the Internet and solicit multiple quotes. This forces the dealers to bid against each other. When you get a satisfactory bid, ask the dealer to send you a worksheet showing all prices, taxes, and fees. Bring this to the dealership when you're ready to buy.

- Order your new car if the one you want is not on the lot. Cars on the lot frequently have options you don't want, which jack up the price.

- Don't make a deposit on a vehicle before the dealership has accepted your offer.

- If a rebate is offered, negotiate the price as if the rebate didn't exist. And have the rebate sent to your home—don't allow the dealership to "apply" it to the amount you owe. Rebates come from the manufacturer and shouldn't be a reason to pay the dealer more for the car.

- Don't discuss the possibility of a trade-in until you fix the price for your new car.

- Don't trade in your old vehicle without doing your homework. A dealer will give you the low *Kelley Blue Book* value, at most. (The *Kelley Blue Book* lists wholesale and retail prices for cars by year and model. You can find it in libraries, bookstores, or online at www.kbb.com.) Take a look at classified ads to get an idea of how much you could get if you sold your car yourself. Or, order a used car price report from *Consumer Reports* magazine (www.consumerreports.org or 800-888-8275). Don't accept less than what you can get on the street. If the dealer won't pay you what the car is worth, forget the trade-in and sell your old car yourself.

- You might want to read up on the sales tactics dealerships use to get you to pay top dollar. Armed with this information, you will be better able to deflect the tactics and get a good deal. There are lots of books on this subject. One of the best is *Don't Get Taken Every Time,* by Remar Sutton (Penguin Books).

What other information do I need to know before I buy my new car?

Before you sign any contract, find out:

- what the warranty covers and how long it lasts
- how you might lose warranty coverage (such as by driving off-road)
- whether an extended warranty is available to you, and if so:
- what it will cost
- what it covers
- how long it lasts
- whether it duplicates coverage provided by the manufacturer's warranty, and
- how likely it is that you'll need it (whether the covered parts have a history of problems)
- the vehicle's estimated miles per gallon for city and highway driving, and
- the dealer's suggested maintenance schedule.

Is there anything I should do when my new car is delivered?

Yes. Before signing a receipt and paying for your new vehicle, do the following:

- Check the vehicle against your order, item by item. Make sure all features are included.
- Inspect the vehicle for damage. Some new vehicles are damaged during manufacturing or in transit. Because of this, you should never take delivery of a new vehicle at night or in the rain. Even in good artificial light, it's hard to see nicks or dents. You'll also miss subtle changes in paint that may indicate the car was damaged in transit and was repainted. Look especially for chips in the windshield

- Test drive the vehicle and pay attention to odd noises, smells, or vibrations.
- Make sure the warranty matches what the dealer agreed to.

If I change my mind after I buy a new car, do I have the right to cancel the contract?

No. Unfortunately, many people think they have a right to change their mind, drive the car back to the dealer a day or two after buying, and cancel the contract. But the truth is, the dealer doesn't have to take the car back and probably won't, and you'll be stuck with a car you no longer want or cannot afford.

Soon after I brought my new car home, it started having problems. How do I know if it's a lemon?

Although the precise definition of a lemon varies by state, in general, a new car is a lemon if a number of attempts have been made to repair a "substantial defect" and the car continues to have this defect. A substantial defect is one that impairs the car's use, value, or safety, such as faulty brakes or turn signals. Minor defects, such as loose radio and door knobs, don't qualify.

In all states, the defect must occur within a certain period of time (usually one or two years) or within a certain number of miles (usually 12,000 or 24,000). And you must usually meet one of the following standards for repair attempts:

- the defect is a serious safety defect involving brakes or steering and remains unfixed after one repair attempt
- the defect is not a serious safety defect and remains unfixed after three or four repair attempts (the number depends on the state), or

• the vehicle is in the shop for a certain number of days (usually 30) in a one-year period.

How to Find Your State's Lemon Law

To find out whether your car qualifies as a lemon in your state, get a copy of your state's lemon law. If you have access to the Internet, www.autopedia.com has links to each state's lemon law. Or, see this book's appendix for information on how to find the law in the library. For a summary of each state's lemon law, check out *Return to Sender,* by Nancy Barron (National Consumer Law Center). The book is available in bookstores, or you can order it from NCLC at www.consumerlaw.org or 617-542-9595.

What should I do if my new car is a lemon?

If you think your new car is a lemon, you must notify the manufacturer and give its authorized dealer the opportunity to make repairs. When contacting the manufacturer, follow your state's notice requirements. (These are contained in your state's lemon law, which you can find at www.lemonlawamerica.com or www.autopedia.com.) If possible, notify the manufacturer before you bring the car to the dealer. Then, deliver a copy of the notice to the dealer when you bring the car in for repair.

During the repair process, keep detailed records. (If you had your car repaired by a non-dealer mechanic before notifying the manufacturer of the problem, keep records of those repairs, too.) Track the number of repair attempts and the time your car is out of service. Each time you bring your car in for repair, prepare a written, dated, list of specific problems. Insist on receiving a detailed repair order from the dealer that includes symptoms, repairs done, parts replaced, and time your car was in the shop.

After you have taken the steps above, you can ask the manufacturer for a refund or replacement vehicle. (The dealer may be entitled to a small offset for your use of the car.) In most states, if the manufacturer has established a qualifying arbitration program, it can require you go to arbitration before it pays you anything.

There are several different types of arbitration programs. You probably won't get to choose which one to use—that's usually up to the manufacturer. But if you are given a choice, pick one that is run by a state consumer protection agency rather than an in-house program administered by the manufacturer.

What happens at a lemon law arbitration?

At the arbitration hearing, the arbitrator hears both sides of the dispute. The arbitrator has a certain amount of time (often 40 or 60 days) to decide whether your car is a lemon and whether you're entitled to a refund or a replacement. Ask for a copy of the arbitration procedures and make sure they are followed.

Consumers who bring substantial documentation to the hearing tend to do better than those with little evidence to back up their claims. The types of documentation that can help include:

• brochures and ads about the vehicle —an arbitration panel is likely to make the manufacturer live up to its claims

• vehicle service records showing how often you took the car into the shop, and

• any other documents showing your attempts to get the dealer to repair your car, including old calendars and phone records.

It is important to take the arbitration seriously and be as prepared as possible. Although you can usually appeal a bad arbitration decision in court, or sue the manufacturer if the arbitration isn't binding, the arbitration decision could be used against you in court.

If I continue to drive my car while I wait for a decision, will it hurt my case?

Because it often takes a long time to get relief, most lemon laws allow you to keep using your car while pursuing a claim. But keep in mind that some courts may look less favorably on your case if you are able to drive your car. And, of course, you should never drive your car if it is unsafe to do so.

What if I don't like the arbitrator's decision?

If you don't like the ruling and the arbitration wasn't binding, you can usually sue the manufacturer in court. You may want to do this if you have substantial "consequential" damages—that is, damages that resulted from owning the lemon, such as the cost of renting a car while your lemon was in the shop or time off from work every time your car broke down. For a list of lawyers with experience in these kinds of cases, see the Center for Auto Safety website, at www.autosafety.org.

"Secret" Warranty Adjustments

Many automobile manufacturers have "secret warranty," or warranty adjustment, programs. Under these programs, a manufacturer makes repairs for free on defects that occur after a warranty expires in order to avoid a recall and bad press. According to the Center for Auto Safety, at any given time there are about 500 secret adjustment warranty programs available through automobile manufacturers.

Unfortunately, in most states, manufacturers are not required to disclose the existence of a secret warranty program for a particular vehicle defect. This makes it very difficult for consumers to know when a defect may be covered. A few states, including California, Connecticut, Virginia, and Wisconsin, require manufacturers to tell eligible consumers when they adopt a secret warranty adjustment, usually within 90 days of adopting the program.

To learn more about secret warranty programs, including how to find them, see the Center for Auto Safety's website at www.autosafety.org.

More Information About Lemons

If you think your new car is a lemon, an excellent book to help you sort out your rights and remedies is *Return to Sender,* by Nancy Barron (National Consumer Law Center). Find it in bookstores or order it from NCLC at www.consumerlaw.org or 617-542-9595.

Leasing a Car

About one-quarter of new car owners lease, rather than purchase, their vehicles. Although leasing isn't for everyone, some people swear by it. Before you sign on the dotted line, be sure you know what you're getting into.

What are the advantages of leasing a new car?

There are three main reasons people lease, rather than buy, a new vehicle:

- People who like to drive a new car every few years will pay much less to lease than to buy. They also don't have to deal with getting rid of their old car—they just turn it in at the end of the lease period.
- Lease payments are lower than loan payments for any given car.
- Leasing gives people the opportunity to drive a more expensive car than they could afford to buy.

Are there any obvious disadvantages to leasing?

Yes—there are many.

- If you continually lease your cars, you will have never-ending car payments. If you look forward to paying off your car and owning it free and clear, don't lease.
- If you decide to buy the car when the lease ends, you'll pay several thousand dollars more than if you had bought initially. For example, if you buy a car, paying $500 a month for four years, you'll pay a total of $24,000. You might be able to lease it for only $400 a month (total payments of $19,200), but you'll probably have to pay another $8,000 to keep it—and if you finance that $8,000, you'll pay even more.

- Most leases charge you as much as 25¢ a mile if you exceed the annual mileage limit—usually between 12,000 and 15,000 miles. If you plan to do extensive driving, leasing probably isn't for you.
- It's very, very expensive to break a lease early. If you no longer want, or can afford, to keep your car—for example, because you lost your job or your financial situation changed—you are stuck.
- If you lease a lemon, the leasing company has to do the complaining (remember, you don't own the car) in order to get redress.

Are all leasing costs disclosed up front?

Not necessarily. While the federal Consumer Leasing Act requires lease agreements to include a statement of costs (such as the number and amount of regular payments), insurance requirements, the penalty for defaulting, and whether you'll have a balloon payment at the end, many lease agreements bury key provisions in the fine print.

If you want to lease, you'll have to be a diligent consumer willing to read all the fine print. Also, ask a lot of questions and demand that the answers be put in writing.

Is there any way to find out the interest rate on a lease?

Yes. Ask the dealer for something called the "money factor" or "leasing factor." Multiply that factor by 24, and you'll get the approximate interest rate.

Are there any good leasing deals?

Yes—especially those heavily advertised by car manufacturers. Those deals usually offer low monthly payments or a high value for the vehicle at the end (so that you're not paying for a lot of depreciation during the lease term), and offer to lock in the price you'd have to pay at lease-end if you want to keep the vehicle.

To get these good deals, you cannot deviate from the advertised terms. If you want air-conditioning, a larger engine, or any other feature that's not in the ad, the dealer will throw out the entire lease offer and you'll wind up paying a bundle.

Another way to get a good deal is to explore financing through an independent lease company. Look in the telephone Yellow Pages under "Automotive—Leasing" or peruse the Internet. For example, the National Vehicle Leasing Association (at www.nvla.org) provides a state-by-state list of both dealer and independent leasing companies. Also, if you belong to a credit union or the AAA, ask about the possibility of financing your lease through them. Finally, if you are not taking advantage of a specific advertised leasing deal, treat your lease like a vehicle purchase. Shop around, compare lease terms between dealers, and negotiate lease terms before signing the contract. Keep your eye on the agreed-upon value of the vehicle (a lower value means lower monthly payments), up-front costs, lease length, monthly payments, and end-of-lease fees and charges.

I usually shop for a new car in the fall, when dealers are trying to get rid of old inventory. Does this strategy work for leasing?

In general, no. Because dealers lose money on cars sitting in their lots, they often increase the monthly lease payments to make up for lost revenue.

If I do lease a vehicle, who pays for maintenance and repairs?

Your lease agreement will specify who must pay. In addition, the agreement should come with a manufacturer's warranty. Ideally, it will cover the entire length of the lease and the number of miles you are likely to drive.

Most lease agreements obligate you to pay for "excessive wear and tear." This means that when you return the vehicle at lease-end, the dealer could charge you to fix anything deemed "excessive." You should insist that the dealer specify in writing exactly what is meant by "excessive" before you sign the lease contract.

Finally, look for a deal that includes "gap" insurance. If the vehicle is stolen or totaled, gap insurance will pay the difference between what you owe under the lease and what the dealer can recover on the vehicle (assuming it's not stolen)—a difference that could amount to thousands of dollars.

Can I cancel my lease agreement early?

Probably not, unless you're willing to pay a substantial penalty. If you want to cancel your lease, look carefully at the provision describing what happens if you default or terminate the lease early. The provision may state that you'll owe an enormous sum of money, or may use a complex formula to calculate what you owe.

Auto Leasing: The Art of the Deal's Lease Kit explains the legal language in your contract regarding early lease termination and includes information on your options if you want to end a lease early. You can purchase the Lease Kit at www.leaseguide.com.

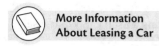

**More Information
About Leasing a Car**

Both the Federal Trade Commission (at www.ftc.gov) and the Federal Reserve Board (at www.federalreserve.gov) publish brochures to help you understand your rights when leasing a car.

Buying a Used Car

Horsepower was a wonderful thing when only horses had it.

—**ANONYMOUS**

While buying a used car is often a sound financial decision, the transaction itself can be ripe with potential disaster. We probably all know someone who bought a used car—assured that "my grandmother drove it to church once a week"—only to have it need lots of expensive repairs shortly after bringing it home. But, with diligence and caution, you can minimize the risks associated with buying a used car and save a bundle of money in the process.

What are the advantages and disadvantages of buying a used car?

Buying a used car can be a smart financial decision. Not only do used cars cost less, but you also pay less in taxes, registration fees, and insurance. In addition, new cars depreciate rapidly during the first few years of ownership—usually between 25% and 45% in the first three years, depending on the make and model. So when you buy a used car, it has already taken the depreciation "hit." You pay less and your car depreciates more slowly during the years you own it.

But buying a used car has its risks. Most new cars have few problems during the first few years and are covered by warranty. Not so for used cars. Older cars have more problems and, usually, expired warranties. Also, the car could be a lemon or have hidden damage. Following the suggestions below will help you minimize these risks.

How do I go about finding a used car?

It's best if you have some idea of the make, model, and year that you're interested in. There are many good sources to help you compare cars. *Consumer Reports* magazine publishes an annual car-buying issue, comparing price, features, service histories, resale values, and reliability. Other sources of information are *Motor Trend* magazine and *The Insider's Guide to Buying a New or Used Car,* by Burke and Stephanie Leon (Betterway Books).

Once you've made this preliminary decision, look at the listings in your local newspaper and Internet classifieds. Don't forget weekly advertising papers or local automobile publications as well. Call any mechanics that you trust to see which cars they recommend—and to find out whether they know of any available vehicles. Finally, check with car dealers; they often have used cars that people have traded in, which the dealers recondition and sell at a premium.

How much should I spend on a used car?

Check the wholesale and retail values of the cars that interest you. Bookstores and libraries have copies of the *Kelley Blue Book* (which lists wholesale and retail prices), or you can find it online at www.kbb.com.

For a small fee, *Consumer Reports* (www.con-sumerreports.org or 800-258-1169) will tell you how much a particular car is worth, taking into consideration the car's mileage, condition, and additional equipment (such as power windows or compact disc player). You can also get most of this information from the *Kelley Blue Book* website at www.kbb.com.

How do I negotiate a good price?

After you've checked wholesale and retail prices of the car you want and thoroughly explored its condition, you are ready to negotiate. Often, the listed wholesale price of the car is a good opening bid, assuming the car is in decent condition. The seller will probably aim for retail price. The final price will depend on many factors, including the condition of the car and the circumstances of the person from whom you buy it.

The Buyers Guide

Federal law requires an automobile dealer to post a Buyers Guide in every used car it offers for sale (motorcycles and most recreational vehicles are exempt from this requirement). Among other things, the Buyers Guide tells you whether the vehicle is sold "as is" or with a warranty and describes the warranty. Be sure to get the Buyers Guide when you buy a used car, and make sure it reflects any changes to warranty coverage that you negotiated with the dealer. The Buyers Guide becomes part of the sales contract—if the dealer refuses to make good on the warranty, you'll need it as proof of your original agreement.

Obviously, price isn't the only factor to consider when buying a used car. What else do I need to know?

With used cars, reliability is as important as price. Before you buy, you should:

- Have the car checked out by a mechanic you trust.
- Have the car inspected by a diagnostic center. These businesses will check virtually every aspect and component of a car. They're more expensive—but more thorough—than a mechanic.
- Ask for copies of the maintenance records for the life of the car.
- From your state motor vehicle department, you can often get a printed history of the car's previous ownership. It won't include the names or addresses of previous owners, but it will tell you the mileage each time it was sold and all states (other than where you live) where the car has been registered. You can get similar information from www.carfax.com (for about $20). If this information doesn't match up or looks fishy, don't buy the car.
- Do your own visual inspection—you'll want to look for oddities that might indicate damage (such as scratches or new paint).

Also, look at the vehicle identification number (VIN) on the lower left-hand side of the front windshield. If it shows any signs of tampering, the car may be stolen. And finally, if you're buying the car from a private party (as opposed to a car dealer), make sure the person selling the car actually holds title. Ask to see the seller's driver's license (or other form of ID) and the title certificate for the vehicle.

Will a warranty protect me if I get a bad deal on a used car?

If you're buying a used car from a dealer, the dealer will probably offer you an extended warranty. Before buying, be sure you know exactly what is covered and what isn't, and for how long. You'll also need to know the types of problems the car has had in the past, and the types of problems that particular make of car is likely to have in the future. (You can get this kind of information from *Consumer Reports*, at www.consumerreports.org.) It makes no sense to buy an extended warranty that doesn't cover emissions, for example, if the type of car you're buying is likely to have emission problems in a year or so.

If you're buying a car from a private party, check to see whether the car is still under a factory warranty or whether the original owner purchased an extended warranty—and whether either of these warranties can be transferred to you as the new owner.

Used Car "Lemon Laws"

Some states have lemon laws or warranty coverage for used cars. To find out about your state, contact the state attorney general or department of consumer affairs. Or, you can look up your state's lemon law at www.autopedia.com or www.autosafety.org and check to see whether it covers used cars.

Financing a Vehicle Purchase

If you are like most people, you don't have a large sum of cash to plunk down for a new or used car. This means you'll have to finance your purchase. Of course, after you spend time shopping for a car and negotiating a good deal, the last thing you'll want to do is haggle over financing terms. But if you don't shop around for the best financing deal and read the finance contract carefully, you could end up paying lots more for a loan than you should.

I want to buy a car, but I'm not sure how to finance my purchase. Do you have any general advice?

If you can pay for the purchase outright, you'll save money by avoiding interest charges. But if you need to borrow money to buy the car, consider the following sources:

- **The car dealer.** Many offer generous terms—for example, interest at 1.5% or 2%—especially in the early fall when dealers are eager to clear out stock to make room for new models. Be careful that these low-interest loans don't require you to buy upgraded features—such as air-conditioning or rust protection—or credit insurance. And don't assume you are getting the best deal around. Always compare dealer terms to those of banks and credit unions.

- **Banks you do business with.** Dealer financing isn't your only option. Before you buy, contact the banks where you have your savings, checking, credit card, or business accounts. Ask about the going rate for car loans. Also ask about discount rates for loans tied to your other accounts.

- **Credit unions.** If you're a member of a credit union (or are eligible to join one), be sure to investigate its car loans. Historically, credit unions have offered some of the best loan terms.

Regardless of who finances the contract, if you want a good interest rate but have a poor credit history, you'll need to either make a substantial down payment or get a cosigner.

Do You Need Credit Insurance?

Many dealers and lenders will ask you to buy credit insurance—insurance that will pay off your loan if you die or become disabled. (This is just like the dealer asking you to buy an extended warranty—he'd love for you to buy it, but he'll sell you the car without it if you refuse.) Before you add this cost to your contract, consider whether you really need it. Remember, you can always sell the car and use the proceeds to pay off the loan. In fact, most financial experts say credit insurance is unnecessary and advise consumers not to buy it. If you do decide you want this protection, you can almost always buy it from an outside source at a much better price.

If I borrow money for the purchase, what should the lender tell me about my loan?

If you get a car loan from a bank, credit union, or car dealer, the federal Truth in Lending Act requires that the lender disclose, in writing, important information about your loan, including:

- your right to a written itemization of the amount borrowed
- the total amount of the loan
- the monthly finance charge
- the annual percentage rate (APR)
- the number, amount, and due dates of all payments, and
- whether any late payment fee or penalty may be imposed.

Insuring Your Car

Certainly those so inclined can have lots of fun imagining possible needs for insurance.

—HAYDEN CURRY

Almost every state requires every registered vehicle or licensed driver to have some vehicle liability insurance. And all states have financial responsibility laws, which require drivers to either carry insurance that will pay certain minimum amounts or have sufficient assets to pay any claims resulting from an accident. To find out your state's requirements, check out the Insurance Information Institute's website, at www.iii.org.

Even where it's not required by law, most drivers have some liability coverage. Before you buy auto insurance, you must decide how much coverage you need and what types of coverage are appropriate for you. And, of course, you'll want to find ways to cut your insurance costs.

Who is usually covered under an auto insurance liability policy?

An auto insurance liability policy usually covers the following people no matter what car they are driving:

- **Named insured**—the person or people named in the policy.

- **Spouse**—a spouse not named in the policy, unless he or she does not live with the named insured.

- **Other relative**—anyone living in the household with the named insured who is related by blood, marriage, or adoption, usually including a legal ward or foster child.

Auto insurance liability policies also cover anyone driving the insured vehicle with permission. Someone who steals the car is not covered.

Which vehicles are normally covered under an auto insurance liability policy?

- **Named vehicles**—an accident in a non-named vehicle is covered only if a named insured (see above) was driving.

- **Added vehicles**—any vehicle that the named insured uses as a replacement for the original named vehicle, and any additional vehicle the named insured acquires during the policy period (you may be required to notify the company of the new or different vehicle within 30 days after you acquire it).

- **Temporary vehicles**—any vehicle, including a rental vehicle, that substitutes for an insured vehicle that is out of use because it needs repair or service, or has been destroyed.

What kinds of damage are covered under an auto insurance liability policy?

Liability insurance covers money owed when a driver is at fault for hurting another person or damaging another car. Coverage includes medical costs for diagnosis and treatment of injuries, property damage, loss of use of damaged property, expenses incurred (such as the cost of renting a replacement vehicle), lost income, and costs of defending a lawsuit.

In addition, an injured person is entitled to a certain amount of "general damages," also referred to as pain and suffering.

What is collision coverage?

Collision coverage pays for property damage to your vehicle resulting from a collision with another car or object or from flipping over.

What is comprehensive coverage?

Comprehensive coverage pays for property damage to your vehicle resulting from anything other than a collision, such as a theft or a break-in.

What is uninsured motorist coverage?

If you have an accident with an uninsured vehicle or hit-and-run driver, the place to turn for compensation for your injuries is the uninsured motorist (UM) coverage of your own vehicle insurance policy. Normally, UM covers only bodily injury and not property damage to your vehicle. Vehicle damage would be covered by the collision coverage of your own policy.

Are there any limits on my ability to collect under an uninsured motorist provision?

Most insurance policies impose a few rules for collecting under your UM coverage:

- If your accident involves a hit-and-run driver, you must notify the police within 24 hours of the accident.

- If your accident involves a hit-and-run driver, the driver's car must have actually hit you—being forced off the road by a driver who disappears is not sufficient.

- Your UM coverage will be reduced by any amounts you receive under other insurance coverage, such as your personal medical insurance or any applicable workers' compensation coverage.

- If you or your family members are injured by an uninsured motorist while you are in someone else's car, your UM coverage will be secondary to the UM coverage of that other car's owner.

What is no-fault automobile insurance?

Under no-fault insurance, each person's own insurance company pays for his or her medical bills and lost wages—up to certain dollar amounts—regardless of who was at fault.

About a quarter of the states have mandatory no-fault laws. Other states allow you to "add on" no-fault coverage to your existing policy (though it's not required). The advantage of no-fault insurance is prompt payment of medical bills and lost wages without any arguments about who caused the accident. But most no-fault insurance provides extremely limited coverage:

- No-fault pays benefits for medical bills and lost income only. It provides no compensation for pain, suffering, emotional distress, inconvenience, or lost opportunities.

- No-fault coverage does not pay for medical bills and lost income higher than the limits of each person's policy. No-fault benefits often fail to reimburse fully for medical bills and lost income.

- No-fault often does not apply to vehicle damage; those claims are paid under the liability insurance of the person at fault, or by your own collision insurance.

When No-Fault Benefits Aren't Enough

All no-fault laws permit an injured driver to file a liability claim, and a lawsuit if necessary, against another driver who was at fault in an accident. The liability claim permits an injured driver to obtain compensation for medical and income losses above what the no-fault policy paid, as well as compensation for pain, suffering, and other general damages.

Whether and when you can file a liability claim for further damages against the person at fault in your accident depends on the specifics of the no-fault law in your state. In some states, you can always file a liability claim for all damages in excess of your no-fault benefits. In others you must meet a monetary threshold, a serious injury threshold, or both, before you can file a liability claim.

My auto insurance rates keep going up. How can I cut some of the cost?

Here are a few suggestions for ways to reduce your premiums:

- Shop around for insurance. Just because your current company once offered you the best deal doesn't mean it's still competitive.

- Increase your deductibles.

- Reduce your collision or comprehensive coverage on older cars.

- Find out what discounts are available from your company (or from a different company). Discounts are often given to people who:

  - use public transit or carpool to work

  - take a class in defensive driving (especially if you are older)

  - own a car with safety features such as airbags or antilock brakes

  - install antitheft devices

  - are students with good academic records

  - have no accidents or moving violations, or

  - have multiple insurance policies with the same company—such as automobile and homeowner's insurance.

- Find out which vehicles cost more to insure. If you're looking to buy a new car, call your insurance agent and find out which cars are expensive to repair, targeted by thieves, or involved in a higher rate of accidents. These vehicles all have higher insurance rates.

- Consolidate your policies. Most of the time you will pay less if all owners or drivers who live in the same household are on one policy or at least are insured with the same company.

**More Information
About Insuring Your Car**

How to Insure Your Car, by The Merritt Editors (Merritt Publishing), is a step-by-step guide to buying the right kind of auto insurance at a price you can afford.

Your Driver's License

To a teenager, a driver's license seems magical—a ticket to freedom. For the rest of us, driver's licenses aren't much more than scraps of paper or plastic bearing bad pictures. But every now and then a question may arise about a license: Is it still good if I move to another state? What if I take a trip to a foreign country? And how do I know if I'm in danger of losing my license?

State laws governing how you can get, use, and lose your driver's license vary tremendously. We can't answer every question here, but we do discuss some of the bigger issues that arise in connection with driving privileges.

Is my driver's license good in every state?

If you have a valid license from one state, you may use it in other states that you visit. But if you make a permanent move to another state, you'll have to get a driver's license there, usually within 30 days of your move. Most states will issue your new license without requiring tests, though some may ask you to take a vision test and a written exam covering basic driving rules.

If you make frequent business trips to another state, or even if you attend school in a state away from home, there's no need to get another driver's license. But when you set up housekeeping and pay taxes in the new state, it's time to apply.

Young Drivers Who Cross State Lines

Adults who visit another state may rely on their driver's licenses, but the same may not be true for young drivers. The driving age varies significantly from state to state (from 15 to 21), and a state that makes young people wait longer to drive may not honor a license from a state that issues licenses to younger folks. For example, if you are 16 and legally allowed to drive in your home state, but travel to another state where the legal age limit for driving is 17, you may not be permitted to drive in that state. A young driver who plans to drive in another state where the legal limit is above his or her age should contact that state's department of motor vehicles to find out what the rules are.

If I get a ticket in another state, will it affect my license?

Forty-eight states belong either to an agreement called the "Driver's License Compact" or to the "Non-Resident Violator Compact." (The only states that don't are Michigan and Wisconsin.) When you get a ticket in one of these states, the department of motor vehicles will relay the information to your state—and the violation will affect your driving record as if the ticket had been issued in your home state.

Can I use my license in a foreign country?

Many countries, including the United States, have signed an international agreement allowing visitors to use their own licenses in other nations. Before traveling to another country, contact its consulate office or embassy to find out whether your license will be sufficient. Look in the telephone book under the name of the country or check the Internet. Other good sources of information are foreign government tourism offices (find them at www.towd.com) and car rental offices in the foreign country.

In addition, you may want to obtain an International Driving Permit, issued by the American Automobile Association. This document translates the information on your driver's license into ten languages. Many countries require the permit, not because it meets their requirements for a license but because it is a ready-made translation of the important information on your American license.

Finally, if you intend to stay in another country for an extended period of time, you should check with the consulate to find out whether you'll need to apply for a license in that country. Every country has its own rules about when a "visit" turns into something more permanent.

When can my driver's license be suspended or revoked?

Driving a car is considered a privilege—and a state won't hesitate to take it away if a driver behaves irresponsibly on the road. A state may temporarily suspend your driving privileges for a number of reasons, including:

• driving under the influence of alcohol or drugs

- refusing to take a blood-alcohol test
- driving without liability insurance
- speeding
- reckless driving
- leaving the scene of an injury accident
- failing to pay a driving-related fine
- failing to answer a traffic summons, or
- failing to file an accident report.

In addition, many states use a "point" system to keep track of a driver's moving violations. Each moving violation is assigned a certain number of points. If a driver accumulates too many points within a given period of time, the department of motor vehicles suspends the license.

If you have too many serious problems as a driver, your state may take away (revoke) your license altogether. If this happens, you'll have to wait a certain period of time before you can apply for another license. Your state may deny your application if you have a poor driving record or fail to pass required tests.

Finally, a few states revoke or refuse to renew the driver's licenses of parents who owe back child support.

My elderly friend is becoming unsafe behind the wheel. Will her license be taken away?

The number of drivers over 65 years old has more than doubled in the last 20 years. At present, there are 13 million older drivers; by the year 2020 there will be 30 million. Studies show that, as a group, older drivers drive less than younger drivers, but have more accidents per mile.

Elderly, unsafe drivers often do not come to the attention of the state until the driver is stopped for erratic driving or, worse, is involved in an accident. A few states try to screen out unsafe older drivers by requiring more frequent written tests. But the added tests are expensive and don't always identify unsafe driving habits.

All licensing departments accept information from police officers, families, and physicians about a driver's abilities. If a licensing agency moves to cancel someone's license as the result of an officer's observations, an accident, or the report of family members or a doctor, the driver usually has an opportunity to protest.

What will happen if I'm caught driving with a suspended or revoked license?

You'll probably be arrested. Usually, driving with a suspended or revoked license is considered a crime that carries a heavy fine and possibly even jail time. At worst, it may be a felony; you'll end up in state prison or with an obligation to perform many hours of community service. The penalties will probably be heaviest if the suspension or revocation was the result of a conviction for driving under the influence of alcohol or drugs (DUI).

The Whole Truth and Nothing but the Truth

Many states will ask you specific questions regarding your health when you renew your driver's license. For example, you might receive a questionnaire that asks whether you have ever had seizures, strokes, heart problems, dizziness, eyesight problems, or other medical troubles. If you have medical problems and answer the questions truthfully, an examiner may question you further and may even deny you a license. If you don't tell the truth, you may get your license—but you're setting yourself up for big legal trouble if you are in an accident caused by one of these impairments. It's not that different from driving a car when you know the brakes are bad: If you go out on the road with defective equipment that you know about (including the driver), you greatly increase the chance that you will be held responsible if the defect causes an accident.

If You're Stopped by the Police

Most of us know the fear of being pulled over by the police. An officer may stop your car for any number of reasons, including an equipment defect (such as a burned-out headlight), expired registration tags, a moving violation, or your car's resemblance to a crime suspect's car. You may also have to stop at a police roadblock or sobriety checkpoint.

What should I do if a police officer pulls me over?

Remain as calm as possible and pull over to the side of the road as quickly and safely as you can. Roll down your window, but stay in the car—don't get out unless the officer directs you to do so. It's a good idea to turn on the interior light, turn off the engine, put your keys on the dash, and place your hands on top of the steering wheel. In short, make yourself visible and do nothing that can be mistaken for a dangerous move. For example, don't reach for a purse or backpack or open the glove box unless you've asked the officer's permission, even if you are just looking for your license and registration card. The officer may think you're reaching for a weapon.

When the officer approaches your window, you may want to ask (with all the politeness you can muster) why you were stopped. If you are at all concerned that the person who stopped you is not actually a police officer (for example, if the car that pulled you over is unmarked), you should ask to see the officer's photo identification and badge. If you still have doubts, you can ask that the officer call a supervisor to the scene or you can request that you be allowed to follow the officer to a police station.

Can an officer pull me over for a traffic violation and search me or my car?

In most cases, no. Just because an officer has a justifiable reason for making a traffic stop—and even if he or she issues you a valid ticket for a traffic violation—that does not automatically give the officer authority to search you or your car. If the officer has a reasonable suspicion (based on observable facts, and not just a "hunch") that you are armed and dangerous or involved in criminal activity, then the officer can do a "pat-down" search of you, and can search the passenger compartment of your car. The officer can frisk any purses, bags, or other objects within the car that might reasonably contain a weapon. The officer can also search if something illegal (such as drugs) is in plain view—sitting on your passenger seat, for example. The officer does have the authority, however, to ask you and any passengers to exit the car during a traffic stop.

If my car is towed and impounded, can the police search it?

Yes. If your car is impounded, the police are allowed to conduct a thorough search of it, including its trunk and any closed containers that they find inside. This is true even if your car was towed after you parked it illegally, or if the police recover your car after it is stolen.

The police are required, however, to follow fair and standardized procedures when they search your car. They may not stop you and impound your car simply to perform a search.

I was pulled over at a roadblock and asked to wait and answer an officer's questions. Is this legal?

Yes, as long as the police use a neutral policy when stopping cars (such as stopping all cars or stopping every third car) and minimize any inconvenience to you and the other drivers. The police can't single out your car unless they have good reason to believe that you've broken the law.

Drunk Driving

If you're caught while driving drunk or under the influence of drugs, you'll face serious legal penalties. Many states will put you in jail, even for a first offense, and almost all will impose hefty fines. If you're convicted more than once, you may also lose your driver's license.

How drunk or high does someone have to be before he can be convicted of driving under the influence?

In most states, it's illegal to drive a car while "impaired" by the effects of alcohol or drugs (including prescription drugs). This means that there must be enough alcohol or drugs in the driver's body to prevent him or her from thinking clearly or driving safely. Many people reach this level well before they'd be considered "drunk" or "stoned."

How can the police find out whether a driver is under the influence?

Police typically use three methods of determining whether a driver has had too much to be driving:

- **Observation.** A police officer who notices that you are driving erratically—swerving, speeding, failing to stop, or even driving too slowly— can pull you over. Of course, you may have a good explanation for your driving (tiredness, for example), but an officer is unlikely to buy your story if you smell like alcohol, slur your words, or can't seem to think straight.

- **Sobriety tests.** An officer who suspects that you are under the influence will probably ask you to get out of the car and perform a series of balance and speech tests, such as standing on one leg, walking a straight line heel-to-toe, or reciting a line of letters or numbers. The officer will look closely at your eyes, checking for pupil enlargement or constriction, which can be evidence of intoxication. If you fail these tests, the officer may arrest you or ask you to take a chemical test.

- **Blood-alcohol level.** The amount of alcohol in your body is determined by measuring the amount of alcohol in your blood. This measurement can be taken directly, by drawing a sample of your blood, or it can be calculated by applying a mathematical formula to the amount of alcohol in your breath or urine. Some states give you a choice of whether to take a breath, blood, or urine test—others do not. Defense attorneys often question the validity of the conversion formula when driver's alcohol levels are based on breath or urine tests. All states have adopted the National Drunk Driving Standard, which defines drunk driving as having a blood alcohol concentration (BAC) of .08%. In many states if you test at or above this level, you may be charged with two offenses: driving under the influence and driving with a BAC over .08%. For the first charge, a BAC of .08% creates a presumption that you were driving under the influence. You can beat the charge only if you can convince a judge or jury that your judgment was not impaired and you were not driving dangerously.

However, with the second charge, a BAC of .08% or more means automatic guilt. There is no defense but to attack the reliability of the test. In many states, this level is even lower for young drivers. (In California, the level is .01% for drivers under 21.)

Do I have to take a blood, breath, or urine test if asked to do so by the police?

No, but it may be in your best interests to take the test. Many states will automatically suspend your license if you refuse to take a chemical test. And if your drunk driving case goes to trial, the prosecutor can tell the jury that you wouldn't take the test, which may lead the jury members to conclude that you refused because you were, in fact, drunk or stoned.

Am I entitled to talk to an attorney before I decide which chemical test to take?

The answer depends on where you live. In California, for example, you don't have the right to speak with an attorney first. But many other states allow you to talk to a lawyer before you take a chemical test. If you are unsure of the law in your state, it's a good idea to ask for an attorney before you submit to a chemical test.

If I am pulled over, does the officer have to read me my rights before asking how much I had to drink?

No. During a traffic stop, an officer does not have to read you your rights until you are under arrest. (See Chapter 17 for a description of *Miranda* rights.) Determining whether you are "under arrest" can be tricky—you can be under arrest even before a police officer says you are. But if an officer is just asking you questions at the side of the road or even if you are detained in the officer's car for a few minutes, you are probably not under arrest. Keep in mind that you don't have to answer an officer's questions, whether you are under arrest or not—and whether or not the officer has read your rights to you. Of course, sometimes it is wise to answer a few questions, as long as you don't say anything that can be used against you.

When to Get a Lawyer

Defending against a charge of drunk driving is tricky business. To prevail, you'll need someone who understands scientific and medical concepts and can question tough witnesses, including scientists and police officers. If you want to challenge your DUI charge, you're well advised to hire an attorney who specializes in these types of cases.

Traffic Accidents

Anyone who drives or rides in a car long enough is likely to be involved in at least one minor fender-bender. Bicycle or motorcycle riders know the roads are even more dangerous for two-wheelers. And on our crowded streets, pedestrians, too, are often involved in accidents with buses, cars, and bikes. Knowing a few laws of the road, and the best steps to take when an accident occurs, can help ease the pain of any accident—and help make the insurance claims process less painful too.

What should I do if I'm involved in a traffic accident?

The most important thing to do is document the entire situation by taking careful notes soon after the accident. Taking good notes (rather than relying on your memory) will help with the claim process—and increase your chances of receiving full compensation for your injuries and vehicle damage.

Write things down as soon as you can. Begin with what you were doing and where you were going, the people you were with, the time, and the weather. Include every detail of what you saw, heard, and felt. Be sure to include everything that others—those involved in the accident or witnesses—said about the accident.

Finally, take daily notes of the effects of your injuries. Include pain, discomfort, anxiety, loss of sleep, or other problems resulting from your innjuries.

Reporting to the DMV

In many states, you must report a vehicle accident resulting in physical injury or a certain amount of property damage to the state department of motor vehicles. Check with your insurance agent or your local department of motor vehicles to find out the time limits for filing this report; you might have just a few days. Be sure to ask whether you'll need a particular form for the report.

If you must file a report, and the report asks for a statement about how the accident occurred, make it very brief—and admit no responsibility for the accident. Similarly, if the official form asks what your injuries are, list every injury, not just the most serious or obvious. An insurance company may later gain access to the report, and if you have admitted some fault in it or failed to mention an injury, it might affect your claim.

What determines who is responsible for a traffic accident?

Figuring out who is at fault in a traffic accident is a matter of deciding who was careless. Each state has traffic rules (which apply to automobiles, motorcycles, bicycles, and pedestrians) that tell people how they are supposed to drive and provide guidelines for determining liability.

Sometimes it is obvious that one driver violated a traffic rule that caused the accident—for example, one driver runs a stop sign and crashes into another. In other situations, whether or not there was a violation will be less obvious. Sometimes, neither driver violated a traffic rule, although one driver may still have been careless.

Finding Your State's Traffic Rules

The traffic rules are contained in each state's Motor Vehicle Code. You can usually obtain a simplified version of these rules—often called the "Rules of the Road"—from the department of motor vehicles (DMV). Most DMV offices also have the complete Motor Vehicle Code. Or, you can find the Motor Vehicle Code in a public library, in a law library, or on the Internet. (See the appendix for more information on how to find state laws.)

What if the cause of the accident is not clear?

It is sometimes difficult to say that one particular act caused an accident. This is especially true if what you claim the other driver did is vague or seems minor. But if you can show that the other driver made several minor driving errors or committed several minor traffic violations, you can argue that the combination of those actions caused the accident.

Special Rules for No-Fault Policyholders

Almost half the states have some form of no-fault auto insurance, also called personal injury protection. (See *Insuring Your Car*, above.)

Under no-fault insurance, the injured person's own insurance company pays medical bills and lost wages (up to certain amounts) in smaller accidents, regardless of who caused the accident. This eliminates injury liability claims and lawsuits. Usually, no-fault does not cover vehicle damage; those claims are still handled by filing a liability claim against the person who is responsible for the accident, or through your own collision insurance.

Who is liable if my car is rear-ended in a crash?

The driver who hit you from behind is almost always at fault, regardless of your reason for stopping. Traffic rules require that a driver travel at a speed at which he or she can stop safely if a vehicle ahead stops suddenly. In rear-end accidents, the vehicle damage provides strong proof of liability. If the other car's front end and your car's rear end are both damaged, there is no doubt that you were struck from behind.

In some situations, both you and the car behind you are stopped when a third car runs into the car behind you, pushing it into the rear of your car. In that case, the driver of the third car is at fault, and you should file a claim against that driver's insurance.

Are there any other clear patterns of liability in traffic accidents?

A car making a left turn is almost always liable to a car coming straight in the other direction. According to traffic rules, a car making a left turn must wait until it can safely complete the turn before moving in front of oncoming traffic. There may be exceptions to this rule if:

- the car going straight was going too fast (this is usually difficult to prove)
- the car going straight went through a red light, or
- the left-turning car began its turn when it was safe but something unexpected happened that forced the driver to slow down or stop the turn.

Police Reports: Powerful Evidence

If the police responded to the scene of your accident, they probably made a written accident report (particularly if someone was injured).

Sometimes a police report will plainly state that a driver violated a specific section of the state's motor vehicle laws and that the violation caused the accident. It may even indicate that the officer issued a citation. Other times, the report merely describes or briefly mentions negligent driving.

Any mention in a police report of a legal violation or other evidence of careless driving will provide support for your claim that the other driver was at fault.

 Online Help

www.nolo.com
Nolo offers information about a wide variety of legal topics, including what to do if you're in an accident.

www.kbb.com
Kelley Blue Book gives you the resale and wholesale values of your vehicle, as well as new car prices.

www.edmunds.com
Edmunds offers information about buying a new car, including reviews, comparisons, prices, and strategies.

www.bbb.org
The Better Business Bureau offers tips on buying new and used cars, including financing suggestions.

www.autopedia.com
Autopedia is an encyclopedia of automotive-related information. In addition to articles on many topics, it includes links to each state's lemon law.

www.consumerreports.org
Consumer Reports provides articles on how to buy or lease a car and, for a small fee, a price service for both new and used cars.

www.nhtsa.dot.gov
The National Highway Traffic Safety Administration provides recall notices, service bulletins, defect investigations, consumer complaints, and other data about vehicle problems.

www.leaseguide.com
Auto Leasing: The Art of the Deal offers information about leasing a car, including frequently asked questions, an auto consumer's lease kit, and tips for getting a good deal.

www.iii.org

The Insurance Information Institute provides information on automobile insurance, including how to choose a policy and file a claim.

www.dui.com

The Driver Performance Institutes provide information about driving under the influence.

www.motorists.org

The National Motorists Association offers information on fighting traffic tickets. ●

Wills and Estate Planning

It's not that I'm afraid to die.
I just don't want to be there when it happens.

—WOODY ALLEN

The first thing that comes to many people's minds when they think of estate planning is property: Who gets what you own when you die? But estate planning encompasses much more—for example, minimizing probate court costs and estate taxes, deciding who will care for your minor children if you can't, appointing people to handle your medical and financial affairs if necessary, and expressing your wishes regarding memorial services and burial. While none of us relish thinking about these things, taking some time to do so now can save your loved ones a great deal of money, pain, and confusion later on.

This chapter answers often-asked questions about estate planning, from basic wills to organ donation. Along the way we consider probate and the many ways to avoid it, methods for eliminating or reducing death taxes, and funeral planning. For information about arranging for someone to make your medical and financial decisions should you become unable to handle them yourself, see Chapter 12.

Wills

Though most Americans are aware that they need a will, the majority—an estimated 70% of us—don't have one. There are lots of reasons we put off making our wills, from fear of lawyers' fees to fear of death. But writing a will doesn't have to be expensive or even terribly complicated. And once it's done, you can rest a little easier, knowing that your wishes are known and will be followed after your death.

What happens if I die without a will?

If you don't make a will or use some other legal method to transfer your property when you die, state law will determine what happens to your property. (This process is called "intestate succession.") Your property will be distributed to your spouse and children or, if you have neither, to other relatives according to state law. If no relatives can be found to inherit your property, it will go into your state's treasury. Also, in the absence of a will, a court will determine who will care for your young children and their property if the other parent is unavailable or unfit.

Do I need a lawyer to make my will?

Probably not. Making a will rarely involves complicated legal rules, and most people can draft their own will with the aid of a good do-it-yourself book or software program. If you know what you own and whom you care about, and you have a good, clear, plain-English resource to guide you, you should be fine.

But you shouldn't approach the task of will drafting absolutely determined not to consult a lawyer. If you have questions that aren't answered by the resource you're using, a lawyer's services are warranted. Even so, you don't have to turn over the whole project; you can simply ask your questions and then finish making your own will.

For example, you may want to consult a lawyer if:

- You have questions about your will or other options for leaving your property.
- You expect to leave a very large amount of assets—over $2 million—that will be subject to estate taxes unless you engage in tax planning. (But first read up on tax-saving strategies.)
- You own a small business and have questions as to the rights of surviving owners or your ownership share.

- You want to make arrangements for long-term care of a beneficiary—for example, a disabled child.
- You fear someone will contest your will on grounds of fraud or claim that you were unduly influenced or weren't of sound mind when you signed it.
- You wish to leave no property, or very little property, to your spouse. It's usually not possible to do this unless you live in a community property state where your spouse already owns half of most assets acquired during marriage. (See "Can I disinherit relatives I don't like?" below.) A lawyer can explain exactly what your spouse is entitled to claim from your estate.

Also, some people simply feel more comfortable having a lawyer review their will, even though their situation has no apparent legal complications.

I don't have much property. Can't I just make a handwritten will?

Handwritten wills that are not signed in front of witnesses are called "holographic" wills. They are legal in about 25 states. To be valid, a holographic will must be written, dated, and signed in the handwriting of the person making the will. Some states allow will writers to use a fill-in-the-blanks form if the rest of the will is handwritten and the will is properly dated and signed.

If you have very little property, and you want to make just a few specific bequests, a holographic will is better than nothing if it's valid in your state. But because holographic wills are not witnessed, if your will goes before a probate court, the court may be unusually strict when examining it to be sure it's legitimate. It's better to take a little extra time now to get yourself a will that will easily pass muster when the time comes.

Making Your Will Legal

Any adult of sound mind is entitled to make a will. (And if you're reading this book, you're of sound mind.) Beyond that, there are just a few technical requirements:

- The document must expressly state that it's your will.
- You must date and sign the will.
- The will must be signed by at least two, or in some states three, witnesses. They must watch you sign the will, though they don't need to read it. Your witnesses should be people who won't inherit anything under the will.

You don't have to have your will notarized. In many states, though, if you and your witnesses sign an affidavit (sworn statement) before a notary public, you can help simplify the court procedures required to prove the validity of the will after you die.

Do I need to file my will with a court or in public records somewhere?

No. A will doesn't need to be recorded or filed with any government agency, although it can be in a few states. Just keep your will in a safe, accessible place, and be sure the person in charge of winding up your affairs (your executor) knows where it is.

Can I use my will to name somebody to care for my young children, in case my spouse and I both die suddenly?

Yes. If both parents of a child die while the child is still a minor, another adult—called a "personal guardian"—must step in. You and the child's other parent can use your wills to nominate someone to fill this position. To avert conflicts, you and the other parent should each name the same guardian for a child. (If you have more than one child, however, you do not need to name the same guardian for all of your children.) If a guardian is needed, a judge will appoint your nominee unless the judge concludes that it is not in the best interest of your children.

The personal guardian will be responsible for raising your children until they become legal adults. Of course, you should have complete confidence in the person you nominate, and you should be certain that your nominee is willing to accept the responsibility of raising your children should the need actually arise.

I'm raising a child on my own. Do I have to name the other biological parent as personal guardian, or can I name someone who I think will do a better job?

If one parent dies, the other legal parent usually takes responsibility for raising the child. But if you and the other parent have parted ways, you may feel strongly that he or she shouldn't have custody if something happens to you. A judge will grant custody to someone else only if the surviving parent:

- has legally abandoned the child by not providing for or visiting the child for an extended period, or
- is clearly unfit as a parent.

In most cases, it is difficult to prove that a parent is unfit, absent serious problems such as chronic drug or alcohol use, mental illness, or a history of child abuse.

If you honestly believe the other parent is incapable of caring for your child properly or simply won't assume the responsibility, you should write a letter explaining why and attach it to your will. The judge will take it into account, and may appoint the person you choose as guardian instead of the other parent.

How to Leave Property to Young Children

Except for property of little value, the law requires that an adult manage property inherited by children until they turn 18. You can use your will to name someone to manage property inherited by minors, thus avoiding the need for a more complicated court-appointed guardianship. There are many ways to structure a property-management arrangement. Here are four of the simplest and most useful:

1. Name a custodian under the Uniform Transfers to Minors Act

The Uniform Transfers to Minors Act (UTMA) is a law that has been adopted in every state except South Carolina and Vermont. Under the UTMA, you can choose someone, called a custodian, to manage property you are leaving to a child. If you die when the child is under the age set by your state's law—18 in a few states, 21 in most, 25 in several others—the custodian will step in to manage the property. An UTMA custodianship must end by the age specified by your state's law (18, 21, or up to 25). At that time, your child receives what's left of the trust property outright. If, however, you want to extend property management beyond the age set by your state, you may want to use one of the next three methods.

2. Set up a trust for each child

You can use your will to name someone (called a trustee) who will handle any property the child inherits until the child reaches the age you specify. When the child reaches that age, the trustee ends the trust and gives whatever is left of the trust property to the child.

3. Set up a pot trust for your children

If you have more than one child, you may want to set up just one trust for all of them. This arrangement is usually called a pot or family trust. In your will, you establish the trust and appoint a trustee. The trustee doesn't have to spend the same amount on each child; instead, the trustee decides what each child needs, and spends money accordingly. When the youngest child reaches a certain age, usually 18, the trust ends. At that time, any property left in the trust will be distributed as you direct in the trust document.

4. Name a property guardian

If you wish, you can simply use your will to name a property guardian for your child. Then, if at your death your child needs the guardian, the court will appoint the person you chose. The property guardian will manage whatever property the child inherits, from you or others, if there's no other mechanism (a trust, for example) to handle it. Property management ends when your child becomes a legal adult.

Can I disinherit relatives I don't like?

It depends on whom you want to disinherit. If it's anyone other than your spouse or child, the rule is very simple: Don't mention that person in your will, and he or she won't receive any of your property. Rules for spouses and children are somewhat more complex.

Spouses. It is not usually possible to disinherit your spouse completely. If you live in a community property state (Arizona, California, Idaho, Louisiana, Nevada, New Mexico, Texas, Washington, or Wisconsin), your spouse automatically owns half of all the property and earnings (with a few exceptions) acquired by either of you during your marriage. You can, however, leave your half of the community property, and your separate property (generally considered to be all property you owned before marriage or received via gift or inheritance during marriage), to anyone you choose.

In all other states, there is no rule that property acquired during marriage is owned by both spouses. To protect spouses from being disinherited, these states give your spouse a legal right to claim a portion of your estate, no matter what your will provides. But keep in mind that these provisions kick in only if your spouse challenges your will. If your will leaves your spouse less than the statutory share and he or she doesn't object, the document will be honored as written.

These rules also apply to registered domestic partners in California, Connecticut, Hawaii, Maine, New Hampshire, New Jersey, Vermont, and Washington. If you don't plan to leave at least half of your property to your spouse or registered domestic partner, you should consult a lawyer—unless your spouse or partner willingly consents in writing to your plan.

Children. Generally, it's legal to disinherit a child. Some states, however, protect minor children against the loss of a family residence. For example, the Florida Constitution prohibits the head of a family from leaving his residence to anyone other than a spouse if he is survived by a spouse or minor child.

Most states have laws—called "pretermitted heir" statutes—to protect children of any age from being accidentally disinherited. If a child is neither named in your will or specifically disinherited, these laws assume that you accidentally forgot to include that child. In many states, these laws apply only to children born after you made your will. The overlooked child has a right to the same share of your estate as he or she would have received if you'd left no will. The share usually depends on whether you leave a spouse and on how many other children you have, but it is likely to be a significant percentage of your property. In some states, these laws apply not only to your children but also to any of your grandchildren by a child who has died.

To avoid any legal battles after your death, if you decide to disinherit a child, or the child of a deceased child, expressly state this in your will. And if you have a new child after you've made your will, remember to make a new will to include, or specifically disinherit, that child.

What happens to my will when I die?

After you die, your executor (the person you appointed in your will) is responsible for seeing that your wishes are carried out as directed by your will. The executor may hire an attorney to help wind up your affairs, especially if probate court proceedings are required. Probate and executors are discussed in more detail in the next three sets of questions.

Make Your Will and Records Accessible

Your executor's first task is to locate your will, and you can help by keeping the original in a fairly obvious place. Here are some suggestions:

- Store your will in an envelope on which you have typed your name and the word "Will."

- Place the envelope in a fireproof metal box, file cabinet, or home safe. An alternative is to place the original in a safe deposit box. But before doing that, learn the bank's policy about access to the box after your death. If, for instance, the safe deposit box is in your name alone, the box can probably be opened only by a person authorized by a court, and then only in the presence of a bank employee. An inventory may even be required if any person enters the box or for state tax purposes. All of this takes time, and in the meantime, your document will be locked away from those who need access to it.

- Wherever you choose to keep your will, make sure your executor (and at least one other person you trust) knows where to find it.

What if someone challenges my will after I die?

Very few wills are ever challenged in court. When they are, it's usually by a close relative who feels somehow cheated out of his or her rightful share of the deceased person's property.

Generally speaking, only spouses are legally entitled to a share of your property. Your children aren't entitled to anything unless you unintentionally overlooked them in your will. (See "Can I disinherit relatives I don't like?" above.)

To get an entire will thrown out as invalid, someone must go to court and prove that it suffers from a fatal flaw: the signature was forged, you weren't of sound mind when you made the will, or you were unduly influenced by someone.

 More Information About Wills

Quicken WillMaker Plus (Nolo) (software), lets you create a valid will and many other important estate planning documents.

The Quick & Legal Will Book, by Denis Clifford (Nolo), contains forms and instructions for creating a basic will.

Nolo's Simple Will Book, by Denis Clifford (Nolo), contains a detailed discussion of wills and all the forms you need to create one.

The Busy Family's Guide to Estate Planning: 10 Steps to Peace of Mind, by Liza Weiman Hanks (Nolo), leads you through ten simple steps to take to plan your estate, including lots of information on how to write your will.

Probate

There is only one way you can beat a lawyer in a death case. That is to die with nothing. Then you can't get a lawyer within ten miles of your house.

—WILL ROGERS

When a person dies, someone must step in to wind up the deceased person's affairs. Bills must be paid, property must be accounted for, and items must be passed on to the people chosen by the deceased person. If state law requires that all this be handled through court proceedings, the process can take many months.

What is probate?

Probate is a legal process that includes:

- if there's a will, proving in court that it is valid (usually a routine matter)
- if there is no will, determining who inherits under state law
- identifying and inventorying the deceased person's property
- having the property appraised
- paying debts and taxes, and
- distributing the remaining property as the will or state law directs.

Typically, probate involves paperwork and court appearances by lawyers, who are paid from estate property that would otherwise go to the people who inherit the deceased person's property. Property left by the will cannot be distributed to beneficiaries until the process is complete.

Probate rarely benefits your beneficiaries, and it certainly costs them money and time. Pro-bate makes sense only if your estate will have complicated problems, such as many debts that can't easily be paid from the property you leave.

Property That Avoids Probate

Not all property has to go through probate. Most states allow a certain amount of property to pass free of probate, or through a simplified probate procedure. In California, for example, you can pass up to $100,000 of property without probate, and there's a simple transfer procedure for any property left to a surviving spouse.

In addition, property that passes outside of your will—say, through joint tenancy or a living trust—is not subject to probate. See *Avoiding Probate*, below

---

Who is responsible for handling probate?

In most circumstances, the executor named in the will takes this job. If there isn't any will, or if the will maker fails to name an executor, the probate court names someone (commonly called an administrator) to handle the pro-cess—most often a surviving spouse (or domestic partner) or the closest capable relative.

If no formal probate proceeding is necessary, the court does not appoint an estate adminis-trator. Instead, a close relative or friend serves as an informal estate representative. Normally, families and friends choose this person, and it is not uncommon for several people to share the responsibilities of paying debts, filing a final income tax return, and distributing property to the people who are supposed to get it.

Executors

An executor is the person you name in your will to handle your property after death. The executor—called a personal representative in many states—must be prepared to carry out a long list of tasks prudently and promptly.

How do I choose an executor?

The most important factor in naming an executor is trust. The person you choose should be honest, with good organizational skills and the ability to keep track of details. If possible, name someone who lives nearby and who is familiar with your financial matters; that will make it easier to do chores like collecting mail and locating important records and papers.

Many people select someone who will inherit a substantial amount of their property. This makes sense, because a person with an interest in how your property is distributed is likely to do a conscientious job of managing your affairs after your death. This person may also come equipped with knowledge of where your records are kept and an understanding of why you want your property left as you have directed.

Whomever you select, make sure the person is willing to do the job. Discuss the position with the person you've chosen before you make your will.

Are there restrictions on whom I may choose as my executor?

Your state may impose some restrictions on who can act as executor. You can't name a minor, a convicted felon, or someone who is not a U.S. citizen. Most states allow you to name someone who lives in another state, but some require that out-of-state executors be a relative or a primary beneficiary under your will. Some states also require that nonresident executors obtain a bond (an insurance policy that protects your beneficiaries in the event of the executor's wrongful use of your estate's property) or name an in-state resident to act as the executor's representative. These complexities underscore the benefits of naming someone who lives nearby. If you feel strongly about naming an executor who lives out of state, be sure to familiarize yourself with your state's rules.

Is it difficult to serve as executor?

Serving as an executor can be a tedious job, but it doesn't require special financial or legal knowledge. Common sense, conscientiousness, and honesty are the main requirements. An executor who needs help can hire lawyers, accountants, or other experts and pay them from the assets of the deceased person's estate.

Essentially, the executor's job is to protect the deceased person's property until all debts and taxes have been paid, and see that what's left is transferred to the people who are entitled to it. The law does not require an executor to display more than reasonable prudence and judgment, but it does require the highest degree of honesty, impartiality, and diligence. This is called a "fiduciary duty"—the duty to act with scrupulous good faith and candor on behalf of someone else.

Does the person named in a will as executor have to serve?

No. When it comes time, an executor can accept or decline this responsibility. And someone who agrees to serve can resign at any time. That's why many wills name an alternate executor, who takes over if necessary. If no one is available, the court will appoint someone to step in.

An Executor's Duties

Executors have a number of duties, depending on the complexity of the deceased person's estate. Typically, an executor must:

Decide whether or not probate court proceedings are needed. If the deceased person's property is worth less than a certain amount (it depends on state law), formal probate may not be required.

Figure out who inherits property. If the deceased person left a will, the executor will read it to determine who gets what. If there's no will, the administrator will have to look at state law (called "intestate succession" statutes) to find out who the deceased person's heirs are.

Decide whether or not it's legally permissible to transfer certain items immediately to the people named to inherit them, even if probate is required for other property.

If probate is required, file the will (if any) and all required legal papers in the local probate court.

Find the deceased person's assets and manage them during the probate process, which may take up to a year. This may involve deciding whether to sell real estate or securities owned by the deceased person.

Handle day-to-day details, such as terminating leases and credit cards, and notifying banks and government agencies—such as Social Security, the post office, Medicare, and the Department of Veterans Affairs—of the death.

Set up an estate bank account to hold money that is owed to the deceased person—for example, paychecks or stock dividends.

Pay continuing expenses—for example, mortgage payments, utility bills, and homeowners' insurance premiums.

Pay debts. As part of this process, the executor must officially notify creditors of the probate proceeding, following the procedure set out by state law.

Pay taxes. A final income tax return must be filed, covering the period from the beginning of the tax year to the date of death. State and federal estate tax returns may also be required, depending on how much property the deceased person owned at death and to whom the property was left.

Supervise the distribution of the deceased person's property to the people or organizations named in the will.

Does the executor get paid?

Obviously, the main reason for serving as an executor is to honor the deceased person's request. But the executor is also entitled to payment. The exact amount is regulated by state law and is affected by factors such as the value of the deceased person's property and what the probate court decides is reasonable under the circumstances. Commonly, close relatives and close friends (especially those who are inheriting a substantial amount anyway) don't charge the estate for their services.

Is a lawyer necessary?

Not always. An executor should definitely consider handling the paperwork without a lawyer if he or she is the main beneficiary, the deceased person's property consists of common kinds of assets (house, bank accounts, insurance), the will seems straightforward, and good resource materials are at hand. Essentially, shepherding a case through probate court requires shuffling a lot of papers. In the vast majority of cases, there are no disputes that require a decision by a judge. So the executor may never see the inside of a courtroom but will probably become familiar with the court clerk's office. The executor may even be able to do everything by mail. Doing a good job requires persistence and attention to tedious detail, but not necessarily a law degree.

If, however, the estate has many types of property, significant tax liability, or potential disputes among inheritors, an executor may want some help.

There are two ways for an executor to get help from a lawyer:

- **Hire a lawyer to answer legal questions as they come up.** The lawyer might also do some research, look over documents before the executor files them, or prepare an estate tax return.

- **Turn the probate over to the lawyer.** If the executor just doesn't want to deal with the probate process, a lawyer can do everything. The lawyer will be paid out of the estate. In most states, lawyers charge by the hour ($200 or more is common) or charge a lump sum. But in a few places, including Arkansas, California, Delaware, Hawaii, Iowa, Missouri, Montana, and Wyoming, state law authorizes the lawyer to take a certain percentage of the gross value of the deceased

person's estate unless the executor makes a written agreement calling for less. An executor can probably find a competent lawyer who will agree to a lower fee.

Where can an executor get help?

Lawyers aren't the only source of information and assistance. Here are some others:

- **The court.** Probate court clerks will probably answer basic questions about court procedure, but they staunchly avoid saying anything that could possibly be construed as "legal advice." Some courts, however, have lawyers on staff who look over probate documents; they may point out errors in the papers and explain how to fix them.

- **Other professionals.** For certain tasks, an executor may be better off hiring an accountant or appraiser than a lawyer. For example, a CPA may be a big help on some estate tax matters.

- **Paralegals.** In many law offices, lawyers delegate all the probate paperwork to paralegals (nonlawyers who have training or experience in preparing legal documents). Now, in some areas of the country, experienced paralegals have set up shop to help people directly with probate paperwork. These paralegals don't offer legal advice; they just prepare documents as the executor instructs them, and file them with the court. To find a probate paralegal, an executor can look in the Yellow Pages under "Legal Document Preparer" or "Attorney Services." The executor should hire someone only if that person has substantial experience in this field and provides references that check out.

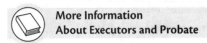

**More Information
About Executors and Probate**

The Executor's Guide, by Mary Randolph (Nolo), explains what executors can expect and how to deal with legal and practical issues such as insurance, benefits, wills, trusts, probate, debts, and taxes.

Social Security, Medicare & Government Pensions, by Joseph Matthews and Dorothy Matthews Berman (Nolo), explains how to make claims for survivors benefits from the Social Security Administration, Federal Civil Service, and the Department of Veterans Affairs.

How to Probate an Estate in California, by Julia Nissley (Nolo), leads you through the California probate process step by step. It contains tearout copies of all necessary court forms, and instructions for filling them out. Although the forms are used only in California, the book contains much information that would be valuable background in any state.

Avoiding Probate

Because probate is time-consuming, expensive, and usually unnecessary, many people plan in advance to avoid it. There are a number of ways to pass property to your inheritors without probate. Some of these probate-avoidance methods are quite simple to set up; others take more time and effort.

Should I plan to avoid probate?

Whether to spend your time and effort planning to avoid probate depends on a number of factors, most notably your age, your health, and your wealth. If you're young and in good health, a simple will may be all you need—

adopting a complex probate-avoidance plan now may mean you'll have to redo it as your life situation changes. And if you have very little property, you won't want to spend your time planning to avoid probate. Your property may even fall under your state's probate exemption; most states have laws that allow a certain amount of property to pass free of probate, or through a simplified probate procedure.

But if you're older (say, over 50), in ill health, or own a significant amount of property, you'll probably want to do some planning to avoid probate.

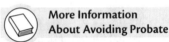

**More Information
About Avoiding Probate**

8 Ways to Avoid Probate, by Mary Randolph (Nolo), explains eight simple and inexpensive methods of sparing your family the hassle and expense of probate after your death.

Plan Your Estate, by Denis Clifford and Cora Jordan (Nolo), offers an in-depth discussion of almost all aspects of estate planning, including probate avoidance.

Living Trusts

If you're considering setting up a living trust to avoid probate, there's no shortage of advice out there, much of it contradictory. Personal finance columnists, lawyers, your Uncle Harry—everybody's got an opinion.

Whether or not a living trust is right for you depends on exactly what you want to accomplish and how much paperwork you're willing to put up with. Living trusts work wonderfully for many people, but not everyone needs one.

How to Avoid Probate

No one probate-avoidance method is right for all people. Which methods, if any, you should use depends on your personal and financial situation. Here are some common techniques to consider:

Pay-on-death designations. Designating a pay-on-death beneficiary is a simple way to avoid probate for bank accounts, government bonds, individual retirement accounts, and in most states, stocks and other securities. In a few states, you can even transfer your car or your real estate through such an arrangement. All you need to do is name someone to inherit the property at your death. You retain complete control of your property when you are alive, and you can change the beneficiary if you choose. When you die, the property is transferred to the person you named, free of probate.

Joint tenancy. Joint tenancy is a form of shared ownership where the surviving owner(s) automatically inherits the share of the owner who dies. Joint tenancy is often a good choice for couples who purchase property together and want the survivor to inherit. (Many states also have a very similar type of ownership, called "tenancy by the entirety," just for married couples or, in a few states, same-sex domestic partners.) Adding another owner to property you already own, however, can create problems.

The new co-owner can sell or borrow against his or her share. Also, there are negative tax consequences of giving appreciated property to a joint tenant shortly before death.

A living trust. A revocable living trust is a popular probate-avoidance device. You create the trust by preparing and signing a trust document. Once the trust is created, you can hold property in trust, without giving up any control over the trust property. When you die, the trust property can be distributed directly to the beneficiaries you named in the trust document, without the blessing of the probate court. Living trusts are discussed in more detail in the next set of questions.

Insurance. If you buy life insurance, you can designate a specific beneficiary in your policy. The proceeds of the policy won't go through probate unless you name your own estate as the beneficiary.

Gifts. Anything you give away during your life doesn't have to go through probate. Making nontaxable gifts (up to $12,000 per recipient per year, or to a tax-exempt entity) can also reduce eventual federal estate taxes. So if you can afford it, a gift-giving program can save on both probate costs and estate taxes.

What is a living trust?

A trust is an arrangement under which one person, called the trustee, holds legal title to property on behalf of another. You can be the trustee of your own living trust, keeping full control over all property held in trust.

There are many kinds of trusts. A "living trust" (also called an "inter vivos" trust by lawyers who can't give up Latin) is simply a trust you create while you're alive, rather than one that is created at your death under the terms of your will.

All living trusts are designed to avoid probate. Some also help you save on death taxes, and others let you set up long-term property management.

Why do I need a living trust?

If you don't take steps to avoid probate, after your death your property will probably have to detour through probate court before it reaches the people you want to inherit it. In a nutshell, probate is the court-supervised process of paying your debts and distributing your property to the people who inherit it. (For more information see *Probate* and *Executors,* above.)

The average probate drags on for months before the inheritors get anything. And by that time, there's less for them to get: In many cases, about 5% of the property has been eaten up by lawyer and court fees. The exact amount depends on state law and the rates of the lawyer hired by the executor.

Don't Forget Your Will!

Even if you make a living trust, you still need a will. Here's why:

A will is an essential backup device for property that you don't transfer to your living trust. For example, if you acquire property shortly before you die, you may not think to transfer ownership of it to your trust—which means that it won't pass under the terms of the trust document. But in your backup will, you can include a clause that names someone to get any property that you don't leave to a particular person or entity.

If you don't have a will, any property that isn't transferred by your living trust or other probate-avoidance device (such as joint tenancy) will go to your closest relatives in an order determined by state law. These laws may not distribute property in the way you would have chosen.

How does a living trust avoid probate?

Property held in a living trust before your death doesn't go through probate. The successor trustee—the person you appointed to handle the trust after your death—simply transfers ownership to the beneficiaries you named in the trust. In many cases, the whole process takes only a few weeks, and there are no lawyer or court fees to pay. When the property has all been transferred to the beneficiaries, the living trust ceases to exist.

Is it expensive to create a living trust?

The expense of a living trust comes up front. Lawyers charge high fees—much higher than for wills—for living trusts. They commonly charge upwards of $1,000 to draw up a simple trust. If you're going to hire a lawyer to draw up your living trust, you might pay as much now as your heirs would have to pay for probate after your death—which means the trust offers no net savings.

But you don't have to pay a lawyer to create a living trust. With a good book or software program written for nonlawyers, you can create a valid Declaration of Trust (the document that creates a trust) yourself. If you run into questions that a do-it-yourself publication doesn't answer, you may need to consult a lawyer, but you probably won't need to turn the whole job over to an expensive expert.

Isn't it a hassle to own property in a trust?

Making a living trust work for you does require some crucial paperwork. For example, if you want to leave your house through the trust, you must sign a new deed showing that you now own the house as trustee of your living trust. And in a few states, you may need to use special language in your trust document to avoid wrinkles in your state's income tax laws. This paperwork can be tedious, but the hassles are fewer these days because living trusts are quite commonplace.

Is a trust document ever made public, like a will?

A will becomes a matter of public record when it is submitted to a probate court, as do all the other documents associated with probate—inventories of the deceased person's assets and debts, for example. The terms of a living trust, however, need not be made public.

Does a trust protect property from creditors?

Holding assets in a revocable trust doesn't shelter them from creditors. A creditor who wins a lawsuit against you can go after the trust property just as if you still owned it in your own name.

After your death, however, property in a living trust can be quickly and quietly distributed to the beneficiaries (unlike property that must go through probate). That complicates matters for creditors; by the time they find out about your death, your property may already be dispersed, and the creditors have no way of knowing exactly what you owned (except for real estate, which is always a matter of public record). It may not be worth the creditor's time and effort to try to track down the property and demand that the new owners use it to pay your debts.

On the other hand, probate can offer a kind of protection from creditors. During probate, known creditors must be notified of the death and given a chance to file claims. If they miss the deadline to file, they're out of luck forever.

I'm young and healthy. Do I really need a trust now?

Probably not. At this stage in your life, your main estate planning goals are probably making sure that in the unlikely event of your early death, your property is distributed as you want it to be and, if you have young children, that they are cared for. You don't need a trust to accomplish those ends; writing a will, and perhaps buying some life insurance, would be simpler.

Can a living trust save on estate taxes?

A simple probate-avoidance living trust has no effect on taxes. More complicated living trusts, however, can greatly reduce your federal estate tax bill. Federal estate taxes are collected only from large estates—so few people need to worry about them. (See *Estate and Gift Taxes*, below.)

One tax-saving living trust is designed primarily for married couples with children. It's commonly called a bypass or AB trust, though it goes by many other names. For more information about how an AB trust works, see the next set of questions, *Estate and Gift Taxes*.

 More Information About Living Trusts

Quicken WillMaker Plus (Nolo) (software), lets you make a basic probate-avoidance trust or tax-saving AB trust using your computer.

Make Your Own Living Trust, by Denis Clifford (Nolo), contains forms and instructions for preparing two kinds of living trusts: a basic probate-avoidance trust and a tax-saving AB trust.

Plan Your Estate, by Denis Clifford and Cora Jordan (Nolo), is a detailed guide to estate planning, including information about living trusts.

Estate and Gift Taxes

In this world nothing can be said to be certain, except death and taxes.

—BENJAMIN FRANKLIN

It's a universal truth that you can't take it with you. But will your inheritors have to pay for what you leave behind? Most people who consider estate planning are understandably concerned with estate and inheritance taxes. The good news is that most people's estates won't have to pay any death taxes—federal or state.

Will my estate have to pay taxes after I die?

Probably not. The federal government imposes estate taxes only if your property is worth more than a certain amount at your death. All property left to a spouse is exempt from the tax, as long as the spouse is a U.S. citizen. And estate taxes won't be assessed on any property you leave to a tax-exempt charity.

Currently, the amount that you can leave that is exempt from estate tax is $2 million. The exemption rises to $3.5 million in 2009 and in 2010 the estate tax will no longer be imposed at all. But unless Congress extends the estate tax repeal, the tax will pop up again in 2011 with a $1 million exemption.

The Estate Tax Exemption	
Year	**Amount**
2008	$2 million
2009	$3.5 million
2010	Estate tax repealed
2011	$1 million
	unless Congress extends repeal

Don't some states also impose taxes at death?

A handful of states impose inheritance or estate taxes.

Inheritance taxes are paid by your inheritors, not your estate. Typically, how much they pay depends on their relationship to you. For example, Nebraska imposes a 15% tax if you leave $25,000 to a friend, but only 1% if you leave the money to your child. But tax rates vary from state to state. If you live in Maryland, your child wouldn't owe any taxes on a $25,000 inheritance, but your friend could owe 10%.

States That Impose Inheritance Taxes	
Indiana	Nebraska
Iowa	New Jersey
Kentucky	Pennsylvania
Maryland	Tennessee

Estate taxes collected by states are similar to the estate tax imposed by the federal government. Your estate must pay this tax no matter who your beneficiaries are. Estates may now have to pay state tax even if they aren't large enough to owe federal estate tax. That's because Congress changed the tax rules, no longer allowing states to claim any of the federal tax. To make up for this loss of revenue, some states have enacted their own estate taxes, which are no longer connected to the federal system.

If you're concerned about state taxes, see a tax lawyer in your state (and in any other state where you own real estate) who can bring you up to date on this rapidly changing area of the law.

You can find a listing of your state's death tax laws in Nolo's *Plan Your Estate*, by Denis Clifford and Cora Jordan, and *The Executor's Guide*, by Mary Randolph.

What are the rates for federal estate taxes?

The maximum estate tax rate is is 45% for deaths in 2007 through 2009. In 2010, the estate tax is repealed. If it returns in 2011, the tax rate will be 55%.

Are there ways to avoid federal estate taxes?

Yes, although there are fewer ways than many people think, or hope, there are.

The most popular method is frequently used by married couples with grown children. It's called an AB trust, though it's sometimes known as a "credit shelter trust," "exemption trust," or "marital bypass trust." Spouses put their property in the trust, and then, when one spouse dies, his or her half of the property goes to the children—with the crucial condition that the surviving spouse gets the right to use it for life and is entitled to any income it generates. When the second spouse dies, the property goes to the children outright. Using this kind of trust keeps the second spouse's taxable estate half the size it would be if the property were left entirely to the spouse, which means that estate taxes may be avoided altogether.

Unlike a probate-avoidance revocable living trust, an AB trust controls what happens to property for years after the first spouse's death. A couple that makes one must be sure that the surviving spouse will be financially and emotionally comfortable receiving only the income from the money or property placed in trust, with the children as the actual owners of the property.

How an AB Trust Works: An Example

Ellen and Jack have been married for nearly 50 years. They have one grown son, Robert, who is 39. Ellen and Jack create an AB trust and transfer all their major items of property to it. They name each other as life beneficiaries, and Robert as the final beneficiary.

Ellen dies first. The trust splits into two parts: Trust A, which is irrevocable, contains Ellen's share of the property. Trust B is Jack's trust, and it stays revocable as long as he is alive.

The property in Trust A legally belongs to Robert, but with one very important condition: His father, Jack, is entitled to use the property, and collect any income it generates, for the rest of his life. When Jack dies, the property will go to Robert free and clear.

Now let's take a look at the tax savings: Ellen's half of the trust property is worth $1.2 million when she dies.

At Ellen's death

Taxable estate .... $1.2 million

Estate tax $0

(*because of the personal exemption*)

At Jack's death

Taxable estate .... $1.2 million

Estate tax $0

If Ellen had left all her property to Jack outright, his estate would have been worth $2.4 million at his death—which would have resulted in thousands of dollars of estate tax if he died before 2009.

Are there other ways to save on estate taxes?

Yes. Common ones include what's called a "QTIP" trust, which enables a surviving spouse to postpone estate taxes that would otherwise be due when the other spouse dies. And there are many different types of charitable trusts, which involve making a sizable gift to a tax-exempt charity. Some of them provide both income tax and estate tax advantages.

Can I avoid paying state taxes?

If your state imposes estate or inheritance taxes, there probably isn't much you can do. But if you live in two states—winter here, summer there—your inheritors may save if you can make your legal residence in the state with lower, or no, taxes.

Can't I just give all my property away before I die and avoid estate taxes?

No. The government long anticipated this one. If you give away more than $12,000 per year to any one person or noncharitable institution, you are assessed federal "gift tax," which applies at the same rate as the estate tax. There are, however, a few exceptions to this rule. You can give an unlimited amount of property to your spouse, unless your spouse is not a U.S. citizen, in which case you can give him or her up to $125,000 per year free of gift tax. Any property given to a tax-exempt charity avoids federal gift taxes. And money spent directly for someone's medical bills or school tuition is exempt as well.

The federal gift tax will not be repealed in 2010 with the estate tax. Instead, it will survive, but with a $1 million exemption. In other words, you'll still be able to give away $1 million in taxable gifts (and most ordinary gifts aren't taxable) without owing any tax.

But I've heard that people save on estate taxes by making gifts. How?

You can achieve substantial estate tax savings by making use of the annual gift-tax exclusion for gifts to people and nonexempt organizations. If you give away $12,000 a year for four years, you've removed $48,000 from your taxable estate. And each member of a couple has a separate exclusion. So a couple can give $24,000 a year to a child free of gift tax. If you have a few children, or other people you want to make gifts to (such as your sons- or daughters-in-law), you can use this method to significantly reduce the size of your taxable estate over a few years.

Consider a couple with combined assets worth $2.5 million and four children. Each year they give each child $24,000 tax free, for a total of $96,000 per year. In seven years, the couple has given away $672,000 and has reduced their estate below the federal estate tax threshold.

Of course, there are risks with this kind of gift-giving program. The most obvious is that you are legally transferring your wealth. Gift giving to reduce eventual estate taxes must be carefully evaluated to see if you can comfortably afford to give away your property during your lifetime.

More Information About Estate and Gift Taxes

Plan Your Estate, by Denis Clifford (Nolo), is a detailed guide to estate planning, including all major methods of reducing or avoiding estate and gift taxes.

Funeral Planning and Other Final Arrangements

Many of us are squeamish when it comes to thinking and talking about death, particularly our own. But there are many good reasons to spend some time considering what you want to have happen to your body after death, including any ceremonies and observances you'd like.

Why should I leave written instructions about my final ceremonies and the disposition of my body?

Letting your survivors know your wishes saves them the difficulties of making these decisions at a painful time. And many family members and friends find that discussing these matters ahead of time is a great relief—especially if a person is elderly or in poor health and death is expected soon.

Planning some of these details in advance can also help save money. For many people, death goods and services cost more than anything they bought during their lives except homes and cars. Some wise comparison shopping in advance can help ensure that costs will be controlled or kept to a minimum.

Why not leave these instructions in my will?

A will is not a good place to express your death and burial preferences for one simple reason: Your will probably won't be located and read until several weeks after you die—long after decisions must be made.

A will should be reserved for directions on how to divide and distribute your property and, if applicable, who should get care and custody of your children if you die while they're still young.

What happens if I don't leave written instructions?

If you die without leaving written instructions about your preferences, state law will determine who will have the right to decide how your remains will be handled. In most states, the right—and the responsibility to pay for the reasonable costs of disposing of remains—rests with the following people, in order:

- spouse or registered domestic partner
- child or children
- parent or parents
- the next of kin, or
- a public administrator, who is appointed by a court.

Disputes may arise if two or more people—the deceased person's children, for example—share responsibility for a fundamental decision, such as whether the body of a parent should be buried or cremated. But such disputes can be avoided if you are willing to do some planning and to put your wishes in writing.

What details should I include in a final arrangements document?

What you choose to include is a personal matter, likely to be dictated by custom, religious preference, or simply your own whims. A typical final arrangements document might include:

- the name of the mortuary or other institution that will handle burial or cremation
- whether or not you wish to be embalmed

- the type of casket or container in which your remains will be buried or cremated, including whether you want it present at any after-death ceremony
- who your pallbearers will be if you wish to have some
- how your remains will be transported to the cemetery and gravesite
- where your remains will be buried, stored, or scattered
- the details of any marker you want to show where your remains are buried or interred, and
- the details of any ceremonies you want before, at the time of, or following your burial, interment, or scattering.

What services can I expect from a mortuary?

Most mortuaries or funeral homes are equipped to handle many of the details related to disposing of a person's remains. These include:

- collecting the body from the place of death
- storing the body until it is buried or cremated
- making burial arrangements with a cemetery
- conducting ceremonies related to the burial
- preparing the body for burial, and
- arranging to have the body transported for burial.

Where can I turn for help in making final arrangements?

From an economic standpoint, choosing the institution to handle your burial is probably the most important final arrangement that you can make. For this reason, many people join nonprofit memorial or funeral societies, which help them find local mortuaries that will deal

Going Green

Burials and cremations can be hard on the environment. Embalming chemicals, metal caskets, concrete burial vaults, and cremation facility emissions take a surprising toll. If you want to make plans that minimize environmental effects, here are some options:

Choose a green cemetery. The Green Burial Council can help you find providers that avoid toxins, use biodegradable materials, and even help to preserve open space. Visit www.ethical-burial.org for more information.

Say no to embalming. Embalming fluid contains toxic chemicals—including up to three gallons of formaldehyde—that can seep into soil and ground water. Embalming rarely serves a legitimate purpose and is almost never required.

Ask for a biodegradable container. You can use a simple wood casket, cardboard box, or shroud for burial. There are also biodegradable urns for ashes that will be buried.

Avoid vaults. Vaults are large containers, usually made from reinforced concrete, that are placed in the ground before a burial. They're not required by law, but many cemeteries demand them because they make it easier to maintain the landscape. The result is that, every year, more than 1.5 million tons of reinforced concrete are buried along with caskets and bodies.

You can look for a cemetery that doesn't require vaults. In a few states, you can even refuse a vault on religious grounds. You may be required to pay an extra fee for grave maintenance.

Cremation conservation. Cremation uses the fewest resources, but it's not entirely clean. It burns fossil fuels and carries the risk of mercury pollution from incinerated fillings. Newer cremation facilities are more efficient, using about half the fuel. If you have amalgam fillings in your teeth, you can ask that they be removed before cremation.

honestly with their survivors and charge reasonable prices.

Society members are free to choose whatever final arrangements they wish. Most societies, however, emphasize simple arrangements over the costly services often promoted by the funeral industry. The services offered by each society differ, but most societies distribute information on options and explain the legal rules that apply to final arrangements.

If you join a society, you will receive a form that allows you to plan for the goods and services you want—and to get them for a pre-determined cost. Many societies also serve as watchdogs, making sure that you get and pay for only the services you choose.

The cost for joining these organizations is low—usually from $20 to $40 for a lifetime membership, although some societies periodically charge a small renewal fee.

To find a funeral or memorial society near you, contact the Funeral Consumers Alliance (information is below).

If you don't want to join a society, you can shop around to find the mortuary or funeral home that best meets your needs in terms of style, proximity, and cost.

Can my family handle my final arrangements independently, without a mortuary?

There is a slowly growing trend in America for people to care for their own dead, minimizing or even eliminating the involvement of funeral industry personnel. This can mean everything from preparing the body to burying it or transporting it to the cremation facility.

Most states do allow individuals to act completely on their own. But there are rules about how people may proceed—for example, most states have laws that regulate the depth of a site for a body burial. A few states throw up roadblocks to acting independently, requiring that a funeral director handle body disposition.

If you want to ask a family member or friend to handle your disposition independently, the following resources can help you make your plans:

- *Caring for the Dead: Your Final Act of Love*, by Lisa Carlson (Upper Access Press). This book will help you understand how to take care of a body and what laws may apply. It includes a state-by-state guide to funeral and burial practices, as well as directories of cremation facilities and nonprofit funeral consumer groups.
- *Coming to Rest: A Guide to Caring for Our Own Dead*, by Richard Spiegel and Julie Wiskind (Dovetail). This guide covers details from preparing a body to complying with legal requirements and completing paperwork.
- The Funeral Consumers Alliance website (listed just below) offers extensive resources to help you make your own plans.

How can I arrange payment for my final arrangements?

Whatever arrangements you make, you have two main options for covering costs. You can:

- pay everything up front (in a lump sum or installments), or
- decide what you want and leave enough money for your survivors to pay the bills.

If you don't do either of these things, and your estate doesn't have enough money to cover the costs, your survivors will have to pay for any final expenses.

Paying in advance. If you want to pay in advance, either all at once or under a payment plan, be sure you're dealing with a reputable provider of goods and services, and document your arrangements very clearly.

There are reasons to be cautious about paying up front. Though there are a number of legal controls on how the funeral industry can handle and invest funds earmarked for future services, there have been many reported instances of mismanaged and stolen funds. A great many other abuses go unreported by family members too embarrassed or grief-stricken to complain.

In addition, when mortuaries go out of business, customers who have prepaid may be left without a refund and without recourse. Also, many individuals who move during their lifetimes discover that their prepayment funds are nonrefundable—or that there is a substantial financial penalty for withdrawing or transferring them. In addition, money paid now may not cover inflated costs of the future, meaning that survivors will be left to cover what's left.

Setting aside funds. A safe, simple, and flexible option is to set aside funds that your survivors can use to cover the costs of your final plans.

After making your plans and estimating the cost, you can tuck away that sum (perhaps adding a bit to cover inflation or unexpected expenses) in a money market or other accessible fund. Tell the bank or financial institution that you want to set up a payable-on-death account. You can designate a beneficiary—a good choice might be the executor of your will or successor trustee of your living trust—who can claim the money immediately upon your death. One warning: The beneficiary will have no legal obligation to use these funds for your final arrangements, so be sure that person understands what the funds are for and that you trust him or her to do as you ask.

**More Information
About Final Arrangements**

The Funeral Consumers Alliance, a nonprofit organization, can help you locate a funeral or memorial society near you. Call 800-765-0107 or reach FCA online at www.funerals.org.

Quicken WillMaker Plus (Nolo) (software), lets you use your computer to create a final arrangements document, in addition to a valid will, living trust, health care directives, a durable power of attorney for finances, and other documents.

Body and Organ Donations

In addition to making other arrangements for your funeral and burial or cremation, you may want to arrange to donate some or all of your organs.

How can I arrange to donate my body for education or scientific research after my death?

Arrangements for whole body donations must usually be made while you are alive, although some medical schools will accept a cadaver through arrangements made after death.

The best place to contact to arrange a whole body donation is the nearest medical school. If you live in a state with no medical school or one that has very strict requirements for whole body donations, you may wish to find out more about your body donation options from the National Anatomical Service at 800-727-0700.

How can I arrange to donate my body organs for others to use after my death?

The principal method for donating organs is by indicating your intent to do so on donor card or in a health care directive (see the next chapter).

In most states, you can obtain an organ donation card from the department of motor vehicles. Depending on where you live, you can check a box, affix a stamp or seal, or attach a separate card to your license, indicating your wish to donate one or more organs.

Even if you have not signed a card or other document indicating your intent to donate your organs, your next of kin can approve a donation after you die. If you do put your intent in writing, make sure you tell family members you have done so. Even if you have indicated in writing that you want to donate your organs, an objection by your next of kin will often defeat your wishes; medical personnel usually do not proceed in the face of an objection from relatives. The best safeguard is to discuss your wishes with close friends and relatives, emphasizing your strong feelings about donating your organs.

Online Help

www.nolo.com
Nolo offers extensive information about wills and estate planning.

www.estateplanninglinks.com
This site contains a very thorough list of websites that cover almost every imaginable estate planning issue.

Health Care Directives and Powers of Attorney

*There is no mortal whom
sorrow and disease do not touch.*

—EURIPIDES

Many of us fear that we may someday become seriously ill and unable to handle our own affairs. Who would act on our behalf to pay bills, make bank deposits, watch over investments, and deal with the paperwork required to collect insurance and government benefits? Who would make arrangements for our medical care and see that our wishes for treatment are carried out?

Preparing a few simple documents—health care directives and a durable power of attorney for finances—can ease these worries by ensuring that your affairs will stay in the hands of the trusted people you choose. This chapter answers your questions about these documents and how they work, as well as what happens if a court appoints a conservator—that is, a person who will manage your affairs if you haven't drafted legally valid instructions naming someone to take over.

Health Care Directives

If you're like most people, you aren't eager to spend time thinking about what would happen if you became unable to direct your own medical care because of illness, an accident, or advanced age. But if you don't do at least a little bit of planning—writing down your wishes about the kinds of treatment you do or don't want to receive and naming someone you trust to oversee your care—these important matters could wind up in the hands of estranged family members, doctors, or sometimes even judges, who may know very little about what you would prefer.

There are two basic documents that allow you to set out your wishes for medical care: a living will and a durable power of attorney for health care. It's wise to prepare both. In some states, the living will and the power of attorney are combined into a single form—often called an advance directive. In fact, all of these documents are types of health care directives—that is, documents that let you specify your wishes for health care in the event that you become unable to speak for yourself.

What is a living will?

A living will—sometimes called a health care declaration or something similar—is a written statement that details the type of medical care you want (or don't want) if you become incapacitated. A living will bears no relation to the conventional will or living trust used to leave property at death; it's strictly a place to spell out your health care preferences.

You can use your living will to say as much or as little as you wish about the kind of health care you want to receive.

What is a durable power of attorney for health care?

A durable power of attorney for health care gives another person authority to make medical decisions for you if you are unable to make them for yourself. This person is usually called your agent but, depending on your state, your health care representative may also be called your proxy, patient advocate, surrogate, or something similar.

If you make a living will, part of your health care agent's job will be making sure that your wishes are carried out as you intend. Your agent can also make any necessary health care decisions for you that your living will does not cover.

If you don't know anyone you trust enough to name as your health care agent, it is still important to complete and finalize a living will recording your wishes for health care. That way,

your doctors will still know what kind of medical care you do or do not want.

Do Not Resuscitate (DNR) Orders

Some people who do not wish to receive life-prolonging treatment when close to death—most likely those who are already critically ill—may also want to prepare a "do not resuscitate" order, or DNR order. If a medical emergency occurs, this form alerts emergency personnel that you do not wish to receive cardiopulmonary resuscitation (CPR).

If you are in the hospital, your doctor can add a DNR order to your medical record. If you are not hospitalized, you can make what's called a "prehospital DNR order," to alert paramedics who come to your home or care facility. In addition to preparing a prehospital DNR order, you should also obtain an easily identifiable Medic Alert bracelet, anklet, or necklace. If you think you might want to make a DNR order, talk to your doctor or a hospital representative.

What happens if I don't have any health care documents?

If you do not make a living will or durable power of attorney for health care, the doctors who attend you will decide what kind of medical care you will receive. For consent, they will turn to a close relative—usually your spouse, registered domestic partner, parent, or adult child.

Problems may arise if those closest to you disagree about what treatment is proper. In the most extreme circumstances, these battles end up in court, where a judge—who usually has little medical knowledge and no familiarity with you—is called upon to decide the course of your treatment. Legal battles can be avoided if you take the time to make a document expressing your wishes.

What should I cover in my living will?

You don't need to become a medical expert to complete your living will, but it's a good idea to become familiar with the kinds of medical procedures that are commonly administered to patients who are seriously ill.

Life-prolonging medical care. In most states, living wills ask you whether or not you want to receive life-prolonging treatments at the end of life. Such procedures typically include:

- transfusions of blood and blood products
- cardiopulmonary resuscitation (CPR)
- diagnostic tests
- dialysis
- administration of drugs
- use of a respirator, and
- surgery.

If you want more information, you can discuss these treatments with your doctor or a patient representative at a hospital or health insurance plan office, or you can turn to self-help resources for more detailed information.

Food and water. If you are permanently comatose or close to death from a serious illness, you may not be able to survive without the administration of food and water. Unless you indicate that treatment should be withheld, doctors will use intravenous (IV) feeding or tubes to provide you with a mix of nutrients and fluids. IV feeding, where fluids are introduced through a vein in an arm or a leg, is a short-term procedure. Tube feeding, however, can be carried on indefinitely.

Permanently unconscious patients can sometimes live for years with artificial feeding and hydration without regaining consciousness. If food and water are removed, death will occur in a relatively short time due to dehydration, rather than starvation. Such a course of action generally includes a plan of medication to keep the patient comfortable.

When you make your health care documents, you can choose whether you want artificially administered food and water withheld or provided. This decision is difficult for many people. Keep in mind that as long as you are able to communicate your wishes, by whatever means, you will not be denied food and water if you want it.

Palliative care—or pain relief. If you want death to occur naturally—without life-prolonging intervention—it does not mean you must forgo treatment to alleviate pain or keep you comfortable. This type of care is often called "palliative care."

Rather than focusing on a cure or prolonging life, palliative care emphasizes quality of life and dignity by helping a patient remain comfortable and free from pain until life ends naturally. Palliative care may be administered at home, in a hospice facility, or at a hospital.

You may wish to spend some time educating yourself about palliative care. You can include your feelings and preferences about such care in your living will.

> ### How Pregnancy May Affect Your Health Care Directives
>
> There is one situation in which your specific health care directions might be challenged or ignored completely: when you are pregnant. If you may become pregnant, it's a good idea to explicitly state what you want if your health care documents go into effect while you are carrying a child.
>
> Whether or not doctors will honor your wishes depends on several factors, including how far along you are in your pregnancy, the risks to you and the unborn child, and the policies of individual doctors and health care facilities. If you are in your second or third trimester, doctors are likely to administer all medical care they deem necessary to keep you and the fetus alive.

Do doctors have to follow my wishes?

Health care providers are generally required to comply with the wishes you set out in your health care documents—and to honor your health care agent's authority as long as the agent's directions are a reasonable interpretation of your wishes.

In some situations, however, a health care provider is permitted to reject a medical decision made by you or your agent. This may be true if:

- the decision goes against the conscience of the individual health care provider
- the decision goes against a policy of a health care institution that is based on reasons of conscience, or
- the decision would lead to medically ineffective health care or health care that

violates generally accepted health care standards applied by the health care provider or institution.

But this doesn't mean that your health care instructions can be ignored. A health care provider who refuses to comply with your wishes or the directions of your health care agent must promptly inform you or your agent. And if you or your agent wishes, the provider must immediately take steps to transfer you to another provider or institution that will honor your directive. In some states, a health care provider who intentionally violates these rules may be legally liable for damages.

When will my health care documents take effect?

Your health care documents take effect if your doctor determines that you lack the ability—often called the "capacity"—to make your own health care decisions. Lacking capacity usually means that:

- you can't understand the nature and consequences of the health care choices that are available to you, and
- you are unable to communicate your own wishes for care, either orally, in writing, or through gestures.

Practically speaking, this means that if you are so ill or injured that you cannot express your health care wishes in any way, your documents will spring immediately into effect. If, however, there is some question about your ability to understand your treatment choices and communicate clearly, your doctor (with the input of your health care agent or close relatives) will decide whether it is time for your health care documents to become operative.

In some states, it is possible to give your health care agent the authority to manage your medical care immediately. If your state allows this option, you may prefer to make an immediately effective document so that your agent can step in to act for you at any time, without the need to involve a doctor in the question of whether or not your health care document should take effect.

Making your document effective immediately will not give your agent the authority to override what you want in terms of treatment; you will always be able to dictate your own medical care if you have the ability to do so. And even when you are no longer capable of making your own decisions, your health care agent must always act in your best interests and diligently try to follow any health care wishes you've expressed in your health care declaration or otherwise.

How do I choose a health care agent ?

The person you name as your health care agent should be someone you trust—and someone with whom you feel confident discussing your wishes. Though your agent need not agree with your wishes for your medical care, you should believe that the person you choose respects your right to get the kind of medical care you want.

The person you appoint to oversee your health care wishes could be a spouse or partner, relative, or close friend. Keep in mind that your agent may have to fight to assert your wishes in the face of a stubborn medical establishment—and against the wishes of family members who may be driven by their own beliefs and interests, rather than yours. If you foresee the possibility of a conflict in enforcing your wishes, be sure to choose an agent who is strong-willed and assertive.

While you need not name someone who lives in the same state as you do, proximity may be an important factor. The reality is that the person you name may be called upon to spend weeks or months near your bedside, making sure medical personnel abide by your health care wishes. If you name someone who lives far away, make sure that person is willing to travel and stay with you a while. The agent's job may demand it.

You should not choose your doctor or an employee of a hospital or nursing home where you receive treatment to be your agent. In fact, the laws in many states prevent you from naming such a person. In a few instances, this legal constraint may frustrate your wishes. For example, you may wish to name your spouse or partner as your representative, but if he or she works as a hospital employee, that alone may rule him or her out. Many states have created exceptions to allow close family members who work in medical facilities to serve as agents. However, if the law in your state bans your first choice, you will have to name another person to serve.

How much power will my health care agent have?

In most states, your agent will have the authority to make all health care decisions for you unless you specifically limit your agent's authority in your power of attorney document. This means that your agent will normally be permitted to:

- consent or refuse consent to any medical treatment that affects your physical or mental health (there are usually exceptions to this rule for situations such as extreme psychiatric treatments and termination of pregnancy, and your agent is not permitted to authorize any act that violates the wishes you've stated in your living will)

• hire or fire medical personnel

• make decisions about the best medical facilities for you

• visit you in the hospital or other facility even when other visiting is restricted

• gain access to medical records and other personal information, and

• get court authorization, if required to obtain or withhold medical treatment, if for any reason a hospital or doctor does not honor your living will or the authority of your health care agent.

Keep in mind that as long as you are able to understand and communicate your own wishes, your agent cannot override what you want. Your agent steps in only if you can no longer manage on your own.

Organ Donation and Body Disposition

Most of your agent's authority under a durable power of attorney for health care will end upon your death. In an increasing number of states, however, you can give your agent permission to oversee the disposition of your body, including authorizing an autopsy or carrying out your wishes for organ donation. If you want your agent to have these powers, you should say so in your power of attorney document.

If you have specific wishes about these matters, your living will is a good place to write them down. Your agent is legally required to follow your instructions whenever possible.

Where can I get health care directive forms?

There are a number of ways to find the proper health care documents for your state; you don't need to consult a lawyer to obtain or prepare them.

Here are some likely sources for forms and instructions:

• local senior centers

• local hospitals (ask to speak with the patient representative; by law, any hospital that receives federal funds must provide patients with appropriate forms for directing health care)

• your regular physician

• your state's medical association

• Caring Connections lets you download free health care directives for your state at www.caringinfo.org/advancedirectives. You can also call the organization's HelpLine at 800-658-8898.

• *Quicken WillMaker Plus* software from Nolo walks you step by step through the process of writing your own health care directives. In addition, you can use the program to prepare a valid will, living trust, durable power of attorney for finances, and other important legal documents.

Make Your Documents Legal

There are a few requirements you must meet to make valid health care directives. In most states, you must be 18 years old, though a few states allow parents to make health care directives for their minor children. All states require that the person making a health care directive be able to understand what the document means, what it contains, and how it works.

Also, every state requires that you sign your documents. If you are physically unable to sign them yourself, you can direct another person to sign them for you.

You must sign your documents, or have them signed for you, in the presence of witnesses or a notary public—sometimes both, depending on your state's law. The purpose of this additional formality is to make sure that at least one other person can confirm that you were of sound mind and of legal age when you made the documents.

Durable Powers of Attorney for Finances

A durable power of attorney for finances is a simple, inexpensive, and reliable way to arrange for someone to make your financial decisions should you become unable to do so yourself. It's also a wonderful thing to do for your family members. If you do become incapacitated, the durable power of attorney will likely appear as a minor miracle to those close to you.

How does a durable power of attorney work?

When you create and sign a power of attorney, you give another person legal authority to act on your behalf. This person is called your attorney-in-fact or, sometimes, your agent. The word "attorney" here means anyone authorized to act on another's behalf; it's most definitely not restricted to lawyers.

A "durable" power of attorney stays valid even if you become unable to handle your own affairs (incapacitated). If you don't specify that you want your power of attorney to be durable, it will automatically end if you later become incapacitated.

When does a durable power of attorney take effect?

There are two kinds of durable powers of attorney for finances: those that take effect immediately and those that don't take effect unless and until a doctor (or two, in some states) declares that you can no longer manage your financial affairs. Which kind you should make depends, in part, on when you want your attorney-in-fact to start handling tasks for you.

If you want someone to take over some or all of your affairs now, you should make your document effective as soon as you sign it. Then, your attorney-in-fact can begin helping you with your financial tasks right away—and can continue to do so if you later become incapacitated.

On the other hand, you may feel strongly that your attorney-in-fact should not take over unless you are incapacitated. In this case, you have two options. If you trust your attorney-in-fact to act only when it's absolutely necessary, you can go ahead and make an immediately effective document. Legally, your attorney-in-fact will then have the authority to act on your behalf—but won't do so unless he or she ever decides that you can't handle your affairs yourself.

If you're uncomfortable giving your attorney-in-fact authority now, you can add language to your durable power of attorney to make what's known as a "springing" document. It won't take effect until at least one physician examines you and declares, in writing, that you can't manage your finances.

There are some real inconveniences involved in creating a springing power of attorney, however. First, the process of obtaining the doctors' statements can be time-consuming and complicated for your attorney-in-fact, and may delay the handling of your affairs. (You may even be required to prepare special release forms under a law called HIPAA, authorizing doctors to release information to your attorney-in-fact.) Second, some people may be reluctant to accept a springing power of attorney, even though your attorney-in-fact has obtained the required doctors' statements and your document is perfectly legal. A bank, for example, might question whether you have, in fact, become incapacitated. These hassles could further disrupt the handling of your finances. For these reasons, many experts recommend against making a springing document. If you truly trust your attorney-in-fact, it makes more sense to create a document that takes effect immediately, and then tell your attorney-in-fact when to actually step in.

How do I create a durable power of attorney for finances?

To create a legally valid durable power of attorney, all you need to do is properly complete and sign a fill-in-the-blanks form that's a few pages long. Some states have their own forms.

After you fill out the form, you must sign it in front of a notary public. In some states, witnesses must also watch you sign the document. If your attorney-in-fact will have authority to deal with your real estate, you must put a copy on file at the local land records office. (In just two states, North and South Carolina, you must record your power of attorney for it to be durable.)

Some banks, title companies, insurance companies, brokerage companies, and other financial institutions have their own durable power of attorney forms. If you want your attorney-in-fact to have an easy time with these institutions, you may need to prepare two (or more) durable powers of attorney: your own form and forms provided by the institutions with which you do business.

What happens if I don't have a durable power of attorney for finances?

If you become incapacitated and you haven't prepared a durable power of attorney for finances, a court proceeding is probably inescapable. Your spouse, closest relatives, or companion will have to ask a court for authority over at least some of your financial affairs.

If you are married, your spouse does have some authority over property you own together—to pay bills from a joint bank account, for example. There are limits, however, on your spouse's right to handle property owned by both of you. And, of course, your spouse has no authority over property you own alone.

If your relatives go to court to get someone appointed to manage your financial affairs, they must ask a judge to rule that you cannot take care of your own affairs—a public airing of a very private matter. And like any court proceeding, it can be expensive if your relatives must hire a lawyer. Depending on where you live, the person appointed may be called a conservator of the estate, guardian of the estate, committee, or curator. When this person is appointed, you lose the right to control your own money and property.

The appointment of a conservator is usually just the beginning of your family's days in court. Often the conservator must:

- post a bond—a kind of insurance policy that pays if the conservator steals or misuses property
- prepare (or hire a lawyer or accountant to prepare) detailed financial reports and periodically file them with the court, and
- get court approval for certain transactions, such as selling real estate or making slightly risky investments.

A conservatorship isn't necessarily permanent, but it may be ended only by the court. Conservatorships are discussed in more detail in the next set of questions.

I have a living trust. Do I still need a durable power of attorney for finances?

A revocable living trust can be useful if you become incapable of taking care of your financial affairs. That's because the person who will distribute trust property after your death (the successor trustee) can also, in most cases, take over management of the trust property if you become incapacitated.

Few people, however, transfer all their property to a living trust, and the successor trustee has no authority over property that the trust doesn't own. So a living trust isn't a complete substitute for a durable power of attorney for finances.

The Attorney-in-Fact's Duties

Commonly, people give an attorney-in-fact broad power over their finances. But you can give your attorney-in-fact as much or as little power as you wish. You may want to give your attorney-in-fact authority to do some or all of the following:

- use your assets to pay your everyday expenses and those of your family
- buy, sell, maintain, pay taxes on, and mortgage real estate and other property
- collect benefits from Social Security, Medicare, or other government programs or civil or military service
- invest your money in stocks, bonds, and mutual funds
- handle transactions with banks and other financial institutions
- buy and sell insurance policies and annuities for you
- file and pay your taxes
- operate your small business
- claim property you inherit or are otherwise entitled to
- transfer property into your living trust
- represent you in court or hire someone to represent you, and
- manage your retirement accounts.

Whatever powers you give the attorney-in-fact, the attorney-in-fact must act in your best interests, keep accurate records, keep your property separate from his or hers, and avoid conflicts of interest.

Can my attorney-in-fact make medical decisions on my behalf?

A durable power of attorney for finances does not give your attorney-in-fact legal authority to make medical decisions for you.

You can, however, prepare a durable power of attorney for health care, a document that lets you choose someone to make medical decisions on your behalf if you can't. In most states, you'll also want to write out your wishes in a living will, which tells your doctors your preferences about certain kinds of medical treatments if you can't communicate your wishes.

Health care documents are discussed in the previous section of this chapter.

When does the durable power of attorney end?

It ends at your death. That means that you can't give your attorney-in-fact authority to handle things after your death, such as paying your debts, making funeral or burial arrangements, or transferring your property to the people who inherit it. If you want your attorney-in-fact to have authority to wind up your affairs after your death, use a will to name that person as your executor.

Your durable power of attorney also ends if:

- **You revoke it.** As long as you are mentally competent, you can revoke a durable power of attorney at any time.

- **A court invalidates your document.** This happens rarely, but a court may declare your document invalid if it concludes that you were not mentally competent when you signed it, or that you were the victim of fraud or undue influence.

- **You get a divorce.** In a handful of states, including Alabama, California, Colorado,

Illinois, Indiana, Kansas, Minnesota, Missouri, Ohio, Pennsylvania, Texas, Washington, and Wisconsin, if your spouse is your attorney-in-fact and you divorce, your ex-spouse's authority is automatically terminated. In any state, however, it is wise to revoke your durable power of attorney after a divorce and make a new one.

- **No attorney-in-fact is available.** A durable power of attorney must end if there's no one to serve as attorney-in-fact. To avoid this problem, you can name an alternate attorney-in-fact in your document.

 More Information About Durable Powers of Attorney for Finances

Quicken WillMaker Plus (software from Nolo), walks you step by step through the process of writing your own durable power of attorney for finances. You can also use the program to prepare a valid will, living trust, health care directives, and other useful legal documents.

Conservatorships

A conservatorship is a legal arrangement that gives an adult the court-ordered authority and responsibility to manage another adult's financial affairs. Many states use the terms "conservator" and "guardian" interchangeably, or use other terms such as "custodian" or "curator." In this book, we use the term "guardian" for a person who makes personal decisions for a child or an incapacitated adult, and "conservator" for someone who takes care of financial matters for an incapacitated adult. The adult who needs help is called the "conservatee."

If you need information about guardianships for children, see Chapter 15.

When is a conservatorship necessary?

Conservatorships are permitted only for those who are so incapacitated that they cannot manage their own financial affairs. Generally, conservatorships are established for people who are in comas, suffer from advanced stages of Alzheimer's disease, or have other serious illnesses or injuries.

Conservatorships are rarely needed for people who have made—or can knowingly sign—financial documents, such as a durable power of attorney for finances. (See the previous set of questions.)

Adults May Need Guardians, Too

In addition to help with finances, an incapacitated adult may also need assistance with personal matters, such as medical decisions (if the adult has not prepared a health care directive) and decisions about where the adult will live and what his or her daily activities will be. If a court appoints someone to take care of these things, that person is usually called a "guardian" or "conservator of the person." The incapacitated adult is often called the "ward." An incapacitated adult may need a guardian, a conservator, or both. The same person can be appointed to take both jobs. As with conservators, guardians are supervised by, and held accountable to, a court.

What are the advantages of a conservatorship?

Conservatorships are subject to court supervision, which provides a powerful safeguard for an incapacitated adult's property. To prevent a conservator from mismanaging the property of the person he or she is helping (the conservatee), most courts require the conservator to provide periodic reports and accountings that give details about the conservatee's assets and how the conservatee's money was spent. Many courts also require the conservator to seek permission before making major decisions about the conservatee's property, such as whether to sell real estate.

What are the downsides to a conservatorship?

Conservatorships are time-consuming and expensive; they often require court hearings and the ongoing assistance of a lawyer. The paperwork can also be a hassle because, as mentioned above, the conservator must keep detailed records and file court papers on a regular basis.

In addition, a conservator must usually post a bond (a kind of insurance policy that protects the conservatee's estate from mishandling). The bond premiums are paid by the conservatee's estate—and are an unnecessary expense if the conservator is competent and trustworthy.

Occasionally, however, a conservator will mismanage a conservatee's assets. Common abuses range from reckless handling of the conservatee's assets to outright theft. Although each state has rules and procedures designed to prevent mishandling of assets, few have the resources to keep an eye on conservators and follow through if they spot trouble. Many cases of incompetence or abuse go unnoticed.

Finally, a conservatorship can be emotionally trying for the conservatee. All court proceedings and documents are public records, which can be embarrassing for someone who values independence and privacy.

How are conservators compensated for their services?

The conservatee's estate must reimburse the conservator for necessary expenses and must usually pay for the conservator's services—if these payments are "reasonable" in the eyes of a court. Generally, payments are made to professional or public conservators, but a family member who has been appointed conservator may also seek compensation by making a request to the court.

Are there ways to block a conservatorship?

Before a court approves a conservatorship, notice must be given to the proposed conservatee and his or her close family members. Anyone—including the proposed conservatee, family members, and friends—may object to the conservatorship in general, or to the specific choice of conservator. The person who wants to block the conservatorship must file papers with the court, inform all interested parties (the proposed conservatee, family members, and possibly close friends), and attend a legal hearing. The final decision is up to a judge.

The best way to avoid a conservatorship is to prepare a durable power of attorney for finances before a health crisis occurs. That way, someone you've handpicked will be able to step in and make decisions for you if necessary. (For information about preparing a durable power of attorney, see the previous set of questions.)

How does a judge choose a conservator?

When a conservatorship petition is filed in court, a judge must decide whom to appoint. Often, just one person is interested in taking on the role of conservator—but sometimes several family members or friends vie for the position. If no one suitable is available to serve as conservator, the judge may appoint a public or other professional conservator.

When appointing a conservator, a judge follows certain preferences established by state law. Most states give preference to the conservatee's spouse, adult children, adult siblings, or other blood relatives—and some states now give priority to a registered domestic partner. But a judge has the discretion to pick the person he or she thinks is best for the job. Without strong evidence of what the conservatee would have wanted, however, it is unlikely that a nonrelative would be appointed over a relative. Because of this, conservatorship proceedings may cause great heartache if an estranged relative is chosen as conservator over the conservatee's partner or close friend.

Who financially supports the conservatee?

If the conservatee has the means, money for support will come from his or her own assets. But a conservator should seek all financial benefits and coverage for which the conservatee may qualify. These benefits may include Social Security, medical insurance, Veterans Administration benefits, pension and retirement benefits, disability benefits, public assistance, and Supplemental Security Income. When needed, close family members (including the conservator) often contribute their own money to help support a conservatee.

When does a conservatorship end?

A conservator must care for the conservatee's finances until the court issues an order ending the arrangement. This ordinarily happens when:

- the conservatee dies
- the conservatorship estate is used up
- the conservatee regains the ability to handle financial matters, or
- the conservator becomes unable or unwilling to handle the responsibilities. In this situation, the conservatorship itself does not end, but someone else takes over the conservator's duties.

 Online Help

www.nolo.com

Nolo offers information on a wide variety of legal topics, including health care directives, powers of attorney, and conservatorships.

http://www.nhpco.org

The National Hospice and Palliative Care Organization provides extensive information on end-of-life health care options and choices. They also provide access to free health care directive forms.

www.pbs.org/wnet/onourownterms

On Our Own Terms is a website created in conjunction with a Bill Moyers public television documentary on end-of-life medical treatment. The site features interviews with professionals, patients, and loved ones—all of whom share insights and perspectives on making difficult health care choices.

www.hardchoices.com

This website offers a free downloadable book titled *Hard Choices for Loving People: CPR, Artificial Feeding, Comfort Care and the Patient With a Life-Threatening Illness*, by Hank Dunn (A & A Publishers). The book is a well-written resource that features a particularly good discussion of the issues surrounding artificial nutrition and hydration.

www.growthhouse.org

Growth House is a gateway to helpful resources and information on life-threatening illnesses and end-of-life care.

Older Americans

*To be seventy years young is sometimes far
more cheerful and hopeful than to be forty years old.*

—OLIVER WENDELL HOLMES, JR.

For many older Americans, the final years are no longer the Golden Years. Worries over limited incomes—and the real threat of being financially ruined by any extended bout with the medical system—crowd out thoughts of leisure and fulfillment.

There is help available for supplementing limited incomes and covering medical care in your later years, but you have to take some initiative to find it. The sooner you start planning, the better.

Retirement Plans

In the world of retirement planning, there are two broad categories of plans that are potentially available to you: individual plans and employer plans. There are only two types of individual plans: traditional individual retirement accounts (IRAs) and Roth individual retirement accounts (Roth IRAs). There are lots of types of employer plans, the most common of which are profit-sharing plans (including 401(k)s), SEPs, SIMPLEs, and defined-benefits plans—you can read more about each of these types of plans below.

Congress created these plans to provide an incentive for individuals to save for their own retirement—and to encourage employers to chip in as well. To make the pot as sweet as possible, both categories offer tax breaks to those who participate.

Of course, too much sugar can be bad for you, and Congress, ever mindful of our well-being, put some penalties in the mix as well. It wanted to make sure that people actually used the money for retirement (and not for, say, a trip to Maui). As a result, the rules can be strict about how much you can take out of the plans and when you can do it. These rules vary depending on the type of plan at issue, but one thing is always true: You should educate yourself about the dos and don'ts before taking money out of your plan. Otherwise, you could face stiff penalties and back taxes.

What is an individual retirement plan?

Individual retirement plans are accounts that you can set up for yourself, without any connection to your employer, using income you have earned. Regardless of where you work or whether you change jobs, the individual plan always belongs to you. And you can establish an individual plan even if your employer also provides a separate employer retirement plan for you. Think of it as your own personal retirement savings account, separate from anything your employer funds or makes available.

There are two types of individual plans: traditional IRAs and Roth IRAs. Traditional IRAs are available to everyone. In a traditional IRA, you can contribute a maximum of $4,000 for 2007, or $5,000 if you reach age 50 by the end of the year. These figures rise to $5,000 and $6,000 respectively, beginning in 2008. To make a contribution, you must have earned at least that much in taxable compensation during the year. The exact amount you are allowed to contribute will depend on whether you also contribute to a Roth IRA. (See below.) That money can then grow, sheltered in the account, temporarily free of taxes. If you meet certain income requirements, you can even get a tax break on the money you contribute. You don't have to worry about taxes again until you take the money out.

Roth IRAs are available only to people who meet certain income requirements. The contribution limits for Roth IRAs are the same as those described above for traditional IRAs. The money will grow tax free. The exact amount you can contribute will depend on whether you also contribute to a traditional IRA. (See below.) Although you will pay taxes on the money you contribute, you won't pay taxes on any of the growth, nor will you pay taxes on the money when you take it out of the account.

How can I establish an IRA for myself?

Opening an IRA—be it a traditional IRA or a Roth IRA—is no more complicated than opening an ordinary bank account. The first step is to find a financial institution (such as a bank or a brokerage firm) to hold the assets for you. Then contact the institution to request the necessary paperwork. Many institutions even allow you to download the paperwork online. The paperwork is very simple —usually one or two pages requesting basic information. Send the paperwork and a check for your contribution amount back to the institution. That's it. Depending on the institution you choose, you may have to take the additional step of selecting a mutual fund in which to invest your money.

What is an employer retirement plan?

An employer retirement plan is just what it sounds like: a plan set up by your employer to fund your retirement. Beyond that general similarity, however, employer plans can vary greatly. In some employer plans, the employer contributes all of the money and guarantees you a set amount of income during your retirement. On the other end of the spectrum, other types of plans might not require the employer to contribute anything—or even guarantee that there will be money in the plan when you need it.

There are many types of employer plans; two of the most common are defined-benefit plans and defined-contribution plans.

Defined-benefit plans promise a specific dollar amount to each participant beginning at retirement. The promised payment is usually based on a combination of factors, such as the employee's earnings and years of service to the company. Generally speaking, the employer is the one who contributes money to the plan. When people speak of "pensions," they are usually thinking of defined-benefit plans. These types of plans are becoming very rare indeed.

In a defined-contribution plan, there is no guarantee of money at retirement, and the employer does not bear the full burden of contributing to the plan. Rather, the employer establishes the framework of the plan so that you, the employee, can contribute some of your income to the plan. Sometimes, but not always, the employer contributes money to your account as well. Both you and the employer get tax breaks on whatever money you contribute, and the money grows in the plan tax deferred. That means you pay taxes on the money only when you withdraw it from the plan. The risk of defined-contribution plans is that they don't guarantee that there will be money in the account when you retire. If you manage the account well, and if luck is with you, your assets will grow in the account and be there when you retire. If you manage the account poorly, however, or if you have bad luck, you could end up with far less than you need—or nothing at all.

What is a 401(k) plan?

A 401(k) is the most common type of employer defined-contribution plan. The employer establishes the program in which employees can contribute a portion of their salary to the account. The employer can contribute money to the account as well, but it doesn't have to. The employees then direct the investment of the account funds into various investment vehicles (such as stock mutual funds, money market accounts, and bond funds) chosen by the employer. As with all defined-contribution plans, there is no guarantee that a participant will receive a particular amount of money at retirement. It all depends on how the investments do.

What is a Roth 401(k) plan?

A Roth 401(k) plan is an option that can be added to a traditional 401(k) plan; it cannot exist on its own. If your employer wants to establish a Roth 401(k) plan, it must establish a regular 401(k) plan and then add a provision to the plan documents that would establish a separate Roth 401(k) account. You could then contribute part of your salary to either the regular 401(k) plan or the Roth 401(k) plan—or perhaps split the contribution between the two accounts.

You may only deposit after-tax salary deferral contributions to the Roth 401(k) account. No employer contributions and no pretax employee contributions are permitted. Therefore, the entire account will contain only after-tax contributions from your salary plus pretax earnings on those contributions.

Because the Roth 401(k) is part of a regular 401(k) plan, most of the rules that apply to a regular 401(k) plan also apply to a Roth 401(k) plan. For example, the vesting rules and the contribution limits are the same. But there are significant differences in how the contributions will be taxed when they come out of the plan. Typically, you won't pay taxes on the Roth 401(k) money when you take it out of the account in retirement.

What are SEP and SIMPLE IRAs?

SEP and SIMPLE IRAs have misleading names. Even though they have "IRA" as part of their moniker, they really are employer plans, not individual plans. In other words, these plans can only be established by business entities, not individuals.

If I am self-employed, what kinds of retirement plans are available to me?

Self-employed people—like everyone else—can participate in individual plans (that is, a Roth IRA and a traditional IRA). They can also participate in special types of employer plans that are commonly called Keoghs.

Keoghs include most of the usual types of employer plans—such as 401(k) plans—but with rules designed specifically for businesses owned by self-employed individuals.

What does it mean to be vested in my retirement plan?

If you are vested in your company's retirement plan, you can take it with you when you leave your job. For example, if you are 50% vested, then you can take 50% of the account with you when you go.

In the case of a defined-contribution plan (such as a 401(k) plan), you are always 100% vested in the money that you have contributed to the plan. How vested you are in the money your employer has contributed, however, depends on the plan's terms. For example, the plan may allow you to vest over time—perhaps 50% for your first year of employment and 50% for your second.

Is my retirement plan protected from creditors?

Most employer plans are safe from creditors thanks to a federal law called the Employee Retirement Income Security Act (ERISA). This law requires all plans under its control to include provisions that prohibit the assignment of plan assets to a creditor. The U.S. Supreme Court has ruled that ERISA protects plans from creditors even when the plan participant is in bankruptcy.

Unfortunately, Keogh plans that cover only self-employed business owners (that is, plans that do not also cover employees) are not protected from creditors by ERISA. Neither are IRAs, whether traditional, Roth, SEP, or SIMPLE.

Even though IRAs are not protected by ERISA, many states have laws in place that protect them from creditors.

When can I start taking money out of my retirement plan?

When Congress created the various types of retirement plans, it intended for you to keep the money in the plan until you retired. And it also intended you to actually use the money during retirement, not to sock it away it to pass down to your children or grandchildren.

As a result, there are two broad sets of rules that govern taking money out of a retirement plan: One set requires you to start taking money out beginning at age 70½. The other set penalizes you if you try to take money out before you reach age 59½—unless your withdrawal meets one of the exceptions to the rule against early withdrawals (for example, to buy a new house).

If you take money out too early, or if you fail to take money out when the rules require you to, then you will have to pay a penalty and, depending on the circumstances, back taxes.

The details of the rules depend on what type of plan is at issue (for example, a 401(k), a SEP, or a traditional IRA) and the rules of your particular plan (for example, your company can make its own 401(k) more restrictive than the law requires).

If you have questions about taking money out of your retirement plan, ask your plan administrator.

 **More Information
About Retirement Plans**

IRAs, 401(k)s and Other Retirement Plans: Taking Your Money Out, also by Twila Slesnick and John Suttle (Nolo), explains the different types of retirement plans and the rules that apply when you want to withdraw funds.

The Essential Guide to Federal Employment Laws, by Amy DelPo and Lisa Guerin (Nolo), contains an entire chapter devoted to ERISA.

 Online Help

www.irs.gov
The IRS's website offers a number of helpful fact sheets and publications on retirement accounts, including Publication 590, *Individual Retirement Arrangements*.

www.morningstar.com
This investment site offers lots of information on planning for retirement and setting up and managing retirement accounts.

Social Security

Social Security is the general term for a number of related programs—retirement, disability, dependents, and survivors benefits. Together, these programs provide workers and their families with money when their normal flow of income shrinks because of retirement, disability, or death.

Unfortunately, the amount of money these programs provide rarely fills the gap. The combination of rising living costs, stagnating benefit amounts, and penalties for older people who continue to work, make the amount of support offered by Social Security less adequate with each passing year. This shrinking of the Social Security safety net makes it that much more important for you to learn how to get the maximum benefits to which you are entitled.

How much can I expect to get in Social Security benefits?

There is no easy answer to this question. The amount of benefits to which you are entitled under any Social Security program is based not on need but on how much income you earned during your years of working. In most jobs, both you and your employer must pay Social Security taxes on the amounts you earned. Since 1951, workers have also had to pay Social Security taxes on reported self-employment income. Social Security keeps a record of these earnings over your working lifetime and pays benefits based upon the average amount earned.

Who is eligible to collect benefits?

The specific requirements vary depending on the type of benefits, the age of the person filing the claim, and if you are claiming as a dependent or survivor, the age of the worker. However, there is one general requirement that everyone must meet: The worker on whose earnings record the benefit is to be paid must have worked in "covered employment" for a sufficient number of years—that is, earned what Social Security calls "work credits"—by the time he or she claims retirement benefits, becomes disabled, or dies. To find out about your eligibility, call the Social Security Administration (SSA), 800-772-1213, or visit its website at www.ssa.gov to request a Social Security Statement. (Click "Your Statement.")

Social Security Benefits: A Guide to the Basics

Four basic categories of Social Security benefits are paid based upon the record of your earnings: retirement, disability, dependents, and survivors benefits.

Retirement benefits. You may choose to begin receiving retirement benefits at any time after you reach age 62; the amount of benefits will increase for each year you wait until age 70. The increase in delayed benefits varies from 4% to 8%, depending on the year in which you were born. But no matter how long you wait to begin collecting benefits, the amount you receive will probably be only a small percentage of what you were earning.

Because so many variables are thrown into the mix in computing benefit amounts—some of them based on your individual work record and retirement plans, some of them based on changes and convolutions in Social Security rules—it is impossible to give you what you want most: a solid estimate of the amount that will appear on your retirement benefit check.

For a 65-year-old single person first claiming retirement benefits in 2007, the average monthly benefit is about $1,050. But these numbers are just averages. Benefits change yearly as the cost of living changes.

Disability benefits. If you are under 65 but have met the work requirements and are considered disabled under the program's medical guidelines, you can receive benefits roughly equal to what your retirement benefits would be.

Dependents' benefits. If you are the spouse of a retired or disabled worker who qualifies for retirement or disability benefits, you and your minor or disabled children may be entitled to benefits based on the worker's earning record. This is true whether or not you actually depend on your spouse for your support.

Survivors benefits. If you are the surviving spouse of a worker who qualified for retirement or disability benefits, you and your minor or disabled children may be entitled to benefits based on your deceased spouse's earnings record.

Special Social Security eligibility rules apply to some specific types of workers, including federal, state, and local government workers; workers for nonprofit organizations; members of the military; household workers; and farmworkers. If you have been employed for some time in one of these jobs, check with the SSA for more information.

How are my benefit amounts calculated?

The amount of any benefit is determined by a formula based on the average of your yearly reported earnings in covered employment since you began working. To further complicate matters, the SSA computes the average of earnings differently depending on your age. If you reached age 62 or became disabled on or before December 31, 1978, the computation is simple: Social Security averages the actual dollar value of your total past earnings and bases your monthly benefits on that amount.

If you turned 62 or became disabled on or after January 1, 1979, Social Security divides your earnings into two categories: earnings from before 1951 are credited with their actual dollar amount, up to a maximum of $3,000 per year; and from 1951 on, yearly limits are placed on earnings credits, no matter how much you actually earned in those years.

How can I find out what I've earned so far?

The SSA keeps a running computer tally of your earnings record and work credits, tracking both through your Social Security number. The SSA mails out copies of individual Social Security records on what is called a Social Security Statement. The statement is mailed to everyone age 40 and over (unless you're already receiving Social Security benefits).

If you are age 40 or over but have not received your statement, or you are under age 60 and want to check your statement now, you can request a copy by filing out a simple form, SSA 7004, called a *Request for Social Security Statement*. You can get this form at your local Social Security office or by calling 800-772-1213. You can also make your request online at www.ssa.gov. However, you will have to wait to receive your answer by mail.

Can I collect more than one type of benefit at a time?

No. Even if you technically qualify for more than one type of Social Security benefit, you can collect just one. For example, you might meet the requirements for both retirement and disability, or you might be eligible for benefits based on both your own retirement and that of your retired spouse. You may choose to collect whichever one of these benefits is higher, but you can't claim both.

Can I claim spousal benefits if I'm divorced?

You are eligible for dependents' benefits if both you and your former spouse have reached age 62, your marriage lasted at least ten years, and you have been divorced for at least two years. This two-year waiting period does not apply if your former spouse was already collecting retirement benefits before the divorce.

You can collect benefits as soon as your former spouse is eligible for retirement benefits. He or she does not actually have to be collecting those benefits for you to collect your dependent's benefits.

If You Find an Error

Some government watchers estimate that the SSA makes mistakes on at least 4% of the total official earnings records it keeps. It is always wise to check the SSA's work. Make sure that the Social Security Number noted on your earnings statement is your own. Also make sure the earned income amounts listed on the agency's records mesh with your own records of earnings as listed on your income tax forms or pay stubs.

If you have evidence that the SSA has made an error, call its helpline at 800-772-1213, Monday through Friday from 7 a.m. to 7 p.m. This line takes all kinds of Social Security questions and is often swamped, so be patient. It is best to call early in the morning or late in the afternoon, late in the week, or late in the month. Have all your documents on hand when you call.

If you would rather speak with someone in person, call your local Social Security office and make an appointment, or drop in during regular business hours. Bring two copies of your benefits statement and the evidence that supports your claim of higher income. That way, you can leave one copy with the Social Security worker. Write down the name of the person with whom you speak so that you can reach the same person when you follow up.

It may take several months to have the corrections made in your record. And once the SSA confirms that it has corrected your record, request another benefits statement to make sure the correct information is in your file.

If you are collecting dependent's benefits on your former spouse's work record and then marry someone else, you lose your right to those benefits. You may, however, be eligible to collect dependent's benefits based on your new spouse's work record. If you divorce again, you can return to collecting benefits on your first spouse's record, or on your second spouse's record if you were married for at least ten years the second time around.

Can I keep a job even after I start collecting retirement benefits?

Yes—and many people do just that. But if you plan to work after retirement, be aware that the money you earn may cause a reduction in the amount of your Social Security benefits. The amount of income you're allowed to earn without losing a portion of your benefits depends on your age and yearly changes in the amounts allowed.

If you are under full retirement age and you earn income over the year's limit, your Social Security retirement benefits are reduced by one dollar for every two dollars over the limit. In 2007, the limit on earned income was $12,960 per year.

How do I claim my Social Security benefits?

You can apply for benefits at your local Social Security office, by phone, or on the Internet at www.ssa.gov.

A Social Security worker in your local office is usually the best source of help for filing your claim. Find the office closest to you in your telephone directory under the listing for U.S. Government, Social Security Administration, or under U.S. Government, Department of Health and Human Services, Social Security Administration. Alternately, call the SSA at 800-772-1213, or go to www.ssa.gov.

If illness or disability prevents you from visiting your local office, call for accommodations. The most important thing is to act promptly and apply for the benefits to which you are entitled.

Social Security workers should also be able to answer general questions about benefits and rules over the phone—including what type of paperwork must be completed and what documentation is required to claim each kind of benefit.

Sign Up Three Months Before Your Birthday

If you need to receive benefit payments at the youngest eligibility age, file your claim three months before the birthday on which you will become eligible. This will give the SSA time to process your claim so that you will receive the benefits on time. If you file a claim later, you cannot get benefits retroactively for months during which you were eligible but before you applied.

Anyone who is eligible for Social Security benefits is also eligible for Medicare coverage at age 65. (For more information about Medicare, see the next series of questions.) Even if you are not going to claim Social Security benefits at age 65—because your benefit amount will be higher if you wait—you should sign up for Medicare coverage three months before your 65th birthday. There is no reason to delay signing up for Medicare, and waiting until after your 65th birthday will delay coverage.

What should I do if I feel I've been wrongly denied my benefits?

If your application for benefits is denied, don't despair. Many decisions are changed on appeal. For example, almost half of all disability appeals, which are by far the most common, are favorably changed during the appeal process.

There are four possible levels of appeal following any Social Security decision. The first is called reconsideration; it is an informal review that takes place in the local Social Security office where your claim was filed. The second level is a hearing before an administrative law judge; this is an independent review of what the local Social Security office decided, made by someone outside the local office. The third level is an appeal to the Social Security national appeals council in Washington, DC. And the final level is filing a lawsuit in federal court.

Appealing a Social Security claim need not be terribly difficult, as long as you properly organized and prepared your original claim. In many situations, the appeal is simply another opportunity to explain why you qualify for a benefit. In other cases, you'll need to present a few more pieces of information that better explain your situation. The key is to figure out why there was a misunderstanding or error, and put forth your most compelling evidence and arguments to overcome it.

Begin your appeal by completing a simple, one-page form you can get from the Social Security office or download at www.ssa.gov. It is called a *Request for Reconsideration* (SSA 561-U2). You'll be asked for basic information such as your name and Social Security number. Then you will need to state, very briefly, the reasons why you think you were unfairly denied benefits or were allotted lower benefits than you believe you earned.

When you submit your form, attach any other material you want the administrators to consider, such as recent medical records or a letter from a doctor or employer about your ability to work. You must send in the completed *Request for Reconsideration* within 60 days after you receive written notice that you were denied benefits.

More Information
About Social Security

Social Security, Medicare & Government Pensions, by Joseph Matthews with Dorothy Matthews Berman (Nolo), explains Social Security rules and offers strategies for dealing with the Social Security system.

The Social Security Administration, 800-772-1213, answers general questions about eligibility and applications over the phone. It also operates a helpful website at www.ssa.gov.

In every state, there is a department or commission on aging that gives information and provides advice about problems with Social Security claims. Check the phone book under Aging or Elderly for the service in your state.

Medicare

Give me health and a day and I will make the pomp of emperors ridiculous.

—RALPH WALDO EMERSON

Over the last several decades, Medicare has been carving an inroad into the mountain of consumer health care costs. At present, the Medicare system provides some coverage for almost 40 million people, most of them seniors. Medicare pays for most of the cost of hospitalization and much other medical care for older Americans—about half of all medical costs for people over 65.

Despite its broad coverage, Medicare does not pay for many types of medical services, and it pays only a portion of the costs of other services. To take maximum advantage of the benefits Medicare does provide, to protect yourself against the gaps in Medicare coverage, and to understand the current political debate about the program's future, you must become well informed about how the Medicare system works.

Medicare, Medicaid: What's the Difference?

People are sometimes confused about the differences between Medicare and Medicaid. Medicare was created to address the fact that older citizens have medical bills significantly higher than the rest of the population, while they have less opportunity to earn enough money to cover those bills. Eligibility for Medicare is not tied to individual need. Rather, it is an entitlement program; you are entitled to it because you or your spouse paid for it through Social Security taxes.

Medicaid, on the other hand, is a federal program for low-income people, set up by the federal government and administered differently in each state.

Although you may qualify and receive coverage from both Medicare and Medicaid, there are separate eligibility requirements for each program; being eligible for one program does not necessarily mean you are eligible for the other. If you qualify for both, Medicaid will pay for most Medicare Part A and B premiums, deductibles, and copayments.

Inpatient Care Covered by Medicare Part A

The following list gives you an idea of what Medicare Part A does, and does not, cover during your stay in a participating hospital or skilled-nursing facility. However, even when Part A pays for something, there are significant financial limitations on its coverage.

Medicare Part A hospital insurance covers:

- a semiprivate room (two to four beds per room); a private room if medically necessary
- all meals, including medically required diets
- regular nursing services
- special-care units, such as intensive care and coronary care
- drugs, medical supplies, and appliances furnished by the facility, such as casts, splints, or a wheelchair; also, outpatient drugs and medical supplies if they let you leave the hospital or facility sooner
- hospital lab tests, X-rays, and radiation treatment billed by the hospital
- operating and recovery room costs
- blood transfusions; you pay for the first three pints of blood, unless you arrange to have them replaced by an outside donation of blood to the hospital, and
- rehabilitation services, such as physical therapy, occupational therapy, and speech pathology provided while you are in the hospital or nursing facility.

Medicare Part A hospital insurance does not cover:

- personal convenience items such as television, radio, or telephone
- private-duty nurses, or
- a private room, unless medically necessary.

What is Medicare?

Medicare is a federal government program that helps older and some disabled people pay their medical bills. The program is divided into three parts: Part A, Part B, and Part D. Part A is called hospital insurance and covers most of the costs of a stay in the hospital, as well as some follow-up costs after time in the hospital. Part B, medical insurance, pays some of the cost of doctors and outpatient medical care. And Part D, prescription drug coverage, covers some of the cost of prescription medications taken at home.

Who is eligible for Medicare Part A coverage?

Most people age 65 and over receive free Medicare coverage, based on their work records or on their spouse's work records. However, people over 65 who are not eligible for free Medicare Part A coverage can enroll in it and pay a monthly fee for the same coverage—at least $206 per month according to current rules.

If you enroll in paid Part A hospital insurance, you must also enroll in Part B medical insurance, for which you pay an additional monthly premium.

How much of my bill will Medicare Part A pay?

All rules about how much Medicare Part A pays depend on how many days of inpatient care you have during what is called a "benefit period" or "spell of illness." The benefit period begins the day you enter the hospital or skilled-nursing facility as an inpatient and continues until you have been out for 60 consecutive days. If you are in and out of the hospital or nursing facility several times but have not stayed out completely for 60 consecutive days, all your inpatient bills for that time will be figured as part of the same benefit period.

Medicare Part A pays only certain amounts of a hospital bill for any one benefit period—and the rules are slightly different depending on whether you receive care in a hospital, psychiatric hospital, skilled-nursing facility, or at home or through a hospice. You must also pay an initial deductible—currently $992 per benefit period (2007)—before Medicare will pay anything.

What kinds of costs does Medicare Part B cover?

Part B is medical insurance. It is intended to help pay doctor bills for treatment in or out of the hospital. It also covers many other medical expenses when you are not in the hospital, such as medical equipment and tests.

The rules of eligibility for Part B medical insurance are much simpler than for Part A: If you are age 65 or over and are either a U.S. citizen or a U.S. lawful permanent resident who has been here for five consecutive years, you are eligible to enroll in Medicare Part B medical insurance. This is true whether or not you are eligible for Part A hospital insurance. You will have to pay a monthly premium—$93.50 in 2007. And a surcharge is added for people with high incomes. The amount of the surcharge depends on your adjusted gross income.

How much of my bill will Medicare Part B pay?

When all of your medical bills are added up, you will see that Medicare pays, on average, only about half the total. There are three major reasons why Part B medical insurance pays for so little.

First, Medicare does not cover a number of major medical expenses, such as routine physical examinations, medications, glasses, hearing aids, and dentures.

States With Limits on Billing

Several states—Connecticut, Massachusetts, Minnesota, New York, Ohio, Pennsylvania, Rhode Island, and Vermont—have passed balance billing or charge-limit laws. These laws forbid a doctor from billing patients for the balance of the bill above the amount Medicare approves. The patient is still responsible for the 20% of the approved charge not paid by Medicare Part B.

The specifics of these patient-protection laws vary from state to state: Some forbid balance billing to any Medicare patient, others apply the restriction only to patients with limited incomes or assets. To find out the rules in your state, contact the following agencies:

Connecticut Medicare Assignment Program: 800-443-9946; www.ctelderlaw.org

Massachusetts Executive Office of Elder Affairs: 800-882-2003; www.800ageinfo.com

Minnesota Board on Aging: 800-882-6262; www.mnaging.org

New York State Office for the Aging: 800-342-9871; http://aging.state.ny.us

Ohio Department of Aging: 800-266-4346; www.goldenbuckeye.com

Pennsylvania Department of Aging: 717-783-1550; www.aging.state.pa.us

Rhode Island Department of Elderly Affairs: 401-222-2858; www.dea.state.ri.us

Vermont Department of Disabilities, Aging, and Independent Living: 800-241-2400; www.dail.vermont.gov.

Second, Medicare pays only a portion of what it decides is the proper amount—called the approved charges—for medical services. When Medicare decides that a particular service is covered and determines the approved charges for it, Part B medical insurance usually pays only 80% of those approved charges; you are responsible for the remaining 20%.

However, there are now several types of treatments and medical providers for which Medicare Part B pays 100% of the approved charges rather than the usual 80%. These categories of care include: home health care, clinical laboratory services, and flu and pneumonia vaccines.

Finally, the approved amount may seem reasonable to Medicare, but it is often considerably less than what doctors actually charge. If your doctor or other medical provider does not accept assignment of the Medicare charges, you are personally responsible for paying the difference.

Services Covered by Medicare Part B

Part B medical insurance is intended to cover basic medical services provided by doctors, clinics, and laboratories. The lists of services specifically covered and not covered are long, and do not always make a lot of sense.

Part B insurance pays for:

- doctors' services (including surgery) provided at a hospital, doctor's office, or your home
- some screening tests, such as colorectal cancer screening, bone-density tests, mammograms, and Pap smears
- medical services provided by nurses, surgical assistants, or laboratory or X-ray technicians
- an annual flu shot
- a one-time physical (called a "wellness exam") done within six months after you enroll in Medicare Part B
- services provided by pathologists or radiologists while you're an inpatient at a hospital
- outpatient hospital treatment, such as emergency room or clinic charges, X-rays, tests, and injections
- an ambulance, if medically required for a trip to or from a hospital or skilled-nursing facility
- medicine administered to you at a hospital or doctor's office
- medical equipment and supplies, such as splints, casts, prosthetic devices, body braces, heart pacemakers, corrective lenses after a cataract operation, oxygen equipment, glucose-monitoring equipment and therapeutic shoes for diabetics, wheelchairs, and hospital beds
- some kinds of oral surgery
- some of the cost of outpatient physical and speech therapy
- manual manipulation of out-of-place vertebrae by a chiropractor
- part-time skilled nursing care, physical therapy, and speech therapy provided in your home
- Alzheimer's-related treatments
- limited counseling by a clinical psychologist or social worker or mental health day treatment
- limited services by podiatrists and optometrists, and
- scientifically proven obesity therapies and treatments.

What do I need to know about Medicare Part D?

In 2006, Medicare began covering some of the costs of prescription medications taken at home. Medicare Part D is administered through private insurance companies that offer Medicare-approved prescription drug plans. The Part D prescription drug program replaces drug coverage that was previously available through Medigap plans, most Medicaid coverage, and most managed care plans.

If you are entitled to Medicare Part A or enrolled in Medicare Part B, you may join a Part D prescription drug plan. Participation is voluntary, but if you delay signing up for a Part D plan, you will pay a penalty in the form of a larger premium for each month you were eligible to enroll but didn't.

How much will my prescriptions cost under a Medicare Part D plan?

Your cost for prescription drugs under a Part D plan can vary widely depending on a number of factors. The following figures are for 2007:

Premium. Monthly premiums vary depending on the plans available in your area and the particular plan you choose—premiums range from $0 to $50 per month.

Deductible. You pay the first $265 per year of the cost of your prescription medications. A few high-premium plans waive this deductible.

Copayment. Once your total annual drug expense reaches $265 (and before it reaches $2,400), you pay 25% of your drug costs as a copayment. Your copayment may be higher for brand-name drugs or less for generics, depending on your plan.

Coverage gap. Once your total drug expense reaches $2,400 (and before it reaches $5,451), you must pay the entire amount of your drug costs. Your plan generally pays no part of your prescription drug costs within this coverage gap, although a few high-premium plans may pay some portion of your costs.

Catastrophic coverage. If your total annual prescription drug cost exceeds $5,541, the plan will pay 95% of all further costs; you'll pay the remaining 5%.

Low-income subsidies. There are several categories of low-income subsidies available to help pay some or all of your Part D coverage. To find out if you qualify for a low-income subsidy, visit www.ssa.gov. (Click "Medicare Prescription Drug Plan" then click "Apply for help.")

How do I choose the right plan?

Not all plans are alike, and choosing the best plan for you involves several steps. Look carefully at the plans you are considering and choose a plan that covers most, if not all, of your regular medications. Consider your overall costs under each plan you're considering, including the amount you'll pay for premiums, deductibles, and copayments. And find out whether any plan you're considering offers coverage within the coverage gap.

Finding a Part D Plan

You may enroll only in a plan that operates in the state where you live. To find out about plans in your area, contact one of these agencies:

- The Centers for Medicare and Medicaid Services at 800-MEDICARE (800-633-4227) or at www.medicare.gov.

- The State Health Insurance Assistance Program (SHIP) in your state—sometimes called the Health Insurance Counseling and Advocacy Program (HICAP). For the nearest SHIP or HICAP office, check the business listings of your white pages phone directory.
- Your state department of insurance.

 More Information About Medicare

Social Security, Medicare & Government Pensions, by Joseph Matthews with Dorothy Matthews Berman (Nolo), explains Medicare rules and offers strategies for dealing with the Medicare system.

The Social Security Administration website, at www.socialsecurity.gov, provides a variety of informative publications. Also check out www. medicare.gov.

Finding a Caregiver or Residential Care Facility

As Americans live increasingly longer lives, many require ongoing, long-term care. Elders may need help with daily activities—grooming, bathing, preparing meals, or just getting around. Or, they may need full-time care in a residential treatment facility. Whether you are thinking about your own future or seeking care for a relative who needs help, you have many options to consider.

How do I choose between in-home care and a residential facility?

It may depend on the type of care that you or your loved one requires. Much of the care seniors need is not medical or nursing care, but help with day-to-day activities. These may include bathing, using the toilet, getting dressed, eating, getting in and out of bed or a chair, and walking around. For people with Alzheimer's disease or other cognitive impairment, home care may consist primarily of making sure that the person does not become lost, disoriented, or injured.

For this type of help, home care is often better than residential care. Home care is provided one-to-one, whereas residential facilities have staff-to-resident ratios of one-to-ten or more. And by choosing and monitoring a home care agency or individual home care providers, you may be better able to control the quality of care. On the other hand, tracking the effectiveness of home care is primarily up to the family, whereas residential facilities have professional staff members who are supposed to check regularly on the quality of nonmedical care provided.

Cost is another consideration in the type of care you choose. There is a significant range in nursing home costs, depending on location, size, and facilities. It is an expensive level of care: You can expect to pay an average of $50,000 annually for nursing home care (or $115 per day). Assisted living facilities range widely in cost, from $1,000 to $5,000 per month, depending on what level of care is needed. And nonmedical home care averages $20 per hour or, for 24-hour care, about $100 per day.

What types of in-home care are available?

Home care providers can help with of a variety of medical and personal needs, including:

- **Health care**—nursing, physical and other rehabilitative therapy, medicating, monitoring, and medical equipment
- **Personal care**—assistance with personal hygiene, dressing, getting in and out of a bed or chair, bathing, and exercise
- **Nutrition**—meal planning, cooking, meal delivery, or driving the senior to meals away from home
- **Homemaking**—housekeeping, shopping, home repair, and household paperwork
- **Social and safety needs**—escort and transportation services, companions, overall planning, and program coordination service.

If you're not sure whether a particular type of care can be safely and adequately delivered at home, consult a doctor that you trust.

How do I find a good in-home caregiver?

The best way to find a good caregiver is by referral. Ask your family physician about getting in-home help, or consult a public health nurse. These professionals should be able to put you in touch with reputable home-care services. And don't forget to ask family, friends, and neighbors for referrals.

Caregivers who provide medical care must be licensed or certified by your state's home care licensing agency. So when you need medical or nursing care—not just assistance with daily activities—you should seek help from certified agencies rather than independent caregivers.

If you need nonmedical care, you can hire an independent caregiver or an agency—your caregiver does not need to be licensed or certified to provide care. Because of this, it is very important to check references carefully and to find out what credentials a potential caregiver has. For example, ask whether the caregiver has had CPR and first aid training or any other health care training. Also, be sure to define the tasks that you need the caregiver to perform and make sure that he or she is willing and able to do them.

Finally, after you've hired a caregiver, be sure to have a backup plan in place just in case your caregiver gets sick or needs to take time off.

What types of care are available from residential care facilities?

If you need full-time assistance, a residential care facility may be the right choice. There are many levels of care available in long-term residential facilities. Care ranges from intensive 24-hour care for the seriously ill (called skilled nursing care) to long-term personal assistance and health monitoring with very little active nursing (often called custodial care). Some facilities provide only one level of care, while others provide several levels at the same location.

Skilled nursing facilities provide short-term, intensive medical care and monitoring for people recovering from acute illness or injury. Other facilities—called nursing homes, board and care homes, sheltered care homes, or something similar—provide custodial care, long-term room and board, and 24-hour assistance with personal care and other health care monitoring, but not intensive medical treatment or daily nursing.

For someone with severe physical or mental limitations, it is crucial to find a facility that provides the kind of attention and care that meets the individual's specific needs. For people who need little or no actual nursing care, the task is to find a facility that provides physical, mental, and social stimulation rather than merely bed and board.

Special Considerations for People with Alzheimer's

People with Alzheimer's disease have special needs when it comes to residential care:

- **Space.** Look for a facility that allows active residents to move about freely, while keeping the space safe.

- **Other residents.** Alzheimer's-only facilities often have educational programs, family counseling, and support groups that might not be available elsewhere. And the staff can organize meals, activities, and care solely with Alzheimer's residents in mind.

- **Staff.** Try visiting at different times of day, including meal times, to see how well the staff interacts with the residents. Is the staff calm and soothing, treating the residents with respect and acknowledging their comments and requests? Do the residents seem comfortable with the staff?

- **Special programs.** People with Alzheimer's can benefit from programs to help residents stay mentally alert, such as arts and crafts work, reading, word games, and outings. Find out what special programs are offered.

- **Medication and medical care.** Find out whether the facility is licensed to administer drugs by injection and deliver other types of medical care that a patient cannot self-administer. People with Alzheimer's may need regular medical attention so having a facility that can assist with medical care is important.

How do I find a good residential care facility?

We've all heard about poor facilities that provide substandard living conditions or even a dangerous lack of care. But there are also excellent long-term care facilities that provide high-quality care while assisting residents to maintain active lives with a full measure of dignity. Because there are many levels and types of nursing and personal care, your task is to find a good, affordable facility that provides the services you need.

As with finding an in-home caregiver, your best bet is to ask for referrals. Here are some good places to start:

- **Relatives, friends, and neighbors.** They may have had experience with a long-term care facility or know someone who has, and are often your best sources of information.

- **Hospital discharge planner.** The discharge planner may help if you or your loved one is going straight from a hospital to a long-term care facility.

- **Your doctor.** Ask your doctor about personal experience with any facilities in your area.

- **Organizations focusing on specific illness.** Check with organizations that focus on the illness or disability at issue, such as the American Heart Association, the American Cancer Society, the American Diabetes Association, or the Alzheimer's Disease Foundation.

- **National long-term care organizations.** A number of private organizations, such as the American Association of Homes for the Aging, specialize in long-term care and give referrals to local facilities.

- **Government agencies.** You can often get targeted referrals from the federal Area Agencies on Aging, or from state and local agencies found through Senior Referral and Information numbers in the white pages of the phone book or your local county social services or family services agency.

- **Church, ethnic, or fraternal organizations.** Ask about long-term care facilities that members have used successfully or that are operated by or affiliated with the church or organization.

Is financial assistance available to help pay for a caregiver or nursing home?

Under certain conditions, you may be able to get financial assistance to help pay for care.

Medicare. Medicare will pay some nursing home costs for Medicare beneficiaries who require skilled nursing or rehabilitation services. To be covered, you must receive the services from a Medicare certified skilled nursing home after a qualifying hospital stay (generally a stay of at least three days is required). To learn more about Medicare payment for skilled nursing home costs, visit www.medicare.gov or call 800-MEDICARE.

If a doctor prescribes medically necessary home health care for a homebound senior, Medicare will cover some of the costs if you use a Medicare-approved home health agency. Medicare will not, however, pay for a caregiver who provides nonmedical assistance.

Medicaid. Medicaid is a state and federal program that will pay most nursing home costs for people with very low income and few assets. Eligibility varies by state—check your state's requirements to find out whether you are eligible.

Medicaid will pay only for nursing home care provided in a facility certified by the government to provide service to Medicaid recipients. For more information about Medicaid payments, call your state's Medicaid office.

Other financial assistance. Here are some additional options for financial assistance:

- **Long-term care insurance.** The benefits and costs of these private insurance plans vary widely. For those who have this type of insurance, it may cover some costs of custodial care.

- **Medicare Supplemental Insurance.** This private insurance is often called Medigap because it helps pay for gaps in Medicare coverage such as deductibles and copayments. Most Medigap plans will help pay for skilled nursing care, but only when that care is covered by Medicare.

- **Managed care plans.** A managed care plan will not help pay for care unless the nursing home has a contract with the plan. If the home is approved by your plan, find out whether the plan also monitors the home for quality of nursing care.

- **Counseling and assistance.** The State Health Insurance Assistance Program (SHIP) in your state, sometimes called the Health Insurance Counseling and Advocacy Program (HICAP), provides counselors who can review your existing coverage and find any government programs that may help with your expenses. For the nearest SHIP or HICAP office, check the business listings of your white pages phone directory.

- **Help for veterans.** Some veterans may find coverage for custodial care through the Veterans Administration.

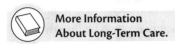

More Information About Long-Term Care.

Long-Term Care: How to Plan & Pay for It, by Joseph Matthews, helps you understand the alternatives to nursing facilities and shows you how to find the best care you can afford.

Online Help

www.nolo.com
Nolo offers information about a wide variety of legal topics, including issues affecting older Americans.

www.aarp.org
The American Association of Retired People offers helpful information on a range of issues for older people—including family, health, money matters, housing, and crime prevention.

www.aoa.dhhs.gov/elderpage.html
The Administration on Aging's ElderPage provides directories of resources that can help with aging issues—along with a host of articles covering topics such as retirement planning, housing alterations, and Medicare fraud.

www.pbgc.gov
The Pension Benefit Guaranty Corporation (PBGC) was established to protect pension benefits, primarily by giving financial assistance to some types of plans that have become insolvent. Its site provides information on pension rights and benefits, including what to expect if your pension plan changes hands and how to appeal an adverse pension decision.

Spouses and Partners

Love is love's reward.

—JOHN DRYDEN

We all know how the story goes: Boy meets girl, boy and girl fall in love, get married, and live happily ever after. Or, sometimes boy meets boy, or girl meets girl—and the fairy tale hopes remain largely unchanged.

What we often don't see are the details: Where do boy and girl get a marriage license, and do they need blood tests first? What should girl and girl do if they can't get married, but they want to buy a house together? And what if the fairy tale turns into a horror story, and one partner wants to end it?

Our intimate relationships aren't usually the stuff of childhood tales. There are a lot of real-world concerns—emotional and practical—that need attention every day. The questions and answers in this chapter will help you with some of the legal questions, tasks, and troubles that may surface during the course of your relationship. Keep in mind that laws in this area vary, sometimes dramatically, from state to state. We've put together an overview to get you started, but be certain to confirm your state's law before you act on any of the information given here.

Living Together— Gay or Straight

Many laws are designed to govern and protect the property ownership rights of married couples. In most states, no such laws exist for unmarried couples. If you and your partner are unmarried, you must take steps to protect your relationship and define your property rights. You will also face special concerns if you are raising children together.

When we refer to "unmarried" couples, we mean straight and gay couples who aren't married and same-sex couples who aren't in a registered domestic partnership or civil union. For those same-sex couples who are in a marriage-like relationship in one of the states that offer them, special rules apply. These are covered separately in *Domestic Partnership and Civil Unions,* below.

My partner and I don't own much property. Do we really need a written contract covering who owns what?

If you haven't been together long and don't own much, it's probably not necessary. But the longer you live together, the more important it is to prepare a written contract making it clear who owns what—especially if you begin to accumulate a lot of property. Otherwise, you might face a serious (and potentially expensive) battle if you split up and can't agree on how to divide what you've acquired. And when things are good, taking the time to draft a well-thought-out contract helps you clarify your intentions.

My partner makes a lot more money than I do. Should our property agreements cover who is entitled to her income and the items we purchase with it?

Absolutely. Although each person starts out owning all of his or her job-related income, many states allow couples to change this arrangement by an oral contract or even a contract implied from the circumstances of how you live. These oral or implied contracts often lead to misunderstandings during a breakup. For example, if you don't have a written agreement stating whether income will be shared or kept separate, one partner might falsely claim the other promised to split his income 50-50. Although this can be tough to prove in court, the very fact that the

partner can bring a lawsuit creates a huge problem. For obvious reasons, it's an especially good idea to make a written agreement if a person with a big income is living with and supporting someone with little or no income.

What is palimony?

"Palimony" is a word coined by journalists—not a legal concept—to describe the division of property or alimony-like support paid by one unmarried partner to the other after a breakup. Members of unmarried couples are not legally entitled to such payments unless they have an agreement. In the famous case of *Marvin v. Marvin,* the California Supreme Court ruled that a person who cohabitated and later sued for support could argue that an *implied* contract existed between the partners. To avoid a cry for palimony, it's best to have a written agreement about whether one person will make payments to the other if the relationship ends.

My partner and I have a young son, and I'm thinking of giving up my job to become a full-time parent. How might I be compensated for my loss of income?

This is mostly a personal—not a legal—question. If you and your partner decide that compensation is fair, there are many ways to arrange it. For example, you could make an agreement stating that if you break up while you're still providing child care, your partner will pay an agreed-upon amount to help you make the transition to a new situation. Or, you might agree in writing that your partner will pay you a salary during the time you stay at home, including Social Security and other legally required benefits.

Am I liable for the debts of my partner?

Not unless you have specifically taken on the responsibility to pay a particular debt—for example, you are a cosigner or the debt is charged to a joint account. By contrast, husbands and wives, and, in some cases, domestic partners, are generally liable for all debts incurred during marriage, even those incurred by the other person. The one exception for unmarried couples applies if you have registered as domestic partners in a location where the domestic partner law states that you agree to pay for each other's "basic living expenses" (food, shelter, and clothing). See *Domestic Partnership and Civil Unions*, below.

If one of us dies, how much property will the survivor inherit?

It depends on whether the deceased partner made a will or used another estate planning device such as a living trust or joint tenancy agreement to leave property to the surviving partner. In some states—California, Connecticut, Hawaii, Maine, New Hampshire, New Jersey, Oregon, Vermont, and Washington—registered domestic or civil union partners may automatically inherit a portion of a deceased partner's property, but some of these laws carry numerous restrictions and are by no means the safest or easiest way to plan for inheritances. The bottom line is simple: To protect a person you live with, you must specifically leave property to that person using a will, living trust, or other legal document.

Buying a House? Make an Agreement

It's particularly important to make a written property agreement if you buy a house together; the large financial and emotional commitments involved are good reasons to take extra care with your plans. Your contract should cover at least four major areas:

How is title (ownership) listed on the deed? One choice is as "joint tenants with rights of survivorship," meaning that when one of you dies, the other automatically inherits the whole house. Another option is as "tenants in common," meaning that when one of you dies, that person's share of the house goes to whomever the deceased partner named in a will or trust, or goes to blood relatives if the deceased partner left no estate plan.

How much of the house does each of you own? If it's not 50-50, can the person who owns less than half increase his or her share—for example, by working on the house or paying a larger share of the mortgage?

What happens to the house if you break up? Will one of you have the first right to stay in the house (perhaps to care for a young child) and buy the other out, or will the house be sold and the proceeds divided?

If one of you has a buyout right, how will the house be appraised, and how long will the buyout take? Often, couples agree to use the realtor they used to buy the house to appraise it, and then give the buying partner one to five years to pay off the other.

Parenting Concerns of Unmarried Couples

Unmarried couples face unique concerns when they raise children together.

- Straight couples who have children together should take steps to ensure that both are recognized as the legal parents. Both parents should be listed on the birth certificate, and the father should sign a statement of paternity. Even better, both parents should sign a statement of parentage acknowledging the father's paternity.

- All unmarried couples face potential obstacles when adopting together because all states favor married couples as adoptive parents. For more information about adoption by unmarried couples, see Chapter 15.

- Unmarried partners who have children from former marriages face potential prejudice if they are battling an ex-spouse for custody while living with a partner. In most states, this is a much greater concern for lesbian and gay parents than for straight ones, as judges (with the exception of a few states that come down hard on all unmarried couples) tend to be more tolerant of opposite-sex cohabitation than same-sex cohabitation. Many judges prefer to place children with a parent who is heterosexual and married, if that's an option.

If I am injured or incapacitated, can my partner make medical or financial decisions on my behalf?

Not unless you have executed a document called a "durable power of attorney" (sometimes included in a "Health Care Directive"), giving your partner the specific authority to make those decisions. Without a durable power of attorney, huge emotional and practical problems can result. For example, the fate of a severely ill or injured person could be in the hands of a biological relative who disapproves of the relationship and won't honor the wishes of the ill or injured person. It is far better to prepare the necessary paperwork so the loving and knowing partner will be the primary decision maker. For more information about durable powers of attorney, see Chapter 12.

If my partner and I live together long enough, won't we have a common law marriage?

Probably not. In a handful of states (listed below), heterosexual couples can become legally married without a license or ceremony. This type of marriage is called a common law marriage. Contrary to popular belief, a common law marriage is not created when two people simply live together for a certain number of years. In order to have a valid common law marriage, the couple must do all of the following:

- live together for a significant period of time (not defined in any state)

- hold themselves out as a "married couple"—typically this means using the same last name, referring to the other as "my husband" or "my wife," and filing a joint tax return, and

- intend to be married.

When a common law marriage exists, the spouses receive the same legal treatment given to formally married couples, including the requirement that they go through a legal divorce to end the marriage.

States That Recognize Common Law Marriage

Alabama	New Hampshire*
Colorado	Ohio (if created
District of Columbia	before 10/10/91)
Georgia (if created	Oklahoma
before 1/1/97)	Pennsylvania
Idaho (if created	Rhode Island
before 1/1/96)	South Carolina
Iowa	Texas
Kansas	Utah
Montana	

*For inheritance purposes only.

More Information About Living Together

Living Together: A Legal Guide for Unmarried Couples, by Ralph Warner, Toni Ihara, & Frederick Hertz (Nolo), explains the legal rules that apply to unmarried couples and includes sample contracts about jointly owned property.

A Legal Guide for Lesbian & Gay Couples, by Denis Clifford, Emily Doskow, and Frederick Hertz (Nolo), sets out the law and contains sample agreements for same-sex couples.

Do Your Own California Adoption: Nolo's Guide for Stepparents and Domestic Partners, by Frank Zagone and Emily Doskow (Nolo), leads you, step by step, through the adoption process in California.

Domestic Partnership and Civil Unions

A number of states now have laws creating marriage-like relationships for same-sex and/or unmarried heterosexual couples. Each of these states has different rules, and we can't set them all out in detail here, but this section will explain domestic partnership, reciprocal beneficiaries, and civil union relationships in general. You'll need to check with a lawyer in your state to learn more about how these laws might affect you.

What makes us domestic partners?

Many unmarried couples call themselves "domestic partners" because they live together in a committed relationship. It's a perfectly reasonable thing to do, but if you live in a state where a legal form of domestic partnership is available, just considering yourself domestic partners and referring to yourselves that way isn't enough to make you eligible for the benefits your state offers—you must register formally with the state for that.

Many employers offer domestic partnership benefits to their employees, meaning that the employees' domestic partners, whether registered or not, are treated like spouses for purposes of benefits such as health insurance and paid family leave. The employer can decide what the criteria are for being domestic partners. And, again, if you live in a state with domestic partner benefits, filling out a form with your employer to get health coverage for your partner doesn't mean you are registered with the state.

If your employer doesn't offer domestic partner coverage and you want to get involved in trying to establish a program at your workplace, check out the Alternatives to Marriage website at www.unmarried.org. You can also download a copy of *The Domestic Partnership Organizing Manual for Employee Benefits,* published by the Policy Institute of the National Gay and Lesbian Task Force, from the NGLTF website at www.thetaskforce.org/reports_and_research/dp_manual.

In California and Oregon, the term "domestic partnership" has a very specific legal meaning: Only couples who have registered with the state are domestic partners, and as a result they have a slew of rights and responsibilities that are almost identical to those that come with marriage. Maine and Washington also have state domestic partner registration, but with more limited rights, while Vermont, Connecticut, and New Jersey offer civil unions that confer the rights and responsibilities of marriage. New Hampshire has civil unions that confer fewer rights. Also, most of these states restrict who can register—for example, in California and Washington, only same-sex couples and heterosexual couples in which at least one partner is 62 or older are allowed to register as domestic partners.

Are domestic partnerships and civil unions the same as marriage?

These marriage-like relationships are very similar to marriage in some states, but with one very big difference. Although states might treat couples who register or enter into civil unions like married people for purposes of the laws of those states, the federal government won't recognize any same-sex relationships. (The federal Defense of Marriage Act, or DOMA, mandates this.) This means couples can't file joint tax returns,

apply for Social Security survivors' benefits if one partner dies, or rely on any of the many other federal laws that affect married couples.

If you are a same-sex couple living in one of the states where a marriage-like relationship is available to you, it's a good idea to do some research, consider the issue carefully, and even think about talking to a lawyer before you take the plunge into domestic partnership or a civil union.

If my boyfriend and I become domestic partners, am I responsible for his debts?

In most states, domestic partners aren't responsible for each other's debts (and aren't entitled to share in each other's income, either). But in California, Connecticut, New Hampshire, New Jersey, Oregon, and Vermont, where domestic partnerships or civil unions bring most of the same rights and responsibilities of marriage, it's a different story. Partners are responsible for all debts incurred during the partnership, even those that one person incurred without the other person's knowledge.

Premarital Agreements

Love reasons without reason.

—WILLIAM SHAKESPEARE

A premarital agreement is a written contract created by two people planning to be married—and now, that can include same-sex couples planning to marry in Massachusetts or enter into marriage-like relationships in states that offer registered domestic partnerships or civil unions.

The agreement typically lists all of the property each person owns, as well as their debts, and specifies what each person's property rights will be after they tie the knot. Premarital agreements often specify how property will be divided—and whether spousal support (alimony) will be paid—in the event of a divorce. In addition, an agreement may set out the couple's intentions about distributing property after one of them dies. (This is especially useful for second marriages, when one or both spouses wants to preserve property for children or grandchildren from a former union.) In some states, a premarital agreement is known as an "antenuptial agreement," or in slightly more modern terms, as a "prenuptial agreement" or "prenup."

Are premarital agreements legal?

As divorce and remarriage have become more prevalent, and with growing equality between the sexes, courts and legislatures are increasingly willing to uphold premarital agreements. Today, every state permits them, although a prenup that is judged unfair, that seems to encourage divorce, or that otherwise fails to meet state requirements will still be set aside. And courts won't uphold agreements of a nonmonetary nature. For example, you can agree on how you will divide your property if you divorce, but you can't sue your spouse for refusing to take out the garbage, even if your premarital agreement says that he or she must do so every Tuesday night.

Same-sex couples who are planning to marry in Massachusetts can make a prenup just like heterosexual couples do. And couples planning to enter into a registered domestic partnership or civil union can also make agreements that are the equivalent of prenups—sometimes called prepartnership agreements. These prepartnership agreements ordinarily must comply with all the same rules that apply to prenuptial agreements.

Should my fiancé and I make a premarital agreement?

Whether you should make a premarital agreement depends on your circumstances and on the two of you as individuals. Most premarital agreements are made by couples who want to circumvent the mandates of state law in the event of a divorce or at death. Often this happens when one partner has property that he or she wishes to keep if the marriage ends—for example, a considerable income or a family business. Perhaps most frequently, premarital agreements are made by individuals who have children or grandchildren from prior marriages. The premarital agreement allows the partner to ensure that the bulk of his or her property passes to the children or grandchildren rather than to the current spouse.

Are there rules about what can or cannot be included in a premarital agreement?

A law called the Uniform Premarital Agreement Act provides legal guidelines for people who wish to make agreements before they marry regarding the following: ownership, management, and control of property; property disposition on separation, divorce, and death; alimony; wills; and life insurance beneficiaries.

States that haven't adopted the Act (or that have adopted it with changes) have other laws, which often differ from the Act in minor ways. For example, a few states do not allow premarital agreements to modify or eliminate a spouse's right to receive court-ordered alimony at divorce.

In every state, whether covered by the Act or not, couples are prohibited from making binding provisions about child-support payments.

States That Have Adopted the Uniform Premarital Agreement Act*	
Arizona	Montana
Arkansas	Nebraska
California	Nevada
Connecticut	New Jersey
Delaware	New Mexico
District of Columbia	North Carolina
Hawaii	North Dakota
Idaho	Oregon
Illinois	Rhode Island
Indiana	South Dakota
Iowa	Texas
Kansas	Utah
Maine	Virginia

*Although Wisconsin is typically included in the list of states that have adopted the law, its law bears little resemblance to the Act.

Can my fiancé and I make our premarital agreement without a lawyer?

You and your fiancé can go a long way toward making your own agreement by evaluating your circumstances, agreeing on what you want your agreement to cover, and even writing a draft of the contract. But if you want to end up with a clear and binding premarital agreement, you'll eventually have to enlist a good lawyer to help you. In fact, you will need two lawyers—one for each of you. That may sound like surprising advice from advocates of self-help law, but it's true.

The laws governing marriage contracts vary widely from state to state. Unless you want to invest your time learning the ins and outs of your state's matrimonial laws, you'll want to find a lawyer who can help you put together an agreement that meets state requirements and says what you want it to say.

This explains the desirability of having one lawyer, but why two? Some courts closely scrutinize premarital agreements for fairness. If you want your agreement to pass muster, having an independent lawyer advise each of you will go a long way toward convincing a court that the agreement was negotiated fairly. While most courts don't require that each party to a premarital agreement have a lawyer, the absence of separate independent advice for each party is a red flag to courts.

Finally, on a practical note, having separate legal advisors can help you and your fiancé craft a balanced agreement that you both understand and that doesn't leave either of you feeling that you've been taken advantage of.

To start considering the issues, check out *Prenuptial Agreements: How to Make a Fair & Lasting Contract,* by Katherine E. Stoner and Shae Irving (Nolo). For domestic partners in California, there's also *Prenups for Partners: Essential Agreements for California Domestic Partners,* a Nolo eGuide by Katherine E. Stoner. These resources will help you figure out whether you need an agreement, take you through the steps of deciding what you might want in it, and help you figure out how to find and work with lawyers.

I've been living with someone for several years, and we've decided to get married. Will our existing property agreement be enforceable after we are married?

Probably not. To be enforceable, premarital contracts must be made in contemplation of marriage. This means that unless your living-together contract is made shortly before your marriage, when you both plan to be married, a court will disregard it. In your situation, it's best to review your contract and rewrite it as a premarital agreement.

Marriage

There is more of good nature than of good sense at the bottom of most marriages.

—HENRY DAVID THOREAU

Marriage is the legal union of two people. When you are married, your responsibilities and rights toward your spouse concerning property and support are defined by the laws of the state in which you live. The two of you may be able to modify the rules set up by your state, however, if you want to. See *Premarital Agreements,* above.

Your marriage can only be terminated by a court granting a divorce or an annulment.

What are the legal rights and benefits conferred by marriage?

Marriage brings with it many rights and benefits, including the rights to:

- file joint income tax returns with the IRS and state taxing authorities

- create a "family partnership" under federal tax laws, which allows you to divide business income among family members (this will often lower the total tax on the income)

- create a marital life estate trust (this type of trust is discussed in Chapter 11)

- receive spouse's and dependent's Social Security, disability, unemployment, veterans', pension, and public assistance benefits

- receive a share of your deceased spouse's estate under intestate succession laws

- claim an estate tax marital deduction

- sue a third person for wrongful death and loss of consortium

- sue a third person for offenses that interfere with the success of your marriage, such as alienation of affection and criminal conversation (these lawsuits are available in only a few states)

- receive family rates for insurance

- avoid the deportation of a noncitizen spouse

- enter hospital intensive care units, jails, and other places where visitors are restricted to immediate family

- live in neighborhoods zoned for "families only"

- make medical decisions about your spouse in the event of disability, and

- claim the marital communications privilege, which means a court can't force you to disclose what you and your spouse said to each other confidentially during your marriage.

Requirements for Marriage

You must meet certain requirements in order to marry. These vary slightly from state to state, but essentially require that you:

- are one man and one woman (except in Massachusetts, where same-sex couples can legally marry)
- are at least the age of consent (usually 18, though sometimes you may marry younger with your parents' consent)
- are not too closely related to your intended spouse
- have the mental capacity—that is, you understand what you are doing and the consequences your actions may have
- are sober at the time of the marriage
- are not married to anyone else
- get a blood test (in just a few states), and
- obtain a marriage license.

What's the difference between a "marriage license" and a "marriage certificate"?

The difference is as simple as "before" and "after." A marriage license is the piece of paper that authorizes you to get married. A marriage certificate is the document that proves you are married.

Typically, couples obtain a marriage license, have the wedding ceremony, and then have the person who performed the ceremony file a marriage certificate with the appropriate county office. (This may be the office of the county clerk, recorder, or registrar, depending on where you live.) The county will then send the married couple a certified copy of the marriage certificate within a few weeks after the ceremony.

Most states require both spouses, the person who officiated, and one or two witnesses to sign the marriage certificate; often this is done just after the ceremony.

Where can we get a marriage license?

You may apply for a marriage license from a city or county official—usually the county clerk or recorder, a district or probate court clerk, or a municipal or town clerk—in the state where you want to be married. (In some circumstances, you must apply in the county or town where you intend to be married—this depends on state law.) You'll have to pay a fee for your license (anywhere from $10 to $80), and you may also have to wait a few days before it is issued.

In some states, you'll have to wait a short period of time after you get your license—one to three days—before you tie the knot. In special circumstances, this waiting period can be waived. Licenses are good for 30 days to one year, depending on the state. If your license expires before you get married, you can apply for a new one.

For more specific information about marriage license laws in your state, check your state's website for vital statistics, or your city or county website.

Do all states require blood tests? And why are they required?

A handful of states still require blood tests for couples planning to marry, but most do not.

Premarital blood tests check both partners for venereal disease and women for rubella (measles). The tests may also disclose that someone carries a genetic disorder such as sickle cell anemia or Tay-Sachs disease. You will not be tested for HIV, but in some states the person who tests you will provide you with information about HIV and AIDS. In most states, the blood test may be waived for people over 50 and for other reasons, including pregnancy or sterility.

If either partner tests positive for a venereal disease, what happens depends on the state where you are marrying. Some states may refuse to issue you a marriage license. Other states may allow you to marry as long as you both know that the disease is present.

State Benefits for Same-Sex Couples

If you're a member of a same-sex couple living in one of these states, you can take advantage of laws that allow you to register your partnership and receive many of the benefits granted to married couples. (See *Domestic Partnership and Civil Unions*, above.)

California. To register a domestic partnership in California, visit the California Secretary of State website at www.ss.ca.gov. (Look under "Special Programs Information.") Or call 916-653-3984 for more information.

Connecticut. For information on civil unions in Connecticut, go to the Love Makes a Family website at www.lmfct.org.

Hawaii. To learn about registering your partnership in Hawaii (where it's called a "reciprocal beneficiary relationship"), visit the website of Hawaii's Vital Records office at state.hi.us/doh/records/rbrfaq.htm and click "Vital Records."

Maine. Forms to register as domestic partners are available online at www.maine.gov/dhhs/bohodr/domstprtnerspge.htm or at municipal offices, the Maine Department of Health and Human Services, or any probate court. The telephone number for the Bureau of Health, which administers the domestic partnership program, is 207-287-8016.

New Hampshire. You can learn more about civil unions in New Hampshire by visiting www.glaad.org.

New Jersey. For more information on civil unions and domestic partnerships in New Jersey, see the New Jersey Department of Health website at www.state.nj.us/health (click on the link "Vital Records") or call the domestic partnership hotline at 866-722-8218.

Oregon. A new domestic partnership law takes effect in Oregon on January 1, 2008. After that date, check the licensing page of the Oregon state website at www.licenseinfo.oregon.gov.

Vermont. To read the official guide to Vermont's civil union law, go to www.sec.state.vt.us and click on the link for "Civil Unions/Marriage." You can also call the Vermont Secretary of State office at 802-828-2363.

Washington. A new domestic partnership law took effect in Washington state on July 1, 2007. To learn more, go to the Secretary of State's website at www.secstate.wa.gov/corps/domesticpartnerships.

Who can perform a marriage ceremony?

Nonreligious ceremonies—called civil ceremonies—must be performed by a judge, justice of the peace, or court clerk who has legal authority to perform marriages, or by a person given temporary authority by a judge or court clerk to conduct a marriage ceremony. Religious ceremonies must be conducted by a clergy member—for example, a priest, minister, or rabbi. Native American weddings may be performed by a tribal chief or by another official, as designated by the tribe.

Are there requirements about what the ceremony must include?

Usually, no special words are required as long as the spouses acknowledge their intention to marry each other. Keeping that in mind, you can design whatever type of ceremony you desire.

It is customary to have witnesses to the marriage, although they are not required in all states.

What is a common law marriage?

In 15 states and the District of Columbia, heterosexual couples can become legally married if they:

- live together for a long period of time
- hold themselves out to others as husband and wife, and
- intend to be married.

These marriages are called common law marriages. Contrary to popular belief, two people who live together for a certain number of years do not have a common law marriage unless they intend to be married and act as if they are.

When a common law marriage exists, the spouses receive the same legal treatment given to formally married couples, including the requirement that they go through a legal divorce to end the marriage.

To find out whether your state recognizes common law marriages, see the list earlier in this chapter.

Does any state recognize same-sex marriage?

Massachusetts is currently the only state that recognizes same-sex marriages. Many states have passed laws specifically barring same-sex marriages, and the number of states with such laws is increasing.

Although the U.S. Constitution requires each state to give "full faith and credit" to the laws of other states—for example, by recognizing marriages and divorces across state lines—the federal Defense of Marriage Act (DOMA), passed in 1996, expressly undercuts the full faith and credit requirement in the case of same-sex marriages. Legal challenges to the DOMA nonrecognition rules and to the laws banning same-sex marriage in numerous states are pending. In particular, couples who are married in Massachusetts or who have entered into marriage-like relationships in other states (see above) are seeking federal recognition of their legal relationships. Make sure to keep up to date on same-sex marriage by checking the website of the Lambda Legal Defense and Education Fund's "Marriage Project" for the latest news: www.lambdalegal.org. Another good source of information is the National Center for Lesbian Rights website at www.nclrights.org.

Divorce

There is no disparity in marriage like unsuitablility of mind and purpose.

—CHARLES DICKENS

Divorce is the legal termination of a marriage. In some states, divorce is called dissolution or dissolution of marriage. A divorce usually includes division of marital property and, if necessary, arrangements for child custody and support. It leaves both people free to marry again.

How does an annulment differ from a divorce?

Like a divorce, an annulment is a court procedure that dissolves a marriage. But an annulment treats the marriage as though it never happened. For some people, divorce carries a stigma, and they would prefer their marriage be annulled. Others prefer an annulment because it may be easier to remarry in their church if their marriage ends by annulment rather than divorce.

Grounds for annulment vary slightly from state to state. Generally, an annulment may be obtained for one of the following reasons:

- **misrepresentation or fraud**—for example, a spouse lied about the capacity to have children, falsely stated that he or she had reached the age of consent, or failed to mention that he or she was still married to someone else

- **concealment**—for example, concealing an addiction to alcohol or drugs, conviction of a felony, children from a prior relationship, a sexually transmitted disease, or impotence

- **refusal or inability to consummate the marriage**—that is, refusal or inability to have sexual intercourse with one's spouse, or

- **misunderstanding**—for example, one person wanted children and the other did not.

These are the grounds for civil annulments. Within the Roman Catholic church, a couple may obtain a religious annulment after obtaining a civil divorce, in order for one or both spouses to remarry.

Most annulments take place after a marriage of a very short duration—a few weeks or months—so there are usually no assets or debts to divide or children for whom custody, visitation, and child support are a concern. When a long-term marriage is annulled, however, most states have provisions for dividing property and debts, as well as determining custody, visitation, child support, and alimony. Children of an annulled marriage are *not* considered illegitimate.

When are married people considered separated?

Many people are confused about what it means to be "separated"—and it's no wonder, given that there are four different kinds of separations:

Trial separation. When a couple lives apart for a test period, to decide whether or not to separate permanently, it's called a trial separation. Even if they don't get back together, the assets they accumulate and debts they incur during the trial period are usually considered jointly owned. A trial separation is a personal choice, not a legal status.

Living apart. Spouses who no longer reside in the same dwelling are said to be living apart. In some states, living apart without intending to reunite changes the spouses' property rights. For example, some states consider property accumulated and debts incurred from the time when a couple starts living apart until they divorce to be the separate property or debt of the person who accumulated or incurred it.

Permanent separation. When a couple decides to split up, it's often called a permanent separation. It may follow a trial separation, or may begin immediately when the couple starts living apart. In most states, all assets received and most debts incurred after permanent separation are the separate property or responsibility of the spouse incurring them. In some states, assets and debts are joint until divorce papers are filed, regardless of when you separate.

Legal separation. A legal separation results when parties live separately and a court rules on the division of property, alimony, child support, custody, and visitation—but does not grant a divorce. The money awarded for support of the spouse and children under these circumstances is often called separate maintenance (as opposed to alimony and child support).

What is a "no-fault" divorce?

"No-fault" divorce describes any divorce where the spouse suing for divorce does not have to prove that the other spouse did something wrong. All states allow divorces regardless of who is at "fault," but some states also allow parties to try to prove fault if they want to (see below).

To get a no-fault divorce, one spouse must simply state a reason recognized by the state. In most states, it's enough to declare that the couple cannot get along (this goes by such names as "incompatibility," "irreconcilable differences," or "irremediable breakdown of

the marriage"). In nearly a dozen states, however, the couple must live apart for a period of months or even years in order to obtain a no-fault divorce.

Is a no-fault divorce the only option even when there has been substantial wrongdoing?

In 17 states, yes. The other states allow a spouse to select either a no-fault divorce or a fault divorce. Why choose a fault divorce? Some people don't want to wait out the period of separation required by their state's law for a no-fault divorce. And in some states, a spouse who proves the other's fault may receive a greater share of the marital property or more alimony, or get custody of the children.

The traditional fault grounds are:
- cruelty (inflicting unnecessary emotional or physical pain)—this is the most frequently used ground
- adultery
- desertion for a specified length of time
- confinement in prison for a set number of years, and
- physical inability to engage in sexual intercourse, if it was not disclosed before marriage.

What happens in a fault divorce if both spouses are at fault?

Under a doctrine called "comparative rectitude," a court will grant the spouse who is least at fault a divorce when both parties have shown grounds for divorce. Years ago, when both parties were at fault, neither was entitled to a divorce. The absurdity of this result gave rise to the concept of comparative rectitude.

Grounds for Divorce				
State	Fault	No-fault (other than separation)	Separation	Length of separation
Alabama	x	x	x	2 years
Alaska	x	x		
Arizona		x		
Arkansas	x		x	18 months
California		x		
Colorado		x		
Connecticut	x	x	x	18 months
Delaware	x	x		
District of Columbia			x	6 months if both parties agree; otherwise 1 year
Florida		x		
Georgia	x	x		
Hawaii		x	x	6 months if both parties agree; otherwise 2 years
Idaho	x	x	x	5 years
Illinois	x	x	x	2 years
Indiana		x		
Iowa		x		
Kansas	x	x		
Kentucky		x		
Louisiana	x		x	180 days
Maine	x	x		
Maryland	x		x	12 months if both parties agree; otherwise 2 years
Massachusetts	x	x		
Michigan		x		
Minnesota		x		
Mississippi	x	x		
Missouri	x	x	x	12 months if both parties agree; otherwise 2 years
Montana		x	x	180 days
Nebraska		x		
Nevada		x	x	1 year
New Hampshire	x	x		
New Jersey	x		x	18 months
New Mexico	x	x		

State	Fault	No-fault (other than separation)	Separation	Length of separation
Grounds for Divorce (cont'd.)				
New York	x		x	1 year
North Carolina	x		x	1 year
North Dakota	x	x		
Ohio	x	x[1]	x	1 year
Oklahoma	x	x		
Oregon		x		
Pennsylvania	x	x	x	2 years
Rhode Island	x	x	x	3 years
South Carolina	x		x	1 year
South Dakota	x	x		
Tennessee	x	x	x	2 years
Texas	x	x	x	3 years
Utah	x	x	x	3 years
Vermont	x		x	6 months
Virginia	x		x	1 year[2]
Washington		x		
West Virginia	x	x	x	1 year
Wisconsin		x	x	1 year
Wyoming		x		

[1] No-fault divorce will be denied if one party contests ground of incompatibility.
[2] May be reduced to six months if there are no minor children.

Can a spouse successfully prevent a court from granting a divorce?

One spouse cannot stop a no-fault divorce. Objecting to the other spouse's request for divorce is itself an irreconcilable difference that would justify the divorce.

A spouse can prevent a fault divorce, however, by convincing the court that he or she is not at fault. In addition, several other defenses to a divorce may be possible:

• **Collusion.** If the only no-fault divorce available in a state requires that the couple separate for a long time and the couple doesn't want to wait, they might pretend that one of them was at fault in order to manufacture a ground for divorce. This is collusion because they are cooperating in order to mislead the judge. If, before the divorce, one spouse no longer wants a divorce, that spouse could raise the collusion as a defense.

- **Condonation.** Condonation is someone's approval of another's activities. For example, a wife who does not object to her husband's adultery may be said to condone it. If the wife sues her husband for divorce, claiming he has committed adultery, the husband may argue as a defense that she condoned his behavior.

- **Connivance.** Connivance is the setting up of a situation so that the other person commits a wrongdoing. For example, a wife who invites her husband's lover to the house and then leaves for the weekend may be said to have connived his adultery. If the wife sues her husband for divorce, claiming he has committed adultery, the husband may argue as a defense that she connived—that is, set up—his actions.

- **Provocation.** Provocation is the inciting of another to do a certain act. If a spouse suing for divorce claims that the other spouse abandoned her, her spouse might defend the suit on the ground that she provoked the abandonment.

Keep in mind that although these defenses exist, most courts will eventually grant the divorce. This is because of the strong public policy against forcing people to stay married against their will.

Do you have to live in a state to get a divorce there?

All states except Alaska, South Dakota, Washington, and (with a few exceptions) Massachusetts require a spouse to be a resident of the state for a certain length of time (six weeks to one year, depending on the state) before filing for a divorce there. Someone who files for divorce must offer proof of having lived in the state for the required length of time.

Can one spouse move to a different state or country to get a divorce?

If one spouse meets the residency requirement of a state or country, a divorce obtained there is valid even if the other spouse lives somewhere else. The courts of all states will recognize the divorce.

Any decisions the court makes regarding property division, alimony, custody, and child support, however, may not be valid unless the nonresident spouse consented to the jurisdiction of the court or later acts as if the foreign divorce was valid—for example, by paying court-ordered child support.

I'm a great housekeeper.
I get divorced. I keep the house.

—ZSA ZSA GABOR

How is property divided at divorce?

It is common for a divorcing couple to decide how to divide their property and debts themselves, rather than leave it to the judge. But if a couple cannot agree, they can submit their property dispute to the court, which will use state law to decide how to divide the property.

Division of property does not necessarily mean a physical division. Rather, the court awards each spouse a percentage of the total value of the property. Each spouse gets items whose value adds up to the percentage awarded.

Courts divide property under one of two schemes: equitable distribution or community property.

Durational Residency Requirements for Divorce

The durational residency requirement is the length of time a person filing for divorce must live in that state before he or she can file court papers. In most states, this means a period of continuous residence immediately prior to filing.

State	No Length of Residency Specified	6 Weeks	60 Days	3 Months or 90 Days	6 Months or 180 Days	12 Months or 1 Year
Alabama					x	
Alaska	x					
Arizona				x		
Arkansas			x			
California					x	
Colorado				x		
Connecticut						x
Delaware					x	
District of Columbia					x	
Florida					x	
Georgia					x	
Hawaii					x	
Idaho		x				
Illinois				x		
Indiana					x	
Iowa						x
Kansas			x			
Kentucky					x	
Louisiana					x	
Maine					x	
Maryland						x
Massachusetts	x[1]					x[1]
Michigan					x	
Minnesota					x	
Mississippi					x	
Missouri				x		
Montana				x		
Nebraska						x

[1] If cause for divorce occurred in Massachusetts, no residency requirement; if cause occurred out of state, the requirement is one year.

Durational Residency Requirements for Divorce (cont'd)						
State	No Length of Residency Specified	6 Weeks	60 Days	3 Months or 90 Days	6 Months or 180 Days	12 Months or 1 Year
Nevada		x				
New Hampshire						x
New Jersey						x[2]
New Mexico					x	
New York						x
North Carolina					x	
North Dakota					x	
Ohio					x	
Oklahoma					x	
Oregon					x	
Pennsylvania					x	
Rhode Island						x
South Carolina				x[3]		
South Dakota	x					
Tennessee					x	
Texas					x	
Utah				x		
Vermont					x	
Virginia					x	
Washington	x					
West Virginia						x[4]
Wisconsin					x	
Wyoming			x			

[2] Required for all grounds but adultery.

[3] If only one spouse is a resident of South Carolina, the requirement is one year.

[4] If marriage occurred in West Virginia, no length of time is required as long as one party is a state resident. If the marriage occurred out of state, one party must have lived in West Viriginia for a year prior to filing.

• **Equitable distribution.** Assets and earnings accumulated during marriage are divided equitably (fairly). Sometimes this means the assets are divided equally, but just as often it does not. In practice, often two-thirds of the assets go to the higher wage earner and one-third to the other spouse. Equitable distribution principles are followed everywhere except the community property states listed just below.

• **Community property.** In Arizona, California, Idaho, Louisiana, Nevada, New Mexico, Texas, Washington, and Wisconsin, all property of a married person is classified as either community property (owned equally by both spouses) or as the separate property of one spouse (property that is accumulated prior to the divorce or acquired by gift or inheritance). At divorce, community property is generally divided equally between the spouses, while each spouse keeps his or her separate property. In Alaska, couples can agree in writing to have their property treated as if they lived in a community property state.

Very generally, here are the rules for determining what's community property and what isn't:

Community property includes all earnings during marriage and everything acquired with those earnings. All debts incurred during marriage, unless the creditor was specifically looking to the separate property of one spouse for payment, are community property debts.

Separate property of one spouse includes gifts and inheritances given just to that spouse, personal injury awards received by that spouse, and the proceeds of a pension that vested (that is, the pensioner became legally entitled to receive it) before marriage. Property purchased with the separate funds of a spouse remain that spouse's separate property, though states differ on whether income from separate property (such as rent or dividends) is separate or community property.

A business owned by one spouse before the marriage remains his or her separate property during the marriage, although a portion of it may be considered community property if the business increased in value during the marriage or both spouses contributed to its worth.

Property purchased with a combination of separate and community funds is part community and part separate property, as long as a spouse is able to show that some separate funds were used. Separate property mixed together with community property generally becomes community property.

My spouse and I are thinking of using a divorce mediator. Is there anything we should know before we begin the process?

More and more couples are turning to mediation in order to negotiate divorce agreements. In a divorce mediation, the parties jointly hire a trained, neutral mediator—often a lawyer—to help them negotiate and reach a settlement. Mediation almost always takes less time, is less expensive, and results in a more solid agreement than using a lawyer to take the case to court. Of course, every divorcing spouse should know and understand his or her legal rights before agreeing to a settlement, even one reached through mediation. You might want to consult a lawyer or do some independent legal research early in the process and then have a lawyer review the agreement before signing. (See Chapter 16 for general information on mediation and Chapter 15 for more information on mediating disputes about child custody and visitation. And see *Divorce Without Court: A Guide to Mediation & Collaborative Divorce,* by Katherine E. Stoner (Nolo).)

I've heard some divorces take months or even years to become final. Is there a way I can get child support and access to the family's more reliable car during this time?

If you've already decided to divorce, and you have financial or child-rearing concerns, you may benefit from a *pendente lite* action, which literally means "pending the litigation." In a *pendente lite* procedure, a court may sign orders providing for temporary alimony, child support, and asset distribution if appropriate. A lawyer is usually involved because the paperwork can be complicated. A *pendente lite* order lasts until it is modified by the final divorce judgment. It can even set the tone for the final divorce order, if custody and money arrangements are functioning satisfactorily during the time the divorce is being settled.

More Information About Divorce

Nolo's Essential Guide to Divorce, by Emily Doskow (Nolo), is a thorough 50-state guide to the ins and outs of divorce.

How to Do Your Own Divorce in California, by Charles Sherman (Nolo Occidental), contains step-by-step instructions for obtaining a California divorce without a lawyer.

How to Do Your Own Divorce in Texas, by Charles Sherman (Nolo Occidental), contains step-by-step instructions for obtaining a Texas divorce without a lawyer.

Divorce Without Court: A Guide to Mediation & Collaborative Divorce, by Katherine E. Stoner (Nolo), provides divorcing couples with all the information they need to work with a neutral third party to resolve differences and find solutions.

Divorce & Money: How to Make the Best Financial Decisions During Divorce, by Violet Woodhouse with Dale Fetherling (Nolo), explains the financial aspects of divorce and property division.

Annulment: Your Chance to Remarry Within the Catholic Church, by Joseph P. Zwack (Harper & Row), explains how to get a religious annulment.

Domestic Violence

Domestic violence occurs more often than most of us realize. People who are abused range in age from children to the elderly, and come from all backgrounds and income levels. The majority of those subjected to domestic violence are women abused by men, but women also abuse other women, men abuse men, and women abuse men. If you're being hurt at home, the first thing to do is to get away from the abuser and go to a safe place where you're unlikely to be found. Then, find out about your options for getting help.

What kind of behavior is considered domestic violence?

Domestic violence can take a number of forms, including:

- physical behavior (slapping, punching, pulling hair, or shoving)
- forced or coerced sexual acts or behavior (unwanted fondling or intercourse, or sexual jokes and insults)
- threats of abuse (threatening to hit, harm, or use a weapon)
- psychological abuse (attacks on self-esteem, controlling or limiting another's behavior, repeated insults, or interrogation)

- stalking (following a person, appearing at a person's home or workplace, making repeated phone calls, or leaving written messages), or

- cyberstalking (repeated online action or email that causes substantial emotional distress).

Typically, many kinds of abuse go on at the same time in a household.

If I leave, how can I make sure the abuser won't come near me again?

The most powerful legal tool for stopping domestic violence is the temporary restraining order (TRO). A TRO is a decree issued by a court that requires the violent partner to leave you alone. The order may require, for example, that the perpetrator stay away from the family home, your work place or school, your children's school, and other places you frequent (such as a gym, friend's house, or church). The order will also prohibit further acts of violence.

Many states make it relatively easy for you to obtain a TRO. In New York, California, and some other states, for example, the court clerk will hand you a package of forms and will even assist you in filling them out. In other areas, nonlawyers may be available to help you complete the forms. When you've completed your forms, you'll go before a judge to show evidence of the abuse, such as hospital or police records or photographs. You can also bring in a witness, such as a friend or relative, to testify to the abuse. Judges are often available to issue TROs after normal business hours because violence can occur any time—not just during business hours.

Finding a Safe Place

Many communities have temporary homes called battered women's shelters where women and their children who are victims of domestic violence may stay until the crisis passes or until they are able to find a permanent place to relocate. The best way to find these shelters is to consult the local police, welfare department, neighborhood resource center, or women's center. You can also look in your phone book under Crisis Intervention Services, Human Service Organizations, Social Service Organizations, Family Services, Shelters, or Women's Organizations. In some states, the police are required to provide a battering victim with a list of referrals for emergency housing, legal services, and counseling services.

If you're having trouble finding resources in your area, you can contact the National Coalition Against Domestic Violence (NCADV), 303-839-1852, www.ncadv.org. NCADV provides information and referrals for abused women and their children, and they may know of assistance programs near you. Or you can contact the National Domestic Violence Hotline, 800-799-SAFE (7233), www.ndvh.org. You can also check out the website of the Women's Law Initiative, which provides state-by-state information and resources on domestic violence, at www.womenslaw.org.

In my community, judges don't issue TROs after 5 p.m. How can I get protection?

Contact your local police department. In many communities, the police can issue something called an emergency protective order when court is not in session. An emergency protective order usually lasts only for a brief period of time, such as a weekend or a holiday, but otherwise it is the same as a temporary restraining order. On the next business day, you will need to go to court to obtain a TRO.

Programs for Abusive Men

A number of programs have been established to help abusive men change their behavior. You can get more information from the following organizations:

Abusive Men Exploring New Directions (AMEND)

2727 Bryant Street, Suite 350

Denver, CO 80211

303-832-6363

www.amendinc.org

EMERGE: A Men's Counseling Service

2464 Massachusetts Ave., Suite 101

Cambridge, MA 02140

617-547-9879

www.emergedv.com

Are TROs and emergency protective orders only available when the abuser is a spouse?

No, in most states, the victim of an abusive live-in lover, even of the same sex, can obtain a TRO or emergency protective order. In a few states, the victim of any adult relative, an abusive lover (non-live-in), or even a roommate can obtain such an order. In some states, if victims and abusers do not live in the same household and are not lovers, the domestic violence laws do not apply. However, in this situation, other criminal laws—such as antistalking laws—may come into play. To learn about your state's rule, contact a local crisis intervention center, social service organization, or battered women's shelter.

Help for Abused Gay Men and Lesbians

The following organizations provide information and support for battered gay men and lesbians:

The National Domestic Violence Hotline, at 800-799-SAFE, is a national toll-free number that provides information to callers (gay and straight) about shelters and assistance programs in their area. You can also check out the hotline's website at www.ndvh.org.

The Lambda Gay & Lesbian Anti-Violence Project (AVP), has a website at www.lambda.org.

The New York City Gay & Lesbian Anti-Violence Project maintains a website at www.avp.org, and their 24-hour hotline number is 212-714-1141.

San Francisco's Community United Against Violence has a hotline at 415-333-HELP, and their website address is www.cuav.org.

Massachusetts residents can contact the Gay Men's Domestic Violence Project at 800-832-1901. Their website is located at www.gmdvp.org.

What should I do once I have a TRO?

Register it with the police in the communities where the abuser has been ordered to stay away from you—where you live, work, attend school or church, and where your children go to school. Call the appropriate police stations for information about how to register your order.

What if the abuse continues after I have a TRO?

Although TROs are often effective, a piece of paper obviously cannot stop an enraged spouse or lover from trying to harm or initimidate you.

If the violence continues, contact the police. They can take immediate action and are far more willing to intervene when you have a TRO than when you don't. Of course, if you don't have a TRO or if it has expired, you should also call the police—in all states, domestic violence is a crime whether or not you already have a TRO.

The police should respond to your call by sending out officers. In the past, police officers were reluctant to arrest abusers, but this has changed in many communities where victims' support groups have worked with police departments to increase the number of arrests. You can press criminal charges at the police department, and ask for criminal prosecution. Documentation is crucial if you want to go this route. Be sure to insist that the officer responding to your call makes an official report and takes photographs of your injuries, no matter how slight. Also, get the report's prospective number before the officer leaves the premises.

If you do press charges, keep in mind that only the district attorney decides whether or not to prosecute. If you don't press charges, however, the chance is extremely low that

the district attorney will pursue the matter. In some states, if the injury is severe, the prosecuter may decide to pursue the case and urge your cooperation.

Getting Legal Help

If you want to take legal action against your abuser or you need other legal help related to domestic abuse, the following organizations can refer you to assistance programs in your area:

The National Coalition Against Domestic Violence (NCADV), 303-839-1852, www.ncadv.org.

The National Domestic Violence Hotline, 800-799-SAFE (7233), 800-787-3224 (TTY) www.ndvh.org.

Changing Your Name

You may be thinking of changing your name for any number of reasons—perhaps you're getting married or divorced, or maybe you just want a name that suits you better. Whatever the reason, you'll be glad to know that name changes are common—and usually fairly easy to accomplish.

I'm a woman who is planning to be married soon. Do I have to take my husband's name?

No. When you marry, you are free to keep your own name, take your husband's name, or adopt a completely different name. Your husband can even adopt your name, if that's what you both prefer. Give some careful thought to what name feels best for you. You can save yourself considerable time and trouble by making sure you are happy with your choice of name before you change any records.

Can my husband and I both change our names—to a hyphenated version of our two names or to a brand-new name?

Yes. Some couples want to be known by a hyphenated combination of their last names, and some make up new names that combine elements of each. For example, Ellen Berman and Jack Gendler might become Ellen and Jack Berman-Gendler or, perhaps, Ellen and Jack Bergen. You can also pick a name that's entirely different from the names you have now, just because you like it better. But if you adopt an entirely new name, you'll have to follow the rules discussed below.

Changing Identification and Records

To complete your name change, you'll need to tell others about it. Contact the people and institutions you deal with and ask what type of documentation they require to make your name change official in their records. Different institutions have different rules. Most private institutions (such as banks and insurance companies) will simply require you to complete a form. Public agencies (like the department of motor vehicles) may require a copy of a court order.

It's best to start by getting a driver's license, then a Social Security card in your new name. Once you have those pieces of identification, it's usually fairly simple to acquire others or have records changed to reflect your new name.

Here are the people and institutions to notify of your name change:

- department of motor vehicles
- Social Security Administration
- department of records or vital statistics (issuers of birth certificates)
- banks, brokers, and other financial institutions
- creditors and debtors
- landlords or tenants
- telephone and utility companies
- state taxing authority
- insurance agencies
- friends and family
- employers
- schools
- post office
- registrar of voters
- real estate recorders' offices
- passport office
- public assistance (welfare) office, and
- Veterans Administration.

Many government agencies provide instructions on how to register a name change with the agency via their websites. (For information on how to find government websites, see the appendix.) For example, you can download the form for changing your name on your Social Security card at www.ssa.gov/online/ss-5.html.

What if I do want to take my husband's name? How do I make the change?

If you want to take your husband's name, simply start using the name as soon as you are married. Use your new name consistently, and be sure to change your name on all of your identification, accounts, and important documents (because this type of name change is so embedded in our culture, you generally won't need a court order). To change some of your identification papers—your Social Security card, for example—you'll simply need a certified copy of your marriage certificate, which you should receive within a few weeks after the marriage ceremony.

In many states, a wife may automatically take her new husband's name after marriage, but a husband must go to court for an official name change. And if you both want to change your names to an entirely new, shared last name, you'll have to go to court for that in most states, too.

For a list of people and institutions to contact about your name change, see "Changing Identification and Records," above.

I took my husband's name when I married but now we're getting divorced, and I'd like to return to my former name. How do I do that?

In most states, you can request that the judge handling your divorce make a formal order restoring your former or birth name. If your divorce decree contains such an order, that's all the paperwork you'll need. In some states, you can even have a completed divorce case reopened to provide for a name change. You'll probably want to get certified copies of the order as proof of the name change—check with the court clerk for details. Once you have the necessary documentation, you can use it to have your name changed on your identification and personal records.

If your divorce papers don't show your name change, you can usually still resume your former name without much fuss, especially if it's your birth name and you have a birth certificate to prove it. In many states, you can simply begin using your former name consistently and have it changed on all your personal records (see "Changing Identification and Records," above).

After my husband and I are divorced and I return to my former name, can I change the last name of my children as well?

Traditionally, courts ruled that a father had an automatic right to have his child keep his last name if he continued to actively perform his parental role. But this is no longer true. Now a child's name may be changed by court petition when it is in the best interest of the child to do so. However, it's not your decision alone, and if your ex-husband doesn't agree to the change, you'll have to ask a judge. When deciding to grant a name change, courts consider many factors, such as the length of time the father's name has been used, the strength of the mother-child relationship, and the child's need to identify with a new family unit (if the change involves remarriage). The courts must balance these factors against the strength and importance of the father-child relationship. What this all boils down to is that it's up to the judge to decide which name is in the child's best interest (although most judges won't change a child's name without a very good reason).

Keep in mind that even if you do change your children's last name, you won't be changing paternity—that is, the court's recognition of who is the children's father, and the rights and obligations that come with that recognition. Nor will a name change affect the rights or duties of either parent regarding visitation, child support, or rights of inheritance. Changes such as these occur only if the parental roles are altered by court order—for example, a new custody decree or a legal adoption.

I just don't like my birth name, and I want to change it. Can I choose any name I want?

There are some restrictions on what you may choose as your new name. Generally, the limits are as follows:

- You cannot choose a name with fraudulent intent—meaning you intend to do something illegal. For example, you cannot legally change your name to avoid paying debts, keep from getting sued, or get away with a crime.

- You cannot interfere with the rights of others, which generally means adopting a famous person's name in circumstances likely to create confusion.

- You cannot use a name that would be intentionally confusing. This might be a number or punctuation—for example, "10," "III," or "?".

- You cannot choose a name that is a racial slur.

- You cannot choose a name that could be considered a "fighting word," which includes threatening or obscene words, or words likely to incite violence.

That's "Mr. Three" to You

Minnesota's Supreme Court once ruled that a man who wanted to change his name to the number "1069" could not legally do so, but suggested that "Ten Sixty-Nine" might be acceptable.

Do I have to file forms in court to change my birth name?

Traditionally, most states allowed people to change their names by usage, without court proceedings. A name change by usage is accomplished by consistently using a new name in all aspects of your personal, social, and business life for a significant period of time. No court action is necessary, and it is free. (Minors and prison inmates generally aren't allowed to take advantage of this rule.)

Practically speaking, however, you will probably want to get an official court document changing your name. Especially in this day and age, with concerns about identity theft and national security, having a court order will make it much easier to get everyone to accept your new name. You won't be able to get certain types of identification—such as a new passport, birth certificate attachment, or (in most states) a driver's license—unless you have a court document, so, as a practical matter, a court-ordered name change is much more effective.

You can find out what your state requires by contacting your local clerk of court. Many state courts have name change forms on their websites. Go to the "Courts" or "Judiciary" section of your state's home page and look for "Forms." You can look at your state's statutes in a local law library—start in the index under "Name" or "Change of Name."

How do I implement my name change?

The most important part of accomplishing your name change is to let others know you've taken a new name. Although it may take a little time to contact government agencies and businesses, don't be intimidated by the task—it's a common procedure.

The practical steps of implementing a name change are:

- **Advise officials and businesses.** Contact the various government and business agencies with which you deal and have your name changed on their records. See "Changing Identification and Records," above.

- **Enlist help of family and friends.** Tell your friends and family that you've changed your name and you now want them to use only your new one. It may take those close to you a while to get used it. Some of them might even object to using the new name, perhaps fearing the person they know so well is becoming someone else. Be patient and persistent.

- **Use only your new name.** If you are employed or in school, go by your new name there. Introduce yourself to new acquaintances and business contacts with your new name.

If you've made a will or other estate planning document (such as a living trust), it's best to replace it with a new document using your new name. Your beneficiaries won't lose their inheritances if you don't, but changing the document now will avoid confusion later.

Finally, remember to change your name on other important legal papers. For example, if you've made a durable power of attorney for finances and health care directives in your old name, you should replace them. However, it is usually not necessary to rewrite a contract that you made in your former name—for instance, an agreement to provide or receive services from someone—because both sides are still bound by the agreement's terms. Simply inform the other party to the contract that, going forward, you'd like to conduct all dealings in your new name.

 More Information About Changing Your Name

How to Change Your Name in California, by Lisa Sedano and Emily Doskow (Nolo), provides complete information on changing your name in California.

Many state court websites provide name change forms. A good resource for links to state courts is the National Center for State Courts, at www.ncsc.org.

Local law libraries are good sources of information for name changes. Look under "Name" or "Change of Name" in the index of your state's statutes, or ask the reference librarian for help. You can also research state laws on the Internet. See the appendix for more about doing your own legal research.

Online Help

www.nolo.com
Nolo offers information about a wide variety
of legal topics, including relationships between
spouses and partners.

www.samesexlaw.com
Same Sex Law provides information affecting
lesbian and gay couples.

www.lectlaw.com
The 'Lectric Law Library's Lawcopedia on Family
Law offers articles and other information on a
wide variety of family law issues, including articles
about living together.

www.divorceonline.com
The American Divorce Information Network provides FAQs, articles, and information on a wide
range of divorce issues.

www.ncadv.org
The National Coalition Against Domestic Violence
offers help, information, and links for those affected by domestic violence.

Parents and Children

A child of five could understand this.
Fetch me a child of five.

—GROUCHO MARX

Raising children is a big job, and an emotional subject even when family relationships are well established and running smoothly. An adoption, divorce, or guardianship proceeding adds extra stress, requiring us to juggle law, finance, and our highly charged feelings. Be reassured, however, that there are many people who can help you find your way through family law proceedings, including knowledgeable lawyers, mediators, counselors, and therapists. In this chapter, we get you started by answering common questions about the laws that affect parents and their children.

Adopting a Child

Adoption is a court procedure by which an adult legally becomes the parent of someone who is not the adult's biological child. Adoption creates a parent-child relationship that is recognized for all purposes—including child-support obligations, inheritance rights, and custody. The birth parents' legal relationship to the child is terminated, unless a legal contract allows them to retain or share some rights or the adoption is a stepparent or domestic partner adoption, in which case only the parent without custody, if there is one, loses parental rights.

This section discusses the general legal procedures and issues involved in adopting a child, including the advantages and disadvantages of various types of adoption and some of the special concerns of single people or unmarried couples (gay and straight) who want to adopt a child. Stepparent adoptions and the rights of relatives are discussed later in this chapter.

Who can adopt a child?

As a general rule, any adult who is found to be a "fit parent" may adopt a child. Married or unmarried couples may adopt jointly, and unmarried people may adopt a child through a procedure known as a single-parent adoption.

Some states have special requirements for adoptive parents. A few of these require an adoptive parent to be a certain number of years older than the child. And some states require the adoptive parent to live in the state for a certain length of time before they are allowed to adopt. You will need to check the laws of your state to see whether any special requirements apply to you. And keep in mind that if you're adopting through an agency, you may have to meet strict agency requirements in addition to requirements under state law.

Even if you find no state or agency barriers to adopting a child, remember that some people or couples are likely to have a harder time adopting than others. A single man or a lesbian couple may not legally be prohibited from adopting—although in a few places these prohibitions do exist—but may have a harder time finding a placement than would a married couple.

I'm single, but I'd like to adopt a child. What special concerns will I face?

As a single person, you may have to wait longer to adopt a child, or be flexible about the child you adopt. Agencies often "reserve" healthy infants and younger children for two-parent families, putting single people at the bottom of their waiting lists. And birth parents themselves often want their children to be placed in a two-parent home.

If you're a single person wishing to adopt, you should be prepared to make a good case for your fitness as a parent. You can expect questions from case workers about why you haven't married, how you plan to support and care for the child on your own, what will happen if you do marry, and other questions that will put you

in the position of defending your status as a single person. To many single adoptive parents, such rigorous screening doesn't seem fair, but it is common.

Agencies serving children with special needs may be a good option for single people, as such agencies often cast a wider net when considering adoptive parents. Of course, you shouldn't take a special-needs child unless you feel truly comfortable with the idea of meeting that child's needs—but being flexible will make the obstacles to single-parent adoptions easier to overcome.

My long-term partner and I prefer not to get married, but we'd like to adopt a child together. Will we run into trouble?

There is no specific prohibition against unmarried opposite-sex couples adopting children—sometimes called two-parent adoptions. However, you may find that agencies are biased toward married couples. You may have a longer wait for a child, or you may want to consider adopting a child that is more difficult to place—an older or special-needs child, for example.

Is it still very difficult for lesbians and gay men to adopt children?

A few states have laws that prohibit open lesbians and gay men from adopting children, and Utah prohibits adoption by anyone "cohabitating" outside of marriage. But that doesn't mean it's easy to adopt in other states, and in the wake of the same-sex marriage debate, some states are considering new laws or regulations that limit the opportunities of same-sex couples who wish to adopt. Even if a state adoption statute does not specifically mention sexual orientation, a judge might find that a prospective adoptive parent is unfit just because of the person's sexual orientation. And before a case even gets to court, adoptive parents have to pass muster with a social services agency, which also might be biased against same-sex parents.

On the other hand, many individual gay men and lesbians have been able to adopt children, and an increasing number of states allow gay men and lesbians to adopt a partner's biological or legally adopted child.

There are still only a few states—California, New Jersey, New York, and the District of Columbia—whose courts have ruled that a gay couple may adopt a child together when neither is the child's biological or legal parent. But keep in mind that the legal landscape in all areas affecting gays and lesbians is changing rapidly. There have been successful challenges to laws and practices prohibiting gay and lesbian adoptions. Even in states that do not have favorable laws or decisions currently on the books, individual agencies, counties, and courts may allow adoptions.

One encouraging sign is the American Academy of Pediatrics' February 2002 report that supports second-parent adoptions by gay or lesbian parents. The Academy takes the position that children born to or adopted by gay or lesbian adults "deserve the security of two legally recognized parents." Lesbians and gay men will usually need an experienced attorney to handle an adoption. But you can do your own homework: The National Center for Lesbian Rights (address and phone number listed below) provides information for gay men and lesbians who want to adopt.

Same-Sex Partners and Adoption

Same-sex couples in some states are now subject to marital rules regarding parental rights and responsibilities. For example, California's domestic partnership law provides that a child born into a domestic partnership is the legal child of both partners (the rule doesn't apply to children adopted by only one partner). The same is true for children born to same-sex parents who are married in Massachusetts or legally partnered in Connecticut, Maine, New Jersey, Oregon, or Vermont. In theory, these new rules should make it unnecessary for a nonbiological parent to adopt a partner's biological child in these states. (And some courts have in fact given this recognition to second parents from Vermont.) However, legal experts say that it's possible—and, in this period of hostility toward same-sex families, even likely—that the relationship between the second parent and the child won't be recognized outside the home state. These experts recommend that second parents continue to complete adoptions even in states where marriage-like relationships are available.

In the states that offer marriage or marriage-like relationships, one partner may adopt the other partner's child using stepparent adoption procedures, which is a faster and less-expensive process than second-parent adoption. (See *Stepparent Adoptions*, below.) These partners must register with the state in order to be covered by marriage-equivalent laws.

For more about same-sex relationships and parenting, check out *The Legal Guide for Lesbian & Gay Couples*, by Denis Clifford, Frederick Hertz, and Emily Doskow (Nolo).

Can I adopt a child whose race or ethnic background is different from mine?

Usually, yes. You do not need to be of the same race as the child you want to adopt, although some states do give preference to prospective adoptive parents of the same race or ethnic background as the child. Adoptions of Native American children are governed by a federal law—the Indian Child Welfare Act— that outlines specific rules and procedures that must be followed when adopting a Native American child.

Whose consent is needed for an adoption to take place?

For any adoption to be legal, the birth parents must consent to the adoption, unless their parental rights have been legally terminated for some other reason, such as a finding that they are unfit parents. All states prohibit birth parents from giving their consent to an adoption until after the child's birth, and some states require even more time to pass—typically three to four days after the birth—before the parents are allowed to consent. Some states also allow the birth parents a period of time within which they can revoke their consent—in some cases, up to 30 days. This means that birth parents can legally change their minds about putting their child up for adoption at any point before (or shortly after) the child is born.

What are some of the advantages and disadvantages of an agency adoption?

Using an agency to manage your adoption can be helpful for a number of reasons. Agencies are experienced in finding children, matching them with parents, and satisfying the necessary legal requirements of the adoption. Agencies will do most of the legwork of an adoption, from finding a birth parent to finalizing the papers, and they'll walk adoptive parents through many of the crucial steps in between, such as conducting the home study, obtaining the necessary consents, and advising parents on the state's specific legal requirements.

One key advantage of an agency adoption is the extensive counseling that agencies provide throughout the process. Typically, counseling is available for adoptive parents, birth parents, and the children (if they are older). Careful counseling can help everyone involved weather the emotional, practical, and legal complexities that are likely to arise during the adoption.

Preadoption counseling for a birth mother can also help ensure that she is really committed to giving up her child for adoption and reduce the likelihood that she might change her mind at the last minute, leading to heartbreak for the potential adoptive parents.

Finally, many agencies specialize in certain kinds of children; this may be helpful if you want, for example, to adopt an infant, a child of a different race than yours, or a child with special medical needs. Some agencies also offer international adoption services.

On the down side, private agencies are often extremely selective when choosing adoptive parents. This is because they have a surplus of people who want to adopt and a limited number of available children. Most agencies have long waiting lists of prospective parents, especially for healthy, white infants. Agencies weed out parents using criteria such as age, marital status, income, health, religion, family size, personal history (including criminal records), and residency requirements.

Types of Adoption

Agency Adoptions. In an agency adoption, a child is placed with adoptive parents by a public agency, or by a private agency licensed and/or regulated by the state. Public agencies generally place children who have become wards of the state because they were orphaned, abandoned, or abused. Private agencies are often run by charities or social service organizations. Children placed through private agencies are usually brought to an agency by parents that have or are expecting a child that they want to give up for adoption.

Independent Adoptions. In an independent or private adoption, a child is placed with adoptive parents without the assistance of an agency. Some independent adoptions are arranged directly between the birth parents and the adoptive parents, while others are arranged through an intermediary such as a lawyer, adoption facilitator, doctor, or clergyperson. Whether or not an intermediary is used, a lawyer is essential because of the legal complexities involved. Most states allow independent adoptions, though many regulate them quite carefully. A few states will not allow adoptions arranged through an intermediary; others do not permit advertising in connection with independent adoptions; and many limit how much adoptive parents may pay a birth mother for maternity expenses.

Identified Adoptions. An identified, or designated, adoption is one in which the adopting parents locate a birth mother (or the other way around) and then ask an adoption agency to handle the rest of the adoption process. In this way, an identified adoption is a hybrid of an independent and an agency adoption. Prospective parents are spared the waiting lists of agencies by finding the birth parents themselves, but reap the other benefits of agencies, such as the agency's experience with legal issues and its counseling services. Identified adoptions provide an alternative to parents in states that ban independent adoptions.

International Adoptions. In an international adoption, the adoptive parents take responsibility for a child who is a citizen of a foreign country. In addition to satisfying the adoption requirements of both the foreign country and the parents' home state in the United States, the parents must obtain an immigrant visa for the child through U.S. Citizenship and Immigration Services (USCIS) and the State Department. The USCIS has its own rules for international adoptions, such as the requirement that the adoptive parents of orphans be either married or, if single, at least 25 years old. The USCIS also requires adoptive parents to complete several forms and submit a favorable home study report. You'll find more about international adoption below.

Second-Parent Adoptions. A second-parent adoption (sometimes called a coparent adoption) allows a lesbian or gay man to adopt a partner's biological or adopted child. Many lesbian couples do second-parent adoptions, where one partner has a child through donor insemination and the other partner adopts the child as a second parent. This type of adoption has been recognized in more than 20 states. However, some states—including Colorado, Nebraska, Ohio, and Wisconsin—have expressly disapproved of this type of adoption.

Types of Adoption (cont'd.)

Relative Adoptions. When a child is related to the adoptive parent by blood or marriage, the adoption is a relative adoption—also sometimes called a "kinship adoption." The most common example of this type of adoption is a stepparent adoption, in which a parent's new spouse adopts a child from a previous partner.

Grandparents often adopt their grandchildren if the parents die while the children are minors. These adoptions are usually simpler than nonrelative adoptions.

Stepparent Adoptions. See *Stepparent Adoptions,* below.

Additionally, agencies often wait to place the child in the adoptive home until all necessary consents have been given and become final. Because of this, a child may be placed in foster care for a few days or weeks, depending on the situation and the state's law. This delay concerns many adoptive parents who want the child to have a secure, stable home as soon as possible. Some agencies get around this by placing infants immediately through a type of adoption known as a "legal risk placement": If the birth mother decides she wants her child back before her rights have been legally terminated, the adoptive parents must let the child go.

Public agencies usually have many children ready to be adopted, but they often specialize in older or special-needs children. If you want a newborn, a public agency might not be able to help you. Also, public agencies may not provide many other services such as the much-needed counseling that private agencies offer.

How do I find an adoption agency?

There are an estimated 3,000 adoption agencies in the United States, public and private. If you live in a state like California or New York,

you'll have more options than if you live in a less populated state. But wherever you live, you'll probably have to do some searching to find an agency that meets your needs and is able to work with you. You can call or look online for a national adoption organization for referrals to get you started. The websites, addresses, and phone numbers of several organizations are listed at the end of this section.

Be persistent with the agencies you contact. If they tell you that there are no children, ask whether there is a waiting list. Then ask other questions, such as: Is the waiting list for child placement or a home study? How do you determine who may file an application? Can I fill out an application now? If not, when can I? Do you hold orientation meetings? If so, when will the next one be held? Ask whether you can speak with other parents in circumstances similar to yours who have adopted through the agency. These parents may provide valuable information about the service they received from the agency, how long the process took, and whether they were ultimately happy with the outcome. Screen the agencies as much as they screen you.

How can I check on the reputation of an adoption agency?

As discussed above, you can and should speak with other parents who have adopted through the agency. In addition, you should check out the agency's accreditation. Start with the licensing department of your state. It can tell you whether the agency has been cited for licensing violations, or whether the licensing office has received any complaints about the agency. You can also request a copy of the state's rules governing agencies so that you understand the standards to which your agency is held.

The staff at your state's department of social services may also be able to give you information about the agency. Finally, you can check your state or local department of consumer affairs to see if it handles complaints about adoption agencies.

Are agency adoptions very expensive?

They can be. Agencies charge fees to cover the birth mother's expenses as allowed by state law; these expenses may include medical costs, living expenses during the pregnancy, and costs of counseling. Add to this the agency's staff salaries and overhead, and charges can mount up quickly.

Many agencies charge a flat fee for adoptions, while others add the birth mother's expenses to a fixed rate for the agency's services. Some agencies use a sliding scale that varies with adoptive parents' income levels, usually with a set minimum and maximum fee. Most agencies charge a lower rate for handling special-needs adoptions.

Public agencies generally do not charge fees for placing children in adoptive homes.

You Can't Buy a Baby

It is illegal in all states to buy or sell a baby. All states, however, allow adoptive parents to pay certain "reasonable" costs that are specifically related to the adoption process. Each state has its own laws defining the expenses that may be paid by adoptive parents in any kind of adoption proceeding—agency or independent. If you pursue an independent adoption, you must adhere to these laws when you give any money to the birth mother. And agencies are regulated to make sure that they charge adoptive parents only for the costs that the state allows.

Most states allow the adoptive parents to pay the birth mother's medical expenses, counseling costs, and attorneys' fees. Some states allow payments to cover the birth mother's living expenses such as food, housing, and transportation during pregnancy. Most states require all payments to be itemized and approved by a court before the adoption is finalized. Be sure you know and understand your state's laws, because providing or accepting prohibited financial support may subject you to criminal charges. Furthermore, the adoption itself may be jeopardized if you make improper payments.

What are the costs involved in an independent adoption?

Because each situation is unique, fees for independent adoptions vary widely. Prospective parents must generally cover the costs of finding a birth mother, all costs related to the pregnancy and birth, and the legal costs involved in the adoption process. Some states also include the birth mother's living expenses during the pregnancy. Expenses such as hospital bills, travel costs, phone bills, home study fees, attorneys' fees, and court costs can sometimes exceed $20,000.

What should I keep in mind when deciding whether to pursue an independent adoption?

Birth and adoptive parents are sometimes attracted to independent adoptions because they allow control over the entire adoption process. Rather than relying on an agency as a go-between, the birth parent and adoptive parents can meet, get to know each other, and decide for themselves whether the adoption should take place. Independent adoptions also avoid the long waiting lists and restrictive qualifying criteria that are often involved in agency adoptions. Plus, independent adoptions usually happen much faster than agency adoptions, often within a year of beginning the search for a child.

One major drawback to independent adoptions is that they are heavily regulated in many states and illegal in a few. Some states that allow independent adoptions prohibit adoptive parents from advertising for birth mothers or intermediaries from advertising their adoption services. Be sure to check your state's laws before you proceed. Your state's website will have information on adoption laws and policies. Look for links to the state health and human services agency.

Another concern is that birth parents might not receive adequate counseling during the adoption process. This may leave your agreement more vulnerable to unraveling. Furthermore, some states extend the period in which birth parents may revoke their consent for independent adoptions; this places your agreement at additional risk.

Finally, independent adoptions are a lot of work. Adoptive parents often spend enormous amounts of time—and money—just finding a birth mother, not to mention the efforts required to follow through and bring the adoption to a close. Some parents decide afterwards that pursuing an independent adoption ate up too much time and money, and they hire an agency to do the work for their next adoption.

What's a home study?

All states require adoptive parents to undergo an investigation to make sure that they are fit to raise a child. Typically, the study is conducted by a state agency or a licensed social worker who examines the adoptive parents' home life and prepares a report that the court will review before allowing the adoption to take place. Some states do not require the agency to submit a report to the court. These states allow the agency or social worker to decide whether the prospective parents are fit to adopt. Common areas of inquiry include:

- financial stability
- marital stability
- lifestyles
- other children
- career obligations
- physical and mental health, and
- criminal history.

In recent years, the home-study process has become more than just a method of investigating prospective parents; it serves to educate and inform them as well. The social worker helps to prepare the adoptive parents by discussing issues such as how and when to talk with the child about being adopted, and how to deal with the reaction that friends and family might have to the adoption.

Open Adoptions

An open adoption is one in which there is some degree of contact between the birth parents and the adoptive parents both before and after the adoption. Often this includes contact between the birth parents and the child as well. There is no one standard for open adoptions; each family works out the arrangement that works best for them. Some adoptive parents consider meeting the birth parents just once before the birth of the child, while others form ongoing relationships that may include written correspondence or visits.

Open adoptions often help reduce stress and worry by eliminating the power of the unknown. Rather than fearing the day that a stranger will come knocking on their door to ask for the child back, adoptive parents are reassured by knowing the birth parents personally and dealing with them directly. This openness can be beneficial to the child as well, who will grow up with fewer questions—and misconceptions—than might a child of a "closed" adoption.

If you want your adoption to be open and decide to use an agency, be sure to find out their policies on open placements. Some agencies offer only closed or "semi-open" adoptions and will not provide identifying information about birth or adoptive parents even if both families want the adoption to be open. On the other hand, independent adoptions—where allowed—permit birth and adoptive families to determine what degree of contact is agreeable to all.

Can I adopt a child from another country?

If you're a U.S. citizen (or, in some cases, a green card holder), you can adopt a foreign child through an American agency that specializes in intercountry adoptions—or you can adopt directly (although this is much less common). If you prefer a direct adoption, you will have to adhere not only to the adoption laws of your state but also to U.S. immigration laws and the laws of the country where the child is born. It will be a complex process, so be prepared for some tangles. Do as much research as you can before you fly off to find a child; the more you know about the chosen country's adoption system ahead of time, the better off you'll be when you get there.

For practical reasons, most prospective parents focus on adopting an orphan. If you adopt a child who is not an orphan, the child must be under the age of 16 and must live in your legal custody for two years before you begin the child's immigration process. This means that you'd have to either live overseas for those two years or find a temporary visa that would allow the child to stay in the United States for two years—and there are no visas designated for this purpose. Because of these complexities, we'll limit the remainder of our discussion to orphan adoptions.

U.S. immigration laws require that prospective adoptive parents be married or, if single, at least 25 years old. And the country from which you're adopting probably has it's own requirements as well. If you've already identified the child you want to adopt, you must file a *Petition to Classify Orphan as an Immediate Relative*

(USCIS Form I-600) with the U.S. Citizenship and Immigration Services (USCIS). The form indicates that the child's parents have died, disappeared, or abandoned the child, or that one remaining parent is not able to care for the child and consents to the child's adoption and immigration to the United States. If there are two known parents, the child will not qualify as an orphan under any circumstances.

Along with the I-600, you will need to submit a number of other documents, including a favorable home study report. If the USCIS approves the petition, and there are no disqualifying factors such as a communicable disease, the child can be issued an immigrant visa.

Much of the paperwork for an intercountry adoption can be completed even if you haven't yet identified a specific child to adopt (you must use a different USCIS form, I-600A). Advance preparation is a valuable option because the USCIS paperwork often takes a long time to process and may hold up the child's arrival in the United States even after all foreign requirements have been met.

Finally, be sure to check your own state laws for any preadoption requirements. Some states, for instance, require you to submit the written consent of the birth mother before they approve the entry of the child into the state. Some experts recommend that parents who adopt overseas readopt the child in their own state in order to make sure that the adoption fully conforms to state law.

For more information about intercountry adoptions, see the resource list at the end of this section.

What should my adoption petition say?

A standard adoption petition will generally include five pieces of information:

1. the names, ages, and address of the adoptive parents

2. the relationship between the adoptive parents and the child to be adopted

3. the legal reason that the birth parents' rights are being terminated (usually that they consented to the termination)

4. a statement that the adoptive parents are appropriate people to adopt the child, and

5. a statement that the adoption is in the child's best interests.

Sometimes, the written consent of the birth parents or a court order terminating their parental rights is filed along with the petition. Other times, the termination occurs a bit later in the process. Adoptive parents also often include a request for an official name change for the child.

Do I need an attorney to handle the adoption of my child?

If you do not use an agency, yes. And even if you do use an agency, you will probably need to hire a lawyer to draft the adoption petition and to represent you at the hearing. Although there is no legal requirement that a lawyer be involved in an adoption, the process can be quite complex and should be handled by someone with experience and expertise. The exception is a stepparent adoption, which in most places is quite simple and which you might be able to handle yourself. See *Stepparent Adoptions*, below. When seeking a lawyer, find out how many adoptions the lawyer has handled, and whether any of them were contested or developed other complications.

When is an adoption considered final?

All adoptions—agency or independent—must be approved by a court. The adoptive parents must file a petition to finalize the adoption proceeding; there will also be an adoption hearing.

Before the hearing, anyone who is required to consent to the adoption must receive notice. Usually this includes the biological parents, the adoption agency, the child's legal representative if a court has appointed one, and the child if he or she is old enough (12 to 14 years in most states).

At the hearing, if the court determines that the adoption is in the child's best interest, the judge will issue an order approving and finalizing the adoption. This order, often called a final decree of adoption, legalizes the new parent-child relationship and usually changes the child's name to the name the adoptive parents have chosen.

Stepparent Adoptions

The majority of adoptions in the United States are stepparent adoptions, in which the biological child of one parent is formally adopted by that parent's new spouse. This type of adoption may occur when one biological parent has died or has left the family after a divorce, and the remaining parent remarries. While most stepparents do not formally adopt their stepchildren, those who do obtain the same parental rights as biological parents. This section discusses some of the issues that arise when a stepparent adopts a stepchild.

My new spouse wants to adopt my son from a previous marriage. Are there special adoption rules for stepparents?

Generally speaking, a stepparent adoption is much easier to complete than a nonrelative adoption. The procedure is generally the same as for any adoption, but specific steps are sometimes waived or streamlined. For instance, waiting periods, home studies, and even the adoption hearing are sometimes dispensed with in a stepparent adoption.

In all stepparent adoptions, however, the ex-spouse of the parent will need to consent to the adoption. If the parent's former spouse refuses to consent, the adoption will not be allowed unless the legal parent's parental rights are terminated for some other reason—abandonment or unfitness, for example.

My new husband has a great relationship with my ten-year-old son and wants to adopt him. My son communicates about once or twice a year with his birth father, who will consent to the adoption. Is adoption the right thing to do?

Stepparent adoptions can be complicated when the noncustodial biological parent is still alive and in contact with the child. There may be no legal reason why the adoption cannot take place, but the emotional impact of the adoption also should be considered.

If an adoption will bring stability to your new family and help your son feel more secure, it may be the right choice. But no matter how well your son gets along with your new husband, he may feel conflicting loyalties between his adoptive father and his birth father, and this may be hard for him to handle. Generally speaking, the less contact your son has with his birth father, the more sense it makes to go through with the adoption.

Besides the impact on the child (which should be of primary importance), also make sure your ex-husband understands that giving consent to the adoption means giving up all parental rights to his son, including any right to visit him or make decisions for him regarding issues such as medical treatment or education. In addition, he would no longer be responsible for child support once his parental rights were terminated.

Your new husband should be aware that if he adopts your son, and you and he divorce, he will be responsible for paying child support. Of course, he will also be entitled to visitation or custody.

I had my daughter when I was unmarried, and we haven't heard from her father for several years. I'm now married to another man, and he wants to adopt my daughter. Do I have to find her biological father and get his consent to the adoption before it can take place?

The adoption cannot take place until the absent parent either gives consent or has his parental rights terminated for some other reason. That being said, there are a few specific ways to proceed with an adoption when one biological parent is out of the picture.

First, it is possible to go forward without a biological parent's consent if you can prove that the absent parent has not exercised any parental rights and convince the court that it's appropri-ate to legally terminate that parent-child rela-tionship. Most states' laws allow parental rights to be terminated when a parent has willfully failed to support the child or has abandoned the child for a period of time, usually a year. Generally, abandonment means that the absent parent hasn't communicated with the child or supported the child financially.

If the absent parent is a father, another com-mon way to terminate his parental rights is to show that he is not, legally speaking, the presumed father of the child. Most states have statutes establishing who the presumed father of a child is in certain situations. In this case, you won't have to prove that the father has aban-doned the child. You simply must show that he does not meet the legal definition of presumed father. For instance, in all states, a man who is married to a woman at the time she gives birth is legally presumed to be the child's father. An-other way of establishing presumed fatherhood in many states is by marrying the mother after the child has been born and being named as the father on the child's birth certificate.

If you can show that the father doesn't meet any of the tests in your state for presumed fa-therhood, the court may terminate his rights and allow you to proceed without his consent. If, however, the father meets one of the state's tests for presumed fatherhood, you'll need either to obtain the father's consent to the adoption or have his rights terminated by proving abandon-ment, willful failure to support the child, or parental unfitness—or by giving him notice of the adoption proceeding and hoping he doesn't interfere or object. If he doesn't, you'll be able to complete the adoption.

Adoption Rights: Birth Parents, Grandparents, and Children

The rights of parents to raise and care for their children have traditionally received strong legal protection. Courts have long recognized that the bond between parents and children is a profound one, and the law will not interfere with that bond except in the most carefully defined circumstances. Adoption generally involves creating a parent-child relationship where there previously was none—and sometimes negating someone's parental rights in the process. Balancing the legal rights of the parties involved can sometimes be difficult. This section discusses how the legal rights of birth parents, grandparents, and children can be affected by the adoption process.

Are birth parents allowed to change their minds and take children back even after they've been placed in the adoptive parents' home?

Even after the birth parents have consented to an adoption and the child is living in the adoptive home, many states allow birth parents to change their minds for a set period of time. Depending on the state, the birth parents have the right to withdraw consent weeks or even months after the placement. Though it can be nervewracking—and sometimes devastating—for the adoptive parents who have begun to care for the child, it's important that they understand that birth parents have this right. Adoptive parents should find out how long their state allows for birth parents to legally withdraw consent.

The birth mother of the baby we were going to adopt just decided she wants to keep her child. She's eight months pregnant, and we've paid all of her medical bills during her pregnancy. Can we get our money back?

Unless the mother agrees to pay you back, you're probably out of luck. Especially with independent adoptions, paying a birth mother's allowable costs is a risk for adoptive parents. Birth parents often change their minds, and courts will not force them to pay back the expenses paid by the adoptive parents.

My girlfriend is pregnant and I'm the father. I want to keep the baby, but she wants to give it up for adoption. Can she do that?

No. If you acknowledge that you're the father of the child, your consent is needed before the baby can be adopted. The rights of fathers have gotten much more attention in recent years and are now more strongly protected by the law. However, fathers' rights vary greatly from state to state, and the law in this area is far from settled. If you don't want to see your baby adopted, you should be sure to acknowledge paternity and make it clear to the mother that you won't allow your parental rights to be terminated. You might even want to file a paternity action to establish your parental rights.

My husband and I found an expectant mother who wants us to adopt her baby. But her mother is trying to talk her out of giving up the child. Can a grandparent legally object to an adoption?

No. The parents of a birth mother don't have any legal right to stop her from giving up the baby. Also, grandparents won't necessarily be favored as adoptive parents over nonrelative parents. (One big exception to this rule is the adoption of Native American children, where a special federal law applies.)

That said, however, grandparents often hold a lot of sway over birth parents, and in many cases have convinced them at the last minute not to give up their babies. If you know that the grandparents are actively trying to talk the birth mother out of the adoption, you should consider that there's an increased risk that the adoption might fall through. In this situation, it's especially important to keep in close touch with the birth mother and make extra efforts to encourage open communication. You'll have to judge for yourself how confident you feel about proceeding with a birth mother whose family is opposed to the adoption.

I was adopted as a baby. Now I'm 25 and I want to find my birth parents. Do I have a legal right to obtain my birth records?

In most adoptions, the original birth records and other case documents are "sealed" by the court that finalizes the adoption, which means that no one can see them without the court's permission. But as attitudes toward adoption have become more open, states have come up with a variety of ways for adopted children to find their birth parents, some of which do not require the unsealing of records.

Only a few states offer adult adopted children open access to original birth certificates. More popular is a system called "search and consent," in which an adopted child has an agency contact the birth parent, who then either agrees to be identified or says no. If the birth parent consents, then the agency provides the information to the child. The most common system is a mutual consent registry, used in about

25 states, in which birth parents and adopted children provide identifying information about themselves to the registry. If a birth parent and that parent's adopted child both appear within a registry, the agency in charge of the registry will share the information with each of them, enabling them to contact each other.

If one of these options isn't available or doesn't work for you, it may be possible to obtain your birth records. Generally, a court will unseal a record for "good cause," such as a need for medical or genetic information.

The best way to start your search is to contact a local adoption agency that knows your state's laws and procedures for contacting birth parents. The National Adoption Information Clearinghouse and the North American Council on Adoptable Children are good sources for referrals to local agencies. (See "More Information About Adopting a Child," for contact information.)

Another useful tool in searching for birth parents is the Internet. Dozens of organizations and services designed to help adopted children find their birth families have cropped up on the Web, as well as individuals posting their own searches.

 More Information About Adopting a Child

The Adoption Resource Book, by Lois Gilman (HarperPerennial), is a comprehensive guide for anyone considering adoption.

The Child Welfare Information Gateway, www.childwelfare.gov/adoption/index.cfm. This website provides free information about adoption as well as referrals to local agencies and support groups.

A Legal Guide for Lesbian & Gay Couples, by Denis Clifford, Frederick Hertz, and Emily Doskow (Nolo). Contains a chapter that covers adoption, as well as other issues such as foster parenting and guardianships.

The National Center for Lesbian Rights, 870 Market Street, Suite 370, San Francisco, CA 94102, 415-392-6257, www.nclrights.org, provides help to gay men and lesbians who want to adopt.

The Independent Adoption Center, 800-877-6736, www.adoption help.org, is a national nonprofit organization that specializes in open adoptions.

The North American Council on Adoptable Children (NACAC), 970 Raymond Ave., Suite 106, St. Paul, MN 55114, 651-644-3036, www.nacac.org, can provide you with information about adoption resources in your local area.

Do Your Own California Adoption: Nolo's Guide for Stepparents and Domestic Partners, by Frank Zagone & Emily Doskow (Nolo), leads you, step by step, through the process of adopting your spouse's or partner's child.

The United States State Department, http://travel.state.gov/family/adoption/adoption_485.html and The United States Citizenship and Immigration Services, www.uscis.gov (click on "Services and Benefits") have all the information and forms you will need for an international adoption.

U.S. Immigration Made Easy, by Ilona Bray (Nolo), contains a chapter on international adoptions and citizenship for adopted children, including the necessary INS forms.

Child Custody and Visitation

You can't shake hands with a clenched fist.

—INDIRA GANDHI

When parents separate or divorce, the term "custody" serves as shorthand for "who lives with and cares for the children" under the divorce decree or judgment. In most states, custody is split into two types: physical custody and legal custody. Physical custody refers to the responsibility of actually taking care of the children day to day, while legal custody involves making decisions that affect their interests (such as medical, educational, and religious decisions). In states that don't distinguish between physical and legal custody, the term "custody" implies both types of responsibilities.

For information on how to find your state's custody law, see the appendix. Also, the Legal Information Institute, at www.law.cornell.edu/wex/index.php/child_custody, has an excellent summary of child custody laws, cases, and resources.

Does custody always go to just one parent?

No. Courts frequently award at least some aspects of custody to both parents. This is called joint custody, and it usually takes one of three forms:

- joint physical custody (children spend a relatively equal amount of time with each parent)

- joint legal custody (medical, educational, religious, and other decisions about the children are shared), or

- both joint legal and joint physical custody.

In every state, courts are willing to order joint legal custody, but about half the states are reluctant to order joint physical custody unless both parents agree to it and they appear to be sufficiently able to communicate and cooperate with each other to make it work. In some states, courts automatically award joint legal custody unless the children's best interests—or a parent's health or safety—would be compromised. Many other states expressly allow their courts to order joint custody even if one parent objects to such an arrangement.

Can someone other than the parents have physical or legal custody?

Sometimes neither parent can suitably assume custody of the children, perhaps because of substance abuse or a mental health problem. In these situations, others may be granted custody of the children or be given a temporary guardianship or foster care arrangement by a court.

What factors do courts take into account when deciding who gets custody of the children?

A court gives the "best interests of the child" the highest priority when deciding custody issues. What the best interests of a child are in a given situation depends upon many factors, including:

- the child's age, sex, and mental and physical health

- the mental and physical health of the parents

- the lifestyle and habits of the parents, including whether the child is exposed to secondhand smoke and whether there is any history of child abuse

- the love and emotional ties between the parent and the child, as well as the parent's ability to give the child guidance

- the parent's ability to provide the child with food, shelter, clothing, and medical care

- the child's established living pattern (school, home, community, religious institution)

- the quality of the available schools

- the child's preference, if the child is old enough to weigh the alternatives (children are usually consulted once they reach the age of 12 or so), and

- the ability and willingness of the parent to foster healthy communication and contact between the child and the other parent.

Assuming that none of these factors clearly favors one parent over the other, most courts tend to focus on which parent is likely to provide the children a more stable environment. With younger children, this may mean awarding custody to the parent who has been the child's primary caregiver. With older children, this may mean giving custody to the parent who is best able to foster continuity in education, neighborhood life, religious institutions, and peer relationships.

Are mothers more likely to be awarded custody over fathers?

In the past, most states provided that custody of children of "tender years" (age five and under) had to be awarded to the mother when parents divorced. This rule is now rejected in most states, or relegated to the role of tie-breaker if two fit parents request custody of their preschool children. Most states require their courts to determine custody based only on the children's best interests, without regard to the sex of the parent.

As it turns out, many divorcing parents agree that the mother will have custody after a separation or divorce, and that the father will exercise reasonable visitation.

Are there special issues if a gay or lesbian parent is seeking custody or visitation rights?

Only the District of Columbia has a law on its books stating that a parent's sexual orientation cannot be the sole factor in making a custody or visitation award. In a few states—including Alaska, California, New Mexico, and Pennsylvania—courts have ruled that a parent's homosexuality, in and of itself, cannot be grounds for an automatic denial of custody or visitation rights. In many other states, courts have ruled that judges can deny custody or visitation because of a parent's sexual orientation only if they find that the parent's sexual orientation would harm the child.

In reality, however, a lesbian or gay parent faces a difficult struggle when trying to gain custody in many courtrooms, especially if that parent lives with a partner. Many judges are ignorant about, prejudiced against, or suspicious of gay and lesbian parents. Few judges understand that a parent's sexual orientation, alone, does not affect the best interests of the children.

My partner and I broke up after eight years. During that time I was artificially inseminated, and we raised the child together. Now she wants visitation. Is that possible even if she isn't related by blood to my child and hasn't adopted the child?

The courts are all over the map on this question. In some states, courts have held that a nonbiological parent who has established a psychological parent-child relationship with a partner's biological child is entitled to visitation and, in some cases, to legal status as a parent. In other places, courts have shut out nonbiological parents entirely based on the absence of a genetic or legal relationship between the nonbiological parent and child. The law is certainly not settled, and the best course of action is usually to try to mediate an agreement rather than going to court and fighting over kids you have raised together. There's more about mediation in Chapter 16.

Is race ever an issue in custody or visitation decisions?

The U.S. Supreme Court has ruled it unconstitutional for a court to consider race when a noncustodial parent petitions for a change of custody. In that case, a white couple had divorced, and the mother had been awarded custody of their son. She remarried an African-American man and moved to a predominantly African-American neighborhood. The father filed a request for modification of custody based on the changed circumstances. A Florida court granted the modification, but the U.S.

Supreme Court reversed, ruling that societal stigma, especially one based on race, cannot be the basis for a custody decision. (*Palmore v. Sidoti*, 466 U.S. 429 (1984)).

When a court awards physical custody to one parent and "visitation at reasonable times and places" to the other, who determines what's reasonable?

The parent with physical custody is generally in the driver's seat regarding what is reasonable. This need not be bad if the parents cooperate to see that the kids spend a maximum amount of time with each parent. Unfortunately, it all too often translates into very little visitation time with the noncustodial parent, and lots of bitter disputes over missed visits and inconvenience. To avoid such problems, many courts now prefer for the parties to work out a fairly detailed parenting agreement that sets the visitation schedule and outlines who has responsibility for decisions affecting the children.

The judge in my divorce case has mentioned a parenting agreement. What is that?

A parenting agreement is a detailed, written agreement between divorcing parents that describes how they will deal with visitation, holiday schedules, vacation, religion, education, and other issues related to their child. More and more, courts are encouraging the use of parenting agreements during divorce proceedings. If couples discuss and agree upon how to deal with issues affecting their children—rather than having the judge make an independent ruling on those issues—they are more likely to stick to the terms of the agreement.

I have sole custody of my children. My ex-spouse, who lives in another state, has threatened to go to court in his state and get the custody order changed. Can he do that?

All states and the District of Columbia have enacted the Uniform Child Custody Jurisdiction Act (UCCJA), or the Uniform Child Custody Jurisdiction and Enforcement Act (UCCJEA). These laws determine which court may make a custody determination and which court must defer to an existing determination from another state. Having similar laws in all states helps standardize how custody decrees are treated. It also helps solve many problems created by parental kidnapping or disagreements over custody between parents living in different states.

In general, a state may make a custody decision about a child only if it meets one of these tests (in order of preference):

- The state is the child's home state. This means the child has lived in the state for the six previous months, or was living in the state but is absent because a parent took the child to another state. (A parent who wrongfully removed or retained a child in order to create a "home state" will be denied custody.)

- The child has significant connections in the state with people such as teachers, doctors, and grandparents. (A parent who wrongfully removed or retained a child in order to create "significant connections" will be denied custody.)

- The child is in the state and either has been abandoned or is in danger of being abused or neglected if sent back to the other state.

• No other state can meet one of the above three tests, or a state that can meet at least one test has declined to make a custody decision.

If a state cannot meet one of these tests, the courts of that state cannot make a custody award, even if the child is present in the state. If more than one state meets the above standards, the law specifies that only one state may make custody decisions. This means that once a state makes a custody award, other states must stay out of the dispute.

Can custody and visitation orders be changed?

After a final decree of divorce or other order establishing custody and visitation is filed with a court, parents may agree to modify the custody or visitation terms. This modified agreement (also called a "stipulated modification") may be made without court approval. If one parent later reneges on the agreement, however, the other person may not be able to enforce it unless the court has approved the modification. Thus, it is generally advisable to obtain a court's blessing before relying on such agreements. Courts usually approve modification agreements unless it appears that they are not in the best interests of the child.

If a parent wants to change an existing court order and the other parent won't agree to the change, the parent who wants the change must file a motion (a written request) asking the court that issued the order to modify it. Usually, courts will modify an existing order only if the parent asking for the change can show a "substantial change in circumstances." This requirement encourages stability and helps prevent the court

from becoming overburdened with frequent modification requests. Here are some examples of a substantial change in circumstances:

• **Geographic move.** If a custodial parent makes a move that will seriously disrupt the stability of the child's life, the move may constitute a changed circumstance that justifies the court's modification of a custody or visitation order. Some courts switch custody from one parent to the other, although the increasingly common approach is to ask the parents to work out a plan under which both parents may continue to have significant contact with their children. If no agreement is reached, what the court will do depends on where you live. Courts in some states will permit the move unless the other parent can show that the child will be adversely affected. In other states, the court will carefully examine the best interests of the child—looking at factors such as switching schools and distance from relatives—and make a decision about which parent should have custody.

• **Change in lifestyle.** If substantial changes in a parent's lifestyle threaten or harm the child, the other parent can often succeed in changing custody or visitation rights. If, for example, a custodial parent begins working at night and leaving a nine-year-old child alone, the other parent may request a change in custody. Similarly, if a noncustodial parent begins drinking heavily or taking drugs, the custodial parent may file a request for modification of the visitation order (asking, for example, that visits occur only when the parent is sober, or in the presence of another adult). What constitutes a lifestyle sufficiently detrimental to warrant a change in custody or visitation rights varies tremendously depending on the state and the particular judge deciding the case.

I've heard that mediation is the best approach to solving disagreements about child custody and visitation. Is this true?

Yes, in most cases. Mediation is a nonadversarial process where a neutral person (a mediator) meets with disputing persons to help them settle a dispute. The mediator does not have power to impose a solution on the parties but assists them in creating an agreement of their own. (In a few states, however, the court may ask the mediator to make a recommendation if the parties cannot reach an agreement.)

There are several important reasons why mediation is superior to litigation for resolving custody and visitation disputes:

- Mediation usually does not involve lawyers or expert witnesses (or their astronomical fees).

- Mediation usually produces a settlement after five to ten hours of mediation over a week or two. (Child custody litigation can drag on for months or even years.)

- Mediation enhances communication between the spouses and makes it much more likely that they will be able to cooperate on child-raising issues after the divorce or separation. Experts who have studied the effects of divorce on children universally conclude that children suffer far less when divorcing or separating parents can cooperate.

Custodial Interference

In most states, it's a crime to take a child from his or her parent with the intent to interfere with that parent's physical custody of the child (even if the taker also has custody rights). This crime is commonly referred to as "custodial interference." In most states, the parent deprived of custody may sue the taker for damages and get help from the police to have the child returned.

If a parent without physical custody (who may or may not have visitation rights) removes a child from—or refuses to return a child to—the parent with physical custody, it is considered kidnapping or child concealment in addition to custodial interference. Federal and state laws have been passed to prosecute and punish parents guilty of this type of kidnapping, which is a felony in over 40 states.

In many states, interfering with a parent's custody is a felony if the child is taken out of state. Many states, however, recognize good-cause defenses, including that the taker acted to prevent imminent bodily harm to herself or himself or to the child. In addition, some states let a parent take a child out of state if the parent is requesting custody in court and has notified the court or police of the child's location.

How to Find a Family Law Mediator

Several states require mediation in custody and visitation disputes, and a number of others allow courts to order mediation. In these situations, the court will direct the parents to a mediator and will pay for the services. Parents can also find and pay the mediator themselves. With increasing frequency, family law attorneys are offering mediation services for child custody and other divorce-related disputes, as are a number of nonlawyer community mediators. Two good resources for finding a family law mediator in your area are a website at www.mediate.com, or a national mediation organization called The Association for Conflict Resolution.

Association for Conflict Resolution
1015 18th Street, NW, Suite 1150
Washington, DC 20036
202-464-9700
202-464-9720 (fax)
www.acrnet.org

Things are so bitter between my ex and me that it's hard to see us sitting down together to work things out. How can mediation possibly work?

Mediators are very skilled at getting parents who are bitter enemies to cooperate for the sake of their children. The more parents can agree on the details of separate parenting, the better it will be for them and their children. And mediators are skilled at getting the parents to recognize this fact and move forward toward negotiating a sensible parenting agreement. If the parents initially cannot stand to be in the same room with each other, the mediator can meet with each parent separately and ferry messages back and forth until agreement on at least some issues is reached. At this point, the parties may be willing to meet face to face.

More Information About Child Custody

Building a Parenting Agreement That Works: Putting Your Kids First When Your Marriage Doesn't Last, by Mimi Lyster (Nolo), shows separating or divorcing parents how to create a win-win custody agreement.

National Center for Lesbian Rights, 870 Market Street, Suite 370, San Francisco, CA 94102, 415-392-6257, www.nclrights.org, provides legal information, referrals, and assistance to lesbian and gay parents.

Child Support

Children have more need of models than of critics.

—JOSEPH JOUBERT

Child support is an emotional subject. Parents who are supposed to receive it on behalf of their children often do not. Parents who are supposed to pay it often cannot, or choose not to for a variety of reasons that are not legally recognized. It is the children who suffer the most when child support levels are inadequate or obligations are not met. Therefore, the trend in all states is to increase child support levels and the ways child support obligations can be enforced.

How long must parents support their children?

Biological parents and adoptive parents must support a child until:

- the child reaches the age of majority (and sometimes longer if the child has special needs or is in college)
- the child is on active military duty
- the parents' rights and responsibilities are terminated (for example, when a child is adopted), or
- the child has been declared emancipated by a court. (Emancipation can occur when a minor has demonstrated freedom from parental control or support and an ability to be self-supporting.)

How are child support obligations affected by a divorce or separation?

When one parent is awarded sole custody of a child, the other parent typically is required to fulfill child support obligation by making payments to the custodial parent. The custodial parent meets support obligation through the custody itself. When parents are awarded joint physical custody in a divorce, the support obligation of each is often based on the ratio of each parent's income to their combined incomes, and the percentage of time the child spends with each parent.

Are fathers who never married the mother still required to pay child support?

The short answer to this question is yes. When a mother is not married, however, it's not always clear who the father is. An "acknowledged father" is any biological father of a child born to unmarried parents whose paternity has been established by either his own admission or the agreement of the parents. Acknowledged fathers are required to pay child support.

Additionally, a man may be presumed to be the father of a child if he welcomes the child into his home and openly holds the child out as his own. In some states, the presumption of paternity is considered conclusive, which means it cannot be disproved, even with contradictory blood tests.

The obligation to pay child support does not depend on whether a court ordered it. Most unmarried fathers encounter this principle when the mother seeks public assistance. Sooner or later the welfare department will ask the court to order the father to reimburse it, based on his support obligation and income during the period in question. Sometimes the government catches up with the father many years later, and the father is required to pay thousands of dollars in back support that he never knew he owed.

Do fathers have the same right to child support as mothers?

Yes. If you're a father with custody, you have the right to ask for child support. Each parent has a duty to support his or her children, and that duty doesn't discriminate between genders.

Is a stepparent obligated to support the children of the person to whom he or she is married?

No, unless the stepparent legally adopts the children.

How does the court determine how much child support I can afford to pay?

When evaluating your ability to pay child support, the court looks at your net income. This is your gross income from all sources—such as wages, investment income, rents from real property, or public benefits—minus any mandatory deductions. Mandatory deductions include income taxes, Social Security payments, and health care costs. In most states, courts don't consider other types of automatic deductions from your paycheck (such as wage attachments or credit union payments) or debt obligations (such as loan or credit card payments) when figuring net income. The law places a high priority on child support. Courts would rather see other debts go unpaid than have a child suffer from inadequate support. One exception is other child-support obligations. In some states, courts allow you to deduct the amount of child support you pay for other children from your gross income.

Some courts consider reasonable expenses you incur for the necessities of life—for example, rent, mortgage, food, clothing, and health care. But this usually does not include the cost of tuition, eating in restaurants, or entertainment. Again, the theory is that support of your children should come before these types of personal expenses. In a growing number of states, courts will not consider any personal expenses when determining your ability to pay support.

Can the court base its child-support order on what I am able to earn as opposed to what I'm actually earning?

In most states, the judge is authorized to examine a parent's ability to earn as well as what the parent is actually earning, and order higher child support if there is a discrepancy. Actual earnings are an important factor in determining a person's ability to earn but are not conclusive where there is evidence that a person could earn more.

For example, assume a parent with an obligation to pay child support leaves his current job and enrolls in medical or law school, takes a job with lower pay but good potential for higher pay in the future, or takes a lower-paying job that provides better job satisfaction. In each of these situations, a court may base the child-support award on the income from the original job (ability to earn) rather than on the new income level (ability to pay). The basis for this decision would be that the children's current needs take priority over the parent's career plans and desires.

What happens if a parent falls behind on his or her child-support payments?

Each installment of court-ordered child support is due on the date set out in the order. When a person does not comply with the order, the overdue payments are called arrearages or arrears. Judges have become very strict about enforcing child-support orders and collecting arrearages. While the person with arrears can ask a judge to order lower future payments, the judge will usually insist that the arrearage be paid in full, either immediately or in installments. In fact, judges in most states are prohibited by law from retroactively modifying a child-support obligation.

EXAMPLE: Joe has a child support obligation of $300 per month. Joe is laid off of his job, and six months pass before he finds another one with comparable pay. Although Joe could seek a temporary decrease on the grounds of diminished income, he lets the matter slide and fails to pay any support during the six-month period. Joe's ex-wife later brings Joe into court to collect the $1,800 arrearage; Joe cannot obtain a retroactive ruling excusing him from making the earlier payments.

In addition, back child support cannot be cancelled in a bankruptcy proceeding. This means that once it is owed, it will always be owed until the parent pays.

Calculating Child Support

Each state has guidelines for calculating child support, based on the parents' incomes and expenses and the amount of time each parent spends with the children. These guidelines vary considerably from state to state. In addition, judges in some states have considerable leeway in setting the actual amount, as long as the general state guidelines are followed. But an increasing number of states impose very strict guidelines that leave the judges very little latitude.

In most states, the guidelines specify factors that a court must consider in determining who pays child support, and how much. These factors usually include:

- the needs of the child—including health insurance, education, day care, and special needs
- the income and needs of the custodial parent
- the paying parent's ability to pay, and
- the child's standard of living before divorce or separation.

To find your state's guidelines, check with your state child support enforcement agency (it is usually part of the state department of human services). Most states have this information, along with child-support calculators, on their websites.

My ex-spouse is refusing to pay court-ordered child support. How can I see to it that the order is enforced?

Under the Uniform Interstate Family Support Act (UIFSA), your state's child support enforcement agency (or official) must help you collect the child support your ex-spouse owes, even if your ex has moved out of state. These efforts might range from meeting with your ex and arranging a payment schedule to attaching his salary. If you live in a different state from your ex-spouse, the agency will help you get your state court to issue a support order (sometimes called a petition), which will be forwarded to an agency or court in the state where your ex lives for enforcement. Most of these services are free or low cost.

In recent years, the federal government has taken an aggressive approach to enforcing child support orders. The Child Support Recovery Act of 1992 makes it a federal crime for a parent to willfully refuse to make support payments to a parent living in another state. The support owed must be more than $5,000 and must have gone unpaid for more than a year for criminal sanctions to apply.

The federal government has also made it much easier to track a delinquent parent's assets with resources such as the Federal Parent Locator Services and provisions in the Personal Responsibility and Work Opportunity Reconciliation Act of 1996 (PRWORA). PRWORA requires employers to report all new hires to their state's child support enforcement agency. The agency then forwards this data to the National Directory of New Hires, a centralized registry that matches new employees with parents who owe child support, then quickly sets up wage-withholding orders for these delinquent parents. PRWORA also requires all states to enter into agreements with financial institutions—such as banks, savings and loan institutions, credit unions, insurance companies, and money market funds—to match the account records of parents who owe child support. Under this Financial Institution Data Match Program (FIDM), when a match is identified, the information is sent to the state within 48 hours, so the accounts can be seized. Other methods of child-support enforcement include withholding federal income tax refunds, denying a passport, and suspending or restricting a business, occupational, or driver's license. Many states have also enacted laws that revoke a delinquent parent's hunting, fishing, or boating license.

As a last resort, the court that has issued the child-support order can hold a delinquent ex-spouse in contempt and, in the absence of a reasonable explanation for the delinquency, impose a jail term. This contempt power is exercised sparingly in most states, primarily because most judges would rather keep the payer out of jail and in the workforce—where he or she can earn money to pay child support.

I think our existing child support order is unfair. How can I change it?

You and your child's other parent may agree to modify the child support terms, but even an agreed-upon modification for child support must be approved by a judge to be legally enforceable.

If you and your ex can't agree on a change, you must ask the court to hold a hearing in which each of you can argue your own side of the proposed modification. As a general rule,

the court will not modify an existing order unless the parent proposing the modification can show changed circumstances. This rule encourages stability and helps prevent the court from becoming overburdened with frequent modification requests.

Depending on the circumstances, a modification may be temporary or permanent. Examples of the types of changes that frequently support temporary modification orders are:

- a child's medical emergency
- the payer's temporary inability to pay (for instance, because of illness or an additional financial burden such as a medical emergency or job loss), or
- temporary economic or medical hardship on the part of the parent receiving support.

A permanent modification may be awarded under one of the following circumstances:

- either parent receives additional income from remarriage
- changes in the child-support laws
- job change of either parent
- cost of living increase
- disability of either parent, or
- changes in the needs of the child.

A permanent modification of a child support order will remain in effect until support is no longer required or the order is modified at a later time—again, because of changed circumstances.

Do I have to pay child support if my ex keeps me away from my kids?

Yes. Child support should not be confused with custody and visitation. Every parent has an obligation to support his or her children. With one narrow exception, no state allows a parent to withhold support because of disputes over visitation. The exception? If the custodial parent disappears for a lengthy period so that no visitation is possible, a few courts have ruled that the noncustodial parent's duty to pay child support may be considered temporarily suspended.

No matter what the circumstances, if you believe that your ex is interfering with your visitation rights, the appropriate remedy is to go back to court to have your rights enforced or modified, rather than to stop making support payments.

More Information About Child Support

The following organization can give you information about enforcing child-support orders:

National Child Support
Enforcement Association
444 N. Capitol Street, Suite 414
Washington, DC 20001-1512
202-624-8180
www.ncsea.org

Online Help

www.acf.dhhs.gov
Federal Office of Child Support
Enforcement (OCSE)
370 L'Enfant Promenade, SW
Washington, DC 20447
202-401-9383

http://ocse.acf.hhs.gov/necsrspub
National Electronic Child Support Resource System (NECSRS) has links to each state's resources.

Guardianship of Children

A guardianship is a legal arrangement in which an adult has the court-ordered authority and responsibility to care for a child (someone under 18 in most states) or an incapacitated adult. This section focuses on guardianships of children.

A guardianship may be necessary if a child's parents die or if the child has been abandoned, is not receiving adequate care, or is being abused in some way.

What does a guardian do?

Typically, a guardian takes care of a child's personal needs, including shelter, education, and medical care. A guardian may also provide financial management for a child, though sometimes a second person (often called a "conservator" or "guardian of the estate") is appointed for this purpose.

What is the difference between a guardianship and an adoption?

An adoption permanently changes the relationship between the adults and child involved. The adopting adults legally become the child's parents. The biological parent (if living) gives up all parental rights and obligations to the child, including the responsibility to pay child support. If a biological parent dies without a will, the child who was adopted by someone else has no right to inherit.

Although a guardianship establishes a legal relationship between a child and adult, it does not sever the legal relationship between the biological parents and the child. For example, the biological parents are legally required to provide financial support for the child. And if a biological parent dies without a will, the child has certain automatic inheritance rights.

May I be appointed guardian if the child's parents object?

It depends on how a judge sees the situation. You'll need to start by filing guardianship papers in court. A court investigator will likely interview you, the child, and the child's parents and make a recommendation to the judge. The judge will then review the case and decide whether to appoint you. As a general rule, guardianships are not granted unless:

- the parents voluntarily consent
- the parents have abandoned the child, or
- a judge finds that it would be detrimental to the child for the parents to have custody.

If a child lives with me, do I need a guardianship?

You won't need a guardianship if the child is only staying with you for a few weeks or months. But anyone who anticipates caring for a child for a period of years will probably need a legal guardianship. Without this legal arrangement, you may have trouble registering the child in school, arranging for medical care, and obtaining benefits on the child's behalf. In addition, you'll have no right to keep the child if the parents want to end the arrangement— even if you think they're not capable of caring for the child properly.

If You Want to Avoid a Formal Guardianship

An adult who is taking care of a child may have strong reasons to avoid becoming a legal guardian—for example:

- The caretaker expects that the child's parents will not consent to a legal guardianship.
- Dynamics between family members are such that filing for a guardianship might set off a battle for legal custody. (This would be especially likely where a stepparent and one biological or legal parent care for a child.)
- The caretaker doesn't want his or her personal life scrutinized in court or by a court-appointed investigator.

Some adults try to slide by and raise children (often grandchildren or other relatives) without any legal court authorization. If you go this route, you could run into problems with institutions that want authority from a parent or court-appointed legal guardian. Some communities and institutions are, however, very accommodating of people who are bringing up someone else's children. California, for example, has created a form called a Caregiver's Authorization Affidavit, which gives a nonparent permission to enroll a child in school and make medical decisions on the child's behalf without going to court. Research the laws for your state, or talk to a knowledgeable family law attorney, to find out whether there are ways for you to care for a child short of becoming a legal guardian.

Are You Prepared to Be a Guardian?

An obvious but important question to ask yourself before you take any steps to establish a guardianship is whether you're truly prepared for the job.

- Do you want the ongoing responsibilities of a legal guardianship—including potential liability for the child's actions?
- If you're managing the child's finances, are you willing to keep careful records, provide a court with periodic accountings, and go to court when you need permission to handle certain financial matters?
- What kind of personal relationship do you have with the child? Do you want to act as the legal parent of this child for the duration of the guardianship?
- Will the guardianship adversely affect you or your family because of your own children, health situation, job, age, or other factors?
- Do you have the time and energy to raise a child?

- What is the financial situation? If the child will receive income from Social Security, public assistance programs, welfare, a parent, or the estate of a deceased parent, will this be enough to provide a decent level of support? If not, are you able and willing to spend your own money to raise the child?
- Do you anticipate problems with the child's relatives—including parents—who may suddenly reappear and contest the guardianship? (This is rare, but it can happen.)
- What kind of relationship do you have with the child's parents? Will they support the guardianship, or will they more likely be hostile, antagonistic, or interfering?

It's smart to consider your options carefully before initiating a guardianship proceeding. Honestly answering the questions above may help you with your decision.

When does a guardianship end?

A guardianship ordinarily lasts until the earliest of these events:

- the child reaches the age of majority (often 18)
- the child dies
- the child's assets are used up—if the guardianship was set up solely for the purpose of handling the child's finances, or
- a judge determines that a guardianship is no longer necessary.

Even if a guardianship remains in force, a guardian may step down from the role with permission from the court. In that case, a judge will appoint a replacement guardian.

Who financially supports a child under a guardianship?

Unless a court terminates the biological parents' rights (uncommon in most guardianship situations), the parents remain responsible for supporting their child. In practice, however, financial support often becomes the guardian's responsibility. The guardian may choose to pursue financial benefits, such as public assistance and Social Security, on the child's behalf.

Any funds the guardian receives for the child must be used for that child's benefit. Depending on the amount of money involved, the guardian may be required to file periodic reports with a court showing how much money was received for the child and how it was spent.

Is it true that parents may need a guardianship of their own child?

It's strange but true: Sometimes parents need to establish a particular type of guardianship—called a "guardianship of the estate"—to handle their own child's finances, even if the child lives with them. This situation usually arises when significant amounts of property (at least $5,000 in most states) are given directly to a child.

Understandably, institutions and lawyers are reluctant to turn assets over to parents when they were intended for a child. A guardianship of the estate relieves the institution from liability, and the parents are directly accountable to a court to show how funds are spent and invested.

EXAMPLE: The Thompsons lived next door to an elderly widow, who was extremely fond of their small daughter. When the widow died, she left her house to little Suzy Thompson. The lawyer handling the widow's estate suggests that Suzy's parents go to court to establish a guardianship of their child's estate. The house is then transferred into the name of Suzy's guardianship estate, which her parents manage until she reaches adulthood.

While this system is effective in protecting children's assets from unscrupulous parents, setting up a formal guardianship of the estate involves time and money that well-meaning parents sometimes find burdensome. For this reason, all states have passed laws to make it easier to give money or property to children. These laws provide simple, inexpensive procedures by which gifts to minors (typically up to $10,000) can be managed by their parents without setting up a formal guardianship of the estate. The gift-giver must simply name, in his or her will or in a trust document, someone to manage the gift until the child reaches adulthood. No court involvement is required. (For more information about leaving property to children, see Chapter 11.)

I have young children, and I'm worried about who will care for them if something happens to me. How can I name a guardian?

You can use your will to name a guardian for your children. The specifics are discussed in Chapter 11.

**More Information
About Guardianships**

The Guardianship Book for California, by David Brown and Emily Doskow (Nolo), contains all of the forms and instructions necessary to become a child's guardian in California.

Online Help

www.nolo.com
Nolo offers information about a wide variety of legal topics, including laws that affect parents and their children.

www.adoption.com
This site provides information about adoption agencies, international adoption, and many other adoption issues.

www.divorcenet.com
Divorcenet provides general information, including articles about mediation and child custody and links to state resources. The site also gives answers to frequently asked family law questions.

www.law.cornell.edu/wex/index.php/child_custody
The Legal Information Institute at Cornell Law School provides links to many of the family laws available on the Web, including laws governing adoption, child custody, and children's rights.

16

Courts and Mediation

Ninety percent of our lawyers serve ten percent of our people.
We are over-lawyered and under-represented.

—JIMMY CARTER

The average citizen's ability to gain access to the American justice system is significantly determined by economic status. The wealthy can afford experienced lawyers—the legal system's gatekeepers—while many others are frozen out. Fortunately, there are some alternatives to all-out legal war, which can help to level the legal playing field. Mediation, expanded small claims courts, and family courts that make nonlawyers welcome are all part of the changing landscape. So, too, are public and private websites, many of which provide legal information as well as low-cost forms and the instructions necessary to complete routine legal tasks. Together these changes give hope that all Americans will have improved access to our legal system in the years ahead.

Representing Yourself in Court

A man was arrested in New York for impersonating a lawyer over a lengthy period of time. Assistant Manhattan District Attorney Brian Rosner said one judge told him:

"I should have suspected he wasn't a lawyer. He was always so punctual and polite."

With lawyers' fees often running in excess of $250 an hour, it may make sense to represent yourself in a small civil (noncriminal) lawsuit. The task may seem daunting, but if you have a good self-help resource to guide you and, if possible, someone who knows the ropes to coach you when you need help, you really can act as your own lawyer—safely and efficiently.

Free Legal Help

Before you decide to represent yourself, you may want to explore the possibility of getting free legal assistance. Here are several instances in which you may be able to get an attorney to represent you for free. If none of these matches your situation, or if you simply wish to represent yourself, you'll also want to explore whether your court offers help to the self-represented either in person or on the Internet.

If you face criminal charges.

If you've been charged with a crime and cannot afford to hire your own lawyer, you have a constitutional right to an attorney at government expense. At your request, an attorney, often from a public defender's office, can be appointed to represent you when you are formally charged in court with a criminal offense.

If you've been injured.

If you have been significantly injured and it appears that someone else is at least partially at fault, many lawyers will agree to represent you on a "contingency fee" basis. This means that you pay attorneys' fees only when and if the attorney recovers money for you, in which case the attorney takes an agreed-upon percentage of that total as fees. Be aware, however, that even if a lawyer takes your case on a contingency-fee basis, you still have to pay costs, which can add up to thousands of dollars. Costs include court filing fees, court reporters' fees, expert witness fees, and jury fees. The good news is that if you win your case, the judge will usually order your adversary to pay you back for these costs. And many lawyers agree to pay your costs up front, then get reimbursed when the case settles or ends—so if you win, you won't have to pay these costs out of pocket.

If you qualify for legal aid.

If you can't afford an attorney, you may qualify for free legal assistance. Legal aid lawyers are government-funded lawyers who represent people with low incomes in a variety of legal situations, including eviction defense, denial of unemployment compensation or other benefits, and consumer credit problems. If you think you might qualify, look in your telephone directory or ask a local attorney, lawyer referral service, or elected representative for the nearest legal aid or legal services office.

If your claim involves an issue of social justice.

If your dispute involves a civil rights or social justice issue, an attorney or nonprofit organization with an interest in that issue may represent you on a free or "pro bono" (for the public good) basis. For example, if your claim involves sexual harassment by an employer, abuse by a spouse or partner, discrimination in housing or employment, freedom of speech or religion, or environmental pollution, you may find an attorney or nonprofit organization willing to represent you pro bono. Help is much more likely to be forthcoming if your claim raises new and important issues of law. Call a local bar association or a private organization that deals with the kind of problem you face, such as the American Civil Liberties Union, the NAACP Legal Defense Fund, the Natural Resources Defense Council, the National Women's Law Center, or the Lambda Legal Defense and Education Fund (gay and lesbian rights).

If your claim involves a divorce, child custody or support, domestic violence, or other family law problem.

Increasingly, family courts are providing plain-English information and simplified forms to self-represented litigants. Many have established comprehensive family law centers right at the courthouse, where trained staff help nonlawyers successfully achieve their goals.

Is it ever truly sensible to appear in court without a lawyer?

When it comes to small claims court, which is designed to be accessible to nonlawyers, the answer is yes. But sometimes it also makes sense to represent yourself in a more formal court proceeding. Hiring a lawyer is rarely feasible, economically, for disputes over amounts less than $50,000 and often costs more than it's worth even for disputes in the $50,000 to $100,000 range. If you're fighting over these types of amounts, representing yourself may be your only reasonable option.

Are you saying that for small cases, the cost of hiring a lawyer is too high, given the amount at stake?

Because most lawyers charge hefty hourly fees, and any contested court case can rack up at least dozens of hours of attorney time, it is obvious that attorneys' fees can quickly dwarf what is at stake in many disputes. But the problem is really more fundamental: No matter how important the case, many people just don't have the money to pay a lawyer's hourly rate in the first place. Unless the case is for a personal injury or another type of dispute that lawyers will handle for a contingency fee (a percentage of the total recovery)—or the lawyer quotes a reasonable fixed fee to deal with the dispute from start to finish—the person will either have to go it alone or give up the lawsuit altogether.

Court Information Online

Courts in all 50 states post legal information and useful forms and instructions on the Internet. Generally, small claims and family (divorce) courts provide the most helpful information, but many courts are striving to become more accessible to the general public and those representing themselves. Here's how to find court websites:

- Nolo's website, at www.nolo.com, provides links to federal, state, and local courts around the country. It also provides access to information about small claims court in many states.
- National Center for State Courts, at www .ncsconline.org, has a comprehensive directory of links to state, local, federal, and international courts.
- The Federal Judiciary's website (www. uscourts.gov) lists federal court websites.

If I decide to represent myself, how can I handle the technical rules and complex legal language?

Essentially, you have two choices. Get the dispute diverted to mediation (see *Mediation*, below), where things are done in plain English and procedural rules are kept to a minimum, or take the time to learn how to navigate a formal court proceeding. Getting up to speed on court procedures will take some effort, but it is far from impossible. Fortunately, Nolo publishes an excellent primer, *Represent Yourself in Court*, by Paul Bergman and Sara Berman-Barrett, which covers all the basics.

How to Find a Lawyer Coach

Ten years ago, trying to find a lawyer who would help you find your own way through the legal system was next to impossible. Today, given the surplus of personal service lawyers and a gradual change for the better in the profession's attitude toward self-helpers, it's much easier. Because law is an increasingly specialized field, however, you'll want to find someone who is knowledgeable about your type of problem. Try to get a referral from someone else who has recently worked with lawyers on a similar issue. For example, if you're opening a small business and want to find an appropriate lawyer to provide occasional guidance, you might talk to the owners of excellent local businesses to find out which lawyers they use. Once you have a few names, make and pay for a first appointment (lawyers will respect you far more if you don't beg for a free consultation). Come right out and ask whether the lawyer is prepared to help you help yourself. If you're persistent, you're likely to find a lawyer who meets your needs. For more, see "Finding and Working With a Lawyer," below.

Will I really be able to learn everything I need to know to represent myself competently?

Again, the basics of how to bring or defend a case aren't difficult. But trying to get on top of every nuance of procedure and strategy is tricky. That's why we suggest a two-pronged approach: Learn how to handle routine representation tasks yourself, while hiring a lawyer as a self-help law coach to provide advice on strategy and tactics as needed. In many situations, hiring a lawyer to coach your self-help efforts will cost only about 10% to 20% of what it would cost to hire the lawyer to do the entire job.

How can I decide whether to sue someone?

You need to answer three fundamental questions in order to decide whether it's worthwhile to go forward:

- Do I have a good legal case?
- Can I prove my case?
- Can I collect when I win?

If the answer to any of these questions is no, you probably won't want to sue.

How hard is it to collect a court judgment?

That depends on your opponent. Most reputable businesses and individuals will pay what they owe. But if your opponent tries to stiff you, collecting can be a costly, time-consuming struggle. Unfortunately, the court won't collect your money for you or even provide much help; it will be up to you to identify the assets you are legally entitled to take, and then collect what you're owed.

If an individual is working or owns valuable property—such as land or investments—collection is less difficult; you can instruct your local law enforcement agency (usually the sheriff, marshal, or constable) to garnish the debtor's wages or attach his or her nonexempt property. The same is true of a successful business, especially one that receives cash directly from customers; you can authorize your local sheriff or marshal to collect your judgment right out of the cash register. And in many states, if you are suing a contractor or other businessperson with a state license, you can apply to have the license suspended until the judgment is paid.

But if you can't identify a ready source of funds—for example, you're dealing with an unlicensed contractor of highly doubtful solvency—think twice before suing. A judgment will be of no value to you if the business or individual is insolvent, goes bankrupt, or disappears before you get your money.

How can I tell whether I have a good case?

Lawyers break each type of legal claim ("cause of action," in attorney-speak) into a short list of required elements: the facts you'll have to prove in order to win. As long as you know what the elements are for your type of lawsuit, it's usually fairly easy to determine whether your case is legally sound. For example, a lawsuit against a contractor for doing substandard construction would be for breach of contract (the contractor agreed either orally or in writing to do the job properly). The legal elements for this type of lawsuit are:

Contract formation. You must show that you have a legally binding contract with the contractor. If you have a written agreement, this element is easy to prove. Without a written contract, you will have to show that you had an enforceable oral (spoken) contract, or that an enforceable contract can be implied from the circumstances of your situation.

Performance. You must prove that you did what was required of you under the terms of the contract. Assuming you have made agreed-upon payments and otherwise met the terms of the agreement, you'll have no problems with this element.

Breach. You must show that the contractor failed to meet his or her contractual obligations. This is usually the heart of the case— you'll need to prove, for example, that the contractor failed to do agreed-upon work or did work of poor quality.

Damages. You must show that you suffered an economic loss as a result of the contractor's breach of contract. Assuming the work must be redone or finished, this element is also easy to prove. You also must show evidence of the amount you lost.

The legal elements for other types of lawsuits are different. You can find outlines for the most common in *Represent Yourself in Court,* by Paul Bergman and Sara J. Berman-Barrett (Nolo).

Is it difficult to prepare the paperwork to file a lawsuit?

Actually, it's often fairly easy and inexpensive—especially if you learn how to do basic legal research and prepare drafts of the papers, restricting your lawyer's role to that of checking your work. Initiating a lawsuit is straightforward in many states, where court clerks provide preprinted fill-in-the-blanks forms for many types of lawsuits. And many state and local courts make free forms available on their own websites.

Even in states where lawsuits are filed the old-fashioned way, using paragraphs of appropriate legal jargon on numbered legal paper, the actual wording you'll need to use is almost always available from lawyer "forms books" or CD-ROMs. These information sources, which are routinely used by lawyers, are available at most larger law libraries and are usually fairly easy for the nonlawyer to understand.

I've filed my lawsuit. What do I need to do next?

Before your case is scheduled for trial, you'll need to do a number of things, including meeting with your opponent and filing and responding to paperwork designed to reduce or narrow the issues to be tried. Court rules cover many of these tasks—for example, whether and when a settlement conference must take place, when papers must be filed, and how to place a case on the court's trial calendar. You can get these rules from the court clerk and often on the Web as well. Unfortunately, many clerks are not willing to provide help beyond handing out a copy of often confusing written rules.

In addition to procedural maneuverings, you'll probably have to deal with "discovery"—formally asking people and organizations to give you documents and information relating to your case, and responding to your opponent's requests for documents and information from you. This process is left largely up to you and the other parties to the lawsuit. For example, you might want to take the deposition (oral statement) of the other party and one or more witnesses to find out what they are likely to say at trial. Additional types of discovery include interrogatories (written questions to the other party), a request to hand over documents, or a request that the other party admit certain facts (stipulations).

What are the advantages and disadvantages of taking a deposition?

Depositions—questioning the other party or a witness before trial—have several big advantages as compared to the other types of discovery mentioned above:

- You can learn a great deal about your adversary's case, so as to avoid surprise in the courtroom.

- You can offer a deposition transcript into evidence at trial if the deponent (the person you questioned) is unavailable to give live testimony. This rule explains why you might consider deposing a helpful witness who is seriously ill or planning to move out of the area.

- If a witness says something different at trial than at the deposition, you can read the inconsistent deposition testimony into the trial record to impeach (attack) the deponent's credibility.

EXAMPLE: You have sued your former employer for firing you because you missed work to serve on a jury in a lengthy trial. Before trial you take the deposition of your former supervisor, Paul Chepick. At the deposition, Chepick testified that your work performance had been satisfactory before you took off for jury duty. At trial, Chepick testifies that you were fired not because of your jury service but because of a number of work-related problems. Because Chepick's deposition testimony contradicts his trial testimony, you could read the deposition testimony into the record at trial to show that he changed his story—and call his honesty into question.

- As compared to conducting discovery by asking written questions (interrogatories), depositions allow more flexibility in questioning because you hear a deponent's answer before you ask the next question. For example, assume that a deponent unexpectedly refers to an important business meeting that you didn't know about. In a deposition, you can immediately follow up with questions about what took place during this meeting.

- You can take anyone's deposition. You can depose your adversary, an employee who works for your adversary, a bystander who witnessed a key event, an expert witness hired by your opponent—or even your opponent's attorney! By contrast, you can send written questions (interrogatories) only to your opponent, not to witnesses.

- You hear testimony directly from an individual deponent. While your adversary's lawyer will probably attend the deposition and can consult with the deponent during recesses (breaks in the testimony), the deponent has to answer the questions. By contrast, attorneys often play a major role in preparing the answers to written interrogatories and usually help clients answer them in a way that provides you with as little information as possible.

- You can use a deposition to get and ask about documents (or other tangible items) using a notice of deposition (to depose your opponent) or a subpoena duces tecum (to depose a nonparty witness). In either case, you can list items you want the deponent to bring to the deposition.

Unfortunately, deposing an adversary or a witness who supports your adversary also has some disadvantages. Weigh these considerations very carefully before you decide to take a deposition:

- Depositions are the most expensive discovery tool. Even if you are representing yourself (and therefore not paying an attorney to take or attend a deposition), you must pay a court reporter to transcribe the testimony and prepare a written transcript. While costs vary somewhat by locality, it's not unusual for a court reporter to charge $5 or more per page of transcript. A day of deposition testimony can fill up more than 150 pages, meaning that a day-long deposition may cost you upwards of $750. If you win your case, however, the judge may order your adversary to pay your deposition costs.

- If you are involved in a lawsuit against a good-sized business or governmental entity and don't know which witnesses are most likely to have important information, you may end up paying dearly to depose a witness whose favorite phrase is, "I don't know." By contrast, written interrogatories give you access to "corporate knowledge." This means that when you send interrogatories to a business adversary, you are entitled to answers from any employee who knows them.

- Effective deposition questioning is a difficult skill, even for many attorneys. You have to pose questions carefully in order to be sure that you know how adverse witnesses will testify at trial. If your questions are vague or you forget to cover a topic, you won't be prepared for your opponent's evidence at trial or be able to show that a witness has changed his or her tune (and therefore should not be believed).

- Your adversary's lawyer can be present at a deposition. The attorney may throw you off track by objecting to your questions. Also, an adversary's attorney can help witnesses "refresh their recollections" during recesses. Finally, seeing you in action will allow the attorney to estimate your own credibility and ability to represent your case in court.

And by listening to your questions, the opposing attorney may learn as much about your case as you learn about your adversary's.

- If you depose an adverse witness who becomes unavailable for trial, your adversary will be able to offer the deposition transcript into evidence at trial.

When my case finally makes it to the courtroom, I'm afraid I won't know what to say, when to say it, or even where to stand. How can I learn what to do?

It's not as hard as you might think to learn how to conduct yourself in court. This is especially true if your trial is before a judge without a jury, because many judges make an effort to simplify jargon and procedure for self-represented parties. And there are several practical steps you can take to learn the ropes:

- Attend a few trials involving similar issues. You'll see that it won't be that difficult to present your story and evidence to a judge.
- Carefully read a self-help book such as Nolo's *Represent Yourself in Court,* by Paul Bergman and Sara J. Berman-Barrett, which explains what you'll need to do in great detail. For example, you'll want to prepare and practice a brief but thorough opening statement to tell the judge what your case is about.
- Prepare a trial notebook that outlines each major aspect of your case and what you need to do and say at each point. For example, once you've taken the other side's deposition or asked written questions (interrogatories), you'll probably have a pretty good idea what he or she will say at trial. You can use your trial notebook to prepare a carefully crafted

outline of what you plan to ask in court. Similarly, because you will know before trial who else will testify for the other side, your trial notebook should contain a well-organized list of points you want to cover when you have a chance to question (cross-examine) the witnesses.

A Typical Trial

Most trials begin with each side making an opening statement—each party presents an overview of the case, including what that party expects to prove. The next stage is direct examination, during which the plaintiff (the person who filed the suit) gives testimony about what happened and supports it with witnesses' statements and other relevant evidence. After each of the plaintiff's witnesses testifies, the defendant gets a chance to cross-examine. In doing so, the defendant attempts to produce testimony favorable to the defense version of events and to cast doubt on the reliability or credibility of the plaintiff's witnesses. Finally, both sides get to make a closing argument explaining to the judge or jury why they should win.

What types of evidence win trials?

As mentioned above, in addition to having a legally sound case, you need to be able to prove it before a judge or jury. Technically, this means you have to prove each required legal element of your cause of action by a preponderance (more than 50%) of the evidence. Practically, it usually means focusing on one or two disputed elements of a case (for example, whether your remodeling contractor breached the contract by using substandard materials, doing poor work, or installing equipment not called for in the contract). Unfortunately, too many self-represented litigants try to rely primarily on their own oral rendition of events and overlook the need to back up their story with tangible evidence. Depending on the key issues that must be proved, you will want to present things like photos, contracts, cost estimates to redo the work, or government records. In addition, you'll want to question witnesses who either saw or heard what happened (overheard a boss demanding sex with a subordinate, for example) or are qualified to render an expert opinion on a key aspect of the case (such as a master tile layer's testimony that the installation of the tile floor in your kitchen was botched).

What about actually examining (presenting) witnesses? I'm more than a little intimidated by having to act like Perry Mason.

And well you should be. It's not easy being an actor, especially one who died years ago. But fortunately, appearing in a routine court proceeding isn't that difficult, as long as you know the basic rules. For instance, when you present the testimony of eyewitnesses or expert witnesses, you do so by asking a series of questions. First you need to show that your eyewitness has personal knowledge of the event in question, or that an expert witness is qualified to render an opinion on the issues in dispute. This means you must show that your eyewitness personally observed, heard, smelled, touched, or tasted whatever the witness is testifying to—for example, that your witness was on the spot and overheard the contractor you are suing talking to someone about the details of your garage job. Or, in the case of expert witnesses, that their opinion is based on a careful and accurate review of the facts of the case. Second, you must ask questions that allow witnesses to explain whatever they know without putting words in their mouth (called "leading the witness"). You can learn the basic techniques of how to question a witness and how to object to any improper questions your opponent asks by reading a good self-help book and watching a trial or two.

Do I have a right to have my case heard by a jury?

For some types of civil cases, such as those involving child support or custody, or a request for an injunction (to stop the city from cutting down a tree, for example), you are not entitled to a jury trial. And in some courts, the parties in all small civil cases must first try to resolve the case between themselves via mediation before initiating any type of trial. But in most civil cases, including those involving personal injury, breach of contract, professional malpractice, libel, or slander, you are entitled to a jury trial if you want one.

You may, however, want to think twice before you request a jury trial; it will be more complicated and harder to handle a case on your own before a jury than it would be to represent yourself before a judge. Not only can it be tricky to participate in the jury-selection process, but formal procedural and evidentiary rules will almost surely be more rigorously enforced when a jury is involved. In short, most who go it alone are better off trying their case to a judge and avoiding this added level of complexity. But the other party has a say, too. If that person demands a jury, you will have to try your case before a panel of your peers.

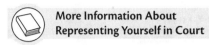

More Information About Representing Yourself in Court

Represent Yourself in Court: How to Prepare & Try a Winning Case, by Paul Bergman and Sara J. Berman-Barrett (Nolo). We have mentioned this book a number of times because it is quite simply the only publication that competently explains all aspects of a civil court trial, including how to determine whether you have a good case, line up persuasive witnesses, present effective testimony in court, cross-examine opponents, and even pick a jury.

Nolo's Deposition Handbook, by Paul Bergman and Albert Moore (Nolo), thoroughly covers the deposition process. Whether you are represented by a lawyer or representing yourself, it explains how to prepare for your deposition, how to respond to questions, and how to cope with the tricks lawyers may use to influence your testimony. It also contains an excellent chapter on deposing expert witnesses.

Win Your Lawsuit: A Judge's Guide to Representing Yourself in California Superior Court, by Judge Roderic Duncan (Nolo), gives California readers all the necessary information, strategic advice, and forms to bring or defend a civil lawsuit worth up to $25,000.

The Lawsuit Survival Guide, by Joseph Matthews (Nolo), is designed to help people who are represented by lawyers understand what's going on in their case and work effectively with their lawyers. Available as an eBook at www.nolo.com.

Small Claims Court

Small claims court judges resolve disputes involving relatively modest amounts of money. The people or businesses involved present their cases to a judge or court commissioner under rules that encourage a minimum of legal and procedural formality. The judge then makes a decision (a judgment) reasonably promptly. Although procedural rules about filing and serving papers differ from state to state, the basic approach to preparing and presenting a small claims case is remarkably similar everywhere.

How much can I sue for in small claims court?

The limit is usually between $2,000 and $10,000, depending on your state. For instance, the maximum is $7,500 in California, $7,500 in Minnesota, $5,000 in New York, and $3,500 in Vermont. (See the chart below for your state's limit.)

Can any kind of case be resolved in small claims court?

No. Small claims courts primarily resolve small monetary disputes. In a few states, however, small claims courts may also rule on a limited range of other types of legal disputes, such as evictions or requests for the return of an item of property (restitution). You cannot use small claims court to file a divorce, guardianship, name change, or bankruptcy, or to ask for emergency relief (such as an injunction to stop someone from doing an illegal act).

Small Claims Court Limits for the 50 states

State	Limit	State	Limit
Alabama	$3,000	Mississippi	$2,500
Alaska	$10,000	Missouri	$3,000
Arizona	$2,500 (small claims division); $5,000 (Justice Court)	Montana	$3,000
		Nebraska	$2,700
Arkansas	$7,500	Nevada	$5,000
California	$7,500 (A plaintiff may not file a claim over $2,500 more than twice a year. The limit for suits involving a surety company or a licensed contractor is $4,000.)	New Hampshire	$5,000
		New Jersey	$3,000 (small claims court); $15,000 (Special Civil Part, Superior Court)
		New Mexico	$10,000
Colorado	$7,500	New York	$5,000 (town and village justice courts, $3,000)
Connecticut	$5,000 (No limit for landlord-tenant cases involving security deposit claims.)	North Carolina	$5,000
		North Dakota	$5,000
		Ohio	$3,000
Delaware	$15,000	Oklahoma	$6,000
District of Columbia	$5,000	Oregon	$5,000
Florida	$5,000	Pennsylvania	$8,000 (small claims court); $10,000 (Philadelphia Municipal Court)
Georgia	$15,000 (No limit for landlord-tenant cases.)		
Hawaii	$3,500 (No limit for landlord-tenant cases involving security deposit claims.)	Rhode Island	$2,500
		South Carolina	$7,500
		South Dakota	$8,000
Idaho	$4,000	Tennessee	$15,000 ($25,000 in Shelby and Anderson counties)
Illinois	$10,000 (Small Claims); ($1,500 Cook County Pro Se Branch)		
		Texas	$5,000
		Utah	$7,500
Indiana	$6,000	Vermont	$3,500
Iowa	$5,000	Virginia	$2,000 (small claims court); $4,500 (General District Court); $15,000 (Circuit Court); no limits on eviction suits in General District Court
Kansas	$4,000		
Kentucky	$1,500		
Louisiana	$3,000		
Maine	$4,500		
Maryland	$5,000	Washington	$4,000
Massachusetts	$2,000 (No limit for property damage caused by a motor vehicle.)	West Virginia	$5,000
		Wisconsin	$5,000 (no limit on eviction suits)
Michigan	$3,000	Wyoming	$5,000 (small claims court); $7,000 (County Circuit Court)
Minnesota	$7,500		

When it comes to disputes involving money, you can usually file in small claims court based on any legal theory that would be allowed in any other court—for example, breach of contract, personal injury, intentional harm, or breach of warranty. A few states do, however, limit or prohibit small claims suits based on libel, slander, false arrest, and a few other legal theories.

Finally, suits against the federal government or a federal agency, or even against a federal employee for actions relating to his or her employment, cannot be brought in small claims court. Suits against the federal government normally must be filed in a federal District Court or another federal court, such as Tax Court or the Court of Claims. Unfortunately, there are no federal small claims procedures available except in federal Tax Court.

Are there time limits for filing a small claims court case?

Yes. States establish rules called "statutes of limitations" that dictate how long you may wait to file a lawsuit after the key event giving rise to the lawsuit occurs or, in some instances, is discovered. Statutes of limitations rules apply to all courts, including small claims.

You'll almost always have at least one year to sue (measured from the event or, sometimes, from its discovery). Often, you'll have much longer. But if you're planning to sue a state or local government agency, you'll usually need to file a formal claim with that agency within three to six months of the incident. Only after your initial complaint is denied are you eligible to file in small claims court. If some time has passed since the incident giving rise to your lawsuit—for example, after the breach of a written contract or a personal injury—you may need to do a little research to determine whether you can still file your claim. Check your state's legal code under the index heading "statute of limitations." (See the appendix for information on how to do this in the library or online.)

Where should I file my small claims lawsuit?

Assuming the other party lives or does business in your state, you probably have to sue in the small claims court district closest to that person's residence or headquarters. In some instances, you also may be able to sue in the court district where a contract was signed or a personal injury (such as an auto accident) occurred. Check with your small claims clerk for detailed rules.

If a defendant has no contact with your state, you'll generally have to sue in the state where the defendant lives or does business. Because most major corporations operate in all states, it's easy to sue most of them almost anywhere. But small businesses typically only conduct business in one or a few states, which means you may have to bring the lawsuit where the defendant is located.

If You Want to Avoid Going to Court

If you are eager to recover what's owed to you but you want to avoid the trouble of bringing a lawsuit, you have a couple of options to consider. First, even if you've been rudely turned down in the past, ask for your money at least once more. This time, make your demand in the form of a straightforward letter that briefly reviews the key facts of the dispute and concludes with the statement that you'll file in small claims court in ten days unless payment is promptly received. Unlike an angry conversation, where the other party may assume you'll never follow up, a polite but direct demand letter is like tossing a cup of cold water in your opponent's face. It really gets the message across that you're serious about getting paid. Because many individuals and small business people have a strong aversion to appearing at a public trial (including the time and inconvenience it will take), making it clear you are prepared to file a lawsuit can be a surprisingly effective way to get the other party to talk settlement. If your letter does get your adversary to the bargaining table, be ready to agree to a reasonable compromise.

There are three good reasons to do so. First, studies show that those who win in small claims court rarely get everything they asked for. Second, by compromising, you save yourself the time and anxiety of preparing and presenting your case in court. And finally, if your case settles, you're more likely to get paid right away, which means that you avoid potential collection problems.

Many states offer, and a few require, community- or court-based mediation designed to help parties settle their small claims disputes. Mediation often works best where the parties have an interest in staying on good terms, as is generally the case with neighbors, family members, or small business people who have done business together for many years. In addition, many defendants are willing to reach a mediated settlement to avoid having an official court judgment appear on their record. For these and other reasons, resolving small disputes through mediation can be remarkably successful. For more information about mediation, see *Mediation*, below.

Will I get paid if I win the lawsuit?

Not necessarily. The court may decide in your favor, but it won't collect your money for you. So before you sue, always ask, "Can I collect if I win?" If not, think twice before suing.

Some people and businesses are "judgment proof"—that is, they have little money or assets and aren't likely to acquire more in the foreseeable future. In short, if they don't pay voluntarily, you may be out of luck. If the person you're suing has a steady job, it should be reasonably easy to collect by garnishing his or her wages if you win. If not, try to identify another collection source, such as a bank account or real property, before going forward. For people who seem to have no job or assets, ask yourself whether they are likely to be more solvent in the future. Court judgments are good for ten to 20 years in many states and can usually be renewed for longer periods. Consider whether the person might inherit money, graduate from college, get a good job, or otherwise have an economic turnaround not too far down the road.

If I'm sued in small claims court but the other party is really at fault, can I countersue?

In some states, you can and must countersue if your claim is based on the same event or transaction that led to the lawsuit. If you don't, you risk losing the right to bring that claim. In other states, these "counterclaims" are not mandatory, and you can sue separately later. No matter what the technical rules, you'll want to countersue promptly.

If the amount you sue for is less than the small claims limit, your case will probably remain in that court. If, however, you want to sue for more, check with your small claims clerk for applicable rules. Often, you'll need to have the case transferred to a different court that has the power to decide cases involving larger amounts of money.

What should I do to prepare my small claims case?

Whether you are a plaintiff (the person suing) or a defendant (the person being sued), the key to victory is not what you say but the evidence you bring with you to court to back up your story. After all, the judge has no idea who you are and whether your oral (spoken) testimony is reliable. And your opponent is likely to claim that your version is wrong.

It follows that your chances of winning will greatly increase if you carefully collect and present convincing evidence. Depending on the facts of your case, a few of the evidentiary tools you can use to convince the judge you are right include eyewitnesses, photographs, letters from experts, or written contracts.

What's the best way to present my case to a judge?

First, understand that the judge is busy and has heard dozens of stories like yours. To keep the judge's attention, get to the point fast by describing the event that gave rise to your claim. Immediately follow up by stating how much money you are requesting. To be able to do this efficiently, it's best to practice in advance. Here is an example of a good start: "Your Honor, my car was damaged on January 10, 2007, when the defendant ran a red light at Rose and Hyacinth Streets in the town of Saginaw and hit my front fender. I have a canceled check to show it cost me $1,927 to fix the fender."

After you have clearly stated the key event and the amount of your loss, double back and tell the judge what led up to the problem. For example, you might next explain that you were driving below the speed limit and had entered the intersection when the light was green, and when the defendant came barreling through the red light, you did your best to avoid her car. Then it would be time to present any eyewitnesses, police reports, or other evidence that backs up your version of events.

A Court Without Lawyers?

In a handful of states, including California, Michigan, and Nebraska, you must appear in small claims court on your own. In most states, however, you can be represented by a lawyer if you like. But even where it's allowed, hiring a lawyer is rarely cost-efficient. Most lawyers charge too much given the relatively modest amounts of money involved in small claims disputes. Happily, several studies show that people who represent themselves in small claims cases usually do just as well as those who have a lawyer.

Will witnesses need to testify in person?

If possible, it's best to have key witnesses speak their piece in court. But if this isn't convenient, the rules of most small claims courts allow you to present a clearly written memo or letter. (Be sure to check your state's rules—the appendix explains how.) Have the witness start the statement by establishing who he or she is. ("My name is John Lomax. I've owned and managed Reo's Toyota Repair Service for the last 17 years.") In clear, unemotional language, the witness should explain what he or she observed or heard. ("I carefully checked Mary Wilson's engine and found that it has been rebuilt improperly, using worn-out parts.") Finally, the witness should try to anticipate any questions a reasonable person might ask and provide the answers. ("Although it can take a few days to get new parts for older engines, such as the one Mary Wilson owned, it is easy and common practice to do so.")

If I lose my case in small claims court, can I appeal?

The answer depends on where you live. In some states, either party may appeal within a certain period of time, usually between ten and 30 days, and have a new trial in which a new judge hears the case from scratch. In other states, appeals are granted only if the small claims judge made a legal mistake. And some states have their own unique rules. In California, for example, a defendant who loses may appeal to the Superior Court within 30 days. A plaintiff who loses may not appeal at all but can make a motion to correct clerical errors or to correct a decision based on a legal mistake.

To find the appeals rules for your state, call your local small claims court clerk or refer to the appendix for information on how to get them in the library or online.

 More Information About Small Claims Court

Everybody's Guide to Small Claims Court, by Ralph Warner (Nolo) (National and California versions), explains how to evaluate your case, prepare for court, and convince a judge you're right. It also contains a useful section on trying to negotiate or mediate a compromise with the other party without going to court. Best of all, it explains the most useful courtroom techniques and tactics to convincingly present evidence, witnesses, and your own testimony.

Mediation

I'd rather jaw, jaw, jaw, than war, war, war.

—WINSTON CHURCHILL

If you're involved in a legal dispute, you may be able to settle it without going to court. One way to do this is to work out a solution with the help of a mediator—a neutral third person. Unlike a judge or an arbitrator, a mediator will not take sides or make a decision but will help each party evaluate goals and options in order to come up with a solution that works for everyone. One exception to this rule is made for child-custody mediations in a few states (such as California), where a mediator has the power to recommend a solution to a judge if the parties cannot agree.

When you reach an agreement with an opposing party through mediation, you can make it legally binding by writing down your decisions in the form of an enforceable contract.

What kinds of cases can be mediated?

Most civil (noncriminal) disputes can be mediated, including those involving contracts, leases, small business ownership, employment, and divorce. For example, a divorcing couple might engage in mediation to work out a mutually agreeable child-custody agreement. Similarly, estranged business partners might choose mediation to work out an agreement to divide their business. Nonviolent criminal matters, such as claims of verbal or other personal harassment, can also be successfully mediated.

Finally, you may want to consider mediation if you get into a scrape with a neighbor, roommate, spouse, partner, or coworker. Mediation can be particularly useful when the participants have some kind of personal relationship, because it is designed to identify and resolve not just the immediate problem but also the tensions and unresolved issues that led up to it. For example, if one neighbor sues another for making outrageous amounts of noise, the court will usually deal with only that issue—and by declaring neighbor A the winner and neighbor B the loser, may worsen long-term tensions. In mediation, however, each neighbor will be invited to present all issues in dispute. It may turn out that overly loud neighbor B was being obnoxious in part because neighbor A's dog constantly pooped on his lawn or A's son's pickup often blocked a shared driveway. In short, because mediation is designed to surface and solve all problems, it's a far better way to restore long-term peace to the neighborhood, home, or workplace.

How long does mediation take?

People who mediate through programs offered by small claims court are often able to settle their disputes in an hour or less. Slightly more complicated cases (such as consumer claims, small business disputes, or auto accident claims) are usually resolved after a half day or, at most, a full day of mediation. Cases with multiple parties often last longer: Add at least an hour of mediation time for each additional party. Major business disputes—those involving lots of money, complex contracts, or business dissolution—may last several days or more.

Private divorce mediation, where a couple aims to settle all the issues in their divorce—property division and alimony, as well as child custody, visitation, and support—may require half a dozen or more mediation sessions spread over several weeks or months.

How is mediation different from arbitration?

A mediator normally has no authority to render a decision; it's up to the parties themselves—with the mediator's help—to work informally toward their own agreement. An arbitrator, on the other hand, conducts a contested hearing between the parties and then, acting like a judge, makes a legally binding decision. The arbitrator's decision-making power may, however, be limited based on a written agreement between the parties. For example, the parties may agree in advance that the arbitrator is limited to making an award of monetary damages of between $200,000 and $500,000. Arbitration has long been used to resolve commercial and labor disputes. An arbitration proceeding typically resembles a court hearing, with witnesses, evidence, and arguments.

Why should I consider having my case mediated?

If you've given up on negotiating a settlement of your dispute directly with the other party, mediation may be the most painless and efficient way to solve it. Compared to a lawsuit, mediation is swift, confidential, fair, and low cost. And because you must agree to any mediated resolution of your case, you won't be blindsided by an outrageously unfair judgment.

Mediation sessions are usually scheduled quickly, and most sessions last only a few hours or a day, depending on the type of case. In contrast, lawsuits often take many months, or even years, to resolve. Another advantage of mediation is confidentiality. With very few exceptions (for example, where a criminal act or child abuse is involved), what you say during mediation cannot legally be revealed outside the mediation proceedings or used later in a court of law.

Mediating instead of litigating will nearly always save you money. In many parts of the country, nonprofit community mediation centers or mediators employed by a small claims or other court handle relatively minor consumer, neighborhood, workplace, and similar disputes free or for a nominal charge. Private dispute resolution companies tackle more complex cases for a fraction of the cost of bringing a lawsuit. A half-day mediation of a personal injury claim, for example, may cost each side about $500 to $1,000. By comparison, a full-scale court battle could cost $50,000 or more, sometimes much more.

Finally, agreements reached through mediation are more likely to be carried out than those imposed by a judge. After a lawsuit, the losing party is almost always angry and often prone to look for ways to violate the letter or spirit of any judgment. In contrast, a number of studies show that people who have freely arrived at their own solutions through mediation are significantly more likely to follow through.

The Six Stages of Mediation

While mediation is a less formal process than going to court, it is more structured than many people imagine. A full-scale mediation typically involves at least six distinct stages, as discussed below. However, in some small claims, child custody, and other publicly funded mediation procedures, time constraints mean that some of these stages are combined.

1. Mediator's Opening Statement

After the disputants are seated at a table, the mediator introduces everyone, explains the goals and rules of the mediation, and encourages each side to work cooperatively toward a settlement.

2. Disputants' Opening Statements

Each party is invited to tell, in his or her own words, what the dispute is about, how he or she has been affected by it, and how it might be resolved. While one person is speaking, the other is not allowed to interrupt.

3. Joint Discussion

The mediator may try to get the parties talking directly about what was said in the opening statements. This is the time to determine what issues need to be addressed.

4. Private Caucuses

Often considered the guts of mediation, the private caucus gives each party a chance to meet privately with the mediator (usually in a nearby room) to discuss the strengths and weaknesses of his or her position, and to propose new ideas for settlement. The mediator may caucus with each side as many times as seems necessary. In mediation procedures sponsored by small claims courts and other public agencies, where time is short, this step may be shortened or skipped, and the parties move on to joint negotiation. And some mediators don't use private caucuses at all, but keep the parties together for the entire negotiation.

5. Joint Negotiation

After caucuses, the mediator may bring the parties back together to negotiate face to face.

6. Closure

This is the end of the mediation. If an agreement has been reached, the mediator may put its main provisions in writing as the parties listen. The mediator may ask each side to sign the written summary of agreement or suggest they take it to lawyers for review. If the parties want to, they can write up and sign a legally binding contract. If no agreement was reached, the mediator will review whatever progress has been made and advise everyone of their options, such as meeting again later, going to arbitration, or going to court.

How can I be sure mediation will produce a fair result?

In mediation, you and the opposing party will work to craft a solution to your own dispute. Unless you freely agree, there will be no final resolution. This means that you can bring your own sense of fairness into the process—you don't have to rely on a judge or arbitrator to make a decision that may not take all of your concerns into account. It also means that it's possible for both parties to feel that the outcome was fair, as opposed to a court process, which will always result in a winner and a loser.

Mediation also allows you to agree to things that would never be ordered in court, where a judge has only the power to order one person to pay money to the other. In mediation, by contrast, you and the other party can agree to nonmonetary solutions like a written apology, a timeline for doing something (for example, building a new fence), or a conditional solution like payment of money only if one party fails to take certain agreed-upon steps.

For all these reasons, and particularly because you won't have a solution forced on you, it's likely that a successful mediation will result in a solution you think is fair.

A piece of paper, blown by the wind into a law court, may in the end only be drawn out by two oxen.

—CHINESE PROVERB

How can I find a good mediator?

It depends on the type of dispute you're involved in. Many cities have community mediation centers that do an excellent job of handling most types of routine disputes (consumer problems, neighbor disputes, landlord-tenant fights). For more complicated disputes (business termination, personal injury, breach of contract) it is often better to turn to a private mediator or mediation center. Two good online sources of information are the American Arbitration Association, www.adr.org, and the Mediation Information and Resource Center, www.mediate.com. Private divorce mediations are usually handled by sole practitioners or small, local mediation groups. Get a list from the phone book or the Internet and check references carefully.

Are there some cases that should not be mediated?

All parties to a dispute must agree to mediate, so if one party refuses or isn't competent to participate, a dispute cannot be mediated. In addition, mediation may also not be the best choice in certain other types of cases, such as:

- One of the parties is attempting to set a legal precedent that interprets or defines the law —for example, to establish a new civil right. Legal precedents cannot be set in mediation because mediation agreements do not decide who is "right" or "wrong," and are usually not made public.

- A person believes he or she can win a huge verdict against a big company (or even a small company with a big bank account or plenty of insurance). Because of the tendency toward compromise in mediation, hitting a legal "jackpot" is more likely in a jury trial.

- One person feels intimidated or intellectually overwhelmed by the other, in which case it's hard to arrive at a true meeting of the minds. It's often possible, however, to remedy a power imbalance by arranging for the more vulnerable person to participate with an advisor—perhaps a lawyer.

If I choose mediation, will I still need a lawyer?

In most mediations, it's not necessary to have a lawyer participate directly. This is because the parties are trying to work together to solve their problem—not trying to convince a judge or arbitrator of their point of view—and because mediation rules are few and straightforward. If your case involves substantial property or legal rights, however, you may want to consult with a lawyer before the mediation to discuss the legal consequences of possible settlement terms. You may also want to condition any agreement you make on a lawyer's approval.

More Information About Mediation

Mediate, Don't Litigate, by Peter Lovenheim and Lisa Guerin (Nolo), thoroughly explains the mediation process and shows you how to choose a mediator, prepare a case, and conduct yourself during a mediation. This book is available as an eBook only, at www.nolo.com.

Divorce Without Court: A Guide to Mediation & Collaborative Divorce, by Katherine E. Stoner (Nolo), provides divorcing couples with all the information they need to work with a neutral third party to resolve differences and find solutions. By choosing mediation or collaboration, couples can avoid court battles, save money, get through a divorce quickly, and minimize negative effects on children.

Building a Parenting Agreement That Works: Putting Your Kids First When Your Marriage Doesn't Last, by Mimi Lyster (Nolo), provides a step-by-step method for overcoming obstacles and putting together a practical parenting agreement that everyone—especially the children—can live with.

When Push Comes to Shove: A Practical Guide to Resolving Disputes, by Karl Slaikeu (Jossey-Bass), is a how-to mediation guide for lawyers, managers, and human resource professionals.

Getting to Yes: Negotiating Agreement Without Giving In, by Roger Fisher and William Ury (Penguin), is a classic book on negotiating strategy.

Finding and Working With a Lawyer

Although it sometimes makes good economic sense to represent yourself in a lawsuit, there are circumstances in which you might want to hire a lawyer. If you don't have the time or inclination to learn all of the legal rules and procedures that you'll have to follow in court, your case has the potential to win you (or cost you) lots of money, or you simply feel like you're in over your head, hiring a lawyer can be a wise investment. The trick is to find a lawyer who is knowledgeable, professional, and fair—and to do your part to make sure your professional collaboration is productive. This section answers some questions about finding and working with a lawyer. And in case your legal relationship goes south, we also offer some information on handling problems with your lawyer.

How can I find a good lawyer?

Perhaps the best way to find a good lawyer is through referrals—recommendations from friends, family members, business associates, or local trade or bar associations. The goal is to find a lawyer who can provide the right kind of representation for you in a particular dispute. This means you might need to speak with several lawyers before finding one who is right for the job.

Many lawyers charge nothing for an initial meeting to discuss the possibility of representing a client. However, some lawyers require potential clients to pay a consultation fee—a fee for meeting with the lawyer to discuss the facts and law relating to the lawsuit and the possibility of working together. Generally, this fee should cover any time the lawyer spends reviewing documents, researching the law, and meeting with you. If you are unwilling or unable to pay a consultation fee, ask the lawyer to waive the fee. Even lawyers who usually charge a consultation fee will probably meet with you for free if they believe you have a strong case.

Where can I get referrals to an appropriate lawyer?

Lawyer referrals can come from many sources.

Lawyers. Lawyers frequently refer cases to one another. Any lawyer probably knows, or knows some other lawyer who knows, a lawyer who specializes in the area of law that covers your case.

Business associates and trade organizations. If a lawsuit arises out of a business dispute, people in the same or other businesses might have been involved in litigation of their own. If so, they may be able to refer you to lawyers they used and liked, or warn about lawyers with whom they had bad experiences. Trade organizations or local groups that represent the interests of business owners, such as your state or local chamber of commerce, may also have lawyers to recommend.

Friends and acquaintances. As an initial referral device, it can be very useful to canvass friends and acquaintances to get referrals to lawyers whom they found helpful. However, a personal recommendation is never enough. A lawyer who does well for one client, or has the time and energy to devote to one case, won't necessarily do as well on another case.

Lawyer directories. There are many online lawyer directories that can help you find an attorney, including Nolo's directory at www.lawyers.nolo. com. Nolo's directory provides detailed information on the lawyers who participate. Check to see whether the directory covers your state.

Bar association referral service. Many county and city bar associations offer lawyer referral services for the public. You can contact these services by calling the city or county bar association and asking for the lawyer referral line, or, increasingly, through the Internet. Once you describe the type of case for which you're seeking a lawyer, the service provides the names of local lawyers who specialize in that area of the law. However, most bar associations do not screen lawyers for competency or experience, so a referral is *not* the same as a recommendation.

Government agencies. Certain state and federal government agencies are responsible for enforcing laws that protect the public. For example, the Equal Employment Opportunity Commission (EEOC) enforces the laws prohibiting discrimination in the workplace, and the Securities and Exchange Commission (SEC) acts to prevent investors from being defrauded. In some cases, these agencies will get directly involved in a lawsuit, particularly if the lawsuit addresses important and new legal issues in the field. Even if they don't take the case, a few government agencies will refer you to local lawyers who handle similar lawsuits. As with referrals from bar associations, however, these referrals may not be screened.

Once I have some referrals, what should I do next?

The first step when you're shopping for a lawyer is to call the lawyers who have been referred by others. Often, a member of the lawyer's staff will ask you questions about the case and ask who referred you. If the lawyer is available and interested in the case, you can arrange a meeting at the lawyer's office.

How You Can Make a First Meeting Successful

Before your first meeting with a lawyer, gather your thoughts and your paperwork. Think about all the important incidents that led to the dispute. It is a good idea to write down these events, either in timeline form or simply as a description—as if you were telling the story in a letter. If you do make a written summary, bring it with you to the meeting with the lawyer. Also bring the names and addresses of witnesses—anyone who might have information about the dispute. And bring any documents—contracts, letters, business records, plans, or photographs, for example—that relate to the case.

During this meeting, you can ask about the lawyer's litigation experience, find out the lawyer's initial view of the case, discuss fee arrangements and legal strategy, and check out the lawyer's communication skills. All of these factors will help you decide whether to hire this lawyer. Of course, the lawyer will also use this meeting to decide whether to take your case. The lawyer will be thinking about the case's strengths and weaknesses, how lucrative the case might be, how much work the case would require, and whether the two of you are likely to get along during the litigation.

Do lawyers specialize in particular areas of law?

Yes. Like doctors, most lawyers specialize. Some handle divorces, some give tax advice, some work on corporate mergers, some write wills and contracts, some do criminal defense. Some do a little of this and a little of that. But unless a lawyer has at least some experience in the legal area involved in your lawsuit, you'll probably want to keep looking.

The facts in every lawsuit are different. At the same time, every lawsuit has many procedural similarities. This means that it is neither practical nor necessary to look for a lawyer who has experience handling lawsuits that are "exactly" like your case. But the lawyer should at least have some experience in that area of law. For example, if a lawsuit involves the breakup of a partnership that ran a florist business, you don't need to find a lawyer who has previously handled cases dealing with florists or flowers—but you will definitely want a lawyer with experience litigating business partnership disputes.

The lawyer I want to hire works in a law firm. Will other people in the firm also work on my case?

Probably. The individual lawyer who is responsible for all major decisions in the lawsuit—and who actually handles major legal maneuvers and trial if the case gets that far—is known as the lead attorney. But in law offices large and small, a certain amount of work on any lawsuit is done by people other than this primary lawyer. Other lawyers in the office (often called associates), paralegals (trained legal assistants similar to nurses in a doctor's office), and legal secretaries all will perform tasks during the course of litigation.

This division of labor is due in part to erratic demands on lawyers' time. Also, much legal work is routine and therefore can be done equally well by legal workers with less training (and lower salaries). It is a division of labor that can help or hurt a client. You benefit if work gets done more quickly and efficiently by others in the office. This might be the case if the lead attorney would not be able to get to the work right away. If you are paying by the hour, it can be to your financial advantage to have routine work done by people with a lower hourly rate. On the other hand, your case might be harmed if important work is left to members of the office with less training or experience.

You should ask who will work on which parts of the lawsuit. Of course, a lawyer does not know in advance exactly who will do every piece of work. But the lawyer can at least describe how busy he or she is likely to be over the next six months to a year, and therefore how much attention the lawyer can devote to the case. For example, if the lawyer is to begin a big trial within the next few months, the lawyer will have very little time or energy for any other cases during that time.

Also, you should discuss which parts of the litigation the lawyer intends to handle personally, such as the trial, depositions of the opposing parties and key witnesses, and preparing you for your own deposition.

What should I ask potential lawyers about fees and costs?

When choosing a lawyer, one of the most important considerations is the amount of the lawyer's fee and how it will be calculated. You should discuss fee arrangements at the outset, before deciding whether to hire a lawyer. If the lawyer will charge by the hour, you should have an open and honest discussion about how much you can or are willing to pay for the entire litigation. A lawsuit can be conducted in quite different ways—the more aggressively it is waged, the more lawyer hours you will have to underwrite.

You should also ask the lawyer for some general idea—though it might be quite speculative this early in the process—of how much you might receive from, or have to pay to, the other side at the conclusion the lawsuit. Once you've discussed these figures, the lawyer can conduct the lawsuit so that attorneys' fees remain in balance with your potential gains or losses. If fees get too high, you will both know that it's time to consider a settlement rather than to continue headlong with the lawsuit.

How much do lawyers charge per hour?

Lawyers charge in several different ways, some of which are covered in the questions that follow. The most common form of lawyer compensation is the hourly rate. Rates range from $75 to $300 per hour—or more. As with most other services, rates tend to be higher in major urban areas. The hourly rate charged for work by less-experienced lawyers in the same office is usually substantially lower than rates charged by more senior attorneys. If the lawyer's office uses paralegals and charges separately for their time, their hourly rate will probably be in the $35 to $100 per hour range. Most lawyers keep painfully close track of, and charge for, every minute they spend on a case. Lawyers usually mark their work time in tenth-of-an-hour increments (six-minute chunks). So, if they spend even one minute on a case—a quick phone call, reviewing and signing a letter—they bill for a tenth of an hour.

What is a retainer?

A lawyer who will be paid an hourly fee may ask you to pay a lump sum at the beginning of the case to guarantee payment for the lawyer's initial work. Once this "down payment," known as a retainer, is received, the lawyer deposits it in a bank trust account. The lawyer withdraws fees from the retainer as the lawyer works on the case and bills the client for the time. Lawsuit costs—such as copying, long-distance phone charges, or messenger fees—may also be charged against the retainer.

What can I do initially to control hourly fees?

Because paying by the hour can become so expensive so quickly, you might want to discuss money-saving measures with the lawyer at the very beginning of the case. Such measures might include:

- **Discounted rate.** Some lawyers will agree to reduce the hourly rate they charge if they work more than a certain number of hours on a case in any one month. For example, a lawyer might charge $150 per hour for the first 20 hours of work on the case in a month, but then only $100 for every additional hour in that month.

- **Cap on total fee.** By the time most disputes get to the lawsuit stage, both sides have a pretty good idea of how much money is at stake. Based on how much you stand to gain or lose, you and your lawyer might be able to gauge how much (in lawyers' fees) it is worth spending to win, or to protect against losing. For example, if you are suing to recover $50,000 in damages, you might want the lawyer to agree to try to settle the lawsuit once legal fees reach $20,000 or so. Otherwise, legal fees might eat up most of your potential winnings. You should discuss this kind of balancing—legal fees versus the total amount at stake in the lawsuit—at the start of the case. If possible, you and your lawyer should agree on a maximum fee amount. When legal fees near that figure, the lawyer can push to settle the case—even if the settlement is not as good as you might have hoped.

- **Prior approval of legal maneuvers.** You might be able to control some hourly legal fees by making sure the lawyer discusses major legal procedures with you before beginning work on them. A conscientious, client-friendly lawyer will do this anyway—but it doesn't hurt to raise the issue at the outset.

- **Careful billing review.** If you are paying a lawyer by the hour, you must keep abreast of the lawyer's work. Most lawyers' offices send an itemized bill every month. The bill includes, by date, a brief description of the work a lawyer or paralegal has done that month on the case and how long (in tenths of hours) the work took. Make sure there have been no major, time-consuming legal maneuvers that you did not previously hear about from your lawyer. Also, if certain aspects of the case are running up a lot of attorneys' fees, you might want to raise the possibility of cutting down in that area of the litigation. Finally, if the total lawyers' fees will soon become unaffordable or will exceed what you stand to win in the case, you must discuss the possibility of settling the case quickly, rather than continuing with expensive litigation.

A Lawyer's Time Is Your Money

If your lawyer charges by the hour, the meter is running whenever you have a conversation. Before you pick up the phone or make an appointment, think about whether you really need to talk to your lawyer. A secretary might be able to handle scheduling issues, make sure you get copies of important documents, and take care of other basic requests.

If you have questions for your attorney, write them down before you call or visit. This way, you can be sure to get all your questions answered at once and avoid getting charged for a second or third conversation. If you have information you need to share with your lawyer—thoughts about potential witnesses, answers to discovery requests, or comments on a pleading, for example—consider writing them down in a letter. Finally, don't use your lawyer—especially not a lawyer you are paying by the hour—as a shoulder to cry on or an emotional sounding board. Lawyers aren't trained as therapists or counselors—but will charge you for their time if you ask them to act like one.

What is a contingency fee?

In certain kinds of cases, lawyers charge what is called a contingency fee. Instead of billing by the hour, the lawyer waits until the case is over, then takes a certain percentage of the amount won. If you win nothing, the lawyer gets no fee. In this way, the lawyer shares your risk of losing or of winning less than expected. A contingency fee also rewards the lawyer for helping to win a higher amount—the more the lawyer wins for you, the more the lawyer gets. This method of payment was developed to permit lawyers to aggressively represent those people who want to sue for damages but don't have the money to pay a lawyer as the case goes along.

Contingency fees are most often used in personal injury and medical malpractice cases. The person who is suing (the plaintiff) arranges to pay based on the amount of money recovered, while the person being sued (the defendant) pays a lawyer by the hour. You may also be able to use a contingency fee if you are suing a business or organization for potentially high compensation—in cases involving employment discrimination, harassment or wrongful termination, patent or trademark infringement, personal or business fraud, or unfair competition.

How much do lawyers charge as a contingency fee?

The standard contingency fee in personal injury cases is 33% of the amount of compensation the plaintiff obtains in a settlement. Sometimes, the fee rises to 40% at a point around 60 to 90 days before the trial date.

Fees rise whether or not the trial actually takes place. The reason for this increase is that a lawyer's work increases tremendously once the case nears trial. Contingency-fee rates in other cases are similar, though they can range from 25% to 50% depending on the amount of work a lawyer must do, the potential for a large fee, and the risk of getting no fee at all.

Although one-third is the standard contingency fee, some lawyers will consider either a lower rate or a mixture of rates, depending on the case. You might successfully negotiate with a lawyer for a lower rate, perhaps 20% to 25% of any settlement before the case is set for trial, if:

- it seems virtually certain that you will recover damages—the only question is how much the award will be
- you are likely to receive a large award, and
- the attorney will not have to do a lot of complicated or time-consuming legal work.

In cases involving a large potential recovery, you might try to negotiate a sliding scale fee schedule. In these arrangements, the lawyer's rate goes down as the compensation goes up. For example, a lawyer might agree to a sliding fee scale of 33% for recovery of up to $100,000 and 25% for all amounts over $100,000. Or a lawyer might agree to a more graduated scale, with 33% up to $100,000, 25% for $100,000 to $250,000, and 15% for all amounts above $250,000. The better your case, the more willing a lawyer will be to negotiate this type of arrangement.

Should I tell my lawyer things that might hurt my case?

Yes. Under a rule called the attorney-client privilege, a lawyer is under the strictest legal instructions never to reveal anything a client tells the lawyer. The protection provided by this privilege extends to your statements to any member of the lawyer's staff, or to anyone hired by the lawyer to work on the case.

Because the attorney-client privilege is so broad, you should tell your lawyer all negative and potentially damaging information as well as those facts that might help your case. A lawyer who knows about potential problems can develop legal tactics to counter or explain them—that is part of a lawyer's job. It is the things you *don't* tell your lawyer that often cause the most trouble. If the lawyer is caught by surprise by a damaging piece of information, it might be too late for damage control.

How can I help my lawyer do a good job?

There are many things a good lawyer should do to keep your relationship on the right track, such as informing you of important developments in the case, including you in the decision-making process, and preparing you for important lawsuit events, like testifying in court or answering questions in a deposition.

There are also some things you can do to help your lawyer advocate more effectively on your behalf. Following these tips will save you time and money—and may lead to a more successful result in your lawsuit.

- **Keep your lawyer informed.** As soon as you hire a lawyer, tell the lawyer everything that might pertain to the dispute. Hand over any documents or other items that might be rel-

evant. If you aren't sure whether a particular fact is important, err on the side of full disclosure. Lawyers are trained to sift through information and determine what is useful and what is not. Your lawyer might be able to use a fact or document you thought was insignificant as the basis for a creative legal argument. And if the information might harm your case, the lawyer will have plenty of time to prepare defensive maneuvers.

- **Carefully prepare summaries, timelines, and other materials.** At the beginning of a lawsuit, your lawyer may ask you to write down important facts or a summary of events leading up to the lawsuit. Lawyers request this information in different forms—some will ask for a timeline, others for a detailed written summary, and others might simply request a few notes or ask you to tell them all the facts in person. No matter what your lawyer requests, make sure that what you write or say is accurate. Your lawyer will base your claims and defenses on this information.

- **Search thoroughly for documents and information.** During the course of a lawsuit, your lawyer may ask you for a particular document or certain facts relating to an important incident. Remember, you have much easier access to information about your lawsuit than the lawyer does. Try to answer these requests promptly.

- **Promptly respond to your lawyer's requests.** During a lawsuit, lawyers often have to work under very tight deadlines. The more time you give your lawyer to digest the material you provide, the better job your lawyer can do using that material to prepare important legal papers. If you aren't able to respond quickly, let your lawyer know as soon as possible. Your lawyer might be able to get an extension of time from your opponent or the court, or rearrange other matters to accommodate the delay.

• **Keep your lawyer apprised of your schedule.** There are certain events in a lawsuit in which you must participate. Often, these events are scheduled weeks or months in advance. Most of these events can be postponed or moved up to accommodate your schedule, if the lawyer has enough advance warning that you won't be available. But be prepared to change your plans if you must—a judge might insist on holding important events (including your trial) on a particular date, regardless of your availability.

May your life be filled with lawyers.

—MEXICAN CURSE

I've lost confidence in my lawyer. Can I fire him?

You have the right to end a relationship with a lawyer at any time. But if the lawyer you don't like is representing you on a contingency-fee basis (for a percentage of any recovery), it is often better not to part ways unless the lawyer's services really are substandard and you have a better lawyer lined up or feel you can handle the case yourself. That's because unless lots of money is involved, it can often be hard to find a second lawyer who will agree to pick up your case in the middle. Changing lawyers under a contingency-fee arrangement usually means any fee from the recovery you eventually get will have to be split between the two lawyers—something the second lawyer may not want to agree to, especially if that lawyer will have to clean up after the first.

I fired my lawyer, but I need my file. How do I get it?

Ask for it, or sign an authorization allowing your new attorney to get it. Even if you have a fee dispute with your former lawyer or you simply have not paid your bill, you are entitled to your file. If you have decided to represent yourself, demand that the lawyer turn your file over to you. If the lawyer refuses, contact your state's bar association for help.

I'm pretty sure my lawyer screwed up my case. Can I sue for malpractice?

Yes. But unfortunately, it is very hard to win a malpractice case. Malpractice means that the lawyer failed to use the ordinary skill and care that would be used by other lawyers in handling a similar problem or case under similar circumstances.

To win a malpractice case against an attorney, you must prove four basic things:

• duty—that the attorney owed you a duty to act properly
• breach—that the attorney breached the duty, was negligent, made a mistake, or did not do as he or she promised
• causation—that this conduct caused you harm, and
• damages—that you suffered financial losses as a result.

Causation may be your biggest hurdle. To win a malpractice case, you usually must prove not only that your lawyer made a mistake but that you would have won the underlying case if the lawyer hadn't mishandled it. Then, you will have to show that if you had won the underlying case, you would have been able to collect from the defendant. For example, let's say you were hit by a car when you were walking across the street, and you hired a lawyer who didn't file the lawsuit on time, with the result that your claim was legally dead. You sue for malpractice and can easily prove the lawyer's negligence and the driver's liability. But to win the malpractice case against your lawyer, you'd also have to show that the driver had the ability to pay your claim. If you can't show that the driver had the assets to pay the judgment, you won't win your malpractice case, even though the lawyer clearly blew it and the driver was clearly at fault.

It can be tough to find a lawyer to represent you in a legal malpractice case, especially if you want to pay on a contingency-fee basis (that is, the lawyer would get a share of whatever you win). Because these cases can be difficult and time-consuming, lawyers are generally reluctant to accept any but the strongest cases, unless quite a bit of money is involved.

My lawyer seems to have stopped working on my case. Is this malpractice?

The longer your attorney ignores you and your case, the more likely it is to amount to malpractice. You should act quickly to see that your case is properly handled, and get another lawyer if necessary. Writing or faxing a letter expressing your concerns and asking for a meeting is a good first step.

My lawyer originally said my case was worth six figures but now suggests that I settle for peanuts. Can I sue the lawyer for the difference?

No. It's possible that newly discovered facts made your case worth less than first thought. Or, your lawyer may have initially given you an optimistic estimate of the value of your case to get your business. In either case, this does not amount to malpractice. To find out, get your file from your lawyer and get a second opinion as to the value of your case. If another reputable lawyer believes you are being advised to settle for too little, consider changing lawyers.

Can I sue my lawyer for settling my case without my authorization?

Yes, but you would have to prove that your lawyer settled the case for less than it was worth.

I'm worried that my lawyer may have misused money I paid as a retainer. What should I do?

If you seriously suspect your lawyer has misused or misappropriated money held for you in trust, complain to your state's attorney regulatory agency right away. Although regulation of lawyers is lax in most states, complaints about stealing clients' money are almost always taken seriously, so you should get a prompt response.

My Lawyer Won't Call Me Back!

It isn't malpractice if your lawyer fails to return phone calls, but it may be a sign of trouble. Try to find out why your lawyer isn't calling you back. (The lawyer may be busy, rude, sick, or procrastinating.) As you do this, examine the possibility that your lawyer may be avoiding you for a good reason—you may be too demanding. A good way to deal with this situation is to write or fax the lawyer a polite but straightforward letter explaining your difficulty in communicating and asking for a phone call or meeting to reestablish or restore your relationship. If your lawyer really has abandoned you, contact your state's bar association to find out what you can do.

Big Bills

If you receive an unexpectedly large bill, your lawyer may have overcharged you. In this situation, you have six options:

- You can pay the entire bill and vow not to go near that attorney again.

- You can pay the part of the bill you think is reasonable, with a letter explaining why you are refusing to pay the rest.

- You can refuse to pay anything until the lawyer agrees to accept less as full payment.

- In most states and situations, you can request fee arbitration from a state or local bar association, usually before a panel made up of local lawyers and perhaps one or two nonlawyers. Arbitration is a process where a supposedly neutral decision maker resolves your fee dispute. But when it comes to disputes over legal fees, you will normally want to follow this approach only if it is "nonbinding," meaning that you are free to reject the arbitrator's decision. That's because whenever an arbitration is conducted by a panel dominated by lawyers, you risk getting a biased result.

- You can pay the bill and file a complaint with your state attorney disciplinary agency.

- You can pay the bill and sue your attorney for a refund.

While weighing these options, keep in mind that a lawyer who has not been paid has far more motive to settle for a reasonable amount than does a lawyer who has already received half of your fee. So, even if you believe your attorney is entitled to part of the big bill, it often makes sense to try to arrive at a mutually acceptable compromise before you pull out your checkbook.

 More Information About Finding and Working With a Lawyer

The Lawsuit Survival Guide: A Client's Companion to Litigation, by Joseph Matthews (Nolo), is a step-by-step guide for people who are involved in a lawsuit. It can help you find a good lawyer, work successfully with your lawyer, and avoid problems right from the start. Available as a downloadable eBook only at www.nolo.com.

 Online Help

www.nolo.com

Nolo's website offers self-help information about a wide variety of legal topics, including representing yourself in court, small claims court, mediation, and how to handle problems with your lawyer. It also provides links to federal, state, local, and small claims courts around the country.

www.legalethics.com

This site provides links to every state's legal ethics rules (rules of professional conduct), ethics opinions, and rules on lawyer confidentiality and advertising.

www.ncsconline.org

The National Center for State Courts' website provides links to state and local court websites. These sites often contain helpful legal information, court forms, and instructions.

www.uscourts.gov

The federal judiciary's website provides links to federal court websites.

Criminal Law and Procedure

It is a less evil that some criminals should escape than that the government should play an ignoble part.

—OLIVER WENDELL HOLMES

The word "criminal" reflects our society's belief that certain acts are unacceptable and that people who commit these acts should be punished. Because going to jail is such a serious consequence, however, our state and federal constitutions put strict limits on how far a prosecutor can go to obtain a conviction. As a result—and perhaps as a price—the court system sometimes appears to protect the criminal rather than the victim. On the other hand, if the system doesn't place a heavy burden on government prosecutors, we risk sending innocent people to jail and making it easier for our government to slide into totalitarian practices. One thing is certain: No matter what type of system we have for prosecuting and punishing people who commit crimes, it will always be a matter of great controversy.

> **Caution!**
>
> The material in this chapter is designed to give you a general overview of several important criminal law topics. As you read, keep in mind that the criminal justice system differs in many small but important ways from state to state, county to county, and even court to court. This means that some of the material in this chapter may not be applicable in your area.
>
> Because we cannot precisely describe the law in your state and what is likely to happen in any particular case, consider this chapter a place to get started. To get more specific and reliable information, do some research or consult a knowledgeable criminal defense attorney.

Criminal Law and Procedure: An Overview

A crime is any behavior that is punishable by imprisonment or fine (or both). State legislatures have an almost unlimited ability to decide which behaviors are considered crimes, and often their decisions do more than simply define socially unacceptable behaviors—they also reflect the values and judgments of the legislators. For example, most state legislatures define welfare fraud as a crime, and welfare recipients who cheat can end up in jail.

While state legislatures have broad powers to decide what constitutes a crime, Congress can define behavior as a crime only if the U.S. Constitution authorizes Congress to regulate that type of behavior in the first place. For example, the Constitution gives Congress the power to "regulate commerce … among the several States." Congress, therefore, can make many activities—such as racketeering—illegal, if the actions cross state lines or affect commerce that involves more than one state.

Who decides how the criminal justice system works?

Though legislators have relatively unfettered power to decide whether certain behavior should be a crime, many rules limit the ways in which the state or federal government can prosecute someone for a crime. These restrictions start with the U.S. Constitution's Bill of Rights, which provides basic protections—such as the right to refuse to incriminate oneself, the right to confront one's accusers, and the right to a trial by jury—for people charged with crimes. State constitutions may offer more protections

than the federal law, but they cannot take away federal rights. Federal and state legislatures can pass laws governing how criminal procedures work in their jurisdictions, but these laws cannot reduce the protections offered by the federal and state constitutions.

The interplay between constitutional provisions and legislative enactments is regulated by our courts. Courts decide whether or not a particular legislative rule, court practice, or police action is permissible under federal and state constitutional law. What may seem like a slight variation from one case to another can be, in the eyes of a court, the determining factor that leads to a vastly different result. For example, a police officer is frisking a burglary suspect on the street and feels a hard object in the suspect's pocket. Suspecting that the object is a possible weapon, the officer reaches into the pocket and finds both a cardboard cigarette box and a packet of heroin. This action by the police officer—reaching into the pocket to protect the officer's safety—would be a permissible search under the rulings of most courts, and the heroin could be admitted into court as evidence. However, if the officer had initially felt a soft object that obviously was not a weapon, then reaching into the suspect's pocket might be an illegal search, in which case the heroin couldn't be used as evidence.

What's the difference between a felony and a misdemeanor?

Most states break their crimes into two major groups—felonies and misdemeanors. Whether a crime falls into one category or the other depends on the potential punishment. If a law provides for imprisonment for longer than a year, it is usually considered a felony. If the potential punishment is for a year or less, then the crime is usually considered a misdemeanor. In some states, certain crimes, called "wobblers," may be either a misdemeanor or a felony, because under some conditions the punishment may be imprisonment for less than a year, and in other situations, the criminal may go to prison for a year or more.

Behaviors punishable only by fine (such as traffic violations) are usually not considered crimes at all, but infractions. But a legislature may on occasion punish behavior only by fine and still provide that it is a misdemeanor—possession of small amounts of marijuana might fall into this category.

How can I tell from reading a criminal statute whether I'm guilty of the crime it defines?

All criminal statutes define crimes in terms of acts and a required state of mind, usually described as the actor's "intent." These requirements are known as the "elements" of the offense. A prosecutor must convince a judge or jury that the person charged with the crime (the defendant) did the acts and had the intent described in the statute. For example, commercial burglary is commonly defined as entering a structure (such as a store) belonging to another person, with the intent to commit petty or grand theft (that is, to steal) or any felony. To convict a person of this offense, the prosecutor would have to prove three elements:

1. The defendant entered the structure.

2. The structure belonged to another person.

3. The defendant entered the structure intending to commit petty or grand theft or any felony.

To figure out whether you may be found guilty of a crime, parse the crime into its required elements to see if each applies in your situation.

What is the presumption of innocence?

All people accused of a crime are legally presumed to be innocent until they are convicted, either in a trial or as a result of pleading guilty. This presumption means not only that the prosecutor must convince the jury of the defendant's guilt but also that the defendant need not say or do anything in his or her own defense. If the prosecutor can't convince the jury that the defendant is guilty, the defendant goes free.

What does it mean to prove guilt "beyond a reasonable doubt"?

To convict a defendant of a crime, the prosecution must prove the defendant's guilt beyond a reasonable doubt. This does not mean that the prosecution must prove guilt beyond *all* doubt, nor does it mean proof beyond *some* doubt. Rather, it means something in between. What exactly that something is can be hard to define (indeed, courts and lawyers have struggled with this throughout history), but everyone agrees that a jury must possess a high degree of certainty in the defendant's guilt before it can convict.

If I'm accused of a crime, am I guaranteed a trial by a jury?

Yes. The U.S. Constitution guarantees the right to a jury trial to anyone accused of any crime where the maximum punishment is six months or more in jail. Some states (for example, California) guarantee a jury trial for any misdemeanor or felony charge, even where the maximum possible sentence is less than six months. This right has long been interpreted to require a 12-person jury that must arrive at a unanimous decision to convict or acquit. (In most states, a lack of unanimity is called a "hung jury," and the defendant will go free unless the prosecutor decides to retry the case.

If I do not have any witnesses who will testify on my behalf, can I still win at trial?

Yes. Defendants often go to trial without having anyone testify for them. In such a situation, the defendant's lawyer will focus on cross-examining the prosecution witnesses in order to poke holes in the prosecutor's case—thereby showing that reasonable doubt exists. Defense attorneys rely on a variety of arguments to discredit the prosecutor's witnesses. Some common arguments include:

- Prosecution witnesses are biased against the defendant and therefore are lying or grossly exaggerating.
- Prosecution witnesses are mistaken in their observations because the lighting was bad, they were under the influence of drugs or alcohol, or they were too far away.
- Evidence from police laboratories is unreliable because the machines were not properly maintained or the technicians were not properly trained.
- Prosecution witnesses are lying to get a good deal on the criminal charges they are facing (prosecution witnesses are often criminals who have been offered a deal if they testify against the defendant).

What these arguments have in common is that they do not depend on defense evidence. Rather, they rely on the presumption of innocence and the prosecutor's failure to overcome it by proving guilt beyond a reasonable doubt.

Why would an innocent defendant choose not to testify?

A criminal defendant has a right not to testify, and jurors will be told that they cannot assume anything negative if the defendant decides to keep quiet. Of course, some jurors do assume that a defendant who doesn't testify is guilty—and they cast their votes accordingly. On the other hand, there are some excellent reasons why an innocent defendant might remain silent in court:

- If the defendant has previously been convicted of a crime, the prosecutor may be able to ask questions about it—but only if the defendant testifies. Evidence of a previous crime may cause some jurors to think that the defendant is guilty of the current crime too.
- If the defendant testifies, the prosecutor may be able to bring out other information that discredits the defendant's reputation and testimony.
- Some defendants have a poor demeanor when speaking in public. A judge or jury may not believe a defendant who, though telling the truth, is a nervous witness and makes a bad impression.
- The defendant may have a perfectly good story that would nevertheless sound fishy to the average jury in that particular locale.

What is self-defense—and how can a defendant prove it?

Self-defense is a common defense asserted by someone charged with a crime of violence, such as battery (striking someone), assault with a deadly weapon, or murder. The defendant admits committing the act but claims that it was justified by the other person's threatening actions. The core issues in most self-defense cases are:

- Who was the aggressor?
- Did the defendant reasonably believe that self-defense was necessary?
- If so, was the force used by the defendant also reasonable?

Self-defense is rooted in the belief that people should be allowed to protect themselves from physical harm. This means that a person does not have to wait until he or she is actually struck to act in self-defense. Somone who reasonably believes that a physical attack is imminent has the right to strike first and prevent the attack. But someone who uses more force than is reasonable may be guilty of a crime, even though some force was justifiable.

When can a defendant win an acquittal on grounds of insanity?

The insanity defense is based on the principle that punishment is justified only if the defendant is capable of controlling his or her behavior and understanding that what he or she has done is wrong. Because some people suffering from a mental disorder are not capable of knowing or choosing right from wrong, the insanity defense prevents them from being criminally punished.

Despite its ancient origins (it seems to have begun in England in 1505), the insanity defense remains controversial. Victim-oriented critics point out that a person killed by an insane person is just as dead as a person killed by someone who is sane, and they argue that people should be punished for the harm they cause regardless of their mental state. Critics also question the ability of psychiatrists, judges, and jurors to determine whether a person suffers from a mental disorder and to link mental disorders to the commission of crimes.

The insanity defense is an extremely complex topic; many scholarly works are devoted to explaining its nuances. Here are some major points of interest:

- Despite popular perceptions to the contrary, defendants rarely enter pleas of "not guilty by reason of insanity." On the few occasions that the defendant does raise it, judges and jurors rarely support it.
- Because neither the legal system nor psychiatrists can agree on a single meaning of insanity in the criminal law context, various definitions are employed. The most popular definition is the "McNaghten rule," which defines insanity as "the inability to distinguish right from wrong." Another common test is known as "irresistible impulse": A person who acts out of an irresistible impulse knows that an act is wrong, but because of mental illness, cannot control his or her actions.
- Defendants found not guilty by reason of insanity are not automatically set free. They are usually confined to a mental institution and not released until their sanity is established. These defendants can spend more time in a mental institution than they would have spent in prison had they been convicted.
- An insanity defense normally rests on the testimony of a psychiatrist, who testifies after examining the defendant and the facts of the case. Courts appoint psychiatrists at government expense to assist poor defendants who

cannot afford to hire their own psychiatrists. The prosecution will normally hire another psychiatrist, who may offer an opinion different from the defense psychiatrist.

Competency to Stand Trial

Aside from insanity as a defense to criminal charges, the question may arise as to whether a defendant is mentally capable of facing a trial. Defendants cannot be prosecuted if they suffer from a mental disorder that prevents them from understanding the proceedings and assisting in the preparation of their defense. Based on a defendant's unusual behavior, a judge, prosecutor, or defense attorney may ask that trial be delayed until the defendant has been examined and found able to understand the proceedings. If a judge finds that a defendant doesn't understand what's going on, the defendant will probably be placed in a mental institution until his or her competence is reestablished. At that time, the trial will be held.

Can a defendant use drinking or drug use as a defense?

Defendants who commit crimes under the influence of drugs or alcohol sometimes argue that their mental functioning was so impaired that they cannot be held accountable for their actions. Generally, however, voluntary intoxication does not excuse criminal conduct. People know (or should know) that alcohol and drugs affect mental functioning, and thus they are legally responsible if they commit crimes as a result of their voluntary use.

Some states allow an exception to this general rule. If the defendant is accused of committing a crime that requires what's known as "specific intent" (intending the precise consequences, as well as intending to do the physical act that leads up to the consequences), the defendant can argue that he or she was too drunk or high to have that intent. This is only a partial defense, however, because it doesn't entirely excuse the defendant's actions. In this situation, the defendant will usually be convicted of another crime that doesn't require proof of a specific intent—for example, assault with a deadly weapon instead of assault with the intent to commit murder.

If You Are Questioned by the Police

There is plenty of law at the end of a nightstick.

—GROVER A. WHALEN

If a police officer wants to stop and question you, whether or not you must comply depends on the circumstances and the reasons the officer has for questioning you. This section explores some of the common questions people have about their rights and responsibilities when approached by a law enforcement officer.

If an officer wants to stop me while I'm walking on the street and I know I've done nothing wrong, should I comply?

Police officers may interfere with your freedom of movement only if they have observed unusual or received information activity or received information suggesting that criminal activity is afoot and that you are involved. Even if the officers are mistaken, however, you do not have the right to keep walking. As long as the officers have a good faith belief in your connection to criminal activity, they are allowed to detain you. This doesn't mean that you must answer all of the officer's questions. (See below.)

If You Run Away

It is not unusual for people who are approached by the police to run away. Some courts have recognized that people of color, in particular, have a well-founded fear of unfair treatment at the hands of the police, and that many people will avoid contact with the police not because they are guilty of a crime but because they reasonably believe that they may be mistreated or unjustly accused. Other courts view evasive behavior as evidence of guilt, however, and allow the police to rely on the attempt to run away as grounds for a detention.

If I am legally stopped by a police officer on the street, can I be searched?

Yes and no. A police officer is permitted to briefly frisk your outer clothing for weapons if the officer reasonably fears for his or her safety.

A frisk is different from a search, however. A search may be conducted for evidence of a crime or contraband (an illegal item) and may be much more intrusive than a frisk. An officer may not search you unless he or she has good cause to believe that you committed a crime or that you're hiding an illegal item. (See *Searches and Seizures,* below.)

How a Frisk Becomes a Search— And Possibly an Arrest

When frisking a person for weapons, the police are attuned not only to the feel of possible weapons under clothing but also to the feel of packaged drugs. Although a frisk may not turn up a weapon, it may turn up a suspicious package that the officer knows is commonly used to carry illegal drugs or some other illegal substance. A discovery like that may give the officer the right to conduct a more intensive search of the person's clothing. The lesson here is that a frisk often leads to a search. And if a search produces an illegal substance, it may result in an arrest.

If I am questioned by a police officer after being stopped on the street, do I have to respond?

The general rule is that you don't have to answer any questions that the police ask you. This rule comes from the Fifth Amendment to the U.S. Constitution, which protects you from self-incrimination. As with all rules, however, there is an exception. Many local and state governments have antiloitering laws that require people to account for their presence if the police have a reasonable suspicion that they are loitering. Once the police have asked all of their questions about loitering, however, you don't have to answer any others—such as questions about a crime in the neighborhood.

A defense lawyer's most sacred piece of advice is this: Don't talk to the police about a crime unless you clearly weren't involved and you want to help the police solve it. And even then, it's not a bad idea to politely demur until you have your own attorney or a public defender by your side. After all, history is filled with instances in which an innocent person has ineptly talked his or her way into a criminal charge or conviction.

Searches and Seizures

Most people instinctively understand the concept of privacy. At the same time, most of us acknowledge that society is served when the police, in appropriate circumstances, are allowed to look for and seize contraband, stolen goods, and evidence of a crime.

In an attempt to balance our desires for privacy against the legitimate needs of the police, the Fourth Amendment of the U.S. Constitution prohibits only unreasonable searches and seizures by state or federal law officers. Generally, this means that the police may conduct a search of your home, barn, car, boat, office, personal or business documents, bank account records, trash barrel, or any other property if:

- the police can show that it is more likely than not that a crime has occurred and that they will probably find evidence or contraband if they are allowed to search (this requirement is called "probable cause"), and
- a judge agrees there is probable cause and issues a search warrant, or the police are permitted to search without a warrant because of the particular circumstances involved.

So, for a search to be legal under the Constitution, the police must have both probable cause to conduct the search and a search warrant (although the warrant requirement has many exceptions, some of which we discuss below).

When is a police investigation considered a search?

A police investigation is not a search unless it intrudes on a person's privacy. In other words, if a person did not have a legitimate expectation of privacy in the place or thing searched, no search has occurred, at least not for the purpose of determining whether the Fourth Amendment has been violated.

Courts ask two questions to determine whether a person had a legitimate expectation of privacy in the place or things searched:

- Did the person expect some degree of privacy?
- Is the person's expectation reasonable—that is, one that society is willing to recognize?

For example, a person who uses a public restroom expects not to have an audience, and most people—including judges and juries—would consider that expectation to be reasonable. Therefore, if the police install a hidden video camera in a public restroom, the action is considered a search and must meet the Fourth Amendment's requirement of reasonableness.

On the other hand, if the police glance into a car and see a weapon on the front seat, it is not a search because it is unlikely that a person would think that the front seat of a car is private—after all, anyone can look through the car windows and see what's on the seat.

How Private Is Your Property?

Generally, if the police are able to view contraband or evidence on your property without actually entering it, they have not conducted a search. In other words, you cannot have a reasonable expectation of privacy in an area that can legitimately be seen from outside your property. This means that the police can use what they have seen as the basis for getting a warrant to come in and take a closer look. Or, if the situation calls for prompt action (the need to stop a drug deal, for instance), they may enter without a warrant.

Law enforcement officers are allowed to take aerial photographs or come close enough to overhear your conversations—these actions are not considered searches. On the other hand, without a warrant or an exception to the rule requiring a warrant, officers are not allowed to use sophisticated equipment, such as thermal-imaging devices, to discover what is on your property or to eavesdrop on your conversations. In general, if the investigation method is highly artificial and high-tech, it's likely to be considered a search. Where the line is drawn, however, is not clear or consistent from state to state.

What is a search warrant?

A search warrant is a kind of permission slip, signed by a judge, that allows the police to enter private property to look for particular items. It is addressed to the owner of the property, and it tells the owner that a judge has decided that it is reasonably likely that certain contraband, or evidence of criminal activities, will be found in specified locations on the property.

As a general rule, the police are supposed to apply for a warrant before conducting a search of private property; any search that is conducted without a warrant is presumed to be unreasonable—even if there was probable cause to conduct the search. This means that the police officers will later have to justify the search—and why a warrant wasn't obtained first—if the defendant challenges it in court.

What does it take to get a search warrant?

A judge will issue a search warrant if the police can show that:

- it is more likely than not that a crime has taken place, and
- items connected to the crime are likely be found in a specified location on the property.

To convince the judge of these facts, the police tell the judge what they know about the situation. Usually, the information given to the judge is based either on the officers' own observations or on the secondhand observations of an informant.

The police are limited in their ability to use secondhand information. As a general rule, the information must be reliable given the circumstances. A judge will normally deem information to be reliable if it is corroborated by police observation. For example, a citizen's tip that a suspect regularly delivers drugs to a certain location would be corroborated if an officer observes that suspect's routine. But corroboration is not necessary in every case. Sometimes a judge will issue a warrant if the source of the information is known to the police and has provided trustworthy information in the past, and sometimes the judge won't insist upon even that.

What are the police allowed to do after they obtain a search warrant?

Once the police have a search warrant, they are entitled to enter the designated property to search for the items listed on the warrant. Legally, the search is supposed to be confined to the specific areas described in the warrant. For example, if the search warrant includes only the living room, the search should not extend into the kitchen, bathroom, or bedroom. But there are exceptions to this limitation that allow broader searches. For example, the police may search beyond the terms of the warrant in order to:

- ensure their safety and the safety of others
- prevent the destruction of evidence
- discover more about possible evidence or contraband that is in plain view elsewhere on the property, or
- hunt for evidence or contraband that, as a result of their initial search, they believe exists in another location on the property.

For instance, although a warrant might be issued for the search of a house, the sound of a shotgun being loaded in the backyard would justify expanding the search to the yard in order to protect the officers; similarly, a search limited to the ground floor might legitimately expand to the upstairs if the police, searching for illegal drugs, hear toilets being flushed above. And the police can always seize evidence or illegal items if they are in plain view or are discovered while the officers are searching for the items listed in the warrant.

Do the police always need a warrant to conduct a search?

No. In many situations, police may legally conduct a search without first obtaining a warrant.

- **Consent searches.** If the police ask your permission to search your home, purse, briefcase, or other property, and you agree, the search is considered consensual, and they don't need a warrant.
- **Searches that accompany an arrest.** When a person is placed under arrest, the police may search the person and the immediate surroundings for weapons that might be used to harm the officer. If the person is taken to jail, the police may search to make sure that weapons or contraband are not brought into the jail. (This is called an inventory search.) Inventory searches might also involve a search of the arrested person's car (if it is being held by the police) and personal effects on the theory that the police need a precise record of the person's property to avoid claims of theft.
- **Searches necessary to protect the safety of the public.** The police don't need a warrant if they have a reasonable fear that their safety, or that of the public, is in imminent danger. For example, an officer who suspected a bomb-making operation while walking his beat might be justified in entering immediately and seizing the ingredients. And in the famous O.J. Simpson case, the police justified their entry onto O.J. Simpson's property on the grounds that they feared for the safety of other family members.
- **Searches necessary to prevent the imminent destruction of evidence.** A police officer does not need a warrant if he or she has observed illegal items (such as weapons or contraband) and believes that the items will disappear unless the officer takes prompt action. This exception arises most frequently

when the police spot contraband or weapons in a car. Because cars are moved so frequently, the officer is justified in searching the entire vehicle, including the trunk, without obtaining a warrant—if the officer has probable cause. On the other hand, if the police learn about a marijuana-growing operation from a neighbor, they usually would need a warrant, as it is unlikely that the growing plants and other evidence of the operation will disappear quickly enough to justify a warrantless search.

- **"Hot pursuit" searches.** Police may enter private dwellings to search for criminals who are fleeing the scene of a crime.

Can my roommate—or my landlord—give the police permission to search my apartment?

The police may search your apartment if the person in charge of the premises gives permission. If you and your roommate share common areas (such as the kitchen and living room), your roommate can authorize a search of those areas. But your roommate cannot give permission to search your separate bedroom.

Similarly, your landlord cannot give permission to search your apartment. Although the landlord owns the property, your monthly check guarantees your privacy at home. This is true even if you are behind in your rent or your landlord has sued to evict you. Until the landlord has a court order that permits him or her to enter and retake the premises, he cannot come in without your permission. (But keep in mind that many states allow a landlord to enter for inspections, which usually require advance notice of a day or two.) If the police can point to circumstances that would justify immediate entry, however—such as the sound of a ferocious fight or the smell of burning marijuana—they may enter without permission from anyone.

Arrests and Interrogations

I haven't committed a crime.
What I did was fail to comply with the law.

–DAVID DINKINS

An arrest occurs when a police officer armed with an arrest warrant utters the words "you're under arrest," or when a police officer's actions cause you to believe that you are not free to leave. The restraint must be more than a mere detention on the street (discussed above). Although in most situations the police will take you to the police station for booking (photographs and fingerprinting), it is also possible for an officer to arrest and book you at the crime scene, and then release you when you give a written promise to appear in court at a later time.

After the police arrest you, they will often question you in order to find out more about the crime, your role in it, and whether there may be other suspects. There are several constitutional protections that you may invoke during police interrogations.

When do the police need a warrant to make an arrest?

As long as the police have good reason (called "probable cause") to believe that a crime has been committed and that the person they want to arrest committed the crime, they can, with just one exception, make an arrest without asking a judge for a warrant.

The exception? There are few situations in which the adage "a man's home is his castle" still applies, but an arrest at home is one of them. The police must usually have a warrant to arrest a person at home if the arrest is for a nonserious offense—such as a simple assault—and there is no fear that the person they want to arrest will destroy evidence or cause harm to the public.

How do the police obtain an arrest warrant?

An officer must present sworn evidence to a judge that a crime has occurred and that the police have probable cause to believe that the crime was committed by the person they want to arrest. If the judge agrees, he or she will issue a warrant. The police are then entitled to seize the person.

If the police make an arrest that doesn't follow the rules, is the arrested person set free?

Not necessarily. But if a search is conducted during the arrest and turns up incriminating evidence, the evidence may be kept out of the person's trial on the grounds that it is "fruit of the poisonous tree"—that is, the evidence was found as the result of an improper arrest. Also, if the illegally arrested person makes any statements to the police after being arrested, the statements may not be used as evidence. This is true whether or not the arrested person was "read his rights." (See below.)

Can a person who is charged with a crime be forced to give bodily samples?

Yes. You might think that being forced to give bodily samples—such as blood, hair, or fingernail clippings—is a violation of the U.S. Constitution's protection against self-incrimi-

nation, found in the Fifth Amendment. But the U.S. Supreme Court thinks otherwise. It has ruled that the Fifth Amendment protects communications only, and that bodily samples are physical evidence and therefore are not covered by the Constitution.

If I'm arrested, do the police have to "read me my rights"?

No. They don't need to read your rights unless they want to question you. However, if they don't read you your rights, they can't use anything you say in response to custodial questioning as evidence against you at trial. What are these rights? Popularly known as the *Miranda* warning (ordered by the U.S. Supreme Court in *Miranda v. Arizona*), your rights consist of the familiar litany invoked by T.V. police immediately upon arresting a suspect:

- You have the right to remain silent.
- If you do say anything, what you say can be used against you in a court of law.
- You have the right to consult with a lawyer and have that lawyer present during any questioning.
- If you cannot afford a lawyer, one will be appointed for you if you so desire.
- If you choose to talk to the police officer, you have the right to stop the interview at any time. (This part of the warning is usually omitted from the screenplay.)

It doesn't matter whether an interrogation occurs in a jail or at the scene of a crime, on a busy downtown street or in the middle of an open field: If you are in custody (deprived of your freedom of action in any significant way), the police must give a *Miranda* warning if they want to question you and use your answers as evidence at trial. If you are not in police custody, however, no *Miranda* warning is required. This exception most often comes up when the police stop someone on the street to question them about a recent crime, and the person blurts out a confession before the police have an opportunity to deliver the warning.

Will a judge dismiss my case if I was questioned without a *Miranda* warning?

No. Many people mistakenly believe that a case will be thrown out of court if the police fail to give *Miranda* warnings to the arrested person. What *Miranda* actually says is that a warning is necessary if the police interrogate a suspect and want to use any of the suspect's answers as evidence. If the police fail to give you a *Miranda* warning, in most situations nothing you say in response to the questioning can be used as evidence to convict you. In addition, under the "fruit of the poisonous tree" rule, if the police find evidence as a result of an interrogation that violates the *Miranda* rule, that evidence is also inadmissible at trial. For example, if you tell the police where a weapon is hidden and it turns out that you gave this information in response to improper questioning, the police will not be able to use the weapon as evidence unless the police can prove that they would have found the weapon without your statements. If there is sufficient other evidence to convict you beyond any statements you made to the police, you can still be convicted even when the police don't give *Miranda* warnings.

What's the best way to assert my right to remain silent if I am being questioned by the police?

If you're taken into custody by the police, you don't have to use any magic words to let police officers know that you want to remain silent. You can simply say nothing in response to police questions. Or, after an officer gives you a *Miranda* warning, you can stop the questioning by saying something like:

- I want to talk to an attorney.
- I won't say anything until I talk to an attorney.
- I don't have anything to say.
- I don't want to talk to you anymore.
- I claim my *Miranda* rights.

If the police continue to question you after you have asserted your right to remain silent, they have violated *Miranda*. As a result, anything you say after that point—and any evidence gleaned from that conversation—should not ordinarily be admissible at your trial. Once you've invoked your right to silence, however, the best course is to remain silent, instead of counting on a judge to disregard your statements further down the line.

How heavy-handed can the police get when asking questions?

Information that you voluntarily disclose to a police officer (after you have been properly warned) is generally admissible at trial. The key word is "voluntary." Police officers are not allowed to use physical force or psychological coercion to get you to talk to them. If police officers obtain information through any of these illegal means, the information cannot be used by the prosecutor at trial regardless of whether you invoked your *Miranda* rights. In addition, under the "fruit of the poisonous tree" rule, any evidence that the police obtain as the result of a coerced statement is equally inadmissible.

Can the police question me after I ask for a lawyer?

If you tell the police that you want to talk to a lawyer—whether it's a lawyer you've already hired to represent you or a lawyer to be appointed by the court—they must immediately stop the interview. What's more, the police aren't allowed to start questioning you again (in an effort to get you to admit something inadvertently) until you've had the chance to speak to an attorney. You can invoke this right at any time during the interview, even if you've already answered some questions.

However, the U.S. Supreme Court has held that this right doesn't apply to new or different crimes, even if they are related to the crime for which you requested an attorney. For example, if you are arrested for arson and you ask to speak to a lawyer, the police cannot ask you any questions about the fire. However, if they later find a dead body in the charred ruins, they can question you about that without your attorney present. You still have the right to counsel for the new crimes, however. So, if you tell the police that you want to talk to your lawyer before you answer any questions about the dead body, they must stop the interview immediately.

**Reality Check:
Cops Usually Win a Swearing Contest**

Defendants often claim that police officers coerced them into talking. And it's just as common for police officers to say that the defendants spoke voluntarily. If the police physically coerce a defendant into talking, the defendant can try to prove it with photos of marks and bruises. But it may be difficult to provide clear evidence of police brutality, and a defendant cannot usually offer independent evidence to support claims of psychological coercion. Judges, believing that defendants have a greater motivation to lie than do police officers, usually side with the police and conclude that no coercion took place.

Bail

Those who expect to reap the blessings of freedom must ... undergo the fatigue of supporting it.

—THOMAS PAINE

Many people, especially those arrested for minor misdemeanors, are given citations at the scene of an arrest telling them when to appear in court, and then are immediately released. Others, however, are put in jail. Often, a person's first thought upon landing in jail is how to get out—and fast. The usual way to do this is to post bail. This section answers common questions about the bail system, including its version of Monopoly's "Get Out of Jail Free" card—called release O.R.

What does it mean to "post bail"?

Bail is cash or a cash equivalent that an arrested person gives to a court to ensure that he or she will appear in court when ordered to do so. If the defendant appears in court at the proper time, the court refunds the bail. But if the defendant doesn't show up, the court keeps the bail and issues a warrant for the defendant's arrest.

Bail can take any of the following forms:

• cash or check for the full amount of the bail

• property worth the full amount of the bail

• a bond—that is, a guaranteed payment of the full bail amount, or

• a waiver of payment on the condition that the defendant appear in court at the required time, commonly called "release on one's own recognizance" or simply "O.R."

Who decides how much bail I have to pay?

Judges are responsible for setting bail. Because many people want to get out of jail immediately and, depending on when you are arrested, it can take up to five days to see a judge, most jails have standard bail schedules that specify bail amounts for common crimes. You can get out of jail quickly by paying the amount set forth in the bail schedule.

Are there restrictions on how high my bail can be?

The Eighth Amendment to the U.S. Constitution requires that bail not be excessive. This means that bail should not be used to raise money for the government or to punish a person for being suspected of committing a crime. The purpose of bail is to allow an arrested person to be free until convicted of a crime,

and the amount of bail must be no more than is reasonably necessary to keep the defendant from fleeing before a case is over.

So much for theory. In fact, many judges set an impossibly high bail in particular types of cases (such as those receiving a lot of publicity) to keep a suspect in jail until the trial is over. Although bail set for this purpose—called preventive detention—is thought by many to violate the Constitution, it still happens.

What can I do if I can't afford to pay the bail listed on the bail schedule?

If you can't afford the amount of bail on the bail schedule, you can ask a judge to lower it. Depending on the state, your request must be made either in a special bail-setting hearing or when you appear in court for the first time, usually called your arraignment.

How do I pay for bail?

There are two ways to pay your bail. You may either pay the full amount of the bail or buy a bail bond. A bail bond is like a check held in reserve: It represents your promise that you will appear in court when you are supposed to. You pay a bond seller to post a bond (a certain sum of money) with the court, and the court keeps the bond in case you don't show up. You can usually buy a bail bond for about 10% of the amount of your bail; this premium is the bond seller's fee for taking the risk that you won't appear in court.

A bail bond may sound like a good deal, but buying a bond may cost you more in the long run. If you pay the full amount of the bail, you'll get that money back (less a small administrative fee) if you make your scheduled court appearances. On the other hand, the 10% premium you pay to a bond seller is nonrefundable. In addition, the bond seller may require "collateral." This means that you (or the person who pays for your bail bond) must give the bond seller a financial interest in some of your valuable property. The bond seller can cash in this interest if you fail to appear in court.

Nevertheless, if you can't afford your bail and you don't have a friend or relative that can help out, a bond seller may be your only option. You can find one by looking in the Yellow Pages; you're also likely to find bond sellers' offices very close to any jail.

Finally, be ready to pay in cash, a money order, or a cashier's check. Jails and bond sellers usually do not take credit cards or personal checks for bail.

Is it true that a defendant can sometimes get out of jail without posting bail?

Sometimes. This is generally known as releasing someone "on his own recognizance," or "O.R." A defendant released O.R. must simply sign a promise to show up in court. The defendant doesn't have to post bail. A defendant commonly requests release O.R. at his or her first court appearance. If the judge denies the request, the defendant then asks for low bail.

In general, defendants who are released O.R. have strong ties to a community, making them unlikely to flee. Factors that may convince a judge to grant an O.R. release include the following:

- The defendant has other family members (most likely parents, a spouse, or children) living in the community.
- The defendant has resided in the community for many years.

- The defendant has a steady job and owns property in the community.
- The defendant has little or no past criminal record, or any previous criminal problems were minor and occurred many years earlier.
- The defendant has been charged with previous crimes and has always appeared as required.

Getting a Lawyer

Justice oft leans to the side where your purse hangs.

—DANISH PROVERB

If you are accused of a crime, you will probably face the possibility of going to jail. This fact alone will most likely drive you to look for a good lawyer. Unfortunately, private criminal defense lawyers don't come cheap, and you may not be able to afford one. This doesn't mean you'll be completely at the mercy of the government, however. The U.S. Constitution guarantees you the right to be represented by an attorney if the state is trying to deprive you of your liberty. This means that a court may be required to appoint a lawyer to represent you for free—or for a fee you can afford. This section discusses the role of private and court-appointed attorneys in the criminal process and offers suggestions for finding a private attorney if you can afford one.

How can I get a court to appoint a lawyer for me?

Normally, if you want a court to appoint a lawyer for you at government expense, you must:

- ask the court to appoint a lawyer, and
- provide details about your financial situation.

Your first opportunity to ask the court to appoint a lawyer is usually your first court appearance, normally called your arraignment or bail hearing. The judge will probably ask you whether you are represented by a lawyer. If you're not, the judge will then ask whether you want to apply for court-appointed counsel. If you say yes, some courts will appoint a lawyer right on the spot and finish your arraignment. Other courts will delay your case and appoint a lawyer only after reviewing and approving your economic circumstances.

Each state (or even county) makes its own rules about who qualifies for a free lawyer. Also, the seriousness of the charge may affect a judge's decision about whether you are eligible for free legal assistance. For example, a judge may recognize that a wage-earner can afford the cost of representation for a minor crime but not for a crime involving a complicated and lengthy trial.

If you don't qualify for free help but can't afford the full cost of a private lawyer, you may still obtain the services of a court-appointed attorney. Most states provide for "partial indigency," which means that at the conclusion of the case, the judge will require you to reimburse the state or county for a portion of the costs of representation.

Do I need a lawyer at my arraignment?

In most criminal courts the arraignment is where you first appear before a judge and enter a plea of guilty or not guilty to the offense charged. Assuming you enter a plea of not guilty, which almost every defendant does at this early stage, the court will then:

- set a date for the next procedural event in your case
- consider any bail requests that you or the prosecutor make
- appoint your lawyer, and
- ask you to waive time—that is, give up your right to have the trial or other statutory proceedings occur within specified time limits.

Most people can handle this proceeding without a lawyer. However, if you can get the court to appoint a lawyer for you without postponing the arraignment, or you are able to arrange for private representation before your arraignment, it's always better to have a lawyer.

If I'm poor, will a judge appoint a public defender to represent me?

Because most criminal defendants are unable to afford their own attorneys, many states have public defender's offices. Typically, each local office has a chief public defender and a number of assistant public defenders (P.D.s). P.D.s are fully-licensed lawyers whose sole job is to represent poor defendants in criminal cases. Because they appear daily in the same courts, P.D.s can gain a lot of experience in a short period of time. And because they work daily with the same cast of characters, they learn the personalities (and prejudices) of the judges, prosecutors, and local law enforcement officers—important information to know when assessing a case and conducting a trial.

My county doesn't have a public defender's office. How will the court provide an attorney for me?

In areas that don't have a public defender's office, the court maintains a list of attorneys and appoints them on a rotating basis to represent people who can't afford to hire their own lawyers.

Do public defenders provide the same quality of representation as regular lawyers?

Despite the increasingly severe financial constraints on their offices, public defenders often provide representation that is at least as competent as that provided by private defense attorneys. In some public defenders' offices, the representation is the best a defendant could hope for. Many offices are staffed by experienced and dedicated attorneys. Despite good intentions and training, however, public defenders are often asked to perform too much work for not enough money, which can cut into their abilities to be effective.

How can I get a second opinion on my public defender's advice?

Like all attorneys, public defenders are ethically obligated to vigorously defend their clients' interests. Undoubtedly, most lawyers live up to their ethical duties. But defendants who think that their court-appointed attorneys are not representing them adequately can buy advice from a private defense attorney. Even a low-income person may be able to pay for a short "second opinion" consultation.

How can I find a private defense lawyer?

Recently arrested people often need to talk to a lawyer as soon as possible. The most urgent priority is often getting a lawyer to help arrange release and provide some information about what's to come in the days ahead.

If you have been represented by a criminal defense lawyer in the past, that is usually the lawyer to call—as long as you were satisfied the last time around. If you have no previous experience with criminal defense lawyers, you can look to the following sources for a referral:

- **Lawyers you know.** Most lawyers do civil (noncriminal) work, such as divorces, drafting wills, filing bankruptcies, or representing people hurt in accidents. If you know any attorney that you trust, ask him or her to recommend a criminal defense lawyer. (Some lawyers who do civil work can also represent clients in criminal matters, at least for the limited purpose of arranging for release from jail following an arrest.)

- **Family members or friends.** Someone close to you may know of a criminal defense lawyer or may have time to look for one.

- **Lawyer directories.** These services provide the names of attorneys who practice in your area. You will probably find several lawyers who specialize in criminal law and will give you an initial consultation for a low fee. You may want to begin with Nolo's lawyer directory at www.lawyers.nolo.com. This directory includes a detailed profile for each attorney with information to help you select the right lawyer for you. Nolo has confirmed that every listed attorney has a valid license and is in good standing with their bar association. (Currently, the directory covers only a handful of states, but new lawyers are being added regularly.) You may also want to check out West's Legal Directory, which lists most lawyers in the United States. You can find the directory at http://lawyers.findlaw.com or in your local law library. Be sure to take the time to check out the credentials and experience of any lawyer who is listed.

- **Courthouses.** You can visit a local courthouse and sit through a few criminal hearings. If a particular lawyer impresses you, ask for his or her card after the hearing is over, then call for an appointment.

Should I expect a lawyer to guarantee a good result?

Toasters come with guarantees; attorneys don't. Steer clear of lawyers who guarantee satisfactory outcomes. A lawyer who guarantees a good result may simply be trying a hard-sell tactic to get your business—and promising to win is against the legal code of ethics.

What is a private lawyer likely to cost?

It's impossible to give a definitive answer. Attorneys set their own fees, which vary according to a number of factors:

- **The complexity of a case.** Most attorneys charge more for felonies than for misdemeanors because felonies are likely to involve more work for the attorney.

- **The attorney's experience.** Generally, less-experienced attorneys set lower fees than their more-experienced colleagues.

- **Geography.** Just as gasoline and butter cost more in some parts of the country than others, so do lawyers.

A defendant charged with a misdemeanor should not be surprised by a legal fee in the neighborhood of $3,000 to $5,000; an attorney may want $25,000 or more in a felony case. And most attorneys want all or a substantial portion of the fee paid up front.

Can I arrange for a contingency fee in a criminal case?

No. A contingency fee is an arrangement where the lawyer gets paid only if he or she wins the case. These arrangements are not allowed in criminal cases.

Can I change lawyers if I'm unhappy with the one I hired?

Generally, defendants who hire their own attorneys have the right to fire them at any time, without court approval. A defendant doesn't have to show "good cause" or even justify the firing. Of course, changing lawyers will probably be costly. In addition to paying the new lawyer, the defendant will have to pay the original lawyer whatever portion of the fee the original lawyer has earned.

Limits on Your Right to Change Lawyers

Your right to change lawyers is limited by the prosecutor's right to keep cases moving on schedule. If you want to change attorneys on the eve of trial, for example, your new attorney is likely to agree to represent you only if the trial is delayed so he or she can prepare. The prosecutor may oppose delay, possibly because witnesses won't be available to testify later on. In these circumstances, the judge is likely to deny your request to change lawyers.

What if I'm not happy with my court-appointed lawyer? Can I get a new one?

Probably not. Defendants with court-appointed lawyers often ask for new ones. Sometimes the problems are the same as those that would be encountered with any retained lawyer: inability to communicate, personality conflicts, or dissatisfaction with the strategy. In addition, clients who are represented by court-appointed lawyers often assume that the representation is substandard.

Requests for a new court-appointed lawyer are rarely granted. A defendant would have to prove that the attorney is truly incompetent before a judge would grant the request.

Why do some defendants choose to represent themselves?

Defendants choose to represent themselves for a variety of reasons:

- Some defendants can afford to hire a lawyer but don't do so because they think the likely punishment is not severe enough to justify the expense.

- Some defendants believe (often mistakenly) that an attorney who represented them previously was ineffective, and figure they can do just as well on their own.

- Some defendants believe that lawyers are part of an overall oppressive system and seek to make a political statement by representing themselves.

- Some defendants want to take responsibility for their own destiny.

- Some defendants who are in jail can gain privileges through self-representation, such as access to the jail's law library. Also, not bound by lawyers' ethical codes, self-represented defendants can delay proceedings by overloading the court with paperwork.

How can I tell whether I should represent myself or not?

The most obvious rule is that the more severe the charged crime, the less sensible it is to represent yourself. Defendants charged with minor traffic offenses should rarely hire an attorney, while defendants charged with serious felonies

should rarely be without one. The most difficult decisions involve misdemeanors such as drunk driving, possession of drugs, or shoplifting. Hiring an attorney in these situations may be wise because jail time and a fine are possibilities, and convictions may carry hidden costs, such as more severe punishment for a second conviction or vastly increased insurance rates. On the other hand, first-time offenders charged with nonviolent crimes are not usually sentenced to jail, and judges and prosecutors often offer standard deals to all defendants, whether or not they are represented by an attorney. Thus, the most critical piece of information that defendants should try to learn before deciding whether to hire an attorney is what the punishment is likely to be if they are convicted.

How to Find Out What Your Punishment Is Likely to Be

It can be difficult to learn about judges' common sentencing practices. Typical sentences aren't usually listed in statutes or court rules. If you want to find out what your punishment is likely to be if you're convicted, you might take the following steps:

- Pay a private defense attorney for an hour of consultation. An experienced defense attorney can often make accurate predictions as to likely punishment.

- Ask a relative or close friend who is or who knows an attorney for informal, unpaid advice.

- Call the public defender's office and ask if they have an "attorney of the day" or "duty attorney" who can answer your questions.

Can I represent myself and pay a lawyer to advise me as I go?

Yes. If you're thinking about representing yourself, you might want to seek out an attorney willing to serve as a "legal coach." The goal of hiring a legal coach is to combine a lawyer's knowledge with your time. Because you pay for the lawyer's help only occasionally, the cost of a legal coach can be far less than turning the entire case over to a private attorney.

Not all attorneys are willing to serve as legal coaches. Some are worried about their liability if they give wrong advice based on incomplete information; others do not want to be involved with a case unless they are in the driver's seat. Thus, if you're considering going it alone and you think you'll want a lawyer's help, you should try to line up your legal coach before you make your final decision.

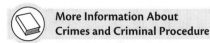

More Information About Crimes and Criminal Procedure

The Criminal Law Handbook, by Paul Bergmann and Sarah Berman-Barrett (Nolo), answers common questions on every aspect of the criminal justice system, including searches, lineups, arraignments, plea bargains, sentencing, and more.

There are many books and publications devoted to explaining state and federal criminal law and procedure. Although most of them are written for lawyers, nonlawyers will find them useful too. Because the practice of criminal law is so intimately tied to state and local laws, we cannot list every resource here. Your best bet is to go to your local law library and ask for practice manuals or digests on the subject. See the appendix for more information on finding state law and practice manuals and digests.

Online Help

www.nolo.com
Nolo's website offers information about a wide variety of legal topics, including criminal law and procedure.

www.findlaw.com
Most states have put their statutes, including their criminal and criminal procedure codes, on the Internet. You can find links to these laws at the FindLaw site, as well as helpful articles on criminal law and procedure.

Glossary

401(k) plan A deferred-compensation savings program in which employees invest part of their pretax wages, sometimes with added employer contributions. Income taxes on the amounts invested and earned are not due until the employee withdraws money from the fund, usually at retirement.

A

AB trust A trust that allows couples to reduce or avoid estate taxes. When the first spouse dies, his or her half of the property held in an AB trust goes to the beneficiaries named in the trust, with the condition that the surviving spouse has the right to use the property for life and is entitled to any income it generates. This keeps the property out of the surviving spouse's estate, reducing the likelihood that estate tax will be due when the surviving spouse dies.

acquittal A decision by a judge or jury that a defendant in a criminal case is not guilty of a crime.

adjustable rate mortgage (ARM) A mortgage loan with an interest rate that fluctuates in accordance with a designated market indicator—such as the weekly average of one-year U.S. Treasury Bills—over the life of the loan.

administration (of an estate) The court-supervised distribution of a deceased person's property.

adoption A court procedure by which an adult becomes the legal parent of someone who is not his or her biological child.

annuity A purchased policy that pays a fixed amount of benefits every year for the life of the person who is entitled to those benefits under the policy.

annulment A court procedure that dissolves a marriage and treats it as if it never happened—except that children of an annulled marriage are still considered "legitimate."

appeal A written request to a higher court to modify or reverse the judgment of a trial court or intermediate-level appellate court.

appellate court A higher court that reviews the decision of a lower court when a losing party files an appeal.

arbitration A procedure for resolving disputes out of court in which one or more neutral third parties—called the arbitrator or arbitration panel—hears evidence and renders a decision, like a judge.

arraignment A court appearance in which a criminal defendant is formally charged with a crime and asked to respond by entering a plea, most commonly "guilty," "not guilty," or "nolo contendere."

arrest A situation in which the police detain someone in a manner that would lead a reasonable person to believe that he or she is not free to leave.

arrest warrant A document issued by a judge or magistrate that authorizes the police to arrest someone.

articles of incorporation A document filed with state authorities to form a corporation.

assault The crime of attempting to physically harm another person in a way that makes the person under attack feel immediately threatened. Actual physical contact is not necessary.

attorney-in-fact A person, also called an "agent," named in a written power of attorney document to act on behalf of the person who signs the document, called the principal.

audit An examination of the financial records of a person, business, or organization, typically undertaken to clean up careless or improper bookkeeping, or to verify that proper records are being kept. Audits are also conducted by the IRS in order to determine whether a person or business owes taxes.

B

bail The money paid to the court, usually at arraignment or shortly thereafter, to ensure that an arrested person who is released from jail will show up at all required court appearances.

bail bond Money posted for a defendant who cannot afford bail. The defendant pays a certain portion (usually 10%) of the bond as a fee.

balloon payment A large final payment due at the end of a loan, typically a home or car loan, to pay off the amount remaining on the loan.

bankruptcy trustee A person appointed by a bankruptcy court to oversee the case of a person or business that has filed for bankruptcy.

battery The crime of making physical contact with someone with the intention to harm him or her. Unintentional harmful contact is not battery, no matter how careless the behavior or how severe the injury.

beneficiary A person or organization that is legally entitled to receive benefits through a legal device, such as a will, trust, or life insurance policy.

bylaws The rules that govern the internal affairs or actions of a corporation.

C

C corporation Common business slang to describe a corporation whose profits are taxed separately from its owners under Subchapter C of the Internal Revenue Code.

capital gains The profit on the sale of a capital asset, such as stock or real estate.

capitalized interest Accrued interest that is added to the principal balance of a loan while you are not making payments or when your payments are insufficient to cover both the principal and interest due.

case A term that most often refers to a lawsuit—for example, "I filed my small claims case." "Case" also refers to a written decision by a court.

certification mark A name, symbol, or other device used by an organization to vouch for the quality of products and services provided by others.

child support Money paid by a parent to support his or her children until the children reach the age of majority or become emancipated—usually by getting married, entering the armed forces, or living independently.

circuit court In many states, the name used for the principal trial court. In the federal system, the name for the appellate courts, which are organized into thirteen circuits.

civil case A noncriminal lawsuit in which an individual, business, or government entity sues another to protect, enforce, or redress private rights. There are hundreds of varieties of civil cases, including suits for breach of contract, probate, divorce, negligence, and copyright violations.

collateral Property that guarantees payment of a secured debt.

collection agency A company hired by a creditor to collect a debt.

collective mark A name, symbol, or other device used by members of a group or organization to identify the goods or services it provides.

collision damage waiver See "loss damage waiver."

collision insurance coverage A component of car insurance that pays for damages to the insured vehicle that result from a collision with another vehicle or object.

common law Rules that are established by court decisions and not by statutes, regulations, or ordinances.

common law marriage In some states, a type of marriage in which couples can become legally married (without a license or ceremony) by living together for a long period of time, representing themselves as a married couple, and intending to be married.

community property A method used in some states to define the ownership of property acquired and the responsibility for debts incurred during marriage. In states with community property laws, all earnings during marriage and all property acquired with those earnings are considered community property that belongs equally to each spouse. Likewise, all debts incurred during marriage are community property debts.

conservator Someone appointed by a judge to oversee the affairs of an incapacitated person. A conservator may also be called a guardian, committee, or curator.

constitution The system of fundamental laws and principles that lay down the nature, functions, and limitations of a government body. The United States Constitution is the supreme law of the United States. States also have constitutions. State constitutions can give people *more* rights than does the U.S. Constitution but cannot take away rights provided in the U.S. Constitution.

contingency fee A method of paying a lawyer for legal representation by which, instead of an hourly or per-job fee, the lawyer receives a percentage of the money his or her client obtains after settling or winning the case.

cooling-off rule A rule that allows a consumer to cancel certain contracts within a specified time period (typically three days) after signing.

copyright The right to control how a creative work is used.

corporation A legal structure authorized by state law that allows a business to organize as a separate legal entity from its owners, thereby shielding them from personal liability from business debts and obligations, and allowing the business to take advantage of corporate tax rules.

counterclaim A defendant's court papers that claim that the plaintiff—not the defendant—committed legal wrongs, and the defendant is entitled to money damages or other relief. In some states, a counterclaim is called a cross-complaint.

covenants, conditions, & restrictions (CC&Rs) Restrictions governing the use of real estate, usually enforced by a homeowners' association and passed on to the new owners of property.

credit bureau A private, for-profit company that collects and sells information about a person's credit history.

credit insurance Insurance that pays off a loan if the person who owes the money dies or becomes disabled.

credit report An account of your credit history, prepared by a credit bureau.

creditor A person or entity (such as a bank) to whom a debt is owed.

crime A type of behavior that has been defined by the state or federal government as deserving of punishment. The punishment for a crime may include imprisonment.

custody (of a child) The legal authority to make decisions affecting a child's interests (legal custody) and the responsibility to take care of the child (physical custody).

D

death taxes Taxes levied at death, based on the value of property left behind. Federal death taxes are called estate taxes. Some states also levy death taxes, sometimes called inheritance taxes, on people who inherit property.

debtor A person or entity (such as a bank) that owes money.

deductible Something that is taken away or subtracted. Under an insurance policy, for example, the deductible is the maximum amount that an insured person must pay toward his or her own losses before beginning to collect money from the insurer.

deed A document that transfers ownership of real estate.

deed in lieu of foreclosure A method of avoiding foreclosure by which the lender accepts ownership of the property in place of the money owed on the mortgage.

default The failure to perform a legal duty. For example, a borrower defaults on a mortgage or car loan by failing to make the loan payments on time, failing to maintain adequate insurance, or violating some other provision of the agreement.

defendant The person against whom a lawsuit is filed. In certain states, and in certain types of lawsuits, the defendant is called the respondent.

defined-benefit plan A type of pension plan that pays a definite, predetermined amount of money when the worker retires or becomes disabled. The amount received is based on length of service with a particular employer.

defined-contribution plan A type of pension plan that does not guarantee any particular pension amount upon retirement. Instead, the employer pays a certain amount into the pension fund every month, or every year, for each employee.

dependents benefits A type of Social Security benefit available to the spouse and minor or disabled children of a retired or disabled worker who qualifies for either retirement or disability benefits under the program's rigorous guidelines.

deposition A tool used by one party in pretrial case investigation (called "discovery") to question the other party or a witness in the case. All questions are answered under oath and recorded by a court reporter, who creates a deposition transcript.

design patent A patent issued on a new design, used for purely aesthetic reasons, that does not affect the functioning of the underlying device.

disability benefits Money paid from Social Security to those under 65 who qualify because of their work and earnings record and who meet the program's medical guidelines defining disability.

dischargeable debts Debts that can be erased by going through bankruptcy.

discovery A formal investigation—governed by court rules—that is conducted before a trial. Discovery allows one party to question other parties and sometimes witnesses and to force others to disclose documents or other physical evidence relating to the lawsuit.

dissolution A term used instead of divorce in some states.

district court In federal court and in some states, the name of the main trial court.

divorce The legal termination of marriage.

doing business as (DBA) A situation in which a business owner operates a company under a name different from his or her real name.

domain name A combination of letters and numbers that identifies a specific website on the Internet, followed by an identifier such as .com or .org.

down payment A lump sum cash payment made by a buyer when he or she purchases a major piece of property, such as a car or house.

durable power of attorney A power of attorney that remains in effect if the maker becomes incapacitated. If a power of attorney is not specifically made durable, it automatically expires upon incapacity.

durable power of attorney for finances A legal document that gives someone authority to manage the maker's financial affairs if he or she becomes incapacitated.

durable power of attorney for health care A legal document that names someone to make medical decisions if the person who makes the document is unable to express his or her wishes for care.

E

emergency protective order Any court-issued order meant to protect a person from harm or harassment. This type of order is a stop gap measure, usually lasting only for a weekend or holiday.

escrow A document (such as a grant deed to real property) or sum of money that, by agreement of parties to a transaction, is held by a neutral third party until certain conditions are met. Once the conditions are met, the third party releases the funds or document from escrow.

estate Generally, all the property a person owns when he or she dies.

estate taxes Taxes imposed by the federal government on property as it passes from the dead to the living. Some states also impose "inheritance taxes" on the people who inherit the property.

eviction Removal of a tenant from rental property by a law enforcement officer.

evidence The many types of information presented to a judge or jury designed to convince them of the truth or falsity of the key facts in a case. Evidence may include testimony of witnesses, documents, photographs, items of damaged property, government records, videos, or laboratory reports.

executor The person named in a will to handle the property of someone who has died.

exempt property The items of property a debtor is allowed to keep if a creditor wins a lawsuit against him or her or if the debtor files for Chapter 7 bankruptcy.

express warranty A guarantee made by a seller about the quality of goods or services provided. An express warranty is explicitly stated, either orally or in writing.

extended warranty contract Warranty coverage on an item that takes effect after the warranty coverage provided by the manufacturer or seller expires.

F

federal court A branch of the United States government with power derived directly from the U.S. Constitution. Federal courts decide cases involving the U.S. Constitution, federal law, and some cases where the parties are from different states.

felony A serious crime, usually punishable by a prison term of more than one year or, in some cases, by death.

fictitious business name The name under which a business operates or by which it is commonly known. See also "doing business as."

fixed rate mortgage A mortgage loan with an interest rate that remains constant throughout the life of the loan, so the person taking out the loan pays the same amount each month over the entire mortgage term.

for sale by owner (FSBO) A type of house sale in which the owner acts alone, without a real estate broker.

forbearance Voluntarily refraining from doing something, such as asserting a legal right. For example, a creditor may forbear on its right to collect a debt by temporarily postponing or reducing the borrower's payments.

foreclosure The forced sale of real estate to pay off a home loan on which the owner of the property has defaulted.

G

garnishment A court-ordered process that takes property from a person to satisfy a debt. For example, a creditor may garnish a debtor's wages if the debtor loses a lawsuit filed by the creditor.

general partnership A business that is owned and managed by two or more people (called partners or general partners) who are personally liable for all business debts.

gift taxes Federal taxes assessed on any gift, or combination of gifts, from one person to another that exceeds $12,000 in one year. There are some exceptions to this tax.

grace period A period of time during which a borrower is not required to make payments on a debt.

grant deed A deed containing an implied promise that the person transferring the property actually owns the title and that it is not encumbered in any way, except as described in the deed.

guarantor A person who makes a legally binding promise to either pay another person's debt or perform another person's duty if that person defaults or fails to perform.

guardian An adult who has been given the legal right by a court to control and care for someone known as a "ward." The ward may be either a minor child or an incapacitated adult. The guardian may make personal decisions on behalf of the ward (a "personal guardian"), manage the ward's property (a "property guardian" or "guardian of the estate"), or both.

guardian of the estate See "guardian."

guardianship A legal relationship created by a court between a guardian and his ward—either a minor child or an incapacitated adult. The guardian has a legal right and duty to care for the ward.

H

health care agent A person named in a health care directive or durable power of attorney for health care to make medical decisions for the person who signed the document, called the principal. A health care agent may also be known as an attorney-in-fact, proxy, surrogate or patient advocate.

health care directive A document in which you write out the health care instructions that will take effect if you are unable to speak for yourself. See "durable power of attorney for health care" and "living will."

holographic will A will that is completely handwritten, dated, and signed by the person making it. Holographic wills are generally not witnessed.

home warranty A service contract that covers a major housing system—for example, plumbing or electrical wiring—for a set period of time from the date a house is sold. The warranty guarantees repairs to the covered system and is renewable.

homeowners' association An organization of neighbors concerned with managing the common areas of a subdivision or condominium complex. The homeowners' association is also responsible for enforcing any covenants, conditions, and restrictions (CC&Rs) that apply to the property.

hung jury A jury unable to come to a final decision, resulting in a mistrial.

I

implied warranty A guarantee about the quality of goods or services purchased. An implied warranty is not written down or explicitly spoken but is provided to consumers by law.

implied warranty of fitness An implied warranty that applies when someone buys an item for a specific purpose. If the buyer notifies the seller of his or her specific needs, this warranty guarantees that the item will meet those needs.

implied warranty of habitability A legal doctrine that requires landlords to offer and maintain livable premises for their tenants.

implied warranty of merchantability An implied warranty that a new item will work for its specified purpose.

independent contractor A self-employed person, as defined by the IRS. Unlike employees, independent contractors retain control over how they do their work. The person or company paying the independent contractor controls only the outcome—the final product or service.

individual retirement account (IRA) A savings or brokerage account to which a person may contribute up to a specified amount of earned income each year. There are several types of IRAs. The most common are traditional contributory IRAs and Roth IRAs. With a traditional contributory IRA, contributions and interest earned are not taxed until the participant withdraws funds at retirement. With Roth IRAs, contributions are taxed, but most distributions (investment returns and withdrawals at retirement) are not.

infraction A minor violation of the law that is punishable only by a fine—for example, a traffic or parking ticket.

infringement (of copyright, patent, or trademark) The violation of a patent, copyright, or trademark owner's rights. Usually, this occurs when someone uses or benefits from a patented or copyrighted work, or a trademark or servicemark, without the owner's permission.

inheritance taxes Taxes levied by some states on people who inherit property (compare with "estate taxes").

interest A commission that a borrower pays to a bank or other creditor for lending the borrower money or extending credit. An interest rate represents the annual percentage that is added to the balance of a loan or credit line. This means that if a loan has an interest rate of 8%, the creditor adds 8% to the balance each year.

interrogatories Written questions that one party to a lawsuit asks an opposing party. Interrogatories are designed to discover key facts about an opponent's case and are a common part of pretrial case investigation (discovery).

intestate succession The method by which property is distributed when a person dies without a valid will. Usually, the property is distributed to the closest surviving relatives.

irrevocable trust A permanent trust. Once the trust is created, it cannot be revoked, amended, or changed in any way.

J

joint custody An arrangement by which parents who do not live together share the upbringing of a child. Joint custody can be joint legal custody (in which both parents have a say in decisions affecting the child), joint physical custody (in which the child spends a significant amount of time with both parents), or both.

joint tenancy A way for two or more people to share ownership of real estate or other property. When property is held in joint tenancy and one owner dies, the other owners automatically receive the deceased owner's share.

judgment A final court ruling resolving the key questions in a lawsuit and determining the rights and obligations of the opposing parties.

judgment-proof A term used to describe a person from whom nothing can be collected because he or she has little income and no property, or is protected from collection of the judgment by law—for example, a law preventing the collection of exempt property.

jury A group of people selected to apply the law, as stated by a judge, to the facts of a case and render a decision, called the verdict.

jury nullification A decision made by a jury to acquit a defendant who has violated a law that the jury believes is unjust or wrong.

L

landlord The owner of any real estate, such as a house, apartment building, or land, that is leased or rented to another person, called the tenant.

lease An oral or written agreement between two people concerning the use by one of the property of the other. A person can lease either real estate (such as an apartment or business property) or personal property (such as a car or a boat).

legal custody The right and obligation to make decisions about a child's upbringing, including schooling and medical care. Compare "physical custody."

legislature The branch of government that has the responsibility and power to make laws. A state legislature makes state laws, and the federal legislature (the U.S. Congress) makes federal laws.

lemon A car that gives you serious trouble soon after you buy it.

liability (1) Legal responsibility for an act or omission. (2) Something for which a person is liable. For example, a debt is often called a liability.

liability insurance A contract that provides compensation to third parties who are injured or whose property is damaged due to the fault of the insurance policyholder.

license (of invention, copyright, or trademark) A contract giving written permission to use an invention, creative work, or trademark.

lien The right of a secured creditor to take a specific item of property if the borrower doesn't pay a debt.

life estate A property interest that provides the right to live in or use, but not own, a specific piece of real estate until death.

life insurance A contract under which an insurance company agrees to pay money to a designated beneficiary upon the death of the policyholder. In exchange, the policyholder pays a regularly scheduled fee, known as the insurance premiums.

limited liability Restrictions on the amount a business owner can lose if the business is subject to debts, claims, or other liabilities. One of the primary advantages of forming a corporation or limited liability company (LLC) is that the business owners stand to lose only the amount of money invested in the business—creditors can't come after an owner's personal assets.

limited liability company (LLC) A business ownership structure that offers limited personal liability for business obligations and a choice of how the business will be taxed: either as a separate entity or as a partnership-like structure in which profits are taxed on the owners' personal income tax returns.

limited liability partnership (LLP) A type of partnership recognized in a majority of states that protects a partner from personal liability for negligent acts committed by other partners or by employees not under his or her direct control.

limited partnership A business structure that allows some partners (called limited partners) to enjoy limited personal liability for partnership debts while other partners (called general partners) have unlimited personal liability. Limited partners are usually passive investors; they are not allowed to make day-to-day business decisions.

living trust A trust created during the trustmaker's life to avoid probate after death. Property transferred into the trust during life passes directly to the trust beneficiaries after death, without probate.

living will A legal document that allows you to set out written wishes for health care. The document takes effect only if you are unable to make decisions for yourself.

loan broker A person who specializes in matching home buyers with appropriate mortgage lenders.

loan consolidation Combining a number of loans into a single new loan.

loss damage waiver (LDW) Rental car insurance that makes the rental car company responsible for damage to or theft of a rental car. Also called a "collision damage waiver."

M

malpractice (by an attorney) The delivery of substandard services by a lawyer. Generally, malpractice occurs when a lawyer fails to provide the quality of service that should reasonably be expected in the circumstances, with the result that the lawyer's client is harmed.

marital property Most of the property accumulated by spouses during a marriage, called "community property" in some states.

marriage certificate A document that provides proof of a marriage, typically issued to newlyweds a few weeks after they file for the certificate in a county office.

marriage license A document that authorizes a couple to get married, usually available from a city or county office in the state where the marriage will take place.

mediation A dispute-resolution method designed to help people resolve disputes without going to court. In mediation, a neutral third party (the mediator) meets with the opposing sides to help them find a mutually satisfactory solution.

Medicaid A federal program that provides health insurance for financially needy people. The program is administered by each state.

Medicare A federal program that provides health insurance to elderly and disabled people.

meeting of creditors A meeting held with a bankruptcy trustee about a month after a debtor files for bankruptcy.

Miranda warning A warning that the police must give to a suspect before conducting an interrogation; otherwise, the suspect's answers may not be used as evidence in a trial. Also known as "reading a suspect his rights."

misdemeanor A crime, less serious than a felony, punishable by no more than one year in jail.

mortgage A loan in which the borrower puts up the title to real estate as security (collateral) for the loan. If the borrower doesn't pay back the debt on time, the lender can foreclose on the real estate and have it sold to pay off the loan.

N

no-fault divorce Any divorce in which the spouse who wants to split up does not have to accuse the other of wrongdoing, but can simply state that the couple no longer gets along.

no-fault insurance Car insurance laws that require the insurance company of each person involved in an accident to pay for the medical bills and lost wages of its insured, up to a certain amount, regardless of who was at fault.

nolo contendere A plea entered by the defendant in response to being charged with a crime. A defendant who pleads nolo contendere neither admits nor denies commiting the crime but agrees to a punishment (usually a fine or jail time).

nondischargeable debts Debts that cannot be erased by filing for bankruptcy.

nondisclosure agreement A legally binding contract in which a person or business promises not to disclose specific information to others without proper authorization.

nonexempt property The property that a debtor risks losing to creditors when he or she files for Chapter 7 bankruptcy or when a creditor sues the debtor and wins a judgment.

nonprofit corporation A business structure that allows people to come together to obtain support for an organization (such as a club) or for some public purpose (such as a hospital or environmental organization). Nonprofits receive benefits—for instance, reduced filing fees and tax exemptions—that are not available to regular corporations.

notarize The act of certification by a notary public that establishes the authenticity of a signature on a legal document.

notary public A licensed public officer who administers oaths, certifies signatures on documents, and performs other specified functions.

nuisance Something that interferes with the use of property by being irritating, offensive, obstructive, or dangerous. Nuisances include a wide range of conditions, from a chemical plant's noxious odors to a neighbor's dog barking.

O

open adoption An adoption in which there is some degree of contact between the birth parents and the adoptive parents and sometimes with the child as well.

order A decision issued by a court. It can be a simple command—for example, ordering a recalcitrant witness to answer a proper question during a trial—or it can be a complicated and reasoned decision made after a hearing, directing that a party either do or refrain from doing some act.

ordinance A law passed by a county or city government.

own recognizance (O.R.) A way for a criminal defendant to get out of jail, without paying bail, by promising to appear in court when next required to be there. Only those defendants with strong ties to the community, such as a steady job, local family, and no history of failing to appear in court, are good candidates for "O.R." release.

P

parenting agreement A detailed written agreement between a divorcing couple that describes how they will deal with visitation, holiday schedules, vacation, education, religion, and other issues related to their child.

partnership When used without a qualifier such as "limited" or "limited liability," this term usually refers to a legal structure called a general partnership: a business that is owned and managed by two or more people who are personally liable for all business debts.

party A person, corporation, or other legal entity that files a lawsuit (a plaintiff or petitioner) or defends against one (a defendant or respondent).

patent A legal monopoly, granted by the U.S. Patent and Trademark Office (PTO), on the right to use, manufacture, and sell an invention.

pay-on-death (POD) designation A way to avoid probate for bank accounts, government bonds, individual retirement accounts, and in many states, securities or a car. A pay-on-death designation is created when the property owner names someone on the ownership document—such as the registration card for a bank account—to inherit the property at the owner's death.

pension A retirement fund for employees paid for or contributed to by an employer as part of a package of compensation for the employees' work.

personal property All property other than land and buildings attached to land. Cars, bank accounts, wages, securities, a small business, furniture, insurance policies, jewelry, patents, pets, and season baseball tickets are all examples of personal property.

petition A formal written request made to a court, asking for an order or ruling on a particular matter.

petitioner A person who initiates a lawsuit. The term is a synonym for plaintiff. It is used almost universally in some states and used in others only for certain types of lawsuits, most commonly divorce and other family law cases.

physical custody The right and obligation of a parent to provide a home for his or her child. Compare "legal custody."

plaintiff The person, corporation, or other legal entity that initiates a lawsuit. In certain states and for some types of lawsuits, the term "petitioner" is used instead of "plaintiff."

plant patent A patent issued for new strains of asexually reproducing plants.

plea The defendant's formal answer to criminal charges. Typically defendants enter one of the following pleas: guilty, not guilty, or nolo contendere.

plea bargain A negotiation between the defense and prosecution (and sometimes the judge) that settles a criminal case. The defendant typically pleads guilty to a lesser crime (or fewer charges) than originally charged, in exchange for a guaranteed sentence that is shorter than what the defendant could face if convicted at trial.

pocket part The paper supplement found in the front or back of a book of laws—such as state statutes—that contains annual changes to the law that are not included in the hardcover version of the book.

pot trust A trust for children—typically established in a will or living trust—in which the trustee decides how to spend money on each child, taking money out of the trust to meet each child's specific needs.

power of attorney A document that gives another person (called the "attorney-in-fact" or "agent") legal authority to act on behalf of the person who makes the document, called the principal.

premarital agreement An agreement made by a couple before marriage that controls certain aspects of their relationship, usually the management and ownership of property, and sometimes whether alimony will be paid if the couple later divorces.

preponderance of the evidence Evidence sufficient to convince a jury that one party's version of events is "more likely than not." In many civil lawsuits, the plaintiff must prove each element of his or her claim by a preponderance of the evidence in order to prevail.

private mortgage insurance (PMI) Insurance that reimburses a mortgage lender if the buyer defaults on the loan and the foreclosure sale price is less than the amount owed the lender (the mortgage plus the costs of the sale).

pro per A term derived from the Latin in propria persona, meaning "for one's self," used in some states to describe a person who handles his or her own case without a lawyer. In other states, the term "pro se" is used.

pro se See "pro per."

probable cause The amount and quality of information a judge must have before signing a warrant allowing the police to conduct a search or arrest a suspect. If the police have presented reliable information that convinces the judge that it's more likely than not that a crime has occurred and the suspect is involved, the judge will conclude that there is "probable cause" and will issue the warrant.

probate The court process following a person's death that includes proving the authenticity of the deceased person's will, appointing someone to handle the deceased person's affairs, identifying and inventorying the deceased person's property, paying debts and taxes, identifying heirs, and distributing the deceased person's property.

property guardian See "guardian."

prosecutor A lawyer who works for the local, state, or federal government to bring and litigate criminal cases.

provisional patent application (PPA) An interim patent application that has the legal effect of providing the inventor with an early filing date for his or her invention. The PPA does not take the place of a regular patent application, but it does confer patent pending status on the underlying invention.

public defender A lawyer appointed by the court and paid by the county, state, or federal government to represent clients who are charged with violations of criminal law and are unable to pay for their own defense.

Q

QTIP trust A marital trust for wealthy couples designed to reduce estate taxes. The surviving spouse receives only a "life estate" in the trust property, which passes to the trust's final beneficiaries after the surviving spouse's death. No estate taxes are assessed on the trust property until the surviving spouse dies.

quitclaim deed A deed that transfers whatever ownership interest the transferor has in a particular property. The deed does not make any guarantees about what is being transferred.

R

real estate agent A foot soldier of the real estate business who shows houses and does most of the other nitty-gritty tasks associated with selling real estate in exchange for a commission on the sale.

real estate broker A real estate professional one step up from a real estate agent. A broker has more training and can supervise agents.

real property Another term for real estate. It includes land and things permanently attached to the land, such as trees, buildings, and stationary mobile homes.

recording The process of filing a copy of a deed or other document concerning real estate with the land records office in the county where the land is located. Recording creates a public record of changes in ownership for all property in the state.

regulation A law issued by a state or federal administrative agency for the purpose of implementing and enforcing a statute.

rent control Laws that limit the amount of rent landlords may charge—and state when and by how much rent can be raised. Most rent control laws also require a landlord to provide a good reason, such as repeatedly late rent payments, for evicting a tenant.

rental agreement A contract, either oral or written, between a landlord and tenant that sets forth the terms of a tenancy.

renter's insurance Insurance that covers those who rent residential property against losses to their belongings that occur as a result of fire or theft.

repossession A creditor's taking of property that has been pledged as collateral for a loan. Lenders most often repossess cars when the buyer has missed loan payments and has not attempted to work with the lender to resolve the problem.

request for admissions A procedure in which one party to a lawsuit asks the opposing party to admit that certain facts are true. This occurs in the pretrial case-investigation phase of a lawsuit, known as "discovery."

request to produce (documents or things) A procedure in which one party to a lawsuit asks an opposing party to turn over certain documents or physical objects. Like a "request for admissions," this procedure is part of the pretrial case-investigation phase of a lawsuit, called "discovery."

respondent A term used instead of "defendant" in some states—especially for divorce and other family law cases—to identify the party who is being sued.

restraining order A court order directing a person not to do something, such as make contact with another specified person, enter the family home, or remove a child from the state.

Roth IRA See "individual retirement account."

ruling Any decision a judge makes during the course of a lawsuit.

S

S corporation A corporation organized under Subchapter S of the Internal Revenue Code in which shareholders enjoy limited liability status but are taxed on their individual tax returns in the same way as sole proprietors or owners of a partnership.

search warrant An order signed by a judge that directs the owners of private property to allow the police to enter and search for items named in the warrant.

secret warranty program A program under which a car manufacturer will make repairs for free on vehicles with persistent problems, even after the warranty has expired, in order to avoid a recall and the accompanying bad press.

secured debt A debt on which a creditor has a lien. The creditor can initiate a foreclosure or repossession to take the property identified by the lien, called the collateral, to satisfy the debt if the borrower defaults.

security deposit A payment required by a landlord to ensure that a tenant pays rent on time and keeps the rental unit in good condition.

sentence Punishment in a criminal case. A sentence can range from a fine and community service to life imprisonment or death.

separate property In community property states, property owned and controlled entirely by one spouse in a marriage.

service contract Another term for "extended warranty contract."

service mark A word, phrase, logo, symbol, color, sound, or smell used by a business to identify a service and distinguish it from those of its competitors.

settlement An agreement resolving a dispute between the parties in a lawsuit without a trial.

severance pay Funds, often amounting to one or two months' salary, that some employers offer to workers who are laid off.

sexual harassment Unwelcome sexual advances or conduct on the job that creates an intimidating, hostile, or offensive working environment.

shared custody See "joint custody."

shareholder An owner of a corporation whose ownership interest is represented by shares of stock in the corporation. Also called a "stockholder."

short sale (of a house) The sale of a house in which the proceeds fall short of what the owner still owes on the mortgage. Many lenders will agree to accept the proceeds of a short sale and forgive the rest of what is owed on the mortgage if the owner cannot make the mortgage payments.

sick leave Time off work for illness.

small claims court A state court that resolves disputes involving relatively small amounts of money. Adversaries usually appear without lawyers—in fact, some states forbid lawyers in small claims court.

Social Security The general term that describes a number of related programs administered by the federal government, including retirement, disability, and dependents and survivors benefits. These programs operate together to provide workers and their families with some monthly income when their normal flow of income shrinks because of the retirement, disability, or death of the person who earned that income.

sole custody An arrangement in which only one parent has physical and legal custody of a child and the other parent often has visitation rights.

sole proprietorship A business owned and managed by one person. Business profits are reported and taxed on the owner's personal tax return, and the owner is personally liable for all business debts.

state court A court that decides cases involving state law or the state constitution. State courts have jurisdiction to consider disputes involving individual defendants who reside in that state or have minimum contacts with the state, such as using its highways, owning real property in the state, or doing business in the state.

statute A written law passed by Congress or a state legislature and signed into law by the president or a state governor.

statute of limitations The legally prescribed time limit in which a lawsuit must be filed.

subpoena A court order that requires a witness to appear in court. Subpoenas may be issued at the request of a party to a lawsuit. Also spelled "subpena."

subpoena duces tecum A type of subpoena, usually issued at the request of a party to a lawsuit, by which a court orders a witness to produce certain documents at a deposition or trial.

Supreme Court The United States Supreme Court is this country's highest court, which has the final power to decide cases involving the interpretation of the U.S. Constitution, certain legal areas set forth in the Constitution (called federal questions), and federal laws. It can also make final decisions in certain lawsuits between parties from different states. Most states also have a supreme court, which is the final arbiter of the state's constitution and state laws. In several states, the highest court uses a different name.

surviving spouse A widow or widower.

survivors benefits An amount of money available to the surviving spouse and minor or disabled children of a deceased worker who qualified for Social Security retirement or disability benefits.

T

temporary restraining order (TRO) An order that tells one person to stop harassing or harming another, issued after the aggrieved party appears before a judge.

tenant Anyone, including a corporation, who rents real property, with or without a house or structure, from the owner (called the landlord). A tenant may also be called the "lessee."

trade dress The distinctive packaging or design of a product that promotes the product and distinguishes it from other products in the marketplace.

trade name The official name of a business, the one it uses on its letterhead and bank account when not dealing with consumers.

trade secret In most states, a formula, pattern, physical device, idea, process, compilation of information, or other information that provides a business with a competitive advantage, and that is treated in a way that can reasonably be expected to prevent the public or competitors from learning about it.

trademark A word, phrase, logo, symbol, color, sound, or smell used by a business to identify a product and distinguish it from those of its competitors. Compare "trade dress," "service mark," "certification mark," and "collective mark."

treatise An extensive book or series of books written about a particular legal topic.

trial court The first court to hear a lawsuit.

trust A legal device used to manage property—whether real or personal—established by one person for the benefit of another. A third person, called the trustee, manages the trust.

trust deed The most common method of financing real estate purchases in California (most other states use mortgages). The trust deed transfers title to the property to a trustee—often a title company—which holds it as security for a loan. When the loan is paid off, the title is transferred to the borrower.

trustee The person who manages assets owned by a trust under the terms of the trust document. A trustee's purpose is to safeguard the trust and distribute trust income or principal as directed in the trust document.

U

unemployment insurance (UI) A program run jointly by federal and state governments that provides money benefits for a specified time after an employee has been laid off or fired from a job for reasons other than serious misconduct. In some instances, an employee who quits a job for a good reason (for example, because she was being sexually harassed at work) can also collect unemployment insurance benefits.

uninsured motorist coverage The portion of car insurance that provides compensation for any injuries resulting from an accident with an uninsured motorist or a hit-and-run driver.

unlawful detainer An eviction lawsuit.

utility patent A patent issued for inventions that perform useful functions. Most patents issued by the U.S. Patent and Trademark Office (PTO) are utility patents.

V

visitation rights The right to see a child regularly, typically awarded by a court to the parent who does not have physical custody of the child.

W

warranty A guarantee by a seller to stand by its product or services by making repairs or offering replacements if something goes wrong. See "express warranty" and "implied warranty."

warranty deed A seldom-used type of deed that contains express assurances about the legal validity of the title being transferred.

will A document in which a person specifies what is to be done with his or her property at death, names an executor to oversee the distribution of that property, and names a guardian for his or her young children.

witness A person who testifies under oath at a deposition or trial, providing firsthand or expert evidence. In addition, the term also refers to someone who watches another person sign a document and then adds his name to confirm that the signature is genuine; this is called "attesting."

workers' compensation A program that provides replacement income and medical expenses to employees who are injured on the job or become ill as a result of work.

Z

zoning The laws dividing cities into different areas according to use, from single-family residences to industrial plants. Zoning ordinances control the size, location, and use of buildings within these different areas.

Legal Research

Legal research is how you learn about the law. It is not a skill reserved exclusively for lawyers; you can find the answers to your legal questions if you are armed with a little bit of patience and a good road map.

Which legal research method you should use depends on what you need to find out. Usually, people want to research the law in order to:

- understand a particular area of the law

- find and read a statute, regulation, ordinance, court decision, or piece of pending legislation (usually called a bill)

- find the answer to a specific legal question, or

- find a legal form.

This appendix explains how to use legal research to accomplish each of these tasks.

Learning About a Particular Area of the Law

Many people need to understand an area of the law before making an important decision. For example, you might want to know:

- Are there any legal rules I have to follow when selling a business?

- What's the difference between a living trust and a living will?

- Once I divorce, am I entitled to a share of my former spouse's pension?

Questions like these can be answered without regard to your specific circumstances; they involve a general understanding of the law. To find this type of information about a legal topic, you should turn to legal background materials.

Legal background materials are books, articles, and encyclopedia entries in which experts summarize and explain the basic principles of a legal subject area, such as bankruptcy, landlord-tenant law, or criminal law. These materials come in many forms; you can find them in law libraries and public libraries, and many are also available on the Internet.

How to Find a Law Library

Most counties have law libraries in the government buildings or courthouses at the county seat. These libraries are open to the public. County libraries are a good place to go if you're looking for legal encyclopedias, treatises, state laws, and court cases.

Law schools also maintain libraries for their students and staff. Although public access to some law school libraries is restricted, many are open to the general public—especially if the law school is part of a university that receives state funding.

Finally, don't limit yourself to law libraries. Most major public libraries in urban areas contain both local and state laws, self-help law books, and directories of organizations. Public libraries are also good sources of city, county, and state information.

Here are a number of legal background resources that you may find useful:

- **Self-help law books.** Self-help law books, such as those published by Nolo, are written in plain English for a nonlawyer audience. They are an excellent starting point for cracking any legal area that is new to you. Law libraries, public libraries, and bookstores (including Nolo's online bookstore at www.nolo.com) often carry self-help law books. Nolo publishes titles on employment, small business issues, divorce, estate planning, and much more.

- **Organizations and advocacy groups.** Many nonprofit and professional organizations or advocacy groups—such as tenants' rights groups, the American Association of Retired People (AARP), and local business groups—publish articles or booklets on particular legal topics. Think about which groups might have the information you need, and then look for them in the Yellow Pages or on the Web. Most public libraries have reference books that list organizations and associations by topic—these books are an easy way to find leads.

- **Legal encyclopedias.** You can often find a good introduction to your topic in a legal encyclopedia. The legal encyclopedias most commonly found in law libraries are *American Jurisprudence* and *Corpus Juris*. Many states have legal encyclopedias that are state-specific—for example, *Texas Jurisprudence*.

- **The Nutshell series.** Another good introduction to legal topics is the Nutshell series, as in *Torts in a Nutshell* and *Intellectual Property in a Nutshell,* published by West Group. These books are available in most law libraries and some bookstores.

- **Treatises.** If you have the time and patience to delve deeply into a subject, you can find comprehensive books—generally known as treatises—on virtually every legal topic. For example, if you want to know about some aspect of trademark law, you could use *McCarthy on Trademarks*, a multivolume treatise on all aspects of trademark law.

- **West's Legal Desk Reference.** This book, by Statsky, Hussey, Diamond, and Nakamura, lists background materials both by state and by legal topic. In addition, *West's Legal Desk Reference* provides keywords and phrases that will help you use the other resources you may need during your research.

- **Internet resources.** Nolo's website, at www.nolo.com, explains many common legal issues in plain English. The other major legal websites (listed below) also provide helpful information and links to specific areas of the law. Finally, U.S. and local government agency sites provide basic legal information for consumers, such as state marriage license requirements or publications on workplace rights. For example, if you visit the federal judiciary's website at www.uscourts.gov, you can download "Bankruptcy Basics," a pamphlet providing a good overview of bankruptcy. To find government agencies online, see *Finding Court and Government Agency Websites,* below.

Finding a Specific Law

There are many reasons why you might need to find a specific statute, regulation, ordinance, or court decision. For example, you might hear about new state laws governing overtime wages and want to read the laws to see if they apply to your work situation. Or perhaps the city building department has referred you to a particular city ordinance that covers zoning laws in your neighborhood. Whatever the reason, finding a specific law is relatively straightforward. The steps depend on what type of law you seek.

City or County Laws

You can usually get copies of city or county laws (often called "ordinances") from the office of the city or county clerk. The main branch of your public library is also likely to have a collected set of these laws. Once you get there, ask the reference librarian for help.

Your best bet for finding city and county ordinances online is FindLaw. Begin at www.findlaw.com/casecode. Then, scroll down to "U.S. State Laws" and click your state. The next Web page should provide available city and county ordinances for that state.

State or Federal Statutes and Regulations

Rules established by state and federal governments are called statutes and regulations. Federal statutes are passed by the United States Congress, while state statutes are passed by state legislatures. Regulations are issued by state or federal administrative agencies (such as the U.S. Department of Transportation or the State Department of Health) to explain, implement, and enforce statutes.

You can find statutes and regulations in the library or on the Internet. You can also use legal background materials to point the way to the statute or regulation you should read.

Finding Statutes and Regulations at the Library

State and federal statutes and regulations can be found at a law library or the main branch of a public library. Depending on the state, statutes are compiled in books called codes, revised statutes, annotated statutes, or compiled laws. For example, the federal statutes are contained in a series called *United States Code,* and the Vermont statutes are found in a series called *Vermont Statutes Annotated.* (The term "annotated" means that the statutes are accompanied by information about their history and court decisions that have interpreted them.) Once you've located the books you need, search for the specific statute by its citation or by looking up keywords in the index.

After you find a law in the statute books, it's important to look at the update pamphlet in the front or back of the book (called the "pocket part") to make sure your statute hasn't been amended or deleted. Pocket parts are published only once per year, so brand-new statutes often have not yet made it to the pocket part. Law libraries subscribe to services and periodicals that update these books on a more frequent basis than the pocket parts. Ask the law librarian to help you find the most recent version of the statute.

Most federal regulations are published in the *Code of Federal Regulations (C.F.R.),* a well-indexed set of books organized by subject. If you don't have a citation for the regulation you want, check the index. To make sure the regulation is current, look at the monthly pamphlet that accompanies the books, called *C.F.R.-L.S.A. (List of C.F.R. Sections Affected).*

State regulations may be harder to find. If you know which agency publishes the regulation you want, you can usually call and get a copy. Many states also keep a portion of their regulations in a series of books called the "administrative code"; check the table of contents. If the regulation is not in an administrative code, look for loose-leaf manuals published by the individual agency. If you find a regulation in the administrative code or loose-leaf manual, you should still call the agency to make sure the regulation hasn't recently changed.

How to Read a Citation for a Statute or Regulation

A citation is an abbreviated reference that tells you where to find a legal resource. Citations for statutes usually include the name of the set of books where the statute appears, the volume or title number, and the section where you can find the statute. For example:

- 42 U.S.C. § 2000e is the citation of Title VII of the Civil Rights Act, which protects workers from discrimination. You can find the text of the law in title 42 of the United States Code, section 2000e.

- Ariz. Rev. Stat. Ann. § 33-1321 is the citation to Arizona's law on tenant security deposits. You can find the text of the law in title 33 of the Arizona Revised Statutes Annotated, section 1321.

Citations for regulations usually include the name of the code where the regulations can be found, and the volume and section number. For example:

- You can find the regulations interpreting the Fair Credit Reporting Act at 16 C.F.R. § 600.1—volume 16 of the Code of Federal Regulations, section 600.1.

- You can find California's regulations on pregnancy discrimination at 2 C.C.R. §7291.2—title 2 of the California Code of Regulations, Section 7291.2.

Finding Statutes and Regulations Online

What to do depends on the type of law you're looking for:

Federal laws. The easiest way to find federal laws online is to use FindLaw: www.findlaw.com/casecode/uscodes. From this site, you can search the U.S. Code by title, section, or keyword.

You can also use the Google search engine. When using Google, provide the literal name or number of the law, in quotation marks. If the law has a lot of words, it usually works to just use the distinctive elements of the phrase. For example, when looking for the Bankruptcy Abuse Prevention and Reform Act of 2005, the phrase "bankruptcy abuse" would be sufficient for the statute's name. Similarly, if the law has a nickname, you can use that phrase. If you can think of key words that identify the law, provide those as well. For instance, if a new law creates an additional procedure for collecting child support, you could likely find it by typing in the terms: "child support" and "collection." If you know the year that the law was passed, add that as well (so that you don't get an out of date law by the same name).

Federal regulations. To find federal regulations online, the FindLaw website is a good place to start. FindLaw provides a searching system for the federal code of regulations at www.findlaw.com/casecode/cfr.html.

State laws. To find state laws online, use the Cornell Law School website: www.law.cornell.edu/states/listing.html. Here, you will see a state-by-state index. You can also find state laws organized by topic at www.law.cornell.edu/topics/state_statutes.html.

State regulations. You can locate many state regulations by using FindLaw: www.findlaw.com/casecode/state.html.

Using Background Materials to Find Statutes and Regulations

When looking for a particular statute or regulation (state or federal), you may want to consult background materials, which often include relevant laws. For example, *Collier on Bankruptcy,* the leading bankruptcy treatise, contains a complete set of the federal bankruptcy laws. Even if the background resource does not include the text of the statutes or regulations, it will provide citations to the relevant laws and the books in which they are found.

Finding the Latest Legislation

If you are looking for a brand-new statute, you may have to search online for recently enacted legislation, because there is often a delay between the date a statute is passed and the date it shows up in the overall compilation of laws. Almost every state provides links to its legislature, where you can find pending and recently enacted legislation. These sites contain not only the most current version of a bill but also its history. For help locating your state's website, see below. To find out about pending federal legislation or to read the latest version of a bill, go to the United States Congress website at http://thomas.loc.gov.

Finding Court and Government Agency Websites

Many courts and government agencies provide statutes and case law, plus other useful items like forms, answers to frequently asked questions, and downloadable pamphlets on various legal topics. To find your state's website, open your browser and type in www.state.<your state's postal code>.us or www.<your state's postal code>.gov. Your state's postal code is the two-letter abbreviation you use for mailing addresses. For example, NY is the postal code for New York, so to find New York's state website, type in www.state.ny.us or www.ny.gov.

Nolo's website provides links to courts across the country and access to small claims court information for most states. You can also find local, state, and federal court websites on the National Center for State Courts' website at www.ncsconline.org. The federal judiciary's website at www.uscourts.gov lists federal court websites.

State Case Law

State case law consists of the rules established by courts in court decisions (also called "opinions"). Court decisions do one of two things. First, courts interpret statutes, regulations, and ordinances so that we know how they apply to real-life situations. Second, courts make rules that are not found in statutes, regulations, or ordinances. These rules are called the "common law."

Finding State Cases in the Library

State cases are found in a series of books called reporters. For example, California cases are contained in the *California Reporter.* You can also find state cases in books known as "regional reporters." These volumes contain cases from several states in a geographical region. For example, the *Atlantic Reporter* contains cases from several eastern states, including Delaware and Maryland.

Finding Cases Using a Citation

A citation indicates the name of the reporter, the volume number, and the page where the case appears. For example, 21 Cal.App.3d 446 tells you that the case is in California Appellate Reports, 3rd Series, Volume 21, on page 446.

Finding Cases Using the Name

If you don't have a citation but you know the name of one or both of the parties in the case—for instance, in the case named *Jones v. Smith,* Jones and Smith are the names of the parties—you can use a "case digest" to find the citation. There are digests for individual states as well as federal and general digests. Look for the parties' names in the digest's Table of Cases. If you don't know the name of the case or the citation, then it will be very difficult to find the case in the law library.

Finding State Cases on the Web

If the case is recent (within the last ten years), there's a good chance it's available free on the Internet. A good place to start is FindLaw at www.findlaw.com. Also, most state court websites now publish recent cases.

If the case is older, you can still find it on the Internet, but you may have to pay a private company for access to its database. (Your local law library may also have online legal resources available for searching.) VersusLaw, at www. versuslaw.com, maintains an excellent library of older state court cases. You can do unlimited research on Versuslaw for $9.95 per month. You can also get state cases online through Lexis and Westlaw, commercial online legal research services. (For more information, see "Using Westlaw and Lexis to Do Legal Research on the Web," below.)

Federal Case Law

Federal case law consists of the rules established by federal courts. Like state cases, you can find federal case law both in the library and on the Web.

Finding Federal Cases in the Library

Cases decided by the U.S. Supreme Court are published in three different series of reporters. All three contain the same cases. The names of these series are:

- United States Reports
- Supreme Court Reporter; and
- Supreme Court Reports: Lawyers' Edition.

Well-stocked law libraries also have cases from other federal courts, including the Federal Circuit Courts of Appeal (federal appellate courts), U.S. District Courts (federal trial courts), and specialized courts such as bankruptcy or tax court.

To find a case in the Supreme Court reporters or any of the volumes containing other federal cases, follow the guidelines for finding state cases by citation or case name, above.

Finding Federal and State Court Cases on the Web

Where to look depends on the type of case you want to find:

U.S. Supreme Court. Start at the Cornell Law School website: www.law.cornell.edu/supct/index.html. It provides a thorough index of U.S. Supreme Court decisions.

If you want to search for a U.S. Supreme Court case using Google, type "Supreme Court" in quotation marks and then add any combination of the following elements:

- one or both names of the parties to the case (you can include the "v." abbreviation—for example, if you enter "Planned Parenthood v. Casey," you will retrieve a copy of the 1992 Supreme Court Case)
- one or more terms that describe the subject matter of the case (for example, if you enter "Betamax" and "Supreme Court," you will get the 1984 Supreme Court case, *Sony v. Universal*)
- the year of the case.

Federal courts. Start at the Cornell Law School website: www.law.cornell.edu/federal/opinions.html. It provides a thorough index of federal court opinions.

If you want to search for a federal case using Google, type any combination of the elements described for U.S. Supreme Court cases, just above. You may also want to include the name of the court that decided the case, if you know it—for example, "Ninth Circuit Court of Appeals."

Note that cases decided before 1995—that is, before the Internet was used to catalogue court cases—are usually only available in private databases that require a paid subscription.

State courts. Start with the Cornell Law School website: www.law.cornell.edu/opinions. html#state. It provides a thorough index of state court decisions.

If you want to search for a state court case using Google, type any combination of the elements described for U.S. Supreme Court cases, above. You may also want to include the name of the court that decided the case, if you know it—for example, "Vermont Supreme Court."

As with federal court cases, state cases decided before 1995 are usually available only through private databases that charge for a subscription.

Using Lexis and Westlaw to Do Legal Research on the Web

Lexis and Westlaw are the chief electronic legal databases that contain the full text of many of the legal resources found in law libraries, including almost all reported cases from state and federal courts, all federal statutes, the statutes of most states, federal regulations, law review articles, commonly used treatises, and practice manuals.

Although Westlaw and Lexis databases are available over the Internet, subscriptions are pricey. However, both offer some free and some fee-based services to nonsubscribers that are helpful and reasonably priced (between $9 and $12 per document). To find out more about these services, visit Westlaw at www.westlaw.com or Lexis at www.lexis.com.

Finding Answers to Specific Legal Questions

It's one thing to track down information on a recent case or statute or to read up on general information about a legal topic. It's quite another to confidently answer a question about how the law might apply to your own situation, such as:

- I live in North Carolina, and I've been charged with second offense drunk driving. My passenger was injured as a result of the accident. What penalties do I face?

- My brother is the executor of our parents' estate, and I don't like how he's handling things. What can I do?

- Can I run a home school in my state (North Dakota) if I've been convicted of a felony?

These are the types of questions that people have traditionally asked lawyers. To answer such questions, you may need to look at all of the legal resources we have mentioned thus far. You must also make sure that the law you find is current. If you want to undertake this type of legal research on your own, we recommend that you use a comprehensive legal research guide that walks you through the process step by step. (See the list of resources at the end of this appendix.) Here, we can provide just a brief overview of what you'll need to do.

When seeking the answer to a specific legal question, your ultimate goal is to predict, as near as possible, how a judge would rule if presented with the issues and facts of your case. The closer your facts are to the facts in previous cases or the more directly a statute applies to your situation, the more likely you'll be able to predict what a judge would decide. Sometimes, your question is so basic that the answer is easy to find. But often, a statute won't address each facet of your situation, and the facts of other cases won't match up 100%. Because of this, legal research cannot always provide a definitive answer, although it can often give you a good idea of what the answer will be. (That's why lawyers often hem and haw when asked a legal question.)

Basic or Common Legal Questions

If your legal question is basic and general, such as "What does it mean to file for Chapter 7 bankruptcy?" or "What kinds of expenses are child-support payments supposed to cover?" then you should begin your research by consulting one or more of the background resources discussed above. The answers to these types of questions are usually based on general legal information rather than on the nuances of your particular circumstances.

If your question is common and straight-forward (such as "What is the filing fee for a Chapter 7 bankruptcy?" or "Can the state garnish my wages if I fall behind on child-support payments?") then it should be quite easy to find an answer, because these kinds of questions rely on factual information that many people need to know. Finding this kind of information doesn't involve any special legal-research methods. Think of the government branches or agencies that are likely to have the answers. For example, the U.S. Bankruptcy Court for your area probably has filing fees posted on its website, or you can call the court clerk. And every state has an agency that handles child-support payments. Look on your state's home page to find the agency website or a public information number. You can find phone numbers for city, county, state, and U.S. government agencies in the Government Pages section at the front of your local telephone book.

In some cases, the quickest way to find an answer is by contacting an organization or advocacy group that specializes in the subject of your question. Do you want to know the current estate tax rate? An organization that advocates for seniors, such as the American Association of Retired People (AARP), may know the answer. If you're looking for information on evictions, a local advocacy group such as a tenants' rights union should be able to help. You can find almost any organization or advocacy group on the Internet. Most Yellow Pages also include listings of community resources.

Complex Legal Questions

If you can't get an answer to your legal question from a background resource—usually because your question involves unique facts related to your situation—you'll need to do more detailed research. Build on the information you found in the background materials.

To proceed further, first search for statutes, regulations, or ordinances that address your question. If you find relevant statutes, look for cases that have interpreted them. To do this at a law library, you can:

- look at the summaries of cases that follow the statute in an annotated code book
- use *Shepard's Citations for Statutes* (a book that provides a complete list of cases that mention a particular statute, regulation, or constitutional provision), and

- search for cases in "case digests" (books that list cases by subject).

If you can't find a relevant statute or other legislative enactment, you need to look for case law only. To do this at a law library, you can:

- read any relevant cases mentioned in the background materials

- search in case digests by subject area or keywords

- if you find a relevant case, read the cases that it mentions, and

- if you find a relevant case, use *Shepard's Citations for Cases* to find more cases on point. (*Shepard's* provides a complete list of cases that mention your case.)

Making Sure the Law Is Up to Date

Because the law changes rapidly, you must make sure that the principles stated in your cases and statutes are still valid. A case may no longer be helpful to you if a more recent case has questioned its reasoning, ruled a different way, or expressly stated that your case is no longer good law. Likewise, you should check to make sure your statute has not been changed or eliminated.

Updating Your Research in the Library

If you are using the law library, there are a few things you should do to make sure your research is up to date.

- **Background resources.** If you use background materials, be sure to check the pocket part; it contains changes and new developments in the law.

- **Statutes.** Books containing statutes and regulations also contain pocket parts. Be sure to check these as well. Also check law library periodicals that contain more recent statutory updates.

- **Cases.** You can check the validity of every case you find by using *Shepard's Citations for Cases. Shepard's* will list every case that mentions your case, and tell you the reasons why it was mentioned. For example, it might show that a later case overruled your case, which means your case is no longer valid. Using *Shepard's* isn't easy—ask the law librarian for help.

Updating Your Research on the Web

On the Internet, the updating process is easier, but it might cost some money.

- **Statutes.** If you're checking a state statute, visit your state's website for current legislative developments. If you need federal information, track Congress's legislative developments at http://thomas.loc.gov. You can also get the most recent version of a statute (for a fee) through Westlaw or Lexis.

- **Cases.** You can check the validity of cases by using www.westlaw.com or *Shepard's* at www.lexis.com. Each service charges $4.25 for each case you check.

Finding Legal Forms

If you must take care of a legal matter, chances are good that you'll need to use a form of some sort—that is, a preformatted document that contains standard ("boilerplate") language addressing your specific situation. Leases, wills, trusts, and sales agreements are just a few examples of the thousands of legal forms that are used in the course of our daily personal and business affairs.

What Form Do You Need?

Figuring out what form you need is usually simple—someone will tell you. For example, suppose you are handling your own divorce, and when you try to file the papers, the clerk says you are missing a "disclosure" form. If the court can't give it to you, you'll have to find it on your own. Or, suppose you are trying to sell your car, and the buyer wants a bill of sale. Again, you'll have to track one down.

If you haven't been told what form you need, but you want to take care of a matter that you assume requires legal forms, start by trying to find a resource that explains the transaction. For example, if you want to sublet an apartment, you might look for a book about leases and rental agreements. This type of resource often provides the necessary forms and explains how to fill them out.

Keep in mind that some forms used by courts and government agencies are "mandatory." This means that you have to use their form, not a similar form that you or someone else has designed, even if your version contains the same information. If you need a form for a court or government agency, it's wise to ask the clerk whether the court has a mandatory form. Or you can check the court or agency's website—it may have forms you can download.

Finding the Form You Need

Fortunately, forms are readily available from many sources. Here are the best ways to get them.

- **Stationery stores.** Many large stationery stores sell legal forms. However, these forms usually don't come with legal instructions, so you may need some help filling them in.

- **Self-help legal materials.** Self-help legal materials, including those published by Nolo, are a good place to find legal forms. Because self-help law materials are written for nonlawyers, the forms are usually accompanied by detailed instructions in plain English. You can find self-help legal materials in bookstores, law libraries, and on the Internet.

- **Law libraries.** Most law libraries have a large collection of books that contain forms for almost every legal transaction imaginable. They usually contain step-by-step instructions for completing the forms and highlight areas where the boilerplate language might not be appropriate.

- **Government forms on the Web.** The Google search engine (www.google.com) is the easiest way to locate state or federal forms. Try typing any combination of the following elements into the search box:

- the state that issued the form or, if it's a local form, the court where you will use it

- the title of the form or a few unique terms that would likely be in the title—for example, "Petition Administer Estate" for a "Notice of Petition to Administer Estate"

- the subject matter of the form in the absence of a specific name—for example "Summons Eviction"

- the term "form."

Many of these forms are not accompanied by instructions. So, unless you already know what you are doing, you may have to search for additional information to assist you in filling them out.

- **Commercial legal forms on the Web.** You can find almost any legal form you need somewhere on the Internet. There are sites that specialize in specific subjects, such as divorce or real estate, and there are mega sites like Findforms.com, where you can locate free or commercial legal forms, or Lawcommerce.com, which has an extensive collection of actual and sample business forms for sale. Many of our favorite legal-research sites also have links to legal forms (see "The Best Legal Websites," above).

More Information About Legal Research

Legal Research: How to Find & Understand the Law, by Stephen Elias and Susan Levinkind (Nolo), is an easy-to-read book that provides step-by-step instructions on how to find legal information, both in the law library and online. It includes examples, exercises (with answers), and sample legal memos.

Gilbert's Law Summaries: Legal Research, Writing and Analysis, by Peter Honigsberg (Harcourt Brace), is a no-nonsense guide to commonly used law library resources.

Sites for Legal Research

The Virtual Chase, at **www.virtualchase.com,** offers guides to researching various legal topics, as well as general research tips and legal resources.

www.nolo.com
Nolo's website provides links to courts across the country and access to small claims information in many states. It also contains U.S. Supreme Court cases and federal and state statutes.

www.ncsconline.org
The National Center for State Courts provides links to local, state, and federal court websites.

www.uscourts.gov
The federal judiciary's website provides links to federal court websites.

www.versuslaw.com
VersusLaw allows you to search online for state and federal statutes and cases for a low monthly fee.

www.findlaw.com
FindLaw's extensive database allows you to search for state and federal statutes and cases and provides links to many courts around the country.

www.statelocalgov.net
State and Local Government on the Net has links to all states and statewide offices, plus many local government organizations.

Index

Get the Latest in the Law

(1) **Nolo's Legal Updater**
We'll send you an email whenever a new edition of your book is published!
Sign up at **www.nolo.com/legalupdater**.

(2) **Updates at Nolo.com**
Check **www.nolo.com/update** to find recent changes in the law that
affect the current edition of your book.

(3) **Nolo Customer Service**
To make sure that this edition of the book is the most recent one, call us at
800-728-3555 and ask one of our friendly customer service representatives
(7:00 am to 6:00 pm PST, weekdays only). Or find out at **www.nolo.com**.

(4) **Complete the Registration & Comment Card ...**
... and we'll do the work for you! Just indicate your preferences below:

- -

Registration & Comment Card

NAME _____ DATE _____

ADDRESS _____

CITY _____ STATE _____ ZIP _____

PHONE _____ EMAIL _____

COMMENTS _____

WAS THIS BOOK EASY TO USE?   (VERY EASY)   5   4   3   2   1   (VERY DIFFICULT)

☐ Yes, you can quote me in future Nolo promotional materials. *Please include phone number above.*

☐ Yes, send me **Nolo's Legal Updater** via email when a new edition of this book is available.

Yes, I want to sign up for the following email newsletters:

   ☐ **NoloBriefs** (monthly)
   ☐ **Nolo's Special Offer** (monthly)
   ☐ **Nolo's BizBriefs** (monthly)
   ☐ **Every Landlord's Quarterly** (four times a year)

☐ Yes, you can give my contact info to carefully selected
partners whose products may be of interest to me.

NOLO

EVL7

Nolo
950 Parker Street
Berkeley, CA 94710-9867
www.nolo.com

MEET YOUR NEW ATTORNEY

"Loves walking in the rain and drawing up prenuptial agreements."

"Enjoys fine wine and creating living trusts."

"Spends time gardening and doing trademark searches."

Brent
San Francisco

Juliana
Phoenix

Ron
Seattle

Start a great relationship
(you can skip the walks on the beach)

You don't need just any attorney. You need that "special someone" – someone whose personality puts you at ease, whose qualifications match your needs, whose experience can make everything better.

With Nolo's Lawyer Directory, meeting your new attorney is just a click away. Lawyers have created extensive profiles that feature their work histories, credentials, philosophies, fees – and much more.

Check out Nolo's Lawyer Directory to find your attorney – you'll feel as if you've already met, before you ever meet.

Visit us and get a free eBook!
http://lawyers.nolo.com/book

Meet your new attorney   **NOLO'S LAWYER DIRECTORY**

LECTURAS BÁSICAS

A LITERARY READER

THIRD EDITION

GUILLERMO I. CASTILLO-FELIÚ
Winthrop College

HOLT, RINEHART and WINSTON

New York   Chicago   San Francisco   Philadelphia
Montreal   Toronto   London   Sydney
Tokyo   Mexico City   Rio de Janeiro   Madrid

Permissions

We wish to thank the authors, publishers, and copyright holders for their permission to use the reading materials in this book.

Enrique Anderson Imbert, "Las estatuas," from *El gato de Cheshire,* by permission of the author.

Jorge Luis Borges, "Los dos reyes y los dos laberintos," from *Obras completas* (Buenos Aires, 1954), by permission of the author.

Francisco Monterde, "La moneda de oro," from *Cuentos mexicanos,* by permission of the author.

Ricardo Palma, "La camisa de Margarita," from *The Literature of Spanish America,* Vol. 2, N.Y.: Las Américas, 1967, by permission of Angel Flores.

Gregorio López y Fuentes, "Una carta a Dios," from *Cuentos campesinos de México,* by permission of Lic. Angel López Oropeza.

José Donoso, "China," from *Los mejores cuentos* (Santiago: Zig-Zag, 1966).

Manuel González Zeledón, "El Clis de sol," from *La propia y otros tipos y escenas costarricenses* (2 ed. San José: Garcia Monge, 1920).

Rubén Darío, "Las pérdidas de Juan Bueno," from *Cuentos completos* (Mexico: Fondo de Cultura Económica, 1950).

Library of Congress Cataloging in Publication Data

Main entry under title:

Lecturas básicas.

 Pref. in English.
 Contents: Las estatuas / Enrique Anderson Imbert—
Los dos reyes y los dos laberintos / Jorge Luis Borges—
La moneda de oro / Francisco Monterde—[etc.]
 1. Spanish language—Readers. I. Castillo-Feliú,
Guillermo I.
PC4117.L412   1985   468.6'421   84-10493
ISBN 0-03-071031-6

 7 8 9   059   9 8 7 6 5

Holt, Rinehart and Winston
The Dryden Press
Saunders College Publishing

PREFACE

Lecturas básicas: A Literary Reader, third edition, is a beginning
reader designed for use in first-year college Spanish courses. The purpose of this book is to provide materials to develop reading skills for
students at the earliest stages of language learning. Although it is
part of the complete introductory program that accompanies the third
edition of Allen, *¿Habla español?,* this reader may be used in conjunction with any basic grammar book.

The materials in *Lecturas básicas: A Literary Reader* represent a
collection of original writings in Spanish arranged according to several
factors, among them length and level of difficulty. Each story is pre-
ceded by a *Vocabulario activo,* a short introduction to the author, and a
section entitled *Points to consider.* Students should familiarize themselves with the vocabulary list before beginning to read, for the listed
words are featured in the story and are also the backbone of the exercises that immediately follow each selection. There are essentially two
types of exercises: comprehension questions treating story content and
exercises for vocabulary development. Finally, difficult words and
phrases are glossed throughout.

The third edition of *Lecturas básicas: A Literary Reader* represents a
combination of the most successful stories from the second edition and
new stories that I believe will be of interest to first-year college students. These new stories are, of course, accompanied by new introduc-
tions and new exercises.

As a general guideline, students can begin to read these stories after
some familiarization with the past tenses. In Allen, *¿Habla español?,*
third edition, this point is reached between Chapters 9 and 11.

I hope that students will find these authentic stories by some of the
finest writers in the Spanish language a satisfying means of building

their reading skills and a rewarding introduction to the rich literature of the Hispanic world.

I am grateful to the following reviewers, who made constructive comments and suggestions that helped shape this edition: Deanne Flouton-Price, Nassau Community College; Hildebrando Ruiz, University of Georgia; Alain Swietlicki, University of Missouri–Columbia; B. R. Weaver, Washington State University.

G.I.C.-F.

CONTENTS

LECTURAS BÁSICAS
A LITERARY READER

capítulo 1

VOCABULARIO ACTIVO

el **jardín**   *garden, yard*
   colegio   *school* (not *college*)
   estatua   *statue*
   fundar   *to found*
   pintar   *to paint*
   suelo   *floor, ground*
   encontrarse   *to meet (up) with each other*
el **amor**   *love*
la **medianoche**   *midnight*
   broma   *joke*
   huella   *print, trace*
   lavar   *to wash, to wash off*
   sucio   *dirty*

Enrique Anderson Imbert (1910–   ) nació en Argentina. Ha sido profesor en varias universidades norteamericanas y ha escrito muchas novelas y cuentos. «Las estatuas» pertenece a la colección *El gato de Cheshire*. Esta narrativa es un ejemplo de los «casos» del autor: anécdotas o cuentos que en pocas palabras impresionan al lector por su gran ingenuidad y originalidad.

POINTS TO CONSIDER

1. Reality and fantasy in "Las estatuas."
2. Why do you think this brief tale belongs to the collection *El gato de Cheshire*? (Recall Lewis Carroll's *Alice in Wonderland*.)

Las estatuas

Enrique Anderson Imbert

En el jardín de Brighton, colegio de señoritas, hay
dos estatuas: *la de* la fundadora y la del profesor   that of
más famoso. Una noche, una estudiante *traviesa*   mischievous
salió *a escondidas* de su dormitorio y pintó sobre el   secretly
suelo, entre ambos pedestales, *huellas de pasos* de   footprints
mujer y de hombre que se encuentran en la *glorieta*   arbor
y se hacen el amor a medianoche. Después se fue a
esperar la reacción del resto del colegio. Cuando al
día siguiente fue a gozar la broma, vio que las huellas habían sido lavadas y que las manos de la es-
tatua de la fundadora *le habían quedado algo su-*   (in spite of an attempt
cias de pintura.   to wash them they
                                                          were still
                                                          somewhat dirty)

El gato de Cheshire (Buenos Aires: Edit. Losada, 1965.)

EJERCICIOS

A. Fill in the blank with the appropriate word(s) from the column on the right.

1. El _____ en Brighton es para señoritas.

2. Una de las _____ es de la fundadora.

3. Los amantes _____ en la glorieta
   a medianoche.

4. Las manos le quedaron algo _____
   de pintura.

5. Había _____ de hombre y de mujer sobre el suelo.

sucias
dijo
colegio
huellas
estatuas
se encuentran
señoritas

B. Retell parts of the story using the following sequences.

1. jardín / colegio / estatuas
2. estudiante / salir / dormitorio / pintar / huella
3. mujer / hombre / encontrar / glorieta
4. ver / huellas / lavar

C. Translate the following sentences using the appropriate words from the list.

1. The founder's statue approaches the professor's statue.
2. The two meet in the garden's arbor.
3. They make love at midnight.
4. She painted women's footprints on the
   ground.
5. Someone washed off the prints.

pintó
socorrer
se acerca
lavó
se encuentran
decir
se hacen el amor
huellas

D. Answer in Spanish.

1. ¿Dónde hay dos estatuas?
2. ¿Cómo salió la estudiante traviesa?
3. ¿Qué pintó ella en el suelo?
4. ¿A qué hora se encuentran?
5. Al día siguiente, ¿qué vio la estudiante?
6. ¿Cómo le habían quedado las manos a la estatua de la fundadora?

capítulo 2

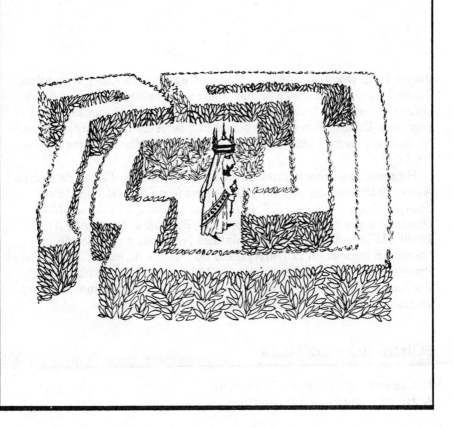

VOCABULARIO ACTIVO

el **rey** *king*
mandar *to have or make someone do something*
laberinto *labyrinth*
perder; perderse *to lose; get lost*
Dios *God*
la **corte** *court*
hacer burla de *to make fun of*
el **huésped** *guest*
hacer *to have, to make, to create*
socorro *help*
dar con *to come across*
dar a conocer *to make known*
desierto *desert*
escalera *stairs*
muro *wall*
tener a bien *to see fit to*

Jorge Luis Borges (1899– 1986) nació en Buenos Aires, Argentina, donde hizo sus primeros estudios. Pasó varios años en Europa donde obtuvo el título de bachiller en el Colegio de Ginebra, Suiza. En 1921 regresó a Buenos Aires donde fundó una serie de importantes revistas literarias: *Prisma* (1921–22), *Proa* (1922–23) y *Martín Fierro* (1924– 1927).

Ha publicado importantes colecciones de poemas (*Fervor de Buenos Aires,* 1923; *Luna de enfrente,* 1925; *Cuaderno San Martín,* 1929), ensayos (*Inquisiciones,* 1925; *Otras inquisiciones,* 1952) y cuentos (*Historia universal de la infamia,* 1935; *Ficciones,* 1944; y *El Aleph,* 1949). Ha sido director de la Biblioteca Nacional y profesor de literatura inglesa en la Universidad de Buenos Aires. En 1957 ganó el Premio Nacional de Literatura y en 1961 compartió con Samuel Beckett el Premio Internacional Formentor. Borges es uno de los más grandes escritores y pensadores de la lengua española.

POINTS TO CONSIDER

1. Comparison of the two labyrinths.
2. He who laughs last laughs best.

Los dos reyes y los dos laberintos

Jorge Luis Borges

Cuentan los hombres dignos de fe (pero *Alá* sabe
más) que en los primeros días *hubo* un rey de las
islas de Babilonia que congregó a sus arquitectos y
magos y les mandó construir un laberinto tan perplejo y sutil que los varones más prudentes no se
aventuraban a entrar, y los que entraban se perdían. Esa *obra* era un escándalo, porque la confusión y la maravilla son operaciones propias de Dios
y no de los hombres. *Con el andar del tiempo* vino
a su corte un rey de los árabes, y el rey de Babilonia (para hacer burla de la simplicidad de su
huésped) lo hizo penetrar en el laberinto, donde
vagó afrentado y confundido hasta la declinación de
la tarde. Entonces imploró socorro divino y dio con
la puerta. Sus labios *no profirieron* queja ninguna,
pero le dijo al rey de Babilonia que él en Arabia
tenía un laberinto mejor y que, si Dios era servido,
se lo daría a conocer algún día. Luego regresó a
Arabia, juntó sus capitanes y sus *alcaides* y *estragó*
los reinos de Babilonia con tan venturosa fortuna
que derribó sus castillos, rompió sus gentes e hizo
cautivo al mismo rey. Lo *amarró* encima de un camello veloz y lo llevó al desierto. *Cabalgaron* tres
días, y le dijo: —¡O, rey del tiempo y substancia y
cifra del siglo!, en Babilonia me *quisiste* perder en
un laberinto de bronce con muchas escaleras, puertas y muros; ahora *el Poderoso ha tenido a bien que
te muestre el mío,* donde no hay escaleras que subir, ni puertas que forzar, ni fatigosas galerías que
recorrer, ni muros *que te veden el paso.*
Luego le *desató* las ligaduras y lo abandonó en
mitad del desierto, donde murió de *hambre* y de *sed.*
La gloria sea con Aquel que no muere.

Obras completas (Buenos Aires, 1954).

Glosses:
- Allah
- there was
- work, piece of work
- With the passage of time
- he wandered ashamed
- he didn't utter
- he would make it known to him / governors / he ruined
- fastened
- They rode
- you tried
- the Almighty has seen fit for me to show you mine
- that block your way
- untied
- hunger / thirst

EJERCICIOS

A. Fill in the blank with the appropriate word from the column on the right.

1. El laberinto tenía muchos _____.

2. Un rey de los árabes imploró _____ divino.

3. El rey quiso perder al árabe en un

   _____.

4. La confusión es operación propia de

   _____.

5. Lo llevó al _____.

6. Los que entraban en el laberinto se

   _____.

7. El rey de los árabes vino a su _____.

8. Les _____ construir un laberinto.

9. Hizo a su _____ penetrar en el laberinto.

10. Hubo un _____ de las islas de Babilonia.

socorro
Dios
laberinto
huésped
hombres
desierto
rey
hicieron burla de
perdían
dieron a conocer
escaleras
mandó
muros
corte

B. Give the feminine form of each of the following nouns.

1. dios	6. vecino
2. rey	7. dependiente
3. huésped	8. indio
4. hombre	9. novio
5. chiquito	10. ladrón

C. Choose the word from the list at the right which corresponds to each definition.

1. persona real
2. persona que viene a visitar
3. pared alta
4. lugar seco
5. resentimiento, disgusto
6. ayuda
7. un lugar enredado
8. pensar que es buena idea
9. lugar donde manda el rey
10. espíritu venerado

desierto
huésped
tener a bien
perder
laberinto
dios
escalera
corte
rey
dar a conocer
queja
socorro
muro
hacer burla de

D. Retell parts of the story using the following sequences.

1. rey / congregar / arquitectos / magos
2. confusión / maravilla / obra / Dios
3. rey / implorar / socorro / dar / puerta
4. rey / amarrar / camello / llevar / desierto

E. Answer in Spanish.

1. ¿Qué mandó construir el rey de las islas de Babilonia?
2. ¿Por qué era un escándalo esa obra?
3. ¿Quién vino a la corte del rey de Babilonia?
4. ¿Qué le hizo al rey de los árabes el rey de Babilonia?
5. Cuando el rey de los árabes regresó a su país, ¿qué hizo?
6. ¿Adónde llevó al rey de Babilonia?
7. ¿Cuántos días cabalgaron?
8. ¿Qué le dijo el rey de los árabes al rey de Babilonia cuando estaban en el desierto?
9. ¿Quién es el Poderoso?
10. ¿Quién muere al final de este cuento?

capítulo 3

VOCABULARIO ACTIVO

la **Navidad** *Christmas*
suelo *ground*
moneda *coin*
oro *gold*
bolsillo *pocket*
por temor a *for fear of*
de seguro *certainly*
rumbo a *towards, in the direction of*
detenerse *to stop*
esquina *corner*
volver *to return*
a punto de *on the point of*
tienda *store*
coser *to sew*
esconder *to hide*
debajo de *beneath, underneath*
por delante *ahead, in front*
chaleco *vest*
saco *coat*
tropezar con *to bump into*
vecino *neighbor*
despedirse de *to say goodbye to*
disculparse *to excuse oneself*
el **dependiente** *clerk*
atreverse a *to dare to*
recoger *to gather, pick up*

Francisco Monterde (1894–   ) nació en la ciudad de México. Se graduó de doctor en Letras Españolas en la Universidad Nacional de México en 1942. Ha cultivado el cuento, la novela, la poesía, el drama y la crítica. Hombre de enorme sabiduría, se ha dedicado casi por completo a la literatura mexicana.

Como narrador, despertó el interés en el período colonial mexicano con *El madrigal de Cetina y el secreto de la escala* (1918) y más tarde con *Moctezuma, el de la silla de oro* (1945). Se trata de uno de los más destacados autores mexicanos.

POINTS TO CONSIDER

1. Andrés's possibilities with the gold coin.
2. The effects of the finding of the coin on the family's life.

La moneda de oro

Francisco Monterde

Aquella Navidad fue alegre para un pobre: Andrés, que no tenía trabajo desde el otoño.

Atravesaba el parque, *al anochecer,* cuando vio en el suelo una moneda que reflejaba la luz fría de la luna. De pronto creyó que era una moneda de *plata;* al cogerla, sorprendido por el peso, cambió de opinión: «Es una medalla, *desprendida* de alguna cadena», pensó. Hacía mucho tiempo que no tenía en sus manos una moneda de oro, y por eso había olvidado cómo eran. Hasta que llegó al fin del parque y pudo examinarla en la claridad, *se convenció de que* realmente era una moneda de oro. nightfall

silver
unfastened from

was convinced that

Palpándola, Andrés comprendía por qué los *avaros* amontonan tesoros, para acariciarlos en la soledad. ¡Era tan agradable su contacto! Touching it / misers

Con la moneda entre los dedos, metió la mano derecha en el bolsillo del pantalón. No se decidía a soltar en él la moneda, por temor a perderla, como el que la dejó en el parque, el que la había poseído antes que él. De seguro no era un pobre; los pobres rara vez tienen monedas de oro. *Sería* rico y aquella moneda *pasaría* inadvertida para él,... Sin embargo, Andrés pensó, como un personaje de cuento moral, que *si supiera* quién la había perdido, rico o pobre, le *devolvería* la moneda, *aunque no lo gratificara...* He probably was
would go

if he knew
he would return /
   even if he didn't
   reward him

Mientras Andrés caminaba apresurado, rumbo a su casa, la moneda de oro saltaba alegremente en el bolsillo...

Una duda asaltó a Andrés: *¿No sería* una moneda falsa? Se detuvo en la próxima esquina, y volvió a examinarla, al pie de un *farol.* Vio sus letras, bien *grabadas; la hizo sonar.* La apariencia y el *timbre* —claro, fino— casi le devolvieron la tranquilidad. Para tranquilizarse por completo, estuvo a punto de entrar a una tienda, comprar algo y pagar con la moneda de oro. Si la aceptaban, indudablemente era buena, si no...; pero era mejor mostrarla a alguien *que le dijera* la verdad. Andrés prefirió llevar la moneda a su casa. Could it be

street lamp
engraved / he made it
   jingle / timber,
   tone

who would tell him

El camino le pareció menos largo que otras noches, en que *volvía* derrotado en la lucha por encontrar empleo, porque ahora pensaba en la sorpresa que *causaría* a su mujer, *cuando le enseñara* la moneda de oro. returned it would cause / when he showed her

Su casa —dos *piezas* humildes— estaba oscura y sola, cuando él llegó. Su mujer había salido, con la niña, a entregar la ropa que cosía diariamente. rooms

Encendió una luz y se sentó a esperarles, junto a la mesa *sin pintar. Con una esquina de mantel a cuadros rojos* frotó la moneda, y cuando oyó cercanas las voces de su mujer y de su hija, la escondió debajo del mantel. unpainted / With the corner of a red-checked tablecloth

La niña entró por delante, corriendo; él la tomó en brazos, la besó en la frente, y la sentó sobre sus piernas. La mujer llegó después; su cara tenía una expresión triste:

—*¿Conseguiste algo?*... Yo no pude comprar el pan, porque no me pagaron la costura que llevé a entregar... Did you get anything (i.e., a job)?

En vez de contestar, Andrés, sonriente, levantó *la punta* del mantel. the tip end

La mujer vio con asombro, la moneda, la tomó en sus manos. Andrés temió que *fuera* a decir: «Es falsa», pero ella dijo: was going to

—¿Quién te la dio?

—Nadie. La encontré.

Y refirió la historia del *hallazgo.* Para explicar mejor colocó la moneda en el piso, retrocedió unos pasos. the find

—Yo venía así, caminando...

La niña se apresuró *a coger* la moneda, la vio sobre la palma extendida; la arrojó al aire; *la hizo rodar por el suelo*... Andrés *se la arrebató,* temeroso... to seize, grasp she made it roll along the floor / snatched it away from her

Guardó la moneda en uno de los bolsillos del chaleco y se sentó junto a la mesa.

—¿Qué compraremos con ella?

—Hay que pagar... ¡Debemos tanto!...—suspiró la mujer.

—Es verdad; pero recuerda que hoy es *Nochebuena.* Tenemos que celebrarla. ¿No te parece? Christmas Eve

La mujer se oponía a ello. *Deberían* pagar, antes... Andrés *malhumorado,* se quitó el saco y el chaleco y los colgó sobre *el respaldo* de la silla. They ought to ill-humored the back

—Está bien—dijo—: pasaremos la Nochebuena sin cenar, a pesar de que tenemos una moneda de oro—. Conciliadora, la mujer propuso:

—*Podrías* ir a comprar algo, guardaremos lo demás.   You could

Andrés aceptó. Volvió a ponerse el chaleco, el saco, y salió de su casa.

En la calle tropezó con Pedro, su vecino.

—¿A dónde vas?... ¿Quieres venir a tomar algo conmigo?

Andrés aceptó. Después de beber y charlar un buen rato, se despidió de Pedro y siguió hacia la tienda. *¿Compraría* sólo alimentos para esa noche o   Should he buy
también dulces para la niña y algún juguete?...

Comenzó por pedir los alimentos. Cuando el paquete estuvo listo, Andrés buscó la moneda, primero en el pantalón, después en el chaleco; pero la moneda de oro no estaba en ninguno de sus bolsillos. *Acongojado,* la buscó en todos, nuevamente   Upset (sad)
—en el pantalón, en el chaleco, en el saco— sin encontrarla. Cuando se convenció de que ya no la tenía, se disculpó con el dependiente y salió de la tienda.

En pocos minutos recorrió, *angustiado,* las calles   distressed, anguished
que lo separaban de su casa. *Al entrar,* vio a la   Upon entering
niña dormida, con la cabeza entre los brazos sobre la mesa y a su mujer, sentada junto a ella, cosiendo. No se atrevía a decir la verdad. Al fin murmuró:

—La moneda...

—¿Qué?

—...*Se me perdió.*   I lost it

—¡Cómo!

La niña, *sobresaltada,* abrió los ojos, bajó los   startled
brazos, y éntonces se oyó, bajo la mesa, el fino *retin-*   tinkling, jingle
tín de la moneda de oro.

Andrés y su mujer riendo, como locos, se inclinaron a recoger la moneda que la niña había *esca-*   stolen
moteado.

Cuentos mexicanos (Santiago: Ediciones Ercilla, 1936).

EJERCICIOS

A. Fill in the blank with the appropriate word from the column on the right.

1. Andrés vio algo en el _____.

2. Metió la mano en el _____.

3. Después de ponerse el chaleco, se puso el _____.

4. Andrés _____ con su vecino.

5. Después de beber, Andrés _____ de Pedro.

6. Está en el bolsillo del _____.

7. Estuvo _____ entrar en la tienda.

8. _____ en la esquina.

9. Andrés caminaba apresurado _____ su casa.

10. Era una _____ de oro.

rumbo a
se atrevió
se despidió
escondió
suelo
saco
chaleco
bolsillo
oro
moneda
tropezó
tienda
se detuvo
a punto de

B. Write the appropriate word to complete each of the following expressions.

1. tropezar _____   *to bump into*

2. por temor _____   *for fear of*

3. rumbo _____   *towards*

4. atreverse _____   *to dare to*

5. _____ seguro   *certainly*

6. _____ delante   *in front*

7. _____ punto de   *on the point of*

8. debajo _____   *underneath*

9. despedirse _____   *to say goodbye to*

10. _____ entrar   *upon entering*

C. Choose the word from the list at the right that corresponds to each related idea.

1. el veinticinco de diciembre	vecino
2. hacer ropa	tienda
3. un metal precioso	chaleco
4. una persona que vive muy cerca	ser inteligente
5. pararse	coser
6. una prenda de vestir	tropezar con
7. donde se puede comprar cosas	esconder
8. encontrar, dar con	estar a punto de
9. estar listo	esquina
10. poner algo donde no se puede verlo	oro
	suelo
	detenerse
	atreverse a
	Navidad

D. Answer in Spanish.

1. ¿Qué vio Andrés en el suelo?
2. ¿Durante qué estación del año tiene lugar *(takes place)* este cuento?
3. Después de hallar *(to find)* la moneda, ¿adónde fue Andrés?
4. ¿Por qué estuvo Andrés a punto de entrar a una tienda y pagar con la moneda?
5. ¿Cómo estaba la casa de Andrés cuando llegó?
6. ¿Con qué frotó la moneda?
7. ¿Qué hizo Andrés cuando oyó cercanas las voces de su mujer y de su hija?
8. ¿Qué hizo la niña con la moneda?
9. ¿Con quién tropezó Andrés en la calle?
10. ¿Dónde buscó Andrés la moneda cuando el paquete estuvo listo?
11. ¿Quién había escamoteado la moneda de oro?

capítulo 4

VOCABULARIO ACTIVO

el **lector**   *reader*
caro   *expensive*
camisa   *shirt, gown*
caballero   *gentleman*
belleza   *beauty*
diablo   *devil*
el **alma (f)**   *soul, heart*
el **solterón**   *(confirmed) bachelor*
pobre   *poor*
conocer   *to meet, to be acquainted*
enamorarse   *to fall in love*
pedir   *to ask for*
joven   *young*
casar(se)   *to marry, to get married*
altivo   *haughty, arrogant*
médico   *physician, medical doctor*
sobrino   *nephew*
jurar   *to swear*
costar   *to cost*
el **brillante**   *diamond*
orgulloso   *proud*

Ricardo Palma (1833–1919) es uno de los maestros del cuento hispanoamericano. Sus *Tradiciones peruanas,* de las cuales el cuento incluido aquí es un buen ejemplo, representan un nuevo género en la narrativa de Hispanoamérica. Las tradiciones se basan en crónicas, anécdotas, refranes o simples noticias curiosas que el autor había encontrado en antiguos manuscritos. Alrededor de estas curiosidades, Palma crea un cuento original como lo es «La camisa de Margarita». La técnica de Palma es sencilla: presenta un documento histórico y luego introduce elementos ficticios, creando un cuento que parece ser real debido a su base auténtica.

POINTS TO CONSIDER

1. The influence of extreme pride on one's behavior.
2. Is the truth what one says or what one does?

La camisa de Margarita

Ricardo Palma

Es probable que mis lectores han oído decir a las viejas de Lima, cuando quieren criticar el precio muy alto de un artículo:

—*¡Qué!* Esto es más caro que la camisa de Margarita Pareja.

My!

I.

Margarita Pareja era (*por los años de* 1765) la hija más *mimada* de don Raimundo Pareja, caballero *de Santiago* y colector general del *Callao*.

(around. . .)
spoiled / Spanish military and religious order / Peru's main port /

La muchacha era una de esas *limeñitas* que, por su belleza, cautivan al mismo diablo y lo hacen *persignarse* y *tirar piedras*. Tenía dos ojos negros que eran como dos torpedos cargados de dinamita y que *hacían explosión* en el alma de los jóvenes limeños.

girls from Lima / cross himself and kick stones (i.e., fall madly in love)
exploded

Llegó por entonces de España un arrogante *mancebo* llamado don Luis Alcázar. Tenía en Lima un tío solterón, rico; un *aragonés* más orgulloso que los hijos de un rey. *Hasta heredar* de su tío, Luis era pobre.

young man

from Spain's Aragón province
Until he inherited

En la procesión de Santa Rosa conoció Alcázar a Margarita. Él con sus *miradas* y ella con sus sonrisitas *se dieron a entender* que se gustaban. Los dos se enamoraron *hasta la raíz del pelo*.

long glances
made it clear
head over heels (to the very roots of their hair) /

Luis no pensó que su presente pobreza iba a ser obstáculo para *el logro* de sus amores y fue *tempranamente* a pedir la mano de Margarita a su padre.

attainment / soon, quickly

A Don Raimundo *no le cayó muy bien* la petición y *despidió al postulante* explicándole que Margarita, de diez y ocho años, era todavía muy joven.

did not suit him very well
dismissed the suitor

Pero ésta no era la verdadera razón para *la negativa* de don Raimundo. En realidad no quería casar a su hija con un *pobretón* y así se lo dijo *en confianza* a sus amigos. Uno de estos amigos le fue a contar *el asunto* a don Honorato, que así se lla-

his saying no

pauper / confidentially

the matter

maba el tío aragonés. Este, que era maś altıvo que el Cid, *trinó de rabia* y dijo: fumed with anger

—¡Cómo *se atreve! ¡Desairar* a mi sobrino! Muchos se alegrarían de casar a su hija con el muchacho, pues no hay uno más gallardo en toda Lima. dare he! / to insult

Margarita, nerviosa como una *damisela* de hoy, *gimoteó, se arrancó* el pelo, y *tuvo pataleta.* Finalmente, gritó: debutante
whined / pulled out /
had a fit

—*¡O de Luis o de Dios!* I'll be Louis' or enter
a convent / nature
healers / had a
tendency toward
consumption

Don Raimundo se alarmó, llamó a médicos y *curanderos.* Todos declararon que Margarita *tiraba a tísica* y que el único remedio no se vendía en ninguna farmacia. El remedio: casarla con el varón, Luis, o *encerrarla en el cajón con palma y corona.* Tal fue el ultimátum médico. place her in a coffin,
wreath and all

Don Raimundo (*¡al fin,* padre!) *se encaminó* como loco a casa de don Honorato y le dijo: after all / went

—Vengo a que consienta usted en que mañana mismo se case su sobrino con Margarita; si no, la muchacha *se nos va de este mundo.* will die on us

—No puede ser —contestó *secamente* el tío—. Mi sobrino es un pobretón; lo que usted necesita es un hombre que sea rico. sternly

El diálogo fue *borrascoso. Mientras más rogaba don Raimundo, más* altivo se ponía don Honorato. Iba ya a *retirarse* aquél cuando Luis apareció y dijo: tempestuous / the
more don
Raimundo begged,
the more / leave

—Tío, acepte usted el *pedido* de don Raimundo. request

—¿*Tú te das por* satisfecho? You are

—*De* todo corazón, tío y señor. With

—Pues bien, muchacho; con una condición consiento y es ésta: don Raimundo me ha de jurar que no le *regalará* un centavo a su hija ni le *dejará* nada en la herencia. give / leave

Más y más argumentos entre todos.

—Pero, hombre —arguyó don Raimundo— mi hija tiene veinte mil duros *de dote.* Sea usted razonable, don Honorato. Permítame darle *siquiera* los muebles y el *ajuar* de novia. in dowry
at least
trousseau

—*Ni* un *alfiler.* Si no le gusta, olvídese de todo y que se muera la chica. Not / pin

—Don Honorato, mi hija necesita *llevar* siquiera una camisa para reemplazar *la puesta.* take with her
the one she is
wearing

—Bien. Consiento en que le regale la camisa de novia, y *san se acabó.* that's all

Al día siguiente don Raimundo y don Honorato

se dirigieron muy temprano a la iglesia de San Francisco y en el momento en que el *sacerdote* elevaba *la Hostia* divina, dijo el padre de Margarita:

went
priest
Holy Eucharist

—Juro no dar a mi hija más que la camisa de novia.

Y don Raimundo cumplió *ad pedem litterae* su juramento: nunca dio nada más a su hija que *valiera* un centavo.

to the letter
was worth

Los encajes de Flandes que adornaban la camisa de la novia costaron dos mil setecientos duros. El *cordoncillo que ajustaba al cuello* era una *cadenita* de brillantes, con un valor de treinta mil pesos.

Flemish lace

the neck drawstring / fine chain

De esto, entonces, el famoso *dicho* sobre la camisa de Margarita.

Hence / saying

Historia y antología del cuento y la novela en Hispanoamérica, Angel Flores, ed. (New York: Las Américas, 1959).

EJERCICIOS

A. Fill in the blank with the appropriate word from the column on the right.

1. El _____ de este cuento es la persona que lo lee.
2. El tío de Luis, don Honorato, era un _____.
3. Don Raimundo _____ no regalar ni un centavo al matrimonio.
4. Luis y Margarita se _____ hasta la raíz del pelo.
5. Margarita era tan bella que el _____ se persignaba y tiraba piedras.
6. El único regalo permitido a don Raimundo era la _____.
7. Don Honorato era un hombre muy _____.
8. Luis _____ a Margarita en una procesión religiosa.
9. Don Raimundo, padre de Margarita, era un _____ de Santiago.
10. Luis le _____ la mano de Margarita a su padre.

pidió
caballero
enamoraron
conoció
juró
joven
orgulloso
caro
brillante
lector
solterón
diablo
camisa

B. Choose the item(s) from the column at the right which can best describe the characters on the left.

1. Luis es _____.
2. Don Honorato es _____.
3. Margarita es _____.
4. Don Raimundo es _____.

una belleza
médico
un diablo
un caballero
rico
joven
solterón
altivo
orgulloso
pobre
sobrino de don Honorato
caro
el brillante

C. Choose the word on the right which best fits the description on the left.

1. una persona sin dinero	caballero
2. un viejo no casado	sobrino
3. el hijo de mi hermano	pedido
4. algo dentro de nosotros	cara
5. así es don Honorato	pobre
6. Margarita es así	lector
7. prometer solemnemente	caro
8. la camisa de Margarita	alma
9. una piedra preciosa	jurar
10. hombre noble y decente	solterón
	altivo
	belleza
	brillante

D. Answer in Spanish.

1. ¿Cuál es la famosa expresión de las viejas de Lima?
2. ¿Cómo era Margarita?
3. ¿Quién llegó a Lima de España?
4. ¿Hasta cuándo iba él a ser pobre?
5. ¿Cómo se dieron a entender los dos jóvenes que se gustaban?
6. ¿Qué excusa le dio don Raimundo a Luis cuando lo despidió?
7. ¿Qué hizo Margarita cuando supo que no podía casarse con Luis?
8. ¿Por qué es difícil para don Raimundo no regalarle nada a su hija?
9. Por fin, ¿qué consiente recibir don Honorato como regalo para Margarita y Luis?
10. ¿Por qué vale tanto el regalo de Margarita?

capítulo 5

VOCABULARIO ACTIVO

el **valle** *valley*
  cerro *hill*
  río *river*
el **maíz** *corn*
el **frijol** *bean*
  cosecha *harvest*
  hacer falta *to be lacking*
  tierra *earth*
  cielo *sky, heaven*
  jugar *to play (a game)*
la **nube** *cloud*
  gota *drop*
  soplar *to blow*
  viento *wind*
  granizo *hail*
  huerta *vegetable garden*

el **árbol** *tree*
  dejar *to leave behind*
  trabajo *work*
el **hambre** *hunger*
  ponerse a *to begin to, start to*
  sembrar *to sow*
  carta *letter*
el **buzón** *mailbox*
la **fe** *faith*
  ayuda *help*
  correo *post office*
el **papel** *paper*
  tinta *ink*
  mojar *to wet*
el **ladrón** *thief*

Gregorio López y Fuentes (1897–1966) nació en Veracruz, México. Gran poeta y novelista, escribió una de las novelas indianistas clásicas *(El indio)* que refleja las bajas condiciones sociales del indio mexicano y que demuestra la influencia de los muralistas de su país. «Una carta a Dios» pertenece a la colección llamada *Cuentos campesinos de México* (1940). En toda esta colección, López y Fuentes muestra su inquietud social, presentando a sus personajes campesinos, indios y soldados, con la esperanza de llamar la atención de la nación hacia su humilde situación social y económica. El protagonista de este cuento es de carácter simple y bonachón pero su absoluta fe en Dios no impide que reconozca las debilidades de sus congéneres.

POINTS TO CONSIDER

1. Faith and distrust in human relationships.
2. The role of irony as seen in the surprise ending.

Una carta a Dios

Gregorio López y Fuentes

La casa —*única* en todo el valle— estaba en un cerro *como* pirámide. Desde allá *se veían* las vegas, el río y la *milpa*. Entre las matas del maíz, se veía el frijol con su florecilla morada que prometía una buena cosecha. *Lo único* que hacía falta a la tierra era una lluvia.

Durante la mañana, Lencho *no había hecho más que* examinar el cielo por el noreste.

—Ahora *sí que viene la lluvia,* vieja.

Y la vieja, que preparaba la comida, le respondió:

—*Dios lo quiera.*

—Los muchachos más grandes *limpiaban de hierba* la siembra, *mientras que* los más pequeños jugaban cerca de la casa, hasta que la mujer les gritó a todos:

—Vengan a comer...

Fue durante la comida cuando, como había dicho Lencho, comenzaron a caer *gruesas* gotas de lluvia. Por el noreste se veían grandes montañas de nubes.

Imagínense, muchachos —exclamaba el hombre—, que no son gotas de agua *las que* están cayendo: son monedas nuevas, las gotas grandes son *de a diez* y las gotas chicas son de a cinco...

Pero, de pronto, comenzó a soplar un fuerte viento y con las gotas de agua comenzaron a caer granizos tan grandes como *bellotas*. Los muchachos, exponiéndose a la lluvia, jugaban y recogían los granizos más grandes.

Durante una hora, el granizo *apedreó* la casa, la huerta, el *monte,* la milpa y todo el valle. El campo estaba muy blanco *debido al* granizo. Los árboles sin hojas y el maíz destruido. El frijol, sin una flor. Lencho, *pasada* la tormenta, decía a sus hijos:

—El granizo no ha dejado nada... La noche *fue* de lamentaciones:

—¡Todo nuestro trabajo, perdido!

—¡Quién nos ayudará!

—Este año *pasaremos* hambre...

Pero en aquella casa solitaria en mitad del valle, había una esperanza: la ayuda de Dios.

the only one
like a / one could see
cornfield

The only thing

had done nothing other than

the rain *is* coming

May God be willing.

weeded
while

thick

those that
ten-centavo ones

acorns

stoned
pasture
due to

after
was one

we'll go

—No te mortifiques tanto, aunque el mal es muy grande. ¡Recuerda que nadie *se muere* de hambre!   dies

—Eso dicen: nadie se muere de hambre...

Lencho era hombre del campo pero sabía escribir. Con la luz del día y *aprovechando* que era domingo, se puso a escribir una carta que él *mismo* llevaría al pueblo para *echarla al correo.*

   taking advantage
   himself
   to mail it

Era nada menos que una carta a Dios.

«Dios —escribió—, si no me ayudas pasaré hambre con toda mi familia durante este año: necesito cien pesos para *volver a sembrar* y vivir mientras viene la otra cosecha, pues el granizo...»

   to seed again

Escribió en el sobre «A Dios», fue al pueblo y, en la oficina de correos, le puso un *timbre* a la carta y la *echó* en el buzón.

   stamp
   put

Un empleado, que era cartero, llegó riendo ante el jefe de correos: le mostraba la carta *dirigida* a Dios. El jefe, hombre gordo y bueno, también su puso a reír pero, bien pronto, se puso serio y dijo:

   addressed

—¡La fe! ¡*Quién tuviera* la fe de *quien* escribió esta carta! ¡Creer como él cree! ¡Esperar con la *confianza* con que él sabe esperar! ¡Tener correspondencia con Dios!

   Who could have / he
    who
   trust

El jefe postal concibió una idea: *contestar* la carta. Pero una vez abierta, vio que necesitaba algo más que buena *voluntad,* tinta y papel. Necesitaba dinero. Pidió ayuda a sus empleados y todos contribuyeron con algo.

   answer

   will

Pero fue imposible para él reunir los cien pesos *solicitados* por Lencho y sólo pudo enviar algo más de la mitad. Puso los billetes en un sobre dirigido a Lencho y con ellos un *pliego* que *no tenía más que* una palabra, como *firma:* Dios.

   asked for

   sheet of paper / only
    had / signature

Al *siguiente* domingo Lencho llegó al correo para ver si había carta para él. El *repartidor* le dio la carta, mientras que el jefe, con la alegría de *quien* ha hecho una buena *acción, espiaba a través de* un vidrio, desde su *despacho.*

   following
   sorter
   someone who
   deed / spied through
   office

Lencho no mostró la menor sorpresa al ver los billetes pero hizo un gesto de *cólera* al contar el dinero... ¡Dios no podía *haberse equivocado!*

   anger
   have made a mistake

Inmediatemente, Lencho *se acercó* a la ventanilla para pedir papel y tinta. Se puso a escribir, demostrando mucho el esfuerzo que hacía. Después, fue a pedir un timbre que *mojó* con la *lengua* y luego puso en el sobre.

   approached

   moistened / tongue

En cuanto la carta cayó al buzón, el jefe de correos fue a *recogerla*. Decía:

«Dios: Del dinero que te pedí, *sólo llegaron* a mis manos sesenta pesos. *Mándame* el resto, que me hace mucha falta; pero no me lo mandes por correo, porque los empleados *son muy ladrones*. —Lencho.»

As soon as
retrieve it
I only got
Send me

are a bunch of thieves

Cuentos campesinos de México (México: Editorial Cima, 1940).

EJERCICIOS

A. Fill in the blank with the appropriate word from the column on the right.

1. Lencho echó la carta en el _____.

2. La lluvia caía en grandes _____.

3. El jefe de _____ primero rió.

4. ¡Quién tuviera la _____ de Lencho!

5. «Este invierno pasaremos _____», dijo Lencho.

6. Mientras los muchachos _____, la lluvia terminó.

7. «¡Vengan a _____!» gritó la vieja.

8. _____ escribir una carta a Dios.

9. Estos empleados son unos _____.

10. El _____ era tan grande como bellotas.

hambre
ladrones
se puso a
frijol
correos
jugaban
Dios lo quiera
comer
dejó
buzón
fe
gotas
escribir
granizo

B. Write a verb that corresponds to each of the following nouns:

1. comida   5. siembra
2. lluvia   6. creencia
3. juego   7. robo
4. trabajo   8. granizo

C. Choose the word from the list on the right which corresponds to each description.

1. el aire que sopla
2. líquido oscuro para escribir
3. el espacio sobre la tierra
4. una planta con tronco
5. lluvia en forma de bellotas
6. una persona que roba
7. lo que sentimos si no comemos
8. correspondencia entre dos personas
9. creer y tener confianza
10. el lugar que envía y recibe cartas

hambre
gota
nube
fe
ladrón
tinta
cielo
correo
huerta
viento
granizo
carta
árbol

D. Answer in Spanish.

1. ¿Dónde estaba la casa de Lencho?
2. ¿Qué hacía falta en el valle?
3. En vez de lluvia, ¿qué cayó?
4. ¿Qué hizo el granizo?
5. ¿A quién se puso a escribir Lencho?
6. ¿Dónde echó la carta Lencho?
7. ¿Qué dijo el jefe de correos cuando vio la carta de Lencho?
8. ¿Cuál fue la idea del jefe de correos?
9. ¿Cuánto dinero quería Lencho y cuánto recibió?
10. ¿Cuál es la opinión que Lencho tiene de los empleados de correo?

capítulo 6

VOCABULARIO ACTIVO

perder *to lose*
enterrar *to bury*
selva *jungle*
el **tigre** *tiger*
cachorro *cub, pup*
dormirse *to fall asleep*
tener miedo *to be afraid*
golpear *to knock*
ocultar *to hide*
mientras *while*
sabio *wise*
llorar *to cry*
la **sangre** *blood*
maestro *teacher*
preguntar *to ask*
extraño *strange*
asustar *to frighten*
el **bosque** *the woods*
rama *branch*
cuerpo *body*
raya *stripe, line*
perro *dog*
mostrar *to show*
quemar *to burn*
dirigirse a *to turn to (someone or something)*

Horacio Quiroga (1878–1937) es considerado por muchos como el más grande cuentista de Hispanoamérica. Aunque nació en el Uruguay, vivió la mayor parte de su vida en la provincia de Misiones, en el norte de la Argentina. Sus cuentos reflejan la fuerte influencia de Edgar Allan Poe y describen lo que el autor mejor conoció: la vida en la selva y los rigores de los hombres que viven en ella. Sobresalen por su penetración psicológica y por las vivas emociones que se definen en ellos. El autor estudia la psicología de los animales y demuestra que éstos son los verdaderos héroes de los cuentos. Resultan ser más humanos que los mismos hombres. Sus *Cuentos de amor, de locura y de muerte* (1917) lo acreditan como gran cuentista; sus *Cuentos de la selva* (1917) lo hacen digno de comparación con el maestro Rudyard Kipling.

POINTS TO CONSIDER

1. The author's attitude toward man and beast.
2. "Juan Darién": a children's story or an adult's story?

Juan Darién

Horacio Quiroga

Una vez, a principios de otoño, la *viruela* visitó un
pueblo de un país lejano y mató a muchas personas.
Los hermanos perdieron a sus hermanitas, y las
criaturas que comenzaban a caminar *quedaron* sin
padre ni madre. Las madres perdieron a sus hijos.
Una pobre mujer joven y viuda enterró a su hijito,
el *único* que tenía en el mundo. Ahora estaba sola.

En la selva había muchos animales feroces que
rugían toda la noche. Y la pobre mujer de repente
vio una cosa chiquita que entraba por la puerta
como un gatito. La mujer *se agachó* y levantó en las
manos un tigrecito de pocos días, con los ojos todavía cerrados. El cachorro *runruneó* de contento porque ya no estaba solo. La mujer llevó al animalito
a su seno y lo *rodeó* con las manos. El tigrecito sintió el calor del pecho y *se acomodó.* Poco después se
durmió.

La mujer entró en la casa contenta sintiendo que
ante la suprema ley del Universo, una vida *equivale*
a otra. Y dio de *mamar* al tigrecito. El cachorro estaba salvado y la madre había encontrado consuelo.
Pero ella tenía miedo de que otra gente *llegara a
saber* del tigrecito.

Un día, un hombre que pasaba *por cerca* de la
casa oyó un pequeño y *ronco gemido* que atemorizó
a este hombre. Se detuvo y golpeó fuertemente a la
puerta de la casa. La mujer trató de ocultar al tigrecito para salvarlo del hombre. Mientras buscaba
dónde esconderlo, *se le apareció* una mansa, vieja y
sabia serpiente. Esta le dijo:

—*Nada temas,* mujer. Tu amor de madre ha salvado a tu hijo. De ahora *en adelante* tendrá forma
humana. Enséñale a ser bueno y ve a la puerta.

La madre creyó a la serpiente porque en todas
las religiones de los hombres la serpiente conoce el
misterio de las vidas que *pueblan* los mundos. Fue,
pues, corriendo a abrir la puerta, y el hombre furioso, entró con el revólver en la mano y buscó por
todas partes sin hallar nada. Cuando salió, la mujer
abrió, temblando, el *rebozo* bajo el cual ocultaba al

Glossary (right margin):
- smallpox
- very young children / were left
- only one
- roared
- reached down
- purred
- held
- made itself comfortable
- before / is equivalent
- breast-feed
- might find out
- near
- hoarse whimper
- there appeared to her
- Fear not
- on
- inhabit
- shawl

tigrecito sobre su seno, y en su lugar vio a un niño
que dormía tranquilo. Lloró largo rato en silencio
sobre su salvaje hijo hecho hombre; lágrimas de
gratitud que doce años más tarde ese mismo hijo
debía pagar con sangre sobre su tumba.   was to pay

Pasó el tiempo. Al nuevo niño se le puso Juan
Darién. La madre le *proporcionó* todas sus necesi-   provided
dades trabajando día y noche para él. Ella lo quería
mucho y Juan Darién era, *efectivamente, digno* de   truly / worthy
ser querido: noble, bueno y generoso como nadie.

Juan Darién iba a la escuela con los chicos de su
edad y ellos *se burlaban* a menudo de él, a causa de   made fun
su pelo *áspero* y su timidez.   coarse

Cuando Juan iba a *cumplir* diez años, su madre   to reach the age of
murió. El niño sufrió mucho, hasta que el tiempo
apaciguó su pena. Pero fue *en adelante* un mu-   abated / from then on
chacho triste, que sólo deseaba *instruirse*.   educate himself

A Juan Darién no lo amaba el pueblo porque el
niño era estudioso y muy generoso y todos *sospe-*   suspected
chaban estas cualidades suyas.

El pueblo iba a celebrar una gran fiesta, y de la
ciudad distante habían mandado *fuegos artificiales*.   fireworks
En la escuela *se dio un repaso general* a los chicos,   a general review was
pues un inspector debía venir a observar las clases.   given
Cuando el inspector llegó, el maestro hizo dar la
lección al primero de todos: a Juan Darién. Juan
Darién era el alumno *más aventajado;* pero con la   most outstanding
emoción del caso, *tartamudeó* y la lengua se le *trabó*   stuttered / stammered
con un sonido extraño. El inspector le preguntó al
maestro:

—¿Quién es ese muchacho?

—Se llama Juan Darién—respondió el maestro
—y lo *crió* una mujer que ya ha muerto; pero nadie   raised
sabe de dónde ha venido.

—Es extraño, muy extraño... —murmuró el ins-
pector, observando el pelo áspero y el reflejo *verdoso*   greenish
que tenían los ojos de Juan Darién cuando estaba
en la sombra. Él sabía que en el mundo hay cosas
mucho más extrañas que las que uno puede inven-
tar y por esta razón decidió *averiguar* quién era el   find out
niño Juan Darién. El inspector subió a la *tarima* y   platform
habló así:

—Bueno. Deseo ahora que uno de ustedes nos
describa la selva. ¿Cómo es la selva? ¿Qué *pasa* en   happens
ella? Esto es lo que quiero saber. Vamos a ver, tú—
añadió dirigiéndose a un alumno cualquiera—.   added

Sube a la tarima y cuéntanos lo que hayas visto.

El chico subió, y *aunque* estaba asustado, habló *un rato.* Dijo que en el bosque hay árboles gigantes, *enredaderas* y florecillas. Después habló otro chico y dos o tres más. Aunque todos conocían bien la selva, respondieron lo mismo, porque los chicos y muchos hombres no cuentan lo que ven, *sino* lo que han leído sobre lo que *acaban de ver.* Al fin el inspector dijo:

—Ahora *le toca al alumno Juan Darién.* Cierra los ojos y dime lo que ves en la selva.

—No veo nada—dijo Juan.

—Pronto vas a ver. Imagínate. Son las tres de la mañana. Hemos concluido de comer, por ejemplo... Estamos en la selva, en la oscuridad... ¿Qué ves?

De pronto Juan Darién *se estremeció,* y con voz lenta, *como si soñara,* dijo:

—Veo las piedras que pasan y las ramas que se doblan... Y el suelo... Veo las hojas secas en la tierra...

—¡Un momento!—le interrumpió el inspector— Las piedras y las hojas que pasan ¿a qué *altura* las ves?

Y Juan Darién, *siempre* con los ojos cerrados, respondió:

—Pasan sobre el suelo... *Rozan* las orejas... las hojas sueltas se mueven con el aliento... y siento la humedad del barro en... —*Su voz se cortó.*

¿En dónde?—preguntó con voz firme el inspector —¿Dónde sientes la humedad del agua?

—¡En los bigotes!—dijo con voz ronca Juan Darién, abriendo los ojos con espanto.

Los alumnos no dijeron nada y miraron a Juan, cuya cara estaba pálida.

La clase había concluido. El inspector no era un mal hombre; pero, como todos los hombres que viven muy cerca de la selva, odiaba *ciegamente* a los tigres. Por eso, dijo en voz baja al maestro:

—Es necesario matar a Juan Darién. Es una fiera del bosque, posiblemente un tigre. Debemos matarlo, porque si no, él, tarde o temprano, nos matará a todos. Pero, no podemos hacerlo mientras tenga forma humana. Conozco a un *domador de fieras* y lo llamaré. Él forzará a Juan Darién a volver a su cuerpo de tigre.

Juan, quien sentía sólo amor hacia todos los

Marginal glosses:

even though
a while
vines

but rather
have just seen

it is student Juan Darién's turn

he shuddered
as if he were dreaming

height

still

they brush by

He stopped speaking abruptly

blindly

wild animal tamer

hombres, no comprendía por qué todos empezaban a *hablar mal* de él. Nadie le hablaba o miraba y lo seguían desde lejos de noche.

speak ill

—¿*Qué tendré?* ¿Por qué son así conmigo?—se preguntaba Juan Darién.

I wonder what's wrong with me?

La misma tarde de la fiesta, mientras Juan se preparaba la pobre sopa que tomaba siempre, llegó a su casa mucha gente y lo *apresó,* llevándoselo a casa del domador.

seized

—¡Aquí está! ¡Es un tigre! ¡Muera Juan Darién!—gritaban todos.

Juan lloraba, protestando su inocencia. Apareció el domador, con sus grandes botas de *charol, levita* roja y un *látigo* en la mano. *Se puso* frente a Juan.

patent leather / frock coat / whip He stood

—¡Ah! —exclamó— ¡te reconozco bien! ¡Te estoy viendo, hijo de tigres! ¡Bajo tu camisa estoy viendo las rayas del tigre! ¡*Quítenle* la camisa y llamen a los perros! ¡Ellos sabrán que eres tigre y no hombre!

Take off

Le arrancaron la camisa a Juan y lo *arrojaron* dentro de la jaula para las fieras. Y cuatro feroces perros de caza fueron lanzados dentro de la jaula.

They ripped off / threw

Pero los perros sólo vieron al buen muchacho Juan Darién y movían la cola apaciblemente al olerlo.

La prueba no había tenido éxito.

—¡Muy bien! —exclamó entonces el domador— Estos son perros bastardos, *de casta de tigre.* No le reconocen. Pero yo te reconozco, Juan Darién.

of the same ilk of tigers

El domador entró en la jaula y con el látigo cruzó una y otra vez el cuerpo del muchacho diciéndole repetidamente:

—¡Tigre! ¡Muestra las rayas!

—¡Por favor! ¡Me muero!—clamaba Juan Darién.

—¡Muestra las rayas!—le decían. Por fin el *suplicio* concluyó. En el fondo de la jaula, *arrinconado,* sólo *quedaba* el cuerpecito sangriento del niño, que había sido Juan Darién.

torture in a corner remained

Lo *sacaron* de la jaula y empujándolo por el medio de la calle, lo *echaron* del pueblo.

took out threw out

En *las afueras* del pueblo, una mujer estaba parada a la puerta de su casa *sosteniendo* a una inocente criatura. Juan Darién, *al caer* al suelo cerca de ella, *tendió sus manos* hacia ella buscando *apoyo.* La mujer gritó:

outskirts holding as he was falling held his hands / support

—¡Me ha querido robar a mi hijo! ¡Ha tendido las manos para matarlo! ¡Es un tigre! ¡Matémosle antes que él mate a nuestros hijos!

He tried to take my son from me!

No era necesaria otra acusación. Apareció el domador y ordenó:

—¡Quemémoslo en los fuegos artificiales!

Ya comenzaba a oscurecer. En la plaza habían levantado un castillo de fuegos artificiales. Ataron *en lo alto* del centro a Juan Darién, y *prendieron la mecha* desde un *extremo.* Rápidamente el fuego creció.

at the highest point / they lit the fuse / end

—¡Es tu último día de hombre, Juan Darién!— *clamaban* todos—¡Muestra las rayas!

cried out

—¡Perdón, perdón!—gritaba el niño, *retorciéndose* entre las *chispas* y el humo—. ¡Yo soy hombre!—*alcanzó* a decir el pobre cuando su cuerpo *se sacudió* convulsivamente; sus gemidos se volvieron profundos y roncos y su cuerpo comenzó a cambiar poco a poco de forma. La *muchedumbre,* con un grito salvaje de triunfo, *pudo* ver por fin, bajo la piel del hombre, las rayas negras, paralelas y fatales del tigre.

Forgive me / writhing
sparks
managed / shook

crowd

was able

Cuando *se apagó* el fuego, la gente arrastró el cuerpo del tigre que había sido Juan Darién hasta el bosque y ahí quedó.

went out

Pero el tigre no había muerto. Con la frescura de la noche *volvió en sí* y poco a poco, durante un mes, descansó y curó sus heridas. Todas *cicatrizaron* por fin, menos una, una profunda quemadura en *el costado,* que no cerraba, y que el tigre vendó con grandes hojas.

came to

healed
his side

Había conservado de su forma recién perdida tres cosas: el recuerdo *vivo* del pasado, la *habilidad* de las manos, que usaba como un hombre, y el lenguaje. Pero en el resto, absolutamente en todo, era una fiera.

vivid / dexterity

Un día en que se sintió completamente curado de sus heridas, llamó a reunión a todos los tigres de la selva. Todos *treparon* a *diversos* árboles a esperar. Al fin apareció por el camino un hombre de grandes botas y levita roja.

climbed / several

El tigre, sin mover una ramita, saltó sobre el domador y lo *derribó desmayado.* Lo cogió entre los dientes por la cintura, y, sin *hacerle daño,* lo llevó hasta el *juncal.* El tigre dijo entonces:

knocked down / unconscious / harming him / stand of reeds

—Hermanos: Yo viví doce años entre los hombres, como uno de ellos. Esta noche rompo el último *lazo* que me une a los hombres y al pasado.   bond

Después de estas palabras, cogió al hombre en la boca y trepó con él a lo más alto del *cañaveral*. Ahí   reeds
lo *dejó* atado entre dos bambúes. Luego prendió   left
fuego a las hojas secas y rápidamente el fuego creció.

—¡Perdón, perdóname!—aulló el domador, retorciéndose—¡Perdón, Juan Darién!

—Aquí no hay nadie que se llama Juan Darién. Éste es un nombre de hombre y aquí somos todos tigres.

Las llamas habían *abrazado* el castillo hasta el   enveloped
cielo. Allá arriba se veía un cuerpo negro que se quemaba *humeando*.   smoking

El nuevo tigre se dirigió a sus compañeros y les dijo: —Sólo me queda una cosa por hacer—Y se dirigió al pueblo. Se detuvo ante un pobre y triste jardín. Saltó la pared y caminó hasta llegar ante un *pedazo de tierra* donde estaba enterrada la mujer a   plot of earth
quien había llamado madre. *Se arrodilló* —se arro-   he knelt
dilló como un hombre— y habló así:

—¡Madre, tú sola comprendiste que el hombre y el tigre *se diferencian únicamente por* el corazón! Tú   are different only / in
me enseñaste a amar, a comprender, a *perdonar*.   to forgive
Madre, soy tu hijo siempre. ¡Adiós, madre mía!

Desde el fondo de la noche *se oyó el estampido de*   was heard the sound
un tiro.   of a shot

—Es en la selva—dijo el tigre a sus compañeros
—Son los hombres. Están cazando, matando, *dego-*   slitting throats
llando.

El tigre se quitó la venda que tenía sobre la herida en el costado y con su misma sangre añadió al nombre de su madre, en la cruz de la tumba:

y
Juan Darién
—Ya estamos en paz—dijo—. Y ahora, a la selva. ¡Y tigre para siempre!

Cuentos (México: Editorial Porrúa, 1968).

EJERCICIOS

A. Fill in the blank with the appropriate word from the column on the right.

1. El domador murió _____ en el cañaveral.

2. El _____ del muchacho se retorcía entre las llamas.

3. La viuda _____ al cachorro bajo su rebozo.

4. El tigrecito _____ contento en las brazos de su nueva madre.

5. Juan estaba muy _____ del domador y su látigo.

6. La muchedumbre continuaba gritándole a Juan—¡Muestra las _____!

7. Este cuento de niños y tigres es ciertamente _____.

8. El inspector _____ a Juan y le preguntó: —¿Cómo es la selva?

9. En el _____ hay muchas fieras salvajes.

10. La gente _____ a Juan con piedras.

enterró
cuerpo
sangre
extraño
asustado
rayas
se dirigió
mientras
golpeó
se durmió
tenía miedo
ocultó
quemado
maestro
bosque
perro
lloró

B. Choose the word from the list at the right which corresponds to each definition.

1. Al madurar el cachorro se vuelve
2. partes de un árbol
3. prender fuego a una cosa
4. lo contrario de encontrar
5. un tigre muy joven y chico
6. se encuentran en el cuerpo del tigre
7. la persona que enseña en la escuela
8. la acción de poner bajo la tierra
9. un animal que usan para cazar al tigre
10. lugar donde hay fieras salvajes

perder
tigre
maestro
selva
sangre
ramas
rayas
tener miedo
cachorro
perro
sabio
enterrar
quemar

C. Choose the items from the right-hand column that are the logical
result of the items on the left.

1. tener miedo	tigre
2. cachorro que crece	sangre
3. fuego	asustado
4. herida	no visto
5. oculto	preguntar
	mientras
	quemado

D. Answer in Spanish.

1. ¿Cuál fue la causa de la muerte de tanta gente en el pueblo?
2. ¿A quién perdió la mujer joven y viuda?
3. ¿Qué entró a la casa de la mujer?
4. ¿Qué transformó al cachorro en niño?
5. ¿Cómo era el niño Juan Darién?
6. ¿Qué deseaba hacer Juan en la vida?
7. ¿Por qué sospecha el inspector de que Juan es una fiera salvaje?
8. ¿Qué cosa confirma para el inspector que Juan es un tigre?
9. ¿Qué tiene Juan Darién debajo de la camisa, según cree el domador?
10. ¿Qué le gritan el domador y la gente a Juan Darién?
11. Cuando queman el niño en el fuego, ¿qué ocurre?
12. Después de un mes, ¿cómo está el nuevo tigre?
13. Aunque era tigre ahora, ¿qué tenía de hombre todavía?
14. ¿Qué hizo el nuevo tigre con el domador?
15. ¿Cuál es la única persona a quién ama todavía el tigre?

capítulo 7

VOCABULARIO ACTIVO

tienda *store*
acera *sidewalk*
la **calle** *street*
la **luz** *light*
sombra *shade, shadow*
la **gente** *people*
distinto *different*
rostro *face*
tocar *to touch*
oler *to smell*
el **paquete** *package*
bolsa *bag*
canasto *basket*
soñar *to dream*
solía (soler) *would, used to*

José Donoso (1924–   ) nació en Santiago, Chile. Fue la «oveja negra» de su familia pero desde joven se interesó por la literatura inglesa y norteamericana. Comenzó escribiendo cuentos, varias novelas, un poco de poesía y hasta una obra de teatro, a fines de 1982. «China» es el primer cuento que publicó el autor.

POINTS TO CONSIDER

1. The reason for the usage of the word "China."
2. The relationship between the protagonist and "China." What do you think is meant by the change in the protagonist's attitude toward "China"?

China

José Donoso

Por un lado el muro gris de la Universidad. Enfrente, la agitación *maloliente* de las *cocinerías* alterna con la tranquilidad de las tiendas de libros de segunda mano. Más allá, las casas *retroceden* y la acera *se ensancha*. Al caer la noche, es la parte más agitada de la calle.

Como todas las calles, ésta también es pública. Para mí, *no siempre lo fue*. Mantuve que yo era el único *ser* extraño que tenía *derecho* a aventurarse entre sus luces y sus sombras.

Cuando pequeño, vivía yo en una calle *cercana*. Allí, había poca gente y era un mundo enteramente distinto. Una tarde, *sin embargo*, acompañé a mi madre a la otra calle. Buscábamos unos *cubiertos* que sospechábamos una *empleada* había *sustraído* para *empeñarlos*. Era invierno y había llovido. *Oscurecía*.

Al entrar por la calle, un tranvía *vino sobre nosotros con estrépito*. Busqué refugio cerca de mi madre. *Yo llevaba los ojos* muy abiertos. Yo quería mirar todos los rostros que pasaban junto a mí, tocarlos y olerlos pues *me parecían* maravillosamente distintos. Muchas personas llevaban paquetes, bolsas, canastos y *toda suerte* de objetos misteriosos. Mi madre rio, diciendo:

—¡Por Dios, esto es como en la China!

No recuerdo qué pasó *con lo de* los cubiertos pero esta calle *quedó marcada* en mi memoria como algo fascinante, distinto. Era la libertad, la aventura. En casa, yo pensaba en «China», el nombre con que bauticé esa calle.

Un día propuse a Fernando, mi hermano menor:
—¿Vamos a «China»?

Sus ojos brillaron. Creyó que íbamos a jugar. *Lo tomé cuidadosamente de la mano* y nos dirigimos a la calle con que yo soñaba. Por fin alcanzamos la primera cuadra de mi calle.

—*Aquí es* —dije, y sentí que mi hermano *se apretaba a mi cuerpo*.

Fernando preguntó:

Glosas (margen):

- *Por un lado* — On one side
- *maloliente / cocinerías* — bad-smelling / eating joints
- *retroceden* — recede
- *se ensancha* — widens
- *no siempre lo fue* — it wasn't always so
- *ser / derecho* — being / the right
- *cercana* — near by
- *sin embargo* — nevertheless
- *cubiertos* — silverware
- *empleada / sustraído* — servant / taken
- *empeñarlos / Oscurecía* — pawn them / It was dusk
- *vino sobre nosotros con estrépito* — brushed by us / noisily
- *Yo llevaba los ojos* — My eyes were
- *me parecían* — they seemed
- *toda suerte* — all sorts
- *con lo de* — with the matter of
- *quedó marcada* — was engraved
- *Lo tomé cuidadosamente de la mano / nos dirigimos a* — I took him carefully by the hand / we went towards
- *Aquí es / se apretaba a mi cuerpo* — This is it / drawing very close to me

—¿Y por qué es «China» aquí?

Me sentí perdido. De pronto, *no supe cómo contentarlo.* Vi *decaer* mi prestigio ante él. Mi hermano jamás volvería a creer en mí. —Vamos al *«Zurcidor Japonés»* —dije— *Ahí sí que es* «China».

I found myself unable to make him happy / fall / Japanese Darner / There it really is / remained stopped

Fuimos a esa tienda y *permanecimos detenidos* ante la cortina metálica del «Zurcidor Japonés».

Se sintió un ruido en el interior. Salió un hombre pequeño y *enjuto,* amarillo, de ojos *tirantes. Pasó a lo largo* y nos sonrió. *Lo seguimos con la vista* hasta que dobló por la calle *próxima.*

We heard

thin / slanted / He went on by / We followed him with our eyes / next

Enmudecimos. Pasó un vendedor de *algodón de dulce* y yo compré dos porciones y le ofrecí una a mi hermano. Él me *agradeció* con la cabeza y volvimos a casa lentamente.

We became silent / cotton candy

thanked

Los años pasaron. «China» solía volver con la imaginación. Poco a poco comencé a olvidar. Más tarde *ingresé* a la Universidad. Compré *gafas de marco oscuro.*

entered / dark-framed glasses

En esa época, solía volver a esa calle. Pero ya no era mi calle. Ya no era «China» aunque nada en ella había cambiado. No recuerdo haber mirado *ni una sola vez* el letrero del «Zurcidor Japonés».

not even once

Más tarde *salí del país.* Un día, *a mi vuelta,* pregunté a mi hermano, quien era estudiante en la Universidad, dónde podía comprar un libro que me interesaba. Sonriendo, Fernando me respondió: —En «China»...

I went abroad / after I returned

Y yo no comprendí.

Los mejores cuentos (Santiago: Zig-Zag, 1966).

EJERCICIOS

A. Fill in the blank with the appropriate word from the column on the right.

1. Donde las casas retroceden la _____ se ensancha.

2. Al caer la noche, las _____ eléctricas producen muchas _____.

3. «China» era una _____ llena de _____ interesantes.

4. «China» era un mundo enteramente _____.

5. El protagonista quería mirar todos los _____ pues eran maravillosamente _____.

6. La _____ que caminaba por «China» llevaba _____, _____ y _____.

7. Con los años, «China» _____ volver a su imaginación.

olía
paquetes
luces
calle
gente
distinto
acera
rostros
distintos
canastos
sombras
bolsas
solía
volvía

B. Arrange the following words in groups of at least two to show some association between them. For example: *calle—avenida*.

diferente   imaginar   calle   oler   canasto   tienda
luz   tocar   cara   rostro   acera   avenida   distinto
soñar   bolsa   ver   mercado   sombra   paquete

C. Create sentences using the following series of words:

1. gente / llevar / paquetes / bolsas
2. «China» / calle / pública
3. luz / sombra / acera
4. cuando / niño / él / soler / pensar / «China»

D. Answer in Spanish.

1. Mientras que hay agitación en las cocinerías, ¿qué existe en las tiendas de libros de segunda mano?
2. ¿Dónde vivía el niño protagonista con relación a «China»?
3. ¿Con quién fue el niño por primera vez a «China»?
4. ¿Cuál fue la razón de esta primera incursión a ese mundo distinto?
5. ¿Qué deseaba hacer el niño al ver los rostros distintos que veía?
6. ¿Quién le dio el nombre de «China» a esta calle? ¿Por qué usó este nombre?
7. ¿A quién llevó el niño en su próximo viaje a «China»?
8. ¿Quién es la persona que confirma para los dos niños que «China» es realmente distinta y maravillosa?
9. Con los años, ¿qué le ocurre al protagonista en cuanto a *(concerning)* «China»?
10. Cuando al final, su hermano le menciona la calle «China», ¿cuál es la reacción del protagonista?

capítulo 8

VOCABULARIO ACTIVO

cuento   *story, tale*
pluma   *pen*
asunto   *matter, affair*
ruhio, a   *blond*
belleza   *beauty*
moreno   *dark-haired or -complexioned*
feo   *homely*
sucio   *dirty, soiled*
orgullo   *pride*
peludo   *hairy*
parecerse   *to resemble*
nacer   *to be born*
reírse   *to laugh*
desasosiego   *restlessness*

Manuel González Zeledón   (1864–1936) fue conocido por el seudónimo de Magón. Escritor costarricense, sus narraciones son perfectos cuadros de costumbres. En ellos, Magón pinta características que identifican a distintos tipos de su país, Costa Rica. El cuento que sigue demuestra claramente el amplio conocimiento que el autor tiene de este tipo campesino.

POINTS TO CONSIDER

1. The attitude of the writer (don Magón) toward Cornelio. Is there disdain, affection, understanding?
2. The possible role of superstition in the story.

El clis de sol

Manuel González Zeledón

No es cuento, es una historia que sale de mi pluma como *ha ido brotando* de los labios de *ñor* Cornelio Cacheda, que es un buen amigo *de tantos como* tengo *por esos campos* de Dios. Me la refirió *hará* cinco meses y quiero contársela a ustedes pues me sorprendió la maravilla del caso.

has been coming out / señor / like many that / in this area / probably

Podría tal vez *entrar en* un análisis serio del asunto, pero *me reservo* para cuando haya oído las opiniones de mis lectores.

get into / I'll wait

Ñor Cornelio vino a verme y trajo un par de niñas de dos años y medio de edad, llamadas María de los Dolores y María del Pilar, ambas rubias como una *espiga,* blancas y rosadas como *durazno* maduro y lindas *como si fueran* «imágenes», según la expresión de ñor Cornelio. Contrastaban notablemente la belleza *infantil* de las gemelas con la incorrección del rostro de ñor Cornelio, feo, moreno y *tosco hasta lo sucio de las uñas.*

spike of grain / peach / as if they were / child-like / coarse down to his dirty fingernails

Naturalmente, se me ocurrió preguntarle por el *progenitor feliz* de aquel par de niñas. El viejo *se llenó de* orgullo, *se limpió las babas con el revés* de la peluda mano y contestó:

happy father / bubbled with / wiped his mouth with the back of his hand / daddy

—¡Pues yo soy el *tata!* ¡No se parecen a mí, pero es que la mama no es tan fea, y para el gran poder de mi Dios no hay nada imposible!

—Pero dígame, ñor Cornelio, ¿su mujer es rubia, o alguno de los abuelos era *así como* las chiquitas?

like

—No, ñor; en toda la familia no ha habido ninguna *gata* ni *canelo;* todos hemos sido *acholaos.*

fair-complexioned / blond / dark-complexioned like a mixed-blood

—Y entonces, ¿cómo se explica usted que las niñas hayan nacido con ese pelo y esos colores?

El viejo soltó una *estrepitosa carcajada.*

a loud guffaw

—¿De qué se ríe, ñor Cornelio?

—Don Magón, veo que un pobre ignorante como yo sabe más que un hombre como usted, que todos dicen que es tan *sabido,* tan *leído* y hasta que *hace leyes* donde el presidente con los ministros.

learned / well-read / you're a legislator

—*A ver,* explíqueme eso.

Let's see

—Usted sabe que ahora *en marzo hizo tres años* que hubo un *clis* de sol. Bueno, pues *como unos*

three years ago this March / eclipse / some

veinte días antes, Lina, mi mujer, *salió habilitada de* esas *chiquillas.* Desde entonces, *le cogió un desasosiego muy grande.* Ella siempre había sido *muy antojada* en todos los partos. *Vea,* cuando nació el mayor, fue *lo mismo,* pero nunca la llegué a ver tan desasosegada como con estas chiquillas. *Como le iba diciendo, le dio por ver para* el cielo día y noche y el día del clis de sol...

> became pregnant with / girls / she became very restless / had always hankered for odd things / You know / the same / As I was telling you, she began to look toward

Para no cansarlo con el cuento, así siguió hasta que nacieron las *muchachitas.*

> the little girls

—No le niego que a mí me sorprendió el verlas tan canelas y tan gatas, pero desde entonces parece que *hubieran traído* la bendición de Dios. La maestra las quiere, el *Cura me las pide* para *pararlas* con *enaguas* de puro lino en el altar para el *Corpus,* y todos los días de la Semana Santa, las sacan en procesión. *¡Bendito sea* mi Dios que las crió de un tata tan feo como yo!

> as though they had brought / the priest asks me for them / stand them up / petticoats / Corpus Christi, a Roman Catholic festival in honor of the Eucharist / Blessed be / discourse would have no end / get back on track / and what else? / because the mother looked at / that is the reason

Interrumpí a ñor Cornelio, temeroso de que el *panegírico no tuviera fin* y lo hice *volver al carril abandonado.*

—Bien, *¿y qué más?*

—Pues, ¿no ve que fue *por haber espiado la mama* el clis de sol *por lo* que son canelas? ¿Usted no sabía eso?

—No lo sabía, y me sorprende que usted *lo hubiera adivinado* sin tener ninguna instrucción.

> that you figured it out

—*Para qué engañarlo,* don Magón. Yo no fui el que adivinó la razón. ¿Usted conoce a un maestro italiano que hizo la torre de la iglesia de la villa? ¿Un hombre *gato,* pelo *colorado,* muy blanco y muy *macizo* que come en casa *hace cuatro años?*

> I won't attempt to deceive you
>
> fair / red
> stocky / for four years

—No, ñor Cornelio.

Pues él fue el que me explicó *la cosa* del clis de sol.

> that thing about

La propia y otros tipos y escenas costarricenses (2 ed. San José: Garcia Monge, 1920).

EJERCICIOS

A. Fill in the blank with the appropriate word from the column on the right.

1. «El clis de sol», nos dice Magón, no es _____, es historia.	cuento pluma
2. La historia de Magón sale de su _____.	feo rieron
3. El _____ de este cuento es el origen de las dos niñas.	rubio orgullo
4. Aunque ñor Cornelio es _____ sus hijas son muy bonitas.	moreno historia nacieron
5. Las _____ de ñor Cornelio están _____.	asunto son sucias
6. Las dos niñas _____ a las imágenes en la iglesia.	rubias se parecen
7. Ñor Cornelio siente mucho _____ por sus dos hijas.	uñas niñas

8. Ñor Cornelio es _____ pero sus

   hijas son _____ como espigas.

9. Las niñas _____ como nueve
   meses después del eclipse de sol.

B. Match the words on the column at the left with their opposites on the column at the right.

1. orgullo   moreno
2. feo   desasosiego
3. llorar   limpio
4. calma   bello
5. sucio   nacer
6. rubio   reírse
7. morir   cuento
8. historia   humildad

D. Answer in Spanish.

1. ¿Con quién está hablando ñor Cornelio?
2. ¿Qué le sorprendió al autor?
3. Describa a las dos niñas.
4. ¿Quién es el «tata», según ñor Cornelio?
5. ¿Quién cree Ud. que es el padre de las niñas?
6. ¿Cuál fue la causa de que las niñas fueran rubias, segun ñor Cornelio? ¿Cuál cree Ud. fue la verdadera razón?
7. ¿Quién le explicó a ñor Cornelio lo del «clis» de sol?

capítulo 9

VOCABULARIO ACTIVO

cara *face*
desde *since, from the time*
entonces *from then on*
cabeza *head*
dulces *sweets*
llegar *arrive*
a ser *come to be*
crecer *to grow*
morir *to die*
gallina *chicken*
sonreír *to smile*
delante de *in front of*
a la derecha *to the right*
pedir *to ask for*
perder *to lose*
encontrar *to find;* **—se** *to find oneself*
volver *to return*
hasta (que) *until*
buscar *to look for*
oreja *ear*

Rubén Darío (1867–1916) nació en Metapa, Nicaragua, pero vivió en varios países de Latinoamérica y en España. Considerado como el poeta máximo de la lírica contemporánea, Darío influyó mucho sobre todas las literaturas en la lengua española. Fue el líder del modernismo, movimiento literario que él originó en América.

POINTS TO CONSIDER

1. Is Juan Bueno a "good" man? What, do you believe, is his problem?
2. Does Darío sympathize with his character?

Las pérdidas de Juan Bueno

Rubén Darío

Érase un hombre que se llamaba Juan Bueno. Se llamaba así porque desde chico, cuando *le pegaban un coscorrón* por un lado, *presentaba* la cabeza por otro lado. Sus compañeros le *despojaban de* sus dulces y bizcochos y, cuando llegaba a su casa, sus padres *a pellizcos, uno a otro le ponían hecho* un San Lázaro. Así *fue* creciendo hasta que llegó a ser hombre. ¡Cuánto sufrió el pobrecito Juan! *Le dieron las viruelas* y no murió, pero *quedó* con la cara como si en ella una docena de gallinas hubieran picoteado. Estuvo *preso* por *culpa* de otro, un Juan Lanas. Todo lo sufría con paciencia. Todo el mundo, cuando lo veía, decía: ¡Allá va Juan Bueno!, y *soltaba la risa*. Al fin, llegó el día en que se casó. [Once upon a time there was / they gave him a rap on the head / he'd present / took away from him] [by pinching him / one or the other / left him like / he continued / He got smallpox / he was left] [jailed / fault] [would laugh]

Una mañana, *vestido con manto* nuevo, sonriente, de buen humor, salió el señor San José *de paseo* por el pueblo en que vivía y *padecía* Juan Bueno. *Al pasar* por una calle oyó unos lamentos y encontró a la mujer de Juan Bueno, pim, pam, pum, *magullando* a su infeliz *consorte*. ¡Alto! —gritó el padre del divino *Salvador*— ¡Delante de mí no hay escándalos! [dressed in robe] [strolling] [suffered] [On passing by] [beating up on / husband / Saviour]

Así fue. Se calmó todo. Juan Bueno le refirió a San José todas sus *cuitas* y él le dijo: [That's how it turned out to be / problems]

—No tengas cuidado. Ya cesarán tus penas. Yo te ayudaré *en lo que pueda.* Ya sabes, cuando me necesites, en la parroquia, en el altar a la derecha. [any way I can]

Juan *quedó* contentísimo. San José fue, desde entonces, su *paño de lágrimas:* Juan pedía todo y todo le era *concedido.* [was] [a shoulder to cry on] [granted]

Un día, Juan llegó con la cara muy *afligida.* [sad]

—Se me ha perdido —gimoteó— una *taleguilla* de plata que tenía. Quiero *que me la encuentres.* [small bag] [that you find it for me]

—Aunque esas son cosas que corresponden a *Antonio,* haré lo que pueda. [St. Anthony of Padua, usually invoked to find lost articles]

Y así fue. Cuando Juan volvió a casa, encontró la taleguilla. En muchas otras ocasiones, *fue igual.* [the same happened]

55

Hasta que en una ocasión el Santo no se encontraba *con* muy buen humor y apareció Juan Bueno con la cara *hecha* un tomate y la cabeza como una *anona*.

— Hum, hum —*hizo* el Santo.

—Señor, vengo a pedir un nuevo favor. *Se me ha ido mi mujer, y como* eres tan bueno...

San José *alzó* el *bastón* florido y *dándole* a Juan *en medio de* las dos orejas, le dijo con voz *airada:*

—¡*Anda* a buscarla al *infierno, zopenco!*

Cuentos completos (Mexico: Fondo de Cultura Económica, 1950).

in a
like
custard-apple
exclaimed
my wife has left me / since
raised / cane / smacking
across / angry
Go / hell / blockhead

EJERCICIOS

A. Fill in the blank with the appropriate word from the column on the right.

1. _____ chico, Juan Bueno presentaba la _____ por otro lado.

2. Cuando _____ a casa, le pellizca-
   ban los padres.

3. El pobre Juan _____ preso por
   culpa de otro.

4. ¡_____ no hay escándalos!—dijo el
   padre del Salvador.

5. A Juan le dieron las viruelas pero no

   _____.

6. Se me ha perdido la taleguilla de plata.

   Quiero que me la _____.

7. _____ en una ocasión, el Santo no
   quiso ayudar más a Juan.

8. Juan le _____ favores al Santo

   cuando _____ en dificultades.

muere
delante de mí
pedía
desde
encuentres
gallina
llegaba
hasta que
estuvo
perdido
murió
cabeza
se encontraba
a la derecha

B. True or false.

1. Juan Bueno era víctima de todos.
2. Cuando llegó a ser hombre, le dieron las viruelas y murió.
3. Juan era un hombre de mucha paciencia.
4. Juan fue el paño de lágrimas del Santo.
5. El Santo se encontraba en un altar de la parroquia.

C. Arrange the following words in groups of at least two to show some logical association between them. For example: *perder—encontrar*.

buscar   morir   nacer   encontrar   salir   querer   pedir
orejas   volver   cara   llegar   cabeza   crecer   recibir

D. Answer in Spanish.

1. ¿Por qué es que el protagonista se llama Juan Bueno?
2. ¿Qué hacían sus compañeros?
3. Después de que le dieron las viruelas, ¿cómo le quedó la cara?
4. ¿Cómo llegó a conocer Juan Bueno a San José?
5. ¿Qué promesa le hizo San José a Juan Bueno?
6. ¿Cuál fue la primera cosa que le pidió Juan al Santo?
7. ¿Quién, según San José, era el santo al que corresponden las cosas perdidas?
8. ¿Quién dejó la cara de Juan como un tomate?
9. ¿Cuál es la última queja de Juan?
10. ¿Qué hace San José, al fin, con Juan Bueno?

vocabulario

adj	adjective	*inter adv*	interrogative adverb
adv	adverb	*inter pron*	interrogative pronoun
conj	conjunction	*n*	noun
def art	definite article	*pl*	plural
exclam	exclamation	*pp*	past participle
f	feminine	*prep*	preposition
indef art	indefinite article	*pron*	pronoun
inf	infinitive	*reflex pron*	reflexive pronoun
interj	interjection	*rel pron*	relative pronoun

A

a *prep* to
abajo *adv* below
la **abeja** bee
abierto *adj & pp* open, opened
el **abogado** lawyer
los **aborigenes** native inhabitants
abortarse to be aborted; to fail
abrir to open
el **abuelo** grandfather; **abuelos** grandparents
abundar to abound, be plentiful
aburridero *adj* boring
aburrido *adj & pp* bored, boring
el **aburrimiento** boredom
acabar to finish; **acabar de** + *inf* to have just
acariciar to fondle, caress
acaso *adv* maybe, perhaps
el **acaso** chance, accident; **por si acaso** just in case
la **acción** action
la **aceptación** acceptance, approval
aceptar to accept
la **acera** sidewalk
acercarse to approach, come near

acertar to hit the mark; to be right
aclaratorio *adj* clarifying
acometer to attack, assault
acomodado *adj* rich, well-to-do
acomodar to accommodate, put up
acompañar to accompany
acongojado *adj & pp* sad, distressed
acordarse to remember
acorralar to corral, surround
acostarse to go to bed
acostumbrarse to get used to
la **actriz** actress
la **actualidad** actuality, present time
actualmente *adv* presently, nowadays
el **acuerdo** agreement; **ponerse de acuerdo** to agree
acurrucado *adj* curled up
acústicamente *adv* acoustically
adelantado *adj & pp* advanced, early
adelantarse to get ahead of oneself
además *adv* moreover
adiós *interj* good-bye
adivinar to guess, foretell

el **administrador** administrator, manager

admirado *adj & pp* astonished, admired

el **adobe** unburnt brick dried in the sun

adolecerse to be suffering from

adolescente *adj* adolescent

¿**adónde?** *interj & adv* where to; where

adorar to adore

adúltero *adj* adulterous

el **afecto** affection

la **afición** love, affection, fondness

afortunadamente *adv* fortunately

afrentado *adj & pp* shamed, insulted

afuera *adv* outside

agacharse to stoop

agarrar to grasp, seize

ágil *adj* agile

agitar to agitate, disturb

agradable *adj* pleasant

agregar to annex, add to, join, attach

agrícola *adj* agricultural

el **agricultor** farmer

el **agua** *f* water

aguantar to sustain; to bear, endure

ahí *adv* there

ahogado *adj & pp* suffocated, drowned

ahogar to choke; to drown

ahora *adv* now

el **ahorro** frugality, saving

el **aire** air

al *prep* upon

alabar to praise

alarmado *adj & pp* alarmed

alarmar to alarm

el **alboroto** tumult, hubbub, uproar

el **alcaide** governor of a castle, warden

el **alcalde** mayor

alegrar to make happy, gladden; **alegrarse** to be glad, rejoice

alegre *adj* happy, merry

alegremente *adv* happily

alejarse to go away from, move away

aletargado *adj* lethargic, drowsy

algo *pron* something; *adv* somewhat

alguien *pron* someone

algun(o) *adj* some, any; *pron* someone

aligerado *adj & pp* lightened, hastened

el **alimento** food

el **alivio** relief

el **alma** *f* soul, spirit

la **almendra** almond

almorzar to eat lunch

el **alrededor** surroundings; **alrededor de** *prep* around

altivo *adj* haughty, arrogant

alto *adj* high, tall

alzado *adj & pp* raised

alzar to raise, lift

allá *adv* there; **más allá** farther

allí *adv* there

amable *adj* kind, affable

amado *adj & pp* loved

amanecer to dawn; to wake up; el **amanecer** dawn, sunrise

el (la) **amante** lover

la **amapola** poppy

amar to love

amarillo *adj* yellow

amarrar to tie

el **ambiente** environment, atmosphere

ambos *adj & pron* both

el **amigo** friend
amontonar to heap, pile
el **amor** love
el **anciano** old man
la **andanza** event, good or bad
fortune
andar to walk; el **andar**
walking, passage
la **anécdota** anecdote
anglosajón *adj & n* Anglo-
Saxon
angustiado *adj & pp*
anguished, worried
el **anillo** ring
el **animal** animal
el **ánimo** *f* spirit, mind; courage
anoche *adv* last night
anochecer to grow dark,
become night
anónimo *adj* anonymous
anotar to write down; to
note, remark
antes *adv* before; **antes que**
conj before
el **año** year
apagar to extinguish; to
turn off (lights); **apa-
garse** to be extinguished
aparecer to appear
la **apariencia** appearance
apartar to part, separate
el **apellido** last name, surname
apenas *adv* hardly, scarcely
aprender to learn
apresurado *adj & pp* hur-
riedly, quickly
apresurarse to hurry up
apretar to squeeze; to
tighten
aproximarse to approach
la **apuesta** bet
apurarse to worry; to hurry
up
aquél *pron* that one;
aquella *adj* that;
aquellas *adj* those

aquí *adv* here
el **árabe** Arab
el **árbol** tree
la **Argentina** Argentina
el **argentino** Argentine
el **argumento** plot of a story
el **arma** *f* weapon
armarse to prepare oneself;
to arm oneself
el **arquitecto** architect
arrebatar to carry; to
snatch
¡**arriba**! hurry up, hurrah;
de arriba abajo from top
to bottom
arrodillarse to kneel
arrojar to throw
el **arroyo** stream, brook
el **arte** *m & f* art; skill
el **artificio** contrivance, trick
artístico *adj* artistic
asaltar to assault; to occur
suddenly
la **asamblea** assembly,
group
así *adv* thus, in this way,
like this; **así como** in the
same way, just as, like
asistir to attend
asomarse to become visible,
appear; to look out (of a
window)
el **asombro** amazement
el **aspecto** aspect, manner,
appearance
áspero rough
la **aspiración** aspiration
el **asunto** matter, affair, business
asustar to frighten
asustado *adj & pp* frightened
asustarse to be afraid
el **ataque** attack
atar to tie
atraerse to be attracted

atrás *adv* backwards, past,
  behind
atravesar to cross, cross
  over
atreverse to dare to
el **aula** *f* classroom
el **aumento** increase, magnify-
  ing
aun *adv* still, even, yet
aunque *conj* although,
  though
la **ausencia** absence
ausente *adj* absent
el **auto** car
el **autor** author
el **avaro** miser
la **avellana** hazelnut
la **avenida** avenue
la **aventura** adventure
aventurarse a to venture,
  risk
ávidamente *adv* avidly,
  eagerly
avisar to warn; to inform; to
  advise
el **aviso** information, notice,
  warning
la **ayuda** help, aid
azotar to beat
azul *adj* blue

B

el **bachiller** bachelor degree
bajar(se) to go down, de-
  scend; to lower; to get out of
  a vehicle
bajo *prep* underneath, below
el **balcón** balcony
la **banda** band
el **bandido** outlaw, bandit
la **barba** beard; chin
el **barquinazo** violent swaying
  or jumping of a vehicle;
  lurch

el **barranco** precipice, ravine,
  cliff
el **barrio** neighborhood
el **barro** mud
el **basquetbol** basketball
bastante *adj* enough, quite
bastar to be enough, suffice
el **bastón** cane
beber to drink
la **belleza** beauty
bello *adj* pretty, beautiful
bendecido *adj & pp* blessed
el **beneficio** benefit, profit
besar to kiss
bíblico *adj* biblical
la **biblioteca** library
bien *adv* well
el **bigote** moustache;
  bigotazo large
  moustache
el **bizcocho** biscuit
blanco *adj* white; el **blanco**
  white man
la **blasfemia** blasphemy
la **boca** mouth
la **bocina** horn
la **bolsa** bag
el **bolsillo** pocket
bonito *adj* pretty
borracho *adj* drunk
el **bosque** woods, forest; el
  bosquecillo small forest
la **bota** boot
la **botica** pharmacy
el **boticario** pharmacist,
  druggist
bravio *adj* ferocious, savage
el **brazo** arm
breve *adj* brief, short
el **breviario** breviary
brillante *adj* brilliant,
  bright
el **brillante** diamond
brillar to shine
la **broma** joke
el **bronce** bronze

bruces *adv*   face downwards
bueno *adj*   good
la **burla**   jest, mockery; **hacer
burla de**   to make fun of
burlar   to mock
buscar   to look for
el **buzón**   mailbox

C

cabalgar   to ride; to mount
el **caballero**   gentleman
el **caballo**   horse
la **cabaña**   cabin
la **cabellera**   long hair
la **cabeza**   head
el **cabo**   tip, end; **al cabo de**
at the end of; after
la **cacería**   hunting-party,
hunting
el **cachorro**   cub, pup
cada *adj*   each, every
el **cadáver**   body, corpse
la **cadena**   chain
caer   to fall
el **cahita**   name of the language
of the Yaqui Indians
la **calamidad**   calamity, misfor-
tune
el **calendario**   calendar;
almanac
caliente *adj*   warm, hot
callado *adj & pp*   quiet,
silent
callar   to be silent
la **calle**   street
la **cama**   bed
cambiar   to change
el **cambio**   change; **en cambio**   on the other hand
el **camello**   camel
caminar   to walk; to travel
el **camino**   road, way
la **camisa**   shirt, gown
el **campamento**   camp, field

el **campeón**   champion
el **campesino**   peasant; *adj*
rural, country, rustic
el **campo**   country, field
el **can**   dog
el **canasto**   basket
el **candado**   padlock
cano *adj*   grey-haired
cansado *adj & pp*   tired
cansarse   to get tired
cantar   to sing
la **caña**   sugar cane
el **caos**   chaos
el **capitán**   captain
la **cara**   face
la **carabina**   carbine
caracterizarse   to be charac-
terized
el **caramelo**   caramel
la **cárcel**   jail
cargar   to burden; to load
el **cariño**   love, affection, fondness
cariñosamente *adv*   affec-
tionately
caritativo *adj*   charitable,
loving
la **carne**   meat, flesh
caro *adj*   expensive
la **carrera**   career
la **carretera**   highway, main
road
el **carro**   car; cart
la **carta**   letter
la **cartera**   wallet
la **casa**   house
casado *adj & pp*   married
casar(se)   to marry; to get
married
el **cascabel**   rattling sound;
jingle
casi *adv*   almost
el **caso**   case
la **casta**   caste, social rank
el **castellano**   Castilian or
Spanish language

el **castillo** castle
el **católico** Catholic
la **causa** cause; **a causa de**
  prep because of
el **cautivo** captive
la **caverna** cavern, cave
la **caza** game (hunting)
el **cazador** hunter
  cazar to hunt
la **cebolla** onion
  celebrar to celebrate
  celoso *adj* jealous
  cenar to eat supper
  cenceño *adj* thin, slender
  cenizoso *adj* ashy, gray
  cerca *adv* near
  cercano *adj* nearby
  cerrado *adj & pp* closed
  cerrar to close
el **cerro** hill
la **cerveza** beer
  cesar to cease
el **césped** lawn
  cicatrizar to heal
el **cielo** heaven, sky
  científico *adj* scientific
la **cifra** number, cipher; code
la **cima** top
el **cine** movie theatre
el **cinto** waist; belt
la **ciudad** city
  civil *adj* civil; polite
la **claridad** clarity; light
  claro *adj* bright, clear, light
  (color)
la **clase** class
  clavar to nail; to stick, prick
la **cobija** shawl; bedclothes;
  blanket
  cobrado *pp & adj* collected;
  gained
  cobrar to collect, to gain
la **cocina** kitchen
la **cocinera** cook
el **coco** bogeyman
  coger to grab, grasp

la **col** cabbage
la **colaboración** collaboration,
  mutual help
  colaborar to collaborate,
  work together
la **colección** collection
el **colegio** school (*not* college)
la **cólera** anger
  colgar to hang
  colocar to place, put
  colonial *adj* colonial
el **colono** colonist; planter
el **color** color
  colorado *adj* ruddy, reddish
el **comandante** commander;
  chief, major
la **comarca** territory, district
el **combatiente** warrior,
  fighter
  comentar to comment
  comenzar to begin
  comer to eat
  cómico *adj* funny
  como *conj & adj* as, like,
  such as; if, since, when;
  cómo *exclam* what;
  ¿Cómo? *interr adv* how
el **compañero** companion,
  friend
  compartir to share
  completo *adj* complete; **por
  completo** *adv* completely
  comprar to buy
  comprender to understand
  comulgar to receive commu-
  nion
  común *adj* common
  comunicar to communicate
la **comunidad** community
  con *prep* with
la **concepción** conception
el **concepto** concept, idea
  conciliador *adj* conciliating
  condensarse to be con-
  densed
el **cóndor** condor, vulture

conducir to lead; to drive
confesar to confess
confiado *adj* confident, secure
la **confianza** confidence, faith
el **conflicto** conflict
confundido *adj & pp* confused
confundir to confuse, mix up
la **confusión** confusion
confuso *adj* confused
el **congénere** fellow being
congregar to bring together
conmover to affect, move to pity
conocer to know
conocido *adj & pp* known
el **conocimiento** knowledge
la **consecuencia** consequence; result; **en consecuencia** as a consequence, therefore
conseguir to obtain; to get
el **consejo** advice, counsel
la **conservación** conservation, preservation
considerado *adj & pp* considered; considerate; thoughtful
considerar to consider
consolar to console
el **consorte** husband
construir to construct
el **contacto** contact
contar to count; to tell, relate
contento *adj* happy
contestar to answer
la **continuación** continuation
continuar to continue
contra *prep* against
convencerse to be convinced
convencido *adj & pp* convinced
la **conversación** conversation

conversar to converse, talk
convertir to convert
el **corazón** heart
el **coronel** colonel
el **correo** mail; **a vuelta de correo** by return post
correr to run
el **corresponsal** correspondent
la **corriente** current, flow; movement
cortado *adj & pp* cut
la **corte** court
cortés *adj* polite
la **cortesía** courtesy, politeness
cortesmente *adv* politely
la **cortina** curtain
corto *adj* short
el **coscorrón** a rap on the head
la **cosecha** harvest
coser to sew
la **costa** cost
costar to cost
la **costumbre** custom
la **costura** sewing
el **creador** creator
crecer to grow, increase
creer to believe
creyente *adj* believing
la **criada** maid
criar to raise, breed; to educate
la **criatura** creature; baby
el **crimen** crime
criollo *adj* Creole; native of Spanish America
el **cristal** crystal, glass, water
la **crítica** criticism
el **crítico** critic; judge
la **crónica** chronicle, history
la **cruz** cross
cruzar to cross
el **cuaderno** notebook
cuadrado *adj* square
el **cuadro** square; picture
cualquier *adj & pron* any, anyone

cuando *conj* when
cuántos *adj* how many
la **cuaresma** Lent
el **cuarto** room; el **cuartito** little room
los **cubiertos** silverware
el **cuello** neck; collar
la **cuenta** count; bill; account; **darse cuenta de** to realize
el (la) **cuentista** short story writer
el **cuento** story
la **cuerda** cord, string; **dar cuerda** to wind
el **cuero** leather
el **cuerpo** body
la **cuesta** hill
la **cuestión** question
el **cuidado** care; ¡**cuidado!** be careful; **tener cuidado** to be careful
cuidar to take care of
la **cuita** problem
el **culantro** coriander
la **culpa** blame, fault
culpar to blame
cultivar to cultivate
el **culto** religion, worship
la **cultura** culture
la **cuñada** sister-in-law
el **cura** priest
curioso *adj* curious; peculiar; neat
el **curso** course
cuyo *adj* whose

CH

el **chaleco** vest
el **charco** puddle
charlar to chat, talk
la **chica** girl
el **chiquito** little boy, youngest
el **chisme** gossip, rumor

chismoso *adj* gossipy, tale-bearing
la **choza** hut, cabin

D

el **daño** harm, damage; **hacer daño** to hurt
dar to give; **dar con** to meet, come upon
de *prep* from, of, about
debajo de *prep* underneath
deber to owe; should, ought to; **deber de** must, should
el **deber** duty, obligation
débil *adj* weak
el **decano** dean
decidir to decide
decir to tell, say
la **declinación** descent, falling
el **decorado** decoration, ornamentation
decrépito *adj* decrepit, old, feeble
dedicarse to dedicate oneself, apply oneself
el **dedo** finger
dejar to let, allow; to leave behind; to drop
delante *adv* before, in front; **delante de** in front of; **por delante** ahead
la **delicia** delight
delinearse to be sketched, be described
el **delito** crime, fault
demás *adj & pp* other; **lo demás** the rest
demasiado *adv* too much, too
dentro *adv* inside, within
el **dependiente** clerk
deplorar to lament
derecha right; **a la derecha** to the right
derecho *adj* right; straight

derramar   to pour; to spill
derribar   to demolish, tear down
desafiar   to challenge; to oppose
desasirse   to free oneself
desasosiego   restlessness
desatar   to untie
descansar   to rest
el descanso   rest
descargar   to unload; to strike
descepar   to pull up by the roots
descifrar   to interpret, decipher
desconfiado *adj*   distrustful
desconocido *adj*   unknown, strange; el desconocido stranger
descubrir   to discover
desde *prep*   from, since
desempeñar   to discharge an office or duty
desfallecido *adj & pp*   fainted
desfilar   to march past, file past
desgraciado *adj*   wretched, unfortunate
el desierto   desert
desinteresado *adj*   disinterested
deslizarse   to slide; to slip away
despachar   to perform; to discharge
despacito *adv*   very slowly
despectivo *adj*   depreciatory
despedirse   to say goodbye
despertarse   to wake up
despierto *adj*   awake
despojar   to strip, deprive of
el desprecio   scorn, contempt
desprendido *adj & pp*   unfastened, loose
después *adv*   after, later;
   después de *prep*   after

destacado *adj & pp*   outstanding
desterrado *adj & pp*   exiled, banished
destrozar   to destroy
el detalle   detail
detenerse   to stop, stay
la determinación   determination
devolver   to give back, return
devuelto *pp*   returned, given back
el día   day
el diablo   devil
el diálogo   dialogue
diariamente *adv*   daily
el diario   daily newspaper
dictar   to dictate; to direct
dicho *pp*   said, told
la diferencia   difference
difícil *adj*   difficult
dificultarse   to become difficult
digno *adj*   worthy
el dinero   money
el dios   god
diplomático *adj*   diplomatic, tactful
directamente *adv*   directly
dirigirse   to direct oneself; to speak to
la disciplina   discipline
disculparse   to excuse oneself
discutir   to discuss
el diseño   design, sketch
disfrazado *adj & pp*   disguised
disparar   to shoot
disputar   to dispute
la distancia   distance
distante *adj*   distant
distinto *adj*   different
diverso   diverse
divino *adj*   divine
el doctor   doctor

doctoral *adj* doctoral
doctorarse to get a doctor's degree
dolido *adj & pp* hurt
el **dolor** pain
domesticar to domesticate
dominar to dominate, control
el **domingo** Sunday
donde *adv* where
dormido *adj & pp* asleep
dormirse to fall asleep
el **dormitorio** bedroom
dos *adj* two; **los dos** both
doscientos *adj* two hundred
el **drama** drama
la **duda** doubt
dulce *adj* sweet; los **dulces** candy
el **duque** duke
durante *prep* during
durar to last
el **durazno** peach
duro *adj* hard, difficult

E

e *conj* and
el **ébano** ebony
ebrio *adj* drunk
el **eco** echo
echar to throw; **echar a** to begin
la **edad** age
educarse to be educated
el **efecto** effect, result; **en efecto** in fact, actually; indeed
el **ejemplo** example
ejercer to exercise; to practice (a profession)
el **ejército** army
el que *pron* he who, the one who
ello *pron* it
embarrado *adj & pp*

smeared with mud
embarrarse to be smeared with mud
embriagarse to get drunk
la **emoción** emotion
empeorarse to become worse
empezar to begin
en *prep* in, on, upon
la **enagua** petticoat
enamorarse to fall in love
encadenarse to be linked together
el **encanto** enchantment, delight, charm
encender to put on lights; to light
encerrado *adj & pp* enclosed
encima de *prep* on top of
encogido *adj & pp* timid, bashful, fearful
el **encogimiento** bashfulness, awkwardness; **encogimiento de hombros** shrug
encontrar to find, to meet; **encontrarse** to meet each other; to find oneself
el **enemigo** enemy
enfermarse to become sick
la **enfermedad** sickness
enfermo *adj* sick
enfrente *adv* opposite, facing, in front
engañar to deceive
engendrar to create; to produce; to cause
enlazar to tie, bind; to interlock; to join
enorme *adj* enormous
enraizado *adj & pp* rooted
el **ensayo** essay; attempt
enseñar to show; to teach
entender to understand
enterarse de to be informed; to find out

enternecido *adj* moved to compassion
entero *adj* entire, whole
enterrar to bury
entonces *adv* then
entrar to enter
entre *prep* between, among
entregar to hand over, deliver; to pay
entretanto *adv* meanwhile
el **entusiasmo** enthusiasm
envejecer to grow old
enviar to send
la **envidia** envy
épico *adj* epic
episódico *adj* episodic
el **episodio** episode
el **equipo** team
el **error** error, mistake
esbelto *adj* slim, slender
escabullirse to escape, slip away
la **escala** ladder, scale
la **escalera** stairs
el **escándalo** scandal
escamoteado *pp & adj* made to disappear from the hands; whisked out of sight
escandinavo *adj* Scandinavian
escaparse to escape
el **esclavo** slave
escolar *adj* scholastic, academic
esconder to hide; **esconderse** to hide, go into hiding
escondidas; a escondidas *adv* hidden, on the sly
escondido *adj & pp* hidden
escribir to write
el **escritor** writer
escuchar to listen to
la **escuela** school
escurrirse to slip; to glide, pass slowly
el **escusado** water closet,

toilet-room
eso *dem pron* that; **a eso de** at about; **por eso** therefore
el **espacio** space
espantar to frighten
el **espanto** fright
España Spain
el **español** Spanish language; Spaniard
especial *adj* special
especializado *adj & pp* specialized
especialmente *adv* specially
la **especie** species
el **espectro** spectre, phantom, ghost
el **espejo** mirror
esperar to wait for; to hope; to expect
el **espía** (la **espía**) spy
espiar to spy (on)
la **espiga** spike of grain
la **esposa** *f* wife
el **esposo** *m* husband
la **esquina** corner of a street
la **estaca** picket, stake
el **estado** state, condition
los **Estados Unidos** United States
el **estaño** tin
estar to be
la **estatua** statue
el **estilo** style
estimar to esteem
estirarse to stretch out
el **estómago** stomach
el **estorbo** hindrance, nuisance
estragar to ravage; to corrupt
estrecho *adj* narrow
el **estuco** stucco, plaster
el (la) **estudiante** student
estudiantil *adj* student
estudiar to study
el **estudio** study
estudioso *adj* studious

estupefacto *adj* stunned, speechless
estúpido *adj* stupid
la **Europa** Europe
europeo *adj* European
exacto *adj* exact; mere
exagerado *adj & pp* exaggerated
examinar to examine
la **excepción** exception
exclusivo *adj* exclusive
exhausto *adj* exhausted
la **existencia** existence
existir to exist
el **éxito** success
la **experiencia** experience
la **explicación** explanation
explicar to explain
el **explorador** explorer, scout
la **explotación** exploitation
exponer to expose
expresar to express
la **expresión** expression
la **expropiación** expropriation
expropiar to expropriate
extasiado *adj* delighted, enraptured
extendido *adj* extended, stretched out
extenso *adj* extensive, with full particulars
el **extranjero** foreigner
extrañar to wonder at
extraño *adj* strange, foreign
extraordinario *adj* extraordinary
extravagante *adj* extravagant
extremamente *adv* extremely
el **extremo** extreme

F

fabricarse to contrive; to manufacture

facilitar to facilitate, make easy
la **facha** appearance, look, face
la **faena** work, task, job, duty
falso *adj* false
la **falta** lack
faltar to be lacking, need
la **fama** fame, reputation
la **familia** family
famoso *adj* famous
la **fantasía** fantasy
el **farol** street light
fatigoso *adj* tiresome, wearisome
la **fe** faith
federal *adj* federal
la **felicidad** happiness
el **fenómeno** phenomenon
feo *adj* ugly
feroz *adj* ferocious
fértil *adj* fertile
festejar to entertain; to feast
la **ficción** fiction
la **fiebre** fever
la **fiera** wild animal
la **fiereza** fierceness, ferocity
la **fiesta** party, holiday, feast
figurar to shape; to represent
la **figurilla** little figure
fijarse to rivet one's attention on something, notice
la **filosofía** philosophy
el **filósofo** philosopher
el **fin** end; **al fin** at last, finally; **al fin y al cabo** at last, in the end; **en fin** in conclusion, in short; **por fin** finally
el **final** ending
fingir to feign, pretend
fino *adj* fine, elegant, subtle, delicate
la **firma** signature
firme *adj* firm, strong
físicamente *adv* physically

flaquear to weaken
la **flauta** flute
la **flor** flower
fluir to flow; el **fluir** flowing, running
el **folklore** folklore
folklórico *adj* folklore
el **fondo** bottom; background
la **forma** form, shape
formar to form, make; **formarse** to take form; to be molded
formular to formulate; to word
la **fortuna** fortune, luck
forzar to force
forzosamente *adv* forcibly
la **fotografía** photography
el **francés** French language; Frenchman
la **frecuencia** frequency
frenar to break
la **frente** forehead; **frente a** in front of
el **frijol** bean
el **frío** cold, coldness; *adj* cold
la **fruta** fruit
el **fuego** fire
fuera de *prep* outside of
fuerte *adj* strong
la **fuerza** force, strength; **a fuerza de** by dint of
la **fuga** escape, flight
el **fundador** founder
fundar to found, to establish
furioso *adj* furious, angry
el **fusil** rifle, gun
el **fútbol** football, soccer
el **futuro** future

G

las **gafas** glasses
la **galería** gallery, corridor
la **gallina** hen, chicken
ganar to gain, win; to earn

la **gata** cat
el **gato** cat; fair
el **general** general
el **género** genre; kind, sort
la **génesis** genesis, origin
la **gente** people
el **gesto** gesture, movement; expression
el **gigante** giant
la **gloria** glory
la **glorieta** arbor
el **gobierno** government
el **golpe** hit, smack, blow
golpear to knock
gordo *adj* fat
la **gota** drop (of liquid)
grabado *adj* engraved
gracias thanks
graduarse to graduate
gran *adj* great
grande *adj* big
el **granizo** hail
gratificar to please, gratify
gris *adj* gray
gritar to shout
el **grupo** group
la **gruta** cavity between rocks, cavern
guardar to keep, protect, watch over
la **guerra** war
guiñar to wink
gustar to like, be pleasing
el **gusto** taste, pleasure, delight, liking

H

haber to have; **haber de +** *inf* must
había there was, there were
la **habitación** room
el **habitante** inhabitant
habitar to live, dwell, reside
habrá there will be; there must be

hace + *time expression* ago
hacer to do; to make
hacer falta to be lacking
hacia *prep* towards
la **hacienda** farm, ranch
hallar to find
el **hallazgo** *m* act of finding;
  discovery
el **hambre** *f* hunger
hambriento *adj* hungry
hasta *prep* even, until;
  hasta que until
hay there is, there are; **hay
  que** + *inf* it is necessary
  to
el **hecho** deed, fact; *pp* made,
  done
herir to wound
el **hermano** brother
hermoso *adj* pretty,
  beautiful
el **hielo** ice
la **hija** daughter
el **hijo** son
hispánico *adj* Hispanic,
  Spanish
hispanoamericano *adj*
  Spanish-American
la **historia** history; story
el **historiador** historian
el **hogar** home; hearth
la **hoja** leaf
la **hojarasca** leaves, foliage
el **hombre** man
el **hombro** shoulder
la **hora** hour, time
la **hortaliza** vegetables
hosco *adj* dark colored
hoy *adv* today
hubo there was, there were
la **huella** print, trace
el **huérfano** orphan
la **huerta** vegetable garden
el **hueso** bone
el **huésped** guest
el **huevo** egg

huir to flee
la **humanidad** humanity
humanitario *adj* humani-
  tarian
humilde *adj* humble, poor
el **humo** smoke
el **humor** humor; mood
humorístico *adj* humorous
hundirse to sink, collapse

I

el **idioma** language
el **idiota** idiot, fool
el **ídolo** idol
ignorante *adj* ignorant,
  stupid
igual *adj* equal
la **imagen** image
imaginarse to imagine
imbécil *adj* imbecile
implorar to implore, beg
importante *adj* important
importar to be important,
  matter
imposible *adj* impossible
la **impresión** impression
la **imprudencia** imprudence,
  recklessness
inaccesible *adj* inaccessible
inadvertido *adj* unnoticed,
  unseen; careless
la **inauguración** commence-
  ment
el **incendio** fire
inclinarse to bend over
incluir to include
incluso including
la **indemnización** indemnity,
  reimbursement
la **independencia** independence
la **indiada** group or crowd of
  Indians

indígena *adj* indigenous, native
el **indio** Indian
indomable *adj* indomitable, unconquerable
indudablemente *adv* undoubtedly
infantil *adj* infantile, childlike
infeliz *adj* unhappy
inferior *adj* inferior
el **infierno** hell
la **influencia** influence
la **información** information, report
informar to inform
el **informe** report
ingenuo *adj* open, candid
el **inglés** English language; Englishman
ingresar to enter; to join
el **iniciador** initiator
iniciar to begin
la **injusticia** injustice
inmediatamente *adv* immediately
inmenso *adj* large
inmóvil *adj* motionless
innecesario *adj* unnecessary
inocente *adj* innocent
inquieto *adj* restless, uneasy
la **inquisición** inquisition; inquiry
insignificante *adj* insignificant
insistir to insist on
la **insolación** sunstroke
inspeccionar to inspect
el **instante** instant; **al instante** immediately
el **instinto** instinct
la **instrucción** instruction
intelectual *adj* intellectual
el **interés** interest

interesante *adj* interesting
interesarse to be interested
interminable *adj* unending
el **intérprete** interpreter
intraducible *adj* untranslatable
intricado *adj* intricate
la **invención** invention, fiction, artifice
inventar to invent
el **investigador** investigator
invitar to invite
ir to go; **irse** to go away
la **ira** anger
irónico *adj* ironical
la **irrealidad** unreality
la **isla** island
izquierdo *adj* left

J

jamás *adv* never
el **jardín** garden, yard
la **jaula** cage
el **jefe** chief, leader
joven *adj* young
el **judío** Jew
el **juego** game
jugar to play
el **juguete** toy
el **juicio** judgment, sense
julio July
juntamente *adv* jointly, together
juntar to join, unite; **juntarse** to come together
junto *adj* joined, united; **junto a** next to
jurar to swear
justamente *adv* exactly, precisely
la **justicia** justice
justo *adj* just, fair, right
la **juventud** youth

K

el **kilómetro**   kilometer

L

la *def art*   the; **la que** *rel pron*   she who, the one who
el **laberinto**   labyrinth
el **labio**   lip
la **labor**   work
el **labrador**   worker; farmer; peasant
el **lado**   side; **al lado**   beside, near
el **ladrón**   thief, robber
lamentar   to lament, regret, mourn
lamer   to lick
la **lámpara**   lamp
lampiño *adj*   beardless
largo *adj*   long
el **latín**   Latin language
latir   to palpitate, throb
lavar   to wash; **lavarse**   to get washed
el **lector**   reader
leer   to read
lejos *adv*   far, far away
la **lengua**   tongue
lentamente *adv*   slowly
el **lente** (la **lente**)   lens
el **leñador**   woodcutter, woodsman
la **letra**   letter of the alphabet; **letras**   letters, learning
el **letrero**   sign
levantar   to raise, pick up; **levantarse**   to get up
el **levitón**   big coat
la **ley**   law
la **leyenda**   legend
liar   to tie
el **libro**   book
la **ligadura**   binding
ligero *adj*   light

limitar   to limit
la **limosna**   alms, offering to the poor
el **limosnero**   beggar
lindo *adj*   pretty
la **línea**   line; limit
listo *adj*   ready
literario *adj*   literary
la **literatura**   literature
lívido *adj*   livid, black and blue; pale
lo que *rel pron*   what
el **lobo**   wolf
el **loco**   madman, insane person
la **locura**   madness, insanity
lograr   to succeed
los que *rel pron*   those who
el **lucero**   morning-star, Venus
lucir   to shine
la **lucha**   fight
luego *conj*   then
el **lugar**   place
el **lujo**   luxury, finery
la **luna**   moon
el **lunes**   Monday
la **luz**   light

LL

llamar   to call; **llamarse**   to be called
llamarada   flash
llegar   to arrive
lleno *adj*   full
llevar   to take, carry, take away; to wear
llorar   to cry
llover   to rain

M

macizo *adj*   stocky
la **madera**   wood
la **madre**   mother
madrileño   person from Madrid

madrugar   to get up at dawn
madurar   to mature
el **maestro**   (la **maestra**)
  teacher
mágico *adj*   magical
el **mago**   sage, magician
el **maíz**   corn
mal *adv*   badly
malhumorado *adj*   in a bad
  mood; ill-humored
la **malicia**   malice
maloliente   smelly
malviviente *adj*   decadent,
  degenerate
el **manantial**   spring
mandar   to command, order;
  to send
la **manera**   manner, way,
  method
la **manga**   sleeve
manifestarse   to show itself
la **mano**   hand
el **mantel**   tablecloth
mantener   to maintain, keep
el **manto**   robe
la **mañana**   morning; *adv*
  tomorrow
la **maravilla**   wonder
marcharse   to go away
el **marido**   husband
más *adj*   more, most; **no**
  más   only
el **masonite**   masonite
matar   to kill
las **matemáticas**   mathematics
el **matrimonio**   marriage
máximo *adj*   very great,
  maximum
mayor *adj*   older, oldest
la **mayoría**   majority
mecánico *adj*   mechanical
la **medalla**   medal
la **medianoche**   midnight
la **medicina**   medicine
el **médico**   physician, medical
  doctor
la **medida**   measurement

medio *adj*   half, middle; **el**
  medio   middle, center; **por**
  medio de   by means of
el **mediodía**   noon
la **meditación**   meditation
la **mejilla**   cheek
mejor *adj*   better, best
la **memoria** *f*   memory, recollec-
  tion
mencionar   to mention
menor *adj*   younger, youngest
menos *adj & pron*   less,
  least; **a menos que**   unless
menudo *adj*   small, slender;
  a menudo *adv*   often
el **mercado**   market
merecer   to merit, deserve
el **mes**   month
la **mesa**   table
meter   to place, put in; **me-**
  terse   to meddle, interfere
mexicano *adj & n*   Mexican
el **México**   Mexico
mezclarse   to be mixed
mi *adj*   my
el **miedo**   fear; **tener miedo**
  to be afraid
mientras *conj*   while
la **milla**   mile
el **ministerio**   ministry, office
el **minuto**   minute
mío *pron*   mine
la **mirada**   glance, gaze, look
mirar   to look at
el **mirlo**   blackbird
la **misa**   mass
miserable *adj*   miserable,
  wretched, unhappy, mean
la **miseria**   calamity
mismo *adj*   same; **lo mismo**
  the same thing; **sí**
  mismos   themselves
misterioso *adj*   mysterious
la **mitad**   half
modestamente *adv*   mod-
  estly

el **modo**   way; **de modo que**
 so that
mojar   to wet, to moisten
moler   to beat, flog
molestar   to bother
la **molestia**   bother, annoyance
molido *adj & pp*   beaten
el **momento**   moment
la **moneda**   coin
la **montaña**   mountain
el **monte**   mountain, hill
moral *adj*   moral
moreno *adj*   brown, dark
 skinned
moribundo *adj*   dying, near
 death
morir   to die
mostrar   to show
moverse   to move
el **movimiento**   movement
el **mozo**   servant, boy, waiter;
 youth
la **muchacha**   girl
el **muchacho**   boy
mucho *adv & adj*   much, a
 lot
mudarse   to move
los **muebles**   furniture
la **muerte**   death
muerto *adj*   dead; *pp* died
la **mujer**   wife, woman
el **mundo**   world
murmurar   to murmur,
 whisper
el **muro**   wall
musical *adj*   musical
muy *adv*   very

N

nacer   to be born
nacional *adj*   national
nada *indef pron*   nothing;
 nada más   only
nadie *pron*   nobody

la **nalga**   buttock, rump
la **nariz**   nose; las **narices**
 nostrils
la **narración**   narration
el **narrador**   narrator
natural *adj*   natural
naturalmente *adv*   naturally
la **Navidad**   Christmas
necesario *adj*   necessary
la **necesidad**   necessity
negarse   to refuse
el **negocio**   business, business
 deal
negro *adj*   black; el **negro**
 black person
nervioso *adj*   nervous
ni *conj & adj*   nor; neither;
 ni siquiera   not even
el **nieto**   grandson
ninguno *adj & pron*   no,
 none; nobody
la **niña**   girl
la **niñez**   childhood
el **niño**   child
nocturno *adj*   nocturnal
la **noche**   night
la **nochebuena**   Christmas Eve
nórdico *adj*   nordic
normal *adj*   normal
norteamericano *adj*
 American
nostálgico *adj*   sad
notar   to note, notice,
 observe; to write down
la **noticia**   news
la **novela**   novel
el **novelador**   novelist
el **novelista** (la **novelista**)
 novelist
la **novia**   fiancee, sweetheart
el **novio**   fiancé
la **nube**   cloud
nuestro *adj*   our
nuevamente   again
nuevo *adj*   new
nunca *adv*   never

O

o *conj* or, either
el **objeto** object, article
la **obra** work
obscuro *adj* dark
observar to observe
la **obsesión** obsession
obstante; no obstante *conj* nevertheless
obstinadamente *adv* obstinately
obstinarse to be obstinate
obtener to obtain
la **ocasión** occasion
ocultar(se) to hide
ocupado *adj & pp* busy
ocurrir to occur, happen
el **oficio** office, work, occupation
oír to hear
el **ojo** eye
oler to smell
olvidar to forget; **olvidarse de** to forget
omitir to omit
la **onda** wave
la **ópera** opera
la **operación** operation
la **opinión** opinion
oponerse a to be opposed
oral *adj* oral
la **orden** order, command; **a la orden** at your service
la **oreja** ear
el **orgullo** pride
orgulloso *adj* proud
la **orilla** shore, bank
el **oro** gold
oscuro *adj* dark
el **otate** species of bamboo
el **otoño** autumn
otro *adj* another, other
el **oxímoron** combination of contradictory or incongruous words

P

la **paciencia** patience
pacífico *adj* peaceful, calm
el **padre** father; los **padres** parents
pagar to pay
el **país** country, nation
el **paisaje** countryside, landscape
la **palabra** word
palidecer to turn pale
la **palma** palm tree; palm of hand
el **palo** stick
palpar to touch
el **pan** bread
el **pantalón** pants; los **pantalones** pants
la **pantera** panther
el **pañuelo** handkerchief
el **papel** paper
el **paquete** package
el **par** pair
para *prep* for; in order to; **para que** *conj* so that
parado *adj & pp* stopped, standing
el **paraguas** umbrella
el **paraíso** paradise
pardo *adj* brown
parecer to seem, appear; **parecerse** to resemble
parecido *adj* similar
la **pared** wall
la **parentela** parentage, kindred, relations
el **pariente** relative
el **párpado** eyelid
el **parque** park
la **parte** part, place
participar to participate
particular *adj* particular, peculiar, odd, individual
particularmente *adv* particularly

el **partido** game
partir to leave
la **parroquia** church, parish
el **pasaje** passage
pasar to happen, pass; to
spend time
pasearse to take a ride
el **paseo** drive, ride
el **pasillo** hallway
el **paso** step, way, passage
patear to kick
la **patria** country, homeland
la **paz** peace
el **pedazo** piece
pedir to ask for, request
pegar to hit; to stick
pelado *adj & pp* bare
la **película** film
el **peligro** danger
el **pelo** hair
peludo *adj* hairy
pellizcar to pinch, nip
la **pena** pain
penetrante *adj* penetrating
penetrar to penetrate, go in
el **pensador** thinker
el **pensamiento** thought
pensar to think
la **peña** rock
peor *adj & adv* worse, worst
pequeño *adj* small
perder to lose; **perderse**
to get lost
el **perdido** lost person; vagabond
el **perdón** pardon
perfecto *adj* perfect
el **periódico** newspaper
el **periodismo** journalism; el
periodista (la **periodista**)
journalist; **periodístico** *adj*
journalistic
permanecer to remain
permitir to permit
pero *conj* but
perplejo *adj* perplexed,
uncertain

el **perro** dog
el **perseguidor** follower, pur-
suer
la **persona** person
el **personaje** character
pertenecer to belong to
la **pesadilla** nightmare
pesar to weigh; **a pesar de**
prep in spite of
el **peso** weight; monetary unit
in Mexico and Argentina
piadoso *adj* pious, merciful
pícaro *adj* mischievous,
roguish
el **pie** foot
la **piedra** rock; stone
la **pierna** leg
la **pieza** room
pintar to paint
pisar to step on
el **piso** floor
la **pistola** pistol
la **plata** silver
la **plaza** square
la **pluma** pen
la **población** population
pobre *adj* poor
poco *adj* little; **poco a
poco** slowly, little by
little; **pocos** few
poder to be able to
poderoso *adj* powerful
la **poesía** poetry
el **poeta** poet
poético *adj* poetical
político *adj* political
poner to put; **ponerse** to
put on; to become; **ponerse
a** + *inf* to begin
popular *adj* popular
por for; by; **¿por qué?** why
porque *conj* because
portarse to behave, conduct
oneself
portátil *adj* portable
posarse to settle, lodge
poseer to possess

poseído *pp* possessed
la **posesión** possession
positivo *adj* positive, sure
practicante practitioner
precisamente *adv* precisely, exactly
el **predominio** predominance
preferir to prefer
preguntar to ask
el **premio** award, prize
la **prensa** press
la **preocupación** worry
preocuparse to worry
preparado *adj* prepared
preparatorio *adj* preparatory
la **presencia** presence
presentable *adj* presentable
el **presente** present
preso *adj* jailed
primario *adj* grammar school
primero *adj* first
el **primo** cousin
principalmente *adv* principally
el **principio** beginning; **a principios de** at the beginning; **al principio** at first
la **prisa** speed; **de prisa** quickly
el **procedimiento** procedure, method
la **procesión** procession
proferir to pronounce, express
el **profesor** teacher
profundo *adj* profound
el **progenitor** father
el **programa** program
prohibido *adj & pp* prohibited
el **prólogo** prologue
prolongarse to be extended, be lengthened
pronto *adv* soon; **de pronto** suddenly

pronunciable *adj* pronounceable
el **propietario** owner
propio *adj* suitable, exact, original, one's own, peculiar, proper
proponer to propose
el **protector** protector
el **protestante** Protestant
provenir to arise; to proceed; to originate
el **proverbio** proverb
próximo *adj* next
el **proyecto** project
prudente *adj* prudent, wise
la **prueba** proof
el **pseudónimo** pseudonym
publicado *adj & pp* published
publicar to publish
público *adj & n* public
el **pueblo** town
el **puente** bridge
la **puerta** door
el **puerto** port
pues *adv* well, then
puesto *pp* placed, put
pulcro *adj* beautiful, neat, tidy
la **punta** point, corner
el **punto** point; **a punto de** *prep* on the point of, about to
la **puntuación** punctuation

Q

que *rel pron* that, which, who, whom
qué *interr pron* what; **¿qué tal?** hi, how are you?
quedar to remain; to be; **quedarse** to stay, remain; to be
los **quehaceres** chores

la **queja** complaint
quemar(se) to burn (up)
querer to want
quien *pron* who, whom; he
who; **quién** *interr pron*
who? whom?; **¿de quién?**
whose?
quieto *adj* tranquil, peaceful
la **quincena** fortnight
la **quinina** quinine
quitarse to take off
quizá *conj* perhaps, maybe

R

el **rábano** radish
rabioso *adj* rabid, mad,
raging
el **rabo** tail; hind part; train
radical *adj* radical; fundamental, basic
la **raíz** root
la **rama** branch
raramente *adv* rarely
raro *adj* rare, strange; **rara
vez** rarely
el **raso** satin
rasurarse to shave
el **rato** short time, while; el
ratito little while; **ratos**
times
la **raya** stripe, line
la **raza** race
la **razón** reason
la **realidad** reality; **en
realidad** *adv* really
realmente *adv* really
la **recámara** bedroom, ward-
robe
recetar to prescribe
recibido *pp* received
recibir to receive
recientemente *adv* recently
recoger to gather, pick,
collect

reconocer to recognize
recordar to remember; to
remind
recortado *adj* cut out
recortar to outline, delin-
eate
recorrer to examine; to pass
over; survey
rectificar to rectify, amend,
make right
recto *adj* straight
el **recuerdo** remembrance
recuperar to recover, regain
recurrir to resort to
la **redacción** editorial office,
editing
el **redactor** editor
el **rededor** surroundings; **en
rededor de** *prep* around,
about
la **redonda** neighborhood; **a la
redonda** round about
redondeado *adj & pp*
rounded
redondo *adj* round
referir to refer
refinado *adj & pp* refined
reflejar to reflect;
reflejarse to be reflected
refrescarse to be refreshed,
be cooled
la **región** region
regresar to return
el **reino** kingdom
reír to laugh; **reírse** to
laugh
la **relación** story, relation
relacionado *adj & pp*
related
el **relámpago** lightning
relatar to tell, relate
el **relato** story
religiosamente *adv* reli-
giously
la **reliquia** relic
el **reloj** watch, clock
remoto *adj* remote, far away

removerse to move; to remove

repartido *adj* & *pp* spread, scattered; distributed

el **repente** sudden movement; **de repente** suddenly

repetir to repeat

la **represa** dam

reprochar to reproach, blame

la **república** republic

resbalar to slip

la **residencia** residence

residir to reside

resistir to resist

respaldado *adj* & *pp* supported, backed

el **respaldo** back of a chair

respetuoso *adj* respectful

responder to answer

la **respuesta** answer

resucitar to resurrect

resuelto *pp* resolved

resultar to follow; to result; to proceed

el **retintín** jingle, clink

retirarse to withdraw, go away from

retorcerse to twist, wriggle

retratar to portray; to imitate

el **retrato** portrait

retroceder to recede, go backwards

reunirse to meet

revelar to reveal

la **reverencia** reverence

reverendo *adj* reverend

el **revés** reverse

la **revista** magazine

la **revolución** revolution

el **rey** king

el **rezo** prayer

rico *adj* rich, wealthy

el **rincón** corner

el **río** river

la **risa** laugh, laughter; **de risa** laughing

la **roca** rock

rodar to roll, revolve

rogar to beg

rojo *adj* red

romper to break

la **ropa** clothing

el **ropero** closet (for clothing)

rosado *adj* pink

el **rostro** face

rubicundo *adj* reddish-blonde, rosy with health

rubio *adj* blonde

la **rueda** wheel

rugoso *adj* corrugated

el **rumbo** direction; **rumbo a** towards, in the direction of

el **rumor** rumor, murmur

S

el **sábado** Saturday

saber to know

la **sabiduría** wisdom

sabio *adj* wise

sacar to take out, remove

el **saco** suit jacket

el **sacrificio** sacrifice

la **sala** room, living room; la **salita** little room

salir to leave; **salir bien** to pass (a subject in school), to turn out well

el **salón** salon, drawing-room

saltar to jump

saludar to greet

el **saludo** greeting

salvaje *adj* savage

la **sandía** watermelon

sangrar to bleed

la **sangre** blood

el **sargento** sergeant

la **satisfacción** satisfaction

secarse to get dry

el **secreto** secret

la **sed**   thirst
la **seguida**   succession; series;
   en seguida   immediately
seguir   to continue; to follow
según *prep*   according to
segundo *adj & n*   second
seguro *adj*   sure, certain; **de
   seguro**   truly, certainly,
   surely
la **selva**   jungle; forest
la **semana**   week
el **semanario**   weekly publication
sembrar   to sow
el **seminario**   seminary
sencillamente *adv*   simply
sencillo *adj*   simple; easy;
   plain
el **sendero**   path
el **seno**   bosom, breast
sentado *adj*   seated, sitting
sentar   to seat; **sentarse**   to
   sit down
el **sentido**   sense, feeling
sentir   to feel; to be sorry, to
   regret; **sentirse**   to feel
   (well; sad)
señalar   to point out
el **señor**   man, sir, mister, gentleman
la **señora**   lady, Mrs.
separar   to separate
septiembre   September
el **sepulcro**   tomb, grave
sepultar   to bury
ser   to be; el **ser**   being
la **serie**   series
el **sermón**   sermon
serpentearse   to meander,
   wriggle
la **serpiente**   snake
servido *pp*   served
el **sexo**   sex
   si *conj*   if, whether
   sí *adv*   yes; *refl pron used af-
      ter a prep*   himself, herself,
      yourself, themselves; **sí**

mismos   themselves
siempre *adv*   always
la **sierra**   mountain range
el **siglo**   century
significar   to mean, signify
siguiente *adj*   following
el **silencio**   silence
silenciosamente *adv*   si-
   lently
la **silla**   chair
el **sillón**   armchair
simple *adj*   simple
la **simplicidad**   simplicity; candor
el **simulacro**   image, idol; vision
sin *prep*   without; **sin embargo**   however
sino *conj*   but
siquiera *conj*   even though;
   adv   even
el **sitio**   place; location
la **situación**   situation
sobrar   to exceed; to have
   over much
sobre *prep*   on, over, above;
   sobre todo   especially,
   above all
sobreponerse   to overcome,
   overpower
sobresaltado *adj & pp*   surprised
el **sobresalto**   surprise, sudden
   fear
sobrevivir   to survive
la **sobrina**   niece
el **sobrino**   nephew
la **sociedad**   society
socorrer   to help
el **socorro**   help
el **sofá**   sofa
el **sol**   sun
el **soldado**   soldier
la **soledad**   solitude
la **solemnidad**   solemnity
soler   to be accustomed to
solo *adj*   alone; **sólo** *adv*   only

soltar to let go, set free
el **solterón** (confirmed) bachelor
la **sombra** shadow
el **sombrero** hat
sonar to sound, ring
sonreír to smile
sonriente *adj* smiling
la **sonrisa** smile
soñar to dream
soñoliento *adj* sleepy, dreamy
soplar to blow
la **sordina** mute (of a musical instrument)
sorprender to surprise; **sorprenderse** to be surprised
sorprendido *adj & pp* surprised
la **sorpresa** surprise
sostener to sustain
la **sotana** cassock
su *adv* his, her, your, their
suavemente *adv* gently, softly
la **suavidad** sweetness, kindness
subir to ascend, go up; to get in (a vehicle)
la **substancia** substance, being
suceder to happen
el **suceso** event, happening
sucio *adj* dirty
el **sudoeste** southwest
el **suelo** ground, floor
el **sueño** dream; sleep
la **suerte** luck
el **sufrimiento** suffering
sufrir to suffer; el **sufrir** suffering
la **suma** sum, total, quantity
la **superficie** surface; area
la **superstición** superstition
suplicar to entreat, beg
suponer to suppose
el **sur** south

suspirar to sigh
sutil *adj* subtle, cunning
suyo *adj & pron* his, of his; her, of hers; your, of yours; their, of theirs; las **suyas** his, hers, theirs

T

la **taberna** tavern
tal *adj* such, such a; **tal vez** maybe, perhaps
el **tamaño** size
también *adv* also
tampoco *conj* neither
tan *adv* so, as
tanto *adj* so much; **tanto como** as much as; **tanto... como** both . . . and
tapar to cover; to hide; to obstruct
la **tapia** mud wall, wall fence
la **tarde** afternoon; *adv* late; **más tarde** later
el **tema** theme, topic
temblar to shake
temer to fear
temeroso *adj* afraid, frightened
el **temor** fear
temprano *adj* early
la **tenacidad** tenacity; perseverance
tenderse to lie down
tener to have; **tener miedo** to be afraid; **tener que** + *inf* to have to
el **teniente** lieutenant
la **tentación** temptation
la **teología** theology
terminante *adj* ending, closing
el **término** term
el **terrateniente** (la **terrateniente**) landowner, landholder

terrible *adj* terrible
el **terruño** territory, native
   country
la **tesis** thesis
el **tesoro** treasure
el **testimonio** testimony
la **tía** aunt
el **tiempo** time, weather
la **tienda** store, shop
la **tierra** earth, land; **tierrita**
   little land
el **tigre** tiger
la **tinta** ink
el **timbre** tine; bell
el **tío** uncle
   tirar to throw
el **título** title
el **tocador** dresser
   tocar to touch; to play (an
   instrument)
   todavía *adv* still, yet; even
   todo *adj* all; **sobre todo**
   especially, above all
   tomar to take
el **tono** tone, tune
   torcerse to be dislocated; to
   twist
el **torno** turn; **en torno**
   round about; around
   tosco *adj* coarse
   tortuoso *adj* winding
la **torre** tower
   trabajar to work
el **trabajo** work
la **tradición** tradition
el **traductor** translator
   traer to bring
   traidor *adj* treacherous
el **traje** suit
la **trama** plot
la **trampa** trap
la **tranquera** palisade, fence
   tranquilamente *adv* peacefully
la **tranquilidad** tranquility,
   peacefulness

   tranquilizarse to relax
   tranquilo *adj* peaceful, calm
   transformarse to be trans-
   formed, be changed
   transmitir to transmit
   tras *prep* behind, after
el **tratamiento** treatment
   tratar to try; to treat
el **través** crossbeam; **a través**
   de along, through, across
   treinta *adj* thirty
   tremendo *adj* tremendous,
   awful, terrible
   trepar to climb
la **tribu** tribe
el **trigo** wheat
el **trique** poor household goods,
   things, junk
   triste *adj* sad
la **tristeza** sadness
el **tronco** tree trunk
   tropezar to trip; **tropezar**
   con to come upon; to meet
el **trueno** thunder

U

   último *adj* last
   un(o) *indef art* one; a, an;
   unos some
   únicamente *adv* only
   único *adj* only
la **universidad** university
la **uña** nail
   usted *pron* you

V

las **vacaciones** vacation
   vacío *adj* empty
   vagabundo vagabond,
   rover, tramp
   vagamente *adv* vaguely

vagar to wander
vago *adj* vagrant; roaming
valeroso *adj* brave
el **valle** valley
varios *adj pl* several
el **varón** man, male
la **vecindad** neighborhood
el **vecindario** neighborhood
el **vecino** neighbor
vedar to hinder, impede; to prohibit
veinte twenty
la **vejez** old age
veloz *adj* fast
el **venado** deer
vencer to conquer
vengarse to avenge
venir to come
la **ventana** window; **ventanilla** little window
venturoso *adj* lucky, successful
ver to see; **a ver** let's see
veranear to spend the summer
el **verano** summer
las **veras** reality, truth; **de veras** truly
la **verdad** truth
verdadero *adj* real, true
verde *adj* green
el **verdugo** executioner
la **vereda** path
la **vergüenza** shame
el **vericueto** rough and roadless place
la **versión** version
el **versito** little verse
la **vez** time; **en vez de** instead of; **una vez** once; **a veces** sometimes
viajar to travel
el **viaje** trip
vibrar to vibrate
la **vida** life
viejo *adj* old; **viejísimo**
adj extremely old; el **viejo** old man
el **viento** wind
el **viernes** Friday
la **violencia** violence
viril *adj* virile, manly
la **viruela** small pox
visitar to visit
la **vista** sight, view
visto *adj & pp* seen
visualizar to visualize
visualmente *adv* visually
vivir to live
vivo *adj* live, alive, lively
vocacional *adj* vocational
volar to fly
la **voluntad** will
volver to return; **volver a**
+ *inf* to do something again
la **voz** voice
la **vuelta** turn; return; repetition; **darse una vuelta** to take a walk; **a vuelta de correo** by return post
vuestro *adj* your

Y

y *conj* and
ya *adv* already; now; **ya que** now that; since; although
yacer to lie down
el **yaqui** (la **yaqui**) Indian tribe of Mexico
la **yarda** yard

Z

el **zapato** shoe
zoológico *adv* zoological
zopenco blockhead
zumbar to buzz, hum